READINGS IN

Applied English Linguistics

READINGS IN

Applied English Linguistics

Edited by
HAROLD BYRON ALLEN
University of Minnesota

SECOND EDITION

APPLETON-CENTURY-CROFTS

DIVISION OF MEREDITH CORPORATION

New York

PREFACE

SOMETIMES THE PREFACE to an anthology appears to have been written merely to provide the editor a chance to say something himself. But since I have unabashedly included two articles of my own, this preface must have another reason for existence. It does, and that reason appears in what can be pertinently repeated from the preface to the first edition in 1958:

"Not many years ago it seemed enough for a person concerned with the teaching of English to know something of a fairly settled corpus of information about the language. For the secondary school teacher this usually meant a compact presentation of systematic traditional grammar, with perhaps—if he were lucky—a brief history of the English language. For the college teacher this meant Old English grammar, with perhaps some attention to early Germanic phonology and the grammar of Gothic or Old Norse and such ancillary language data as would inhere in the study of Chaucer and Shakespeare. The undergraduate English major not headed for teaching rarely was expected to acquire any organized knowledge of his language at all, except for the unrealistic grammatical rules of his freshman English handbook.

"This ostensibly happy situation no longer exists. The far-reaching advances in the relatively new discipline of linguistics in the past few years are now being matched by specific developments in the study of our own language. The general English major and the undergraduate and the graduate student preparing to teach English are beginning to find that some knowledge of English linguistics is basic to their understanding of usage, to composition, and even to the criticism of literature. Further, so active are workers in English linguistics today, so rapid are the advances, that the student needs not only the synthesized information in a textbook or a series of lectures but also the content and points of view in current articles by these workers and by those seeking to apply their findings.

"Experience over more than a dozen years has convinced me of the value of sending students to these current articles. While a teacher, or a single textbook, carries a certain weight in persuading the student of the validity of materials which may contradict deeply entrenched but uncritically accepted attitudes, the weight is multiplied when the student reads article after article presenting additional evidence and further cogent analysis. When a student is confronted with a new approach, he is entitled to know whether it is only the individualistic bent of his instructor or of his single textbook or whether, on the contrary, it is that of contemporary scholars in the field. He is, in brief, entitled to learn what is going on in that part of the world of study and teaching in which he expects to do his own work.

"But the student cannot easily learn this when the library lacks some of the needed publications, when a number of other students are trying to read the same articles in the publications it does have, when his time in the library is limited and current journals may not be removed, and when the library's having only one copy of a given journal prevents his reading articles in any kind of reasonable sequence. And with the recent rapid increase in the quantity of desirable articles which the student should read, the problem has become more and more serious. Hence this collection as a workable solution."

What I said in 1958 I could say even more emphatically today, for during these five years the advances in linguistic science and its applications have been greatly accelerated. Much more has been done in applying linguistics to the teaching of English as a foreign language; linguistics itself has developed esoteric concerns with mathematics and psychology; transformation grammar has introduced a new and still controversial dimension; lexicostatistics—or glottochronology—has drawn the interest of an ever-growing number of scholars; reading specialists are learning that linguistics has basic importance for them.

Conspicuous almost beyond the limits of what could have been predicted ten years ago is the expanded attention of the whole teaching profession. The need for including sound linguistic content in the English curriculum was insisted upon in a 1959 report, *The Basic Issues in the Teaching of English,* prepared after three conferences held jointly by representatives of the Modern Language Association, the National Council of Teachers of English, and the American Studies Association. Evidence of the need appeared in 1961 when the NCTE issued its detailed survey of English teaching in the United States, *The National Interest and the Teaching of English.* This document, prepared for the Congress of the United States, showed that only one-half of the secondary teachers of English were minimally prepared in their subject and that only a small proportion of these were adequately trained in knowledge of the history and the structure of their language.

But current activity is likely to make that report obsolete within a short time. An immediate result was that the NCTE created a new Commission on the English Language, with responsible concern for improving the situation in every possible way. With the International Reading Association the NCTE formed a joint Committee on Linguistics and Reading. Special institutes, in-service programs, summer workshops sponsored by the College Entrance Examination Board, major research and curriculum projects set up by grants from the U.S. Office of Education, inclusion of English language requirements in state teacher certification standards—these are only some of the developments that are appearing as focal points of action as the imperative need for sounder preparation in the English language becomes more widely accepted.

This collection of articles, then, is intended to meet the need for representation of current linguistic thought and applications, representation more diversified and more immediate than would be much of the content of a single textbook.

Whose need is this? Specifically, it is the need of everyone teaching or intending to teach English, whether in the elementary school or in the graduate seminar, or somewhere in between those extremes. But while I have had this group particularly in mind in selecting articles for inclusion, I have never yielded my belief that it is not too much to insist that some knowledge of how his language works can reasonably be expected of a liberally educated person. These articles can provide some of that information.

For the selection of the contents of the first edition helpful advice came from about two dozen colleagues concerned with teaching the English Language. In this second edition such advice has come from a number of those college teachers who have used the book in their classes during the past two or three years. They have indicated which of the original articles they wanted kept; and they checked items in a tentative list of new articles. For this help I am very grateful. Several times I accepted their major judgment when I might have chosen otherwise. But when they disagreed, as they did more often than not, I had to make the decision.

So much good new material has been published recently that the first winnowing left articles which would fill two volumes the size of this one. Ruthlessly some of these articles had to be excluded; even more ruthlessly some of the good original articles had to be removed to make way for more recent ones. Users of the first edition will miss some of their favorites, I am sure.

But I have sought carefully to make the second edition better balanced and less uneven than the first was. Two Parts especially are much stronger, those on the dictionary and on the relation of linguistics and the study of literature. Of the new developments in linguistics, one in particular, transformation grammar, has already had such impact upon the thinking of English teachers that it could not be ignored. Nine articles deal with it: six in Part Two and three in Part Five. All the changes which seemed to me desirable have finally produced a volume of sixty-two selections, three fewer than in the previous edition. Twenty-four of these have been retained, and thirty-eight are new. All articles except those by Trevor Hill and Miss Norris are complete.

The order of articles is conservative and systematic. Although they may be read in the order as presented, many teachers undoubtedly will find other sequences more consistent with their own order of materials in a course in the English language. Familiarity with the contents, furthermore, will enable teachers to assign articles in other groupings which to them may seem more reasonable. This is not a basic textbook; it is a source book, and it may be used in many ways. It is simply my hope that no matter how it is used it will contribute to the reader's understanding of the English language and deepen his appreciation of its subtle and intricate structural wealth.

Whatever contribution this book can make would clearly not occur without the primary work of the authors who have generously granted permission to reprint. For that consent I am most appreciative. I am grateful as well to the publishers and other copyright holders who likewise have extended their permission. Specific acknowledgment is to be found with each article.

University of Minnesota   H.B.A.

CONTENTS

Preface

Part I. THE HISTORICAL BACKGROUND

Part II. ENGLISH LINGUISTICS TODAY

Part III. LINGUISTIC GEOGRAPHY

Part IV. LINGUISTICS AND USAGE

Part V. LINGUISTICS AND THE TEACHING OF GRAMMAR AND COMPOSITION

Part VI. LINGUISTICS AND THE DICTIONARY

Part VII. Linguistics and the Study of Literature

Part I

THE HISTORICAL BACKGROUND

INTRODUCTION

ANTHROPOLOGISTS TELL US that widespread among both primitive and non-primitive people is the belief that language is something mystical if not sacrosanct. Much evidence — verbal taboos, attitudes to various semantic and grammatical changes, popular reaction to a great new dictionary — indicates that in perhaps a modified form this notion persists with considerable vigor in the English-speaking world. If so, then a likely contributing factor would be lack of easily available information about the variegated, if not shady, history of the grammatical ideas still commonly accepted.

Perhaps the best conspectus of this complex history is that by R. H. Robins, *Ancient and Mediaeval Grammatical Theory in Europe* (Bell, London, 1951). Robins, a reader in linguistics in the School of Oriental and African Studies of the University of London, provides in that small volume an excellent overview through the eyes of a modern linguist. For the teacher a good synoptic treatment is included in Robert C. Pooley's *Teaching English Grammar* (Appleton-Century-Crofts, 1957).

In the opening part of this second edition of the *Readings* Dykema first outlines the Graeco-Latinate origins of the still prevalent grammatical tradition. Hartung then seeks to relate this persistent tradition to the transitional work of the language scholars of two generations ago before he epitomizes the contribution of a leader in structural linguistics, Charles C. Fries. If a grammar may be considered in linguistic parlance as a description of the

1

structure of a language, then for ease of reference the Graeco-Latinate description of English may be identified as Grammar A, the description produced by 19th century philology as Grammar B, and that of the present-day structuralist as Grammar C. Some writers fail to distinguish between Grammar A and Grammar B, calling each "traditional grammar."

McMillan then offers a brief look at the chief accomplishments of that 19th century language study from which came Grammar B as represented in the books of Sweet and Jespersen, Curme and Poutsma. Fuller summaries of 19th century developments appear in several general books on linguistics, notably Leonard Bloomfield's *Language* (Holt, 1933) and Louis H. Gray's *Foundations of Language* (Macmillan, 1939), but the most detailed account is that by Holger Pedersen (translated by John Spargo as *Linguistic Science in the Nineteenth Century,* Harvard University Press, 1939, and currently reprinted as a paperback). One matter referred to by McMillan, the repeated confusing of philology and linguistics, has been carefully treated by George Melville Bolling in "Linguistics and Philology," *Language,* 5.27-32 (1928).

Without here specifying the contributions of various scholars Fries next provides a kind of theoretical synthesis of the principles of English linguistics. The specific history of these contributions in recent years would indeed be too long for inclusion here, but the serious student wishing to see English language study in its total context will find two admirable summaries available. One is by Robert A. Hall, Jr.: "American Linguistics, 1925–50," *Archivum Linguisticum,* 3.101-125 (1951) and 4.1-16 (1952). The other is a series of articles contributed to *Trends in European and American Linguistics, 1930–1960* (Spectrum, Utrecht, 1961) by the following: William G. Moulton ("Linguistics and Language Teaching in the United States, 1940–1960"), Schofield Andrews, Jr., and Joshua Whatmough ("Comparative and Historical Linguistics in the United States, 1930–1960"), Eric P. Hamp ("General Linguistics — The United States in the Fifties"), and Charles C. Fries ("The Bloomfield School").

Faced with the co-existence of "traditional" grammar and Grammar C, Levin ends this part with a comparison of the two in historical terms and thus provides a transition to the synchronic descriptions in Part II.

1

Where Our Grammar Came From

KARL W. DYKEMA

THE TITLE OF THIS PAPER is too brief to be quite accurate. Perhaps with the following subtitle it does not promise too much: A partial account of the origin and development of the attitudes which commonly pass for grammatical in Western culture and particularly in English-speaking societies.

The etymology of *grammar* shows rather sharp changes in meaning: It starts with Greek *gramma, letter* (of the alphabet), itself a development from *graphein, draw* or *write.* The plural *grammata* develops in meaning through *letters* to *alphabet* to the *rudiments of writing,* to *the rudiments of learning.* The adjective form *grammatike* with *techne* meant the art of knowing one's letters. From this form comes the Latin *grammaticus.* The medieval vernacular forms with *r* are something of a mystery, appearing first in Old Provençal as *gramaira* and developing in English with a variety of spellings, often with only one *m* and ending in *er.* One of the more amusing forms is that with the first *r* dissimilated to *l, glamour.*

In present usage at least four senses can be distinguished which have an application to language: (1) The complete structural pattern of a language learned unconsciously by the child as he acquires his native tongue; (2) an attempt to describe objectively and systematically this fundamental structure, usually called descriptive grammar; (3) a partial description of the language based on puristic or pedagogical objectives, usually called prescriptive grammar, (4) a conviction held by a good many people that somewhere there is an authoritative book called a grammar, the conscientious memorization of which will eliminate all difficulties from their use of language. This I call grammar as remedy. It is mainly with the last two of these notions of grammar that I shall concern myself, prescriptive grammar and grammar as remedy, and how the earlier conceptions of grammar were metamorphosed into them.

As the etymology of the word suggests, Western grammar begins with the ancient Greeks. As early as Plato we find in the *Sophist* the statement that a

Reprinted by permission from *College English,* 22.455–65 (April, 1961). Professor Dykema is Director of the Division of Languages and Literature, Youngstown University.

word describing action is a verb (rhema), one which performs the action is a noun (onoma). Aristotle adds conjunctions (syndesmoi), recognizes that sentences have predicates, and is aware of three genders and of inflection (*Rhetoric*, etc.). The Stoics attempted to separate linguistic study from philosophy and made important contributions to the discipline. In their writings we find terms which are approximately equivalent to *noun, verb, conjunction, article, number, gender, case, voice, mood,* and *tense.*[1] But the direct source of most of our widely used grammatical terms is Dionysius Thrax's little *Techne Grammatike,* which Gilbert Murray recollects his great-uncle still using at the Merchants Taylors' School in the nineteenth century to learn Greek from.[2]

A few quotations from this little work will illustrate how close many of our school grammars still are to their source of more than 2000 years ago:

> A sentence is a combination of words, either in prose or verse, making complete sense . . . . Of discourse there are eight parts: noun, verb, participle, article, pronoun, preposition, adverb, and conjunction . . . . A noun is a part of discourse having cases, indicating a body (as 'stone') or a thing (as 'education'), and is used in a common and a peculiar way (i.e., is common or proper) . . . . A verb is a word without case, admitting tenses, persons, and numbers, and indicating action and passion (i.e., being-acted-upon) . . . . A pronoun is a word indicative of definite persons and is used in place of a noun . . . . The adverb is an uninflected part of discourse, used of a verb or subjoined to a verb . . . . The conjunction is a word conjoining or connecting thought in some order and filling a gap in the expression.[3]

The few examples I have given emphasize analysis by meaning, because that is the aspect of classical grammar which our traditional grammar has dwelt upon. But the definitions of noun and verb, it should be observed, begin with formal distinctions—case and tense—and throughout the work there is clearly an awareness of the importance of structure in the functioning of the language. The contribution of the Greeks to linguistics was a great one, as Gilbert Murray and others have pointed out. But for twenty centuries their work was carried on by slavish and unimaginative imitators incapable of developing the work of their predecessors. Especially in the less highly inflected languages like English and French it did not occur to them that the inflectional devices of Latin and Greek must have some counterpart in the structure of the modern language.

Though today there are a few scholars in universities who assert that they pursue grammar for its own sake as an academic discipline, most people conceive of grammar only as a utilitarian thing, as a means of learning to use a

[1] R. H. Robins, *Ancient and Medieval Grammatical Theory in Europe* (London, 1951), pp. 20–35.

[2] Gilbert Murray, *Greek Studies* (Oxford, 1946), p. 181.

[3] "The Grammar of Dionysius Thrax," translated . . . by Thos. Davidson, *Journal of Speculative Philosophy,* VIII (1874), 326–339.

language correctly. This notion was certainly completely absent from the thinking of Plato, Aristotle, and the Stoics, and probably from that of Dionysius Thrax. Grammar began as a philosophical inquiry into the nature of language. Now, for most people, it is merely a dogmatic means of achieving correctness. It is this transformation that I am mainly concerned with.

How the transformation took place is not easy to document. Perhaps the most plausible explanation lies in the familiar desire of younger teachers to regurgitate undigested fragments of what they have swallowed in the course of their higher education. All too often a high school teacher just out of college will use his college lecture notes as the foundation of his high school teaching, or a teacher of undergraduates tries to give them exactly what he got in his graduate seminar.

Then there is the fundamental difference between the prevailing purposes of elementary and advanced instruction. Primary education is severely utilitarian; and though it can hardly be denied that, especially in our society, graduate instruction is often infected by utilitarianism, the speculative approach does persist, and inquiry for its own sake plays a major role. The curriculum at all levels of education is and has been determined partly by tradition, partly by immediate utilitarian objectives, partly by a desire to perpetuate the best elements of the cultural heritage. The application of these criteria is of ascending difficulty. Easiest is to accept without question the practice of one's predecessors; not much harder is to accept a limited practical goal and provide instruction intended to achieve it. Most difficult is to select critically what is most valuable in the cultural heritage, and the Romans weren't up to it.

Because of Greek prestige in the ancient world, less developed cultures borrowed extensively from that of Greece. The influence of Greek art, philosophy, and literature on Rome is familiar, but Greek grammar was quite as influential and became the model not only for grammars of Latin but of Syriac, Armenian, Hebrew, and possibly Arabic as well.

It could not be a good model. The structure of every language is peculiar to itself—though there are, of course, similarities between members of the same linguistic family—and the best description of it derives from a careful examination of the language itself, not from an attempt to fit it into the pattern of another. To be sure, both Greek and Latin are rich in inflections and the Latin of Varro was not much further away from the parent Indo-European than was the Greek of Dionysius Thrax; so the deformation imposed by the model was less distorting than when the same procedure was followed many centuries later and attempts were made to strait-jacket the modern vernaculars of Europe within the model of Latin grammar. For example, Greek had a definite article, Latin had none, though in Varro's *De Lingua Latina,* the term *articuli* is applied to the demonstratives *is* and *hic* (VIII, 45, 51). Latin has more cases but a different tense system and no dual. English has only two inflected active tenses against six for Latin, but many more periphrastic verbal constructions than had Latin.

The attention given to grammar by the ancients seems to have been considerable. Susemihl in his *History of Greek Literature in the Alexandrian Period* discusses over fifty grammarians. One of them, Aristophanes of Byzantium (ca. 257-ca. 180 B.C.), was librarian to Ptolomy Epiphanius, who imprisoned him to prevent the king of Pergamum from hiring him away.

Among the Romans, grammarians were also in demand. The slave Lutatius Daphnis, a grammarian, was bought for 700,000 sesterces, perhaps $35,000, which puts him about in the class of a lesser baseball player. Caesar put this Lutatius Daphnis in charge of the public libraries, though it was not until much later, according to Suetonius, that a regular salary of 100,000 sesterces was paid from the privy purse for Latin and Greek teachers of rhetoric (Suetonius, *Lives of the Caesars,* VIII, xviii). Caesar himself took part in one of the persisting grammatical quarrels of the time, that of the analogists and the anomalists, by producing a work called *De Analogia,* known to us only in fragments. Though he favored the analogists, who demanded complete inflectional consistency, it is significant that he wanted no radical departures from usage.[4] Suetonius also states that Claudius "invented three new letters and added them to the [Latin] alphabet, maintaining that they were greatly needed; he published a book on their theory when he was still in private life, and when he became emperor had no difficulty in bringing about their general use" (Suetonius, *Lives of the Caesars,* V, xli). Theodore Roosevelt was less successful when he tried to impose a few spelling reforms on the Government Printing Office; Congress refused to permit the changes.

Though Caesar favored the analogists, he was unwilling to depart from established usage. His position was that of many of his cultivated contemporaries, as it has been of many cultivated people ever since. The appeal of analogy is the appeal of logic, a creation of the Greeks and a tool that has been used with interesting and surprising effects in most areas of Western thought ever since. The foundation of Aristotelian logic is the syllogism. As the analogists applied the syllogism to language it worked like this: The form of the personal pronoun determines the form of the verb of which the pronoun is the subject. The form *you* is plural; therefore the form of the verb *be* which follows it must be plural; hence *you were,* not *you was.* So we have in cultivated English today only *you were.* But the cultivated dare not apply this syllogism to the intensive or reflexive, where the eighteenth-century practice of agreement with the notional number of the pronoun still persists. The eighteenth century had both *you was there yourself* and *you were there yourselves;* while we have *you were there yourselves* when the notional number of *you* is plural, but *you were there yourself* when it is singular.

Language has its own logic, which it is the function of the descriptive grammarian to discover if he can. Whatever it may be, it is not Aristotelian

[4] Jean Collart, *Varron, Grammairien Latin* (Paris, 1954), pp. 10, 19, 146; Robins, p. 58.

logic. But for two millennia our attitudes toward language have been colored by the assumption that the system of a language can be analyzed and prescribed by an intellectual tool that is inapplicable.

Conformity to a standard, or correctness if you like, is, of course, socially of the greatest importance. There is a long record of the penalties imposed on those who deviate from the standard, the earliest I know of being the account given in *Judges* (12, 4-6) of the forty and two thousand Ephraimites who were slain by the Gileadites because they pronounced *shibboleth sibboleth*. Later examples are less gory. Aristophanes in the *Lysistrata* (lines 81-206) ridicules the dialect of the Spartan women, though they are the allies of the Athenian women in their campaign of sexual frustration. Stephen Runciman in his *Byzantine Civilization* says "the Patriarch Nicetas in the Eleventh Century was laughed at for his Slavonic accent, and the statesman Margarites treated with disrespect in the Thirteenth because he spoke with a rough rustic voice."[5] And Chaucer's nun spoke the provincial French of the Benedictine nunnery of Stratford-Bow, the French of Paris—standard French—being to her unknown.

Conformity to the standard is what matters. But how is the standard to be determined? Quintilian, whom Professor T. W. Baldwin calls "The Supreme Authority" in his *Shakespeare's Small Latine and Lesse Greeke,* provides a most illuminating basis for discussion. In the *Institutes* Quintilian tells us that:

> Language is based on reason, antiquity, authority and usage. Reason finds its chief support in analogy and sometimes in etymology. As for antiquity, it is commended to us by the possession of a certain majesty, I might almost say sanctity. Authority as a rule we derive from orators and historians. For poets, owing to the necessities of metre, are allowed a certain licence . . . . The judgment of a supreme orator is placed on the same level as reason, and even error brings no disgrace, if it results from treading in the footsteps of such distinguished guides. Usage however is the surest pilot in speaking, and we should treat language as currency minted with the public stamp. But in all cases we have need of a critical judgment, ...(I.vi.1-3)

This is fuller than Horace's neater statement: "Use is the judge, and law, and rule of speech" (*De Arte Poetica, 72: Quem [usus] penes arbitrium est et ius et norma loquendi.*) and shows more clearly why we have troubles. Usage "is the surest pilot" but "we have need of a critical judgment."

Quintilian has more to say on the matter:

> Usage remains to be discussed. For it would be almost laughable to prefer the language of the past to that of the present day, and what is ancient speech but ancient usage of speaking? But even here the critical faculty is necessary, and we must make up our minds what we mean by usage. If it be defined

[5] Stephen Runciman, *Byzantine Civilization* (Meridian Books, New York, 1956), pp. 173, 176.

merely as the practice of the majority, we shall have a very dangerous rule affecting not merely style but life as well, a far more serious matter. For where is so much good to be found that what is right should please the majority? The practices of depilation, of dressing the hair in tiers, or of drinking to excess at the baths, although they may have thrust their way into society, cannot claim the support of usage, since there is something to blame in all of them (although we have usage on our side when we bathe or have our hair cut or take our meals together). So too in speech we must not accept as a rule of language words and phrases that have become a vicious habit with a number of persons. To say nothing of the language of the uneducated, so we are all of us well aware that whole theatres and the entire crowd of spectators will often commit *barbarisms* in the cries which they utter as one man. I will therefore define usage in speech as the agreed practice of educated men, just as where our way of life is concerned I should define it as the agreed practice of all good men. (I.vi. 43-45)

But Quintilian makes it quite apparent from the many examples he cites that educated men are not entirely agreed on their practice, and that they lean heavily on the authority of Greek usage:

More recent scholars have instituted the practice of giving Greek nouns their Greek declension, although this is not always possible. Personally I prefer to follow the Latin method, so far as grace of diction will permit. For I should not like to say *Calypsonem* on the analogy of *Iunonem*, although Gaius Caesar in deference to antiquity does adopt this way of declining it. Current practice has however prevailed over his authority. In other words which can be declined in either way without impropriety, those who prefer it can employ the Greek form: they will not be speaking Latin, but will not on the other hand deserve censure. (I.v. 63-64)

A thorough knowledge of Greek, learned from slave-tutors, had long been common among educated Romans, but it was Varro who transferred the entire body of Greek grammatical scholarship to Latin in his *De Lingua Latina*, written between 57 and 45 B.C. Though of the original 25 books of that work only V through X survive relatively intact, we have a fairly good account of what was in the rest because Varro is the source which all later Latin grammarians follow, and they have apparently borrowed from him most faithfully.

Greek grammar, is, then, a development of Greek philosophy, an attempt to treat systematically an important aspect of human behavior. It is a late development which in Alexandrian culture is given a practical application through its use in the editing, elucidation, and interpretation of texts, especially that of Homer; and in the correction of solecisms. Since there was little of the speculative in the Romans, Varro's encyclopedic treatment of Latin language and literature was the ultimate source of a host of school texts.

What has been presented so far is a partial account of the development of philology, though this ancient term has been an ambiguous one for almost as long as it has existed—naturally enough, since it derives from the Greek roots usually translated as *love* and *word*. Some people love words as the means of argument, others because they are the foundation of literature, others still for their forms and relations in discourse. All these senses have been designated by the word since it first appeared in Greek, and in nineteenth-century France and Germany it normally included literary history, textual and literary criticism, and linguistics. (We might well revive the word; it would provide a single term by which we could describe ourselves along with chemists, historians, and the rest; we are philologists.)

The ancients called the various aspects of this study by a variety of names: *philologos, grammatikos, grammatistes, kritikos* in Greek; *philologus, grammaticus, litterator, criticus* in Latin. They were evidently no more certain of exactly what the terms signified than we are today with similar terms. Suetonius writes:

The term *grammaticus* became prevalent through Greek influence, but at first such men were called *litterati*. Cornelius Nepos, too, in a little book in which he explains the difference between *litteratus* and *eruditus* says that the former is commonly applied to those who can speak or write on any subject accurately, cleverly and with authority; but that it should strictly be used of interpreters of the poets, whom the Greeks call *grammatici*. That these were also called *litteratores* is shown by Messala Corvinus in one of his letters, in which he says, "I am not concerned with Furius Bibaculus, nor with Ticidas either, or with the *litterator* Cato." For he unquestionably refers to Valerius Cato, who was famous both as a poet and as a grammarian. Some however make a distinction between *litteratus* and *litterator*, as the Greeks do between *grammaticus* and *grammatista*, using the former of a master of his subject, the latter of one moderately proficient. Orbilius too supports this view by examples, saying: "In the days of our forefathers, when anyone's slaves were offered for sale, it was not usual except in special cases to advertise any one of them as *litteratus* but rather as *litterator*, implying that he had a smattering af letters, but was not a finished scholar."
The grammarians of early days taught rhetoric as well, and we have treatises from many men on both subjects. It was this custom, I think, which led those of later times also, although the two professions had now become distinct, nevertheless either to retain or to introduce certain kinds of exercises suited to the training of orators, such as problems, paraphrases, addresses, character sketches and similar things; doubtless that they might not turn over their pupils to the rhetoricians wholly ignorant and unprepared. But I observe that such instruction is now given up, because of the lack of application and the youth of some of the pupils; for I do not believe that it is because the subjects are underrated. I remember that at any rate when I was a young man, one of these teachers, Princeps by name, used to declaim and engage in discussion on alternate days; and that sometimes he would

give instruction in the morning, and in the afternoon remove his desk and declaim. I used to hear, too, that within the memory of our forefathers some passed directly from the grammar school to the Forum and took their place among the most eminent advocates. (*On Grammarians,* iv)

Another writer who provides evidence on the Roman attitudes towards language is Aulus Gellius in his *Attic Nights.* Gellius represents the aristocrat's conviction that what he himself does must be right coupled with the conservative attitude that older practice is to be preferred:

> Valerius Probus was once asked, as I learned from one of his friends, whether one ought to say *has urbis* or *has urbes* and *hanc turrem* or *hanc turrim.* "If," he replied, "you are either composing verse or writing prose and have to use those words, pay no attention to the musty, fusty rules of the grammarians, but consult your own ear as to what is to be said in any given place. What it favours will surely be the best." Then the one who had asked the question said: "What do you mean by 'consult my ear'?" and he told me that Probus answered: "Just as Vergil did his, when in different passages he has used *urbis* and *urbes,* following the taste and judgment of his ear. For in the first *Georgic,* which," said he, "I have read in a copy corrected by the poet's own hand, he wrote *urbis* with an *i.* . . .
> But turn and change it so as to read *urbes,* and somehow you will make it duller and heavier. On the other hand, in the third *Aeneid* he wrote *urbes* with an *e:* . . .
> Change this too so as to read *urbis* and the word will be too slender and colourless, so great indeed is the different effect of combination in the harmony of neighbouring sounds. . . .
> These words have, I think, a more agreeable lightness than if you should use the form in *e* in both places." But the one who had asked the question, a boorish fellow surely and with untrained ear, said: "I don't just understand why you say that one form is better and more correct in one place and the other in the other." Then Probus, now somewhat impatient, retorted: "Don't trouble then to inquire whether you ought to say *urbis* or *urbes.* For since you are the kind of man that I see you are and err without detriment to yourself, you will lose nothing whichever you say." (XIII. xxi. 3-8)

And his attitude towards grammarians is expressed quite as explicitly in this passage:

> Within my memory Aelius Melissus held the highest rank among the grammarians of his day at Rome; but in literary criticism he showed greater boastfulness and sophistry than real merit. Besides many other works which he wrote, he made a book which at the time when it was issued seemed to be one of remarkable learning. The title of the book was designed to be especially attractive to readers, for it was called *On Correctness in Speech.* Who, then would suppose that he could speak correctly or with propriety unless he had learned those rules of Melissus?

From that book I take these words: *"Matrona,* 'a matron,' is a woman who has given birth once; she who has done so more than once is called *mater familias,* 'mother of a family'; just so a sow which has had one litter is called *porcetra;* one which has had more, *scrofa."* But to decide whether Melissus thought out this distinction between *matrona* and *mater familias* and that it was his own conjecture, or whether he read what someone else had written, surely requires soothsayers. For with regard to *porcetra* he has, it is true, the authority of Pomponius in the Atellan farce which bears that very title; but that "matron" was applied only to a woman who had given birth once, and "mother of the family" only to one who had done so more than once, can be proved by the authority of no ancient writer. . . . (XVIII. vi. 1-7)

By the Middles Ages the aristocrats were unlikely to have had much education, and the classical heritage was perpetuated by the grammarians, whose dogmatic victory was complete. Donatus (fl. 400) and Priscian (fl. 500) are the dominating figures. The name of the first, shortened to Donat or Donet, became synonymous with 'grammar' or 'lesson' in Old French and Middle English, and the grammar of the second survives in over a thousand manuscripts.[6] He also has the distinction of being consigned to Hell by Dante (*Inferno,* 15:110).

As an example of Priscian, here is the beginning of an analysis of the *Aeneid*—this is not from his big grammar, which was in eighteen books, but from a smaller one, *Partitiones Duodecim Versuum Aeneidos Principalium:*

Scan the verse, *Arma vi/rumque ca/no Tro/iae qui/primus ab/oris.* How many caesuras does it have? Two. What are they? Semiquinaria (penthemimeral) and semiseptenaria (hephthemimeral). How? The semiquinaria is *arma virumque cano* and the semiseptenaria is *arma virumque cano Troiae.* How many figures are there? Ten. For what reason? Because it consists of three dactyls and two spondees. How many parts of speech has this verse? Nine. How many nouns? Six: *arma, virum, Troiae, qui, primus, oris.* How many verbs? One: *cano.* How many prepositions? One: *ab.* How many conjunctions? One, *que.* Discuss each word; *arma,* what part of speech is it? Noun. Of what sort? Appelative (or common). What is its species? General. Its gender? Neuter. Why neuter? Because all nouns which end in *a* in the plural are unquestionably of neuter gender. Why is the singular not used? Because this noun signifies many and various things. . . .'

And this is not the end of the catechism on the opening line of Virgil. Evidently this sort of drill was to accompany the study of the poem from beginning to end, if the end was ever reached.

Increasingly in the Middle Ages the written heritage of Greece and Rome was accepted unquestioningly because literate men did not have a cultural

---

⁶ John Edwin Sandys, *A History of Classical Scholarship* (Cambridge, 1920), vol. 1, p. 230, note; p. 274.

ᵀ Heinrich Keil, *Grammatici Latini* (Leipzig, 1859), vol. 3, p. 459.

background which would permit them to ask pertinent questions. We learn, for example, that one of the best sources for the text of Diogenes Laertius is a manuscript of about 1200 written by a scribe "who obviously knew no Greek."[8] To be sure, there were sometimes conflicts between the Christian heritage and the classical, usually resolved in favor of the Christian. In a medieval manuscript is the comment: "Concerning the words *scala* (step), and *scopa* (broom), we do not follow Donatus and the others who claim they are plural because we know that the Holy Ghost has ruled that they are singular." And it was comforting when the traditions of classical grammar could be given divine corroboration. For example: "The verb has three persons. This I hold to be divinely inspired, for our belief in the Trinity is thereby manifested in words." Or this: "Some maintain that there are more, some that there are fewer parts of speech. But the world-encircling church has only eight offices [Presumably Ostiariat, Lektorat, Exorzistat, Akolythat, Subdiakonat, Diakonat, Presbyterat, Episkopat]. I am convinced that this is through divine inspiration. Since it is through Latin that those who are chosen come most quickly to a knowledge of the Trinity and under its guidance find their way along the royal road into their heavenly home, it was necessary that the Latin language should be created with eight parts of speech."[9]

On the other hand, St. Boniface's (675–754) "sense of grammatical accuracy was so deeply shocked when he heard an ignorant priest administering the rite of baptism *in nomine Patria et Filia et Spiritus sancti* [that is, with complete disregard of the required case endings] that he almost doubted the validity of the rite."[10].

Up to about the twelfth century Donatus and Priscian, whose grammars were based ultimately on classical Latin, were followed unquestioningly except where there seemed to be a conflict with sacred texts. The Vulgate and various theological writings were in a later Latin which might disagree with classical grammar, as in the more frequent use of the personal pronouns.[11]

But in the twelfth century the reintroduction of Greek philosophy had a tremendous impact on medieval thought, as is best illustrated by the Aristotelianism of Aquinas. And St. Thomas, as might be expected, deals with philological matters in the *Summa Theologica,* and again as might be expected through the syllogism:

> It seems that in Holy Writ a word cannot have several senses, historical or literal, allegorical, tropological or moral, and anagogical. For many dif-

[8] Diogenes Laertius. *Lives of Eminent Philosophers,* with an English translation by R. D. Hicks (Loeb Classical Library) (Cambridge & London, 1925), vol. 1, p. xxxv. (The quotations from Suetonius, Varro, Quintilian, and Aulus Gellius are from the translations in the Loeb Classical Library editions.)

[9] J. J. Baebler, *Beiträge zu einer Geschichte der lateinischen Grammatik im Mittelalter,* (Halle a. S., 1885), p. 22/Hans Arens, *Sprachwissenschaft, der Gang ihrer Entwicklung von der Antike bis zur Gegenwart* (Munich, 1955), pp. 30, 31.

[10] Sandys, p. 469.

[11] Baebler, p. 22.

ferent senses in one text produce confusion and deception and destroy all force of argument. Hence no argument, but only fallacies, can be deduced from a multiplicity of propositions. But Holy Writ ought to be able to state the truth without any fallacy. Therefore in it there cannot be several senses to a word. (First Part, Question One, Article 10, Objection 1)

A more explicitly grammatical example is this one from the thirteenth century:

> For a complete sentence, two things are necessary, namely a subject and a predicate. The subject is that which is being discussed; it is what determines the person of the verb. The predicate is that which is expressed by the subject. Nouns were invented to provide subjects. . . . Verbs were invented to provide predicates.

This concept of grammar being something created is found in another thirteenth-century writer:

> Was he who invented grammar a grammarian? No, because the creation of grammar cannot be based on teaching since that would presuppose its existence. Grammar was invented. For the invention of grammar must precede grammar. So it was not the grammarian but the philosopher who created grammar, for the philosopher studies the nature of things and recognizes their essential qualities.[12]

The authority of the grammarian was occasionally challenged. In a seventeenth-century German satirical treatment of schoolmasters is this account of a fifteenth-century episode:

> The Emperor Sigismund came to the Council of Constance and said: "Videte patres, ut eradicetis schismam Hussitarium." There sat an old Bohemian pedant in the Council who was convinced that with this box on the ear to Priscian the Emperor had sinned against the Catholic Church as gravely as had John Hus and Hieronymus of Prague. So he said [in Latin]: Most Serene Highness, *schisma* is neuter gender." The emperor said [in German]: "How do you know that?" The old Bohemian pedant answered [now in German]: "Alexander Gallus says so." The emperor said: "Who is Alexander Gallus?" The Bohemian pedant answered: "He is a monk." "Yes," said Sigismund, "I am the Roman emperor, and my word is worth at least that of a monk." (Joh. Balthaser Schupp, *Der Teutsche Schulmeister,* 1663) [13]

It now remains to consider the transfer of these attitudes to the modern vernacular languages. But first a brief review of the three preceding stages. The first is the unique situation in Greece, which differed from that of any of the succeeding cultures in two significant ways: It was essentially a monolingual society, and at least during the period of its greatest intellectual and artistic achievement it knew nothing of formal grammar. Rome differed in both essentials. The cultivated Roman was educated in Greek, and formal

[12] Arens, pp. 34, 32.
[13] Baebler, p. 118.

grammar was a part of his Latin education, though this does not mean that he learned Greek through formal grammar. In the Middle Ages the two-language requirement for the educated, which was characteristic of Rome, was continued, but with an important difference. Whereas for the Roman, Latin was a respectable language with a respectable literature, for the educated man of the Middle Ages his native vernacular was not respectable and at least at first had no important literature. Also he learned the language of scholarship and literature in a way quite different from that used by the Roman. He learned it with the aid of formal grammar.

Of these three stages, the third, the medieval, is much the longest; in formal education and scholarship it lasts well into the eighteenth century and therefore has a duration of well over a thousand years. Of course during the last two or three hundred of those years a great change had come over Europe, due partly to an intimate reacquaintance with the heritage of Greece and Rome. But in the field of philology this meant largely a return to the attitudes of the ancients. It also meant the transference of the whole philological approach—ancient and medieval—to the modern vernacular languages.

The history of vernacular grammars and of English grammars in particular comes next in this development, but there is no space for it here.

One consequence of this transfer must be illustrated: The ambivalence it has given us toward language. Here are some examples. Trollope in his *Autobiography* writes:

> The ordinary talk of ordinary people is carried on in short sharp expressive sentences, which very frequently are never completed,—the language of which even among educated people is often incorrect. The novel-writer in constructing his dialogue must so steer between absolute accuracy of language— which would give to his conversation an air of pedantry, and the slovenly inaccuracy of ordinary talkers, which if closely followed would offend by an appearance of grimace—as to produce upon the ear of his readers a sense of reality. If he be quite real he will seem to attempt to be funny. If he be quite correct he will seem to be unreal.[14]

The nineteenth-century German philologist Wilhelm Scherer, discussing the great dramatist Heinrich Kleist, remarks that "he did distinguished work in all forms. There dwells in his language an individual magic, though he has an uncertain control of German grammar."[15] And in a recent review in the *TLS* is this sentence: "He [Leonard Clark] died after completing the first draft of his book, *Yucatan Adventure,* which would have gained some grammar, while losing some of the punch of its author's virile enthusiasm, if it had been more carefully revised."[16]

[14] Anthony Trollope, *An Autobiography* (World's Classics, Oxford, 1953), p. 206.
[15] Wilhelm Scherer, *Geschichte der deutschen Literatur* (Knaur, Berlin, n. d.), p. 752.
[16] *Times Literary Supplement,* March 20, 1959, p. 156.

In a detective story, Rex Stout has Archie Goodwin make this comment after one of the principal characters has said, "Yes. . . . We shall see.": "But what really settled it was her saying, "We shall see." He [Nero Wolfe] will always stretch a point, within reason, for people who use words as he thinks they should be used."[17] But in another story Wolfe is made to say, "If it's her again. . ."[18]

And Mark Twain, who took Cooper severely to task for his "ungrammatical" English, did what was perhaps his best work, in *Huckleberry Finn,* by using a narrative device which relieved him of all responsibility for conforming to standard usage.

One of the most eloquent and emphatic in condemnation of the Latin grammatical tradition was Macaulay but, as you might guess, he is much too long to quote here.[19]

I conclude by returning to the four senses of the term grammar outlined at the beginning. Contemporary philologists who specialize in linguistics have, it seems to me, attempted to strip away the accretions of two thousand years and are turning to a rigorously descriptive approach, the seeds of which are to be found in the Greeks. Other philologists have other interests, such as literary history, literary criticism, and, of course, the problem of getting freshmen to write better. As an inescapable burden of their academic heritage, they have to bear the weight of the ancient and medieval grammatical tradition, which survives in the other two senses, prescriptive grammar and grammar as remedy. What I have tried to do is to give some account of how that tradition developed, how it was transmitted, and why much of it is essentially irrelevant to the problems the philologist faces today.[20]

[17] Rex Stout, "Murder Is No Joke," *And Four to Go, A Nero Wolfe Foursome* (Viking, New York, 1958), p. 155.

[18] Rex Stout, "Too Many Women," *All Aces, A Nero Wolfe Omnibus* (Viking, New York, 1958), p. 237.

[19] T. B. Macaulay, "The London University", Edinburgh Review, February, 1826, in *Critical, Historical and Miscellaneous Essays and Poems* (Porter and Coats, Philadelphia, n. d.), vol. 3, pp. 631–634.

[20] A somewhat shorter version of this paper was read to the Northeastern Ohio College English Group, Akron, 5 November 1960.

2

The Persistence of Tradition in Grammar

CHARLES V. HARTUNG

RECENT PROCLAMATIONS of a "revolution in grammar"[1] have sought to define a sharp break between the traditional grammar and the new linguistics. The basic problems persist, however, and the solutions of traditional grammarians have to be understood and judged before we can see new approaches to grammar in their proper perspective.

Historically, the term *grammar* has referred to both the study and the art of language. The Alexandrian grammarians incorporated in the art of grammar the separate verbal disciplines that we now refer to as philology, literary criticism, rhetoric, and linguistics. The Roman rhetorician Quintilian began the process of specialization. He divided grammar into two main branches— the broad study of literature and the more specialized art of speaking and writing correctly.[2] The latter conception was adopted by European grammarians and prevailed until late in the nineteenth century, when grammar became defined more specifically as the science of the sentence.

But even the most eminent nineteenth-century spokesmen for grammar as a science did not agree about either the scope or the purpose of grammar. We can observe this division in the thinking of the two greatest philologists of the English-speaking world, Henry Sweet and William Dwight Whitney. Sweet recognized the inclusive nature of grammar when he said, "Grammar in the widest sense of the word is . . . both the science and the art of language."[3] But Sweet did not think that study of grammar as a corrective of "what are called 'ungrammatical' expressions" was of much practical value. He also considered this practice theoretically unsound because he thought that rules of grammar have no value except as statements of fact. Consequently, the business of grammar as a science was to observe the facts of

Reprinted by permission from the *Quarterly Journal of Speech*, 48.174–86 (April, 1962). Professor Hartung is a member of the English department of the University of California, Los Angeles.
[1] See W. Nelson Francis, "Revolution in Grammar," *QJS*, XL (October, 1954), 299–312.

[2] *Institutes of Oratory*, trans. J. S. Watson (London. 1907), I, 29 (1. 4. 1–3).

[3] Henry Sweet, *A New English Grammar* (Oxford, 1891), Part I, p. 4.

language and then to classify and state them methodically.[4] Whitney was also an eminent advocate of grammar as a science. He declared that grammar did not make rules and laws for language, but only reported the facts of good language in an orderly way.[5] But as a reading of Whitney's *Essentials of English Grammar* soon reveals, he judged goodness and orderliness by degree of adherence to the standard rules. The opposing attitudes of Whitney and Sweet may be exemplified briefly by their judgments on *it is me*, a linguistic shibboleth of their time. Whitney says: "Careless and inaccurate speakers . . . often use such expressions as *it is them, it was us, if it were her;* and in the case of *it is me* the practice has become so common that it is even regarded as good English by respectable authorities."[6] Sweet says: "I confine myself to the statement and explanation of facts, without attempting to settle the relative correctness of divergent usages. If an 'ungrammatical' expression such as *it is me* is in general use among educated people, I accept it as such, simply adding that it is avoided in the literary language."[7]

We see in these contrasting attitudes the transition from the ancient prescriptive use of grammar to the modern practice of scientific description. Despite the different ideas Whitney and Sweet had about the purpose of grammar, their methods of analysis were similar. They both followed the traditional practice of classifying words into parts of speech and sentences into kinds of discourse. Although modern scientific grammarians have developed somewhat different approaches, the parts of speech approach is still widely used. C. C. Fries in 1952 produced in his *Structure of English*[8] a scheme of analysis that incorporates modern attitudes and techniques but is nevertheless in basic ways traditional. James Sledd's *A Short Introduction to English Grammar,*[9] published in 1959, has introduced modern techniques while retaining the essential framework of the traditional approach.

Although the traditional parts of speech approach to grammar has been condemned by many modern scientific grammarians, it is still by far the most widely taught and studied system of linguistic methodology. The reasons for this are clear. Parts of speech classification has behind it a tradition of over two thousand years of practical use. During this time it has been subjected to rigorous intellectual examination by some of the best minds in European culture. This examination has not solved the theoretical problems posed by the method, but it has enabled the method to be used in the practical mastery of languages. Greek, Latin, and then the vernacular languages were learned for practical purposes by means of systems of rules devised by prescriptive grammarians. Moreover, throughout the Middle Ages and the Renaissance

[4] *Ibid.,* p. 1.
[5] William Dwight Whitney, *Essentials of English Grammar* (Boston, 1877), p. 4.
[6] *Ibid.,* p. 160.
[7] Sweet, p. xi.
[8] C. C. Fries, *The Structure of English* (New York, 1952).
[9] James Sledd, *A Short Introduction to English Grammar* (Chicago, 1959).

the study of Greek and Latin grammar was the main agency for keeping alive the cultural heritage of Greece and Rome.

In addition to making these solid contributions, the study of grammar has also served as a basis for the theoretical examination of language. The parts of speech grammarians are open to charges of unsoundness in their speculative efforts, but they have also suggested ways for grammarians to deal with language as a whole. Modern scientific grammarians have developed methods that are more precise and more theoretically consistent than the older methods, but they have often done so by rigidly limiting the scope of linguistic analysis. They still have to find solutions for many basic problems that traditional grammarians have tried for so long to solve.

The major problem in classifying the parts of speech has been that of setting up a logically consistent system of definitions. This problem has arisen largely because grammarians have tried to find distinct classes for all of the functionally different kinds of words used in connected discourse. Because of the inherent complexity of language the classes have been developed through the consideration of four contrasting bases for definition: (1) the lexical meaning of the word apart from its grammatical use; (2) the logical function of the word in the structure of thought; (3) the syntactical position of the word in connected discourse; and (4) the inflectional capacity of the word to change its form in a system of paradigms.

Aristotle made the first substantial effort to devise a system of parts of speech. The noun he defined as "a sound significant by convention, which has no reference to time, and of which no part is significant apart from the rest."[10] A notable feature of this definition is its concentration on the semantic (i. e., lexical) properties of the word. As a result of this stress on positive semantic value Aristotle denied to the negative term *not-man* the substantival characteristics of the noun. For reasons of logic he also considered only the nominative form to be a noun proper. Case declensions other than the nominative were not to be classed as nouns, for they could not be coupled with finite forms of verbs to form propositions that could be judged to be either true or false. From this logical extension of his definition we infer that Aristotle conceived that a noun must be a complete word unit possessing positive semantic value and logically capable of functioning as the subject of a finite verb.

The verb Aristotle defined as "that which, in addition to its proper meaning, carries with it the notion of time. No part of it has independent meaning, and it is a sign of something said of something else."[11] The verb, then, is similar to the noun in that it has substantival meaning, but it differs from the noun in carrying a notion of present existence. "Health," according to Aristotle, is a noun; "is healthy," a verb. The verb proper in Aristotle's scheme is limited to words indicating present time; words indicating past and

[10] See Aristotle, *De Interpretatione*, trans. E. M. Edghill, *The Works of Aristotle*, ed. W. D. Ross (London, 1928), I, 16a.
[11] *Ibid.*, 16b.

future are not verbs proper but tenses of a verb. Moreover, the verb proper is characterized by its capacity for combining with a noun to form a predication.

Since in *De Interpretatione* Aristotle was concerned only with the logically necessary parts of discourse, he defined only the noun and the verb. In *De Poetica*[12] he added definitions of other elements. The conjunction, literally "ligament," is defined as a non-significant sound serving to connect two or more significant sounds; it includes not only the regular connectives recognized by later grammarians but also particles that were later to be classified as prepositions. The article, literally "joint," is defined as a non-significant sound serving to mark the beginning, end, or dividing-point of a sentence; it includes words that were later to be defined as personal and relative pronouns. It is notable that the conjunction and the article are defined purely by reference to their syntactical positions in discourse. Since they have no independent semantic value and serve no necessary logical function, they are not to be considered as parts of speech on the same level as the noun and the verb.

In the definitions of the noun and verb in *De Poetica,* Aristotle does not repeat those parts of his definitions in *De Interpretatione* referring to the complementary logical functions of these two parts of speech. This omission may be due to corruption of the text, but it is more likely that he was limiting discussion to the lexical as opposed to the non-lexical properties of units of discourse. In *De Poetica* he is specifically concerned with diction and therefore centers his attention on lexical matters. His definitions of the noun and verb stress semantic properties. His definitions of the article and conjunction indicate that these words have no semantic significance and serve a purely syntactical function. Discussions of the various properties of language occur in contexts specifically concerned with matters of logic, rhetoric, and diction. In these various contexts he centers on features relevant to the topic discussed. In none of his extant works is there a systematic discussion of grammar as an autonomous discipline. He had no special occasion to work out a logically consistent scheme of specifically grammatical definitions. As a result of his many-sided approach to grammatical matters, he found some use for all four of the major criteria for defining the parts of speech, lexical, logical, and morphological criteria to define the different properties of the noun and verb, and syntactical criteria for the article and conjunction. Despite the fact that Aristotle provided no systematic treatment of grammar in any one place, his scattered comments do provide a basis for a reasonably comprehensive scheme. Later grammarians were able to base ambitious philosophical treatments of language on his definitions. For example, James Harris,[13] an English grammarian and linguistic theorist of the eighteenth

---

[12] See Aristotle, *De Poetica,* trans. Ingram Bywater in *Introduction to Aristotle,* ed. Richard McKeon (New York, 1947), 1456b–58a.

[13] James Harris, *Hermes or A Philosophical Inquiry Concerning Universal Grammar* [1751], 5th ed. (London, 1794).

century, found it possible to use Aristotle's definitions of the four parts of speech as a framework for an impressive statement of linguistic theory.

After the death of Aristotle there was much inconclusive discussion of grammar by philosophers of the Athenian world, particularly the Stoics, but the most substantial contributions were made by Alexandrian grammarians. These contributions were summed up in Dionysius Thrax's quintessential *Art of Grammar*,[14] the first comprehensive textbook of Greek grammar and probably the most influential grammar of any language ever published. Gilbert Murray, the English classical scholar, attests that it was used as a basic text in English schools until the second half of the nineteenth century.[15] In keeping with Alexandrian practice, Dionysius conceived the art of grammar quite broadly, including the arts usually assigned to poetics, rhetoric, and philology. Despite this very comprehensive scheme, most of Dionysius's *techne* is concerned with what we now recognize as strictly grammatical matters; definitions of the parts of speech receive the most attention. Since Dionysius was an Analogist, believing in the fundamental regularity of language, he limited his body of data to examples taken from classical literature and constructed a normative grammar.

The major contribution of Dionysius to the methodology of grammar was in analytical procedure. He extended definitions of the parts of speech to eight, using formal criteria to define the pronoun, the participle, the preposition, and the adverb. His scheme of classification is a model of deductive procedure. He begins with a definition of the word as "the smallest part of an ordered sentence," then defines the sentence as a combination of words expressing a thought complete in itself, next lists the eight parts of speech (noun, verb, participle, article, pronoun, preposition, adverb, and conjunction), and finally defines and exemplifies the separate parts of speech by examples taken from the best classical literature. In defining the parts of speech, Dionysius uses formal, lexical, and syntactical criteria but does not attempt to apply the three sets of criteria consistently to all eight parts of speech. He defines the noun and verb by their lexical properties and their capacity for inflection. A noun, for example, indicates a concrete body, "stone," or an abstract thing, "education," and is characterized by case and number. A verb lacks case, admits tense, person, and number, and indicates action and passion. The participle shares the properties of both nouns and verbs with the exception of person and mood. The article is capable of inflection similar to a noun and is distinguished also by its syntactical position preceding the noun. The pronoun indicates definite persons and serves as a substitute for the noun. Prepositions and conjunctions serve syntactical functions as connectives. Adverbs are uninflected parts of speech defined by relations to the verb. As we can see from this summary, Dionysius takes

[14] "The Grammar of Dionysios Thrax," trans. Thos. Davidson, *Journal of Speculative Philosophy*, VIII (1874), 326–339.
[15] Gilbert Murray, *Greek Studies* (Oxford, 1946), p. 181.

that patience is praiseworthy. In practical grammatical analysis the Port Royal grammarians did not go so far as the third step. They considered the central grammatical process that of forming a proposition by means of stating a judgment. Any proposition they conceived to include two terms, a subject and an attribute. The subject is that about which one makes an affirmation, e. g. *earth*; an attribute is that which one affirms about the subject, e. g. *round*. The link between the two terms is expressed by *is*. Our thoughts may be distinguished into two parts—objects and form or manner. The principal manner is that of making judgments. But we must also take into account such mental processes as combining and separating, and we need to distinguish the structural characteristics of such mental impulses as desires, commands, and questions. Words that signify objects of thought are called nouns (substantives and adjectives), participles, pronouns, particles, prepositions, and adverbs. Those signifying form and manner are verbs, conjunctions, and interjections.

The major assumption of the Port Royal approach is that grammar is essentially logical. In the Port Royal system the purely formal elements of accidence and syntax as well as the lexical properties of words are not considered essential. The verb, for example, is defined as a word whose principal function is to signify affirmation, and definitions based on formal and lexical criteria are dismissed as false. That part of Aristotle's definition referring to the verb as a word significant with tense is considered irrelevant because it does not state what the verb signifies, but merely the means of signification. Definitions based on the inflectional capacity of the verb are dismissed for the same reason. Lexical definitions of the verb as a word signifying action and passion or that which passes are also dismissed as invalid. These definitions are considered logically unsound because they neither fit all of the thing defined nor fit it alone; there are verbs which do not signify action or passion or that which passes, and there are words other than verbs that do signify these meanings. The participle *flowing,* for example, signifies a thing that passes just as well as the finite verb *flows.* By such reasoning the Port Royal grammarians discounted the importance of form and lexical meaning as criteria for defining the parts of speech, and pointed up the importance of the logical relationships of words in the structure of thought.

The Port Royal grammarians had a great influence on the methodology of grammatical analysis, especially on syntax. Their influence was particularly strong in Europe and can be seen in such a comparatively modern grammar as the monumental work of Poutsma,[19] still the most ambitiously executed study of the structure of English. But the Port Royal definitions of the parts of speech were by no means universally accepted. In England the classical tradition of Dionysius and Donatus, as carried on in such a Latin grammar as that of John Lily,[20] maintained its dominance. The reasons are relatively

[19] H. Poutsma, *A Grammar of Modern English* (Groningen, 1904–26).
[20] John Lily, *Brevissima Institutio seu Ratio Grammatices cognoscendae* [etc.] (Londini, 1668).

fully into account grammatical matters such as inflection and syn
position (i. e., form), but he also uses lexical criteria to define word
nominal and verbal properties. He does not refer to such logical rela
categories as subject, predicate, and complement.

Dionysius's framework of classification, even though it does appl
ferent criteria to different parts of speech, is admirably designed for de
ing Greek, the language on which it was based. Because the scheme w
effective, it was later used, with some experimental revisions, to des
other languages. Grammarians of Latin dropped the article, as inapplic
to Latin, and added the interjection. The participle was alternately droj
and added. As late as the nineteenth century Goold Brown's English gr
mar[16] included both the article and the participle as separate parts of spe
The noun was subdivided by eighteenth-century grammarians into s
stantive and adjective. But for the most part the scheme of the parts
speech has remained essentially as Dionysius worked it out.

Later changes, such as separation of noun from adjective and dropping
the participle, were foreshadowed by distinctions to be found in his defi
tions. Even when medieval grammarians modified the standard grammars
Donatus and Priscian to describe medieval instead of classical Latin, the
did not find it necessary to make drastic changes in the criteria of classifica
tion.[17] The difficulties arising from the use of different bases of definitio
became acute only when the scheme of Dionysius was applied to language
differing structurally from the classical languages. Before the rise of modern
linguistic science European grammarians sought to devise logically consistent
systems of grammar. Medieval scholastic philosophers, for example, reintro-
duced into grammatical analysis the Aristotelean categories; and Arnauld
and Lancelot, the grammarians and logicians of Port Royal, made grammar
a branch of logic.

The general and philosophical grammar of Port Royal[18] is a full-fledged
attempt to define parts of speech by logical categories based on a hierarchy
of such mental operations as conception, judgment, and reasoning. Conception is defined as simple apprehension of ideas such as *being* and *God* and of
material images such as *circles, dogs,* and *horses.* Judgment is the making of
an affirmation that something is or is not so, e. g., *the earth is round.* Reasoning is the use of two judgments to form a third. For example, if we assume
that virtues are praiseworthy and patience is a virtue, we must also assume

---

[16] Goold Brown, *Grammar of English Grammars* (New York, 1862).

[17] See Petrus Helyas, *Summa Prisciani* in Vincentius Beluacensis, *Speculum Doc-
trinale* (Venetiis, 1494).

[18] A. Arnauld and C. Lancelot, *Grammaire générale et raisonnée de Port-Royal*
(Paris, 1660). Port Royal was a Cistercian convent near Versailles. It was noted
particularly as a center of Jansenism, a doctrine brilliantly defended by Arnauld and
Pascal. At Port Royal a school was established for the sons of Jansenist parents. For
this school a number of important textbooks were written, including the famous *Logic
of Port Royal* and the grammar cited above.

simple. Whereas the Port Royal grammarians were interested primarily in demonstrating the general philosophical functions of linguistic form, practical grammarians were concerned mainly with devising prescriptive rules that would provide a guide to usage. For this reason they preferred simple categorical statements supported by examples of correct and incorrect usage to abstract reasoning based on principles of logic. Bishop Lowth might praise a philosophical grammar such as the *Hermes* of James Harris,[21] which was in the tradition of Aristotle, the Medieval scholastics, and the Port Royal grammarians, but for practical reasons he wrote his own grammar according to the pattern of the most commonly used elementary Latin grammars of his time.

Lowth's definitions of the parts of speech are even more simple than those to be found in the Latin grammars. He explains the reasons for this in the preface to his grammar. Because of the relative simplicity of the English scheme of inflections, Lowth could omit references to inflection in his definitions of the parts of speech. His definitions are made up of rather loosely phrased, simple statements based on lexical and syntactical criteria. They make no attempt to account for the morphological or logical properties of parts of speech. They are, in fact, hardly more than labels used for the organization of prescriptive statements. Their limitations were pointed out even by early nineteenth-century prescriptive grammarians such as William Cobbett and Goold Brown.[22] Nevertheless, they did succeed in becoming the standard definitions that are most commonly used even today in school grammars.

For over a hundred years, until Henry Sweet's *A New English Grammar* in 1891, Bishop Lowth dominated linguistic discussion in England. Popularizations of his grammar by such copyists as Lindley Murray and Samuel Kirkham[23] were sold in the millions. As a result of the popularity of such grammars, the nineteenth century has been termed the midsummer madness of grammar. But in the late nineteenth century, Henry Sweet introduced the scientific spirit into English grammar. Sweet adopted the parts of speech approach to the methodology of grammar, but his purpose was full analytical description rather than dogmatic prescription. Influenced by the Port Royal approach and by Hermann Paul's demonstration of the logical weaknesses resulting from inconsistent use of the categories of form, function, and meaning,[24] Sweet made a full use of all three criteria in defining the traditionally accepted parts of speech. He not only applied his threefold method of analysis to nouns, verbs, adjectives, and adverbs, but to pronouns, propositions, and

[21] Robert Lowth, *A Short Introduction to English Grammar, A New Ed.* (London, 1783), pp. xiii-xiv.

[22] William Cobbett, *A Grammar of the English Language* (London, 1833); Goold Brown cited in n. 16 above.

[23] Lindley Murray, *English Grammar, adapted to the Different Classes of Learners* (New York, 1802); Samuel Kirkham, *English Grammar in Familiar Lectures* (New York, 1857).

[24] Hermann Paul, *Prinzipien der Sprachgeschichte* (Halle, 1880).

conjunctions, which up until his time had been discussed almost entirely from the standpoint of their syntactical relations.

Although Sweet analyzed the standard parts of speech under the separate headings of form, function, and meaning, he made no consistent effort to keep his categories distinct. Under any one of his headings he introduced analysis that pertained more logically to either or both of his other two categories. Moreover, he did not distinguish the logical properties of discourse from grammatical and semantic properties. For example, he discusses the logical uses of the noun under the heading of form, those of the adjective under the heading of meaning, and those of the verb under the heading of function. Such disregard for consistent analytical procedure was probably due to Sweet's basic evaluation of language. He was fond of saying that language is an imperfect instrument of thought, and he provided numerous examples of the imperfect correspondence between grammatical and logical categories. More basically, however, Sweet considered any sharp distinction between form and meaning artificial. The concern of grammar, he believed, is not with form and meaning separately but with connections between the two. To describe these connections, the grammarian may start either with form or with meaning:

> Syntax may be studied from two points of view. We can either start from the grammatical forms, and explain their uses, as when we describe the meanings and functions of the genitive case, or the subjunctive mood; or we may take a grammatical category, and describe the different forms by which it is expressed, as when we give an account of the different ways in which predication is expressed—by a single verb, by the verb *to be* with an adjective or noun-word, etc. We distinguish these as *formal* and *logical* syntax respectively.[25]

In this passage Sweet explicitly recognizes the distinction between the formal and logical approaches to syntax, and he implies that either approach is legitimate as long as the grammarian accounts for the functional relationship between form and meaning. But Sweet did not always hold to this principle. His contrast of the functions of accidence and syntax is a case in point. Accidence, he wrote, concerns itself as much as possible with form and as little as possible with meaning, whereas syntax ignores formal distinctions as much as possible and concentrates on meaning. For this sharply drawn distinction Sweet was criticized by Otto Jespersen,[26] who thought the grammarian should always keep in mind that form and function are inseparable in the life of language. Actually, Jespersen owed a great deal to Sweet, and the difference between his view and Sweet's is more a matter of degree than of essence. Jespersen merely developed somewhat more rigorously than Sweet the exposition of the dual orientation of language

[25] Sweet, p. 205.
[26] Otto Jespersen, *The Philosophy of Grammar* (London, 1924), p. 40.

to outer form and inner logical meanings. Specifically, Jespersen worked out with greater precision and detail Sweet's distinction between the contrasting points of view of speaker and hearer. The speaker starts with inner notional categories for which he finds outer verbal forms; the hearer translates outer forms into inner meanings. The middle point in each transaction is that of function, a term used by Jespersen to designate the specific forms of such grammatical categories as number, case, and tense.[27]

Although Jespersen, like Sweet, based his analysis of the parts of speech on the threefold division of form, function, and meaning, he greatly reduced the importance of specific definitions of the parts of speech. He denied, in fact, the possibility of basing a satisfactory classification of words on short and easily applicable definitions. Instead he assumed that there is sufficient empirical evidence to identify word-classes and then examined in detail the arguments for and against certain principles of classification. For instance, he used the word *noun* as a general heading for substantives and adjectives, and then examined in detail such traditional concepts as substance, quality, specialization, and generalization to determine whether these concepts are useful in distinguishing substantives from adjectives. He concluded that there is an element of truth in such logical distinctions, but that ultimately any practical division of one part of speech from another must be determined by formal criteria that differ from one language to another.[28]

Because of the importance Jespersen gave to formal criteria, he saw no point in making in English such a distinction as that between dative and accusative.[29] To him this was merely one more instance of the application to English of distinctions that pertain to Latin. For his emphasis on formal criteria that were applicable especially to individual languages, Jespersen was widely criticized by traditional grammarians, who also looked askance at many of his innovations in terminology and analytical techniques. Today we recognize that Jespersen did not depart radically from the traditional approach to grammar; his introduction of new analytical techniques was evidently intended to buttress the traditional parts of speech grammar by providing it with a more resourceful methodology.

Jespersen fully recognized the difficulties inherent in defining parts of speech, but he still felt that there was justification for retaining much of the traditional scheme. He refused to join the ranks of such of his contemporaries as Brunot, De Saussure, Sapir, and Bloomfield,[30] who were sceptical of the utility of the parts of speech approach. Jespersen held that the main difficulty with the approach was a pedagogical one, which could be obviated, partic-

---

[27] *Ibid.,* pp. 39–46.

[28] *Ibid.,* pp. 58–63.

[29] *Ibid.,* p. 174.

[30] F. Brunot, *La pensée et la langue* (Paris, 1922); Ferdinand de Saussure, *Cours de linguistique générale* [1916], 5th ed. (Paris, 1960); Edward Sapir, *Language: an Introduction to the Study of Speech* (New York, 1921); Leonard Bloomfield, *Language* (New York, 1933).

ularly at the elementary level, if the teacher depended upon examples rather than brief definitions. In his *Essentials of English Grammar*[31] Jespersen provided a demonstration of how he would reduce the importance of explicit definitions. Under the headings of the parts of speech he lists groups of words with short identifying labels. Substantives such as *God, devil, man, John,* et cetera are labeled parenthetically as living beings and plants; *star, stone, mountain,* et cetera as things; *iron, air, tea,* et cetera as substances; *lightning, death, laughter,* et cetera as happenings, acts, states; *year, inch, bushel,* et cetera as measures, indications of quantity; *beauty, kindness, poverty,* et cetera as qualities. This practice of listing examples with parenthetical labels is followed for the other word-classes—adjectives, verbs, pronouns, and particles. In his class of particles Jespersen included all words that would not fit into his primary classes.

The plan of organization in *Essentials of English Grammar* is evidently designed to keep parts of speech classification in the background. Only one short chapter out of thirty-six is devoted explicitly to defining word-classes, and no chapter is headed by the traditional names of the parts of speech. But this practice is somewhat misleading. Actually, Jespersen has merely abandoned parts of speech classification as an obvious principle of organization. His detailed discussions of grammatical categories and syntactical structures assume the premises and follow in analytical detail the traditional parts of speech methodology. That these discussions have been distributed in a new arrangement may be regarded in some ways as more of a loss than a gain. The richly detailed analyses often lose much of their cogency because they do not fall readily into a systematic framework. The *Philosophy of Grammar* makes clear why Jespersen has tried to reduce the role of parts of speech methodology. With grammatical evidence drawn from many of the same sources as those used by modern linguists, he shows the difficulties of applying the parts of speech approach to languages that exhibit principles of structure different from those of the Indo-European languages.

Jespersen emphasized the need to investigate the inter-relations of form, function, and meaning in defining the parts of speech, but also recognized the particular importance of formal criteria in grammatical analysis. Modern parts of speech grammarians have placed even greater stress on formal criteria for defining the parts of speech. C. C. Fries, in his work on the structure of the sentence,[32] constantly emphasizes form and disassociates his analysis of the parts of speech from the traditional terminology by using such neutral designations as Class 1, Class 2, Class 3, and Class 4 words. James Sledd retains the traditional terms but scrupulously attempts to eliminate semantic and logical criteria from his definitions.[33] Examination of salient

[31] Otto Jespersen, *Essentials of English Grammar* (New York, 1933).

[32] Fries, p. 56.

[33] Sledd, see n. 9 above.

points of analysis in the works of these two modern grammarians will reveal the present status of the parts of speech approach.

To Fries "the grammar of a language consists of the devices that signal structural meaning."[34] Structural meaning is to be carefully distinguished from lexical meaning, which is the province of the dictionary rather than of the grammar. The total meaning of any utterance consists, to be sure, of the two kinds of meaning in combination. But the concern of the grammarian is not with the total meaning but with the special contribution of structural elements to the total meaning. He therefore is concerned not with words as lexical units but with the arrangements of words as parts of speech. To identify the parts of speech, the grammarian considers three main sets of structural signals: the forms of individual words, the correlations of these forms, and the order in which the words are arranged.

In *The Structure of English* Fries demonstrates the central importance of a word's position as a clue to determining its class affiliation. By examining many examples and setting up typical frames of positional relations, he shows that in English certain classes of words normally precede or follow other classes of words. When the function word *the* is present, for example, it regularly precedes and marks the presence of a particular word-class, which can be designated as Class 1. A Class 1 word typically occupies certain positional relations to another word-class, which can be designated as Class 2. Other Classes, 3 and 4, can be identified by their relations to Classes 1 and 2. We can see how this positional principle works by examining the lexically meaningless construction Fries has provided: *the vapy koobs dasaked the citar molently.*[35] By applying his typical frames to this construction, Fries can assume that *the* marks the presence of a Class 1 word. But even if there were no *the,* he could still identify the Class 1 word by its positional relations to the other words in the construction. By such clues he can identify *koobs* and *citar* as Class 1 words, *dasaked* as a Class 2 word, *vapy* as a Class 3 word, and *molently* as a Class 4 word. The fact that *vapy* might also occur in Class 1 frames poses no great problem. In this particular instance it is in a Class 3 frame, identifiable as a Class 3 word.

In addition to word position, Fries uses formal correlations among words that help to identify structural functions. He provides a number of ingenious ways to illustrate such correlations, particularly the use of material replete with structural clues but lacking in lexical significance. An example is the previously quoted construction: *the vapy koobs dasaked the citar molently.* At the outset we must assume with Fries that this sequence of sounds occurs in an English context, and that the morphemes—minimum meaningful units—have been identified and have indicated the probability that the sounds

---

[34] Fries, p. 56.
[35] *Ibid.,* p. 111.

are divisible into the words that we see on the written page. Since we do not know the lexical meanings of the individual words, we must assign the words to parts of speech by those structural clues that are evident. Each word does by itself provide certain formal clues, but for more certain assignment we must depend on correlation and position. The *s* ending on *koobs,* for example, may be assigned to different morphemes, resulting in different structural meanings. The one we select will depend on how we correlate the word as a unit with other words in the group. One correlation would result in two word groups, *the vapy koobs,* and *dasaked the citar molently.* This correlation allows us to look upon *the vapy koobs* by itself as a grammatically complete utterance. But the other group cannot be so considered with the clues we have available. Of course, if we had a complete phonetic transcription of the cited construction, indications of juncture would indicate immediately the probable construction. We would also have little difficulty if we were given a completely punctuated construction with both structural and lexical meaning. Such a sentence would be "The musty stinks polluted the air completely."

In Fries' grammar positional and correlational data provide the main criteria for identifying word classes. But he also demonstrates in rich detail the ways in which the forms of individual words provide clues to probable structural uses. Words like *arrival, departure, deliver, catcher,* and *applicant,* for example, form regular patterns of contrast with such forms as *arrive, depart, deliver, accept, catch,* and *apply.* Word forms like *bigness, activity, bag, truth,* and *book* contrast regularly with such forms as *big, active, baggy, true,* and *bookish. Way, day,* and *sea* contrast with *away, daily,* and *seaward.* Systematic notation of such similarities and differences in the forms of words provides one set of clues to use as a basis of parts of speech classification. We must keep in mind, however, that in English, the position of the word in relation to other words in the sentence is the most positive clue to its structural use and word-class.

Defining word-classes depends in this system on the structural use of the word in the sentence. Fries, therefore, is faced with the need to find a definition of the sentence as a structural unit. In searching for such a definition he examines and dismisses in turn definitions which are based on semantic, intuitive, psychological, and logical grounds. The first to be dismissed as scientifically inadequate is the traditional definition of the sentence as the expression of a complete thought. Definitions based on logical relations follow in short order. By a process of elimination he finally accepts Bloomfield's definition: "Each sentence is an independent linguistic form, not included by virtue of any grammatical construction in any larger linguistic form."[36]

[36] *Ibid.,* p. 21 (Bloomfield, p. 170).

By applying this definition to his data, transcribed telephone conversations, Fries finds that he can classify utterance units into three kinds: (1) a single minimum free utterance; (2) a single free utterance, not minimum but expanded; (3) a sequence of two or more free utterances. To define the limits of utterance units, Fries accepts Bloomfield's assumption that language consists of speaker-hearer relationships in which both speaker and hearer respond to stimuli in the total situation. As a result of this he classifies utterances according to responses evoked:

Communicative Utterances

  I. Utterances regularly eliciting "oral" responses only:
     A. *Greetings.* B. *Calls.* C. *Questions.*
 II. Utterances regularly eliciting "action" responses, sometimes accompanied by one of a limited list of oral responses: *requests* or *commands.*
III. Utterances regularly eliciting convention signals of attention to continuous discourse. . . .

Non-communicative Utterances

  Utterances characteristic of situations such as surprise, sudden pain, prolonged pain, disgust, anger, laughter, sorrow.[37]

What strikes one about this scheme is the attempt to describe by formal clues linguistic functions that more traditional grammarians have defined in terms of semantic, logical, and formal properties of language. In this scheme Fries has found a place for the traditional terms, *statements, questions,* and *commands.* But for the usual rubric *exclamations* he substitutes the phrase *non-communicative utterances.* This phrase evidently is based upon Bloomfield's conception of language as "the use of sound waves to bridge the gap between two nervous systems."[38] The distinct phases of this process are: (1) a speaker stimulated to produce sounds possessing symbolic value; (2) the speech sounds; (3) a hearer making a practical response to the sounds. This formula obviously does not cover the full range of language situations. The behavioristic assumption that the "meaning" of a speech situation necessarily calls for a practical response in an individual other than speaker fails to account for those instances when communication takes place without an overt response. And most importantly, it fails to account for the speculative and expressive uses of language involving only one person. These semantic limitations do not, however, invalidate Fries' structural analysis of his word groups. Within the limits of his assumptions he has made a solid contribution to the description of the structure of the English sentence. The use of his

[37] *Ibid.,* p. 53.
[38] *Ibid.,* p. 33, n. 8. The quotation is Fries' summary of the theory set forth in Leonard Bloomfield's *Language,* chs. 2 and 9, pp. 21–41, 139–157. Fries refers specifically to these pages as the basis for his summary statement.

descriptive methods by such popularizers as Lloyd and Warfel, and Paul Roberts,[39] provides testimony to their effectiveness.

In some ways Sledd's grammar is even more traditional than Fries.[40] It retains, for example, such traditional terms as noun, verb, adverb, adjective, predicate, and complement, although these are redefined to fit structural criteria. The most notable innovation by Sledd is his distinction between parts of speech identified by form and parts of speech identified by position. The parts of speech identified by form are noun, pronoun, verb, adjective, and adverb. The parts of speech identified by position—nominal, verbal, adjectival, and adverbial—are identical with Fries' four primary classes. We can see how the distinction works by examining Sledd's treatment of adjectives.[41] Thus *poor* is always an adjective because it fits into the inflectional series *poor, poorer, poorest*. But whenever any one of these forms occurs in the normal position of a noun, as in the sentence *the poor are always with us*, it is also a nominal. A word like *beautiful* is not considered an adjective because it cannot be fitted into an inflectional series. Instead it is classified as an adjectival. By a similar process of reasoning Sledd distinguishes between the noun and the nominal, the verb and the verbal. The pronoun is identified by its form; by position it is a nominal. For the distinction between the adverb and the adverbial he introduces a slightly different criterion. He points out that in the traditional scheme many adverbs differ in form from adjectives only by the addition of the suffix—*ly*, e. g., *quick* and *quickly*. Consequently, he restricts the term adverb to the member of such pairs having the—*ly* ending. All other words appearing in the position of the adverb are adverbials.

Fries and Sledd seem to have carried structural parts of speech classification to its ultimate stage. It is difficult to see how any future grammarian can add essentially to their results. Any further development in the parts of speech approach would need, it seems, to return to a broader base of classification and find ways to interrelate lexical, logical, and formal criteria more consistently and systematically than grammarians have been able to do in the past. Possibly if Henry Sweet had made a more systematic distinction between the formal and the logical properties of syntax he might have demonstrated more conclusively the possibilities of a comprehensive system for defining word-classes. Some future grammarian may be able to accomplish what Sweet did not. It is more likely, however, that the grammar of the future will develop away from parts of speech analysis toward one of the newer systems. The traditional system of word classification was developed specifically to describe the structure of Indo-European languages

[39] Donald J. Lloyd and Harry R. Warfel, *American English in Its Cultural Setting* (New York, 1956); Paul Roberts, *Patterns of English* (New York, 1956) and *Understanding English* (New York, 1958).

[40] See Sledd, p. 10, for reasons.

[41] *Ibid.*, p. 81.

and has not proved effective for languages of other family groups. At present the major efforts in linguistic study are being directed toward developing a methodology of analysis that will apply effectively to radically different kinds of languages.

At any rate, the course before the general student of language is clear. He should understand the strengths and limitations of the traditional methodology. He should appreciate what the new methodology is contributing to a solid knowledge of language. Moreover, he should keep in mind that the study of grammar is influenced by the general intellectual climate. In the past it has developed as a normative discipline in close touch with logic and philosophy. In its latest form it is developing as a descriptive science. It is probable that the future study of grammar will be enriched by advancements in the behavioral sciences. In such an event it will again be a broad humanistic study.

3

Summary of Nineteenth-Century Historical and Comparative Linguistics

JAMES B. McMILLAN

THE MAIN DEVELOPMENTS in the study of language in our culture during the last century can be summarized, it seems to me, under three heads. Two are positive: (1) a drastic revision of the orthodox concept of language to include such assumptions as (a) language is speech, (b) language has system, (c) language has variety, and (d) language changes, and (2) an accumulation of an enormous mass of facts about the English language and the refinement of methods for collecting and classifying facts. One is negative: there was a confusion of levels of discourse (failure to separate linguistics and rhetoric), a confusion of description and history, and a confusion of linguistics and psychology.

A paper given at the CCCC Spring Meeting, 1954, in St. Louis, as part of a panel discussion on the general subject, "Modern Linguistics and the Teaching of Freshman English." Reprinted by permission from *College Composition and Communication* 5.140–149 (December, 1954). The author is chairman of the Department of English. University of Alabama.

Before elaborating, I wish to stipulate several definitions in the interest of clear communication. (1) A language is an arbitrary system of vocal signals by means of which groups of human beings interact. This definition excludes writing, gesture, animal noises, and visual and auditory and tactile code systems, and it does not limit language to particular groups or kinds of human beings. (2) Linguistics is the scientific study of language. It is inductive, objective, tentative, and systematic; it is concerned with reportable facts, methods, and principles; it works by means of observations, hypotheses, experiments, postulates, and inferences; its products are descriptive verbal or algebraic statements about language. Strict linguistics does not include statements about physiology or non-verbal culture. The correlation of linguistic statements with statements about non-verbal culture belongs in a discipline which has been called metalinguistics or exolinguistics. (3) Philology is the study of written documents (usually belletristic writings) to determine authorship, authenticity, provenience, dating, or meaning. Philology may use linguistic statements, just as it may use paleographic, bibliographic, astrological, and archaeological statements, but philology as here used is not co-extensive with linguistics. (4) Rhetoric is the art of speaking or writing effectively. It may be the practical art of communication (with experimental tests) or the fine art of speaking or writing with aesthetic effects. Rhetoric may include and use linguistic statements. But these statements come from workers in separate disciplines and must be authenticated by different means (although it is common for one person to work as an expert in more than one discipline).

In addition to stipulating definitions, I would insist that to talk sense we must discriminate levels of discourse, just as we discriminate physics, chemistry, and biology, or as we discriminate novels, prose fiction, and prose. In the hierarchy philology and rhetoric may be considered above linguistics, since they include bigger units of phenomena, just as biology may be considered above chemistry. Or, to put it differently, linguistics is more basic than rhetoric in the sense that chemistry is more basic than biology.

For example, the sentence *It ain't hisn!* may be examined by a rhetorician for its communicability, its appropriateness, or its aesthetic effect. He may ask the linguist for a full statement about the utterance, and the linguist can find and report many facts about the phonology, morphology, syntax, and lexicography involved (in terms of the same and other utterances by the same speaker or other speakers), but the linguist cannot *on linguistic grounds* make philological or rhetorical statements or judgments about a locution. Just as a physician can ask a pharmacist whether a certain powder can be dissolved in water, so can the rhetorician ask the linguist about the intra-verbal characteristics of *It ain't hisn;* but just as the pharmacist would not venture an opinion on whether the powder would be good for a patient, so the linguist has no right *as a linguist* to say that the locution is good or bad.

Sometimes, of course, the physician is his own pharmacist, and very frequently the rhetorician is his own linguist, but the levels of operation and discourse need not be blurred by this overlapping. In considering the contributions of the nineteenth century, we must remember that science operates through specializations, compartments, and hierarchies.

Now to look specifically at what language study in the last century was and what it contributed to us as teachers. The study of language was made a science in the nineteenth century. The development of this science has been related by Pedersen, and it was codified by Hermann Paul in his *Prinzipien der Sprachgeschichte* (1880), which was translated into English by H. A. Strong in 1889. Benjamin Ide Wheeler, in the preface to the American edition of Paul, said, "The rapid increase of the materials for a science of language within the last few decades has acted on the one hand to repress amateurism, and on the other to check arbitrariness of method on the part of professional linguists." The method applied was that of observation, collection, classification, hypotheses, postulates, and systematic statements. Paul, at least, saw the necessity for strict attention to the pertinent materials. He said (p. 11), "The picture of a particular condition of language is often blurred when the beholder happens to be acquainted with a language nearly related to the object of his consideration, or with an older or more recent stage of its development. The greatest care . . . is necessary to prevent the intrusion of any foreign material." The confusion of linguistic and extra-linguistic facts and the confusion of linguistics, rhetoric, and philology was not unnoticed in 1880.

The definition of language as speech (vocal signals) was explicit; Paul said (p. 433), "No philologist should ever disregard the fact that whatever is written is not language itself; that speech rendered into writing always needs to be rendered back into speech before it can be dealt with." And (p. 37) "A further source of deception is the habit of starting not from the spoken, but from the written word." Again (p. 39) "A word is not a united compound of a definite number of independent sounds, of which each can be expressed by an alphabetical sign; but it is essentially a continuous series of infinitely numerous sounds, and alphabetical symbols do no more than bring out certain characteristic points of this series in an imperfect way." Contemporary stump-speakers who decry the linguists' definition of language as speech obviously have not done their home-work in classical nineteenth century philology.

The definition of language as structured (a system) was elemental in 1880, and formal (as opposed to semantic) classification was common. Quoting Paul (p. 406): "The division into parts of speech most capable of being systematically carried out is that which starts from the mode of flexion." And (p. 417) "The formation of a comparative and superlative may be regarded as a test for the transformation of the participle into an adjective pure and simple."

Nineteenth century scientific language study rejected the arm-chair notion of a standard norm, and recognized variety in language. Paul insisted (p. 21) that ". . . we have, strictly speaking, to differentiate as many languages as there are individuals . . . at any given moment within any given community there are as many dialects spoken as there are individuals to speak them . . . each having its own historical development." The term *idiolect* had not been coined, but the concept was there, clean and sharp.

The eighteenth-century notion of "fixing" a language was rejected in the nineteenth century. Paul said that each individual's dialect (p. 21) is ". . . in a state of perpetual change." And (p. 481) "A written language to serve any practical purpose must change with the times, just like a living dialect." Professional students of language have not just recently invented the notion that language by its nature cannot remain static; the fact was commonplace and never seriously debated in professional circles in nineteenth century philology. (The practice of textbook writers is, of course, something else; rarely did they seem aware that language was being studied). Because value-judgments and ethnolinguistic statements were not rigidly excluded from linguistic statements, the notion that change was "corruption" lingered for many years, but the fact of change was universally recognized. Grimm, Verner, Grassmann, and other historical and comparative philologists discovered the regularity of linguistic change and, as a correlate, the regularity and system making the structure.

The first great contribution of historical and comparative study, then, was the recognition of linguistics as a science, and the changed concept of language that scientific study produced.

The second great contribution was the great quantity of ordered and classified information about English, both past and present. We need recall merely the Oxford Dictionary, the works on phonetics of Ellis, Sweet, Sievers, and others, the grammars of Sweet, Jespersen, Luick, Poutsma, Curme, and Kruisinga, and the countless special treatises that are recorded in Kennedy's bibliography to realize the amount of data that was produced. Some of this work was written, or at least published, in the twentieth century, but most of our recording and classification was a product of nineteenth century language study. Much of the misinformation epidemic in textbooks was produced in the last century, granted, but not in the framework of professional linguistics or philology.

The third bequest of the last century was a set of handicaps. First, historical philologists simply could not divorce language from language history. Paul said (p. xlvi), "What is explained as an unhistorical and still scientific observation of language is at bottom nothing but one incompletely historical

. . ." And ". . . it is the task of science not merely to determine what reciprocally corresponds in the different languages or dialects, but as far as possible to reconstruct the fundamental forms and meanings which have not come down to us." Paul and his contemporaries realized that diachronic statements must be based on full and accurate synchronic statements, but they insisted on regarding the descriptive statements as subordinate and not worth making for their own sake.

Second, the dominant workers insisted on explaining linguistic phenomena in terms of psychology. True, they gave up logic, but they merely substituted psychology. Although Paul noted that observed speech is the only datum we can use without inferences, he repeatedly used such definitions as the following (p. 111): "The sentence is the linguistic expression or symbol, denoting that the combination of several ideas or groups of ideas has been effected in the mind of the speaker." Similar remarks occur on page after page of his work, but not one of his psychological explanations is actually useful in attempting to describe or account for linguistic phenomena.

The third handicap was the failure of philology to distinguish itself explicitly and formally from linguistics and from rhetoric. Probably because the same people studied language and rhetoric, and probably because the three disciplines have much overlapping terminology, confusion was deep-seated and widespread. Because a man had studied the history and structure of English and also taught people rhetoric it was perhaps inevitable that he should find it hard to keep his linguistics and his rhetoric separate. The confusion was further compounded when people brought up on an authoritarian doctrine of correctness found that they could use the terminology of linguistics and philology to phrase their *dicta* and so (perhaps unintentionally) claimed undeserved sanctions. Let us consider a typical example. When a rhetorician considers a sentence like "The president knowed that the senator had broke his promise" he may want to tell the writer to change *knowed* to *knew* and *broke* to *broken,* and he has a perfect right to do so. But if he cites linguistics or the English language as his authority, he is confusing levels of discourse. The linguist knows and will report that both *knowed* and *broke* are formed normally within the structure of English, that they do not prevent communication, and that they are not structurally ambiguous. He can find the history of each form and he can relate each to other regular forms of the same classes. If we keep our levels of discourse straight, there is no reason *derived from English grammar* to object to these locutions. But if the rhetorician tries correlating *knowed* (pret.) and *broke* (past ptc.) with non-linguistic phenomena (such as the education and socio-economic status of people who use and who do not use the forms), he will certainly find reasons to advise the writer. These reasons are based on metalinguistic (or exolinguistic or ethnolinguistic) facts that are irrelevant to linguistics.

This is as simple and easy-to-apply a distinction as that between medicine and pharmacy, but it has profound implications, is potentially of tremendous use to the teaching of composition, and is the source of the senseless arguments between linguists and "traditionalists." When rhetoricians generally learn that linguists do not object to their conclusions but violently object to misstatements about language to justify those conclusions, both linguistics and rhetoric will profit, become mutually more agreeable, and finally throw off the handicap imposed a hundred years ago.

4

Advances in Linguistics

CHARLES C. FRIES

FOR MANY OF THE PRESENT MEMBERS of the National Council of Teachers of English the term *linguistic science* (often interchanged with the term *linguistics*) has the ring of something very new. It seems to stand for something that has grown up quite recently and for something concerning which the writers of articles recently published in the Council's journals show the most violent disagreement.

Now, as a matter of fact, matters pertaining to the more scientific study of the English language are, by no means, new to the National Council. The first President of this Council (the only President to be elected for two terms), one of the prominent founders of this organization, fifty years ago, combined his chief center of study, Literary Criticism, with a broad and very active interest in the knowledge and understanding won by modern linguistic science. This was Professor Fred Newton Scott (in whose seminar in Literary Criticism I studied in 1915). Let me recommend to you the address he made to this Council 44 years ago, in 1916, entitled *The Standard of American Speech.*[1]

What we call "modern" linguistic science is, however, a young science, but by no means an infant. At the time of the founding of the Council, fifty

Reprinted by permission from *College English,* 25.30–37 (October, 1961). The author is Professor Emeritus of English and Director Emeritus of the English Language Institute, University of Michigan.

[1] It appeared afterward in the *English Journal* and was reprinted in a little volume of twenty-four of his articles published at the end of his career, entitled *The Standard of American Speech and Other Articles.* Of these articles half must be counted as linguistic.

years ago, the beginnings of the techniques which made a *science* of linguistics were already ninety years old. I am assuming that the mark of a "science" is its *cumulative* and *impersonal* nature,—*impersonal* in the sense that the techniques used must lead to generalizations that are verifiable by all competent persons, and *cumulative* in the sense that all new contributions must build upon or take cognizance of all that has preceded.

Every now and then, in the efforts to push out the boundaries of our cumulative knowledge, a break-through into new understanding necessitates a reorientation of the knowledge gained previously. In linguistic science such break-throughs have occurred several times.

(1) With Erasmus Rask's paper (1819), and with Grimm's Germanic Grammar (1821), the beginnings of the new techniques in Indo-European comparative study made the first great advance in language study from the time of the Greek philosophers. It introduced the period of linguistic science characterized by the exploration of genetic relationships between languages, and the beginnings of language history. This period of linguistics saw the start of work upon the great historical dictionaries—for German, Grimm's *Wörterbuch* undertaken in 1837 (and still in progress): for English, *The Oxford English Dictionary* undertaken in 1858 (finished in 1928). The first period of Modern Linguistic Science, thus, was from 1820 to 1875.

(2) In 1875, Karl Verner's paper and the work of Leskien (and of the other Jung-Grammatiker, or Neo-Grammarians) introduced a period of much greater rigor in dealing with the generalizations concerning "sound-change." This period saw also the development (a) of phonetics (the scientific analysis of speech sounds both in respect to the muscular movements, the articulations, by which they are made, and in respect to the vibrations that produce their acoustical effect), (b) of linguistic geography, (c) of the recording and analysis of unwritten languages. This, the second period of Modern Linguistic Science, extended from 1875–1925.

(3) In 1925 Sapir's paper on *Sound Patterns in Language* in America (and de Saussure's lectures in Switzerland) introduced the beginnings of structural linguistics.

I have noted the chronology of these periods of special development in Modern Linguistic Science in order to make certain that no one (in this audience, at least) will any longer believe that what we call Modern Linguistic Science is the private theory of a small group of irresponsible radicals devoted to a program of undermining all the defenses of "accurate and elegant expression," who hold as their first principle "Accept what comes and in time we shall have a classless speech corresponding to the usage of the most numerous."[2]

For each of the three periods of the development of Modern Linguistic Science we have had men of international reputation who have attempted to

[2] Jacques Barzun, *The House of Intellect*, p. 241.

sum up and explain for the educated lay reader the progress in linguistic knowledge that has been achieved. For the first period we have two books by William Dwight Whitney, Professor of Sanskrit at Yale during the third quarter of the nineteenth century. *Language and the Study of Language: Twelve lectures on the principles of Linguistic Science* was delivered first at the Smithsonian Institution in Washington early in 1864, then at the Lowell Institute in Boston in December 1864 and January 1865, and first published in 1867. There were at least five editions of this book. A second book by Whitney, published in 1875 was *Life and Growth of Language: An Outline of Linguistic Science.* For the second period there were Hermann Paul's *Prinzipien der Sprachgeschichte* (Principles of Language History) first published in 1880, with the fifth edition in 1920, Otto Jespersen's *Language: Its Nature, Development and Origin,* in 1923, and Holger Pedersen's *Linguistic Science in the Nineteenth Century,* (tr. by Spargo) 1931. For the third period there have been Edward Sapir's *Language* 1921; Leonard Bloomfield's *Language* 1933, and now Kenneth Pike's *Language (in Relation to a Unified Theory of the Structure of Human Behavior),* Part I in 1954; Part II in 1955; and Part III in 1960.

Scholars devoted to Modern Linguistic Science in this country founded the Linguistic Society of America in 1924. That society has grown from a body of 270 members to a membership of over 1600. Abroad there have been the Linguistic Circle of Prague (Czechoslovakia) and the Linguistic Circle of Copenhagen (Denmark). The International Congress of Linguists, organized in the late twenties, at its eighth meeting in Oslo, Norway in 1957, was attended by 525 invited linguists from 43 different countries, from Japan and Australia to the West Indies, from Ghana and South Africa to Russia and Scotland, and from Argentina to the United States and Canada.

What then is this linguistic science and what is a linguist? A linguist is one whose special field of scholarship is linguistic science. Linguistic science is here understood to be a body of knowledge and understanding concerning the nature and functioning of human language, built up out of information about the structure, the operation, and the history of a wide range of very diverse human languages by means of those techniques and procedures that have proved most successful in establishing verifiable generalizations concerning relationships among linguistic phenomena.

In this much loaded and complicated definition there are five essential features that cannot be separated, for each succeeding feature is a qualifier of what has preceded. Perhaps the following arrangement of the parts of this definition may serve to give these important features their relative prominence.

Linguistic Science is

1. a body of knowledge and understanding

2. (knowledge and understanding) concerning the nature and functioning of human language

3. (this knowledge and understanding) built up out of information about the structure, the operation, and the history of a wide range of very diverse human languages

4. (this knowledge and understanding built up) by means of those techniques and procedures that have proved most successful in establishing verifiable generalizations

5. (verifiable generalizations) concerning relationships among linguistic phenomena.[3]

Every science has developed its own special techniques for investigation, analysis, and the testing of generalizations concerning the data it accumulates. Modern linguistic science began early in the nineteenth century with the use of sets of phonological correspondence as a means of exploring and proving genetic relationships between different languages. These techniques became more refined and more rigorously controlled after 1875. Later came the development of sound techniques for language history, for linguistic geography, for the analysis and description of unwritten language, for finding and checking the structurally significant contrasts that make the special signals of each different language. The validity of the basic approach to language through these techniques has been verified again and again, and the techniques themselves have been and are being constantly improved by rigorous experimentation and criticism. But the *heart and substance of linguistic science is not simply in the techniques of operation—not in the tools of linguistic analysis. The heart and substance of linguistic science is rather in the growing understanding of certain features of the nature and functioning of human language itself, that have become clear as the unexpected results of the use of these techniques and tools, in the study of a great variety of languages.*

Some of these results that constitute our present knowledge are the following.

1. It became clear that all the languages investigated were always, and had been always in a state of constant change. There has, for example, never been a time in English during the last thousand years when the recorded materials do not show evidence of change in progress—evidence of divided usage in some features of the language.

2. It became clear that these changes could not have been accidental and lawless corruptions arising from the ignorance of the speakers. These changes

[3] Only as the study of language turned away from introspection and chance observation to seek a broad informational basis of verifiable facts, and, away from the attempt to establish relationships between linguistic phenomena and such matters as race, climate, and nationality, to the effort to find verifiable relationships within the linguistic phenomena themselves, did that study begin to make real scientific progress.

have shown themselves to be astonishingly regular and systematic—large patterns of change that stretched over long periods of time.

It may be urged that change in language is due ultimately to the deviations of individuals from the rigid system. But it appears that even here individual deviations are ineffective; whole groups of speakers must, for some reason unknown to us, coincide in a deviation, if it is to result in a linguistic change. Change in language does not reflect individual variability, but seems to be a massive, uniform, and gradual alteration, at every moment of which the system is just as rigid as at any other time.[4]

The facts of language history destroyed the myth of a golden age of a language in perfection at some time in the past, a perfection from which it has deteriorated.

3. It became clear that the most stable features of a language were its sounds—not its vocabulary, not its grammar. Linguistic science in the first period of its modern development set up "laws" or generalizations of "sound change." These were generalizations concerning correspondences of "sound" features between several languages, or between different periods of a single language. They were correspondences that could be grasped in statements applicable to the whole body of the native words in the languages concerned. It was these correspondences of "sound" features that established a rigorous basis for the treatment of etymology.

4. It became clear that the only basis for "correctness" in a language had to be the usage of the native speakers of that language. Perhaps the best example of the gathering of the facts of usage is the *Oxford English Dictionary,* earlier named *A New English Dictionary on Historical Principles.*[5] Language history provided the evidence to identify new forms and older forms. The studies in linguistic geography showed the language characteristics of different language and dialect areas, and the centers of language dispersion. Together, linguistic history and linguistic geography led to a much clearer understanding of the significance of dialect differences in a language and of the basis for the special prestige through which one regional dialect out of many becomes the "standard" language.

5. It became clear that "standard" and "literary" languages are not the bases from which "dialects" diverge through mistakes, lawlessness, and in-

[4] Leonard Bloomfield, Review of Jespersen's *Philosophy of Grammar,* in *Journal of English and Germanic Philology,* Vol. 26, (1927) 444–446.

[5] "... It was proposed that materials should be collected for a Dictionary which, by the completeness of its vocabulary, and by the application of the historical method to the life and use of words, might be worthy of the English language and of English scholarship. With this view, it was resolved to begin at the beginning, and extract anew typical quotations for the use of words, from all the great English writers of all ages and from all the writers on special subjects whose works might illustrate the history of words employed in special senses, from all writers whatever before the 16th century, and from as many as possible of the more important writers of later times. ..." (*Oxford English Dictionary,* Vol. I [1888], p. v.)

complete learning. "Standard" language arises out of a "dialect." On the whole, the language forms of colonists tend to keep more of the older patterns than do the speakers who stay in the homeland. In similar fashion, the differing grammatical forms of the uneducated are often more conservative or older than those of the educated.

6. It became clear, from the more than seventy-five years of work upon the great historical dictionaries, that multiple meaning for words is normal, not "queer." We must everywhere in a language expect to find that the most frequently used words have a variety of meanings—not just one literal meaning and a few so-called "figurative" meanings. Words cover whole areas of meaning, and, except for highly technical words, there are no words in two languages that cover precisely the same areas. The number of different meanings for each of the commonly used words in English, as recorded and illustrated by verifiable quotations in *The Oxford Dictionary,* is just unbelievable.

7. It became clear, with the development of the work in phonetics, that all the "mysterious" qualities of the sounds and "accents" of human language are matters that can be analyzed and described in terms of the physical movements by which they are produced, and also in terms of the specific kinds of vibrations that make up their acoustic characteristics.[6] The increasing accuracy and completeness of the recording, reproduction, and transmission of vocal sounds grew out of the work of the phonetics laboratories. In other words, linguistic science, through the techniques of phonetics, has now successfully been able to isolate, describe, produce, and control mechanically a great many of the specific features that comprise the total complex of human speech sounds.

8. It has become clear, with the developments in linguistic science during the last forty years, that the habits that constitute the control of one's own native language are not habits concerning items of language as separate items—i.e. of separate segments of sound as represented by the letters of an alphabet or of individual grammatical forms. Practical language habits are always habits concerning contrastive shapes of linguistic items, in structural patterns, functioning in a system. No item has linguistic significance by itself. Its significance can arise only out of its contrast with other items in the structural patterns that function as signals in a particular language system. "Structural" linguistics has attempted to discover and describe

(a) the basic contrastive sound features that function in identifying or separating the various meaning units (morphemes or words) in a linguistic community—*pan* from *pen* and *pin* and *pun.*

[6] See Kenneth L. Pike, *Phonetics: A critical analysis of phonetic theory and a technic for the practical description of sound,* University of Michigan Publications in Language and Literature, XXI, (1943); and Martin Joos, *Acoustic Phonetics,* Linguistic Society of America, Language Monograph No. 23, (1948).

(b) the basic contrastive features that identify and separate the grammatical units that function in the patterns that signal structural meanings.

(c) the basic contrastive arrangements and forms of these functioning grammatical units that identify and separate the patterns that signal the structural meanings of a language.

It is assumed that all the significant materials that signal linguistic meanings are matters of contrast within a limited number of patterns.

9. It has become clear, then, that that which is objectively the same uttered sound will be perceived and responded to very differently, in accord with the specific patterns of the particular native language of the hearer. Or, in other words, the same phonetic differences may have (usually do have) entirely different structural values from language to language. In general, there are no language sounds that are easy or difficult in themselves. Ease or difficulty of pronunciation or of hearing turns out to be a function of the way the phonetic material patterns in a person's native language. Native speakers of English respond easily to the sound contrasts which distinguish *river* from *liver, pray* from *play, correction* from *collection, variable* from *valuable, storing* from *string.* Native speakers of Japanese, in the first stages of learning English, not only find it difficult to produce these significant differences consistently; they cannot hear them. The child in learning his native language must not only develop great facility and accuracy in responding to the limited number of contrastive physical features that identify the functioning units of the structural patterns of his particular language; he must learn to ignore all those physical features that are not relevant to those patterns. His great facility and accuracy in recognizing and producing the signalling patterns of his native language is thus bought at a price. He develops blind spots for a whole range of physical differences that form the signalling devices of other languages. Thus the power or force in the structural arrangements of the first language (our native language) makes the learning of a second language as an adult a very different matter from the learning of the first language.

Altogether a tremendous body of knowledge and understanding has been won by linguistic science during the last 140 years. In this cumulative body of basic knowledge concerning the nature and functioning of language there is much that ought to be of use in helping to deal with practical teaching problems that have not yet been satisfactorily analyzed. Considerable resistance to its use arises out of the fact that it contradicts many of the older views of language which are still vigorously maintained. But the path from the knowledge and understanding of the nature and functioning of human language to the using of this knowledge in dealing with the practical problems of teaching is a very thorny and difficult one, and we have made comparatively little real progress along that path. There exists a great gap between knowing and doing.

Linguistic science like all science is concerned with knowing and understanding, not with doing. As science, linguistics is not concerned with the teaching of English or of foreign language or of reading. In the other fields also, science, as science, does not concern itself with building better machines for transportation or for mass communication, nor with improving the food supply, nor with the curing of diseases. Of course the knowledge and understanding won by science in its various fields has been of the greatest use to man in his struggle to control the conditions of his living. Some scientists have at times helped to interpret the significance of the knowledge they have won and have often filled the double role of both scientist and engineer. But it is the function, not of the scientists but of our professions—the doctor, the teacher, the engineer—to take the knowledge and understanding that has been achieved by science and to explore its usefulness for man. We must not assume or expect that the scientists themselves can or should be able to lead the way in practical applications of the knowledge of their science, or even to take the responsibility for explaining its practical significance. The applications of scientific knowledge to the practical problems of invention, of construction, of disease, of learning and teaching, demand their own types of research and must be done by those who know and understand both the practical problems and the results of science.

Thus to insist upon the separation of science, as the search for knowledge and understanding, from the struggle to make full use of all that is known, is not to belittle the importance of either. In our modern society, however, technology, the application of science, "doing," receives much greater consideration than "mere knowing." We tend to measure the worth of what we know only in terms of doing, not in terms of understanding or intellectual freedom. And modern linguistic science is no exception. We must in some way learn to make this application.[7]

I shall not here enumerate all the obstacles that lie in the way. Let me just name one, in passing to something more important. There are the overly enthusiastic assertions of those with very little direct contact with the productions in linguistic science, who, in the manner of science fiction, imaginatively project the claims for linguistic science far beyond anything that science is at present able to deliver. This linguistic-science fiction helps to stimulate an even more extravagant anti-linguistic-science fiction from those in greater

[7] "The National Council of Teachers of English supports the scientific study of the English language, and, realizing the importance of the results of that study in freeing our teaching from wasteful and harmful practices, recommends that in the training of teachers, both prospective and in service, opportunities be provided to acquaint English teachers with the principles, methods, results, and applications of modern linguistic science. Furthermore, the National Council of Teachers of English believes that the schools should teach those forms of the English language which sound descriptive research has shown to be the practice of Standard English in the United States." *Resolution Passed by the National Council of Teachers of English* at the general business meeting November 22, 1951.

ignorance of the facts who have built up a hideous mask to hide the real face of the linguistic scientist. This anti-linguistic-science fiction is doing much to muddy the stream of discussion and thus to help keep away from the teachers the aid they need.[8] But there are those real leaders of the teaching profession who have patiently tried to understand the not always easy writing of the linguistic scholars and to find in it helpful materials to report and explain to class-room teachers.[9] These must form the nucleus of the group we need to undertake the cooperative task of using to the full the solid achievements of more than a century of lingustic research. For this cooperative effort we must have

(a) some of the producing scholars in the English language who are willing to struggle hard to understand the practical problems of the broad field of English teaching,

(b) some of the leaders of the teaching profession devoted to the task of understanding both the problems of English teaching and the contributions of linguists,

(c) some of the best class-room teachers who will try to understand the significance of the work of both the linguistic scholars and the professional leaders and then assume the chief burden of the task of putting the results of that work into specific materials for the guidance of text-book writers. This will be a long hard task but one worthy of a top level commission.

Such a group must have available for their work those who have achieved understanding and control of the tremendous body of material produced by a host of workers in the field of English language—from Old English to and including the descriptive analysis of present-day English. This material is not all easily available and nicely laid out. Great masses of it are in a form that needs to be reworked and restudied in the terms of our recent developments in "structural" linguistics.

Teachers can *not* be equipped to provide the "applications of linguistic science" to the problems of teaching English by taking "one or two courses in linguistics." It seems to have been assumed that everybody knew what subject-matter content any course of study labelled "linguistics" would include, and that any course with a "linguistics" label would provide the necessary enlightenment. As a matter of fact, however, "linguistics" covers a very wide range of material and one cannot predict even what an introductory course will stress. Very frequently, "training in linguistics" as recommended to language teachers has meant mastering only the tools, techniques and procedures of linguistic analysis. Many "introductory" courses are set up to offer what is thought to be the necessary first steps for those who aim to become practitioners in the analysis of an unknown language. Some "linguists" seem

[8] See *College English* for February, 1960.
[9] See W. W. Hatfield, "Will Structural Grammar Help?" in *College English*, Dec., 1958.

to believe, or they act as if they believed, that the tools, techniques, and classificatory definitions alone constituted the substance of the science of linguistics. I do not want to belittle the scientific importance of adequate tools, sound techniques, and sharp classifications. I should like, however, to insist that one can achieve a sufficient mastery of these tools and techniques of linguistic analysis without any real understanding of the significance of the achievements of linguistic science. Perhaps this is the reason that some of those teachers of English who have earnestly sought help in linguistic courses have come away greatly disappointed because they found nothing directly applicable to their needs.

The Conference of 1958, in the pamphlet *The Basic Issues in the Teaching of English* ("Issue" 13, p. 9), raises the question of the part linguistics should have in the teaching of English, in the following manner.

> Up to the present only a few textbooks have attempted *to adapt the approach of the structural linguists to use in the classroom.* Nevertheless, we must ask whether *this new method offers a clue to a better correlation of the knowledge of language structure with writing ability.* How much, if any, *of such linguistic knowledge is appropriate for each level?* How may readers best be trained *to develop this knowledge in their pupils?* [The italics are mine.]

This paragraph seems to suggest that "the approach of the structural linguist," his methods and techniques, might be adapted "to use in the classroom" as "a new method" for achieving "a better correlation of the knowledge of language structure with writing ability." It then raises the question of "how much, if any, of such knowledge" of language structure "is appropriate for each level," and how best to train teachers to pass on "this knowledge" to their pupils. I believe we need something quite different. In my view, it is *not the tools and the techniques of linguistic science* that should be brought into the classroom; but, in some way, *the substance of the knowledge and understanding won by linguistic science* must be *thoroughly assimilated* and *then used to shed new light upon the problems that arise wherever language is concerned.*

5

Comparing Traditional and Structural Grammar

SAMUEL R. LEVIN

IN THE LAST FEW DECADES, a significant change has developed in the attitudes of people interested in the study of language. This change results from a different way of looking at language—the structural way. In this paper, I should like to discuss what a comparison of traditional and structural grammar[1] reveals about their respective adequacies, specifically as each is applied to a description of English. I may say, at the outset, that in my opinion the traditional grammar often fails to satisfactorily explain the linguistic facts, whereas structural grammar does not fail in this way—precisely because it deals with them.

The differences between the traditional and the structural approaches to grammar are manifold. I think, however, that their fundamental difference emerges from the following statement—that structuralists, unlike traditionalists, are interested in making only what have been called "vulnerable" statements about grammar. It is primarily in this respect that structural linguistics has a right to be called a science. By "vulnerable" statements is meant simply statements whose claim to being true can be either verified or disproved. In order that statements may have this property of vulnerability, their terms and predicates must be open to everyone's inspection. This is a way of saying that structural statements are made only about observable, formal features of a language.

Traditional grammar does not so restrict itself. Its departures from the above principle may be grouped under several heads—what might be called fallacies. There is first the semantic fallacy. This is exhibited in statements

Reprinted by permission from *College English,* 21.260–65 (February, 1960). Professor Levin is a member of the Department of English, Hunter College.

[1] The term "grammar" has several senses; it can mean, among other things, the actual linguistic material which is under observation, or it can mean the body of statements made about the linguistic material. Cf. W. Nelson Francis, *The Structure of American English,* with a separate chapter on American dialects by Raven I. McDavid, Jr. (1958), pp. 222 ff. Here I use it in the latter sense, as referring to the respective ways in which traditional and structural grammarians describe the English language.

like "A noun is the name of a person, place, or thing," or "An interrogative sentence is one that asks a question." Such statements are unsatisfactory for several reasons. In the first place, items like *fire, happiness, charity* may be adduced forcing us to enlarge the definition of a noun so as to include notions like "process or activity," "state," "abstraction," and so on. This enlarging procedure can be further forced by adducing additional forms, to the point where the definition becomes so particular that it is no longer a general statement but merely a list. It would seem that when semantic statements have the generality that would justify making them as statements they must be inadequate, whereas if statements of such a type are made adequate, they are no longer general.

This lack of fit between grammatical statements couched in semantic terms and the linguistic facts that they presume to cover is not surprising, if we agree that the grammar of a language consists entirely of linguistic forms and their arrangements. Semantic statements are statements made about the relation between language and the world about us (including ourselves). This relation—what we generally call meaning—is certainly of great interest to us but, unfortunately, we cannot control the objects and events of the world in a manner that would be rigorous enough for their use in grammatical analysis.

This lack of control is essentially what we have in mind when we speak of the indeterminacy of meaning, and it points to another difficulty inherent in semantic statements. That is, it is impossible to be certain that what I mean by "person," "place," or "thing" is the same as what someone else means by these terms. Linguistic forms like *him, there, it* might thus qualify for me as nouns and not for someone else, and conversely. It is in this sense that semantic statements are not vulnerable. No satisfactory means can be devised to ascertain their truth or falsity.

The definition given above for an interrogative sentence is likewise fallacious. It presupposes the knowledge of what a question is. All semantic definitions or explanations have this circular property. They may serve as rough-and-ready aids, but they have no claim to being precise or, in fact, actually explaining anything. The same objection holds for the customary explanations of restrictive and non-restrictive clauses, of dependent and independent constructions, and so forth.

We may speak next of the logical fallacy. Under this head are comprehended all such statements about grammar as are made on the supposition that laws of logic govern the universe—with the corollary that language perfectly mirrors that universe. This fallacy, which is at least as old at Plato, looks for order in language corresponding to the putative order in the universe. If we say that English has three primary grammatical tenses, on the basis of the way we cut up the time continuum, we are committing this fallacy. English certainly expresses past, present, and future time, as well as various aspects of these times, but the manner by which future time is expressed in

English is not the same, grammatically, as the manner by which past and present time are expressed. We might just as well say that English has the dual number category, since we can say "I saw both of them."

If we say that the word *man* has masculine gender in English because it refers to a male being, we are committing this fallacy. The structuralist would say that *man* has masculine gender in English because it elicits *he* as its personal pronoun. We should notice that, although we can say also of *he* that it is masculine on logical grounds, we can say further that it belongs to a class of words which has a three-way formal division of a kind that the nominal class does not display.

Fallacious also are statements to the effect that double negatives are incorrect because two negatives make a positive; that sentences may not begin with *and* or *or* since these words logically indicate the conjunction and disjunction of sentences. This approach disallows, also on logical grounds, expressions like *rounder, more perfect, none are,* and so forth. I am not suggesting that all these illustrations of the logical fallacy lead to unacceptable conclusions. I am merely suggesting that the criterion used in judging these grammatical questions is inappropriate.

There is then the normative fallacy. Grammarians proceeding under this fallacy believe that it is possible and necessary to set up prescriptive norms for usage. Such grammarians purport to advance a model of correctness. If asked where the model comes from, they appeal to some earlier authority. Such appeals, if resolutely maintained, are of course invulnerable. The attempt to set up such norms is not of itself reprehensible, however. Under certain circumstances, primarily those embodied in the teaching situation, it is absolutely necessary to teach norms. To my mind, nothing is further from the truth than the common belief that orientation toward usage leads to grammatical anarchy. It is not at all necessary to condone all usage. In fact, teachers of English would be derelict to do so. But it is necessary to study usage in order to know what norms to prescribe. The fallacy of the prescriptivists consists in deriving their norms from sources, chiefly derivative handbooks, which often display little or no recognition of the actual state of the language for which they are making prescriptions. The perennial questions of *shall/will,* of ending sentences with prepositions, of the split infinitive, can all be resolved by observing how qualified users of the language actually handle these matters. I am not suggesting that this would be easy to accomplish. "Qualified users" must be defined, and their different functional varieties must be distinguished. But I think that only in this way—by a careful examination of what the linguistic facts are, not what we hope or imagine them to be—can we teach norms that will be at all realistic.

It would be possible to extend the discussion of these three fallacies; it would also be possible to add others, such as the fallacy represented by discussing the grammar of English on the basis of preconceptions derived from the grammar of another language (say Latin), or the fallacy represented by the misuse of historical considerations in discussing present-day English grammar, or the fallacy represented by extreme purism. I think, however, that what has already been said presents the major deficiences of the traditional approach to grammar.

It is not part of my intention here to dwell on the considerable virtues of traditional grammar. One thing should be mentioned, however. It would be a mistake to think that traditional grammarians paid no attention to formal features.[2] The expansion of the definition of a noun, mentioned earlier, so as to comprehend words like *fire, happiness, charity,* etc., is due to their recognition of the role that formal features play in grammar. That is, the traditionalists recognize certain features as being common to names of persons, places, and things and to words like *fire, happiness,* and *charity.* These are formal features. *Fire, happiness,* and *charity* occur as plurals, just as do the names of persons, places, and things; they co-occur in a restricted way with articles and possessive pronouns as do the names of persons, places, and things; they may occur in the possessive case; and so on. In short, the traditionalist is something of a structuralist himself.

The difference between the two, however, is more than one of mere degree. The structuralist has made a *total* commitment. He believes and proceeds on the assumption that the grammar of a language consists of the linguistic facts of that language and nothing else. This commitment entails a certain cost. Large areas that are customarily regarded as parts of the grammarian's domain are excluded or curtailed. Thus, considerations of meaning are restricted. It is incorrect, however, to think that structuralists are not interested in meaning. They are very much interested in it. It is only that they feel more or less unable to make statements about meaning, as that term is generally understood, of a kind that would satisfy them. They thus resort to things like "differential meaning" and "distributional meaning," not because they think that these types of meaning are more significant than what we may call "semantic meaning," but simply because their wish to make none but verifiable statements makes meaning of only the former types admissible.

Likewise in questions of correctness. These questions involve value judgments which the linguist, as structuralist, does not reckon himself qualified to make. This is not to say that he may not make them. Very few people are exclusively structuralists. They teach, for example. In this latter capacity, a structuralist may make decisions as to correctness but, while such decisions are made, in his case, on the basis of structural analysis, they are not in themselves structural statements. As structuralist he is also not interested

[2] One of the reasons for the continuing appeal and importance of men like Jespersen and Sweet, in addition to the fact that they were extremely learned and brilliant, is that they so clearly perceived the importance of formal features. One other virtue may be mentioned: the completeness of their coverage, particularly in the field of syntax.

in questions of rhetoric, philology, or style, although in his capacity as teacher, scholar, or writer he very well may be.

Such stringent delimitation of the structuralist's area of interest would seem misguided or perverse if there were not compensations. I think, however, that there are. By focusing exclusively on the structure of the language, the structuralist has discovered more and more of the features that play significant roles in the function of the language, namely those features that signal meaning differences, these being the most important features in any language. The fact that *pit* and *bit* mean two different things in English causes the structuralist to look for the formal correlates of this meaning difference. He thus analyzes two bilabial plosive sounds, voiceless and voiced respectively, which have the potential function of distinguishing, by themselves, a meaning contrast in English. Such sounds are phonemic in status. The meaning differences between *differ* and *defér, grêen hóuse* and *gréen-hòuse* cause him to analyze different stresses as being phonemic in status. Comparable examples could be adduced which have led to the analysis of pitch and pause features as phonemic.

In all these operations we have not said what the words in question mean. We have asked only whether the pairs tested mean the same or different things. Meaning is thus used only as a kind of litmus paper check.[3] If a meaning difference exists between two forms, then the structuralist looks for the structural correlates of that difference.

Of course, the structuralist proceeds on the assumption that all meaning differences produced in the language will *have* structural correlates. This may or may not be true in fact.[4] I believe, however, that the structuralist must proceed as if his assumption were, in fact, true.

The history of comparative linguistics provides us with an interesting analogue to this assumption of the structuralists. Among some German comparativists of the late nineteenth century, the so-called *Junggrammatiker,* there developed the notion that sound-laws admit of no exception; i.e., if a sound-change took place which shifted the quality of a vowel sound or a consonant sound, that shift took place wherever the vowel or consonant in question occurred. Some notion of regularity in sound-change was inescapable when one examined correspondences between related languages or between two stages of the same language. Bitter differences of opinion developed in the 1870's and 1880's, however, between those scholars who believed that sound-laws admitted of no exceptions and those scholars who,

---

[3] This figure is used by Francis, *Structure of American English,* p. 229.

[4] Idiomatic meanings, such as that of "He went west," compared with the non-idiomatic meaning of the same expression, pose a problem here. Some of the meanings obtained from a reading of poetry might also be offered by way of contradicting our assertion. There is no denying that these questions, and others like them, represent troublesome problems, nor is it possible to predict whether such problems will eventually yield to more refined linguistic techniques.

agreeing that there was some degree of consistency between correspondences, would not agree that the operation of sound-laws worked according to inexorable laws. These latter scholars saw too many apparent exceptions to the regularity of sound-change. Seeing these exceptions, they argued that the law of regular sound-change must be abandoned.

The *Junggrammatiker,* however, on seeing the apparent exceptions, felt only that the statements regarding the conditions under which a sound-change took place might have to be modified. The interesting thing is that by adhering to the principle, they were able to reveal more and more of the structure of languages. A classic instance vindicating this approach is the so-called Verner's Law. Faced with the fact that the correspondences between Indo-European and Germanic consonants described by Rask and Grimm held in most cases but not in all, some scholars maintained that this fact invalidated the notion of regularity in sound-change. Verner, however, proceeding on the assumption that sound-laws admit of no exception, was able to find the structural conditions under which the variants subsumed by his law occurred. Grimm's Law was thus preserved, with an amendment. That is the typical procedure: when "aberrant" forms occur, they can be comprehended under the sound-law if the particular environments in which they occur are consistently different from the environments in which the change is regular. In this sense, all such changes are regular.

The question of whether sound-laws do or do not admit of exceptions is still a live one. It seems to me, however, that rigorous work in comparative and historical linguistics can only be carried out on the assumption that they do not. The alternative is to admit all kinds of unsystematic, ad hoc explanations of what takes place in the historical development of languages. By the same token I believe that we must commit ourselves to the proposition that the mechanism whereby a language works may be explained entirely in terms of its structural elements. This structural approach has already led to the discovery of the phoneme as the minimal linguistic unit capable of signaling differences in meaning, of the morpheme as the minimal linguistic unit having meaning, of the role that features of stress, pitch, and pause play in communication, and many more things. It has by no means discovered all that structure has to yield, nor has it succeeded in describing precisely all of the features that it has discovered, but I believe that significant further progress in understanding grammar can only come along structural lines.

I would like now to sketch one or two procedures of structural grammar and suggest the ways in which these are superior to the procedures of the traditional grammarians. Let us consider the noun as a part of speech. We will assume that we don't know what a noun is, but we know what a word is. We find, in analyzing the structure of English, that a certain group of words behave in a markedly consistent way. By "behave" here, I am referring to the way in which these words combine and concatenate with other linguistic forms, or to those features that we generally have in mind when we speak of morphology and syntax. That is, of all the structural environments in which a word may find itself in English, this group is found always in only a limited portion of those environments. We find that this group of words may occur with the plural suffix and with the possessive suffix; we find that they co-occur in a restricted way with articles and with possessive pronouns; we find that they pattern with prepositions, occur in certain relations to verbs; and so on. We observe further that only these certain words, from among the total number in English, enjoy precisely these privileges of grammatical domain. We decide that we have here a class of English words, defined as belonging to this class because they have similarities in common which are not shared by any other English words.

It will be noticed that we have used terms like "preposition," "article," "verb," in the analysis of this English word class, and there may be a question as to where these terms came from. Using these terms is merely a short-hand way of discussing the procedure; we could simply make lists of the environing forms and use those lists in describing the patterning habits of the word class we are diagnosing, but since we know something of the structure of English before we begin analysis, such a short-cut, carefully followed, will not lead us astray. When we have isolated this particular class of English words, there is no reason why we should not call them nouns. What we call them is unimportant; the important thing is the way we have defined them. We have defined them in a way that makes it possible for anyone knowing the definition to determine whether any given word in English is a noun or not. Perhaps this last claim is too strong on the basis only of the sketchy way in which the procedure has been described, but if the analysis is exact enough, the claim is valid.

The fact that we can call this class of words nouns without causing too much confusion is interesting. It suggests that there is not too great a difference between the results of traditional and structural analysis. This is, in fact, the case. The rival analyses coincide over, at a guess, 95 percent of the linguistic facts. Our problems, however, are precisely in this marginal area, and now in this marginal area we will not need to attempt determinations on the basis of finer and finer semantic distinctions; we will have our objective criteria ready to hand.

Another illustration of the different procedures and results of traditional and structural grammar may be seen in comparing their respective definitions of the interrogative sentence. The traditional definition, as I have tried to show, is clearly inadequate. We instead try to find out what are the structural features that correlate with a particular type of response—one that we customarily associate with questions.[5] This response is usually the giving of information by reply. We find that these structural features are essentially of three types: when words like *who, what, where, why,* and *how* begin certain sentences; when a particular collocation of verb and subject occur; and when, in the absence or presence of either of these other two features, a particular pitch contour is on the sentence. That is, these three types of grammatical arrangement signal questions in English: "Who are you?" "Are you coming?" and "You're coming?" It will come as no surprise to anyone to learn that these three utterances are questions in English, but again it should be noted that our definition of these three utterances as question sentences depends on nothing but observable, hence verifiable, linguistic facts.

Further examples of the foregoing type could be added. What they will all have in common, if they are based on structural facts, is that their statements of definition or explanation will be expressed in terms that anyone can test for himself. It is this fact which essentially constitutes the great superiority of structural over traditional grammar.

---

[5] It may be objected here that "questions" are what we are trying to define and that, therefore, we are not entitled to use the notion in our definition. This again is merely a short-cut; we could avoid this circularity by listing the types of responses, and say that the unlabeled linguistic forms (described in what follows) correlate with the types of behavior contained in the list. On noticing the consistent and restricted correspondence between the forms and the responses, however, there is no reason why we cannot then call the linguistic forms question or interrogative sentences. "Question" is then not part of the definition, but merely a classificatory index.

Part II

ENGLISH LINGUISTICS TODAY

INTRODUCTION

PART II MAY WELL BE THOUGHT OF as the heart of this book. Although since the preparation of the First Edition at least three important college textbooks in structural English linguistics have appeared, those by Francis, Hill, and Sledd, it has remained important to offer several articles further explicating various aspects and details of what earlier I called Grammar C. These articles constitute the first section of this Part. Then, beginning with the articles by Lees, there is the second section dealing with that revolutionary and controversial newcomer to the linguistic scene, transformation grammar, what may be called Grammar D.

Strictly speaking, the first article in Part II, that by the late Benjamin Lee Whorf, is not directed at English language study, but Whorf's daring and controversial theories of language and nonlanguage cultural relationships have affected English linguistic research and provide here the basis for an immediate realization that a descriptive statement about one language is unlikely to be equally true of another. The structure of English is not the structure of Latin, or of French or of German.

Francis specifically applies this truth in his useful introduction to English structural grammar derived from one of the two seminal books in English linguistics, Charles C. Fries's *The Structure of English* (Harcourt, Brace, 1952). The second seminal work, *An Outline of English Structure* by George L. Trager and Henry Lee Smith, Jr. (Battenberg Press, 1951), then provides material for the two clarifying articles by Faust. The latter's explication abundantly demonstrates the linguist's need for at least a few new terms to name new ideas and new concepts.

Fries meets directly the several misapprehensions concerning the attitude of the linguistic scholar toward word meaning. His insistence that the linguist must begin his analysis with the formal and structural features of the language and only later proceed to study relationship to function and to meaning is generally accepted by American linguists, but among them there is some disagreement as to the manner and extent in which meaning may be involved. Stageberg offers a number of cases of ambiguous meaning to be found in current English and, at least by implication, suggests that structural analysis is inadequate to deal with such cases. Marchand next seeks a procedure for identification of lexical compounds through the formal criterion of stress but finds himself forced to accord some weight to functional and notional meaning as well. Marchand's thesis has been expanded by Anne Granville Hatcher in "An Introduction to the Analysis of English Noun Compounds," *Word,* 16.356–373 (December, 1960). Another correlation between formal feature and lexical meaning appears in Taha's study of that rapidly multiplying phenomenon, the verb-adverb combination functioning as a single grammatical and semantic unit. Such a study may well suggest to the teacher and student other areas of investigation for short or long projects. The teacher will find many reports of studies of specific linguistic features, of course, in such journals as *Language, Word, Studies in Linguistics,* and *American Speech.*

Just at the time the First Edition of these Readings was being readied for the printer there was quietly published in Holland a little book, *Syntactic Structures,* by Noam Chomsky of the Massachusetts Institute of Technology (Mouton, The Hague, 1957). Its inconspicuous launching gave no sign of the impact it would have and the arguments it would raise. Chomsky, turning away from descriptive analysis, especially in terms of immediate constituents, and treating phonemics only marginally, focused his attention upon devising a series of steps by which all "grammatical" sentences of the language are developed from a few basic or kernel sentences.

Paul Roberts, who already had pioneered in applying structural principles in a secondary textbook (*Patterns of English,* Harcourt, Brace, 1956), felt that Chomsky's "transformation" grammar answered questions which had been left unanswered by earlier analysis. He accordingly sought to apply transformation principles in another secondary text (*English Sentences,* Harcourt, Brace, 1962). In the meantime transformation grammar drew the attention of other text writers and project researchers, and it became the object of study in summer workshops and regular classes in the English language. So provocative has been Chomsky's theory that even though it is still highly controversial the noticeable trend in linguistic criticism is toward recognition of transformationalism as a reorienting force with permanent influence.

Because Chomsky's theory offers difficulties to the beginner, the reader of this book may wish to be introduced to it through the article by Owen Thomas in Part V. A clear and more detailed explication is Chapter 12 of H. A. Gleason: *An Introductory Course in Linguistics* (revised edition), Holt, Rinehart, and Winston, 1961.

In this Part Lees begins the section on transformation grammar by pointing to areas of inadequacy in the structural analysis presented in 1952 by Fries. In his second article Lees goes on to show what are the essential and supposedly superior features of transformation grammar. A third article by Lees, which had to be excluded from the Readings because of its length, is well worth reading also: "A Multiply Ambiguous Adjectival Construction in English," *Language,* 36.207–221 (April–June, 1960), as is his longer work, *The Grammar of English Nominalizations* (Indiana University Research Center in Anthropology, Folklore, and Linguistics, 1960). The Chomsky view that structural grammar fails to provide an adequate analysis is found again in Norman's article, in which the latter draws upon transformation theory in altering the classification of English nominals.

Essential in Chomsky's grammar is the concept of "grammaticalness" or "grammaticality." Although probably not intended itself as a point of controversy, this concept has been challenged in various ways by both sympathetic and skeptical critics, whether because of fundamental disagreement or because of misunderstanding. Hill here gives one cogent objection to this concept as it seems to him described in *Syntactic Structures.* Chomsky, in turn, denies Hill's interpretation and offers additional explication to meet various other adverse criticisms. The section ends with Stockwell's description of one feature of the final step in Chomsky's series of transformations, that by which the complete spoken utterance is derived by a transformation rule from the ultimate written form.

To the user of this book, it seems to me, what is stimulating, even exciting, about the work of Noam Chomsky is not so much in its specifics as in the indubitable evidence it provides that the study of language is tremendously dynamic. Constantly the student and the teacher are challenged to keep abreast of new thinking and new facts in linguistic thinking and in the applications to the study of English. No student of the language can fairly consider himself adequately prepared if his thinking about English is still in terms of 1900, or 1930, or even of 1950.

6

Science and Linguistics

NOTIONS ABOUT TALKING AND THINKING, WHICH COMPOSE A
SYSTEM OF NATURAL LOGIC, GO WRONG IN TWO WAYS;
HOW WORDS AND CUSTOMS AFFECT REASONING

BENJAMIN LEE WHORF

EVERY NORMAL PERSON in the world, past infancy in years, can and does
talk. By virtue of that fact, every person—civilized or uncivilized—carries
through life certain naive but deeply rooted ideas about talking and its
relation to thinking. Because of their firm connection with speech habits
that have become unconscious and automatic, these notions tend to be
rather intolerant of opposition. They are by no means entirely personal and
haphazard; their basis is definitely systematic, so that we are justified in
calling them a system of natural logic—a term that seems to me preferable
to the term common sense, often used for the same thing.

According to natural logic, the fact that every person has talked fluently
since infancy makes every man his own authority on the process by which
he formulates and communicates. He has merely to consult a common substratum of logic or reason which he and everyone else are supposed to
possess. Natural logic says that talking is merely an incidental process concerned strictly with communication, not with formulation of ideas. Talking,
or the use of language, is supposed only to "express" what is essentially already formulated nonlinguistically. Formulation is an independent process,
called thought or thinking, and is supposed to be largely indifferent to the
nature of particular languages. Languages have grammars, which are assumed to be merely norms of conventional and social correctness, but the
use of language is supposed to be guided not so much by them as by correct, rational, or intelligent *thinking*.

Thought, in this view, does not depend on grammar but on laws of logic
or reason which are supposed to be the same for all observers of the uni-

First published in *The Technology Review*, 42.229–231, 247–248 (April, 1940),
this article is here reprinted by permission from a collection of Whorf's writings titled
Language, Thought, and Reality (copyright © 1956 by Massachusetts Institute of
Technology Press).

verse—to represent a rationale in the universe that can be "found" independently by all intelligent observers, whether they speak Chinese or Choctaw. In our own culture, the formulations of mathematics and of formal logic have acquired the reputation of dealing with this order of things, i.e., with the realm and laws of pure thought. Natural logic holds that different languages are essentially parallel methods for expressing this one-and-the-same rationale of thought and, hence, differ really in but minor ways which may seem important only because they are seen at close range. It holds that mathematics, symbolic logic, philosophy, and so on, are systems contrasted with language which deal directly with this realm of thought, not that they are themselves specialized extensions of language. The attitude of natural logic is well shown in an old quip about a German grammarian who devoted his whole life to the study of the dative case. From the point of view of natural logic, the dative case and grammar in general are an extremely minor issue. A different attitude is said to have been held by the ancient Arabians: Two princes, so the story goes, quarreled over the honor of putting on the shoes of the most learned grammarian of the realm; whereupon their father, the caliph, is said to have remarked that it was the glory of his kingdom that great grammarians were honored even above kings.

The familiar saying that the exception proves the rule contains a good deal of wisdom, though from the standpoint of formal logic it became an absurdity as soon as "prove" no longer meant "put on trial." The old saw began to be profound psychology from the time it ceased to have standing in logic. What it might well suggest to us today is that if a rule has absolutely no exceptions, it is not recognized as a rule or as anything else; it is then part of the background of experience of which we tend to remain unconscious. Never having experienced anything in contrast to it, we cannot isolate it and formulate it as a rule until we so enlarge our experiences and expand our base of reference that we encounter an interruption of its regularity. The situation is somewhat analogous to that of not missing the water till the well runs dry, or not realizing that we need air till we are choking.

For instance, if a race of people had the physiological defect of being able to see only the color blue, they would hardly be able to formulate the rule that they saw only blue. The term blue would convey no meaning to them, their language would lack color terms, and their words denoting their various sensations of blue would answer to, and translate, our words light, dark, white, black, and so on, not our word blue. In order to formulate the rule or norm of seeing only blue, they would need exceptional moments in which they saw other colors. The phenomenon of gravitation forms a rule without exceptions; needless to say, the untutored person is utterly unaware of any law of gravitation, for it would never enter his head to conceive of a universe in which bodies behaved otherwise than they do at the earth's surface. Like the color blue with our hypothetical race, the law of gravitation is a part of the untutored individual's background, not something he isolates from that background. The law could not be formulated until bodies that always fell were seen in terms of a wider astronomical world in which bodies moved in orbits or went this way and that.

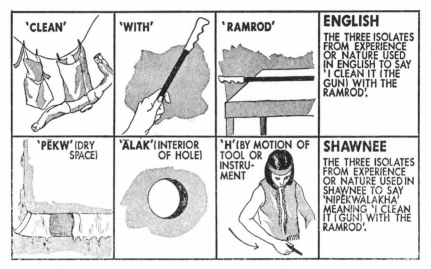

Fig. 1. Languages dissect nature differently. The different isolates of meaning (thoughts) used by English and Shawnee in reporting the same experience, that of cleaning a gun by running the ramrod through it. The pronouns "I" and "it" are not shown by symbols, as they have the same meaning in each case. In Shawnee "ni-" equals "I"; "-a" equals "it."

Similarly, whenever we turn our heads, the image of the scene passes across our retinas exactly as it would if the scene turned around us. But this effect is background, and we do not recognize it; we do not see a room turn around us but are conscious only of having turned our heads in a stationary room. If we observe critically while turning the head or eyes quickly, we shall see, no motion it is true, yet a blurring of the scene between two clear views. Normally we are quite unconscious of this continual blurring but seem to be looking about in an unblurred world. Whenever we walk past a tree or house, its image on the retina changes just as if the tree or house were turning on an axis; yet we do not see trees or houses turn as we travel about at ordinary speeds. Sometimes ill-fitting glasses will reveal queer movements in the scene as we look about, but normally we do not see the relative motion of the environment when we move; our psychic make-up is somehow adjusted to disregard whole realms of phenomena that are so all-pervasive as to be irrelevant to our daily lives and needs.

Natural logic contains two fallacies: First, it does not see that the phenomena of a language are to its own speakers largely of a background character and so are outside the critical consciousness and control of the speaker who is expounding natural logic. Hence, when anyone, as a natural logician, is talking about reason, logic, and the laws of correct thinking, he is apt to be simply marching in step with purely grammatical facts that have somewhat of a background character in his own language or family of languages but are by no means universal in all languages and in no sense a common substratum of reason. Second, natural logic confuses agreement about subject matter, attained through use of language, with knowledge of the linguistic process by which agreement is attained, i.e., with the province of the despised (and to its notion superfluous) grammarian. Two fluent speakers, of English let us say, quickly reach a point of assent about the subject matter of this speech; they agree about what their language refers to. One of them, A, can give directions that will be carried out by the other, B, to A's complete satisfaction. Because they thus understand each other so perfectly, A and B, as natural logicians, suppose they must of course know how it is all done. They think, e.g., that it is simply a matter of choosing words to express thoughts. If you ask A to explain how he got B's agreement so readily, he will simply repeat to you, with more or less elaboration or abbreviation, what he said to B. He has no notion of the process involved. The amazingly complex system of linguistic patterns and classifications which A and B must have in common before they can adjust to each other at all, is all background to A and B.

These background phenomena are the province of the grammarian—or of the linguist, to give him his more modern name as a scientist. The word linguist in common, and especially newspaper, parlance means something entirely different, namely, a person who can quickly attain agreement about subject matter with different people speaking a number of different languages. Such a person is better termed a polyglot or a multilingual. Scientific linguists have long understood that ability to speak a language fluently does not necessarily confer a linguistic knowledge of it, i.e., understanding of its background phenomena and its systematic processes and structure, any more than ability to play a good game of billiards confers or requires any knowledge of the laws of mechanics that operate upon the billiard table.

The situation here is not unlike that in any other field of science. All real scientists have their eyes primarily on background phenomena that cut very little ice, as such, in our daily lives; and yet their studies have a way of bringing out a close relation between these unsuspected realms of fact and such decidedly foreground activities as transporting goods, preparing food, treating the sick, or growing potatoes, which in time may become very much modified simply because of pure scientific investigation in no way concerned with these brute matters themselves. Linguistics is in quite similar case; the background phenomena with which it deals are involved in all our foreground activities of talking and of reaching agreement, in all reasoning and arguing of cases, in all law, arbitration, conciliation, contracts, treaties, public opinion, weighing of scientific theories, formulation of scientific results. Whenever agreement or assent is arrived at in human affairs, and whether or not mathematics or other specialized symbolisms are made part of the procedure, *this agreement is reached by linguistic processes, or else it is not reached.*

As we have seen, an overt knowledge of the linguistic processes by which agreement is attained is not necessary to reaching some sort of agreement, but it is certainly no bar thereto; the more complicated and difficult the matter, the more such knowledge is a distinct aid, till the point may be reached—I suspect the modern world has about arrived at it—when the knowledge becomes not only an aid but a necessity. The situation may be likened to that of navigation. Every boat that sails is in the lap of planetary forces; yet a boy can pilot his small craft around a harbor without benefit of geography, astronomy, mathematics, or international politics. To the captain of an ocean liner, however, some knowledge of all these subjects is essential.

When linguists became able to examine critically and scientifically a large number of languages of widely different patterns, their base of reference was expanded; they experienced an interruption of phenomena hitherto held universal, and a whole new order of significances came into their ken. It was found that the background linguistic system (in other words, the grammar) of each language is not merely a reproducing instrument for voicing ideas but rather is itself the shaper of ideas, the program and guide for the individual's mental activity, for his analysis of impressions, for his synthesis of his mental stock in trade. Formulation of ideas is not an independent process, strictly rational in the old sense, but is part of a particular grammar and differs, from slightly to greatly, as between different grammars. We dissect nature along lines laid down by our native languages. The categories and types that we isolate from the world of phenomena we do not find there because they stare every observer in the face; on the contrary, the world is presented in a kaleidoscopic flux of impressions which has to be organized by our minds—and this means largely by the linguistic systems in our minds. We cut nature up, organize it into concepts, and ascribe significances as we do, largely because we are parties to an agreement to organize it in this way —an agreement that holds throughout our speech community and is codified in the patterns of our language. The agreement is, of course, an implicit and unstated one, *but its terms are absolutely obligatory;* we cannot talk at all except by subscribing to the organization and classification of data which the agreement decrees.

This fact is very significant for modern science, for it means that no individual is free to describe nature with absolute impartiality but is con-

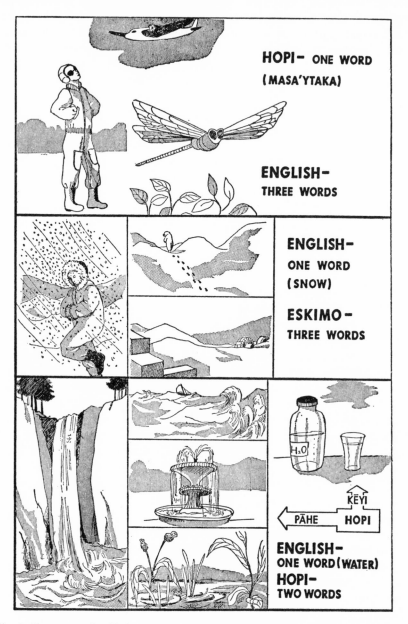

Fig. 2. Languages classify items of experience differently. The class corresponding to one word and one thought in language A may be regarded by language B as two or more classes corresponding to two or more words and thoughts.

strained to certain modes of interpretation even while he thinks himself most free. The person most nearly free in such respects would be a linguist familiar with very many widely different linguistic systems. As yet no linguist even is in any such position. We are thus introduced to a new principle of relativity, which holds that all observers are not led by the same physical evidence to the same picture of the universe, unless their linguistic backgrounds are similar, or can in some way be calibrated.

This rather startling conclusion is not so apparent if we compare only our modern European languages, with perhaps Latin and Greek thrown in for good measure. Among these tongues there is a unanimity of major pattern which at first seems to bear out natural logic. But this unanimity exists only because these tongues are all Indo-European dialects cut to the same basic plan, being historically transmitted from what was long ago one speech community; because the modern dialects have long shared in building up a common culture; and because much of this culture, on the more intellectual side, is derived from the linguistic backgrounds of Latin and Greek. Thus this group of languages satisfies the special case of the clause beginning "unless" in the statement of the linguistic relativity principle at the end of the preceding paragraph. From this condition follows the unanimity of description of the world in the community of modern scientists. But it must be emphasized that "all modern Indo-European-speaking observers" is not the same thing as "all observers." That modern Chinese or Turkish scientists describe the world in the same terms as Western scientists means, of course, only that they have taken over bodily the entire Western system of rationalizations, not that they have corroborated that system from their native posts of observation.

When Semitic, Chinese, Tibetan, or African languages are contrasted with our own, the divergence in analysis of the world becomes more apparent; and when we bring in the native languages of the Americas, where speech communities for many millenniums have gone their ways independently of each other and of the Old World, the fact that languages dissect nature in many different ways becomes patent. The relativity of all conceptual systems, ours included, and their dependence upon language stand revealed. That American Indians speaking only their native tongues are never called upon to act as scientific observers is in no wise to the point. To exclude the evidence which their languages offer as to what the human mind can do is like expecting botanists to study nothing but food plants and hothouse roses and then tell us what the plant world is like!

Let us consider a few examples. In English we divide most of our words into two classes, which have different grammatical and logical properties. Class I we call nouns, e.g., "house," "man"; Class 2, verbs, e.g., "hit," "run." Many words of one class can act secondarily as of the other class, e.g., "a hit," "a run," or "to man" the boat, but on the primary level the division between the classes is absolute. Our language thus gives us a bipolar division of nature. But nature herself is not thus polarized. If it be said that strike, turn, run, are verbs because they denote temporary or short-lasting events, i.e., actions, why then is fist a noun? It also is a temporary event. Why are lightning, spark, wave, eddy, pulsation, flame, storm, phase, cycle, spasm, noise, emotion, nouns? They are temporary events. If man and house are nouns because they are long-lasting and stable events, i.e., things, what then are keep, adhere, extend, project, continue, persist, grow, dwell, and so on, doing among the verbs? If it be objected that possess, adhere, are verbs because they are stable relationships rather than stable percepts, why then should equilibrium, pressure, current, peace, group, nation, society, tribe, sister, or any kinship term, be among the nouns? It will be found that an "event" to *us* means "what our language classes as a verb" or something analogized therefrom. And it will be found that it is not possible to define event, thing, object, relationship, and so on, from nature, but that to define them always involves a circuitous return to the grammatical categories of the definer's language.

In the Hopi language, lightning, wave, flame, meteor, puff of smoke, pulsation, are verbs—events of necessarily brief duration cannot be anything but verbs. Cloud and storm are at about the lower limit of duration for nouns. Hopi, you see, actually has a classification of events (or linguistic isoiates) by duration type, something strange to our modes of thought. On the other hand, in Nootka, a language of Vancouver Island, all words seem to us to be verbs, but really there are no Classes 1 and 2; we have, as it were, a monistic view of nature that gives us only one class of word for all kinds of events. "A house occurs" or "it houses" is the way of saying "house," exactly like "a flame occurs" or "it burns." These terms seem to us like verbs because they are inflected for durational and temporal nuances, so that the suffixes of the word for house event make it mean long-lasting house, temporary house, future house, house that used to be, what started out to be a house, and so on.

Hopi has a noun that covers every thing or being that flies, with the exception of birds, which class is denoted by another noun. The former noun may be said to denote the class (FC–B)—flying class minus bird. The Hopi actually call insect, airplane, and aviator all by the same word, and feel no difficulty about it. The situation, of course, decides any possible confusion among very disparate members of a broad linguistic class, such as this class (FC–B). This class seems to us too large and inclusive, but so would our class "snow" to an Eskimo. We have the same word for falling snow, snow on the ground, snow packed hard like ice, slushy snow, wind-driven flying snow—whatever the situation may be. To an Eskimo, this all-inclusive word would be almost unthinkable; he would say that falling snow, slushy snow, and so on, are sensuously and operationally different, different things to contend with; he uses different words for them and for other kinds of snow. The Aztecs go even farther than we in the opposite direction, with cold, ice, and snow all represented by the same basic word with different terminations; ice is the noun form; cold, the adjectival form; and for snow, "ice mist."

What surprises most is to find that various grand generalizations of the Western world, such as time, velocity, and matter, are not essential to the construction of a consistent picture of the universe. The psychic experiences that we class under these headings are, of course, not destroyed; rather, categories derived from other kinds of experiences take over the rulership of the cosmology and seem to function just as well. Hopi may be called a timeless language. It recognizes psychological time, which is much like Bergson's "duration," but this "time" is quite unlike the mathematical time, T, used by our physicists. Among the peculiar properties of Hopi time are that it varies with each observer, does not permit of simultaneity, and has zero dimensions, i.e., it cannot be given a number greater than one. The Hopi do not say, "I stayed five days," but "I left on the fifth day." A word referring to this kind of time, like the word day, can have no plural. The puzzle picture in Figure 3 will give mental exercise to anyone who would like to figure out how the Hopi verb gets along without tenses. Actually, the only practical use of our tenses, in one-verb sentences, is to distinguish among five typical situations, which are symbolized in the picture. The timeless Hopi verb does not distinguish between the present, past, and future of the event itself but must always indicate what type of validity the *speaker* intends the statement to have: (a) report of an event (situations 1, 2, 3 in the picture); (b) expectation of an event (situation 4); (c) generalization or law about events (situation 5). Situation 1, where the speaker and listener are in contact with the same objective field, is divided by our language into the two conditions, 1a and 1b, which it calls present and past, respectively. This division is unnecessary for a language which assures one that the statement is a report.

Hopi grammar, by means of its forms called aspects and modes, also makes it easy to distinguish between momentary, continued, and repeated occurrences, and to indicate the actual sequence of reported events. Thus the universe can be described without recourse to a concept of dimensional time. How would a physics constructed along these lines work, with no T (time) in its equations? Perfectly, as far as I can see, though of course it would require different ideology and perhaps different mathematics. Of course V (velocity) would have to go too. The Hopi language has no word really equivalent to our "speed" or "rapid." What translates these terms is usually a word meaning intense or very, accompanying any verb of motion. Here is a clew to the nature of our new physics. We may have to introduce a new term I, intensity. Every thing and event will have an I, whether we regard the thing or event as moving or as just enduring or being. Perhaps the

OBJECTIVE FIELD	SPEAKER (SENDER)	HEARER (RECEIVER)	HANDLING OF TOPIC RUNNING OF THIRD PERSON
SITUATION 1a			ENGLISH–"HE IS RUNNING" HOPI– "WARI" (RUNNING, STATEMENT OF FACT)
SITUATION 1b OBJECTIVE FIELD BLANK DEVOID OF RUNNING			ENGLISH–"HE RAN" HOPI–"WARI" (RUNNING, STATEMENT OF FACT)
SITUATION 2			ENGLISH–"HE IS RUNNING" HOPI–"WARI" (RUNNING, STATEMENT OF FACT)
SITUATION 3 OBJECTIVE FIELD BLANK			ENGLISH–"HE RAN" HOPI–"ERA WARI" (RUNNING, STATEMENT OF FACT FROM MEMORY
SITUATION 4 OBJECTIVE FIELD BLANK			ENGLISH–"HE WILL RUN" HOPI–"WARIKNI" (RUNNING, STATEMENT OF EX-PECTATION)
SITUATION 5 OBJECTIVE FIELD BLANK			ENGLISH–"HE RUNS" (E.G. ON THE TRACK TEAM) HOPI–"WARIKNGWE" (RUN-NING, STATEMENT OF LAW)

Fig. 3. Contrast between a "temporal" language (English) and a "timeless" language (Hopi). What are to English differences of time are to Hopi differences in the kind of validity.

I of an electric charge will turn out to be its voltage, or potential. We shall use clocks to measure some intensities, or, rather, some *relative* intensities, for the absolute intensity of anything will be meaningless. Our old friend acceleration will still be there but doubtless under a new name. We shall perhaps call it *V,* meaning not velocity but variation. Perhaps all growths and accumulations will be regarded as *V*'s. We should not have the concept of rate in the temporal sense, since, like velocity, rate introduces a mathematical and linguistic time. Of course we know that all measurements are ratios, but the measurements of intensities made by comparison with the standard intensity of a clock or a planet we do not treat as ratios, any more than we so treat a distance made by comparison with a yardstick.

A scientist from another culture that used time and velocity would have great difficulty in getting us to understand these concepts. We should talk about the intensity of a chemical reaction; he would speak of its velocity or its rate, which words we should at first think were simply words for intensity in his language. Likewise, he at first would think that intensity was simply our own word for velocity. At first we should agree, later we should begin to disagree, and it might dawn upon both sides that different systems of rationalization were being used. He would find it very hard to make us understand what he really meant by velocity of a chemical reaction. We should have no words that would fit. He would try to explain it by likening it to a running horse, to the difference between a good horse and a lazy horse. We should try to show him, with a superior laugh, that his analogy also was a matter of different intensities, aside from which there was little similarity between a horse and a chemical reaction in a beaker. We should point out that a running horse is moving relative to the ground, whereas the material in the beaker is at rest.

One significant contribution to science from the linguistic point of view may be the greater development of our sense of perspective. We shall no longer be able to see a few recent dialects of the Indo-European family, and the rationalizing techniques elaborated from their patterns, as the apex of the evolution of the human mind; nor their present wide spread as due to any survival from fitness or to anything but a few events of history—events that could be called fortunate only from the parochial point of view of the favored parties. They, and our own thought processes with them, can no longer be envisioned as spanning the gamut of reason and knowledge but only as one constellation in a galactic expanse. A fair realization of the incredible degree of diversity of linguistic system that ranges over the globe leaves one with an inescapable feeling that the human spirit is inconceivably old; that the few thousand years of history covered by our written records are no more than the thickness of a pencil mark on the scale that measures our past experience on this planet; that the events of these recent millenniums spell nothing in any evolutionary wise, that the race has taken no sudden spurt, achieved no commanding synthesis during recent millenniums, but has only played a little with a few of the linguistic formulations and views of nature bequeathed from an inexpressibly longer past. Yet neither this feeling nor the sense of precarious dependence of all we know upon linguistic tools which themselves are largely unknown need be discouraging to science but should, rather, foster that humility which accompanies the true scientific spirit, and thus forbid that arrogance of the mind which hinders real scientific curiosity and detachment.

7

Revolution in Grammar

W. NELSON FRANCIS

I

A LONG OVERDUE revolution is at present taking place in the study of English grammar—a revolution as sweeping in its consequences as the Darwinian revolution in biology. It is the result of the application to English of methods of descriptive analysis originally developed for use with languages of primitive people. To anyone at all interested in language, it is challenging; to those concerned with the teaching of English (including parents), it presents the necessity of radically revising both the substance and the methods of their teaching.

A curious paradox exists in regard to grammar. On the one hand it is felt to be the dullest and driest of academic subjects, fit only for those in whose veins the red blood of life has long since turned to ink. On the other, it is a subject upon which people who would scorn to be professional grammarians hold very dogmatic opinions, which they will defend with considerable emotion. Much of this prejudice stems from the usual sources of prejudice—ignorance and confusion. Even highly educated people seldom have a clear idea of what grammarians do, and there is an unfortunate confusion about the meaning of the term "grammar" itself.

Hence it would be well to begin with definitions. What do people mean when they use the word "grammar"? Actually the word is used to refer to

Reprinted by permission from the *Quarterly Journal of Speech,* 40.299–312 (October, 1954). The author is Professor of English and Linguistics at Brown University.

three different things, and much of the emotional thinking about matters grammatical arises from confusion among these different meanings.

The first thing we mean by "grammar" is "the set of formal patterns in which the words of a language are arranged in order to convey larger meanings." It is not necessary that we be able to discuss these patterns self-consciously in order to be able to use them. In fact, all speakers of a language above the age of five or six know how to use its complex forms of organization with considerable skill; in this sense of the word—call it "Grammar 1" —they are thoroughly familiar with its grammar.

The second meaning of "grammar"—call it "Grammar 2"—is "the branch of linguistic science which is concerned with the description, analysis, and formulization of formal language patterns." Just as gravity was in full operation before Newton's apple fell, so grammar in the first sense was in full operation before anyone formulated the first rule that began the history of grammar as a study.

The third sense in which people use the word "grammar" is "linguistic etiquette." This we may call "Grammar 3." The word in this sense is often coupled with a derogatory adjective: we say that the expression "he ain't here" is "bad grammar." What we mean is that such an expression is bad linguistic manners in certain circles. From the point of view of "Grammar 1" it is faultless; it conforms just as completely to the structural patterns of English as does "he isn't here." The trouble with it is like the trouble with Prince Hal in Shakespeare's play—it is "bad," not in itself, but in the company it keeps.

As has already been suggested, much confusion arises from mixing these meanings. One hears a good deal of criticism of teachers of English couched in such terms as "they don't teach grammar any more." Criticism of this sort is based on the wholly unproved assumption that teaching Grammar 2 will increase the student's proficiency in Grammar 1 or improve his manners in Grammar 3. Actually, the form of Grammar 2 which is usually taught is a very inaccurate and misleading analysis of the facts of Grammar 1; and it therefore is of highly questionable value in improving a person's ability to handle the structural patterns of his language. It is hardly reasonable to expect that teaching a person some inaccurate grammatical analysis will either improve the effectiveness of his assertions or teach him what expressions are acceptable to use in a given social context.

These, then, are the three meanings of "grammar": Grammar 1, a form of behavior; Grammar 2, a field of study, a science; and Grammar 3, a branch of etiquette.

II

Grammarians have arrived at some basic principles of their science, three of which are fundamental to this discussion. The first is that a language constitutes a set of behavior patterns common to the members of a given community. It is a part of what the anthropologists call the culture of the community. Actually it has complex and intimate relationships with other phases of culture such as myth and ritual. But for purposes of study it may be dealt with as a separate set of phenomena that can be objectively described and analyzed like any other universe of facts. Specifically, its phenomena can be observed, recorded, classified, and compared; and general laws of their behavior can be made by the same inductive process that is used to produce the "laws" of physics, chemistry, and the other sciences.

A second important principle of linguistic science is that each language or dialect has its own unique system of behavior patterns. Parts of this system may show similarities to parts of the systems of other languages, particularly if those languages are genetically related. But different languages solve the problems of expression and communication in different ways, just as the problems of movement through water are solved in different ways by lobsters, fish, seals, and penguins. A couple of corollaries of this principle are important. The first is that there is no such thing as "universal grammar," or at least if there is, it is so general and abstract as to be of little use. The second corollary is that the grammar of each language must be made up on the basis of a study of that particular language—a study that is free from preconceived notions of what a language should contain and how it should operate. The marine biologist does not criticize the octopus for using jet-propulsion to get him through the water instead of the methods of a self-respecting fish. Neither does the linguistic scientist express alarm or distress when he finds a language that seems to get along quite well without any words that correspond to what in English we call verbs.

A third principle on which linguistic science is based is that the analysis and description of a given language must conform to the requirements laid down for any satisfactory scientific theory. These are (1) simplicity, (2) consistency, (3) completeness, and (4) usefulness for predicting the behavior of phenomena not brought under immediate observation when the theory was formed. Linguistic scientists who have recently turned their attention to English have found that, judged by these criteria, the traditional grammar of English is unsatisfactory. It falls down badly on the first two requirements, being unduly complex and glaringly inconsistent within itself. It can be made to work, just as the Ptolemaic earth-centered astronomy can be, but at the cost of great elaboration and complication. The new grammar, like the Copernican sun-centered astronomy, solves the same problems with greater elegance, which is the scientist's word for the simplicity, compactness, and tidiness that characterize a satisfactory theory.

III

A brief look at the history of the traditional grammar of English will make apparent the reasons for its inadequacy. The study of English grammar is actually an outgrowth of the linguistic interest of the Renaissance. It was during the later Middle Ages and early Renaissance that the various vernacular languages of Europe came into their own. They began to be used for many kinds of writing which had previously always been done in Latin. As the vernaculars, in the hands of great writers like Dante and Chaucer, came of age as members of the linguistic family, a concomitant interest in their grammars arose. The earliest important English grammar was written by Shakespeare's contemporary, Ben Jonson.

It is important to observe that not only Ben Jonson himself but also those who followed him in the study of English grammar were men deeply learned in Latin and sometimes in Greek. For all their interest in English, they were conditioned from earliest school days to conceive of the classical languages as superior to the vernaculars. We still sometimes call the elementary school the "grammar school"; historically the term means the school where Latin grammar was taught. By the time the Renaissance or eighteenth-century scholar took his university degree, he was accustomed to use Latin as the normal means of communication with his fellow scholars. Dr. Samuel Johnson, for instance, who had only three years at the university and did not take a degree, wrote poetry in both Latin and Greek. Hence it was natural for these men to take Latin grammar as the norm, and to analyze English in terms of Latin. The grammarians of the seventeenth and eighteenth centuries who formulated the traditional grammar of English looked for the devices and distinctions of Latin grammar in English, and where they did not actually find them they imagined or created them. Of course, since English is a member of the Indo-European family of languages, to which Latin and Greek also belong, it did have many grammatical elements in common with them. But many of these had been obscured or wholly lost as a result of the extensive changes that had taken place in English— changes that the early grammarians inevitably conceived of as degeneration. They felt that it was their function to resist further change, if not to repair the damage already done. So preoccupied were they with the grammar of Latin as the ideal that they overlooked in large part the exceedingly complex and delicate system that English had substituted for the Indo-European grammar it had abandoned. Instead they stretched unhappy English on the Procrustean bed of Latin. It is no wonder that we commonly hear people say, "I didn't really understand grammar until I began to study Latin." This is eloquent testimony to the fact that the grammar "rules" of our present-day textbooks are largely an inheritance from the Latin-based grammar of the eighteenth century.

Meanwhile the extension of linguistic study beyond the Indo-European and Semitic families began to reveal that there are many different ways in which linguistic phenomena are organized—in other words, many different kinds of grammar. The tone-languages of the Orient and of North America, and the complex agglutinative languages of Africa, among others, forced grammarians to abandon the idea of a universal or ideal grammar and to direct their attention more closely to the individual systems employed by the multifarious languages of mankind. With the growth and refinement of the scientific method and its application to the field of anthropology, language came under more rigorous scientific scrutiny. As with anthropology in general, linguistic science at first concerned itself with the primitive. Finally, again following the lead of anthropology, linguistics began to apply its techniques to the old familiar tongues, among them English. Accelerated by the practical need during World War II of teaching languages, including English, to large numbers in a short time, research into the nature of English grammar has moved rapidly in the last fifteen years. The definitive grammar of English is yet to be written, but the results so far achieved are spectacular. It is now as unrealistic to teach "traditional" grammar of English as it is to teach "traditional" (i.e. pre-Darwinian) biology or "traditional" (i.e. four-element) chemistry. Yet nearly all certified teachers of English on all levels are doing so. Here is a cultural lag of major proportions.

IV

Before we can proceed to a sketch of what the new grammar of English looks like, we must take account of a few more of the premises of linguistic science. They must be understood and accepted by anyone who wishes to understand the new grammar.

First, the spoken language is primary, at least for the original study of a language. In many of the primitive languages,[1] of course, where writing is unknown, the spoken language is the *only* form. This is in many ways an advantage to the linguist, because the written language may use conventions that obscure its basic structure. The reason for the primary importance of the spoken language is that language originates as speech, and most of the changes and innovations that occur in the history of a given language begin in the spoken tongue.

Secondly, we must take account of the concept of dialect. I suppose most laymen would define a dialect as "a corrupt form of language spoken in a given region by people who don't know any better." This introduces moral judgments which are repulsive to the linguistic scholar. Let us approach the definition of a dialect from the more objective end, through the notion of a speech community. A speech community is merely a group of people who are in pretty constant intercommunication. There are various types of speech

---

[1] "Primitive languages" here is really an abbreviated statement for "languages used by peoples of relatively primitive culture"; it is not to be taken as implying anything simple or rudimentary about the languages themselves. Many languages included under the term, such as native languages of Africa and Mexico, exhibit grammatical complexities unknown to more "civilized" languages.

communities: local ones, like "the people who live in Tidewater Virginia"; class ones, like "the white-collar class"; occupational ones, like "doctors, nurses, and other people who work in hospitals"; social ones, like "club-women." In a sense, each of these has its own dialect. Each family may be said to have its own dialect; in fact, in so far as each of us has his own vocabulary and particular quirks of speech, each individual has his own dialect. Also, of course, in so far as he is a member of many speech communities, each individual is more or less master of many dialects and shifts easily and almost unconsciously from one to another as he shifts from one social environment to another.

In the light of this concept of dialects, a language can be defined as a group of dialects which have enough of their sound-system, vocabulary, and grammar (Grammar 1, that is) in common to permit their speakers to be mutually intelligible in the ordinary affairs of life. It usually happens that one of the many dialects that make up a language comes to have more prestige than the others; in modern times it has usually been the dialect of the middle-class residents of the capital, like Parisian French and London English, which is so distinguished. This comes to be thought of as the standard dialect; in fact, its speakers become snobbish and succeed in establishing the belief that it is not a dialect at all, but the only proper form of the language. This causes the speakers of other dialects to become self-conscious and ashamed of their speech, or else aggressive and jingoistic about it—either of which is an acknowledgment of their feelings of inferiority. Thus one of the duties of the educational system comes to be that of teaching the standard dialect to all so as to relieve them of feelings of inferiority, and thus relieve society of linguistic neurotics. This is where Grammar 3, linguistic etiquette, comes into the picture.

A third premise arising from the two just discussed is that the difference between the way educated people talk and the way they write is a dialectal difference. The spread between these two dialects may be very narrow, as in present-day America, or very wide, as in Norway, where people often speak local Norwegian dialects but write in the Dano-Norwegian *Riksmaal*. The extreme is the use by writers of an entirely different language, or at least an ancient and no longer spoken form of the language—like Sanskrit in northern India or Latin in western Europe during the Middles Ages. A corollary of this premise is that anyone setting out to write a grammar must know and make clear whether he is dealing with the spoken or the written dialect. Virtually all current English grammars deal with the written language only; evidence for this is that their rules for the plurals of nouns, for instance, are really spelling rules, which say nothing about pronunciation.

This is not the place to go into any sort of detail about the methods of analysis the linguistic scientist uses. Suffice it to say that he begins by breaking up the flow of speech into minimum sound-units, or phones, which he then groups into families called phonemes, the minimum significant sound-units. Most languages have from twenty to sixty of these. American English has forty-one: nine vowels, twenty-four consonants, four degrees of stress, and four levels of pitch. These phonemes group themselves into minimum meaningful units, called morphemes. These fall into two groups: free morphemes, those that can enter freely into many combinations with other free morphemes to make phrases and sentences; and bound morphemes, which are always found tied in a close and often indissoluble relationship with other bound or free morphemes. An example of a free morpheme is "dog"; an example of a bound morpheme is "un-" or "ex-." The linguist usually avoids talking about "words" because the term is very inexact. Is "instead of," for instance, to be considered one, two, or three words? This is purely a matter of opinion; but it is a matter of fact that it is made up of three morphemes.

In any case, our analysis has now brought the linguist to the point where he has some notion of the word-stock (he would call it the "lexicon") of his language. He must then go into the question of how the morphemes are grouped into meaningful utterances, which is the field of grammar proper. At this point in the analysis of English, as of many other languages, it becomes apparent that there are three bases upon which classification and analysis may be built: form, function, and meaning. For illustration let us take the word "boys" in the utterance "the boys are here." From the point of view of form, "boys" is a noun with the plural ending "s" (pronounced like "z"), preceded by the noun-determiner "the," and tied by concord to the verb "are," which it precedes. From the point of view of function, "boys" is the subject of the verb "are" and of the sentence. From the point of view of meaning, "boys" points out or names more than one of the male young of the human species, about whom an assertion is being made.

Of these three bases of classification, the one most amenable to objective description and analysis of a rigorously scientific sort is form. In fact, many conclusions about form can be drawn by a person unable to understand or speak the language. Next comes function. But except as it is revealed by form, function is dependent on knowing the meaning. In a telegraphic sentence like "ship sails today"[2] no one can say whether "ship" is the subject of "sails" or an imperative verb with "sails" as its object until he knows what the sentence means. Most shaky of all bases for grammatical analysis is meaning. Attempts have been made to reduce the phenomena of meaning to objective description, but so far they have not succeeded very well. Meaning is such a subjective quality that it is usually omitted entirely from scientific description. The botanist can describe the forms of plants and the functions of their various parts, but he refuses to concern himself with their

[2] This example is taken from C. C. Fries, *The Structure of English* (New York, 1952), p. 62. This important book will be discussed below.

meaning. It is left to the poet to find symbolic meaning in roses, violets, and lilies.

At this point it is interesting to note that the traditional grammar of English bases some of its key concepts and definitions on this very subjective and shaky foundation of meaning. A recent English grammar defines a sentence as "a group of words which expresses a complete thought through the use of a verb, called its predicate, and a subject, consisting of a noun or pronoun about which the verb has something to say."[3] But what is a complete thought? Actually we do not identify sentences this way at all. If someone says, "I don't know what to do," dropping his voice at the end, and pauses, the hearer will know that it is quite safe for him to make a comment without running the risk of interrupting an unfinished sentence. But if the speaker says the same words and maintains a level pitch at the end, the polite listener will wait for him to finish his sentence. The words are the same, the meaning is the same; the only difference is a slight one in the pitch of the final syllable—a purely formal distinction, which signals that the first utterance is complete, a sentence, while the second is incomplete. In writing we would translate these signals into punctuation: a period or exclamation point at the end of the first, a comma or dash at the end of the second. It is the form of the utterance, not the completeness of the thought, that tells us whether it is a whole sentence or only part of one.

Another favorite definition of the traditional grammar, also based on meaning, is that of "noun" as "the name of a person, place, or thing"; or, as the grammar just quoted has it, "the name of anybody or anything, with or without life, and with or without substance or form."[4] Yet we identify nouns, not by asking if they name something, but by their positions in expressions and by the formal marks they carry. In the sentence, "The slithy toves did gyre and gimble in the wabe," any speaker of English knows that "toves" and "wabe" are nouns, though he cannot tell what they name, if indeed they name anything. How does he know? Actually because they have certain formal marks, like their position in relation to "the" as well as the whole arrangement of the sentence. We know from our practical knowledge of English grammar (Grammar 1), which we have had since before we went to school, that if we were to put meaningful words into this sentence, we would have to put nouns in place of "toves" and "wabe," giving something like "The slithy snakes did gyre and gamble in the wood." The pattern of the sentence simply will not allow us to say "The slithy arounds did gyre and gimble in the wooden."

One trouble with the traditional grammar, then, is that it relies heavily on the most subjective element in language, meaning. Another is that it shifts the ground of its classification and produces the elementary logical

---

[3] Ralph B. Allen, *English Grammar* (New York, 1950), p. 187.
[4] *Ibid.*, p. 1.

error of cross-division. A zoologist who divided animals into invertebrates, mammals, and beasts of burden would not get very far before running into trouble. Yet the traditional grammar is guilty of the same error when it defines three parts of speech on the basis of meaning (noun, verb, and interjection), four more on the basis of function (adjective, adverb, pronoun, conjunction), and one partly on function and partly on form (preposition). The result is that in such an expression as "a dog's life" there can be endless futile argument about whether "dog's" is a noun or an adjective. It is, of course, a noun from the point of view of form and an adjective from the point of view of function, and hence falls into both classes, just as a horse is both a mammal and a beast of burden. No wonder students are bewildered in their attempts to master the traditional grammar. Their natural clearness of mind tells them that it is a crazy patchwork violating the elementary principles of logical thought.

V

If the traditional grammar is so bad, what does the new grammar offer in its place?

It offers a description, analysis, and set of definitions and formulas—rules, if you will—based firmly and consistently on the easiest, or at least the most objective, aspect of language, form. Experts can quibble over whether "dog's" in "a dog's life" is a noun or an adjective, but anyone can see that it is spelled with " 's" and hear that it ends with a "z" sound; likewise anyone can tell that it comes in the middle between "a" and "life." Furthermore he can tell that something important has happened if the expression is changed to "the dog's alive," "the live dogs," or "the dogs lived," even if he doesn't know what the words mean and has never heard of such functions as modifier, subject, or attributive genitive. He cannot, of course, get very far into his analysis without either a knowledge of the language or access to someone with such knowledge. He will also need a minimum technical vocabulary describing grammatical functions. Just so the anatomist is better off for knowing physiology. But the grammarian, like the anatomist, must beware of allowing his preconceived notions to lead him into the error of interpreting before he describes—an error which often results in his finding only what he is looking for.

When the grammarian looks at English objectively, he finds that it conveys its meanings by two broad devices: the denotations and connotations of words separately considered, which the linguist calls "lexical meaning," and the significance of word-forms, word-groups, and arrangements apart from the lexical meanings of the words, which the linguist calls "structural meaning." The first of these is the domain of the lexicographer and the semanticist, and hence is not our present concern. The second, the structural meaning, is the business of the structural linguist, or grammarian.

The importance of this second kind of meaning must be emphasized because it is often overlooked. The man in the street tends to think of the meaning of a sentence as being the aggregate of the dictionary meanings of the words that make it up; hence the widespread fallacy of literal translation—the feeling that if you take a French sentence and a French-English dictionary and write down the English equivalent of each French word you will come out with an intelligible English sentence. How ludicrous the results can be, anyone knows who is familiar with Mark Twain's retranslation from the French of his jumping frog story. One sentence reads, "Eh bien! I no saw not that that frog has nothing of better than each frog." Upon which Mark's comment is, "if that isn't grammar gone to seed, then I count myself no judge."[5]

The second point brought out by a formal analysis of English is that it uses four principal devices of form to signal structural meanings:

1. Word order—the sequence in which words and word-groups are arranged.
2. Function-words—words devoid of lexical meaning which indicate relationships among the meaningful words with which they appear.
3. Inflections—alterations in the forms of words themselves to signal changes in meaning and relationship.
4. Formal contrasts—contrasts in the forms of words signaling greater differences in function and meaning. These could also be considered inflections, but it is more convenient for both the lexicographer and the grammarian to consider them separately.

Usually several of these are present in any utterance, but they can be separately illustrated by means of contrasting expressions involving minimum variation—the kind of controlled experiment used in the scientific laboratory.

To illustrate the structural meaning of word order, let us compare the two sentences "man bites dog" and "dog bites man."—The words are identical in lexical meaning and in form; the only difference is in sequence. It is interesting to note that Latin expresses the difference between these two by changes in the form of the words, without necessarily altering the order: "homo canem mordet" or "hominem canis mordet." Latin grammar is worse than useless in understanding this point of English grammar.

Next, compare the sentences "the dog is the friend of man" and "any dog is a friend of that man." Here the words having lexical meaning are "dog," "is," "friend," and "man," which appear in the same form and the same order in both sentences. The formal differences between them are in

[5] Mark Twain, "The Jumping Frog; the Original Story in English; the Retranslation Clawed Back from the French, into a Civilized Language Once More, by Patient and Unremunerated Toil," *1601 . . . and Sketches Old and New* (n.p., 1933), p. 50.

the substitution of "any" and "a" for "the," and in the insertion of "that." These little words are function-words; they make quite a difference in the meanings of the two sentences, though it is virtually impossible to say what they mean in isolation.

Third, compare the sentences "the dog loves the man" and "the dogs loved the men." Here the words are the same, in the same order, with the same function-words in the same positions. But the forms of the three words having lexical meanings have been changed: "dog" to "dogs," "loves" to "loved," and "man" to "men." These changes are inflections. English has very few of them as compared with Greek, Latin, Russian, or even German. But it still uses them; about one word in four in an ordinary English sentence is inflected.

Fourth, consider the difference between "the dog's friend arrived" and "the dog's friendly arrival." Here the difference lies in the change of "friend" to "friendly," a formal alteration signaling a change of function from subject to modifier, and the change of "arrived" to "arrival," signaling a change of function from predicate to head-word in a noun-modifier group. These changes are of the same formal nature as inflections, but because they produce words of different lexical meaning, classifiable as different parts of speech, it is better to call them formal contrasts than inflections. In other words, it is logically quite defensible to consider "love," "loving," and "loved" as the same word in differing aspects and to consider "friend," "friendly," "friendliness," "friendship," and "befriend" as different words related by formal and semantic similarities. But this is only a matter of convenience of analysis, which permits a more accurate description of English structure. In another language we might find that this kind of distinction is unnecessary but that some other distinction, unnecessary in English, is required. The categories of grammatical description are not sacrosanct; they are as much a part of man's organization of his observations as they are of the nature of things.

If we are considering the spoken variety of English, we must add a fifth device for indicating structural meaning—the various musical and rhythmic patterns which the linguist classifies under juncture, stress, and intonation. Consider the following pair of sentences:

> Alfred, the alligator is sick
> Alfred the alligator is sick.

These are identical in the four respects discussed above—word order, function-words, inflections, and word-form. Yet they have markedly different meanings, as would be revealed by the intonation if they were spoken aloud. These differences in intonation are to a certain extent indicated in the written language by punctuation—that is, in fact, the primary function of punctuation.

VI

The examples so far given were chosen to illustrate in isolation the various kinds of structural devices in English grammar. Much more commonly the structural meaning of a given sentence is indicated by a combination of two or more of these devices: a sort of margin of safety which permits some of the devices to be missed or done away with without obscuring the structural meaning of the sentence, as indeed anyone knows who has ever written a telegram or a newspaper headline. On the other hand, sentences which do not have enough of these formal devices are inevitably ambiguous. Take the example already given, Fries's "ship sails today." This is ambiguous because there is nothing to indicate which of the first two words is performing a noun function and which a verb function. If we mark the noun by putting the noun-determining function-word "the" in front of it, the ambiguity disappears; we have either "the ship sails today" or "ship the sails today." The ambiguity could just as well be resolved by using other devices: consider "ship sailed today," "ship to sail today," "ship sail today," "shipping sails today," "shipment of sails today," and so on. It is simply a question of having enough formal devices in the sentence to indicate its structural meaning clearly.

How powerful the structural meanings of English are is illustrated by so-called "nonsense." In English, nonsense as a literary form often consists of utterances that have a clear structural meaning but use words that either have no lexical meanings, or whose lexical meanings are inconsistent one with another. This will become apparent if we subject a rather famous bit of English nonsense to formal grammatical analysis:

> All mimsy were the borogoves
> And the mome raths outgrabe.

This passage consists of ten words, five of them words that should have lexical meaning but don't, one standard verb, and four function-words. In so far as it is possible to indicate its abstract structure, it would be this:

> All . . . . y were the . . . . s
> And the . . . . . . s . . . .

Although this is a relatively simple formal organization, it signals some rather complicated meanings. The first thing we observe is that the first line presents a conflict: word order seems to signal one thing, and inflections and function-words something else. Specifically, "mimsy" is in the position normally occupied by the subject, but we know that it is not the subject and that "borogroves" is. We know this because there is an inflectional tie between the form "were" and the "s" ending of "borogroves," because there is the noun-determiner "the" before it, and because the alternative candidate for subject, "mimsy," lacks both of these. It is true that "mimsy" does have the function-word "all" before it, which may indicate a noun; but when it does, the noun is either plural (in which case "mimsy" would most likely end in "s"), or else the noun is what grammarians call a mass-word (like "sugar," "coal," "snow"), in which case the verb would have to be "was," not "were." All these formal considerations are sufficient to counteract the effect of word order and show that the sentence is of the type that may be represented thus:

> All gloomy were the Democrats.

Actually there is one other possibility. If "mimsy" belongs to the small group of nouns which don't use "s" to make the plural, and if "borogroves" has been so implied (but not specifically mentioned) in the context as to justify its appearing with the determiner "the," the sentence would then belong to the following type:

> (In the campaign for funds) all alumni were the canvassers.
> (In the drought last summer) all cattle were the sufferers.

But the odds are so much against this that most of us would be prepared to fight for our belief that "borogroves" are things than can be named, and that at the time referred to they were in a complete state of "mimsyness."

Moving on to the second line, "and the mome raths outgrabe," the first thing we note is that the "And" signals another parallel assertion to follow. We are thus prepared to recognize from the noun-determiner "the," the plural inflection "s," and the particular positions of "mome" and "out-grabe," as well as the continuing influence of the "were" of the preceding line, that we are dealing with a sentence of this pattern:

> And the lone rats agreed.

The influence of the "were" is particularly important here; it guides us in selecting among several interpretations of the sentence. Specifically, it requires us to identify "outgrabe" as a verb in the past tense, and thus a "strong" or "irregular" verb, since it lacks the characteristic past-tense ending "d" or "ed." We do this in spite of the fact that there is another strong candidate for the position of verb: that is, "raths," which bears a regular verb inflection and could be tied with "mome" as its subject in the normal noun-verb relationship. In such a case we should have to recognize "outgrabe" as either an adverb of the kind not marked by the form-contrast "ly," an adjective, or the past participle of a strong verb. The sentence would then belong to one of the following types:

> And the moon shines above.
> And the man stays aloof.
> And the fool seems outdone.

But we reject all of these—probably they don't even occur to us—because they all have verbs in the present tense, whereas the "were" of the first line combines with the "And" at the beginning of the second to set the whole in the past.

We might recognize one further possibility for the structural meaning of this second line, particularly in the verse context, since we are used to certain patterns in verse that do not often appear in speech or prose. The "were" of the first line could be understood as doing double duty, its ghost or echo appearing between "raths" and "outgrabe." Then we would have something like this:

> All gloomy were the Democrats
> And the home folks outraged.

But again the odds are pretty heavy against this. I for one am so sure that "outgrabe" is the past tense of a strong verb that I can give its present. In my dialect, at least, it is "outgribe."

The reader may not realize it, but in the last four paragraphs I have been discussing grammar from a purely formal point of view. I have not once called a word a noun because it names something (that is, I have not once resorted to meaning), nor have I called any word an adjective because it modifies a noun (that is, resorted to function). Instead I have been working in the opposite direction, from form toward function and meaning. I have used only criteria which are objectively observable, and I have assumed only a working knowledge of certain structural patterns and devices known to all speakers of English over the age of six. I did use some technical terms like "noun," "verb," and "tense," but only to save time; I could have got along without them.

If one clears his mind of the inconsistencies of the traditional grammar (not so easy a process as it might be), he can proceed with a similarly rigorous formal analysis of a sufficient number of representative utterances in English and come out with a descriptive grammar. This is just what Professor Fries did in gathering and studying the material for the analysis he presents in the remarkable book to which I have already referred, *The Structure of English*. What he actually did was to put a tape recorder into action and record about fifty hours of telephone conversation among the good citizens of Ann Arbor, Michigan. When this material was transcribed, it constituted about a quarter of a million words of perfectly natural speech by educated middle-class Americans. The details of his conclusions cannot be presented here, but they are sufficiently different from the usual grammar to be revolutionary. For instance, he recognizes only four parts of speech among the words with lexical meaning, roughly corresponding to what the traditional grammar calls substantives, verbs, adjectives and adverbs, though to avoid preconceived notions from the traditional grammar Fries calls them Class 1, Class 2, Class 3, and Class 4 words. To these he adds a relatively small group of function-words, 154 in his materials, which he divides into fifteen groups. These must be memorized by anyone learning the language; they are not subject to the same kind of general rules that govern the four parts of speech. Undoubtedly his conclusions will be developed and modified by himself and by other linguistic scholars, but for the present his book remains the most complete treatment extant of English grammar from the point of view of linguistic science.

VII

Two vital questions are raised by this revolution in grammar. The first is, "What is the value of this new system?" In the minds of many who ask it, the implication of this question is, "We have been getting along all these years with traditional grammar, so it can't be so very bad. Why should we go through the painful process of unlearning and relearning grammar just because linguistic scientists have concocted some new theories?"

The first answer to this question is the bravest and most honest. It is that the superseding of vague and sloppy thinking by clear and precise thinking is an exciting experience in and for itself. To acquire insight into the workings of a language, and to recognize the infinitely delicate system of relationship, balance, and interplay that constitutes its grammar, is to become closely acquainted with one of man's most miraculous creations, not unworthy to be set beside the equally beautiful organization of the physical universe. And to find that its most complex effects are produced by the multi-layered organization of relatively simple materials is to bring our thinking about language into accord with modern thought in other fields, which is more and more coming to emphasize the importance of organization—the fact that an organized whole is truly greater than the sum of all its parts.

There are other answers, more practical if less philosophically valid. It is too early to tell, but it seems probable that a realistic, scientific grammar should vastly facilitate the teaching of English, especially as a foreign language. Already results are showing here; it has been found that if intonation contours and other structural patterns are taught quite early, the student has a confidence that allows him to attempt to speak the language much sooner than he otherwise would.

The new grammar can also be of use in improving the native speaker's proficiency in handling the structural devices of his own language. In other words, Grammar 2, if it is accurate and consistent, *can* be of use in improving skill in Grammar 1. An illustration is that famous bugaboo, the dangling participle. Consider a specific instance of it, which once appeared on a college freshman's theme, to the mingled delight and despair of the instructor:

Having eaten our lunch, the steamboat departed.

What is the trouble with this sentence? Clearly there must be something wrong with it, because it makes people laugh, although it was not the intent of the writer to make them laugh. In other words, it produces a completely wrong response, resulting in total breakdown of communication. It is, in fact, "bad grammar" in a much more serious way than are mere dialectal divergences like "he ain't here" or "he never seen none," which produce social reactions but communicate effectively. In the light of the new grammar, the trouble with our dangling participle is that the form, instead of leading to the meaning, is in conflict with it. Into the position which, in this pattern, is reserved for the word naming the eater of the lunch, the writer has inserted the word "steamboat." The resulting tug-of-war between form and meaning is only momentary; meaning quickly wins out, simply because our common sense tells us that steamboats don't eat lunches. But if the pull of the lexical meaning is not given a good deal of help from common sense, the form will conquer the meaning, or the two will remain in ambiguous equilibrium—as, for instance, in "Having eaten our lunch, the passengers boarded the steamboat." Writers will find it easier to avoid such troubles if they know about the forms of English and are taught to use the form to convey the meaning, instead of setting up tensions between form and meaning. This, of course, is what English teachers are already trying to do. The new grammar should be a better weapon in their arsenal than the traditional grammar since it is based on a clear understanding of the realities.

The second and more difficult question is, "How can the change from one grammar to the other be effected?" Here we face obstacles of a formidable nature. When we remember the controversies attending on revolutionary changes in biology and astronomy, we realize what a tenacious hold the race can maintain on anything it has once learned, and the resistance it can offer to new ideas. And remember that neither astronomy nor biology was taught in elementary schools. They were, in fact, rather specialized subjects in advanced education. How then change grammar, which is taught to everybody, from the fifth grade up through college? The vested interest represented by thousands upon thousands of English and Speech teachers who have learned the traditional grammar and taught it for many years is a conservative force comparable to those which keep us still using the chaotic system of English spelling and the unwieldy measuring system of inches and feet, pounds and ounces, quarts, bushels, and acres. Moreover, this army is constantly receiving new recruits. It is possible in my state to become certified to teach English in high school if one has had eighteen credit hours of college English—let us say two semesters of freshman composition (almost all of which is taught by people unfamiliar with the new grammar), two semesters of a survey course in English literature, one semester of Shakespeare, and one semester of the contemporary novel. And since hard-pressed school administrators feel that anyone who can speak English can in a pinch teach it, the result is that many people are called upon to teach grammar whose knowledge of the subject is totally inadequate.

There is, in other words, a battle ahead of the new grammar. It will have to fight not only the apathy of the general public but the ignorance and inertia of those who count themselves competent in the field of grammar. The battle is already on, in fact. Those who try to get the concepts of the new grammar introduced into the curriculum are tagged as "liberal" grammarians—the implication being, I suppose, that one has a free choice between "liberal" and "conservative" grammar, and that the liberals are a bit dangerous, perhaps even a touch subversive. They are accused of undermining standards, of holding that "any way of saying something is just as good as any other," of not teaching the fundamentals of good English. I trust that the readers of this article will see how unfounded these charges are. But the smear campaign is on. So far as I know, neither religion nor patriotism has yet been brought into it. When they are, Professor Fries will have to say to Socrates, Galileo, Darwin, Freud, and the other members of the honorable fraternity of the misunderstood, "Move over, gentlemen, and make room for me."

8

Terms in Phonemics

George P. Faust

By means of phonemic analysis, structural linguists try to discover the sound-system of a language as it is consciously or subconsciously meaningful to the speakers. A new set of terms (and symbols) is forced upon them partly because they have formed new categories and developed new techniques and partly because the familiar terms have an aura of association that would act to block understanding if they were used in new senses. The difficulty is that the new terms themselves have blocked understanding between structuralists and teachers. The problem of this article is to remove

Reprinted by permission from *College Composition and Communication,* 5.30–34 (February, 1954). Professor Faust is a member of the University of Kentucky Department of English.

some of the barriers and show some of the uses teachers can make of the present knowledge of English structure, with no attempt to go beyond phonemics.[1]

But the barriers will not fall automatically with the explanation of a few technical terms. As I have tried to say earlier,[2] we must first persuade ourselves to accept two basic tenets: (1) that speech is the primary form of language and underlies all writing, and (2) that the concern of structuralists is with the mechanisms of language as a medium, not with the "message" (meaning) carried by the medium.

These two tenets accepted, let us start by fastening attention on the *p*-sounds in the possible expression 'rapid pup.' We will follow the general practice of putting phonetic symbols in brackets, e.g., [p], and phonemic symbols between slashes, e.g., /p/. In a phonemic transcription of my speech without stress and intonation marked, we can set our expression down as /ræpid pəp/. This is not phonetic, for among other things any competent phonetician could hear differences among the *p*-sounds as he listened to me. If he took the first as a phonetic norm, he might transcribe them in order as [p], [p‘], and [p’], with [‘] standing for aspiration (a puff of air that can be felt on the back of the hand held close to the mouth) and [’] indicating no release by reopening the lips. All three varieties are called allophones.

To put it as untechnically as I can, ALLOPHONES are phonetically similar sounds that never get in each other's way. As native speakers of English, we have learned to use the proper allophones automatically and to ignore them completely in our own speech and in the speech of others. This means that *if you know that a word has two pronunciations, they differ phonemically, not allophonically.* It is only when a foreigner fails to use the right allophones that we become vaguely conscious that something is wrong: The foreigner, we say, speaks English with an accent. In all this we are reacting quite normally, and no phonetically untrained reader should be disturbed if he fails to hear allophonic differences.

Allophones have COMPLEMENTARY DISTRIBUTION, the technical term that corresponds to "never get in each other's way." This is a tricky term to handle. Allophones tend to be restricted. That is, [p’] simply cannot appear at the beginning of a word because we have to reopen our lips to get on with the word. On the other hand, [p‘] does on occasion replace [p’] at the end of a word. But we speakers react to /pəp/ as the "same" word, no

---

[1] In general, this article will follow the analysis in George L. Trager and Henry Lee Smith, Jr., *An Outline of English Structure* (Studies in Linguistics: Occasional Papers No. 3), 1951. This is a thoroughly technical piece of work *not* recommended for beginners. The best available starting point is Robert A. Hall's *Leave Your Language Alone* (Linguistica: Ithaca, N.Y.), 1950. If you don't like the social attitudes expressed, ignore them and concentrate on the very able exposition of linguistics.

[2] "Basic Tenets of Structural Linguistics," *CCC*, December, 1953, pages 122–126.

matter which allophone is used, and any sense of difference here is likely to be referred to the speaker's attitude, not his dialect. Therefore, the allophones never collide, even when they alternate with one another, and they complement one another in such a way that in sum they take care of all the situations in which their phoneme occurs.

Complementary distribution is one side of the coin, CONTRASTIVE DISTRIBUTION the other. Sounds contrast most obviously when the difference produces different words. Thus /p/ and /f/ contrast because 'pup' is not 'puff' (/pəf/). *And one contrast anywhere in the language is enough to establish separate phonemes everywhere in the language.* It is known quite definitely that [p] between vowels is voiced in normal American speech and is thus very close to [b] in the same situation—at least as close to [b] phonetically as to initial [p']. But since [p] and [b] are assigned by speakers to different phonemes (cf. the contrast between /pet/ and /bet/), the phonetic similarity is inconsequential. You can test this for yourself. Just invite a friend to pat your 'rabid pup' and see whether his reactions are like those of the friends you have invited to pat your 'rapid pup.'

Here it is necessary to insist that the difference in meaning is the *result* of the difference in sound. Strangers who hear my weakly aspirated initial /p/ (an individual peculiarity) quite easily "misunderstand" me and think, for instance, that my middle initial is B instead of P. The sense of "misunderstand" here is that they have misclassified a sound, with resultant change of meaning.

An error of this sort points up one extremely important difference between phonetics and phonemics. In phonetics a sound can be between a /p/ and a /b/ in the sense that it can have certain characteristics of each, such as the voicelessness of an initial /p/ and the relatively weak aspiration of an initial /b/. The phonetician tries to describe the sound actually produced. But in phonemics there are no gradations. *A sound is assigned to one phoneme or another, and there is no in-between stage.* The linguistic evidence goes to show that we hear in terms of phonemes and listen to only as much of a sound as we need to in order to assign it to an established phoneme. This is a fundamental reason why phonemic transcriptions don't need to distinguish among allophones.

We should now be ready for some definitions. A sound produced is a PHONE. It is a unique historical event, in theory as individual as a fingerprint. Obviously, only a microscopic sample of the phones produced ever get recorded, and yet the patterning of language is such that linguists can classify as confidently as though they had a statistically large sample. In great measure, this is because they have occasion to concentrate on only a few variations. The subclasses into which phones are fitted are ALLOPHONES, each of which, though in complementary distribution, is distinct from all others by at least one phonetic feature. At this level we are still in a region where sounds may be symbolized in phonetic transcription. Next, the allophones are gathered into one class, a PHONEME, which is distinguished by the phonetic similarity of its members and by its contrastive distribution with other phonemes.

To tie all three together, any phone may be called a phone (i.e., an individual sound) or an allophone (i.e., a member of an allophone) or a phoneme (i.e., a member of a phoneme). Imagine that I now hear you say 'pup.' The first sound was a phone, already past history. As long as it remains unclassified, I can call it nothing but a phone. Probably I will next classify it as a member of the phoneme /p/, and now I can call it either a phone or a phoneme. When finally I group it with other members of /p/ that have aspiration, I can also call it an allophone of /p/, and I can describe that allophone phonetically as [pʻ]. In the same kind of way, all other vowel-like or consonant-like phones can be identified as belonging to one or another of the thirty-three phonemes that make up this part of the English sound-system.

For teachers, the usefulness of having a working acquaintance with these phonemes is that it sheds valuable light on many spelling problems. All of us already know, in a relatively unsystematic way, that our students tend to reflect their pronunciations in their writing, but the remedies we have offered have sometimes been unrealistic, to a considerable extent because we have confused letters and sounds. One pronunciation of *often*, now well established, is supposed to be due to the letter *t* in the spelling—some people, apparently, never thought of *soften*. Once we realize that *used to* is regularly pronounced /yuwstuw/, not /yuwzd tuw/, we may be more sympathetic to the spelling *use to,* which is really very sensible, if not orthodox. Of course we should try to impress the conventional spelling but not, I suggest, at the cost of a pronunciation which may be unforced for some speakers but which I never happen to have heard attempted except by teachers. Again, probably many of us tear our hair over students who seem unable to pluralize words like *scientist*. But a great many standard speakers have /-s/ at the end of such words instead of /-st/, and to them the plural presumably sounds just like the singular.[3] It would strike an informed teacher as unreasonable to attempt to modify a standard pronunciation; it would be better to show the students that for spelling such words they cannot trust their ears. This is the type of situation which a knowledge of phonemics enables a teacher to handle sensibly.

To return to the sound-system, the set of phonemes referred to so far are called SEGMENTAL PHONEMES to distinguish them from another more recently discovered set, the SUPRASEGMENTAL PHONEMES. These consist of stresses, pitches, and junctures—the last being modes of transition from

---

[3] A structurally more accurate way of putting this is that the final consonant cluster /-sts/ is non-existent in the speech of many Americans.

one speech-segment to another. Of course the fact of their existence is not news; the recent knowledge is of their contrastive distribution into phonemes, which has been worked out in considerable detail during the last ten years by Kenneth Pike and others.

STRESS is familiar as what we call accent in dictionaries, where only three relative degrees are necessary, counting the unmarked as weak. (However, you should not expect dictionaries to be accurate on stress. For example, they leave the second syllable of *cargo* unmarked, though it definitely has more stress than the second syllable of *sofa*—as much, in my speech, as the marked second syllable of *blackbird*.) Connected speech has a fourth degree of stress which overrides the others and which we use to establish word-groups. Customary symbols of stress are

$$/ \prime, \wedge, \backslash, \smile /,$$

called primary, secondary, tertiary, and weak.

Whêre's thĕ cárgò

illustrates the four phonemic stresses.

The very idea that relative levels of PITCH are contrastive is a novelty. Here there is nothing like a familiar dictionary to fall back on, and since the proof is somewhat complicated, about all that can be done here is to make the flat assertion that English has four phonemic pitches. The joke 'What are we having for dinner? Mother?' depends on the misuse of pitch levels. In the commonplace 'What are we having for dinner, Mother?' the vocative can be either at the lowest pitch or the next above, but it can never be at either of the two highest pitches. With next-to-top pitch, as in the joke, 'mother' becomes a separate question.[4]

Pitches are usually symbolized by numbers: $/^1,^2,^3,^4/$. Unfortunately, there are two systems in use, one that numbers from the top and one that begins at the bottom. Other devices, like dotted lines above and below the text, are also in use.

The phonemes of JUNCTURE, or TRANSITION, are classes of the ways we use to pass from one bit or stretch of linguistic material to the next. If this merely seems a clumsy way of saying something like "get from one phrase or sentence to the next," the reason is that the use of juncture helps to define terms like *phrase* and *sentence*. Therefore we cannot, without circular reasoning, use the terms in describing juncture. As a minor digression, let me point out that our standard practice has been to use circularity, though often at one or two removes. We may use *sentence* to help define *verb*, and then turn around and use *verb* to help define *sentence*. The structuralists try very hard not to fall into this sort of trap.

The four phonemes of juncture are symbolized by $/+, |, ||, \#/$, called

---

[4] I am indebted to H. L. Smith, Jr., for this passage, joke included.

plus juncture, single bar juncture, double bar juncture, and double cross juncture respectively. PLUS JUNCTURE, which classically distinguishes 'night rate' from 'nitrate,' can be left behind with the observation that it always occurs at least between secondary stresses, and between a secondary and primary, unless one of the other three junctures is there. (This, of course, like all that follows, is a rule of the language, not of the structuralists; it is a phenomenon observed, not created.) The remaining junctures can be thought of as major, for they serve to establish what is probably the basic rule of English grammar: There is always one, and only one, primary stress between any pair of /|, ||, #/. This rule is completely accurate if the silence before speech is counted as a major juncture and if the speaker is not interrupted. For example, both these versions are accepted by listeners as normal English:

> My ôlder brôther is a plúmber.
> My ôlder bróther | is a plúmber.

SINGLE BAR JUNCTURE can be read as transition across a fairly minor break with pitch sustained to the point of juncture. It is never an uninterrupted speaker's final juncture. DOUBLE BAR JUNCTURE is familiar to use as the rising "question intonation," a thoroughly misleading term. The questions that end in double bar are those without question words, like 'Are you going?' and 'He's here?' In all but perhaps a very few dialects, questions like 'Where are you going?' do not end in double bar. Polite vocatives always end with double bar: 'I'm going, Mother.' Especially in rather slow speech, the rise of double bar is common within the conventional sentence:

> The sôldiers in Koréa || wânted to gêt hóme.

DOUBLE CROSS JUNCTURE is marked by voice fade-out, and usually a lowering of pitch. It appears where periods have been used in the examples, and at the end of 'Where are you going?' It also appears, at least in some reading styles, before what we have been trained to call a non-restrictive subordinate clause at the end of a sentence.

The implications of the suprasegmental phonemes for teachers are important. Almost all marks of punctuation are juncture signals, as we demonstrate again and again by reading aloud mispunctuated student sentences to show that they sound queer. Some of us, perhaps, sometimes even deliberately misread the student's punctuation because it violates an editorial rule, not a linguistic principle. But almost nobody, within my knowledge, is equipped to give students a sensible explanation of punctuation in terms of major junctures and the arbitrary rules of editors.[5]

Reading styles differ within rather narrow limits, but for the sake of illustration we can arbitrarily pick one in which /#/ is symbolized by a

[5] By far the best available explanation is that by A. H. Marckwardt in the Thorndike-Barnhart *Comprehensive Desk Dictionary* (Doubleday, 1951), pp. 21–24.

period and /||/ by a comma. No other junctures are marked by punctua-
tion. If the student gives the reading 'He wasn't there /||/ therefore I didn't
see him,' the comma before *therefore* is right linguistically, however wrong
it may be editorially. If he reads 'I didn't go to the dance /#/ because I was
too tired,' the proper punctuation linguistically is into two sentences. In the
past year and a half, I have marked comma faults and fragments RA for
"Read aloud." When the student's reading has been right linguistically, I
have been able to show him how to identify the situations in which he cannot
trust to his ear for punctuation. Without claiming perfect results, I can say
that I have been astonished at how readily students of all levels have taken
to my explanations and how often they have asked me why punctuation was
never explained to them that way in high school.

Over and above such editorial errors in punctuation, the suprasegmental
phonemes are important in helping students understand why we group
words as we do and how it happens that writing produced by the unwary
is often ambiguous. Students can see (and hear) that junctures enclose
word groups, and when they understand that the number of junctures increases as the pace of reading slows, they can more and more guard their
readers against misunderstanding. 'After eating the baby fell asleep' (which
I owe to a former colleague) tends to disappear. This is not simply a matter
of punctuation, for often the student either alters the word order ('The baby
fell asleep after eating') or makes a substitution ('After its meal the baby
fell asleep'). The reason it disappears is that the student has discovered
that

After êating the báby . . .

is a possible alternative to

After éating . . .

The sound system of English, then, has a rather direct bearing on what
teachers do in the classroom. In particular, familiarity with the segmental
phonemes should make for an understanding of spelling difficulties due to
dialect and should kill once and for all the notion that unconventional phonemic spelling is a sign that the speller "doesn't speak good English" or
"doesn't enunciate his words clearly": When the snow is deep, many of the
best people wear

/ártĭks/, not /árk+tìks/.

And second, acquaintance with the suprasegmental phonemes can help us
realize why naive students punctuate as they do and manage to produce
some of their howlers. It is not a question of studying speech for its own
sake; it is a question of being able to put our fingers quite precisely on what
is amiss and of being in a position to help each student accommodate himself
to our traditional writing system and its editorial expectations.

9

Something of Morphemics

George P. Faust

THE TWO PREVIOUS ARTICLES of this series have mainly tried to explain (1) that the structural linguists give priority to speech over writing for purposes of analysis and concern themselves with language as a medium of communication, and (2) what the most essential terms in phonemics are and how they are used. The present article will by necessity use the earlier two as background, assuming acquaintance with the phonemes of English and some ability to read phonemic transcription. I hope that is not too forbidding.

As we approach morphemics, new terms will concern us, but they will seem like so much abracadabra unless the occasion for them is clear. I myself do not see how they could be dispensed with. Again, familiar terms used in new ways are sure to be traps unless the redefinitions of them are observed and absorbed. But as Professor Fries has observed, "The difference between the [structural] approach used here and the older approach lies much deeper than a mere matter of terminology."[1] There should be no worship of terms, nor fear either, for the terms themselves are not central except as they operate as tools. In general, the structuralists seem to care relatively little for the terms and a great deal for accurate definition and consistent use. What is important is the discovery of a pattern or of a tool, a method, for bringing patterns to light.

MORPHEMICS, which includes everything in language (narrowly defined) from the smallest unit of meaning to the construction of the sentence, takes its name from a useful tool, the morpheme. The first stages of morphemics, up to syntax, are called MORPHOLOGY, and the first two steps in morphology are to identify morphs and classify them. A MORPH can be oversimply defined as an individual linguistic form which is an indivisible unit of meaning. Someone who says 'scramble' has used a morph. It seems to contain several forms—*am, ram, scram, ramble, amble*. But if any one of them is taken out, the remainder of the sounds is meaningless. We are forced to conclude that the 'scramble' we heard is indivisible.

Reprinted by permission from *College Composition and Communication*, 5.65–69 (May, 1954).
[1] *The Structure of English* (Harcourt, Brace & World, Inc., 1952), p. 2.

Any morph can be recorded as a phoneme or a pattern of phonemes. (Here it should be emphasized that no phoneme *qua* phoneme is a morph. To be a morph, a phoneme must in addition carry meaning.) Suppose you render the line "A rose is a rose is . . ." Each occurrence of *a* /ə/, *rose* /rowz/, and *is* /iz/ is a morph, but the second occurrence is not the same morph as the first, for, strictly speaking, no morph is ever repeated. This only means, of course, that the first pin of the paper is never the second, no matter how much alike they may be.

Determining whether a form is meaningful is a technical process that cannot be described here, but it is important to note that the structuralist does not need to be able to put his finger on the meaning. He only needs to know that it is there. And here is a good place to make, briefly, some distinction between referential meaning, which belongs to semantics, and differential meaning, which is a tool of structural linguistics. Given the knowledge that a form has meaning, it *is* important to the linguist to know whether its meaning is "same" or "different" as compared with another form. So, if he hears

'He's still' /hiyz stíl/

on one occasion and

'He's still here' /hiyz stíl híhr/

on another, he will want to find out whether the two forms he has recorded as /still/ are "same" or "different." (As a native speaker, I say, "Different." Do we agree?)

Broadly speaking, structuralists arrive at morphemes by comparing morphs. A MORPHEME can be defined, again oversimply, as a class of morphs that are semantically similar and contrast with morphs belonging to other morphemes. Semantic similarity by itself might gather /red/, /yelow/, /blɪw/[2] into one morpheme of color, but since they all contrast before /dres/, say, they belong to different morphemes.

Often there are differences among the members of a morpheme, usually phonemic, and it is useful to recognize subclasses, called allomorphs. An ALLOMORPH consists of like morphs that are in complementary distribution with all other members of their morpheme. For example, English has a morpheme of plurality which has a great many allomorphs. To take the three simplest and most obvious variants, consider *coats* /kowts/, *gloves* /gləvz/, and *dresses* /dresɪz/. In each case a member of the plural morpheme is present, as we can learn from experiment. The forms /s, z, ɪz/ differ phonemically but are in complementary distribution. That is, we do not say /kowtɪz/, and with our training, we probably cannot say /kowtz/. These three, along with many others also in complementary distribution,

---

[2] /ɪ/ represents the high central vowel.

are set up as allomorphs of the plural morpheme. (The morpheme itself is recorded for conveniences as /Z_1/[3]; every such "cover symbol" should be described in full somewhere.) *Allomorph* is so convenient a term that even morphemes with a single phonemic shape are said to have one allomorph.

The parallel of *morph, allomorph,* and *morpheme* with *phone, allophone,* and *phoneme* is obvious. Any morph may be called a morph (i.e., an individual linguistic form which is an indivisible unit of meaning) or an allomorph (i.e., a member of an allomorph) or a morpheme (i.e., a member of a morpheme). If I hear you say 'Take your coats,' the last meaningful unit, /s/, is a morph that immediately becomes past history. By comparison with other examples of /s/ with the same kind of meaning, I can set up what I think is a class. But a trained structuralist would very soon discover that my supposed class was only a subclass, an allomorph, of a morpheme that has many allomorphs.

The material considered so far has all consisted of segmental phonemes and has given us SEGMENTAL MORPHEMES. The suprasegmental phonemes produce SUPRASEGMENTAL MORPHEMES, whose meanfulness is harder for us to grasp, partly—at a guess—because they have only recently been discovered. But apparently it is impossible for us to say anything in English without using at least three morphemes: one segmental, one of stress, and one of intonation (pitch and major juncture).[4] The full phonemic transcription of one way of saying 'Go' is

$$/^{3}\text{gów}^{1}\#/.$$

One morpheme is the segmental material, /gow/; one is the stress, /′/; and one is the intonation pattern, /$^{3\ 1}$#/. The suprasegmental morphemes need not be examined here; their greatest value is in syntactic analysis.

After the morphemes are accounted for, the next step in morphology is to classify the segmental morphemes in what might be called "the grammar of the word." Briefly, the segments can be grouped into BASES, PREFIXES, and SUFFIXES. Bases are usually "free forms" like *sweet*—forms that occur without any prefix or suffix—but some are not, like *-ceive,* which always occurs with a prefix. Prefixes, which like suffixes are never free forms, need no comment. There are two kinds of suffixes, DERIVATIONAL and GRAMMATICAL. Derivational suffixes, like the *-ness* of *coolness,* tend to limit forms to a particular part of speech. (Does this account for our widespread objection to the use of *suspicion* as a verb?) Grammatical suffixes give us the

---

[3] For simplicity, the customary brackets for morphemes are not used in this article. The subscript distinguishes the plural morpheme from any others that may have any of the same phonemic shapes.

[4] See G. L. Trager and H. L. Smith, Jr., *An Outline of English Structure* (Studies in Linguistics: Occasional Paper No. 3). Pitch is represented /4 (highest), 3, 2, 1 (lowest)/.

inflections of the few remaining paradigms in English. Disregarding supra-segmental features, the WORD can now be defined as a single base with or without prefixes and suffixes. By this definition, *incompatibility*, with its single base, is a word; *shotgun*, with two bases, is not. *It is of no linguistic importance that* shotgun *is written solid.*

The final step in morphology is the establishment of PARADIGMS, which can be viewed as sets of grammatical suffixes. These suffixes follow the base and derivational suffixes (e.g., either *help* or *helpfulness*). English has paradigms for pronouns, nouns, verbs, and adjectives. In at least the last three, "no suffix" must be recognized as a characteristic ending by contrast with the suffixes used. It is a peculiarity of the language that the noun suffixes for "plural" and "possessive" coalesce when they are both present and the plural morpheme is one of /s, z, ɪz/. Thus we get /kidz/ (alongside /menz/ where we might have expected /kidzɪz/.

The paradigm for MORPHOLOGICAL PRONOUNS, a notoriously irregular set, has been the occasion for a good deal of experimenting. The presentation we grew up with emphasizes person, number, gender and case in that order. One of the structural presentations re-works the order to gender, case, person, and number, with really no attention to the last two. The order of cases is also modified to subject, object, 1st possessive, 2nd possessive. Here is the paradigm: *Without Gender:* I, me, my, mine; we, us, our, ours; you, you, your, yours; they, them, their, theirs. *With Gender:* he, him, his, his; she, her, her, hers; it, it, its,—. (Whether the forms of *who* are included is a matter of personal preference.)

The paradigm for NOUNS is: *Common Case:* Sg. (no suffix) /layf/, Pl. (/-Z₁/) /layvz/; *Possessive Case:* Sg. (/-Z₂/) /layfs/, Pl. (/-Z₁/ and /-Z₂/ merged) /layvz/.

The paradigm for VERBS is: *Infinitive and General Present:* (no suffix) /liv/, /rayz/; *3rd Singular Present:* (/-Z₃/) /livz/, /rayzɪz/; *Past:* (/-D₁/) /livd/, /rowz/; *Past Participle:* (/-D₂/) /livd/, /rizɪn/; *Present Participle:* ('-ing') 'living,' 'rising.'

The paradigm for ADJECTIVES is: *positive:* (no suffix) /layv/; *Comparative:* (/-ər/) /layvər/; *Superlative:* (/-ɪst/) /layvɪst/.

The reason for going into the paradigms fully is that they serve as definitions of parts of speech at the morphological level. If an item is inflectible within a paradigm—that is, if it appears with at least two appropriate suffixes (including "no suffix")—it is a member of the part of speech defined by the paradigm.[5] Every item must qualify by this test to be included, which means that *poor (poorer, poorest)* is a MORPHOLOGICAL ADJECTIVE, but

---

[5] It is not true, as sometimes claimed, that morphological parts of speech cannot be identified without the help of syntax. Without anything to go on but 'Boys will be boys' a linguist could find out from a completely naive informant that *boys* is the plural of *boy*. Contrast 'Fuzz will be fuzz.' If the linguist already knows that *they* is plural, he can take a short cut by trying 'They will be boys.'

excellent remains unassigned. A MORPHOLOGICAL NOUN is defined as a linguistic item which is inflectible for singular/plural, or for common case/possessive, or for both. Similarly, a MORPHOLOGICAL VERB is inflectible for present/past, etc. *Man* is a noun because we write *man's* as well as because of *men;* it is also a verb because of *manned* and other verbal suffixation. What any one occurrence of the form *man* itself may be is a question of assigning it to a paradigm.

Roughly speaking, structural linguistics offers the same list of nouns and verbs as traditional grammar. It is not important why this is so. It is not even important what particular words, like *other* (cf. *others*), are included among nouns, say. What is important is the basis for the classification. We are thoroughly used to a system that often starts with philosophical definitions, and freshmen still know that "A noun is the name of . . ." At this point it is hard for me to see why, *philosophically* speaking, *rain* is not just as much of a noun in 'It rained during the night' as in 'Rain fell during the night.' The difference to me now is purely linguistic. In the first, *rain* has a suffix that belongs distinctly to the paradigm labeled *verb*; in the second, *rains,* with the plural morpheme, can be substituted for *rain* and produce an English sentence.

Structural definitions are no panacea in teaching, but my experience with using them has been encouraging. For the present, students who have mastered traditional grammar had better be left alone, unless they are exceptionally bright. But among those who never "learned grammar" in high school, I have found some who can match forms more easily than grasp the traditional definitions.

When we leave morphology for syntax, we come to an area where much has been done and much remains to be done. Professor Fries's analysis is so well known and speaks so adequately for itself that I need do no more than allude to *The Structure of English.* The highly technical Trager-Smith *Outline of English Structure,* which I have been more or less following (but any mistakes are mine), is simply unreadable without training in structural linguistics. Yet it has been extraordinarily influential among structuralists, especially for its insistence on a separation of "levels" in analysis and for its report on how we use suprasegmental morphemes to determine constructions.

Separation of levels means, among other things, that parts of speech morphologically defined are not the same as parts of speech syntactically defined. If you hear 'Today is Sunday,' 'Today's paper just came,' and 'He just came today,' you can tell from the forms in the first two that *today* is a morphological noun. But in the second it is in some respects a SYNTACTIC ADJECTIVE, and in the last, fully a SYNTACTIC ADVERB.[6] It is only at the

---

[6] In terminology, the Trager-Smith analysis distinguishes less clumsily, but introduces more new terms: *morphological adjective=adjective; syntactic adjective=adjectival.* There are no *adverbs*—only *adverbials.*

syntactic level that adverbs, prepositions, conjunctions, question words (e.g., *when, why, what*), some auxiliaries, and some adjectives can be assigned to parts of speech. To avoid confusion, it is always best to prefix either *morphological* or *syntactic,* whichever is proper, to the name of the part.

Traditional definitions have been by meaning, by form, and by function. Definition by meaning is demonstrably unnecessary. By the separation of levels, it is now possible to take care of difficulties and confusions growing out of using a definition by form and definition by function simultaneously. As a resultant, we may well expect an end of such descriptions as "noun used as adjective" (e.g., in *state highway*) and "noun used as adverb" or "adverbial noun" (e.g., *home* in 'He went home'). If the cleavage between levels were consistently represented in our schoolbooks, I feel sure we would be able to teach it easily.

Suprasegmental morphemes are either SUPERFIXES, patterns of stress with or without plus juncture intervening, or INTONATION PATTERNS, patterns of pitch and major juncture. Several superfixes have been discovered to be "phrase-making":

$$/`+´/,/´+`/, \text{ and } /´+ˆ/.$$

(/ˆ+´/ does not make phrases.) Noun compounds have superfixes and are syntactic phrases (e.g., *shotgun*—shót+gùn—which was rejected as a morphological word). 'A blackboard [bláck+bôard] isn't just a black board [blâck+bóard]' illustrates the difference between phrase and non-phrase, and so does 'It's a come-down' (cóme+dôwn) in contrast with 'He's come down' (côme+dówn). Intonation patterns make a number of distinctions, only one of which can be illustrated here. '²He's ³going¹#' uses the commonest morpheme, which can be described as "statement unless qualified by other signals." It contrasts with '²Is he ³góing³||', a pattern associated with questions that use no question-word. ('²He's ³góing³||', is a question because of the pattern; '²Where is he ²góing¹#' is a question because the pattern is qualified by the use of *where*.) Generally speaking, superfixes apply to phrases, while intonation patterns apply to larger constructions that might be called intonation clauses.

It has proved impossible to cover the ground of morphemics in even a simplified way. My apologies are due the reader for a crowded article which has found little room to point to applications useful to us as teachers. One thing is reasonably certain, and that is that many uses will be found as we gather a corps of middlemen—structuralists who know something about our teaching problems and teachers who are at home with structural linguistics.

10

Meaning and Linguistic Analysis

CHARLES C. FRIES

MANY WHO HAVE READ the materials of present-day American linguists and have listened to their discussions have gained the impression that these linguists have cast out 'meaning' altogether.[1] The two statements following are typical.

> Certain leading linguists especially in America find it possible to exclude the study of what they call 'meaning' from scientific linguistics, but only by deliberately excluding anything, in the nature of mind, thought, idea, concept. 'Mentalism' is taboo.[2]

> A general characteristic of the methodology of descriptive linguistics, as practised by American linguists today, is the effort to analyze linguistic structure without reference to meaning.[3]

One can point to a variety of quotations from the writings of our American linguists, that seem to substantiate the views that these linguists not only condemn the 'use of meaning' in linguistic analysis (as indicated in the quotation from Carroll), but (as indicated in the quotation from Firth) even refuse to treat 'meaning.'

Concerning the supposed refusal to treat 'meaning', quotations such as the following have sometimes been offered in evidence.

> The situations which prompt people to utter speech include every object and happening in the universe. In order to give a scientifically accurate definition

Reprinted by permission from *Language,* 30.57–68 (January–March, 1954).

[1] When I set out to challenge anew the conventional uses of meaning as the basic tool of analysis in sentence structure and syntax—the area of linguistic study in which it has had its strongest hold—I felt very keenly an obligation to state as fully and as accurately as I could just what uses I did make of meaning in my procedures. This paper represents the result. Although the materials presented here use general terms, I should like to point out that my experience has dealt primarily with English. This statement of the principles and assumptions that have underlain and guided my studies of English may not have equal relevance to the problems presented by other languages.

[2] J. R. Firth, "General Linguistics and Descriptive Grammar," *Transactions of the Philological Society,* 1950.82 (London, 1951).

[3] John B. Carroll, *A Survey of Linguistics and Related Disciplines,* 15 (Cambridge, Mass., 1950).

of meaning for every form of a language, we should have to have a scientifically accurate knowledge of everything in the speakers' world. The actual extent of human knowledge is very small, compared to this.

The statement of meanings is therefore the weak point in language-study, and will remain so until human knowledge advances very far beyond its present state.

The signals can be analyzed but not the things signaled about. This reinforces the principle that linguistic study must always start from the phonetic form and not from meaning. . . . the meanings . . . could be analyzed or systematically listed only by a well-nigh omniscient observer.[4]

Concerning the alleged condemnation of the 'use of meaning' in linguistic analysis the evidence usually consists of quotations like the following.

Theoretically it would be possible to arrive at the phonemic system of a dialect entirely on the basis of phonetics and distribution, without any appeal to meaning—provided that in the utterance of the dialect not all the possible combinations of phonemes actually occurred.

. . . our approach differs in some respects from Bloomfield's—chiefly in that Bloomfield invokes meaning as a fundamental criterion . . .[5]

In the present state of morphemic analysis it is often convenient to use the meanings of utterance fractions as a general guide and short-cut to the identification of morphemes. This is especially so in the case of languages that are more or less well known to the analyst, and has been true for most morphemic work done up to now. When we are confronted, however, with a language that we know little about in terms of the relations of the linguistic behavior, it becomes clear that meaning can be of little help as a guide. The theoretical basis of analysis then becomes evident: it consists of the recognition of the recurrences and distributions of similar patterns and sequences. The analyst must therefore constantly keep in mind this theoretical basis, and must be aware that his hunches about what goes with what are really short-cut conclusions about distributional facts.[6]

In exact descriptive linguistic work . . . considerations of meaning can only be used heuristically, as a source of hints, and the determining criteria will always have to be stated in distributional terms. The methods presented in the preceding chapters offer distributional investigations as alternatives to meaning considerations.[7]

Some who are counted among our linguistic scholars have so vigorously condemned all 'uses of meaning' that for many linguistic students the word *meaning* itself has almost become anathema.

[4] Leonard Bloomfield, *Language,* pp. 139, 140, 162 (New York, 1933).
[5] Bernard Bloch, "A Set of Postulates for Phonemic Analysis, *Lg.* 24.5 note 8, 24.6 (1948).
[6] George Trager and Henry Lee Smith Jr., *An Outline of English Structure,* p. 54 (Oklahoma, 1951).
[7] Zellig S. Harris, *Methods in Structural Linguistics,* p. 365, note 6 (Chicago, 1951).

On the other hand, those who oppose the recent developments in the methods of linguistic study nearly all assume, as a matter of course, that all use of every type of meaning has been rigidly excluded from the linguistic studies made in accord with these methods, and often make that assumed fact the basis of their opposition and criticism.

Sometimes it is insisted that the so-called 'repudiation of meaning' in the work of American linguists stems from Leonard Bloomfield. This view rests not upon what Bloomfield has said about meaning (which seems to have been overlooked) but upon inferences drawn from a somewhat superficial reading of his discussions of mentalism and mechanism. Thus concerning Bloomfield there have been such assertions as the following.

> Mechanists cannot successfully speak of meaning because they undertake to ignore certain phases of human response.

> The mechanist cannot consider the ethnologic features of meaning, such as connotative colorings or social levels.

> The mechanists' definition of a plant-name . . . cannot . . . extend beyond the definition which appears in a handbook of botany: it cannot deal with ethnically conditioned features of meaning.

Bloomfield's physicalism (mechanism, anti-mentalism), as it is expressed in his linguistic writings, was not a philosophy of the universe nor a psychological system, but solely, as he insisted over and over again, a matter of the method of scientific descriptive statement:

> An individual may base himself upon a purely practical, an artistic, a religious, or a scientific acceptance of the universe, and that aspect which he takes as basic will transcend and include the others. The choice, at the present state of our knowledge, can be made only by an act of faith, and with this the issue of mentalism should not be confounded. It is the belief of the present writer that the scientific description of the universe, whatever this description may be worth, requires none of the mentalistic terms, because the gaps which these terms are intended to bridge exist only so long as language is left out of account.[8]

Bloomfield strove vigorously to avoid mentalistic terms (*concept, idea,* etc.) in the statement of his linguistic materials and believed that every truly 'scientific statement is made in physical terms.'[9] But his efforts to achieve statements in physical rather than 'mentalistic' terms do not lead to the conclusion that he 'ignores meaning' or that 'he takes no account of meaning.' He and many of his followers have pointed to certain uses of meaning in linguistic analysis as constituting unscientific procedures, but he

---

[8] Bloomfield, *Linguistic Aspects of Science,* p. 12 (Chicago, 1944).

[9] Bloomfield, "Language or Ideas?," *Language,* 12.92 note 6. Bloomfield followed Weiss in objecting to the term *behaviorism* and believed that *physicalism* indicated much better the essential quality of the kind of descriptive statements he sought.

and many of his followers have constantly insisted that meaning cannot be ignored. Pertinent quotations from Bloomfield's *Language* are abundant:

> Man utters many kinds of vocal noise and makes use of the variety; under certain types of stimuli he produces certain vocal sounds, and his fellows, hearing these same sounds, make the appropriate response. To put it briefly, in human speech, different sounds have different meanings. To study this coordination of certain sounds with certain meanings is to study language. (27)

> The study of significant speech-sounds is phonology or practical phonetics. Phonology involves the consideration of meanings. (28)

> Only two kinds of linguistic records are scientically relevant. One is a mechanical record of the gross acoustic features, such as is produced in the phonetics laboratory. The other is a record in terms of phonemes, ignoring all features that are not distinctive in the language. Until our knowledge of acoustics has progressed far beyond its present state, only the latter kind of record can be used for any study that takes into consideration the meaning of what is spoken. (85)

> It is important to remember that practical phonetics and phonology presuppose a knowledge of meaning: without this knowledge we could not ascertain the phonemic features. (137)

> Only in this way will a proper analysis (that is, one which takes account of the meanings) lead to the ultimate constituent morphemes. (161)

Let me add to these quotations an excerpt from a letter dated 29 January 1945, written by Bloomfield to a friend of mine:

> It has become painfully common to say that I, or rather, a whole group of language students of whom I am one, pay no attention to meaning or neglect it, or even that we undertake to study language without meaning, simply as meaningless sound. . . . It is not just a personal affair that is involved in the statements to which I have referred, but something which, if allowed to develop, will injure the progress of our science by setting up a fictitious contrast between students who consider meaning and students who neglect or ignore it. The latter class, so far as I know, does not exist.

With Bloomfield, no serious study of human language can or does ignore 'meaning.' It is my thesis here that on all levels of linguistic analysis certain features and types of meaning furnish a necessary portion of the apparatus used. In what I shall say, however, I do not mean to defend the common uses of meaning as the BASIS of analysis and classification, or as determining the content of linguistic definition and descriptive statement, though such uses have characterized much of the study of language since the time of the Greeks. The issue is not an opposition between NO use of meaning whatever, and ANY and ALL uses of meaning.

With many others, I believe that certain uses of meaning in certain specific processes of linguistic analysis and in descriptive statement are unscientific, that is, that they do not lead to satisfactory, verifiable, and useful results. The more one works with the records of actual speech the more impossible it appears to describe the requirements of sentences (for example) in terms of meaning content. The definitive characteristics distinguishing those expressions which occur alone as separate utterances from those which occur only as parts of larger units are not matters of content or meaning, but matters of form, different from language to language. In the defining of 'subjects' and 'objects,' of the 'parts of speech,' of 'negation,' we have not successfully approached the problems by seeking criteria of meaning content. Only as we have been able to find and to describe the contrastive formal characteristics have we been able to grasp grammatical structures in terms that make prediction possible. Structures do signal meanings, it is true, and these meanings must be described. But the meanings cannot serve successfully to identify and distinguish the structures. Not only does each structure usually signal several different meanings, but—what is more important— there is probably in present-day English no structural meaning that is not signalled by a variety of structures.[10]

This challenging of certain uses of meaning, as I have said, does not constitute a repudiation of all meaning in linguistic analysis. Meaning of some kind and of some degree always and inevitably constitutes part of the framework in which we operate. If that is so, then for clarity and understanding, as well as for rigorous procedure on each level of analysis, we must state as completely as possible the precise uses of each type of meaning that our procedures require and assume.[11]

---

[10] The meaning 'performer of the action' is one of the meanings signaled by the structure we call 'subject.' We cannot, however, expect to DEFINE the structure 'subject' as 'performer of the action,' for this meaning is signaled by a variety of other structures that are not 'subjects.' For example, in each of the following sentences, the word *committee* has the meaning 'performer of the action (of recommending)'; but only in the first sentence is this word in the structure of 'subject': *The committee recommended his promotion; His promotion was recommended by the committee; The recommendation of the committee was that he be promoted; The committee's recommendation was that he be promoted; The action of the recommending committee was that he be promoted.* The structure of 'subject,' on the other hand, signals at least five different meanings—four in addition to that of 'performer'—each distinguished by special formal arrangements. See C. C. Fries, *The Structure of English,* pp. 176–83 (New York, 1952).

[11] To accuse linguists of deliberately refusing to treat meaning at all is to ignore the facts. The number of thoroughly trained linguists is very small indeed, and, although there are more positions for such linguists in the academic world than there were twenty years ago, there are not enough such positions to support a sufficient number of linguists to carry on the linguistic studies that are needed in every part of the field. For the past twenty-five years the really live issues that have claimed the attention of linguists have centered about linguistic structure. The new views of the significance of structure and the success of new procedures of structural analysis applied to various aspects of language have aroused such enthusiasm that most linguists have devoted their studies to these matters. Although the present center of liveliest interest in linguistics is structure

How much and just what of linguistic analysis can be accomplished without the use of any kind or degree of meaning at all? Certain meanings seem essential to making the very first step—the setting up of the material to be worked with, to be analyzed and described. There must be a 'meaning frame' within which to operate. We must know or assume, for example, (a) that the sound sequences we attempt to analyze are indeed real language utterances and the utterances of a single language, not those of several languages—a dozen or a hundred; (b) something of the range of possibilities in human language behavior and the significance of certain techniques or methods of procedure for linguistic analysis; and (c) a practical control of a language (usually another language) in which to grasp and record the processes and the results of the analysis. (Many difficulties arise from the fact that often the language of the descriptive record of the analysis differs greatly in its range of meanings and way of grouping experience from that of the language being analyzed.)

Under (b), for example, we assume that all languages have some type of meaningful units—morphemes; that all languages have bundles of contrasts of sound that function in separating or marking out or identifying these morphemes; that generally the lexical items have some contrastive formal features that make possible their classification into structurally functioning units; that all languages have formal arrangements of some sort of these structurally functioning units into contrastive patterns that have significance as structural signals of certain features of meaning; and that the linguistically significant patterns of structural arrangement are limited, much fewer than the total number of morphemes.

We must approach every linguistic analysis with a large body of 'meaning' in hand. The question is not, then, whether we can dispense with all meaning in linguistic analysis but rather, more specifically, whether we can proceed with a valid and useful analysis without some knowledge or some control (e.g. through an informant) of the meanings of the language forms which we are analyzing.

In respect to this specific question, we must face the problem of distinguishing, with some precision if possible, several varieties of meaning. I do not refer especially to the tremendous diversity of meanings which attach

---

rather than meaning, some portions of the general problems of meaning have received attention. (See for example Bloomfield's *Linguistic Aspects of Science,* 1939; *Philosophical Aspects of Language,* 1942; Language or Ideas?, *Lg.* 12.89–95 [1936]; Meaning, *Monatshefte für deutschen Unterricht* 35.101–6 [1943].)

Even with respect to the lexicon, we should, for the record, note that the American linguists whose center of interest has been the English language have given constant support to the labors of those who have been struggling with the problems of producing the various period dictionaries proposed by Sir William Craigie. The *Oxford Dictionary* itself was an effort to apply practically what was at that time called the 'new philological science.

to the word *meaning*[12] itself, although that diversity often prevents fruitful discussion. A few quotations will show a little of this diversity:

> The meaning of any sentence is what the speaker intends to be understood from it by the listener.[13]

> By the meaning of a proposition I mean . . . the ideas which are called to mind when it is asserted.[14]

> What we call the meaning of a proposition embraces every obvious necessary deduction from it.[15]

> Meaning is a relation between two associated ideas, one of which is appreciably more interesting than the other.[16]

> To indicate the situation which verifies a proposition is to indicate what the proposition means.[17]

> The meaning of anything whatsoever is identical with the set of expectations its presence arouses.[18]

> Meaning is the fact of redintegrative sequence . . . the evocation of a total response by a partial stimulus.[19]

> . . . the word 'meaning' has established itself in philosophical discourse because it conveniently covers both reason and value.[20]

> The meaning of certain irregularities in the motion of the moon is found in the slowing up of the motion of the earth around its axis.[21]

> 'Meaning' signifies any and all phases of sign-processes (the status of being a sign, the interpretant, the fact of denoting, the signification) and frequently suggests mental and valuational processes as well.[22]

[12] See Leo Abraham, What is the theory of meaning about?, *The Monist* 46.228–56 (1936). In this article are gathered more than fifty typical quotations from philosophical and psychological writers, in each of which the term *meaning* is used in a different sense. At the end of these quotations he concludes, 'There is clearly nothing both common and peculiar either to all the various disparate senses, or to only the more familiar among them, which itself bears, or should bear, the name "meaning" . . . A subject matter for the "theory of meaning" cannot, accordingly, be obtained by abstraction from all or some of the entities revealed by the linguistic phenomenology of the term "meaning".'

[13] A. Gardiner, "The Definition of the Word and the Sentence, *"British Journal of Psychology,* 1922.361.

[14] N. Campbell, *Physics: The Elements,* p. 132 (1920).

[15] C. S. Peirce, *Collected Papers,* 5.165 (1934).

[16] F. Anderson, "On the Nature of Meaning," *Journal of Philosophy,* 1933.212.

[17] A. J. Ayer, "Demonstration of the Impossibility of Metaphysics," *Mind,* 1934.333.

[18] C. W. Morris, "Pragmatism and Metaphysics," *Philosophical Review,* 1934.557.

[19] H. L. Hollingworth, "Meaning and the Psycho-physical Continuum," *Journal of Philosophy,* 1923.440.

[20] W. E. Hocking, *Philosophical Review,* 1928.142.

[21] M. R. Cohen, *Reason and Nature,* p. 107 (1931).

[22] C. W. Morris, *Signs, Language, and Behavior,* p. 19 (New York, 1946).

We come then to the conclusion that meaning is practically everything. We always see the meaning as we look, think in meanings as we think, act in terms of meaning when we act. Apparently we are never directly conscious of anything but meanings.[23]

As speakers of English have employed it, the word *meaning* has thus represented a great range of content. In English usage the word *meaning* has signified such diverse matters as 'the denotation of a name,' the connotation of a symbol,' 'the implications of a concept,' 'the neuro-muscular and glandular reactions produced by anything,' 'the place of anything in a system,' 'the practical consequences of anything,' 'the usefulness of anything,' 'that to which the interpreter of a symbol does refer,' 'that to which the interpreter of a symbol ought to be referring,' 'that to which the user of a symbol wants the interpreter to infer,' 'any object of consciousness whatever.' This great diversity of statement arises out of an attempt to describe the specific content of the situations in which the word *meaning* appears. Even more difficult and controversial has been the effort to classify and define the various kinds of meaning in terms of the meaning content of utterances in general. Often these various 'meanings' are grouped under two general headings: (1) the scientific, descriptive, representative, referential, denotive, cognitive kind of meaning, and (2) the emotive, expressive, noncognitive kind of meaning.[24]

The following quotation summarizes a portion of an analysis of utterances in terms of meaning content.

Thus in the case of certain sorts of indicative, interrogative, imperative, and optative sentence-utterances . . . it seems possible to distinguish a number of factors, each of which may be and has been referred to as the meaning or part of the meaning of the utterance. These are: (1) the primary conceptual content symbolized, i.e. presented and evoked; (2) the propositional attitude (with regard to this) expressed and evoked; (3) the secondary conceptual content presented and evoked; (4) the propositional attitudes (regarding this) expressed and evoked; (5) the emotions and conative attitudes expressed; (6) the emotional tone; (7) the emotions and attitudes revealed; (8) other kinds of effects; (9) the purpose.[25]

Let me turn away from these attempts to classify and describe the different kinds of meaning in terms of the meaning content itself to a classification

[23] W. B. Pillsbury, "Meaning and Image," *Psychological Review*, 1908.156.
[24] C. L. Stevenson, *Ethics and Language,* p. 33 (New Haven, 1944): 'The emotive meaning of a word is the power that the word acquires, on account of its history in emotional situations, to evoke or directly express attitudes, as distinct from describing or designing them.' Id. 73: 'The independence of emotive meaning can be roughly tested by comparing descriptive synonyms which are not emotive synonyms. Thus to whatever extent the laudatory strength of "democracy" exceeds that of "government where rule is by popular vote," the emotive meaning of the former will be independent.'
[25] William Fankena, "Cognitive and Non-cognitive Aspects of Language," *Language and Symbolism* [unpublished tentative report] 5.27, 28 (1952).

based upon the kinds of signals a language uses in fulfilling its social function. I am concerned here solely with language as it provides a connection between two nervous systems. Such a use of language is not by any means limited to the communication of knowledge; but it provides for all the ways in which the members of a group interact.

A well-known diagram (slightly modified) will furnish a simplified frame for some comments concerning my use here of the term *meaning* as it applies to language content. This diagram must not be taken as implying any psychological theory whatever.

INDIVIDUAL A	INDIVIDUAL B
S ⟶ r . . . . s ⟶ R	
Effective field Sounds as	Sounds as The practical
of the stimulus produced	heard response

The particular speech act which
becomes an effective stimulus
for B through language

The speech act consists of both r, the succession of sound waves as produced by individual A, and s, the succession of sound waves as heard by individual B. Broadly speaking, there never is or can be an exact repetition of any particular succession of sound waves as produced and as heard: precise measurements and accurate recordings always reveal some differences. But in a linguistic community two or more physically different speech acts may fit into a single functioning pattern and thus may be functionally the 'same.'[26] Basically, then, the material that constitutes language must be recurring 'sames' of speech acts. The sum of the speech acts of a community does not, however, constitute its language. Only as sequences of vocal sounds are grasped or recognized[27] as fitting into recurring patterns do they become the stuff of language—only when they are correlated with recurring practical situations in man's experience and thus become the means of eliciting predictable responses.

[26] These 'sames' must not be taken as the engineer's 'norms' with margins of tolerance —statistical norms clustering around averages; see Martin Joos, Language design, *Journal of the Acoustical Society* 22.701–8 (1950). They are 'sames' as the various types of 'strike' in baseball are functionally the same; see Fries, *The Structure of English*, pp. 60–1.

[27] I take *recognition* here to mean not a conscious act of identification, but rather an automatic conditioned response connecting the patterns of vocal sound with recurrent features of experience. Recognition is itself a 'meaning' response. I am assuming that every kind of meaning has this kind of process. On every level, it seems to me, shapes, colors, sizes, smells, tastes have meaning only as they fit into patterns that connect them in some way with recurring features of experience. When stimuli do not fit such patterns of recurring experience they are 'meaningless,' and confuse us. As a matter of fact it is usually the case that only features that do fit such patterns are reacted to at all; the others do not become effective features of stimuli. For adults there seems to be no such thing as 'raw' observation unrelated to any pattern of experience.

The schematic formula above helps to direct attention to three aspects of meaning in language. First, there is the recognition of a sequence of vocal sounds as fitting into some pattern of recurring sames. Second, there is the recognition of the recurring sames of stimulus-situation features with which these sames of vocal sounds occur. Third, there is the recognition of the recurring sames of practical response features which these sames of vocal sounds elicit. A language, then, is a system of recurring sequences or patterns of sames of vocal sounds, which correlate with recurring sames of stimulus-situation features, and which elicit recurring sames of response features.[28]

In general, for linguists,[29] the 'meanings' of an utterance consist of the correlating, regularly recurrent sames of the stimulus-situation features, and the regularly elicited recurring sames of response features.[30] These meanings are tied to the patterns of recurring sames of vocal sounds. In other words, the patterns of recurring sound sequences are the signals of the meanings. The meanings can be separated into various kinds or layers in accord with the several levels of patterns in the recurring sound sequences which do the signaling. Utterances will have then at least the following types or 'modes' of meaning.

(a) There is the automatic recognition of the recurrent sames that constitute the lexical items. The lexical items selected for a particular utterance are distinguished from others that might have been selected by sharp patterns of sequences of sound contrasts. One layer of the meaning of the utterance

[28] A linguistic community consists of those individuals that make the 'same' regular and predictable responses to the 'same' patterns of vocal sounds. The language function is fulfilled only in so far as it is possible to predict the response features that will regularly be elicited by the patterns of vocal sound. For the discussion here I am not concerned with what might be called 'personal' meaning—the special non-recurrent or not regularly recurring response features that mark individual differences.

[29] For many others the meaning of a text or a sequence of utterances has often been considered a function of (a) the 'words' (as items of sound patterns which experience has connected in some way with reality), and (b) the 'context.' This context has included both the so-called 'verbal context' or linguistic context (not specified further) and the 'context of situation'—the circumstances in which the utterance occurs. Firth has pushed the analysis of 'context' much farther in his dealing with 'formal scatter' and 'meaning by collocation.' See his Modes of meaning, *Essays and studies* (English Assn.) 1951.118–49, and General linguistics and descriptive grammar, *Transactions of the Philological Society*, 1951.85–7; cf. his earlier "Technique of Semantics," *Trans. Philol. Soc.* 1935.36–72, and "Personality and Language in Society," *Sociological Review*, 1950.

[30] In the study of the language records of a former time we have, because of the nature of the evidence, usually had to try to arrive at the meanings of the language forms by connecting them with recurring elements of the situations in which they were used. In the study of living languages it is often possible to observe directly the responses which particular language forms elicit in a speech community. We assume that if a particular response regularly follows the utterance of a language pattern, then this pattern 'means' this response. Upon such regular recurrences rests the kind of prediction that makes possible the social functioning of language.

is determined and signaled by the particular lexical items selected and thus recognized. This recognition covers both the identification of the item itself by its contrastive shape, and the situation and response features with which this shape correlates in the linguistic community. If the stress and intonation, as well as the social-cultural situation, are kept constant, the meaning of the utterance *The point of this pen is bent over* differs from that of each of the following only because the lexical items differ: *The point of this pin is bent over, The cover of this pan is bent over, The top of that pen was sent over.* One of the separable layers of the meanings signaled by our utterances is thus the lexical meanings.

One other feature of lexical meaning must be noted. In addition to the recognition of the shape or forms of the lexical item itself, identified by contrastive patterns of sound sequences, there is also the automatic (and sometimes more conscious) recognition of the distribution of each lexical item with 'sets' of other lexical items as they occur in the complete utterance unit.[31] There is a 'lexical scatter' as well as a 'formal scatter.' It is this recognition of the particular set in which the lexical item occurs[32] that stimulates the selection of the specific 'sense' in which that item is to be taken, the specific stimulus-response features for that utterance.

(b) In addition to the layer of lexical meaning there is the automatic recognition of the contrastive features of arrangement in which the lexical items occur.[33] These contrastive features of arrangement regularly correlate with and thus signal a second layer of meanings—structural meanings. The difference in meaning between the following sentences depends solely upon the contrastive features of arrangement, assuming that the stress and intonation as well as the social-cultural situation are kept constant: *There is a book on the table, Is there a book on the table.* Structural meanings are not vague matters of 'context,' so called. They are sharply defined and specifically signaled by a complex system of contrastive patterns.

Together, LEXICAL MEANINGS and STRUCTURAL MEANINGS constitute the LINGUISTIC MEANING of our utterances. Linguistic meaning thus consists of lexical meanings within a frame of structural meanings—that is, of the

---

[31] 'Complete utterance unit' here means the total span of talk of one person in a single conversation or discourse.

[32] As we record more specifically the details of the experience of language learning, we realize increasingly that we 'learn' not only the shape of a lexical item and the recurrent stimulus-response features that correlate with it, but also the sets of other lexical items with which it usually occurs. Perhaps when psychologists explore the 'free association' of words for an individual, they are really dealing with these sets of lexical distribution.

[33] In English the functioning units of the contrastive arrangements that signal meanings are not lexical items as such, but rather classes of these items. A variety of formal features make possible the classification of lexical items into a very small number of form classes the members of which each function as structurally the same. Linguistic analysis must discover and describe these form classes as a means of dealing with the structures themselves.

stimulus-response features that accompany contrastive structural arrangements of lexical items.

But the linguistic meaning is only part of the total meaning of our utterances. In addition to the regularly recurring responses to the lexical items and structural arrangements there are also throughout a linguistic community recurring responses to unique whole utterances or sequences of utterances. Rip Van Winkle's simple utterance, *I am a poor quiet man, a native of the place, and a loyal subject of the King, God bless him!*, almost caused a riot, not because of the linguistic meaning signaled by the lexical items and structures, but because the unique utterance as a whole, now, after the Revolution, meant to the group that he was a confessed enemy of the newly established government. The statement, *Bill Smith swam a hundred yards in forty-five seconds,* would have not only the linguistic meaning attaching to the lexical items and the structures, but also the significance of the unique utterance as a whole, that this man had achieved a new world record. The petulant child's insistence at bed-time that he is hungry often means to the mother simply that he is trying to delay the going to bed. Meanings such as these I call 'social-cultural' meanings.[34] Linguistic meaning without social-cultural meaning constitutes what has been called 'mere verbalism.' The utterances of a language that function practically in a society therefore have both linguistic meaning and social-cultural meaning.

In general the meanings of the utterances are tied to formal patterns as signals.[35] In respect to linguistic meanings, I have assumed as a basis for study, that all the signals are formal features that can be described in physical terms of form, arrangement, and distribution. As I see it, the task of the linguistic analyst is to discover, test, and describe, in the system in which they occur, the formal features of utterances that operate as signals of meaning—specifically, (1) the contrastive features that constitute the recurrent sames of the forms of lexical units—the bundles of contrastive sound features by which morphemes are identified, (2) the contrastive markers by which structurally functioning groups of morphemes can be identified, and (3) the contrastive patterns that constitute the recurrent sames of the structural arrangements in which these structurally functioning classes of morphemes operate. In describing the results of the analysis, only verifiable physical terms of form, of arrangement, and of distribution are necessary. Whenever descriptive statements must depart from such formal matters, the fact is evidence of unsolved problems.

[34] The term 'social-cultural meaning' is not wholly satisfactory, but it is the best I have found to cover all the varieties of predictable meaning other than linguistic meaning. As indicated above, I have excluded from the discussion here the personal meaning of individual differences.

[35] This is true even of many of the varieties of social-cultural meaning—for example, the set of deviations from the norm of the sound segments that signal the meaning that a speaker is drunk, the whispering of an utterance that signals the meaning that the content of it is secret, and the unusual distribution that is the cue to a metaphor.

In the process of discovering just what formal features constitute the linguistic signals I can see no merit in denying ourselves access to any sources of suggestions concerning the nature of the materials that are significant. The more we know of the diverse characteristics of languages in general and of the processes that have marked language history, the more fruitfully prolific will be our suggestions. The less we know about language, the more frequently we may be led into blind alleys or follow the superstitions of the past.

In the process of testing these suggestions, however, and of proving the validity of our insights concerning the precise formal features that are significant, we need all the rigor that scientific procedure can offer. The real question centers upon the validity of the procedures through which we use techniques of distribution and of substitution. There must be some rigorous way of establishing 'sameness' of frame and 'sameness' of focus, as well as what constitutes 'difference' in each case.

In carrying out these tasks certain uses of particular kinds of 'meaning' within the utterance seem necessary and legitimate. (1) In testing the contrastive features that constitute the recurrent sames of lexical forms it is necessary to control in some way enough of the lexical meaning to determine whether forms showing certain differences of sound features are, for the particular language, 'same' or 'different.'[36] (2) In testing the contrastive patterns that constitute the recurrent sames of structural arrangements it is necessary to control in some way enough of the structural meaning to determine whether particular variants are substitutable, leaving the arrangement the 'same' for the language, or constitute such a change as to make the arrangement 'different.' Note that lexical meaning does not form part of the apparatus in which to test structural arrangements.

Social-cultural meanings which attach to the unique utterance as a whole or to a sequence of utterances do not seem to form any part of the frames in which to test either lexical forms or structural forms. Although a certain control of specific kinds of meaning seems to me essential for the various parts of linguistic analysis I should like to insist that as a general principle any use of meaning is unscientific whenever the fact of our knowing the meaning leads us to stop short of finding the precise formal signals that operate to convey that meaning.

[36] Sometimes it is insisted that we use 'differential' meaning, not 'referential' meaning. Perhaps this statement means that the linguistic analyst seeks basically to establish the fact whether two instances differ in meaning content or not. He does not need to know what that content is or in what ways the two may differ. If they differ in meaning he assumes that there must be some difference in formal features, and sets out to find, prove, and describe that difference.

11

Some Structural Ambiguities

Norman C. Stageberg

Many native speakers believe that our language can be manipulated like a boy's mechanical-builder set—with its interchangeable parts that can be put together in every which fashion—and that in English one can say any old thing in any old way. Such a belief is naive, for English is structured with a large number of syntactic patterns that we are compelled to follow. As a quick example, consider this noun group: *Our first large authorized class party.* Each of the five modifiers belongs in a class by itself and takes its predetermined position in the pattern.[1] If you change the order of these modifiers in any way, you will get a non-English sequence. And with many other patterns the same is true. We are pattern-bound in language just as we are culture-bound in mores. Now one would think that the numerous patterns of English, after centuries of development, would have become so refined as to be clear and unequivocal vehicles of thought. But such is not the case. On the contrary, there are many syntactic patterns that are open to ambiguity. It is these ambiguous patterns that I propose to describe—not all of them to be sure, but those that may be of greatest interest to the teacher of composition. At the outset we must be clear on one point: we are dealing with ambiguities in the written, not the spoken, language.

First, it may be useful to distinguish between two kinds of ambiguity, lexical and structural. In lexical ambiguity the multiple meaning resides in the words themselves, as in this news item from a California paper: "Rev. Keith Hammond was congratulated on being able to get his parish plastered." Structural ambiguity, on the other hand, results from the arrangement of the words, that is, from the structure of the utterance. It is sometimes known as syntactic ambiguity and, in older logic books, as amphiboly. Here is an example from a New York paper: "Whatever her thoughts, they were interrupted as the hotel lobby door swung open and a young woman carrying a baby and her husband entered." Our concern here is with the latter type

Reprinted by permission from *The English Journal,* 47.479–86 (November, 1958). The author is Professor of English at The State College of Iowa, Cedar Falls.
[1] There is nothing "natural" about the order of pre-noun modifiers. In Russian, for example, one says "gray two horses" and "two my friends."

of ambiguities, and I will present them in a series of structural situations.

SITUATION 1: *Adjective + noun in possessive case + noun.* As an example we may take *a dull boy's knife.* The trouble here is that the adjective may modify either the noun in the possessive case or the second noun. It is true that in English we tend to interpret an adjective as modifying everything that follows it up to and including the headword; but despite this tendency we often meet ambiguities like a *blond artist's model, a clever reporter's story,* and *a plain man's necktie.* An advertisement in the *New Yorker* played upon this pattern with this legend: "A handsome man's shirt? No, a man's handsome shirt."

SITUATION 2: *Adjective + noun + noun.* A good example occurs on a sign beside an Iowa highway reading *Little Charm Motel.* This is similar to the first situation in that the adjective may modify the immediately following noun or the second noun. We meet ambiguities of this kind often in such expressions as *modern language teaching, big building owners, basic English text, hot evening drink, fresh strawberry ice cream, hot bed covers, heavy hog production,* and *deep love movies.*

SITUATION 3: *Modifier (noun or adjective) + noun.* In this situation the reader must know whether the modifier is a noun or an adjective if he is to understand the sentence. A convenient example is furnished by a headline in the *Waterloo Daily Courier:*

Fleet planes told shoot snooper jet.

What kind of planes do we have here, speedy planes or planes of the fleet? The sentence is ambiguous because we do not know the form-class of the modifier *fleet.* From a trade journal called the *Tire Review* comes a similar case:

A keen edge quickly on rubber knives with Branick electric knife sharpener.

Or suppose you read this headline:

German teachers visit Greensboro.

Would you take this to mean teachers of German or teachers from Germany?

SITUATION 4: *More or most + adjective + noun.* The ambiguity lies in the two possibilities—that the *more* or *most* may modify the adjective or the noun. Of the examples which follow, the first is a comment I once wrote on the paper of a freshman, who demanded clarification:

Give more realistic details.

The defense system should have fewer troops with more modern arms, including field missiles.

Occasionally the words *less* and *least,* because of their use in the sense of *fewer,* and *fewest,* will cause a similar difficulty:

This soap has less harmful effects on the hands.

SITUATION 5: *Noun + noun + noun.* When this pattern occurs it may raise a question of modification, as it does in this newspaper headline:

Study of fish blood system may aid cancer research.

Does the first noun *fish* modify the compound noun *blood system,* or does the compound noun *fish blood* modify *system?* And how do you interpret the next:

Cream cheese cake.

Is this cheese cake with cream or cake with cream cheese? The list of ingredients below the label does not help a bit: "Cheese, sugar, fresh eggs, cream, graham crackers, flour...." Usually when we meet a collocation of three nouns the sense operates to prevent ambiguity, as in *hand garden plow* and *coil bed springs.* When more than three nouns pile up, the result is likely to be confusion, as in this:

New Moscow bus student travel officer.

SITUATION 6: *Adjective + series of nouns.* Here is an example from a student paper:

A baseball player must have good vision, coordination, and speed.

Does the adjective *good* in this sentence modify only *vision,* or the whole series of nouns? If one insists that of course it modifies only *vision,* then what can be said about this sentence, which has exactly the same pattern?

She raised wonderful tulips, hyacinths, and crocuses.

Does *wonderful* here modify only tulips? Thus it seems apparent that the situation itself makes for ambiguity. Of course the lexical compatibility of the words may keep the reading from going wrong. For instance, the first sentence would be clear if the adjective were compatible only with *vision:*

A baseball player must have sharp vision, coordination, and speed.

Here are two more instances:

Bulletin No. 7 contains only a few items on French literature, theology, and philosophy.

For sale: Handwoven towels, table mats, wool shirts, and wool stoles.

SITUATION 7: *Noun + series of adjectives.* This is like Situation 6. It can be illustrated by a quotation from a *New York Times* advertisement. The words describe three colors in which men's socks are available: *heather gray, red,* and *blue.* If one ordered red socks on the basis of this description, what color would he get, red or heather red?

SITUATION 8: *Modifier + past participle + noun*. In this pattern the question is whether the first term modifies the past participle or the noun. Students write expressions like these, without punctuation: *steep pointed gables, heavy padded coat*, and *clean swept room*.

SITUATION 9: *ing verb + noun*. This pattern may sometimes be construed in two ways: as modifier + noun, or as verb + noun object. An AP Story gives us a good example:

> U. S. Sabre jet pilots today shot down one Communist MIG-15 and damaged another in clearing North Korean skies.

From E. A. Nida's *Synopsis of English Syntax* we get another:

> . . . two systems of outlining notation are employed.

A second interpretive possibility for the *-ing verb + noun* pattern is that it may be looked at as either adjective + noun, or as noun + noun. This is fundamentally the same as Situation 3. The following examples will illustrate:

> So you think you have moving problems!

> He joined the standing committee.

> She maintains an entertaining apartment.

SITUATION 10: *Adjective + noun + conjunction + noun*. The question in this pattern is whether the adjective modifies only the first noun or both nouns. An example will make the question clear:

> A new company was formed to handle artificial ice and fuel.

SITUATION 11: *Series of words + modifying word or word-group*. The series usually consists of nouns. The question that arises is whether the modifier refers to all items in the series or only to the last item. A few examples will show the problem:

> . . . a conservative, a Fascist, and an atheist who might be excluded from the teaching profession because of non-conforming beliefs.

> He used an arm stroke and a kick which propelled him through the water.

> Red, yellow, blue, navy, or white with trim.

> At the dress rehearsal she sang, danced, and tumbled very expertly.

SITUATION 12: *Modifier + subject of sentence*. The reader tends to associate an opening modifier with the closest following word, which is usually the subject, whereas this modifier may relate to something further on in the sentence. This is more often a misleading construction than a genuine ambiguity, as these examples will show:

After choosing the college I thought I would like to attend, the student adviser at my high school arranged an interview with a former student.

Whether religious or humorous, the church plays a great part in everyone's Christmas activities.

SITUATION 13: *Modificand + intervening material + modifier.* The difficulty here is that the modifier may appear to modify some part of the intervening material. Here are some cases from student papers:

We must show the world how fallacious the Communist Party is by democratic means.

Zola was able to describe the characters, the places they went, and the things they did very well.

We believe in doing what we do well (motto of Tuskegee Institute).

When the intervening material consists of a noun + relative clause, we have a pattern that frequently occurs:

Every child awaits the time he can go to school with great excitement.

When applying the clay coil to the base, roughen the parts you are joining with a comb.

SITUATION 14: *Modificand + modifier + modificand.* This is our old friend, the squinting modifier, which looks before and after and pines in both directions, as in this sentence:

The club will be open to members only from Monday to Thursday.

A writer sometimes gets into this pickle when he tries to wriggle out of a split infinitive. In the next example a *New York Times* writer placed the modifier before the *to:*

. . . one-way streets had failed completely to relieve cross-town traffic.

And the writer who puts the modifier after the infinitive runs the same risk, as the next exhibit will show. It is from a textbook by a Browning scholar who eschews a split infinitive like ginger ale in his whiskey:

The university man or woman learns to examine critically conflicting points of view.

The last example is from a well-known college textbook of speech:

What we believe profoundly influences our ability to listen fairly to any subject.

SITUATION 15: *Verb-adverb, or preposition.* By verb-adverb is meant such verbs as *put up with* (endure), *turn up* (appear), *turn down* (refuse), *look up to* (admire), *look down on* (scorn), *and prevail on* (induce).

Sometimes a reader cannot be sure whether the second word is part of the verb or a preposition. These two instances will illustrate:

The loud speaker wakes everyone up in the hall.

The amphibious truck will carry over its rated capacity when crossing a stream.

SITUATION 16: *Dual parallel structure.* A sentence element may sometimes be taken to go with either one of two structures already established in the sentence. This ambiguity occurs frequently in student writing, from which these sentences are taken:

We overheard the same cleaning woman who cleans the Rose Lounge and another one.

Some persons, after consuming alcohol, want to fight and become hard to manage.

It seems as though the commander of the ship put very little foresight into a problem which faced him and endangered both men and ships.

This situation not infrequently forms the basis of cretinous humor, as in this TV exchange: "I've always wanted to see Lake Louise and Banff." "Sounds great, but how do you banff?" A special case of this kind that students find hard to see occurs with a professional phrase which contains a series of nouns:

His job is to post changes in address, telephone numbers, and performance ratings.

The course includes the theory of procurement, property accounting, and requisitioning.

SITUATION 17: *Modificand + two modifying word groups.* If we consider the modifying word groups may be of three kinds—prepositional phrases, relative clauses, and verbal phrases—then it is evident that this situation contains nine different patterns. Each of these nine lends itself to possible ambiguity. In all of them the trouble lies in the third term—what does it refer to?

A. *Modificand + prepositional phrase + relative clause.* In this pattern the writer often intends the relative clause to modify the modificand; but but when this clause appears to modify the last word of the preceding phrase, then the sentence is ambiguous. There is no ambiguity, of course, when ties in agreement prevent us from misreading. This is a standard pattern of modification in English, and students frequently run afoul of it. Here are three examples culled out of many:

The life of a movie star that the public sees does look glamorous.

She has cute ideas for parties that are easy to plan.

He has a blue satin ribbon around his neck which is tied in a bow at the top.

The menu of a restaurant in Marshalltown, Iowa, proudly makes this ambiguous pronouncement:

We have a reputation for fine food, quick service, and a friendly atmosphere which amounts to a tradition.

The remaining eight patterns are fundamentally the same, except that only two of them can be protected from ambiguity by ties in agreement. Hence a mere listing, with a single example each, will perhaps suffice to show what they are.

B. *Modificand + prepositional phrase + verbal phrase.*

There was a spotted dog in the group barking at the speeding car.

C. *Modificand + prepositional phrase + prepositional phrase.*

This restatement of the central idea serves as a review for the audience of the entire speech.

D. *Modificand + relative clause + prepositional phrase.*

I was talking about the books I had read in the library.

E. *Modificand + relative clause + verbal phrase.*

We watched the old miner, Maheu, who was feeding his horse, begrimed with dust from the mine.

F. *Modificand + relative clause + relative clause.*

Fred had a second-hand car that he later traded for a motorcycle which he loved to tinker with.

G. *Modificand + verbal phrase + prepositional phrase.*

They stood watching the fireworks in the back yard.

H. *Modificand + verbal phrase + relative clause.*

There is also a theater located near the business district which is crowded every night.

I. *Modificand + verbal phrase + verbal phrase.*

I saw the rake lying against the box stuffed with leaves from my last raking.

SITUATION 18: *Elliptical constructions.* Sometimes the omission of words from a structure will result in ambiguity, as in these cases:

Serve meat when thoroughly stewed.

For sale: Two Dutch rabbits, does, low cost. Breeding age. Will breed if requested.

In this respect *than* and *as well as* are especially troublesome. Here is an example from Noah Webster:

. . . we are less under the influence of reeson [*sic*] than our ancestors.

And students will write sentences like these:

It is more important for me to enter the activities in high school than college.
I like my room mate as well as Janice.

SITUATION 19: *Movable adverbial modifiers.* The different kinds of adverbs and adverbial modifiers have allowable and non-allowable positions in various types of sentences, though this matter has never, to my knowledge, been thoroughly studied. At any rate, such modifiers do move around rather freely, and it is this freedom that betrays students into putting them in positions where they are ambiguous. Student writing contains many ambiguities of this sort:

I repaired the car and returned the following day.

The hostess greeted the girl with a smile.

The crew chief will drive the truck, choose a suitable site, and unload the ammunition with the assistance of two helpers.

The bottle on the table there.

SITUATION 20: *Reference of pronouns, relatives, and demonstratives.* This kind of ambiguity might be considered lexical rather than structural. Words like *he, it, they, her, which, who, this,* and *such* are a constant source of ambiguity in student writing because they often refer to more than one antecedent. The instances that follow are taken from both professional writings and student papers:

At 10 a.m. today the anchor will be carried out into Lake Ontario aboard a naval craft and consigned to the waters. The three chaplains will accompany it.

The local weather bureaus are not permitted to dispute the predictions of the central weather bureau, regardless of whether they are right or not.

The Graf Zepplin was leaving Lakehurst Airport. Among the last to enter was Mrs. J. D. Smith, lone woman passenger. Slowly her huge nose was turned into the wind. Then, like some huge beast, she crawled along the grass.

Men like Brodie and Kolmer discovered vaccines and gave them to the public, but they were not successful . . . .

He had never gone ice-fishing from a hut like that.

The words *this* and *which* are a special source of confusion because they may refer not only to individual words but to word groups. The following cases are typical:

> He was always bringing into the room a strange dog which he had found. This was a nuisance when I was trying to study.

> She told me that Joe had come, which pleased me.

> Biologists have discovered that fragments of chromosomes attach themselves to another chromosome which is called translocation.

> Each room has two study desks and only one study lamp. This is very inconvenient because of poor lighting on one of the desks.

The foregoing twenty situations seem to be the ones responsible for much of the structural ambiguity that we find in student writing.[2] Of those that remain we should take into account one set of situations which need not be described in detail and which can be lumped together in a single omnibus group of form-class ambiguities. These have been emphasized by Professor C. C. Fries in his *Structure of English*.[3] He points out that if one does not know the form-class, that is the part of speech, of a word, then one does not recognize the pattern and as a consequence the word is ambiguous. We have remarked this condition above in situations three, nine, and fifteen. Even the basic sentence pattern of subject-verb-object, Professor Fries reveals, can be ambiguous, as in *Ship sails today,* where we do not know the form-class of *ship* and *sails.*

We frequently meet form-class ambiguities of various types in newspaper headlines, where the demands of space-saving cause the usual signals of form-class to be left out. Here are a few miscellaneous examples: *PW's 1st item on agenda—call girl; babysitter demands rise; police raid gatherings; digs well with bulldozer; complete 31-piece drill outfit.* Now and then form-class ambiguities other than those we have classified will turn up in student papers. Here are a few:

> At last they heard the boat whistle.

> The storm was striking.

> Unlike other Shakespearean plays, *Othello* offers no real complicated personality.

> Students have important experiences in college that prepare them for the future. They are meeting people, gaining new friendships, and learning to get along with different types of people.

---

[2] Sometimes one finds interesting permutations of them, as in *a manned missile launching base,* and in this description of shirts—*blue, tan, or gray stripes or checks.*
[3] New York: Harcourt, Brace, & World, Inc. 1952.

The presence of ambiguity in student writing is easy to understand. In high school the student does not always write to communicate to a known class of readers, as we do in normal writing situations. Instead he often writes writing to fulfill an assignment. The consequence is that he does not develop a reader-awareness: he does not learn to step outside himself and survey his words as with the mind of another person. When he reads over what he has produced, the words mirror what was in his mind as he wrote, and he fails to realize that other readers might get other meanings from these same words.

One way to sensitize the student to the dangers of multiple meaning is to make a direct attack on the structural situations liable to ambiguity. For instance, the teacher can present the situations described above and then have the class write original examples of them with double-track meanings. These examples will furnish material for lively discussions and will offer heady and challenging problems of restatement. Such a procedure will help the student to tool his sentences to a closer tolerance in meaning and to write with greater clearness and precision.

12

Notes on Nominal Compounds in Present-Day English

HANS MARCHAND

1.1. WHEN TWO OR MORE WORDS are combined into a morphological unit, we speak of a compound. The principle of combining two words arises from the natural human tendency to see a thing identical with another one already existing and at the same time different from it. If we take the word *rainbow,* for instance, identity is expressed by the basic *bow:* the phenomenon of a rainbow is fundamentally a bow. But it is a bow connected with the phenomenon rain: hence the differentiating part *rain.* The compound is thus made up of a determining and a determined part. In the system of

Reprinted by permission from *Word,* 11.216–227 (August, 1955), with minor changes by the author, who is Professor of English Philology at the University of Tübingen, Germany.

languages to which English belongs the determinant generally precedes the determinatum. The types which do not conform to this principle are either syntactical compounds (e.g. *father-in-law*) or loan-compounds (e.g. *MacDonald, Fitzgerald*) with the "inner form" of a non-English language. The determinatum is the grammatically dominant part which undergoes the changes of inflection. On the other hand, its semantic range is considerably narrowed as the second word of a compound, determined as it is by the first word.

1.2. A compound, we have said, has two constituent elements, the determinatum and the determinant. There are, however, many combinations which do not seem to fulfill this condition. The essential part of the determinatum as a formal element is obviously missing in such types as *pickpocket, runabout, overall, blackout, dugout*, the bahuvrihi types *hunchback, paleface, fivefinger, scatterbrain*. A pickpocket is neither a pick nor a pocket, a hunchback is neither a hunch nor a back, and so on. In all of the preceding combinations the basis, the determinatum, is implicitly understood, but not formally expressed. The combinations are compounds with a zero determinatum (also called exocentric compounds, as the determinatum lies outside the combination).

1.3. A similar concept underlies combinations of the type *householder*. The analysis of *householder* is parallel to that of *pickpocket:* 'one who holds a house.' The difference is that *householder* has a formal determinatum (*-er*) whereas *pickpocket* has not. However, the conceptual analysis clashes with a word-forming principle in English. *Householder* cannot be considered a suffixal derivative from the basis *household* in the way that *old-timer* or *four-wheeler* are derived from *old time* (*s*) or *four-wheel* (*s*), as there is no compound verb **to household* in English. The modern type *to brainwash* is of quite recent development and is not nearly so well established as the type *householder,* which is very old (in its present form, extended by *-er*, it goes back to late Old English, while the original OE type *man-slaga* 'man-killer' is Indo-European; cf. Latin *armiger, signifer, artifex*). The idea of verb/object relation could combine with the concept of agent substantive only by way of joining an agent noun created ad hoc as a pseudo-basis to a common substantive. We are thus faced with the fact that an analysis which considers the underlying concept only may be disavowed by the formal pattern. The formative basis of combinations of the type *householder* is the agent substantive, however artificial the analysis may sometimes appear. A *skyscraper,* though not naturally analyzable as 'a scraper of the sky' but '(a building which) scrapes the sky,' from the formative point of view must be understood as a compound with *scraper* as the basis. This type of compound therefore is not the primary one which arises from combining two fully independent common substantives (as in the type *rainbow*). Because of their 'forcible' character, such compounds have been termed synthetic compounds (in German they are called *Zusammenbildungen*).

1.4. Parallel to *householder* are the types *housekeeping* (sb.) and *heartbreaking* (adj.). The second words of such combinations do not often exist as independent words: *holder, keeping, breaking* are functional derivatives, being respectively the agent substantive, the action substantive, and the first participle of the underlying verbs. Strictly speaking, they should not figure in a dictionary, which is an assemblage of semantic units. The lexical value of, say, the word *crasher* is nil, as the word represents nothing but the aspect of actor of the verb *crash*, whereas *gate-crasher* is a lexical unit. In the same sense, the second elements of most compound impersonal substantives of the type *housekeeping* and of most compound participles of the type *heartbreaking* are semantic units only in conjunction with their first words, *house* and *heart*. In a similar way, other combinations with participles as second words are synthetic compounds: *cooking, going, working* are not adjectives, but preceded by adjectives or locative particles they form compounds (*quick-cooking, easy-going, hard-working; forthcoming, inrushing, outstanding*). *Eaten, bred, borne, baked, flown, spread* are nothing but participles, but *moth-eaten, home-bred, air-borne* or *fresh-baked, high-flown, widespread* are compounds.

1.5. The non-compound character of extended bahuvrihi combinations is manifest. *Hunchbacked, palefaced, five-fingered, knock-kneed* are not analyzable into the immediate constituents *hunch+backed, pale+faced*, etc.; the determinatum is always *-ed* while the preceding compound basis is the determinant. Extended bahuvrihi adjectives therefore are suffixal derivatives from compounds or syntactic groups. Exactly parallel are combinations of the types *old maidish* and *four-wheeler*.

1.6. One of the constituent members of a compound may itself be a compound. In German, the determinant as well as the determinatum occur as compounds (*Rathaus-keller, Berufsschul-lehrer; Stadt-baurat, Regierungsbaumeister*). The regular pattern in English, however, is that of the determinant being a compound (*aircraft carrier, traffic signal controller, flower pot stand, plainclothes man, milk truck driver* etc.), whereas in the event of a compound determinatum the whole combination becomes a two-stressed syntactic group (*níght wátchman, víllage schóolmaster, hoúse dóorkeeper*). The only case of a compound determinatum in English I can think of is one in which the second constituent is a preparticle compound, as in *báby oùtfit, húnting oùtfit*.

2.1. What is the criterion of a compound? Many scholars have claimed that a compound is determined by the underlying concept; others have advocated stress; some even seek the solution of the problem in spelling.

H. Paul says that "the cause which makes a compound out of a syntactic phrase is to be sought in the fact that the compound is in some manner isolated as compared to its elements."[1] By isolation he understands difference in meaning from a syntactic group with the same words, and treats as compounds such phases as *dicke Milch* or *das goldene Vliess,* which are what Bally terms *groupes locutionnels.* H. Koziol[2] holds that the criterion of a compound is the psychological unity of a combination, adding that there "seems to be" a difference of intonation between a compound and a syntactic group which it is, however, difficult to describe. W. Henzen,[3] who discusses at some length the diverse definitions, decides for "the impossibility of a clear-cut distinction" between a compound and a syntactic group and hesitatingly proposes to consider a compound as "the multi-stem expression of a conceptual unit which is written together." This is a very weak definition and he admits that the German separable verbs do not fit it. Bloch and Trager[4] do not treat the question in detail; they call a compound "a word made up wholly of smaller words," specifying that both of the immediate constituents must be free forms.

2.2. Stress also has been advocated as a criterion. "Wherever we hear lesser or least stress upon a word which would always show high stress in a phrase, we describe it as a compound member: *ice-cream* 'ajs-ˌkrijm is a compound, but *ice cream* 'ajs 'krijm is a phrase, although there is no denotative difference of meaning."[5] Kruisinga[6] makes no difference at all between a compound and a syntactic group, at the same time feeling the need to maintain the traditional concept of compound. He defines the compound as "a combination of two words forming a unit which is not identical with the combined forms or meanings of its elements." In a similar way, Bally defines the compound as a syntagma expressive of a single idea.[7] Jespersen also introduces the criterion of concept, and rejects Bloomfield's criterion of stress. "If we stuck to the criterion of stress, we should have to refuse the name of compound to a large group of two-linked phrases that are generally called so, such as *headmaster* or *stone wall.*" This is certainly no argument, nor is the objection that words such as *sub-committee, non-conductor* have forestress according to Jones, but level stress according to Sweet. The first elements are not independent morphemes, anyway. For

---

[1] H. Paul, *Deutsche Grammatik.* Band V, Teil IV: Wortbildungslehre (Halle, 1920) 4.

[2] H. Koziol, *Handbuch der englischen Wortbildungslehre* (Heidelberg, 1927) 46 f.

[3] W. Henzen, *Deutsche Wortbildung* (Halle, 1947) 44.

[4] B. Bloch and G. L. Trager, *Outline of Linguistic Analysis* (Baltimore, 1942), 54, 68.

[5] L. Bloomfield, *Language* (New York, 1933) 228.

[6] E. Kruisinga, *A Handbook of Present-Day English,* Part II: Accidence and Syntax 3. Fifth edition (Groningen, 1932) 1581.

[7] Ch. Bally, *Linguistique générale et linguistique française,* second edition (Bern, 1944) 94.

this reason it is wrong to argue that "the prefixes *un-* (negative) and *mis-* are often as strongly stressed as the following element; are they, then, independent words?"[8] If it rains, the ground becomes wet. But if the ground is wet, we are not entitled to the conclusion that it has rained. As for the criterion of stress, we shall see that it holds for certain types only.

2.3. That spelling is no help in solving the problem I will add for the sake of completeness only. A perusal of the book *Compounding in the English Language,*[9] which is a painstaking investigation into the spelling variants of dictionaries and newspapers, shows the complete lack of uniformity.

2.4. For a combination to be a compound there is one condition to be fulfilled: the compound must be morphologically isolated from a parallel syntactic group. However much *the Holy Roman Catholic Church* or *the French Revolution* may be semantic or psychological units, they are not morphologically isolated: they are stressed like syntactic groups. *Blackbird* has the morphophonemic stress pattern of a compound, *black market* has not, despite its phrasal meaning; the latter therefore is a syntactic group, morphologically speaking. Stress *is* a criterion here. The same distinction keeps apart the types *strónghòld* and *lóng wáit,* the types *shárpshoòter* and *goód ríder,* the types *búll's-èye* and *rázor's édge,* the types *wríting-tàble* and *fólding doór.*

2.5. On the other hand, there are many combinations with double stress which are undoubtedly compounds. Most combinations with participles as second elements belong here: *eásy-góing, hígh-bórn, mán-máde.* We have already pointed out their synthetic character. Being determined by first elements which syntactically could not be their modifiers, they must be considered compounds. The type *gráss-greén* has two heavy stresses, but again the criterion is that an adjective cannot syntactically be modified by a preceding substantive (the corresponding syntactic construction would be *green as grass*). The adjectival type *ícy-cóld* is isolated in that syntactically the modifier of an adjective can only be an adverb. The corresponding co-ordinative type *Gérman-Rússian (war)* is likewise morphologically distinct. The corresponding syntactic construction would be typified by *long, grey (beard)*, with a pause between *long* and *grey,* whereas the combination *German-Russian* is marked by the absence of such a pause.

3.1. The most important type in which stress is morphophonemic is *raín-bòw*. As it has been the object of much discussion, it will here be given a somewhat detailed treatment. English has at all periods known and made

---

[8] O. Jespersen, *A Modern English Grammar on Historical Principles,* Part VI: Morphology (Copenhagen, 1942) 8.12.
  [9] A. M. Ball, *Compounding in the English Language* (New York, 1939) and *The Compounding and Hyphenation of English Words* (New York, 1951).

use of this Germanic type of word formation. The possibility of combining substantives is today as strong as ever. On the other hand, English has, for at least three centuries, been developing the syntactic group of the type *stóne wáll*,[10] which has two stresses. While the coining of forestressed compounds continues, a new syntactic type has arisen which challenges the privileged position of the type *rainbow*. Though the co-existence of two types of substantive + substantive combination has long been recognized, the conditions under which a combination enters the compound type, *rainbow*, or the syntactic group type, *stóne wáll*, do not seem to have been studied. Sweet, in his chapter on the stressing of compounds,[11] has a few remarks on the subject, but otherwise the problem has not received attention. The following, therefore, can be an attempt only.

3.2. The most important factor is the underlying concept. Some concepts are invariably tied up with forestress pattern. The concept may be grammatical: when the verb/object or subject/verb relation is present, the combination receives forestress. Therefore the following are types of stable compounds: *hóusehòlder, skyscraper, doorkeeper, caretaker; hóusekeèping, sightseeing, mindreading, childbearing; ráttlesnàke, popcorn, sobsister, crybaby*. The first element is the object in the verbal nexus substantives *householder* and *housekeeping*. There are also combinations in which the underlying relation is the same though the formal type be different (*geography teacher, árt crìtic, cár thìef*) and related constructions such as *teá mèrchant, clóth deàler, leáther wòrker, stéel prodùction, tráffic contròl, móney restrìctions, fúr sàle, graín stòrage*. If the second element has acquired the status of an independent word, the predicate/object nexus may have come to be blurred, as in *párty leáder, fúneral diréctor*, which are stressed as syntactic groups. Again, a combination may step out of line, either because the verbal nexus is blurred or because the combination is too long: *cóntract violátions, búsiness administrátion, cóncert perfórmance* always have two stresses.

3.3. As a rule, combinations in which a verbal nexus is expressed have forestress. Most combinations with a verbal stem therefore are compounds: *shówroòm, páydày, dánce flòor, pláybòy, sweátshòp*. But in cases where the verbal stem is used in adjunctal function, i.e. has become a quasi-adjective, equivalent to a past participle, a situation similar to that in *stone wall* has arisen: the two constituents receive full stress. We say *roást beéf, roást mútton*, etc., and *wáste páper, wáste lánd* are often heard though many speakers always give to these combinations the compound stress. The case is the same with combinations whose first constituents are -*ing*

---

[10] O. Jespersen, *A Modern English Grammar on Historical Principles* (Heidelberg, 1909–1914) 1.5.33–37 and 11.13.

[11] H. Sweet, *A New English Grammar* (Oxford, 1892) 889–932.

forms of a verb. Most combinations of type *wríting-tàble* are compounds because the underlying concept is that of destination (*looking-glass, frying-pan*, etc.). But when the verbal *-ing* is apprehended as an adjunct, i.e. a participle, the combination is susceptible of being treated as a syntactic group: *Flýing Dútchman, flýing saúcers, revólving doór*. However, other combinations have forestress owing to the idea of implicit contrast: *humming-bird*, with the frequent constituent *bird*, receives forestress to distinguish it from *bláckbìrd, bluébìrd, mócking-bìrd*.

3.4. Other relations are of a purely semantic nature. The following cases involve forestress pattern:

The underlying concept is that of purpose, destination: *theater ticket, freight train, bread basket, paper clip, reception room, concert hall, windshield, toothbrush*.

The signifié of the second element is naturally dependent on that of the first: *windmill, watermill, water clock, motorcar, motorboat, steam engine, mule cart, sea bird, water rat, lap dog*.

The first element denotes the originator of what is expressed by the second: *rainwater, rainbow, bloodstain, birth right, pipe smoke, smoke screen*.

The underlying concept is that of resemblance: *blockhead, bellflower, goldfish, horse-fish, iron-weed, silkweed, wiregrass*.

3.5. There are other, quite external factors conducive to forestress. The frequent occurrence of a word as second constituent is apt to give combinations with such words compound character. The most frequent word of this kind is probably *man* (the reduction of the vowel and the loss of stress of *man* as a second element is another result of the same phenomenon: *policeman, congressman, gunman, postman, milkman*. A few other words frequent as second constituents of compounds are *ware* (*houseware, hardware, silverware*), *work* (*woodwork, network, wirework*), *shop* (*giftshop, candyshop, hatshop*), *store* (*bookstore, drugstore, foodstore*), *fish* (*bluefish, goldfish, jellyfish*). The forestress of such combinations is thus due to implicit contrast: each *-man, -shop, -store word* is automatically stressed on the first member to distinguish the combination from others of the same series. The case of *-girl* combinations is particularly interesting in this connection. Appositional combinations are usually syntactic groups with two stresses in English (*boy king, woman writer, gentleman farmer*), but *servant girl, slave girl, peasant girl, gipsy girl* have contrastive forestress.

4.1. The criterion of the underlying concept may now be applied to the syntactic group type *stóne wáll*. The grammatical concept which involves syntactic stressing is that of adjunct/primary. All coordinative combinations, additive as in *king-emperor, secretary-stenographer*, or appositional as in *gentleman-farmer, prince consort,* have two heavy stresses. The only copulative combination I know that has forestress is *fíghter-bòmber,* the stress obviously being due to contrast with common bombers. Here belong combinations with sex or age denoting first constituents as *man, woman, boy, girl, baby, embryo,* except that owing to contrast, *boy friend, girl friend, manservant, maidservant* have developed forestress. (It is perhaps interesting to point out that the sex-denoting pronouns *he, she,* as in *he-goat, she-dog,* form forestressed compounds, despite Sweet 904.) Combinations with first constituents denoting relational position, as *top, bottom, average, brother, sister, fellow* likewise have the basic stress pattern of the syntactic group under discussion.

4.2. Combinations with a first member denoting material are treated as adjunct/primary groups and receive two stresses: *gold watch, silver chain, steel door, iron curtain, cotton dress, silk stocking, leather glove, straw hat, paper bag.*

4.3. Incidentally, the treatment of adjunct/primary combinations consisting of two substantives has a parallel in Turkish. Determinative substantive +substantive combinations all receive the determinative group suffix whereas coordinative combinations made up of two substantives do not. Turkish morphologically opposes *kadin terzi-si* (*kadin* 'woman', *terzi* 'tailor, dressmaker', *-si* = the determinative group suffix), women's tailor' to *kadin terzi* '(woman) dressmaker'. Coordinative groups in both languages are treated like syntactic groups of adjective+substantive.

5.1. Often two contradictory principles are at work; then one has to give way. Though material denoting first constituents usually makes a combination into a syntactic group, a frequently used second element may obviate the result, as in *tinware, ironware, silverware,* or contrastive stress may interfere with the normal two-stress pattern of coordinative combinations, as in *fíghter-bòmber, gírl frìend, bóy frìend.*

5.2. When a substantive can also be interpreted as adjective, changed analysis may lead to change in the stress pattern. Though a hospital can be neither mental nor animal, we stress *méntal hóspital, ánimal hóspital,* as against *síck roòm, poór hoùse.* Similar shifts occur also in a more amply inflected language such as German: *ein deutsches Wörterbuch, ein latein isches Heft, die französische Stunde.*

5.3. Many forestressed compounds denote an intimate, permanent relationship between the two signifiés to the extent that the compound is no longer to be understood as the sum of the constituent elements. A summerhouse, for instance, is not merely a house inhabited in summer, but a house of a particular style and construction which make it suitable for the warm season only. Two-stressed combinations of type *stóne wáll* never have this character. A syntactic group is always analyzable as the additive sum of its elements. It is an informal, noncommittal meeting, never a union of the constituents. This is a great advantage which English enjoys, for instance, over German. German cannot express morphologically the opposition 'permanent, intimate relationship' ~ 'occasional, external connection' instanced by *súmmer-hoùse ~ súmmer résidence, Chrístmas trèe ~ Chrístmas tráffic*. English, therefore, has acquired a substantive + substantive combination of a looser, casual kind for groups in which an intimate, permanent relationship between the signifiés is not meant to be expressed: *field artillery, world war, country gentleman, village constable, parish priest, city court, state police, home town, district attorney,* and countless other combinations.

5.4.   On the one hand, the possibilities of coining compounds are much more restricted than in German, where any occasional combination of two substantives automatically becomes a forestressed compound. On the other hand, English compounds are much closer morphologic units which cannot be split up the way German compounds are. In German, it is possible to say, for instance, *Hand- und elektrische Modelle* (*Weltwoche,* Sept. 26, 1947), clipping the *rainbow* type compound and leaving the adjective/substantive syntactic group intact. However, in English as well as in German, serial combinations like *house and shop owners, wind and water mills* occur (Bloomfield, *Language,* 232, restricts them to German).

5.5.   It is nevertheless often difficult to tell why in one case the language has created a compound while in another it has coined a syntactic group. Conceptually, *cóllege président* is in about the same position as *ópera dirèctor,* but the first combination is a syntactic group, the second a compound. Form is one thing, concept is another. On the other hand, the same morphologic pattern does not necessarily involve the same degree of semantic unity: *lípstick* is a closer unit than *recéption roòm*. The morphologic criterion of a compound enables us to do justice to both form and concept.

6.1.   A few words are required about the problem of stress with regard to compounding. With Stanley S. Newman[12] we accept three degrees of phonemic stress: heavy stress (marked′), middle stress (marked‵), and weak stress (which is traditionally and perhaps more appropriately called absence of stress). As a combination of two independent words, basically speaking, a compound combines two elements which are characterized by presence of stress. Absence of stress in general indicates grammaticalization of a morphemic element (as in *políce-man, MacDónald, Fitz-gérald*). The determinant has the heavy, the determinatum the middle stress. Thus the usual pattern is ′‵ (e.g. *raínbòw*), which is also followed by combina-

---

[12] Stanley S. Newman, "On the Stress System of English," *Word* 2. 171–187 (1946).

tions with a zero determinatum (*píckpòcket,* etc., see 1.2). All substantival compounds show this pattern, with the exception of those whose first elements are the pronouns *all* and *self.* Such compounds have double stress (e.g. *áll-soúl, áll-creátor, sélf-respéct, sélf-seéker*). Of adjectival compounds, only two types have the stable stress pattern heavy stress/middle stress: the type *cólor-blìnd,* i.e., adjectives determined by a preceding substantive (unless the underlying concept is that of emphatic comparison, as in *gráss-greén,* where double stress is the rule) and *heárt-breàking.* All other adjectival types are basically double stressed.

6.2. Bloch and Trager[13] posit four degrees of phonemic stress: loud stress, reduced loud stress, medial stress, and weak stress. They find reduced loud stress on the adjunct of a syntactic adjunct/primary group (*old man*) as well as on second elements of forestressed compounds (*bláckbìrd, élevator-òperator*) which are obviously not on the same level. But it seems to be more correct to say that the reduced stress on *old* is rhythmically conditioned by the position of *old* before a likewise heavy stressed word to which *old* stands in the subordinate relation of adjunct. This is a syntactic phenomenon of stress reduction. No change of the underlying concept is involved in a shift from reduced to loud stress, as no oppositional stress pattern ′ ′ ∼ ΄ ′ exists in the case of adjective/substantive combinations. So *ôld mán* is really a free variant of *óld mán. Bláckbìrd* is different: we cannot oppose *bláckbìrd* to *bláck bírd* without changing the underlying concept. The stress pattern ⌢ of *bláckbìrd* is morphophonemic. The case of *élevator-òperator* is similar. A combination of the type *hoúsehòlder* (discussed in 1.3) implies the stress pattern ⌢ as morphophonemically relevant. Though in the particular case of *élevator-òperator* we cannot oppose the heavy/middle stress to a heavy/heavy stress combination, we can conceive of other pairs where change of stress implies change of the underlying concept, as *Frénch teàcher* 'a teacher of French' ∼ *Frénch teácher* 'a teacher who is French', *réd hùnter* 'one who hunts reds' ∼ *réd húnter* 'a hunter who is red', *fát prodùcer* 'one producing fat' ∼ *fát prodúcer* 'a producer who is fat'.

We must therefore assume a relevant degree of stress which distinguishes the phonemic non-heavy stress of *bláckbìrd* and *élevator òperator* from the non-phonemic non-heavy stress of *ôld mán.* While we interpret the reduced loud stress as a positional variant of the heavy stress, we must consider the phonemic secondary stress of *bìrd* and *òperator* as a middle stress. On the other hand, the degree of stress on the third syllable of independent *élevàtor* and *óperàtor* is not different from that on *bird* in *bláckbìrd:* in either case we have a full middle stress. When these words become second elements of compounds, the intensity of the full middle

[13] B. Bloch and G. L. Trager, *op. cit.,* 48.

stress is lessened and shifted to a light middle stress (which, for the sake of convenience, I will here mark ˇ): *élevător òperător*. This light middle stress is non-phonemic. We interpret it as the rhythmically predictable form assumed by the full middle stress in a position before or after a morphophonemic full middle stress. In composition, it chiefly occurs with compounds of type *aírcrăft-càrrier* (see 1.6) on the second element of the determinant, the full middle stress being morpho-phonemically reserved for the determinatum. That full middle stress on the determinatum is morphophonemic is also manifest in the behavior of German compounds: those having a compound determinant are stressed as in *Ráthaŭskèller* whereas those with a compound determinatum are stressed as in *Stádt-baùrăt*.

13

The Structure of Two-Word Verbs in English

Abdul Karim Taha[1]

This is a summary of a study which set out to investigate the structural features of the two-word verb constructions in spoken English. To achieve this objective, a large body of utterances with two-word verbs was obtained directly from native speakers of English. Each of these utterances was carefully recorded with its stress,[2] juncture,[3] and order characteristics.

Reprinted by permission from *Language Learning*, 10.115–22 (1960). The author is a member of the English Department of the University of Baghdad, Iraq.

[1] I should like to express my indebtedness to Professor Archibald A. Hill, my supervisor, who suggested the topic of this study and who helped me through its course. I am profoundly grateful to him, not only for his wise criticism and ever-patient direction of this investigation, but also for much of my instruction and training in descriptive linguistics.

[2] The present study assumes that in English, stress is phonemic, and that there are four different phonemic levels of stress, in descending order: primary /′/, secondary /ˆ/, tertiary /ˋ/, and weak /ˇ/.

[3] This study makes use only of terminal junctures, i.e., the single-bar juncture /|/, the double-bar juncture /||/, and the double-cross juncture /#/. The characteristics of these terminal junctures, according to Trager and Smith, are as follows: /|/ indicates "terminal sustention at the (pitch) level previously marked"; /||/ indicates "terminal rise from the previously marked (pitch) level"; and /#/ indicates "terminal fall from the previously marked (pitch) level". (George L. Trager and Henry Lee Smith, Jr., *An Outline Of English Structure*, p. 42.).

By employing stress as a criterion, two-word verb constructions used in these utterances were classified into: (1) intransitive constructions, and (2) transitive constructions. It was found that the verbal elements of constructions of the former group receive tertiary stress, whereas the adverbial elements receive secondary stress in utterance-medial position, or primary stress before a terminal juncture. This may be indicated by the following sample sentences:

> Jôhn gòt dówn #
>
> Wòuld yòu pléàse sìt dówn #

> Hè fèll dówn | òn thĕ jób #
>
> Ìn thĕ àfternóon | Ì lìe dówn #
>
> Mỳ wâtch hàs rùn dówn #
>
> Gèt dówn | fròm thât cháir #

Constructions of the latter group receive secondary stress on the verbal elements, and secondary or primary on the adverbial elements. When used medially with non-utterance-final pronoun-complement the adverbial elements receive secondary stress, as in:

> Hè *cût dôwn* hìs smóking #
>
> Thĕ hêat *bêat dôwn* hìs énergy #
>
> Hè *bôlted dôwn* thĕ machíne #

> Mâry *bânged dôwn* thĕ stáge #
>
> Thĕ môwer *môwed dôwn* thĕ bánk #
>
> Hè *rôde dôwn* thĕ stréet #

When used before a terminal juncture or before an utterance-final pronoun-complement they receive primary stress, as in:

> Hè *cût* hìs smôking *dówn* #
>
> Thĕ hêat *bêat* hìs ênergy *dówn* #
>
> Hè *bôlted* thĕ machîne *dówn* #

> Mâry *bânged down* ĭt #
>
> Thĕ môwer *môwed dówn* ĭt #
>
> Hè *rôde dówn* ĭt #

Insofar as stress is concerned, therefore, it was observed that each group of two-word constructions falls into certain stress-patterns. Thus the intransitive constructions in the first group may take either the /ˈ^/ stress-pattern,[4] when occupying utterance-medial position, or /ˈˋ/ when occurring before a terminal juncture. The transitive constructions in the second group, on the other hand, may receive the stress-pattern /^ ^/ in medial position with a non-utterance-final pronoun-complement, or /^ˈ/ before a terminal juncture or before an utterance-final pronoun-complement.

The stress-pattern of a transitive verb followed by the adverbial use of the ad-prep[5] contrasts with that of an intransitive verb followed by the prepositional use of the ad-prep. This contrast may occur in utterance-medial position, as in:

Thĕ hôrses *pûlled dówn* thĕ híll # (verb + adverbial use of the ad-prep.)

Thĕ hôrses *púlled* | *dòwn* thĕ híll # (verb + prepositional use of the ad-prep)

Thĕ hôrses *púlled dòwn* thĕ híll #

Thĕ knîght *smôte dówn* | thĕ ênemy's líne # (verb + adverbial use of the ad-prep)

Thĕ knîght *smôte* | *dòwn* thĕ ênemy's líne #(verb + prepositional use of the ad-prep)

Thĕ knîght *smóte dòwn* thĕ ênemy's líne #

Hè *whîttled dôwn* thĕ bránch # (verb + adverbial use of the ad-prep)

Hè *whíttled* | *dòwn* thĕ bránch # (verb + prepositional use of the ad-prep)

Hè *whíttled dòwn* thĕ bránch #

Or it may occur in utterance-final, as in:

Thìs ĭs thĕ híll thĕ hôrses *pûlled dówn* # (verb + adverbial use of the ad-prep)

Thìs ĭs thĕ híll thĕ hôrses *púlled dòwn* # (verb + prepositional use of the ad-prep)

Thìs ĭs thĕ ênemy's lìne thĕ knîght *smôte dówn* # (verb + adverbial use of the ad-prep)

Thìs ĭs thĕ ênemy's lìne thĕ knîght *smóte dòwn* # (verb + prepositional use of the ad-prep)

Thàt ĭs thĕ bránch hĕ *whîttled dówn* # (verb + adverbial use of the ad-prep)

Thàt ĭs thĕ bránch hĕ *whíttled dòwn* # (verb + prepositional use of the ad-prep)

[4] Although no occurrence of the sub-stress pattern /ˈˋ/ appeared in the examples, yet it can occur with intransitive constructions in medial position, as in: Hè fèll dôwn òn thĕ jób #

[5] This term was first used by Professor Archibald A. Hill.

Here, as we have already stated above, the adverbial use of the ad-prep varies in stress according to whether a terminal juncture follows it or not: it gets a primary stress when a terminal juncture immediately follows; when no such juncture follows, it gets a secondary stress. No such variation in stress takes place with the prepositional use of the ad-prep: it always receives a tertiary stress whether it occurs in utterance-final position before a terminal juncture, or in utterance-medial position with or without a terminal juncture preceding. This stress characteristic is one of the significant structural signals by which a distinction can be made between the adverbial use and the prepositional use of the ad-prep.

The stress-pattern /ˈˋ/ characterizes not only a verb and a following prepositional use of the ad-prep, but also a two-word noun construction such as *bréak-dòwn*. Whether a construction as such is verbal or nominal depends on its morphological and syntactic features. Thus, for example, in the utterance: *Thĕ cãr hãd ă bréak-dòwn # bréak-dòwn* is nominal because it is preceded by the function-word *a* which determines its nominal identity.

To show this contrast in stress-pattern between:

1. Verbal constructions consisting of a verb and an adverbial use of the ad-prep,
2. Verbal constructions consisting of a verb and a prepositional use of the ad-prep,
3. Nominal constructions,

the following sentences may be presented in respective order of illustration:

Shè wăs cãlled dówn #

Shè wăs cálled | dòwn thĕ stáirs #

Shĕ gõt ă cáll-dòwn #

The other structural feature of two-word verb constructions is their word-order. Insofar as this feature is concerned, it was found that some constructions always take contiguous order only, others always take noncontiguous order only, and still others may take either the contiguous or the noncontiguous order. Those constructions which take the contiguous order only include all the intransitive constructions, as in:

Hè *fèll dówn* | òn thĕ jób #   Jôhn *gòt dówn* #

Mỳ wâtch hàs *rùn dówn* #   Mâry *sàt dówn* #

and some transitive constructions, as in:

Thĕ môwer *môwed dòwn* thĕ bánk #   Hè *rôde dòwn* thĕ stréet #

Thĕ môwer *môwed dówn* ĭt #   Hè *rôde dòwn* ĭt #

In contrast to this contiguous order-group, there is another noncontiguous order-group which is occupied by some transitive constructions, as in:

Hè trîed tŏ *yêll* hìs wîfe *dówn* #   *Tâke* Jônes *dówn* #

Hè trîed tŏ *yêll* hĕr *dówn* #   *Tâke* hĭm *dówn* #

In addition to these two groups of constructions, there is another group of transitive constructions which can take either the contiguous or the non-contiguous order. In some instances, this choice in order is accompanied by a clear distinction in meaning, as in:

Hè *jûmped dôwn* thĕ hórse #
(i.e., he jumped down from the horse.)

Hè *jûmped* thĕ horse *dówn* #
(i.e., he forced the horse to jump down.)

Dôn't *lêt dôwn* thĕ cóach #
(i.e., don't lower it.)

Dôn't *lêt* thĕ côach *dówn* #
(i.e., don't disappoint him.)

Thĕ trôops *mârched dôwn* thĕ gráss #
(i.e., they marched down a grassy slope.)

Thĕ trôops *mârched* thĕ grâss *dówn* #
(i.e., they trampled it down.)

In other instances, however, no such semantic distinction exists, as in:

Rôll dôwn yòur sléeves #
Rôll yòur sléeves *dówn* #

Gêt dôwn thàt cháir #
Gêt thàt châir *dówn* #

Flâg dôwn thât cár #
Flâg thât câr *dówn* #

Shè *smôothed dôwn* thĕ béd-còver #
Shè *smôothed* thĕ bêd-còver *dówn* #

In transitive constructions where the complement is a long phrase, the contiguous order is the common practice, as in:

Hè *bênt dôwn* thĕ brîm ŏf thĕ hát | thàt hè bôught làst yéar #

Hè *glûed dôwn* thĕ êdge ŏf thĕ bôok-còver wìth gílt òn ĭt #

Hè *plûnked dôwn* thĕ hâlf-dòllar wìth ă hóle ìn ĭt #

Thĕ polîce *brôke dôwn* thĕ críminal's stòry abòut thĕ róbbery #

Pût dôwn yòur nâme ănd addréss | ìn Hóuston #

In cases such as this, the noncontiguous order may also occur, but only with pitch[6] /⁴/ in utterance final position, as in:

$$\overset{2}{\text{Hè}} \; b\hat{e}nt \; \text{thĕ brîm ŏf thĕ hât thàt hè } \overset{\wedge}{\text{boúght}} \; \text{làst } \overset{32}{\text{yéar}} \mid \overset{41}{d\acute{o}wn} \; \#$$

$$\overset{2}{\text{Hè}} \; gl\hat{u}ed \; \text{thĕ êdge ŏf thĕ book-còver wìth } \overset{3}{\text{gílt}} \; \overset{2}{\text{òn}} \; \overset{41}{\text{ĭt}} \mid d\acute{o}wn \; \#$$

$$\overset{2}{\text{Hè}} \; pl\hat{u}nked \; \text{thĕ hâlf-dòllar wìth ă } \overset{3}{\text{hóle}} \; \overset{2}{\text{ĭn}} \; \overset{41}{\text{ĭt}} \mid d\acute{o}wn \; \#$$

$$\overset{2}{\text{Thĕ}} \; \text{polîce } br\hat{o}ke \; \text{thĕ crîminal's stòry abòut thĕ } \overset{3}{\text{ró}} \overset{2}{\text{bbery}} \mid \overset{41}{d\acute{o}wn} \; \#$$

$$\overset{2}{P\hat{u}t} \; \text{yòur nâme ănd addrèss ìn } \overset{3}{\text{Hó}} \overset{2}{\text{uston}} \mid \overset{41}{d\acute{o}wn} \; \#$$

Whatever the order of two-word verb constructions may be, it was noted, as the result of grouping samples of these constructions into their immediate constituents and layers of structure, that the verbal element and the following adverbial use of the ad-prep always fall together in the same layer of structure. In contrast with such constructions, the prepositional use of the ad-prep falls in the same layer of structure with the noun-object rather than with the verb.

This result is revealed and confirmed by the structural signals of stress, juncture, and pitch. Thus in the utterance:

Mâry *rân dôwn* thĕ híll #

the secondary stress on *dôwn* and the absence of a terminal juncture between *rân* and *dôwn* indicate that *dôwn* is here used adverbially and hence should be assigned to the preceding verb rather than to the following noun. But in the contrasting utterance:

Mâry rán | dòwn thĕ híll´#

the tertiary stress on *dòwn* and the presence of the terminal juncture between it and the preceding verb indicate that *dòwn* is used prepositionally and should, therefore, go with the noun which follows rather than with the verb which precedes.

In instances such as:

$$\overset{2}{\text{Hè}} \; pl\hat{u}nked \; \text{thĕ hâlf-dòllar wìth ă } \overset{3}{\text{hóle}} \; \overset{2}{\text{ìn}} \; \overset{41}{\text{ĭt}} \mid d\acute{o}wn \; \#$$

where the adverbial use of the ad-prep *dówn* is widely separated from the verbal element *plûnked* by a long phrase and a terminal juncture, both elements must be grouped together in the same layer of structure, despite

[6] I am using the four pitch levels as used by George L. Trager and Henry L. Smith in *An Outline Of English Structure* (1951): /¹/, /²/, /³/ and /⁴/ for *low, mid, high* and *extra-high* respectively.

the presence of the terminal juncture between them. This unity is signalled both by the primary stress and by the pitch contour /⁴¹/ on the adverbial element *down*.

Other evidence which confirms the unity between the verbal element and the adverbial use of the ad-prep, on the one hand, and the lack of such unity between the verbal element and the prepositional use of the ad-prep, on the other hand, is the fact that the adverbial use of the ad-prep always forms a member of the predicator, whereas the prepositional use of the ad-prep never forms such a member.

All these evidences indicate that a two-word verb construction is a combination of a verb and the adverbial use of an ad-prep.

By way of conclusion, it should be recalled that the analysis of the structure of two-word verb constructions in this study is based on strictly descriptive and formal grounds. The first step was to identify the structural signals present in the utterance which includes a two-word verb construction. Then, according to these formal signalling devices, the structure of the whole utterance was determined. After the structure had been thus determined, the third step was to give the construction proper the lexical meaning that was carried within the utterance.

The sequence of these steps is important; formal signals and structure must be clearly identified before any lexical meaning is given to a two-word verb construction since the meaning of such a construction depends entirely on its structure.

Had this procedure been reversed and lexical meaning employed to determine structural phenomena, the present study would not only have been disqualified and deprived of its objective and scientific merits, but also would have led to contradictory and invalid results.

14

Transformation Grammars and the Fries Framework

ROBERT B. LEES

IF I HAVE READ CORRECTLY the history of modern linguistics and its relation to the study of English grammar, then I believe the following evaluation would be fair: the main contribution of Bloomfieldian structuralism to our understanding of language has been its replacement of vague notional definitions of parts-of-speech by very precise, so-called "formal," definitions of word classes. (One might also have expected that structural linguistics would encourage grammatical analysis of sentences in terms of morphemes instead of words, but this development has not taken place to any significant extent.) It is my personal opinion, and that of some of my colleagues, that this welcome gain in precision has been purchased at an inappropriate price.

The goals of traditional grammatical studies were high, in the sense that the classical grammarian attempted sincerely to account for what kind of knowledge the mature user of a language must have in order to construct correctly formed sentences and to interpret new sentences which he hears. The traditional grammarian was, however, severely handicapped in achieving this goal by his ignorance of the fact that one can actually specify explicitly a finite characterization of a complex infinite set, such as he knew the set of well-formed sentences of a natural language to be, namely by the use of a productive system of ordered rules which recursively enumerate the members of the desired set. He therefore resorted to vague semantic notions in order to specify what could qualify as a well-formed expression.

The structural linguist, in an effort to avoid such "mentalism," has chosen to reduce his goals drastically. Thus he has claimed on occasion simply to give an account of which sequences of words occur in a particular corpus of sentences examined, and linguistic analysis is then said to succeed

Printed by permission of the author, who is Professor of English and Linguistics at the University of Illinois. This paper was read at the meeting of the section on linguistics of the Midwest Modern Language Association, Lincoln, Nebraska, April 27, 1962.

simply in providing brief and efficient ways to state this. On other occasions he has claimed rather that linguistic analysis is a way to construct various kinds of abbreviatory transcription schemes with which utterances can be represented so that certain restricted kinds of redundancy are eliminated; in other words, analysis provides a set of elements, such as morphemes, or phonemes, by means of which one can transcribe sentences as linear sequences of these units. On the other hand, the linguist has sometimes claimed that his science provides, or should provide, exact procedures for constructing automatically a grammatical analysis for any given presented sentence, or for a language as a whole, but with no indication of just what sort of thing a grammatical analysis would have to be. But in any case, the attempt to explain directly the knowledge which the language user has of grammatical well-formedness has been abandoned. Thus, while in certain respects a so-called structural grammar is very precise, it is so just by virtue of the fact that it attempts to accomplish so little of interest.

The main feature of traditional grammatical analysis was that a well-formed sentence was viewed as correctly constructed just when it consisted of a sequence of bona fide words, each one drawn from the members of a particular class of words, and when the given sequence of word-classes was itself a member of some fixed set of allowable sequences. This conception of sentence patterning has for the most part been accepted and continued in the so-called structuralist school; however, now the classes themselves are said to be "formally" defined, and in the most sophisticated treatments it is also often admitted that the class sequences themselves do not quite suffice to characterize well-formedness but that to this notion must be added the idea of "immediate-constituent analysis". In this paper I shall not discuss the dubious advantages of these "formal" definitions of word-classes, the replacement of semantic paradigms by "form-classes" on the basis of inflectional affixes and substitution-in-frames, for I and others have shown elsewhere why definition of parts-of-speech by substitution techniques is illusory. Rather I wish to consider what kinds of regularities can be explained on the basis of the conception of syntax as a fixed set of allowed sequences of word-classes, how much is added by supplementing this conception with constituent-analysis, and what kinds of inadequacies in this conception have led to the development of transformational grammars.

It is clear that, given only a fixed set of words to draw from, the most one can say is that:

(1)   Die Katze sitzt auf der Matte.

is not a sentence of English, but that:

(2)   The cat is on the mat.

is. However, on this simple-minded view, so is:

(3)   *Cat the on is mat the.

Adding the specification that there are, say, eight word-classes, namely the traditional parts of speech, and that the successive words of the sentence must be drawn from only certain of these, we might then eliminate example (3) as having the wrong sequence; however, now there is no way to reject:

(4)   *The cat are on the mat.

This problem is, of course, not difficult to solve, but on the view that sentencehood is exactly characterized by allowed sequences of word-types, it requires us to separate the traditional class of Nouns into two subclasses, Singular Nouns and Plural Nouns, and likewise to split other parts of speech. If we generously stipulate difficulties of this type, or if we accept splitting of the classes just sufficient to account for the few cases of agreement in number and gender, or the like, there will still remain many non-sentences which we cannot eliminate without a wild proliferation of ad hoc classes. For example:

(5)   The event occurred and John vanished.   but not:

(6)   *John occurred and the event vanished.

Again generously stipulating some reasonable ramification of the set of word-classes, notice the following difficulty. In:

(7)   They were entertaining women.

the sequence of word-types, say: Pronoun, Copula, Present Participle, and Noun, or the like, does not reveal why the sentence is really two different sentences, understood or interpreted respectively as:

(8)   They were the entertaining women.

(9)   They were entertaining the women.

This kind of grammatical, or structural, ambiguity is exactly explained however if we assume that sentences consist not only of *sequences* of word-types but also of *groupings* of these into phrases. Then we may construe example (7) as either:

(10)   ((They) ((were) (entertaining women)))   or as:

(11)   ((They) ((were entertaining) (women)))

Of course, this explains why there is an ambiguity, but it does not explain why in (10) we know the Noun *women* to be the "subject" of the Verb *entertain,* though it is the object in (11).

Consider next the ambiguous string of words:

(12)   He assembled them by the new machine.

To account for our knowledge of what is involved here it does not seem to
suffice to place a reasonable bracketing of the elements on the sentence, as
for example:

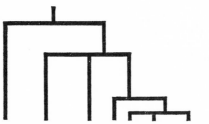

(13)   He assembled them by the new machine.

Whether the sentence is construed as a paraphrase of:

(14)   He assembled them near the new machine.   or of:

(15)   He assembled them by means of the new machine.

the way in which the words are grouped would be the same. But if, in addition to bracketing the words into phrases, we were to distinguish different
types of identically bracketed phrases, just as we were led to distinguish
types of words originally, then the ambiguity becomes transparent. In this
example we have simply an Adverbial of Place, or a Loc(ative), and an
Adverbial of Manner, namely an Inst(rumental), and these two adverbial
elements happen to consist of exactly the same words and phrases. Thus,
we add to the branching-diagram which represents the phrase bracketing
a label to each node, and we now conceive of the sentence as being (literally) "constructed" by successive expansion of syntactic formatives; such
a process of expansion is easily formulated in terms of a finite set of rewrite rules of formation. We have now arrived at the rather sophisticated
view that the infinite set of grammatical descriptions of the well-formed
sentences of a language is recursively enumerated by a finite set of iterative
and ordered rules of formation by a process of successive expansion.[1] And
our particular example can be construed as an instance of the following
kind of derivation:

[1] This paper is intended only to be explanatory and is by no means an original
proposal about the study of grammar. The view presented in the foregoing paragraphs
was first presented in N. A. Chomsky, *Syntactic Structures* (Mouton and Co., 1957);
see especially Chapter 4, The second edition of 1961 contains also a bibliography on
other works.

(16) (a) Sentence = Nominal + Verb Phrase   (Nom + VP)

   (b) Verb Phrase = Verb + Nominal + Adverb   (V + Nom + Adv)

   (c) Adverb = Locative   (Loc)

              Instrumental   (Inst)

   (d) Locative = Locative Preposition + Nominal   (LP + Nom)

   (e) Instrumental = Instrumental Preposition + Nominal (IP + Nom)

   (f) Nominal = Noun Phrase   (NP)

              Personal Pronoun   (PP)

   (g) Noun Phrase = Article + Noun   (T + N)

   (h) PP = he

              they

   (i) v = assemble, choose, make, . . .

   (j) LP = by, on, in, . . .

   (k) IP = by, with

   (l) T = the, a, some, . . .

   (m) N = machine, rabbit, task, . . .

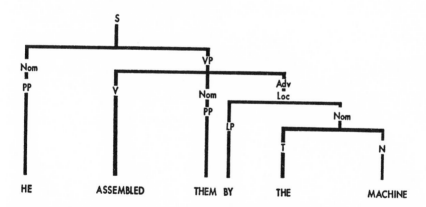

And the derivation for the other, or Instrumental, case would be identical with the exception of a choice of Instr in place of Loc.

Despite the fact that this view of sentence structure, in essence Immediate Constituent Analysis, is quite elaborate, there still remain many obvious deficiencies. I shall consider only a certain kind in this paper.

To introduce the main notion I wish to emphasize, consider first the following:

(17)   Watch me !

(18)   Watch yourself!

(19)   Watch myself!

(20)   Watch you!

We should like to account for this peculiar restriction of the reflexive object in imperative sentences to the 2nd person. But this is not difficult once we note that ordinarily *yourself* occurs as object in simple declarative sentences only when preceded by the pronoun *you*, say as subject; it is, in other words, the normal pro-nominal replacement for the nominal *you* when repeated within the same sentence. Thus, we need only interpret the imperative sentence (18) as a version of:

(21)   You watch yourself!

that is, as being "derived from" the latter.

But this notion of a sentence being derived from another requires an entirely different and radically new conception of syntactic structure—i.e., new to structuralism. (Notice that the traditional analysis of the imperative as containing an "understood subject *you*" is then quite correct, and in a rather literal sense at that, but the implications for grammatical theory are concealed by this psychological terminology.)

Now a sentence is regarded not simply as made up of various constituents, themselves in turn expansions of underlying phrase-type formatives, but it is viewed as "derived from" some other underlying sentence by a process quite different from expansion of phrase-types. Now our branching-diagram, or tree, is regarded not as growing out of its root according to various rules formation but rather as arising by the *trans*-formation of some already constructed underlying tree. Thus, we are now allowed not only to grow trees but also to transmute simple trees into derived trees. There is no reasonable way to construe certain sentence-types other than as permuted, elided, or embedded versions of source-sentences.[2]

In conclusion, let me show how the notion of transformation of underlying sentences can serve to clarify our understanding of certain expressions. Let us begin with an example on p. 24 of Ralph B. Long's recent book *The Sentence and Its Parts*:[3]

(22)   We wanted him to give you more time.

Of it Long, one of the most meticulous and penetrating of traditional grammarians, says: " . . . sometimes . . . a preposition (here *to*) occurs within its object (here *him give you more time*)." Constructions of this kind have not

[2] *Ibid.,* Chapters 5 and 7.

[3] Ralph B. Long, *The Sentence and Its Parts* (University of Chicago Press, 1961).

only forced Long into a rather dubious doctrine; they have caused trouble for English grammarians for a long time. Noting their similarity to other composite verbs in English in which the object intervenes between the verb head and an adverbial particle, as in:

(23)   They *sent* him *away*.

        He was *sent away* by them.,

and also the close parallelism among such cases as:

(24)   Napoleon compelled him to retreat.

(25)   "   wished   (him) "   "

(26)   "   refused   "   "

(27)   "   caught him retreating.

(28)   "   enjoyed (him)   "

(29)   "   avoided   "

(30)   "   appointed him general.

(31)   "   considered " able.

(32)   "   sealed   " in the valley.

N. A. Chomsky proposed that these latter cases also be treated as composite verbs with interposed object. The verb itself consists of a verb stem and a following complement, and in every case the object nominal occurs also as subject in a sentence whose predicate is precisely the complement expression, but now in finite-verb form. E.g., corresponding to:

(33)   Napoleon compelled the enemy to retreat.

there must be a sentence of the form:

(34)   The enemy retreated.

If we separate in the predicate the verb itself, call it the Main Verb, from the verbal tense apparatus, in this case the Past morpheme, call it the Auxiliary, then we see that the complement expression in the sentences in question consists simply of the Main verb and a new non-finite Auxiliary, in some cases the Gerund morpheme *ing*, in others the morpheme *to*. The sentences may be construed as obligatory permutations, each derived (optionally) from two underlying expressions in the following manner:

(35)   Napoleon compelled + Complement the enemy. ⎫
                                                       ⎬ ⟶
(34)   The enemy retreated   ⎭

(36)   Napoleon compelled to retreat the enemy. $\xrightarrow{\text{obl.}}$

(33)   Napoleon compelled the enemy to retreat.

or, to consider another type:

(37)   Napoleon considered + Complement him. ⎫
                                                    ⎬ ⟶
(38)   He was able.   ⎭

(39)   Napoleon considered able him. $\overset{\text{obl.}}{\longrightarrow}$

(31)   Napoleon considered him able.

Thus, we can explain all the pertinent peculiarities of these sentence-types by deriving them from underlying expressions containing an obligatorily replaced element called a Complement.

In my book on English Nominalizations I proposed the use of other Complement-type expressions, and I have time now to present only a brief catalog of these and a few newer proposals.[4]

To explain the differences between the two adjectival expressions in:

(40)   He was easy to understand.

(41)   He was eager to understand.

we can assume that there are Adjectivals which consist of an Adjective plus a Complement, that one such Adjective is *eager* (along with *apt, likely,* etc.), and that the kind of Complement replacement in this case is the one with *to* as Auxiliary; thus:

(42)   He was eager + Comp. ⎫
                              ⎬ ⟶ (41) He was eager to understand.
(43)   He understands.   ⎭

In contrast to this kind of derivation there are others in which an Infinitival Nominal as subject of a copula sentence with predicate adjective *easy* can shift to the end, the empty subject position is filled with the morpheme *it*; but if there is another nominal, say as object, within the Infinitival, then it may remain behind as subject, thus:

(44)   N   was easy. ⎫
            abstract   ⎬ ⟶
                              ⎪
(45)   I understand him.   ⎭

(46)   To understand him was easy. ⟶

(47)   [It was easy to understand him.]   or:

(40)   He was easy to understand.

These derivations show clearly why in Example (40) he is the object of *understand* but in (41) the subject.

[4] R. B. Lees, *The Grammar of English Nominalizations,* Research Center in Anthropology, Folklore, and Linguistics, Publication No. 12 (Indiana University, 1960).

The reversal of an abstract nominalization as subject into the predicate and the resulting empty-subject *it* can also explain the otherwise unaccountable use of a third-person neuter pronoun in other sentence-types, for which I give here only a sketch of the derivations:

(48)   To go there was like Nom.⟶

(49)   It was like Nom to go there.⟶

(50)   What was *it* like to go there?

(51)   For him to do it was so hard because X.⟶

(52)   It was so hard because X for him to do it.⟶

(53)   Why was *it* so hard for him to do it?

(54)   What he wanted became clear then.⟶

(55)   It became clear then what he wanted.⟶

(56)   When did *it* become clear what he wanted?

(57)   Swimming in the pool is a lot of fun.⟶

(58)   It is a lot of fun swimming in the pool.

(59)   Nom didn't find + Comp it.   ⟶

(60)   Nom didn't find it a lot of fun swimming in the pool.⟶

(61)   Who didn't find *it* a lot of fun swimming in the pool?

(62)   To work with him is hard.⟶

(63)   It is hard to work with him.

(64)   He makes + Comp it.   ⟶

(65)   He makes *it* hard to work with him.

And finally, from an unpublished paper of mine on the so-called Cleft-Sentence, we can view emphatic sentences of the form:

(66)   It is the secretary who does all the work.

as being derived from a Complement-sentence thus:

(67)   It is Cleft-Comp.

(68)   *The secretary* does all the work.   ⟶

(69)   It is the secretary WH + the secretary does all the work.

(66) obl.   It is the secretary who does all the work.

This kind of Cleft-complement construction can then explain the appearance of *it* in Ralph B. Long's examples, of which he says (p. 343): "*It* is even usable of human beings generally, without regard either to sex or to number, as a subject in identifications which are begun vaguely":

(70)   Who left just now? I thought *it* was the Smiths.

(71)   If anyone needs help, *it's* George.

(72)   A young woman came to the door when we knocked. *It* was the new secretary.

Rather than attempt to justify the neuter pronoun in (70) on the basis of generality or suspension of sex, I prefer the less provocative explanation that the sentence is an elliptic version of:

(73)   I thought that *it* was the Smiths who left.

derived thus:

(74)   It was Cleft-Complement

(75)   *The Smiths* left. $\Bigg\} \longrightarrow$

(76)   It was the Smiths who left.

(77)   I thought N
                    abst $\Bigg\} \longrightarrow$

(73)   I thought that *it* was the Smiths who left.

15

Some Neglected Aspects of Parsing

Robert B. Lees

IT IS NOT CUSTOMARY for linguists to discuss the parsing of sentences, at least under that name; and I have the impression that among some modern linguists the notion of parsing has been very unfashionable. Perhaps the

Reprinted by permission from *Language Learning*, 11.171–81 (1960). This abstract of Professor Lees's remarks was made by Professor Lois McIntosh of the University of California, Los Angeles.

main reason is that parsing is strongly associated with elementary-school doctrines on grammar, and as is well known by linguists, these are all antediluvian superstitions. But by "neglected aspects of parsing" I mean to refer to aspects which have been neglected not by school teachers alone, but by linguists themselves; and I shall take the truly unorthodox position, in fact, the perhaps traitorous position, that there are some aspects of grammatical structure of which the elementary-school teacher has long been aware but for which the modern so-called "descriptive" linguist has provided little if any explanation or enlightenment.

Let us take note of three main reasons for the linguist's disparaging attitude toward school grammar. First, the school teacher is charged with being prescriptive rather than descriptive, fighting a pointless battle to maintain archaic speech forms in the face of inevitable and natural language change. I suppose that by now most are agreed that children are going to speak the prevailing dialect of their culture or of the most prestigious sector of it perhaps, but that on the other hand, the school is responsible for teaching them the prescriptive rules of good behavior in correct use of the formal *written* dialect if they are to grow up literate.

Second, the teacher is charged with using vague semantic terminology in describing the grammatical features of our language. Most linguists appear to be in agreement that semantic designations are indeed vague and uninformative, especially to children who speak the language natively anyway. In other words, everyone is convinced that, even though it is largely true, it is unilluminating to baptize with the term "noun" the "name of a person, place, or thing." If a person understands English sentences sufficiently well to know which are the names, then it is pointless to replace the term "name" by the technical term "noun." It is equally pointless, though perhaps less vague to employ "formal" definitions like "A noun is any word which can be inflected by the addition of -s." When one knows which words can be so inflected, no new insight is given to the name "noun." Neither the vague nor the precise definition succeeds in capturing the desired concept of "nominal expression in English." If it is possible to capture this idea at all, it requires much deeper insight into the grammatical machinery of English.

The third charge is that the school teacher's attempts to formulate rules for analyzing arbitrarily chosen sentences seem to be easily confutable by readily available counter-examples, or that the exceptions to such rules always outnumber the example sentences successfully analyzed by them. But in every case in which the linguist has attempted to repair the difficulty by giving different or more complicated or formal rather than semantically based rules, the same charge can be leveled fairly against him. For example, the old-fashioned rule that the subject of a sentence may be identified by isolating the expression which refers to whatever the sentence "talks about" is said to be unworkable, not only because it is based on the vague semantic notion of "talk about," but also because even in cases which are not vague, it fails correctly to identify the subject: note sentences like *It is the linguist who is wrong.* The sentence is unambiguously about *the linguist,* but the subject is the word *it.*

The descriptive linguist would seek to avoid this difficulty by formulating a rule to find the subject by locating the nominal expression in the sentence which occupies a certain position with respect to the other constituents. Beside the unjustified assumption in this reformulation that nominal expressions can themselves be identified correctly beforehand, the new rule fails because there *is* no particular position which can be specified explicitly in which subjects of sentences will be found, except for some previously chosen special type of sentence. But anyone who knew beforehand just which expressions the rule applies to correctly would already have that very knowledge of grammatical structure which it is the purpose of the rule to provide.

It is truly curious and a little sad how few linguists have ever come to see where the real trouble lies. It seems very unpromising to attempt any further repair of the old unworkable rules, for all we ever achieve thereby are new unworkable rules. While it is not really known whether there are any exact rules for correctly recognizing every presented example of some English expression type, there should nevertheless be no great difficulty in specifying expression types simply by giving explicit recipes for constructing each one from well chosen elements. This, I take it, has been the major goal of all traditional grammars . . . to tell the reader how to construct sentences correctly. I do not know where or when this goal was lost sight of, but both school teacher and modern structural linguist have been struggling long and perhaps in vain to tell us how to supply each arbitrarily selected utterance with an analysis without having first specified just what a grammatical analysis would be.

Notice furthermore that there are two different demands of this kind which might be made. The linguist often speaks as though he might rationally seek an exact procedure to analyze correctly any presented utterance, given only that utterance and perhaps some others with which to compare it. The school teacher, on the other hand, assumes a weaker demand, namely that there be exact rules to analyze presented utterances, given the utterance and the grammar of the language. It would, however, prove far more enlightening to the student if she were to concentrate her efforts upon explaining the particularities of the grammar; that is, the rules for constructing correct sentences, not the putative rules for analyzing given sentences.

A very small, but growing group of linguists, under the inspiration primarily of N. A. Chomsky, has been attempting in recent years to study such sentence-enumerating sets of grammatical rules, with the conviction that more exact knowledge of grammars would certainly shed much light on a variety of aspects of language behavior. While it has not neglected other languages entirely, this study has achieved its most penetrating results in the analysis of English. Stated succinctly and therefore not too lucidly, this effort might be summarized thus: we seek to formulate explicitly a finite set of grammatical rules, operating on a finite set of grammatical symbols, which exactly enumerates the infinite set of well-formed sentences of English and no non-sentences, and so specifies each one that to it is assigned its correct structural description.

I should now like to explain in some detail what we have come to believe such a set of grammatical rules to look like, and then I shall be able to say how such a theory of linguistic structure can formalize, or explicate, certain neglected aspects of parsing.

Let me begin by mentioning briefly what some of the features of well-formed sentences are which we shall have to account for by means of the grammatical rules we formulate. If by "sentence" we mean a certain pronounceable sequence of sounds, then among our rules there will have to be a set which correctly assigns all those phonetic features which we have chosen for the physical description of speech. Nothing would be a sentence of English which did not consist of a sequence of bona fide words, or more accurately, of bona fide English morphemes, and therefore among our rules there will have to be a set which ensures the selection of such elements only from some given finite list of allowable morphemes, the *lexicon* of the language. The rules will have to be so constructed that the chosen morphemes will appear only in allowable order and will have to distinguish properly between different but grammatically significant orders; in other words, the article must precede the noun, and subject and object of a verb cannot be freely interchanged, etc.

The rules must be so constructed that certain elements of the sentence become *subordinated* to others, certain become *modifiers* of others. In fact, in general, the elements of a sentence may not be a simple string of concatenated words, but rather the successive parts must be thought of as grouped together with one another into superordinate parts; for example, in many cases one must distinguish between that subsequence which belongs to the *subject* and that which comprises the *predicate*. We would say, for instance, that the sentence: *The women students are attempting new subjects* contrasts not only in choice of words, but also in the way they are grouped together, with the sentence: *The women students are tempting new subjects.*

The pronounceable and bona fide words, their order, and the way in which they are bracketed together, however, do not account for all easily perceived grammatical contrasts. Notice the following structurally different sentences, all grouped in the same way:

(1) They were made by the wrong manufacturer.

(2) They were made by the wrong process.

(3) They were made by the wrong side of the building.

Ordinarily, we should say that the prepositional phrase in *by* which ends these sentences is being used in different ways, though labeling the constituents in this final bracketed element with the usually accepted parts of speech does not distinguish these different functions. We shall wish our rules to formulate correctly this aspect of grammatical structure also, although it has never before been adequately treated in language studies. Finally, the grammar should account properly for the fact that certain sentence-types are clearly related to others, it must express this relation exactly, and it must explain our perception that sentences of various contrasting outward shapes are nevertheless instances of the same type, as in the case of "interrogative" sentences.

These then are some of the requirements which one might reasonably set for an adequate theory of English "sentencehood." I am convinced that they can be met in an interesting and significant way, but to construct such an explicatory theory in detail is no trivial task. We seek an explicit formulation of each individual grammatical rule in all detail, and of the exact order in which these rules must be applied to enumerate all the well-formed sentences of the language and to assign to each one its correct structural description. A great deal of progress has been achieved toward this goal, all of it through only the most patient working out of detailed grammatical formulations, trial and error, casting and recasting of rules. I shall now try to convey in a succinct snap-shot version what such a theory of sentencehood, or grammar, appears to be like.

The grammar contains two major components, or distinct sets of rules, called the *syntax* and the *phonology*. The syntax enumerates an infinite set of abstract representations of the sentences as strings of grammatical symbols, the symbols standing for individual morphemes, boundaries, syntactic categories, etc. On each string is automatically imposed a bracketing structure, or parsing in the narrow sense, which can be represented as a branching tree of grammatical categories. The phonology, about which I shall say very little in this presentation, serves to map each such syntactic string into another representation of the sentence in terms of the most detailed phonetic features chosen to transcribe sentences; that is, it serves to provide each sentence with its pronunciation.

The rules of the syntax are again of two kinds; the first set serves to enumerate a finite set of abstract representations of so-called *kernel-sentences,* each with its branching-diagram of constituents; the second set of rules then serves to derive from these an infinite set of representations of all derived, or complex, sentences. The rules of the first component are all of the following form: $XAY \rightarrow XZY$, where A is a single grammatical symbol,

X and Y are arbitrary strings of grammatical symbols, possibly null, and Z is the particular expansion of A in the context X—Y. Thus the string Z is said to "be an A," in just the same sense as we say that the expression *the little, old, brown, church* "is a" nominal, or the abstract representation of certain expressions as *Article + Adjective + Noun* "is a" nominal. Following this example further, if in our grammar of English the category of Nominal is represented by the symbol Nom, and Article = T, Adjective = A, Noun = N, then it is conceivable that the grammar might contain a "rewrite" or "expansion" rule of the form:

$$\text{Nom} \rightarrow \text{T} + \text{A} + \text{N}$$

exactly expressing this perception of grammatical form (in this particular case, the environment strings X and Y are both null). The little sub-tree corresponding to this expansion which appears as a part of the final branching-diagram of each sentence containing the constituent Noun is then:

The syntax operates like a logical or mathematical system consisting of an axiom and a set of rules-of-formation; the latter permit the derivation of theorems from the axiom; if the rules permit a derivation to loop back on itself and pass through some stage again, then the rules-of-derivation will yield from the single axiom an infinite of theorems. In the special case of a natural-language syntax, the axiom is the single symbol S, standing for sentence, and the rules-of-formation are the grammatical rules, such as those of the form XAY → XZY; clearly, the first rule must consist of S alone on the left and on the right a representation of the most general aspect of sentence structure we believe valid for our language. For English this is undoubtedly:

$$\text{S} \rightarrow \text{Subj.} + \text{Pred.}$$

expressing our conviction that all well-formed sentences of English consist of a subject and a predicate in that order. The lexicon of individual morphemes which are allowed in sentences is then simply a very long set of rules of the form:

$$N_{animate} \rightarrow \text{uncle}$$

$$N_{an} \rightarrow \text{oculist}$$

$$V_{tn(transitive)} \rightarrow \text{complete}$$

$$\text{A}_z \qquad\qquad \rightarrow \text{clever}$$

etc., the left-hand sides being representations of the most specific syntactic categories relevant for the language, the right-hand sides the individual morphemes.

Now, clearly, if each string to be expanded appeared only once on the left-hand side of a rule, then there would be only one sentence enumerated by the set of rules, and this would mean that we view all sentences of English to be of exactly the same type and consist of the same morphemes. Thus we must have many rules to expand the same constituent in different ways; for example, we should like to say that the Predicate may be either Transitive-Verb Phrase or an Intransitive Verb:

$$\text{Pred} \longrightarrow \left\{ \begin{matrix} \text{V}_{tr} + \text{Nom} \\ \\ \text{V}_{in} \end{matrix} \right\}$$

In this way, the set of kernel-sentences generated can grow beyond a single theorem. We believe that the set of rules in this expansion part of the syntax does not permit looping back, and that therefore the set of kernel sentences is finite.

Notice how such a set of rules generates recursively all representations of sentences: the axiom "says" that S is a sentence, and the rules of formation "say" successively that if S is a sentence then so is Subj plus Pred, and if Subj + Pred is a sentence then so is Subj plus Transitive Verb plus Object, etc., etc., through increasingly more specific representations until each sentence is enumerated as a string of individual morphemes.

The rules of this expansion, or rewrite, section of the syntax are all so formulated that they apply or fail to apply just on the basis of the shape of the string so far developed. Now to achieve greater generalization it becomes desirable to formulate other rules in such a way that they can take account of not only the shape of a string but also of its derivational history. One of the reasons for this is that in general various paths through the expansion rules can happen to yield identical strings, but because of the way the constituents are grouped we may wish to further derive new expressions only from one of the ambiguous strings involved. There are other compelling reasons to introduce into the grammar a new layer of rules having this power, rules which are defined not on strings but on constituent-structure trees. These rules serve to derive complex sentences from the kernel sentences, and they can effect permutations of elements and ellipses.

In the case of the rewrite rules of the first section of the syntax, the constituent-structure of the resulting expanded expressions was given automatically by the way the expansion rules operated upon the underlying strings. For these new rules, called *grammatical transformations,* it is necessary to specify in a special way how the constituent-structure of the resulting transforms is to be derived from that of the underlying strings and the process which the rule in question subjects these strings to. In general it has been found that the ramified IC-structure of underlying representations is gradually erased by the application of grammatical transformations, especially those which permute elements.

The most characteristic grammatical transformations serve to embed a transformed version of one underlying sentence within another; when the embedded expression replaces a Nominal constituent of the underlying matrix-sentence, the transform sentence contains a Nominalization. The process of nominalizing sentences thus serves to extend the class of nominal expressions from a finite set of noun morphemes to an infinite set of nominalizations. (There are corresponding sets of grammatical transformation rules which extend the set of verbs, adjectives, and adverbs to infinite sets.) As an example, consider the sentence:

We were caught unaware by the committee's appointment of John.

The grammar enumerates this sentence as a complicated transform of the underlying kernel sentences:

(1) The committee appoints John.
(2) X caught + C us. (where X = abstract noun)
(3) We are unaware.

First sentence (1) is nominalized to *The committee's appointment of John* and the result is substituted in for X in sentence (2) to yield

(4) *The committee's appointment of John* caught + C us.

Then the complex verb caught + C is extended to a new verb *caught unaware* by replacement of the "complement" constituent C by the Predicate constituent of Sentence (3) yielding:

(5) The committee's appointment of John caught-unaware us.

Next a Passive transformation reforms Sentence (5):

(6) We were caught unaware by the committee's appointment of John.

This infinite extendability of certain grammatical categories under grammatical transformation serves in turn to define the "major grammatical categories" of the language. Constituents which under expansion were permitted to be chosen optionally can then be viewed as *attributive* to these categories. Thus, for example, the rules which expand the Nominal constituent are of the form (in part):

$$
\text{Nominal} \rightarrow
\left\{
\begin{array}{l}
\text{Noun Phrase} \\
\text{Personal Pronoun} \left\{ \begin{array}{l} \text{Singular} \\ \text{Plural} \end{array} \right\} \\
\text{Proper Noun}
\end{array}
\right\}
$$

Noun Phrase $\rightarrow$ Article Substantive

Substantive $\rightarrow$ Adjective Noun

$$\text{Noun} \rightarrow \left\{ \begin{array}{l} \text{Count Noun} \left\{ \begin{array}{l} \text{Singular} \\ \text{Plural} \end{array} \right\} \\ \text{Uncountable Noun} \end{array} \right\}$$

Thus, the constituent Adjectival is attributive to the major constituent Noun. Later, under certain grammatical transformations this attributive is replaced by transforms of sentences, including especially the Predicate portion of Copula-type sentences, and it thus gives rise to all nominal modifiers such as Relative Clauses, Post-Nominal Modifiers, Adjectives, and the Possessive Genitive. These formal notions are what underlie the intuitive idea of "modifier." Their origins in the Copula Predicate explain the good correlation between modifiers and descriptive meanings.

Let me now point out how the details of a sentence-generating grammar as just described might formalize certain other aspects of sentence parsing. Grammar teachers have been enjoined not to speak of so-called "understood" elements of a sentence. For example, it is perhaps no longer fashionable to say that an Imperative sentence contains an understood subject—*you*. And this is indeed a misleading way to describe the grammatical structure of a sentence. Nevertheless, there is an important, intuitive perception of grammatical form which I believe underlies this mode of description, although modern linguistics has provided no explanation for such intuitions. E. S. Klima has pointed out to me that it is convenient in formulating the rules which enumerate all Imperative sentences to derive the Imperative from a Modal sentence in *will* so that no special apparatus will be required to yield at the same time such echo-question sentences as: *Close the door, will you?* The grammatical transformation which derives Imperatives need only operate upon *will*-sentences, simply deleting the modal, thus:

You will close the door $\rightarrow$ You close the door.

and a later optional rule can then delete the subject. Thus, Imperative sentences of the form *Close the door* do have, in a perfectly clear and formal sense, an underlying subject *you* . . . the old "understood" subject. Despite the murky controversy in recent linguistics about the use of so-called "zero elements" in grammatical analysis, the idea of elliptical constituents in a sentence has a purely formal explication in the automatic deletion of certain grammatical symbols from strings under transformational rules.

Another intuitive notion about Subjects for which there is no reasonable treatment in recent linguistic work is the idea of the so-called "logical" subject as contrasted with the "grammatical" subject of a sentence. Thus in Impersonal sentences like: *It's hard to do that*, or so called Cleft-sentences like: *It's the principle that counts,* one used to say that the grammatical subject of the sentence is *it* but the logical subject some other constituent. The same may have been true for all Passive sentences, though there the practice was, I believe, to distinguish subject/object contrast from actor/action meaning. In any case, the intuitive idea underlying such a distinction of "grammatical" from "logical" subject is purely grammatical and has nothing to do with logic or meaning. Certain sentences are correctly derived in an English grammar from other underlying sentences; in those cases where the subject of the transform is not the same as that of the underlying source-sentence some of the original grammatical relationships of the underlying subjects are, nevertheless, still retained sufficiently strongly that the resulting transform seems, in a certain sense, to have two subjects, the new one, and the underlying source subject. For example, the sentence: *It's hard to do that* is properly derived from: *For X to do that is hard,* and thus there is the "grammatical" subject *it* and also the underlying, so-called "logical" subject *to do that.*

There is a purely formal, or internal, motivation for bracketing sentences into Immediate-Constituents, and this grammatical motivation can then, at least in part, explain the intuition on the part of the user of the language that sentences are correctly analyzed by this kind of segmentation and also that precisely the segmentations chosen were the correct ones.[1]

---

[1] This motivation is, briefly, the ineliminability of certain symbols from the constituent-structure component of the syntax. A grammatical category might appear to be eliminable in general from the grammar since it must appear for the last time in the grammar as the left-hand side of an expansion rule, and the right-hand side, or expansion of it, can then be substituted for the symbol wherever else it occurs previously in the grammar; that last rule can be deleted; and then the symbol in question no longer occurs anywhere in the grammar. But if a certain symbol is expanded in a grammar by means of a context-restricted rule, i.e., by means of a rule of the form $XAZ \rightarrow XYZ$, where A is the symbol in question, Y its expansion in the environment $X\_\_Z$, and X and Z are not both null strings, then there must be some other subsequent occurrence of A on the left, else the context-restriction would not have been required. This later expansion of A, say $A\_\_B + C$, cannot then be used to eliminate A from the previous context-restricted rule without rendering it ambiguous, for if Y had been $D + E$, we should then have obtained $X + B + C + Z \rightarrow X + D + E + Z$, and there is no way to tell which of D and E came from which of B and C. Thus A is ineliminable.

Furthermore, even if a category does not occur in a context-restricted rule it may still be eliminable only with a concomitant decrease in generality of the grammar. This will happen just in case the symbol in question occurs in the grammar N times altogether, it is expanded in its final occurrence into a sequence of m symbols, and N is greater than $2m/(m-1)$, for in this case substituting in the string of m symbols for each of the previous N-1 occurrences of the symbol in question and deleting the final rule results in an increase in the total number of symbols used in the grammar.

Thus, certain intermediate grammatical-category symbols are not in general eliminable and others are not deletable without decreasing the generality of the grammar; and the appearance of these ineliminable categories in derivations imposes a bracketing structure on the derived sentences which is then motivated on purely systemic grounds. This is a formal motivation for the intuitive perception of the bracketing, or grouping of elements, which the native speaker perceives.

16

An Outline of the Subclasses of the English Nominal

Arthur Norman

WHILE THE SYNTAX OF THE ENGLISH NOUN and other nominals is anything but simple, nominals show very limited patterning when they act as subject of minimal sentences. A description of these limited patterns permits us to divide nominals into fairly definite subclasses, which in turn become useful tools for discussing the full range of noun syntax.[1]

In *The Structure of English,* Fries employs as his basic test for nominals (Class I words) the frames

> (The) —— is/was good.
> —— are/were good.

The definite article in the first frame is one of a number of determiners

Reprinted by permission from *American Speech,* 33.83–89 (May, 1958). This article has been slightly amended by the author for reprinting here. Professor Norman is a member of the English Department of the University of Chicago.

[1] Despite the superabundance of material they present, most treatments of the syntax of the English noun are characterized by insufficient organization according to function. Of interest or importance are: Bernard Bloch and George L. Trager, *Outline of Linguistic Analysis* (Baltimore, 1942), pp. 77–78; Leonard Bloomfield, *Language* (New York, 1933), pp. 201–6; George O. Curme, *A Grammar of the English Language* (New York, 1931), III, 549–56; H. A. Gleason, Jr., *An Introduction to Descriptive Linguistics* (New York, 1955), pp. 145–47; Otto Jespersen, *A Modern English Grammar on Historical Principles,* Part II (Heidelberg, 1927), pp. 70–210, and Part VII, completed by Niels Haislund (Copenhagen, 1949), pp. 416–71, 479–579; E. Kruisinga, *A Handbook of Present-Day English* (Utrecht, 1925), II, 3–43, 173–278; Robert B. Lees, *The Grammar of English Nominalizations* (Baltimore, 1960); Ralph B. Long, *The Sentence and Its Parts* (Chicago, 1961), pp. 203–227; Edward Maetzner, *An English Grammar,* trans. Clair James Grece (London, 1874), III, 140–278; H. Poutsma, *A Grammar of Late Modern English,* Part II, *IA* (Groningen, 1914), pp. 112–276, 365–426, 513–699, and Part II, *IB* (Groningen, 1916), pp. 1011–1224; R. W. Zandvoort, *A Handbook of English Grammar* (London, 1957). pp. 90–127.

This outline is based on my own speech. In a briefer version, it was read at the Tenth Kentucky Foreign Language Conference (April, 1957). I am grateful to E. Bagby Atwood, James H. Sledd, Ralph B. Long, and Robert B. Lees for their many suggestions and criticisms; my debt to Mr. Atwood is particularly large.

(Group *A* function words) which can substitute for *the* before nominals. Included by Fries in his list of determiners are:

a/an, all, any, both, each, eighteen, every, few, five, four, her, his, its, John's, many, more, most, much, my, no, one, our, some, that, their, these, this, those, three, thirty-one, twenty, two.[2]

By testing these determiners in the frame

$$^2D\ \hat{N}\ \check{V}\ {}^2\acute{A}^1\ \downarrow$$

where *D* stands for determiner (under all grades of stress), *N* for noun (usually under secondary stress), *V* for verb, *A* for adjective, and space between words for open transition, as for instance:

²Thìs rîce ĭs ²góod¹ ↓
²Thòse stûdents ăre ²góod¹ ↓
²Ăn âpple ĭs ²góod¹ ↓

We see that a number of them (*any, her, his, its, John's, my, no, our, that, the, their, this, what,* and *your*) occur before almost all nouns that can be used in these test frames (except personal names and place names, which will be considered later). Since the remaining determiners do not pattern freely with all nominals, their use or nonuse affords a basis for dividing nominals into subclasses and at the same time grouping determiners into subsets, a procedure roughly comparable to solving simultaneous equations with two unknowns.

The first category into which nominals can thus be divided may be called 'pluralizers.' Examples are *appendage, apple, applicant, arrival, army, collision, colloquialism, gnat, murmur, nation, pearl, potato, ripple, situation, star, student, subject, teacher, truism,* and *wave length*. In the singular a pluralizer may be preceded by the determiners *a/an, another, each, either,*

[2] Charles C. Fries, *The Structure of English; an Introduction to the Construction of English Sentences* (New York, 1952), pp. 76–79, 88–89. Fries states that the numerical determiners go from thirty-one to ninety-nine (information echoed by Donald J. Lloyd and Harry R. Warfel in *American English in Its Cultural Setting* [New York, 1956], p. 111), which implies that numbers greater than ninety-nine are not determiners. Obviously, Fries's list is meant to exemplify, and is further limited by his materials, which seem not to include *another, either,* or *less*."

The determiner *some*, of course, represents more than one morpheme, including /sǝm/, meaning 'an unspecified quantity or number of,' and /sɔ́m/, 'a certain group or certain ones'.

Although the determiners quite often appear under weak or tertiary stress, they also occur with secondary and even primary stress. A more adequate criterion, therefore, for calling a word a determiner is its ability to function in the same way as the definite article in a frame such as

²Thĕ frèsh frûit (s) ĭs/ăre ²chéap¹ ↓

A determiner or determiner cluster (*a hundred, some few, the many, those two,* etc.) can replace the article, but—like the article—cannot appear between the adjective and the noun (with the exception of *enough, John's,* and *little* which, however, show differences in stress).

every, neither, one, whatever, which, and *whichever,* and in the plural by *all, both, certain, enough, few, many, more, most, other, several, some, such, these, those, which,* by zero, and by any numerical determiner from *two* on. This subclass includes nominals which in meaning-based grammars are tagged 'abstract' and 'collective,' as well as the ordinary 'countable' or 'thing noun.'[3]

The second subclass may be called 'nonpluralizers,' examples including *bamboo, bigness, blood, broccoli, clarity, drinking, fame, fun, gold, magic, mathematics, mother-of-pearl, news, radium, rice, smoke, spaghetti, stealth, sweat,* and *wheat.* The nonpluralizer is preceded only by the determiners *all, enough, less, little, more, most, much, other, some, such,* and zero. So far as classification by meaning is concerned, this subclass includes most names of chemicals, many 'abstract nouns,' and the so-called 'mass nouns' or 'material nouns,' which are the usual exemplars of the class.[4]

In contrast with the two highly restricted classes of pluralizers and non-pluralizers, there remains a large group of nominals which patterns freely with all determiners. Examples of these are *absence, amusement, beauty, cabbage, deceit, deformity, disability, fear, ham, hope, light, meaning, rain, refusal, sand, sickness, steak, thought, water,* and *wine.* Any of these words may be preceded in the singular by *a/an, all, another, each, either, every, less, little, more, most, much, neither, one, other, some, such, whatever, which, whichever,* and zero; while as plural forms they may follow *all, both, certain, enough, few, many, more, most, other, several, some, such, these, those, which,* zero, and any numerical determiner.

The table illustrates the occurrence of these three groups of nominals with their several determiners. Since the singular pluralizer is not bounded by zero, statements concerning the abstraction *boy* cannot easily be made

[3] Even at the risk of adding to the onomastic hodgepodge of modern linguistics, it seems better to use expressions like *pluralizer* and *nonpluralizer,* which describe according to form, rather than more familiar terms like *countable, mass noun,* or *uncountable,* which describe according to meaning.

The idea of the 'collective noun' is valid only in describing certain nouns which may in the singular agree with a plural verb (*The jury have made their decision*) and other singular nouns which must agree with a plural verb (*The people have spoken*). The 'abstract noun,' a standard fixture in traditional grammars, has an equally slender basis in formal syntax.

The pluralizing nominals also include zero plurals (*sheep*), replacive plurals (*tooth*), and nunnative plurals (*ox*), as well as non-native plural forms (*alumnus, alumna, bacterium; stigma, phenomenon; cherub*).

Needless to say, not all the determiners pattern the same way for every speaker: *less, whatever, which,* and *whichever* appear to vary especially. When restricted to the test frames, *enough* patterns like *all, more,* and *most;* but in larger utterances, and especially in nonsubject position, it precedes pluralizers which are singular as well as plural: *Is there enough potato in the stew? Was there enough scholar in his publications?*

[4] It may be observed that the referents of some of these 'uncountables' have very definite, regular shapes (*broccoli*), while others (*rice*) are considerably easier to count than many 'countables' (*gnats*).

without modification: (*All*) *boys are good* but not *Boy is good.*[5] The nonpluralizer, on the other hand, does pattern with zero: *Gold is good,* which is as generic as *All gold is good.* When bounded by the definite article (and especially in context), the nonpluralizer implies particularization: *The gold is good.* But in order to particularize further, in the manner of the pluralizer (*The boy is good*), the nonpluralizing nominal must resort to periphrasis: *A nugget of gold is good.*

SUBCLASSES OF THE NOMINAL

A		B	C	D		E	
all, enough, more, most, other, some, such	∅	less, little, much	a/an, another, each, either, every, neither, one, whatever which, whichever	both, certain, few, many, several, these, those, two (three, etc.), which	this, that	any, her, his, its, John's, my, no, our, their, what, your	the
1. potato p		—	s	p	s	s/p	
teacher p		—	s	p	s	s/p	
truism p		—	s	p	s	s/p	
2. bigness s		s	—	—	s	s	
gold s		s	—	—	s	s	
magic s		s	—	—	s	s	
3. beauty s/p		s	s	p	s	s/p	
hope s/p		s	s	p	s	s/p	
steak s/p		s	s	p	s	s/p	

s = singular noun and verb
p = plural noun and verb
s/p = both patterns appear
— = construction does not appear

The table shows how the third group of nominals exhibits all the formal properties of the pluralizing and nonpluralizing nominals. How, then, is it to be treated? Bloomfield would say that such nominals exhibit class cleavage

[5] In newspaper headlines, of course, singular pluralizers are frequently bounded by zero (*Boy meets girl*). Singular pluralizers bounded by the definite article can produce a generic, but not usually in minimal sentences: *The child is father of the man; The oak sends its roots deep.* The third group of nominals, since it can express the generic by patterning with zero (*Water is good*), does not frequently resort to this idiom. But cf. *Do you swear to tell the truth?*

A few phrases, chiefly *a lot of N,* but also *a great deal of N* and *a mess of N,* should perhaps be regarded as units. The subclass to which *N* belongs controls the number of the verb (*A lot of gold was seen; A lot of teachers were seen*), but a pronoun substituted for *N* takes the objective form (*A lot of them were seen*).

and thus belong to both subclasses.[6] Whorf would call a word like *wine* a
'mass noun' (nonpluralizer) in a sentence like *Much wine is good,* but
would consider it an entirely different (pluralizing) lexeme in *These wines
are good.*[7]

If we eliminate homonyms with altogether dissimilar meanings (for instance, *iron* 'metallic element,' and *iron* 'a poker'; or *division* 'military unit,'
and *division* 'mathematical operation'), a third solution to this problem
presents itself. In contrast with those restricted nominals which show only
pluralizing or nonpluralizing patterns, the distributional evidence suggests
that these nominals may be considered a completely distinct subclass of
'unrestricted nominals'—unrestricted in that there are no limitations on
their ability to pattern with determiners and unrestricted in that they pattern
in such a way as to display their allosemes in a manner determined by their
structure within the sentence.

The pluralizers and nonpluralizers, as shown, are quite limited in the
gradations of meaning which each can produce (using only zero and the
definite article with singular and plural forms), even though these shades of
meaning range from the most general in the case of the nonpluralizing to the
most specific in the case of the pluralizing nominal. Since the unrestricted
nominal offers these gradations in a structurally predictable hierarchy, they
can be considered allosemes of a single sememe. For example, the unrestricted nominal *cabbage,* like the nonpluralizer *rice,* can pattern *Cabbage
is good* or *The cabbage is good,* the latter suggesting an indefinite amount.
Like the pluralizer *potato,* it can pattern *Cabbages are good, The cabbages
are good,* or *The cabbage is good,* the final construction suggesting one of a
kind and involving the unrestricted nominal in potential, if minor ambiguity.[8]
Thus indirectly the subclasses of the English nominal offer a way to explore
meaning through structure.

---

[6] Bloomfield, *op. cit.,* p. 205.

[7] Benjamin Lee Whorf, *Language, Thought, and Reality* (New York, 1956), p. 140.

[8] If a word like *wine* is to be called an unrestricted nominal, its pluralizing alloseme
would usually mean 'a certain wine or wines': *some wine* vs. *some wines.*

It is possible that some speakers consistently use the determiner *some* in a way that
shows the class identity of the unrestricted nominals. The stressed morpheme /sɔm/
most frequently occurs in subject position while unstressed /sɔm/ quite often appears
in the complement. In the frames

1. ²I wânt ₂sŏme ³N¹ ↓
2. ²Sóme *N* ĭs/ăre ³góod¹ ↓

both pluralizing and nonpluralizing nominals substitute freely for *N*. But the plural
form of the unrestricted nominal is limited to Frame 2, while the singular usually
occurs with Frame 1 situations: *I want some steak vs. Some steaks are good.*

Class cleavage is here to stay though. Both pluralizers and nonpluralizers show it,
especially in nonsubject position and in expanded sentences:

There is too much boy in him.
I got egg on my suit.
The brooch was made of pearl.
A knowledge of good and evil is a lot to expect.

Because of their restricted environment, names of persons and places are commonly treated as a subclass of nominals traditionally called 'proper nouns.' A given name, like *Mary* for example, most frequently occurs bounded by zero in such frames as

²Mâry ĭs ²góod¹ ↓

²Ī sàw ³Máry¹ ↓

The surname, in the singular, patterns like a given name, but in the plural is bounded by the definite article.

While this is the usual syntax of personal names, it ignores the fact that names do sometimes follow adjectives (*poor Richard*) and various group *E* determiners, such as *her, his, my, our,* and *your*.[9] But when the name is preceded by *a/an, all, every, more, most, some,* or the like, it is most often considered an entirely different lexeme which patterns as a pluralizer. Thus in the phrase *the four Marys,* the word *Marys* would be called a pluralizing nominal meaning 'women who are named Mary.'[10]

Quite possibly the limited patterning of personal names with only zero and the definite article represents usage rather than a real grammatical limitation and, by analogy with the unrestricted nominal, a name like *Mary* and the phonemically identical pluralizer *Mary* could be grouped together into one lexeme with greater freedom of occurrence. Thus *Mary* would signal a personal name when bounded by zero in the singular or with most of the group *E* determiners; an alloseme, generally meaning 'a person named Mary,' would appear when the nominal is bounded by the definite article, the various pluralizing determiners, or when the plural nominal is bounded by zero.

If such a grouping actually predicts the full structural range of personal names, it is reasonable to speculate that the place names (*England, France*), institutional names (*Harvard, Yale*), and names of lakes (*Lake Leman, Lake Travis*) which distribute as do personal names are open to the same possibilities. If so, their formal patterning would also be identical with a limited number of nouns (including *dawn, evening, man, spring,* and *war*) which, when bounded by zero, signal the generic rather than the single specimen of a class, as is the case with names. This new grouping, because it augments the syntax of the pluralizers by its ability to pattern with zero, may be called 'unrestricted pluralizers.'

The custom of treating names as something apart from other nominals has tended to obscure their actual workings. Many place and institutional names (*The Hague, the University of Chicago*) are bounded by the definite article,

[9] Cf. Burns's line 'My Mary, dear departed shade!' and *Tennie's Jim* (in Faulkner's 'The Bear').

[10] In extreme cases there appear such unrelated lexemes as *I'm going to visit John* and *I'm going to visit the john.*

as are the names of rivers, oceans, and ships (*the Mississippi; the Atlantic, the Mayflower*), and some diseases (*the clap, the pip*), among other things. The base form of some of these nouns, whether singular (*the clergy, the police*) or apparently plural (*the blues, the Netherlands*), regularly occurs with a plural verb, and vice versa (*the measles, the United States*). Adjectives and participles also appear in this pattern (*The Naked and the Dead, the wounded and the dying*) usually with a plural verb and the sense of 'animate being.' Only rarely are they bounded by zero (*Handsome is as handsome does*) or do other determiners substitute for the definite article (*Farewell, My Lovely*). Since this is the extent of their syntax, at least in my speech, this subclass may be referred to as 'minimally bounded nominals.' However, the treatment of personal names suggests the possibility that for other speakers these restricted patterns may represent usage rather than a real structural limitation.[11]

Pronouns (except for the first possessive form) and all the morphologically indeterminate words which function as determiners (except *a/an, certain, every, no, other, the,* and zero) also appear as nominals: *He is correct; His is correct; Each is correct.* Since they are seldom modified by determiners, they may be designated 'unbounded nominals.'[12]

The marked infinitive, like the unbounded nominal, is not modified by determiners (*To think is to exist*). Only seldom does the infinitive appear as a nominal in any other pattern (*He made a big to-do over the matter*).

Other categories exist, including nominals like *alms, scissors, suds,* and *trousers.* These may be conveniently regarded as incomplete pluralizers, nonpluralizers, etc.

It should be stressed that the examples given in this study—which is based on only one user's brand of English—do not pattern the same for all speakers. It is possible that the membership of the different subclasses varies

[11] The present participle can appear as a minimally bounded nominal (*The dying were everywhere*), pluralizer (*His writings can be found everywhere*), or nonpluralizer (*His writing us was a good idea*). When it acts as a nonpluralizer, the present participle can retain its verbal characteristics and take an object (as the example shows). There is little need, if any, to set up a special class of gerunds to account for such syntax.

Some people do not hesitate to speak of 'American dead and wounded,' which would make me uncomfortable. The danger of introspective analysis, such as I have used here, is that the investigator will be carried away by his passion for neatness and symmetry and unwittingly prettify the patterns that he finds in his speech—or else that he will fail to recognize the great variation in syntax between his idiolect and the next man's. The ideal investigation of this problem would be through recorded conversation—as developed by Fries and his students—but such a technique isn't easily applied to a study of this kind.

[12] However, they can occasionally be modified by adjectives (*Poor you!*) and can exist independently as pluralizing lexemes: *Both puppies were 'he's'; Give me the others.* Determiner clusters, likewise, appear as determiner plus nominal (*These few seem good*). Other words which do not function primarily as nominals are arbitrarily pluralizers, unbounded nominals, etc., when in nominal position: *Up is this way; Three strikes make an out.*

dialectally, and it is certain that this membership is far from static and even now in the process of change,[13] a change which seems to make unrestricted nominals out of nonpluralizers.

This outlines does not begin to chart the complexities of English nominals. But by limiting itself to a restricted environment, it provides a more adequate description of the nominal than hitherto available and proposes a more efficient way of grouping many nominals that were thought to show class cleavage. This grouping, if valid, provides one of the first explorations of meaning through structure.

17

Grammaticality

Archibald A. Hill

Among transformational analysts, it has become common to state that a grammar must generate all the grammatical sentences of a given language, and no ungrammatical sentences. It is also usual to say that naive expert speakers can be relied upon to reject all ungrammatical sentences, and that this convergent rejection can be used to build a theory of degrees of grammaticality. In the discussion of these beliefs which follows, I shall largely confine myself to Noam Chomsky's readily accessible *Syntactic Structures,* since Chomsky seems to speak for many of his fellow transformationists.[1]

On page 15 Chomsky lists six sentences which I quote verbatim:

    (1) Colorless green ideas sleep furiously.

    (2) Furiously sleep ideas green colorless.

    (3) have you a book on modern music?

    (4) the book seems interesting

    (5) read you a book on modern music?

    (6) the child seems sleeping.

[13] See Conrad T. Logan, 'The Plural of Uncountables,' *American Speech*, XVI (1941), 170–75.

Reprinted by permission from *Word,* 17.1–10 (April, 1961).

[1] Noam Chomsky, *Syntactic Structures,* 'S-Gravenhage, Mouton and Co., 1957. (Janua Linguarum, IV) 116 pp.

Page 16 supplies two more, in the shape of a sentence frame with a blank to be filled by the words "whale," and "of." I have written out the two sentences, numbered them, and slightly changed the punctuation. For the original punctuation, see below.

> (7) I saw a fragile whale.

> (8) I saw a fragile of.

These sentences are accompanied by the following statements:

Sentences (1) and (2) are equally nonsensical, but any speaker of English will recognize that only the former is grammatical. (p. 15)

Similarly, there is no semantic reason to prefer (3) to (5) or (4) to (6), but only (3) and (4) are grammatical sentences of English. (*ibid.*)

. . . there are deep structural reasons for distinguishing (3) and (4) from (5) and (6) . . . (*ibid.*)

Yet (1), though nonsensical, is grammatical while (2) is not. Presented with these sentences, a speaker of English will read (1) with a normal sentence intonation, but he will read (2) with a falling intonation on each word; in fact, with just the intonation pattern given to a sequence of unrelated words. He treats each word in (2) as a separate phrase. Similarly, he will be able to recall (1) much more easily than (2), to learn it more quickly. . . . We cannot, of course, appeal to the fact that sentences such as (1) 'might' be uttered in some sufficiently far-fetched context, while (2) would never be. . . . (p. 16)

. . . in the context "I saw a fragile—," the words "whale" and "of" may have equal (i.e. zero) frequency in the past linguistic experiences of a speaker who will immediately recognize that one of these substitutions, but not the other, gives a grammatical sentence. (p. 16)

These statements, with their categorical pronouncements about the behavior of "any speaker of English," constitute predictions which invite experimental verification. Accordingly the eight sentences were copied onto cards, in exactly the form just given. To round out the number, I added two more sentences concocted by Martin Joos for a similar discussion:

> (9) Those man left yesterday.

> (10) I never heard a green horse smoke a dozen oranges.

The ten cards were shuffled into random order, and then given separately to ten informants. My informants were not, it is true, a reliable sample of the total English-speaking world, but it should be remembered that the statements to be tested applied to "any speaker." My informants were, however, fairly typical of the Academic community. They were professors, graduate students, one undergraduate business major, one secretary. Only three were in any sense linguists. The professors (except for two of the linguists) were teachers of English literature and composition. All were native speakers of English.

The first request to each informant was that he read aloud all the material on the cards. Rather interestingly, a number of the informants commented on the lack of punctuation in some sentences, and asked if they might "supply it" in their reading. They were told that they might do so in any fashion which seemed reasonable. The results of this request sharply contradicted Chomsky's statement that sentence (2) would be read with list intonation. Eight informants read (2) with a simple and single two-three-one double-cross pattern. Two broke the sentence into three phrases, with the breaks setting off *green* as the second phrase. It is interesting that one of those who used this pattern offered the spontaneous comment that the sentence "sounds like Modern Poetry." The second did not do so until questioned, but on the next day wanted the sentence quoted again, and then said "It not only sounds like Modern Poetry, it sounds like good Modern Poetry."

The next request to the informants was to reject any sentences which were ungrammatical, and to accept those which were grammatical. In the results of this voting, (9) 'those man . . .' was the only sentence rejected by all ten informants. Sentence (2) 'Furiously sleep . . .' was rejected by seven, accepted by three. The voting on (8) '. . . fragile of.' was similar, seven rejecting, three (but not the same three) accepting. Sentences (5) 'read you. . . ?' and (6) '. . . seems sleeping.' were each rejected by four, accepted by six. Sentence (10) '. . . green horse . . .' was rejected by three, accepted by seven. Sentence (1) 'Colorless green ideas . . .' was rejected by one, accepted by nine. Sentence (3) 'have you a book . . .' was accepted by all but one informant, who offered the qualification that it would be ungrammatical in his idiolect. This informant was one of the two linguists fully aware of differences in British and American dialects. Sentence (4) 'the book seems . . .' was hesitated over before final acceptance by one informant. All others accepted without hesitation. Sentence (7) '. . . fragile whale,' was accepted without hesitation by all informants.

Next, sentence (2) was read back with the three-phrase intonation pattern to all informants who had rejected the sentence, and these informants were then asked what the sentence now sounded like. Five then said that it sounded poetical. Two said that it sounded all right, but did not mean anything. A third said that it would be correct on one condition, that is, 'if ideas are green, and can sleep.' This informant had not applied the same conditions to (1).

Sentence (8) was also read back to the seven who rejected it, with primary stress and sentence-final intonation on *of*. Two then stated that such a reading made *of* a noun, and a third said that a pertinent question would then be "What's an of?"

There were also a few other comments. The one rejection of sentence (1) was from a student of literature, the informant who had accepted (2) because it sounded like poetry. One of the four who rejected sentence (5) 'read you . . . ?' commented that it would have been grammatical if it had begun with a capital, though he did not offer this comment about (4) which he had accepted. One of those who accepted (6) '. . . seems sleeping.' offered the comment that it would have been rejected by Tennyson because it had too many *s*'s. Of the three who rejected (10) '. . . green horse . . .' two changed their votes when it was pointed out that the sentence was strictly true. The third agreed, but did not change his vote.

While the experiment described here is neither large-scale, nor exhaustive, it still yields significant results. Not only is Chomsky's statement that (2) can only be given as a list contradicted,[2] some of his other statements about it are also not borne out. In my experience informants did not find it hard to remember; they were intrigued by it. I am also told that one reader has even constructed a poem for the purpose of fitting (2) into it. I have not heard of any one who was similarly challenged by (1). As for the comments just given, one informant found (2) more acceptable on stylistic grounds than (1).[3]

Another conclusion is that the intonation-pattern influences acceptance or rejection. I would regard it as significant that a number of informants changed their votes on (2) and (8) when these sentences were read back with possible patterns. Somewhat similar, but less interesting to a linguist, is the fact that pointing out the truth of the negative sentence in (10) also influenced acceptance.

Moreover, the mere recording of these votes on a scale from most to fewest rejections does not tell the whole story. For instance, the extremes ran from one rejection to six. There was only one informant who rejected only one sentence. There were three who rejected only two, but only two of these agreed on the sentences rejected. Of the two who rejected the maximum of six, there was disagreement on two sentences.

A scale of grammaticality for any given group of sentences could, of

[2] It is interesting that Chomsky gives (in footnote 2, pp. 35-6) a rather different statement of the way ungrammatical sequences are read aloud. They are there stated to have "extra long pauses . . . contrastive stress and intonation, failure to reduce vowels and drop final consonants." It is not clear whether this is meant to be the same thing as giving list intonation, or something different. If different, one can be permitted to wonder if "extra long pauses" may not mean terminal junctures, and "contrastive stress" merely successive primary stresses on a sentence of several phrases. Such patterns, of course, occur on many quite grammatical sentences.

[3] It is an interesting, if unimportant, detail that it would be possible to argue that when sentence (2) is pronounced so as to treat both *green* and *colorless* as separate phrases, sentence (2) becomes at least a little more logical than sentence (1). Sentence (2) can be interpreted as meaning that two groups of ideas, one green, the other colorless, sleep furiously. In sentence one, a single group of ideas is stated to be with contradiction, both green and colorless.

course, be constructed by giving the sentences to a sample of naive expert speakers large enough to be statistically reliable. But in view of the idiosyncratic reactions and the many rationalizations having little to do with the real reasons for acceptance or rejection which our informants showed, it is unlikely that a scale built on percentages of acceptance would be very profitable. That is, it is to be doubted if any generally acceptable principles would emerge, and without such principles any new group of sentences would have to be tested afresh. The thought of testing all the sentences, possible and impossible in English, is too horrifying to be entertained for long.

In most of the passages in which Chomsky discusses grammaticality, it is also true that he is ultimately concerned not with sentences in isolation, but with series of sentences to which given transforms may or may not be applied. Thus if the attempt to define ungrammatical sentences in terms of isolated sequences of words is given up, another kind of test immediately suggests itself. The test consists in putting sentences suspected of being ungrammatical in a relational or transformational framework, and testing their suitability to this frame. The test framework looks like this:

(1) The plate is hot. The plate seems hot. The plate seems very hot.

(2) The child is sleeping. The child seems sleeping. The child seems very sleeping.

(3) The book is interesting. The books seems interesting. The book seems very interesting.

(4) This hat is old. This hat seems old. This hat seems very old.

(5) The wine was drunk by the guests. The guests drank the wine.

(6) Golf is played by John. John plays golf.

(7) The pie was eaten by John. John ate the pie.

(8) John was drunk by midnight. Midnight drank John.

(9) John is a man. Is John a man?

(10) You have a book on modern music. Have you a book on modern music?

(11) You read books on modern music. Read you books on modern music?

(12) John can. Can John?

In these sets of sentences, set (2) is found in the series discussed by Chomsky on page 73. Set (3) is an expansion in accord with page 73, of a sentence found on page 15. Sets (1) and (4) were added.

In the second group, set (5) is given by Chomsky on page 80, where it is contrasted with set (8). Set (6) is given by Chomsky on page 78, with the statement that this set is more grammatical than the set "Golf plays John —John is played by golf." Set (7) was added.

In the final group, set (10) is derived from page 15, where it is made clear that Chomsky is concerned with the question as a transform of the declarative. Set (11) is similarly derived, but with a minor modification. Since a satisfactory declarative sentence could not be constructed from the question ("You read a book on modern music," might be taken as an imperative) the question form was revised to "Read you books on modern music?" Set (12) was added. Also, I revised punctuation throughout, to suggest sentence ends, and in some instances, sentence types.

The groups of sentences were then given individually to ten fresh informants. The informants were teachers of literature and composition except for one typist. The informants were told that the sentences were arranged in three groups, and that in each of these groups of four, the relations between sentences were the same throughout. The informants were asked to reject any set in which the relations were unsatisfactory, and the only other direction was that if any one sentence in a set seemed unsatisfactory, the whole set was to be rejected.

In one important way, the results were as expected. Sets (2), (8), and (11) were rejected by all informants, though one (a mediaevalist) rejected (11) only after considerable hesitation, and with a final statement that it was archaic, and so wrong. Still another rejected (11) only because he would not use it himself.

The surprises came in the sentences which were rejected by some informants (though not all), and the reasons given. Thus two informants rejected set (1) on the ground that things must either be hot or not hot, they can not seem hot. One informant rejected all the sets in group two, on the ground that passives are weaker and less direct than actives. It was interesting that this informant then immediately added that sets (2), (8), and (11) were the primary examples of wrongness. Another informant rejected (2), (8), and (11) without hesitation, and then said that (3) seemed 'a trifle odd,' and that (6) was 'awkward.' The mediaevalist who said that (11) was archaic, said that (6) sounded as if it were translated from some foreign language.

It would seem that here also there are some significant results, and it is pleasant to be able to say that they are not all negative. The framework which tells the informant what the relationships are, also tells him how to treat the suspected sentence. Without such a framework he operates as Sapir long ago said we all operate, attempting to wring some kind of pattern, and some kind of meaning, out of the most unlikely material.

What is significant in these results, then, is that sets (2), (8), and (11) were universally rejected, and that this rejection occurred in spite of the fact that the crucial sentences from (2) and (8) had previously been accepted by four informants out of ten, when the sentences had been presented in isolation. I should suggest, therefore, that universal rejection constitutes significant convergence, exactly the sort the analyst needs, and on which Chomsky hoped to found a theory of ungrammaticality. On the other hand, sentences which are not universally rejected do not show ungrammaticality either total, or to a significant degree. What appears here are occasional idiosyncratic and often nonlinguistic objections, like the one that nothing can 'seem hot.' Finally, sets like (9), objected to by no one, are also completely grammatical.

If my experimental results are verifiable, as I believe they are, I am at a loss to account for Chomsky's assertions that all speakers unhesitatingly reject certain sequences or pronounce them as mere lists. Chomsky has stated in an at least semipublic situation that these results are based on experiments several times repeated. I can only guess that there is some misunderstanding between us, or that one set of results is for some reason statistically unreliable.

It is worth pointing out, however, that there is an *a priori* theoretical reason why sentences in isolation would be unlikely to produce convergent rejection of those which are ungrammatical. The number of intonation patterns is small, and no utterance can be given without one of them occurring. It has, for instance, become a sort of commonplace among linguists that a normal child learns all the intonation patterns—and what they mean—before he is five years old. The lexicon of any language is not only so large that the individual speaker never learns it all, it is characteristically open to new coinages at any time. The result is that the normal speaker operates on the tacit assumption that he knows and can recognize all the intonation patterns, and can make full use of them in identifying grammatical structure. With vocabulary items, on the other hand, the equally normal assumption is that anything which turns up in a situation where the surrounding vocabulary items, and the intonation mark it as strange, is merely a word whose meaning is unknown. This second assumption is what explains the response of those informants who heard "I saw a fragile of" read back with primary stress and final sentence-pitch on *of*, and said that such a reading made *of* a noun, or suggested the question "What's an *of?*". In short, a familiar intonation pattern takes precedence in identification over isolated word items made up of vowels and consonants. If the intonation is right, at least enough normal speakers will react to the sentence as grammatical though of unknown meaning, to prevent convergent rejection.

The Chomskyan approach—whether it is found in his writings or those of Lees or even Henry Lee Smith Jr.[4]—is that a sentence can be proved to be ungrammatical on two conditions. The first of these is that the underlying segmental morphemes and words are fully identified, and the second is that the sequence in which these morphemes are presented is an impossible one. It is my contention that the first of these conditions is always unfulfilled when sentences are spoken. Every sentence gets a normal intonation pattern, and consequent irregularity of the sequence then simply contradicts the identification of the segmental morphemes. When a sentence consists of a normal sequence of words and morphemes with the exception of one intruder, and is furthermore provided with normal intonation, the tendency to abandon a semi-etymological identification of the strange morpheme is very strong. That is, we follow the Joos law (cf. *Language,* Vol. 34, 1958; p. 286) and interpret the strange morpheme as the one which would do least violence to the context. Such a tendency also agrees with what lexicologists and other linguists have long known—that the meaning of a word can not be adequately known except in context. Thus a sequence like "look at the cross eyed. . . ." if filled with *of* will in-

[4] The Robert B. Lees passage to which I refer is in *Rules for English Pro-Nominalization,* IBM Research Center, 1960, p. 19, fn. 3

"It is also important to recognize in this connection that, except for utterly impeccable, short sentences or for unintelligible gibberish, absolute judgments on grammatical acceptability cannot be given with assurance unless some independent knowledge has already been acquired about other formal features of English sentences and grammar relevant to the doubtful examples in question. Thus, e.g., we would reject the 'queer sentence': '*John astounded the dark green.' with some conviction since we know from independent analyses that the distinction between 'animate' and 'inanimate' nouns is relevant in English sentence structures."

The example by Henry Lee Smith Jr. is from "Linguistics: A Modern View of Language," in *An Outline of Man's Knowledge of the Modern World,* edited by Lyman Bryson, McGraw-Hill, 1960, pp. 344–72. The example is found at page 355.

" 'The tall man smoked the black cigar' is an acceptable occurrence as a sentence, whereas... 'Tall the man cigar the smoked black' would be palpably impossible as an occurrence *and* as a sentence, since it violates grammatical patterns of the language."

The Lees sentence is the more interesting and important of the two, since it illustrates a belief which I presume to be seriously held. Yet I think it can be shown that the queerness of his sentence depends primarily on previous identification of *green* as the inanimate color adjective. For several hearers to whom I have read the sentence, the identification broke down, and *green* was identified as some other word. Some took it as the proper name *Green,* and some, part of a team-name, *Dark Green,* as in *Light Blue* for Cambridge. A large part of the queerness would disappear, certainly, if the last word, or the last two words, were capitalized.

The Smith example is more nearly trivial. Smith, a leading if not the leading exponent of phonologically based grammar and syntax, seems here to have been hasty, impelled by the necessity of giving an ungrammatical example in a popular article where he could not indicate the intonation. One wonders whether his meaning is not approximately "This is a sequence of words for which it would be difficult to find a suitable intonation pattern." One can be found, however. *Man cigar* can be read with the stress of a nominal compound, and the utterance as a whole read as two linked equations. The fact that the meaning remains unknown is irrelevant.

evitably lead some hearers to reidentify an *of* as some kind of animal. Not until some other principle of ordering (such as alphabetical listing) is evident, can the naive expert speaker be relied upon to reject a sequence of words as being a non-sentence.

The assumption that morphemes and words are fully identifiable without reference either to their syntactic position or the accompanying patterns of pitch, stress, and juncture, explains the ungrammaticality which Chomsky has ascribed to many of his sentences. Furthermore, belief in the absolute identifiability of morphemes forces Chomsky to rely on spelling in a fashion which is more than a little startling. In his "I saw a fragile *of*" it would appear that the letter sequence *o* and *f* is thought of as firmly identifying the preposition. No attention is given to the possibility that this pair of letters might spell a different word with a different pronunciation. There is here a curious parallel to a writer of a very different sort—Charlton Laird. Laird has recently maintained that it is possible to recognize the difference between "I scream" and "ice cream" without attention to the sound, because (among other things) "we guess at once that any word like *I* . . . which comes immediately before a word like *scream* is a subject. . . ."[5] Both Laird and Chomsky are relying upon spelling, both apparently without fully realizing that they are doing so. And both are forced to rely on spelling for the reason that there are only two systems which we can rely on for first identifications of a sentence heard or seen—the system of sound or the system of spelling. If we reject the one, we are forced to accept the other, with results which are confused and confusing if the reliance is not overtly realized.

A belief that sentences are merely strings of words, and that words in turn, are merely sequences of letters surrounded by white spaces, could certainly result in viewing grammaticality as a complex and difficult problem, and give to generative grammar the shakiness of any house without a firm foundation. It could also explain the hostility of many structuralists who maintain that language is basically a system of sound, only secondarily one of writing. But while it is sometimes true that controversy advances knowledge, at least a large part of the present controversy between structuralists and transformationists is unnecessary. It is ironical that transformationists, who are above all interested in processes, applicable to certain items, and giving certain results, should have been so insistent on judging items in isolation, with no attention to what the item was derived from, nor the process of derivation. It would almost appear that the insistence on the ungrammaticality of "Midnight drank John" marks abandonment of interest in transformations. Surely a transformationist ought to demand that such a sentence be judged only in the light of

[5] Charlton Laird, *Thinking About Language,* Rinehart English Pamphlets (New York, 1960). The quotation is on page 56.

transforms of active to passive sentences, and the possible (or impossible) reversal of that process.

The transformationist should not ask whether an isolated sentence is grammatical. He should take sets of superficially similar sentences, and apply an identical transform to all of them, exhibiting the results. The sets, transforms, and results can be submitted to naive expert speakers, and acceptance, rejection, and responses can be expected to be reliable, as they can not when what is submitted to the naive expert speaker are isolated sentences. It is obvious that such a tool for eliciting reliable responses would be a powerful one for the transformationist, and that convergence would give him a foundation for generative grammar. It is less obvious that such testing would be no more than an application of a tool which has been basic in structural linguistics. The question asked by post-Bloomfieldian linguists has always been "are the items the same, or different?" and the answers have enabled structuralists to segment and describe much of language. With a more structural question, set in a more structural frame, the transformationists might reach some of the convergence which now they can only claim.

18

Some Methodological Remarks on Generative Grammar

Noam Chomsky

1. THESE REMARKS ARE PROMPTED by several critical discussions[1] of recent work in descriptive syntax and syntactic theory carried out within the framework of generative grammar.[2] I will try to clarify several issues that have, apparently, been the source of some misunderstanding and confusion as to the purposes and assumptions of this work, and to indicate how it can perhaps be extended into certain important but neglected areas.[3]

It is useful, at the outset, to make a distinction between *data* and *facts*. The linguist's data consist of certain observations about the form and use of utterances. The facts of linguistic structure that he hopes to discover go well beyond these observations. A grammar of a particular language is, in effect, an hypothesis about the principles of sentence formation in this language. It represents a factual claim concerning the rules that underlie the data that have been collected. We judge the truth or falsity of this hypothesis by considering how well the grammar succeeds in organizing the data, how satisfying an explanation it provides for a wealth of empirical observations, how far-reaching are its generalizations, how successfully it accomodates new data. An enormous amount of data is available to any native speaker; the deeper facts of linguistic structure, however, remain hidden to him.

Similarly, a theory of linguistic structure is an hypothesis about linguistic

Reprinted by permission from *Word*, 17.219–39 (August, 1961). Professor Chomsky is a member of the Department of Linguistics at the Massachusetts Institute of Technology.

[1] Hill, "Grammaticality," *Word* XVII (1961) referred to henceforth as [G]); Jakobson, "Boas' view of grammatical meaning," *The Anthropology of Franz Boas, American Anthropologist* (1959) (henceforth, [BVGM]); Bolinger, "Linguistic Science and Linguistic Engineering," *Word* XVI (1960) (henceforth, [LSLE]).

[2] As exemplified, in particular, in my *Syntactic Structures,* The Hague, 1957 (henceforth [SS]).

[3] Much of what I say here is a paraphrase of earlier remarks, e.g., in [SS] and in "A transformational approach to syntax," *Third Texas Conference on Problems in the Analysis of English,* A. A. Hill, editor, Austin, 1962 (henceforth, [TAS]).

universals. It asserts that the grammars of all human languages are constructed on such-and-such a specified plan. Such a theory should explicitly characterize the form of grammars (the schema for grammatical description) and should provide a method for selecting among alternative grammars, each compatible with the available data from some language (and each making a specific set of factual claims concerning this language). A theory of this sort can be verified in an indirect, but quite satisfactory way. We can ask whether, for each language, the most highly valued grammar of the specified form is confirmed in the sense described in the preceding paragraph.

A linguist who is exclusively concerned with linguistic data and not with the facts of language, in this broader sense, has severely limited the scope of his research.[4] A grammatical description that gives nothing more than "a compact one-one representation of the stock of utterances in the corpus"[5] can be challenged only to the extent that the observations it summarizes or rearranges are defective. It claims little, and its interest is correspondingly limited.

In [SS] I was concerned with grammars that make a much stronger factual claim than this. A *generative grammar,* in the sense of [SS], is not a large collection of neatly organized examples, supplemented with comments about these examples and hints as to how to construct similar ones. Nor is it a discussion of efficient and compact notations (e.g., inventories of phonemes, morphemes, categories or construction types) in terms of which the utterances of a corpus can be represented. A generative grammar is a system of explicit rules that assign to each sequence of phones, whether of the observed corpus or not, a structural description that contains all information about how this sequence of phones is represented on each of the several linguistic levels—in particular, information as to whether this

[4] In his [LSLE], Bolinger distinguishes between data-oriented and model-oriented approaches to linguistic description, the implication being that 'model-oriented' studies are less concerned with the facts of language as such. The essential difference between the two approaches that Bolinger describes seems to me, rather, that his 'data-oriented approach' limits its concern to a narrow subset of more immediately accessible facts; it does not attempt the precise formulation of deeper underlying generalizations.

It should be remembered, in this connection, that the most partial and limited set of explicitly formulated recursive (iterative) rules is, literally, far more extensive in coverage than the most immense collection of examples assembled and arranged by the data-oriented linguist. We return to this matter below.

[5] At one point (p. 366) in his *Methods in Structural Linguistics* (Chicago, 1951), Harris describes this as "the over-all purpose of work in descriptive linguistics." Later, however, he remarks (p. 372) that "the work of analysis leads right up to the statements which enable anyone to synthesize or predict utterances in the language." It is this set of statements that I am calling the grammar. I am not convinced that the last-quoted remark is really justified (that is, that any known procedures do provide an adequate grammar), but this is another question. At the moment I am only concerned to make the difference in aim explicit.

sequence of phones is a properly formed or *grammatical* sentence[6] and if not, in what respects it deviates from well-formedness.[7] In particular, then, this grammar distinguishes a class of perfectly well-formed (fully grammatical) sentences. It is designed, in other words, to meet what Hockett has proposed as the basic test of significance for a grammar, namely, that it "generate any number of utterances in the language, above and beyond those observed in advance by the analyst—new utterances most, if not all, of which will pass the test of casual acceptance by a native speaker."[8] To Hockett's remark I should only like to add that a grammar must not merely specify an infinite class of properly formed utterances, but must also assign to each sequence of phones a structural description that provides a basis for explaining how this utterance is used and understood—that provides the structural information without which it is impossible to undertake this further task in a serious way.

Three theories of generative grammar are proposed for comparison and study in [SS]. The first (based on the notion of finite state Markov process or finite automation) was shown to be too weak. The second was a formalized and somewhat generalized version of the theory of immediate constituents, reinterpreted as a theory of generative grammar. The third was a transformational model. I tried to show, by considering several kinds of linguistic data, that the immediate constituent theory was inadequate, and that the transformational theory seemed much more promising. Additional work that has appeared since then[9] seems to me to give support to this claim, which, I should like to emphasize again, is a factual claim concern-

---

[6] In grammars of the type studied in [SS], part of the structural description of a phone sequence is its representation on the phrase structure level by a set of abstract strings that can be presented, equivalently, as a tree with labelled nodes. See [SS], and references there, for details. The fully grammatical sentences generated by the grammar are the ones represented by trees headed by a single node labelled *S*, where *S* is the distinguished initial symbol of the underlying constituent structure grammar. Transformational rules also play a part in assigning a phrase structure representation, in that theory, although the question exactly how they do so has not yet been satisfactorily answered. For discussion of this see my *Logical Structure of Linguistic Theory* (mimeographed, 1955, henceforth, [LSLT]), of which [SS] is essentially an excerpt, and "On the notion 'rule of grammar'," *Proceedings of the Symposia on Applied Mathematics,* XIII (1961).

[7] That is, sentences not generated directly can still be assigned a degree of grammaticalness, and a structural description which will indicate how they are related to directly generated sentences. A chapter of [LSLT] is devoted to this question, which is mentioned only in passing in [SS] (footnotes 2 and 7 of chapter 5). We return to this below in §5.

[8] "Two Models of Grammatical Description," *Word* X (1954), reprinted in Joos, ed., *Readings in Linguistics* (Washington, 1957). See also Hockett's "A Note on 'Structure'," *International Journal of American Linguistics* XIV (1948), also reprinted in Joos' *Readings.*

[9] E.g., [TAS] (which is, again, largely an excerpt from [LSLT]) and Lees' *Grammar of English Nominalizations* (Baltimore, 1960), henceforth referred to as [GEN].

ing English and, more generally, the structure of natural languages—a claim that can be proven false in several ways; e.g., by the construction of grammars of a different form that are more successful in handling data of the kind that originally motivated the theory, by a proof that any grammar of this form must fail, for some natural language, because of certain formal features of utterances in this language, etc.

2. The investigations of generative grammar described in [SS] were motivated in part by an interest in the problem of accounting for the ability of a speaker to produce and understand an indefinite number of new sentences (or for that matter, to recognize them as properly formed, or as deviating from well-formedness in one or another respect) ([SS], p. 15), a task that he performs regularly with great facility. A generative grammar can be regarded as an attempt to characterize certain aspects of this ability, and a particular theory of generative grammar is a proposal concerning its general and universal features.[10] If we hope to make significant progress towards these goals, the grammars we construct must be sufficiently precise so that we can deduce from them consequences that can be confronted directly with linguistic data of a rich and varied sort. This requirement is rarely met by either traditional or modern studies,[11] though this fact may be obscured by the informality of linguistic descriptions, whether traditional or modern.

The study of precise generative grammars with explicit consequences (and the general form of such grammars) is in its infancy. Traditional grammars rely on the intelligence and linguistic intuition of the reader to provide the structural descriptions of items that do not appear in the collection of examples. There is little doubt that deep features of grammatical structure are unexpressed in a grammar addressed to an intelligent human who, in some totally unknown way, acquires the ability to produce and understand new sentences, having absorbed the information presented to him in a compendious traditional grammar. The study of generative

[10] A theory of generative grammars can be regarded quite naturally as a proposal concerning certain fundamental and specific skills that the child brings to language learning. See my "Explanatory Models in Linguistics," *Proceedings of the International Congress on Logic, Methodology and Philosophy of Science* (August 1960), to appear, P. Suppes, editor (henceforth [EML]), for some further discussion.

[11] With some very limited exceptions, e.g., inflectional paradigms of the traditional sort. Given a list of lexical items, a paradigm gives explicit instructions for constructing a finite set of inflected forms. But it is clear that this is a relatively minor success.

It is on the level of syntax, of course, that the intuitive character of grammatical descriptions, and the defects of such descriptions, are most apparent, since it is here that the data cannot be enumerated in a finite list. However, I think that the preoccupation of modern linguistics with inventories rather than rules has had the effect of removing even significant aspects of phonology from the domain of linguistic research; for example, questions of the kind mentioned further below. For further observations on this see [EML], and Halle and Chomsky, *Sound Pattern of English* (forthcoming, henceforth, [SPE]).

grammars is, however, a natural outgrowth of traditional descriptive linguistics. Modern linguistics has, typically, been concerned with the much narrower problem of constructing several inventories of elements in terms of which utterances can be represented, and has given little attention to the rules that generate utterances with structural descriptions.[12]

3. Clearly if our goals are as described in §2, we will bring to bear data of many kinds in attempting to determine the validity of particular generative grammars or, more seriously, particular theories of generative grammar. Thus in [SS], [TAS], and elsewhere, I have been concerned with such data as

(1) (a) phonetic transcriptions;

   (b) judgments of conformity of utterance tokens;

   (c) judgments of well-formedness;

   (d) ambiguity that can be traced to structural origins;

   (e) judgments of sameness or difference of sentence type;

   (f) judgments concerning the propriety of particular classifications or segmentations;

and so on.[13] By (a), I refer to the kind of data given by impressionistic phonetics of the usual kind, e.g., transcriptions of stress contours, etc. Category (b) includes the intuitive sameness-difference judgments that are fundamental to descriptive phonology, e.g., the observation that in my normal speech, *latter* and *ladder* are phonemically identical (i.e., tokens of them are) but *writer* and *rider* are phonemically distinct. To illustrate (c), I gave such examples as

(2)   colorless green ideas sleep furiously

(3)   furiously sleep ideas green colorless

[12] In [TAS] I noted a few exceptions to this. In particular, Harris' morpheme-to-utterance rules can be reinterpreted as a model for generative grammar, and Hockett's Markov process model was explicitly designed as a sentence-generating grammar.

[13] To avoid a possible misunderstanding, notice that I am suggesting that data of these kinds are relevant to determining the validity of grammars and linguistic theory, but not that these data should be utilized in the construction of or choice among grammars, insofar as this is specified by the theory of linguistic structure. The difference is fundamental. See [SS] and [EML] for further discussion. Thus we might try to develop a general theory of linguistic structure powerful enough to lead us from certain data about a language to a generative grammar of this language, limiting the data, in this context, to (a), (b), (c), that is, to the kind of data that we might regard as being available to the child who learns language. This might be a reasonable decision for someone whose motivation in studying generative grammars is to construct some sort of model for language learning. But such a person would still concern himself with such data as (d), (e), (f) in evaluating the success with which his theory of language learning duplicates the performance of the human.

(4)   the child seems sleeping

(5)   the book seems interesting

and several others. Thus I am as certain of the fact that (2) and (5) are well-formed (in a sense in which (3) and (4) are not) as I am of particular impressionistic phonetic transcriptions (e.g., of the various *light house keeper's*) or of particular judgments of sameness and difference. In connection with (d), I was concerned with such forms as *flying planes can be dangerous, I found the boy studying in the library,* etc. Examples of type (e) are of many kinds. Thus I discussed the problem of finding a grammatical explanation for the fact that *did you eat the apple, who ate the apple, what did you eat,* etc. are all naturally regarded as belonging to a special sentence type, as distinct from *you ate the apple,* etc.), and the problem of explaining the intuitively obvious difference between *the police suspected the man behind the bar, . . . questioned the man behind closed doors, . . . put the man behind bars.* Many other questions of the same kind were also raised, e.g., why smôking mén seems to mean "men who are on fire" rather than "men who smoke." Concerning the propriety of segmentation and classification, it would be absurd not to use the fact that

(6)   [it ended late ([įDêndįd + léyt], [D] = alveolar flap)

obviously contains at least four morphemes in evaluating a theory of morphemic analysis, or not to use the fact that *boy, horse, justice* are, in a certain clear sense, words of a different type from *compel, retain, bring,* etc., in determining the success of a theory of word classes.

Considerations of all of these kinds are familiar in traditional grammar. Considerations of kinds (a), (b), (f) are explicit in modern structural linguistics. Thus the methodological studies of American descriptivists are motivated by information of type (f), presumed known. If someone were to propose a theory of morphemic segmentation that led to the conclusion that (6) contains two morphemes, this consequence would, presumably, be regarded as grounds for rejecting the theory. The same is true of proposed methods (e.g., substitution procedures) for finding classes, for defining the phoneme, etc. These methodological studies (and the controversies to which they give rise) become utterly unintelligible if we do not make the perfectly justified assumption that they are an attempt to characterize precisely something that is, in part, intuitively given. The attempts to define 'phoneme', 'morpheme', etc. presuppose a set of clear cases of applicability or non-applicability of these terms, with reference to which the adequacy of the proposed definition can be tested. The same is true of an attempt to define 'well-formed (grammatical) English sentence' (that is, the attempt to construct an English grammar), or the attempt to define 'well-formed (grammatical) sentence in an arbitrary language L'. In terms of the preceding discussion, these are attempts to discover and state the facts that underlie and account for the observed data. A refusal to use data such as (1) would eliminate linguistics as a discipline, just as surely as a refusal to consider what a subject senses or perceives would destroy psychophysics. In both cases, we are trying (though in very different ways) to find a basis for intuitive judgements. In both cases, furthermore, the difficulty of obtaining reliable and relevant reports is quite apparent.

It seems to me perfectly plain that an enormous amount of data of this sort is available to the native speaker (though it does not follow that it is easy to elicit such data). It is pointless to refuse to make use of such data in evaluating the success of a particular attempt to formulate the rules of some grammar (i.e., the rules that the native speaker must somehow have internalized when he has achieved the ability to produce and understand new sentences) or the principles that underlie grammatical structure in general.

It is data of the kinds mentioned above, it seems to me, that we are trying to characterize precisely, to account for and reduce to general underlying principles, when we study grammatical structure. A generative grammar can be thought of as a theory of the language that attempts to characterize and explain data of this sort. This point of view is discussed at length in [SS] (e.g., §§6, 8), [EML] and elsewhere, but I will illustrate what I have in mind by a few examples.

In the case of data of type (1a), a generative grammar will attempt to exhibit general rules that underlie particular phonetic observations. It will try to show how the stress contours of English phrases and words are related to and determined by their immediate constituent structure and segmental phonemes;[14] it will offer an account of vowel reduction (as in the second syllable of *compensation*, but not *condensation,* in my speech) in terms of IC and syllable structure (cf. [EML] and [SPE]); it will try to explain why such items as *telegraph, aristocrat* (in the contexts $\#-\#$, $-+y$, $-+ic$), etc., have a particular set of variants, instead of others, by showing that this is a result of application of independently motivated rules (cf. [EML] and [SPE]); and so on, in innumerable similar cases. A generative grammar will be judged successful—that is, it will be judged to have brought to light the underlying facts of linguistic structure—to the extent that it shows how a relatively small number of simple and systematic rules account for a substantial quantity of such data. Cf. §1, above.

Similarly, in the case of data of the kind (1c), the generative grammar will attempt to exhibit interconnections among apparently independent

---

[14] Cf. Chomsky, Halle, Lukoff, "On Accent and Juncture in English," *For Roman Jakobson* (The Hague, 1956). A new version of this material, simplified, generalized, and incorporated into a much more general study of phonological processes, will appear in [SPE]. It is described in part in [EML] and (in an earlier version), in my contribution to the IVth Texas conference (1959).

judgments as to well-formedness and to state general rules from which a large variety of such judgments (e.g., those mentioned above (6)) can be deduced as consequences. Cf. [SS], [TAS], [GEN], for many examples.

There is a second and independent way of approaching the study of data of kind (1). We can try to discover objective experimental techniques for characterizing these intuitive observations. Thus in the case of impressionistic phonetic observations of type (1a), we can try to discover objective acoustic or articulatory correlates to what the linguist hears as stress level, vowel quality, and so on. And in the case of data of kind (1c), we can try to construct behavioral tests that will correspond, in their results, to the intuitive judgments of well-formedness.[15]

Here, then, are two approaches to the data of linguistics. We can attempt to characterize the data by a generative grammar or by experimental tests. The two approaches are not alternatives. Obviously, both are justified and we should like to pursue them in such a way that they give convergent results. It is important to realize that each approach complements the other and that neither presupposes the other. Whichever approach we are pursuing, the criterion of success is provided by the data that give rise to the investigation; in this case, such data as (1).[16] Suppose, for example, that someone proposes that impressionistic judgments of stress level correspond to physical measures of intensity. He will quickly discover that 'stress' as so defined does not at all correspond to the impressionistic transcriptions that constitute the phonetic record (1a). In the face of just this evidence, it would be absurd for him to conclude that the transcriptions are incorrect, that phonology is built on sand, etc. This lack of correspondence may simply show that he has chosen the wrong test.[17]

[15] Linguists have in general not been much concerned with this approach to linguistic data. Thus even in the case of (1b), where a reasonably good test has been suggested (namely, the paired-utterance test proposed by Harris, op. cit., pp. 32f.), there is not a single paper in the linguistic literature devoted to an objective evaluation of its results, despite the fact that the relation of conformity (sameness-difference) among utterance tokens has been regarded, since the publication of Bloomfield's *Postulates,* as the corner-stone of structural linguistics. There is no doubt that this test will often fail to give the right results, in the form in which it is usually described. Some ways in which it can be improved have been suggested (e.g., in [SS], p. 96), but have not been systematically investigated.

[16] To some extent, of course, theoretical investigations or operational tests may lead us to reject some of the original data as irrelevant, or as probably incorrect or contaminated. We can expect that one result of systematic study, of either kind, will be to improve our understanding of what are the natural bounds of the discipline or what phenomena are relevant to deepening our investigation of linguistic structure.

[17] Continued failure of attempts to find a test might, ultimately, shake our confidence in the phonetic record, but it is not easy to say just when this would be justified. Thus we might discover that what the phonetician hears as stress level is determined in part not by the acoustic event but by an ideal stress pattern that is assigned to the utterance by the rules of a generative grammar—that is, the phonetician may be "hearing" something that is not present in the sound wave in full detail, but that is implied by the grammatical structure of the sound wave that he has understood in a certain way. I think,

Similarly, if the paired utterance test, administered in a certain way, fails to show that *writer* and *rider* are phonemically distinct in my speech, this is evidence that the proposed test requires revision. Or, if a test for grammaticalness (i.e., a test of (1c)) is proposed which fails to make the required distinction between (2), (5) on the one hand and (3), (4) on the other, we can conclude only that the test is poorly constructed.

In other words, we evaluate the success and relevance of an operational test (just as we evaluate the success of a generative grammar) by asking how well it corresponds to the given data. There is no difficulty in constructing a bad grammar. It is just as easy to construct a bad test. There is no interest in either.

4. I would like to turn now to some of the criticisms of [SS]. Consider first Hill's [G]. What Hill shows is that several tests that he has tried are quite bad. I do not see the importance of these negative results, nor do I see any reason to find them at all surprising.[18] Thus if we ask a speaker the question "which of these sentences are grammatical?" giving him no idea how this question is to be interpreted, we will naturally expect the responses to be of no use in characterizing data of type (1c). Similarly, if we were to ask a speaker "what do you hear?" his responses would probably be of little phonetic relevance (they would have little relation to (1a)); or if

---

in fact, that this is not at all out of the question, in the case of stress levels. Cf. [SPE].

Similarly, a continued failure to elicit the judgment that (2), (5) are distinct in some significant way from (3), (4) might ultimately shake our confidence in this particular judgment, at least for certain speakers. It is, I suppose, conceivable that some speakers of English are unaware of the difference between (2), (5) and similar examples, on the one hand, and (3), (4), (or "tall the man cigar the smoked black," with whatever intonation—cf. [G], footnote 4), etc., on the other. Such a person, if he exists, is likely to be about as successful in studying syntax as a deaf man would be as a phonetician.

[18] Hill seems to have the impression that I have suggested these tests as general criteria of grammaticalness or degree of grammaticalness. But this is not the case. In [SS], I made it clear at the outset (p. 13) that I was not proposing any behavioral test. I did assert (p. 16, as an aside, in the context of a discussion of order of approximation) that a speaker of English will treat (3), but not (2), as a sequence of unrelated words, assigning phrase final intonation to each, and that he will be able to recall (2) more easily than (3), to learn it more quickly, etc., despite the fact that they are equally new to him. I was careful *not* to suggest that these remarks offer a general criterion for grammaticalness—they would, for example, no doubt fail in the case of (4), (5). Later, on pp. 35–36, I made some further remarks on phonetic accompaniments to deviation from grammaticalness, again suggesting no general operational criterion. In fact, I know of none.

There is only one apparent conflict between [SS] and Hill's results, namely, he has found that his informants did not assign phrase final intonation to each word in (3), as I did. This lack of correlation is not at all surprising. In such quasi-operational tests as these, the instructions, the setting and so on can have a significant effect on what the subject does. It is for this reason, among others, that neither my comments nor his can be taken seriously as the description of an experimental procedure. Talk of "statistical reliability" ([G], p. 7) in connection with such informal suggestions as these betrays a misconception as to what is a serious scientific experiment. In any event, the question how the particular sequence of words (3) is read (nothing else is at stake) is surely too insignificant to justify a sustained discussion.

we ask "were these utterances the same or different?" not indicating how we intend this question, we would expect the result to correlate poorly with the classification of utterance tokens as phonemically identical or distinct (cf. (1b)). Lack of correspondence, in such cases, demonstrates nothing about the validity of such observations as (1a), (1b), (1c). It merely indicates, as we should have expected in advance, that more subtle means will be necessary if we are to obtain relevant information about the speaker's awareness.[19]

Hill does suggest one test which might yield some useful data. In this test, two sets of utterances are presented to a subject who is asked, essentially, whether the same formal relation holds in the two sets. Hill regards this test as "more structural" than a direct test of grammaticalness, and considers it somehow more relevant to the "transformationist."[20] Insofar as I can reconstruct the reasoning that leads to this conclusion, it seems to me to be based on two confusions. The first has to do with the nature of transformational relations. Thus some of the sets that Hill presented in his test contain sentences that are transformationally related to one another, but others do not. If Hill considers this test particularly relevant to transformational grammar, it may be in part because he has misinterpreted the technical use of the term "grammatical transformation" in [SS], [TAS], [GEN], and elsewhere, taking it to refer to any formally statable relation among sentences. I do not think it has ever been used in this sense.

Secondly, there is apparent in Hill's paper a confusion about the relation between the terms "generative grammar" and "transformational grammar." Hill seems to identify the two. Similarly, Bolinger regards Jakobson's comments about grammaticalness (to which I return below) as having some particular relevance to "transformationalists" ([LSLE], p. 377). In fact, neither Hill's nor Jakobson's comments have any direct bearing on the transformational model for generative grammar. They apply rather to generative grammar as such, that is, to the attempt to construct precise grammars with explicit consequences as to well-formedness of utterances. Grammaticalness is no specific concern of those who happen to think that

[19] This is noted explicitly by Maclay and Sleator in their "Responses to Language: Judgements of Grammaticalness," *International Journal of American Linguistics* XXX (1960), 281. Their tests apparently gave somewhat better and more relevant results than the one that Hill describes. In his "Language, Purposive Behavior and Evolution" (mimeographed, 1958), Eric Lenneberg describes a test of grammaticalness applied to (2) and randomly chosen rearrangements of the words of (2) which, given to M.I.T. undergraduate language students with appropriate instructions (there stated), gave the expected results unequivocally.

[20] It should be observed that this test, as presented, is not yet very useful. Thus it does not tell us which of the two sentences "the child is sleeping," "the child seems sleeping" is to be rejected as deviating from well-formedness. Furthermore, it does not seem to be generalizable to such distinctions as (2)–(3). However, it can perhaps be refined, and it should be considered as one of a battery of tests that may ultimately succeed in giving a characterization of grammaticalness.

the particular transformational theory proposed in [SS], [GEN] and elsewhere is the most promising specific characterization of generative grammars. It is, rather, the concern of anyone who is interested in syntax in
the traditional sense, or in the problems discussed above in §2.

One final set of criticisms of transformational grammar presented in [G]
also requires some clarification. Hill is under the impression that those of
us who are exploring transformational models for generative grammar
believe that sentences are primarily to be regarded as strings of printed
words, and that we reject the view that "language is basically a system of
sound, only secondarily one of writing." This, he believes may "explain
the hostility of many structuralists." In [SS], [GEN], and elsewhere, a
grammar is regarded as consisting of a syntactic component and a morphophonemic component. The former generates an infinite class of strings of
minimal syntactically functioning units. Each such string, furthermore,
automatically receives a structural description. The morphophonemic component converts each item given as output by the syntactic component
into, ultimately, the phonetic representation of an utterance. Both [SS]
and [GEN] are devoted primarily to the syntactic component. Other studies
have been primarily devoted to the morphophonemic component of a
generative transformational grammar.[21] The fact that the output of a
generative grammar is a representation of speech is made quite clear in
[SS] (e.g., p. 46) and [GEN], however.[22]

Jakobson, in his [BVGM], also indicates his dissatisfaction with the use
to which such examples as

(6)   colorless green ideas sleep furiously

(7)   furiously sleep ideas green colorless

[21] In particular, Halle's *Sound Pattern of Russian* (The Hague, 1960). This is also the
central topic in my "Transformational Basis for Syntax," to appear in the *Proceedings*
of the IVth Texas conference, 1959, A. A. Hill, editor; and it is discussed in a section of
[TAS].

[22] What led Hill to conclude that transformational grammar is concerned primarily
with writing rather than speech was apparently my remark in [SS] that "in the context
'I saw a fragile—', the words 'whale' and 'of' may have equal (i.e., zero) frequency in
the past linguistic experience of a speaker who will immediately recognize that one of
these substitutions, but not the other, gives a grammatical sentence" (p. 16). The point
in that context, was to show that judgment of well-formedness is not based on statistical
order of approximation. This is rather obvious, and hardly deserves more than this
casual comment. It is true that the phrasing of this observation makes use of an appeal
to the literacy of the audience. It would have been possible to make the same point,
more elaborately, without this appeal. That is, I could have stated that in the context
Σ — (where Σ stands for a phonetic transcription of "I saw a fragile", with full intonation, etc.), /wéyl/ will be interpreted as the familiar lexical item *whale*, /ɔv/ will
be rejected with stress 4, and, with stress 1, either rejected or treated as a new, unfamiliar lexical item, or as the quotation form *of*. I suppose that one could add even
further qualifications, but there are other places where preciseness and rigor are likely
to be more rewarding.

were put in [SS]. This criticism (which is cited with approval in Bolinger's [LSLE]) I find quite curious and puzzling. What Jakobson says about these examples, and about the question of grammaticalness and degree of grammaticalness in general, seems to me in full support of the position maintained in [SS]—in fact, it is in part no more than a paraphrase, in a slightly different terminology. It seems to me, therefore, that Jakobson (and Bolinger) must have completely misinterpreted the point of view expressed in [SS].

In [SS] examples (6) and (7) were used to illustrate the futility of (a) a search for a semantically based definition of "grammaticalness," or (b) an attempt to define grammaticalness in terms of order of approximation. Thus (6), but not (7), is clearly a well-formed sentence (or, at least, more like one than (7)), although (a) neither (6) nor (7) seems to be "meaningful" in any sense independent of grammatical structure and (b) the two are not differentiated in terms of statistical order of approximation. The same examples could be used to illustrate the impossibility of (c) defining "grammaticalness" in terms of a frame of "grammatical morphemes," since (8) has the same frame as (6) and (9) the same frame as (7) (note that it would be begging the question to argue that the morphemes *ly,* etc., are different in (6) and (8)).

(8)   harmless seem dogs young friendly (—less — —s — —ly)

(9)   friendly young dogs seem harmless (—ly — —s — —less).

What Jakobson points out is that we can recognize the grammatical structure of (6) (but not (7)), and that "these grammatical relations create a meaningful sentence." He also observes that only (6) could appear in a poem,[23] that we know how to question it, that we can recognize in it certain metaphors, etc. These remarks are precisely in support of the argument in [SS] that (6) but not (7) is grammatical, and that the basis for whatever meaningfulness we can assign to it is its independently recognizable grammatical structure. The fact that the independently recognized "grammatical relations create a meaningful sentence" is perfectly consistent

[23] Hill, on the contrary, considers that (7) but not (6) could be a line of modern poetry ([G], p. 4). Both Hill and Jakobson refer to poems written to prove these (opposing) points. In fact, the question whether a sequence of words might appear in a poem is entirely beside the point, since it is perfectly plain that deviation from well-formedness is not only tolerable, in prose or poetry, but can even be effectively used as a literary device. We return to this below. It is by no means a novel observation. Cf., e.g., Empson, *Seven Types of Ambiguity* (Meridian), p. 34: "The demands of metre allow the poet to say something which is not normal colloquial English, so that the reader thinks of the various colloquial forms which are near to it, and puts them together; weighting their probabilities in proportion to their nearness. It is for such reasons as this that poetry can be more compact, while seeming to be less precise, than prose. It is for these reasons, too, among others, that an insensitivity in a poet to the contemporary style of speaking ... is so disastrous ..."

with the claim in [SS] that grammaticalness is not attributed to an utterance by virtue of the fact that the utterance is recognized to be meaningful. To argue against this claim, one would have to maintain that there is an absolute semantic property of "meaningfulness" that can be assigned to utterances quite independently of any consideration of their grammatical structure—a property that can be shown to hold of (6) but not (7). It is difficult to believe that anyone would seriously uphold this view.

From consideration of such examples as (6), (7) (and many others of different kinds—cf. [SS], §9) it seems evident that perception of grammatical relations in a sentence does not depend on a prior and independent identification of semantic properties, and that the study of grammatical structure seems to be, in fact, quite independent of meaning. Furthermore, as noted in [SS], p. 101,

> it seems that the study of meaning is fraught with so many difficulties even after the linguistic meaning-bearing elements and their relations are specified that any attempt to study meaning independently of such specification is out of the question.[24] To put it differently, given the instrument language and its formal devices, we can and should investigate their semantic function (as, e.g., in R. Jakobson, "Beitrag zur allgemeinen Kasuslehre," *TCLP* (1936)); but we cannot, apparently, find semantic absolutes, known in advance of grammar, that can be used to determine the objects of grammar in any way.

Nothing in Jakobson's remarks gives any reason to revise these conclusions. He is saying that having recognized a sentence as grammatical and having identified its grammatical relations, a speaker can proceed to interpret it, determining how these formal elements and constructions are functioning, in this case. It will, in general, be easier to invent some sort of an interpretation for a grammatical than for an ungrammatical sequence, as Jakobson observes. This is basically the point of view expressed in [SS].[25]

In this connection, we can turn to Bolinger's discussion of what he regards as the semantic basis for transformational grammar ([LSLE], p. 377). He asserts that "knowing the meaning of *seem,* we can predict with some

[24] This is taken for granted in investigations that are actually concerned with meaning. Cf., e.g., Ziff, *Semantic Analysis* (Ithaca, 1960).

[25] The temporal implications in this description should not be taken too literally. However, I think that a reasonable perceptual model would have the property that grammatical structure is identified independently of any semantic consideration, and a reasonable model for language learning would have the parallel property. This is a large topic in itself, and I will not attempt to pursue it here. I would merely like to emphasize that those who regard semantics as providing the basis, in some sense, for grammar, may not have realized how extreme and implausible is their claim, if stated quite openly. The claim must be that there are semantic absolutes, identifiable in noises independently of the grammatical structure (in particular, the lexical items) assigned to them. Perhaps some weaker claim than this is intended, but if so, it has never, to my knowledge, been clearly formulated.

assurance that the structure *He is seeming* is not likely to occur." Under
one interpretation, this remark is perfectly true. In just the same way we
could say that knowing the meaning of *seem,* we can predict that this
element will not appear in the context *I saw—boy,* or knowing the meaning
of *in,* we can predict the ungrammaticalness of *I saw in boy,* etc.[26] The
comment is useful, however, only if we are presented with some characterization of the meaning of *seem, in,* etc., stated without reference to their
grammatical function, from which this function can be predicted.[27] In the
absence of this, Bolinger's statement reduces to the observation, mislead-
ingly expressed, that *seem* does not appear in the progressive. In general,
study of the continuing controversy over the reliance of grammar on
meaning seems to me to show that the issue is only verbal—that no substantive claim is being made by those who claim that such reliance is
essential.

In apparent conflict with [SS], Jakobson also argues that the notion
"degree of grammaticalness" is untenable. Here too, however, I can find
only a terminological issue. Jakobson recognizes ([BVMG], final paragraph) that there is some sort of scale of "obliteration" of "syntactic forms
and the relational concepts which they carry," and he would, of course,
insist on the importance of the distinction between literal and figurative
usage. It is precisely such observations as these that motivate the study of
deviation from grammaticalness to which he expresses his objection. Clearly
the only question is whether the study of these problems is a natural
outgrowth of grammatical investigations—that is, the question is to what
extent considerations of the kind that are fundamental to the study of
principles of sentence formation can provide some systematic account of
such phenomena. I think that to some extent they can, and the investigation
of degrees of grammaticalness (or, if one prefers, the scale of obliteration
of syntactic forms . . .) is an attempt to show how a simple generalization
of some familiar notions can give some insight into these problems.

5. Since the point has been widely misunderstood, I would like to
emphasize that I am using the terms 'grammatical' and 'degree of grammaticalness' in a technical sense (which is, however, not unrelated to the
ordinary one). In particular, when a sentence is referred to as semi-grammatical or as deviating from some grammatical regularity, there is no
implication that this sentence is being "censored" ([BVGM], p. 144) or

---

[26] The phrase "likely to occur" is often used in place of some such technical term as
"grammatical." Its use gives an appearance of objectivity which is, however, quite misleading. In the literal sense of these words, practically nothing can be predicted about
what is likely to occur in speech.

[27] It should be emphasized again that in studies devoted to meaning, the argument is
usually reversed. Thus it is common to find the claim that knowing, seeing, etc., are not
processes supported by the observation that *know, see* (like *seem*) do not naturally
occur in the progressive, in their usual senses.

ruled out, or that its use is being forbidden. Nor, so far as I can see, are there any "ontological" considerations involved ([LSLE], p. 377, [BVGM], p. 144), except insofar as these are reflected in grammatical categories and subcategories. Use of a sentence that is in some way semi-grammatical is no more to be censured than use of a transform that is remote from the kernel. In both cases, what we are attempting to do is to develop a more refined analysis of sentence structure that will be able to support more sophisticated study of the use and interpretation of utterances. There are circumstances in which the use of grammatically deviant sentences is very much in place. Consider, e.g., such phrases as Dylan Thomas' "a grief ago,"[28] or Veblen's ironic "perform leisure." In such cases, and innumerable others, a striking effect is achieved precisely by means of a departure from a grammatical regularity.

Given a grammatically deviant utterance, we attempt to impose an interpretation on it, exploiting whatever features of grammatical structure it preserves and whatever analogies we can construct with perfectly well-formed utterances. We do not, in this way, impose an interpretation on a perfectly grammatical utterance (it is precisely for this reason that a well-chosen deviant utterance may be richer and more effective—cf. footnote 23). Linguists, when presented with examples of semi-grammatical, deviant utterances, often respond by contriving possible interpretations in constructed contexts, concluding that the examples do not illustrate departure from grammatical regularities. This line of argument completely misses the point. It blurs an important distinction between a class of utterances that need no analogic or imposed interpretation, and others that can receive an interpretation by virtue of their relations to properly selected members of this class. Thus, e.g., when Jakobson observes ([BVGM], p. 144) that "golf plays John" can be a perfectly perspicuous utterance, he is quite correct. But when he concludes that it is therefore as fully in accord with the grammatical rules of English as "John plays golf," he is insisting on much too narrow an interpretation of the notion "grammatical rule"—an interpretation that makes it impossible to mark the fundamental distinction between the two phrases. The former is a perspicuous utterance precisely because of the series of steps that we must take in interpreting it—a series of steps that is initiated by the recognition that this phrase deviates from a certain grammatical rule of English, in this case, a selectional rule that determines the grammatical categories of the subject and object of the verb "play." No such steps are necessary in the case of the nondeviant (and uninteresting) "'John plays golf."

I am not, of course, suggesting that every difficult, interesting or figurative expression is semi-grammatical (or conversely). The important ques-

---

[28] One of the examples analyzed in Ziff's interesting study of the problem of deviation from grammaticalness, "On Understanding 'Understanding' " (mimeographed, 1960).

tion, as always, is to what extent significant aspects of the use and understanding of utterances can be illuminated by refining and generalizing the notions of grammar. In the cases just mentioned, and many others, I think that they can. If this is true, it would be arbitrary and pointless to insist that the theory of grammatical structure be restricted to the study of such relatively superficial matters as agreement, inflectionally marked categories, and so on.[29]

In short, it seems to me no more justifiable to ignore the distinctions of subcategory that give the series "John plays golf," "golf plays John," "John plays and," than to ignore the rather similar distinctions between seeing a man in the flesh, in an abstract painting, and in an inkblot. The fact that we can impose an interpretation in the second case and sometimes even the third, using whatever cues are present, does not obliterate the distinction between these three strata.

Examples such as these provide a motive for the study of degrees of grammaticalness. Thus in addition to such data as (1), we can try to account for the observation that such phrases as (10) are not as extreme in their violation of grammatical rules as (11), though they do not conform to the rules of the language as strictly as (12):

(10)   a grief ago; perform leisure; golf plays John; colorless green ideas sleep furiously; misery loves company; John frightens sincerity; what did you do to the book, understand it?

(11)   a the ago; perform compel; golf plays aggressive; furiously sleep ideas green colorless; abundant loves company; John sincerity frightens; what did you do to the book, justice it?

(12)   a year ago; perform the task; John plays golf; revolutionary new ideas appear infrequently; John loves company; sincerity frightens John; what did you do to the book, bite it?

Here too, we can find innumerable relatively clear cases, and we can attempt to express these distinctions in a generative grammar (and, more importantly, we can try to find some basis for them through the study of generative grammar).

The question then arises: by what mechanism can a grammar assign to an arbitrary phone sequence a structural description that indicates its

---

[29] Notice that if we do, arbitrarily, limit the study of grammar in this way, we cannot even account for the difference between (6) and (9), on the one hand, and (7) and (8), on the other, since this difference can be expressed only in terms of categories that are established in terms of syntactic considerations that go well beyond inflection. But if we distinguish (6) from (9) by rules involving such syntactic categories as Adjective, Noun, etc., we can just as well distinguish "John plays golf" from "golf plays John" by rules involving such syntactic subcategories as Animate Noun, etc. These are simply a refinement of familiar categories. I do not see any fundamental difference between them. No general procedure has ever been offered for isolating such categories as Noun, Adjective, etc., that would not equally well apply to such subcategories as are necessary to make finer distinctions. I return to this below.

degree of grammaticalness, the degree of its deviation from grammatical regularities, and the manner of its deviation (cf. §1). This is a natural question to ask within the framework of §2.

Suppose that we have a grammar that generates an infinite set of utterances with structural descriptions. Let us call the units in terms of which these utterances are represented by the neutral term *formatives* (following a suggestion of Bolinger's). Suppose, in addition, that we have an m-level hierarchy of categories of formatives with the following structure. On level one we have a single category denoted C_1^1, the category of all formatives. On level two, we have categories labelled $C_1^2, \ldots, C_{n_2}^2$. On level three, we have categories $C_1^3, \ldots, C_{n_3}^3$, where $n_3 > n_2$, and so on, until we reach the mth level with categories $C_1^m, \ldots, C_{n_m}^m$ ($1 < n_2 < \ldots < n_m$). On each level, the categories are exhaustive in the sense that each formative belongs to at least one, perhaps more (in the case of grammatical homonymy). We might also require that each level be a refinement of the preceding one i.e., a classification into subcategories of the categories of the preceding level.

Let us assume, furthermore, that the mth level categories are the smallest categories that appear in the rules of the generative grammar. That is, the members of C_1^m are mutually substitutable in the set of generated utterances. Many of them may contain just a single formative.

For concreteness, think of the formatives as English words.[30] Suppose we have a three-level hierarchy. Then C_1^1 is the class of all words. Let $C_1^2 = $ Nouns, $C_2^2 = $ Verbs, $C_3^2 = $ Adjectives, $C_4^2 = $ everything else. Let $C_3^1, \ldots, C_j^3$ be subcategories of Verbs (pure transitives, those with inanimate objects, etc); subcategories of Nouns, and so on. Every sequence of words can now be represented by the sequence of first level, second level, third level categories to which these words belong. Thus "misery loves company" is represented $C_1^1 C_1^1 C_1^1$ on level one, $C_1^2 C_2^2 C_1^2$ (i.e., NVN) on level two, $N_{abstr} V_k N_{abstr}$ on level three (where these are the appropriate C_i^3's). One of the selectional rules of the generative grammars (i.e., in the transformational model of [SS], one of the context-restricted constituent structure rules) will specify that V_k occurs only with animate subjects. Thus "misery loves company" will not be generated by the grammar, though "John loves company" will. However, "misery loves company" has a level two representation in common with a generated utterance, namely, NVN. We therefore call it semi-grammatical, on level two. "Abundant loves company," on the other hand, has only a level one representation in common with a generated utterance, and is therefore labelled completely ungrammatical.

Without going into details, it is obvious how, in a similar way, a degree of grammaticalness can be assigned to any sequence of formatives when

---

[30] This is merely an illustrative example.

the generative grammar is supplemented by a hierarchy of categories. The degree of grammaticalness is a measure of the remoteness of an utterance from the generated set of perfectly well-formed sentences, and the common representing category sequence will indicate in what respects the utterance in question is deviant.[31] The more narrowly the mth level categories circumscribe the generated language (i.e., the more detailed the specification of selectional restrictions) the more elaborate will be the stratification of utterances into degrees of grammaticalness. No utterances are "lost" as we refine a grammatical description by noting more detailed restrictions on occurrence in natural sentences. By adding a refinement to the hierarchy of categories, we simply subdivide the same utterances into more degrees of grammaticalness, thus increasing the power of the grammar to mark distinctions among utterances.[32]

Thus a generative grammar supplemented with a hierarchy of categories can assign a degree of grammaticalness to each sequence of formatives. If we could show how a hierarchy of categories can be derived from a generative grammar, then the latter alone would assign degree of grammaticalness. There are, in fact, several ways in which this might be possible.

Notice, first, that a transformational grammar will have such symbols as Noun, Adjective, . . . (in addition to much narrower subcategories) at intermediate levels of representation, even if it is designed to generate only a narrow class of highly grammatical sentences, since these larger categories will simplify the descriptions of the domains of transformational rules. Thus we can expect to find a hierarchy of categories embedded within the constituent structure rules of the transformational grammar. This might be the appropriate hierarchy, or a step towards its construction.[33]

We might approach the question of projecting a hierarchy of categories from a set of utterances in a different way, by defining "optimal k-category analysis," for arbitrary k. Suppose, for simplicity, that we have a corpus

[31] We can represent only one "dimension" of deviation from grammaticalness in this way. There are others. Cf., e.g., [SS], §5, footnote 2. In obvious ways, we could give a more refined stratification of utterances by considering their parts, but I will not go into this.

[32] What is the natural point where continued refinement of the category hierarchy should come to an end? This is not obvious. As the grammatical rules become more detailed, we may find that grammar is converging with what has been called logical grammar. That is, we seem to be studying small overlapping categories of formatives, where each category can be characterized by what we can now (given the grammar) recognize as a semantic feature of some sort. If this turns out to be true in some interesting sense when the problem is studied more seriously, so much the better. This will show that the study of principles of sentence formation does lead to increasingly deeper insights into the use and understanding of utterances, as it is continually refined.

[33] This possibility was suggested by some remarks of R. B. Lees.

of sentences all of the same length. Let $C_1, . ., C_k$ be (perhaps overlapping) categories that give an exhaustive classification of the formatives appearing in the corpus. Each sentence is now represented by at least one category sequence. Each such category sequence, in turn, is the representation of many sequences of formatives, in particular, of many that may not be in the original corpus. Thus a choice of k categories extends the corpus to a set of sentences that are not distinguishable, in terms of these categories, from sentences of the corpus. It is natural to define the optimal k-category analysis as that which extends the corpus the least, i.e., which best reflects substitutability relations within the corpus. Given, for each k, the optimal k-category analysis, we might select the optimal k-category analysis as a level of the hierarchy if it offers a considerable improvement over the optimal k-l-category analysis, but is not much worse than the optimal k+l-category analysis (this could be made precise, in various ways). It is easy to see that there are circumstances under which the optimal k-category analysis might contain overlapping classes (homonyms).[34] It is also easy to drop the restriction that all sentences be of the same length, and that the corpus be finite. Such suggestions as these, when made precise,[35] offer an alternative way in which the generative grammar itself may impose degrees of grammaticalness on utterances that are not directly generated, through the intermediary of the category hierarchy projected from the set of generated sentences.

This suggestion is schematic and no doubt very much oversimplified. Nevertheless, such an approach as this to the problem of defining syntactic categories has many suggestive features, and offers some important ad-

[34] In general, it is to be expected that overlapping of categories will lead to an extension of the set of generated sentences, since categories will now be larger. Therefore, in general an analysis with disjoint categories will be preferred, by the evaluation procedure suggested above, over an analysis with an equal number of overlapping categories. Suppose, however, that the overlap includes true homonyms—suppose, e.g., that the categories N and V are allowed to overlap in such elements as /riyd/ (read, reed), etc. We now have two ways of representing the sentences *read the book* (namely, VTN or NTN), *the reed looks tall* (TNVA or TVVA), and so on, instead of just one (e.g., VTN and TVVA, if /riyd/ is assigned to V). We can select, in each case, the representation which is required, on independent ground, by other sentences, i.e., VTN and TNVA, in this example. In this way we can reduce the number of generated sentences by allowing categories to overlap. Overlapping of categories will be permitted, then, when the gain that can be achieved in this way more than compensates for the loss resulting from the fact that categories are larger. We might inquire then whether homonyms can be defined as elements that are in the overlaps in the optimal set of categories on some level. Some evidence in favor of this assumption is presented in [LSLT].

[35] This approach to degrees of grammaticalness was described in more detail in [LSLT]. It was presented, with some supporting empirical evidence, in a Linguistic Institute lecture in Chicago in 1954, and again in the discussions of the IVth Texas conference, 1959.

vantages over the alternatives (e.g., substitution procedures)[36] that have been described in the literature (cf. [LSLT] for a detailed discussion—in particular, it allows for the possibility of setting up a hierarchy of categories and subcategories and for a principled and general solution to the problem of recognizing homonyms). I mention it here to indicate one way in which the further investigation of deviation from grammaticalness might be systematically pursued.

19

The Place of Intonation in a Generative Grammar of English

ROBERT P. STOCKWELL

CHOMSKY'S RULES[1] do not at present generate intonation patterns as elements in terminal strings, nor do they show the optional and obligatory choices of intonation patterns that are available with any given sequence of formatives. The following modifications of his rules are suggested as a way of incorporating intonation patterns.

(1) $S \rightarrow Nuc + IP$

This is Hockett's first IC cut,[2] *Nuc*leus plus *I*ntonation *P*attern. The follow-up rule for *Nuc* is Chomsky's first rule, specifically

$$Nuc \rightarrow NP + VP$$

His subsequent rules characterize the terminal strings which lead by morphophonemic rules to kernel sentences. The details of the expansion of *Nuc* are irrelevant here, since in every instance *IP* will appear at the end of the strings

---

[36] It is often proposed that categories be defined in terms of particular sets of inflectional morphemes, but unless some general method is given for selecting the relevant sets (none has ever been proposed, to my knowledge), such definitions are completely ad hoc, and simply avoid the problem of discovering the basis for categorization.

Reprinted by permission from *Language*, 36.360–67 (July–September, 1960). Professor Stockwell is in the Department of English, University of California, Los Angeles.
[1] *Syntactic Structures* (1957), the Third Texas Conference on English (1958), and the Fourth Texas Conference on English (1959).
[2] *Manual of Phonology* (1955).

by virtue of rule (1). The rules which expand *IP* and specify its shape appear below.

(2) $$IP \rightarrow C + JP$$

It is necessary to divide *IP* into Contour and Juncture Point because whereas the *C* can be relocated by a variety of transformations, the end point of the *C* remains unchanged by such relocations. This end point is marked by *JP*, which is an entity set up to locate the end of a morpheme *C* which is spread throughout the preceding string.

(3) $$C \rightarrow \left\{ \begin{matrix} Cont \\ Disc \end{matrix} \right\}$$

This specifies that the two basic functions of intonation contours are those of *Disc*ontinuity and *Cont*inuity—i.e. that the grammar offers a choice at this point between a pattern which disjoins a segmental sequence of elements from any following sequence, or joins it to such a sequence.

(4) $$Disc \rightarrow 001 \downarrow {}^{3}$$

001↓ is a specification of all possible English intonation morphemes which end in pitch /1/ and terminal fade. It specifies morpheme types with a maximum of three digits, since the present discussion is programmatic in any case. Five digit morphemes would be specified as *00001↓*; I believe, in fact, that these can be specified fairly simply[4]. For the moment, however, the rules are constructed as if there were no four-digit and five-digit contours. Typical *001↓* morphemes are *231↓, 241↓, 111↓, 331↓*.

(5) $$Cont \rightarrow \left\{ \begin{matrix} \left\{ \begin{matrix} 002\downarrow \\ 003\downarrow \\ 004\downarrow \end{matrix} \right\} \\ \left\{ \begin{matrix} 021\uparrow \\ 032-\uparrow \\ 043-\uparrow \end{matrix} \right\} \end{matrix} \right\}$$

The first group in (5) includes all terminal-fading morphemes which do not have pitch /1/ as the last phoneme. By a low-level morphophonemic rule (a phonetic rule), terminal fade will become terminal sustain. That is, these rules are constructed with only two terminal junctures, fading and rising. Sustained juncture is treated as an allophone of fading juncture, environmentally predictable. I have not been able to find an unarguable instance of minimal contrast between sustain and fade. Repeated though small-scale

[3] In symbolizing intonation morphemes I use the following conventions: *O* means any pitch phoneme, /1 2 3 4/. A plus sign means the last digit or any higher digit; e.g. 001 + ↑ means /001↑/, /002 ↑/, /003 ↑/, or /004 ↑/. A minus sign means the last digit or any lower digit.

[4] See my discussion of five-digit intonation patterns in the report of the Second Texas Conference on English (1957).

attempts to establish the contrast by pair-test have failed. If I am wrong, and there are clear contrasts, the above rule will have the following shape:

(5a)

$$Cont \rightarrow \left[\begin{array}{l} \left\{ \begin{array}{l} \{000|\} \\ 002\downarrow \\ 003\downarrow \\ 004\downarrow \end{array} \right\} \\ \left\{ \begin{array}{l} 021\uparrow \\ 032-\uparrow \\ 043-\uparrow \end{array} \right\} \end{array} \right]$$

The second group in (5) specifies contours ending in rising juncture with the final digit lower than the middle digit. The list in (5) excludes two groups: those in (4), and those which end with two identical digits and rising juncture, or with the last digit higher than the middle digit and rising juncture, which are generated by the interrogative transformation, the list transformation, and no doubt others.

The above five rules are all that seem to me to be needed to introduce a full range of choice of *IP*'s into the constituent structure rules. It should be recalled that the constituent structure rules will generate only simple terminal strings, which by morphophonemic rules and obligatory transformations become kernel sentences. By the above rules, all such terminal strings will have only one *IP,* and the position of that *IP* will always be final. The location of the contour phonemes (the pitches, the juncture, and the primary stress) in the sequence of formative elements which make up the phrase is specified by a simple morphophonemic rule of expansion, discussed below. This set of rules, it seems to me, gives us among other things a way of specifying what we mean by a 'colorless' or 'normal' intonation pattern: it is that pattern which emerges from the application of constituent structure rules and those optional transformations which do not operate specifically to shift the position of the *IP* in the string. 'Normal' intonation is, in effect, the consequence of failing to elect an optional transformation of shift. We think of it as the 'normal' pattern because it is the obligatory pattern equivalent to zero, in the sense that it occurs automatically if the *IP* rules are, so to speak, left alone (i.e. not modified by the optional choice of explicitly intonation-shifting transformations).

There is only one obligatory transformation which has any effect on the *IP*. Since it is obligatory, everything said above about 'normal' intonation applies also to the strings which result from this transformation.

(6)   *C* with *Prep* and *Pronoun.*

Structural Description X, $\left\{ \begin{array}{l} Pro \ (+m) \\ Prep \end{array} \right\}$, *C, Y*

Structural Change. 1, 2, 3, 4 $\Rightarrow$ 1, 3, 2, 4

Condition: Position of *C* does not result from $T_{emphatic}$.

Thus, a sequence like *give it to, him, C, JP* becomes *give it, to, C, him JP*, which still fits the SD and therefore becomes *give, it, C, to him JP*, which still fits the SD and therefore becomes *give C it to him JP*. The final string no longer fits the SD of (6); by morphophonemic rules it is ultimately the sentence

(i)   /gív it tùw im↓/

It is important to note the condition under which this transformation applies: the position of *C* has not been fixed by the emphatic transformation. If it has, this transformation does not apply, so that such a sentence as the following results only from $T_{emphatic}$:

(ii)   /gîv it túw im↓/

In general, then, the six rules above generate with 'normal' intonation (colorless, unemphatic, noncontrastive) those kernel sentences in which the primary stress and the middle digit of the contour coincide on the last item that is neither a pronoun nor a proposition. (Note that the SD of (6) allows either subject or object form of the pronoun, but not the two possessive forms.) These rules generate sentences with pitch /4/, but not as specifically contrastive sentences, for the reason that this is (at best) a sentence-generating grammar which is still unable to specify relations between two sentences. Contrastive stress or pitch within a single complex sentence can easily be specified in two-string transformations ('generalized' transformations) by requiring that the pitch or stress pattern of one string or the other be of a certain shape in the SD, but it is still ncessary to allow pitch /4/ to be generated by the constituent structure rules in order to have such patterns available to the SD's of the two-string transformational rules.

There is one instance in which Chomsky's rules (at least in one of their forms as I know them) need to be modified. It is possible to generate two adverbs (place and time, in that order) from his constituent structure rules— say, *I went home yesterday*. The IP rules formulated above require that this turn out to be the sentence

(iii)   /ày wênt hôwm yéstərdiy ↓/.

Now in fact this is emphatic or contrastive: it means 'yesterday' as opposed to 'day before yesterday' or the like. I am reasonably certain that the uncolored pattern is either

(iv)   /ày wênt hówm | yêstərdiy ↓/

or, as a reduction of (iv) in more rapid speech (specifiable by a series of tempo-reduction transformations or the like),[5]

(v) /ày wênt hówm yéstərdiy ↓/.

(pitch numbers above: 2 over "ày", 3 over "hówm", 1 over "yéstərdiy")

If in fact (iv) is 'normal' in intonation, then sentences with two adverbs must be generated by generalized transformations (in this instance from the two strings *I went home* and *I went yesterday*), or the rules do not work very well. But if, as I expect most scholars will agree, sequences of adverbs, like sequences of adjectives, are best generated by transformations operating on two or more strings starting from one adverb in each, then (iii) above is the result of the emphatic transformation applied to the result of such a two-string transformation, (iv) is the normal result of such a transformation, and (v) is a further result generated by a tempo-reduction transformation.

If the programmatic simplification of intonation contours into three-digit morphemes is allowed, then two straightforward morphophonemic expansion rules are all that are needed to place the pitches, the terminal juncture, and the 'phrase stress', i.e. the primary. The rules are written on the assumption that we have three stresses ('word stresses') already given on the formative elements from the lexicon. If, in some such way as that attempted by Chomsky, Halle, and Lukoff,[6] or by Chomsky at the 1959 Texas conference, one, two, or even all three of these stress levels can be predicted in terms of vowel quality and syllabic sequence, so much the better. In any case there is a maximally prominent syllable in any phrase which is correlatable with the center (the middle digit) of the intonation contour, and that syllable is the last syllable before the *C* which carries maximum lexical stress. All such maximum lexical stresses will turn out, by these rules, to be what Trager and Smith, along with many others, call secondaries, except the last one before *C*, which will be what they call a primary. Besides assuming word stress, these rules also assume 'idiom stress'—i.e. the stresses on constructs like *White House* which are generated from what Householder has called[7] the 'idiom grammar' rather than from the sentence grammar. Items from the idiom grammar are, in other words, viewed simply as part of the available lexicon.

The two morphophonemic expansion rules, then, are these:

(7) $\acute{X}_n, \acute{Y}, 0_1 0_2 0_3 \mid, \acute{Z}_n, JP^m_{\rightarrow} 0_1 + \hat{X}_n, 0_2 + \acute{Y}, \hat{Z}_n + 0_3 + \mid$

(8) $\acute{Y}, 0_1 0_2 0_3 \mid, \acute{Z}_n, JP^m_{\rightarrow} 0_2 + \acute{Y}, \hat{Z}_n + 0_3 + \mid$

[5] For convenience, I follow the transcription conventions of Trager and Smith; as noted earlier, I no longer believe that the phoneme /|/ is needed. Also, the intonation pattern *231* ↓ is arbitrarily chosen for illustration; it can be replaced by any other *Disc.* contour.

[6] *On accent and juncture in English, For Roman Jacobson* (1956).

[7] In his review of Hockett, *Lg.* 35.503–26 (1959).

Here X_n represents any number of formative elements appearing in a terminal or T-terminal string introduced from the lexicon or from the idiom grammar with acute accent, with lower-stressed formatives interspersed and unmodified by the rule; $\acute{Y}$ is the last of the string $\acute{X}_n$ preceding C; 000 | is a C of three digits and a terminal juncture, with subscripts marking the first, second, and third digits of the three pitch phonemes represented as 000; and $\acute{Z}_n$ represents any number of formatives appearing with acute accent in a terminal or T-terminal string between C and JP, with lower-stressed formatives again interspersed and unmodified by the rule.

What rules (7) and (8) accomplish is simply this: they take a contour formative, a C, which is generated in such a way that it has a position in a string, just as any other formative has a position, and they distribute the components (pitches and junctures) of this C over the whole sequence back as far as the beginning (or last JP) and up as far as the next JP—in other words, through the whole phrase. It is the POSITION of the contour in the sequence of formatives that determines which segmental formative receives the acute accent (phrase primary) and which receive the circumflex (word primary). The grave accent (medial) and the unmarked (weak) are lexically fixed except in compounds, where they are fixed presumably by the compounding rules of the idiom grammar and from there enter into the lexical potential.

So far I have tried to show (a) that a large number of intonation patterns can be generated in the constituent structure rules; (b) that they are formative elements with a position in the sequential string like other formative elements; (c) that the phonetic occurrence of the C over the whole phrase is specificable by a simple phonetic rule, not essentially different from the rule that changes *go + past* into *went;* and (d) that 'normal' intonation can be given a well-motivated definition, which provides a zero-line for opposition with various contrastive patterns. 'Normal' is a function, not of what particular pattern is chosen (no C is emphatic or contrastive by virtue of its shape alone, though this assumption creates a special difficulty discussed below), but of what its position is in the string of formatives. Suppose, however, that one chooses to emphasize the last formative that can be the center of a contour, say *tomorrow* in *I'll do it tomorrow.* By rules (1) to (6), C occurs after *tomorrow,* its regular nonemphatic position. The tradition of Trager and Smith has at least by implication stated that the nonemphatic utterance is

(vi)   /àyl dûwit t¡máròw↓/

and that the emphatic utterance is

(vii)   /àyl dûwit t¡máròw↓/

But by present rules, either *C* can equally well be chosen: it is simply part of the MEANING of *241*↓ that it is more emphatic than *231*↓. That is, neither (vi) nor (vii) is the result of a shift transformation, nor is the POSITION of *C* emphatic or contrastive, in spite of the fact that special emphasis is present by virtue of the meaning of *241*↓ in (vii) as opposed to that of *231*↓ in (vi). This distinction is an important one: special emphasis, calling extra attention to a given item, can be achieved either by dislocating the normal position of *C* in the string or by selecting a *C* which is more emphatic in its meaning than others. The notion of shift, by these rules, is restricted to positional dislocations.

The inclusion of *IP* among the constituent structure rules has interesting consequences for the transformations. This is especially true among the two-string transformations, where more and more intonationally marked phrase breaks are introduced as the sentence becomes more and more complex in its derivation from more and more source strings, each with its own *IP*. Thus Chomsky's derivation[8] of *This event prompted me to try to visualize myself forcing him to come* from *This event prompted comp it, I tried comp it, I visualized comp it, I forced comp it, he came* has potentially five phrases, deriving, as it does, from five underlying strings, each with an *IP*. I find that as I say it only four of these five remain:

$$/ \,\overset{2}{\eth\text{îs}} \; \text{i̯vênt} \; \overset{3}{\text{prámptịd}} \; \text{miy} \mid \overset{2}{\text{ti̯trâyt}} \text{ə} \; \overset{2}{\text{víẑuwəlàyz}} \; \overset{4}{\text{màysêlf}} \uparrow \; \overset{2}{\text{fórsị}} \text{ŋ} \; \overset{3}{\text{hìm}} \mid \overset{2}{\text{ti̯k}} \text{əm} \; \overset{2}{\underset{41}{\downarrow}} \; / $$

The one which has disappeared is the one we might expect after *try*. The dropping appears to be an optional result of the shortness of the phrase *to try* that would precede the juncture, though I cannot formulate it neatly. The phrase break before *to come* can easily disappear, apparently for similar reasons. That anything but exceptionally rapid speech would reduce the sentence to fewer than three intonationally marked phrases, I seriously doubt. The interesting fact is not that the phrase breaks appear, but that they appear precisely where the transformational rules, modified to include an *IP* as the last element of each unemphatic underlying string, would quite naturally generate them. This seems to me to indicate that there is a point where phonologically oriented syntax, worked out most fully by Hill,[9] and the generative syntax of Chomsky come together and reinforce each other extremely well. It also seems to me that the validity of transformations which do not thus neatly predict intonational breaks may be seriously questioned. In this way, intonation can become one of the many criteria needed to assist us in arriving at the simplest set of generative rules for English.

I cite three sample transformations to show how Chomsky's published transformations can be reworked to include intonation. Instead of Chom-

---

[8] 1958 Texas Conference, pp. 42–3 of the mimeographed paper.
[9] In his *Introduction to Linguistic Structures* (1958).

sky's *C* for 'tense' I use *Te;* otherwise all symbols are those defined in his publications.

(9) T_{intrg} SD. $NP, \begin{cases} Te\,(n't),\, VP_1\,(X) \\ Te + M\,(n't),\, X \\ Te + have\,(n't),\, X \\ Te + be\,(n't),\, X \end{cases}, IP$

SC. $1, 2, 3, 4 \Rightarrow 2, 1, 3, Intrg + JP$

$Intrg = 011 + \uparrow,\, 022 + \uparrow,\, 033 + \uparrow,\, 044\uparrow$

This transformation generates simple yes-no interrogatives with a rising intonation:

$$\overset{2}{} \quad \overset{3}{} \overset{3}{} \qquad \overset{2}{} \qquad \overset{33}{}$$
/ìziy gówiŋ ↑ /,/ wòwntiy íyt ↑ /,

and the like. The *Wh*-question transformation, which starts from a string to which T_{intrg} has been applied, inverts the intonation pattern by converting *Intrg* to *C*, giving

$$\overset{2}{} \quad \overset{3}{} \overset{1}{} \qquad \overset{2}{} \qquad \overset{31}{}$$
/ hùwz gówiŋ ↓ /,/ hùw wòwnt íyt ↓ /.

This pattern may be inverted again by the echo-question transformation, giving

$$\overset{2}{} \quad \overset{3}{} \overset{3}{} \qquad \overset{2}{} \qquad \overset{33}{}$$
/ hùwz gówiŋ ↑ /,/ hùw wòwnt íyt ↑ /.

The following is one of several types of nominalizing transformations; the others are similar.

(10) T_{nom} SD. $T + it, VP + IP$

$NP, Aux, V, X + Cont + JP$

$1, 2, 3, 4, 5, 6 \Rightarrow (3 + S^2) + ing + 5, 6, 2$

To illustrate this, we take Chomsky's example, *It was a surprise* plus *John proved the theorem,* which results in *(John's) proving the theorem was a surprise*. X_6 contains the *IP* of the second string (which I call the SOURCE string, the first being the CONSUMER string). The *SD* of the source string specifies that its *IP* be one of the *Cont* types. The resulting sentence, therefore, will have either terminal sustain or terminal rise after *theorem* and the pitch sequence will be any one of those allowed by the constituent structure rules (specifically, (5) above). The final *IP* of the sentence is of course contained in X_2 and remains as in the consumer string. Here is a reason for my doubt that there are more than two terminal junctures in English: in order to have *Cont* appear internally in the resulting sentence, it must first have been final in the source string. I do not believe I have ever heard a final terminal sustaining juncture—indeed, I cannot imagine what it would sound like in contrast with final terminal fade. It is easy to formulate a phonetic rule that / ↓ / has the allophone [|] whenever it is not followed by a pause or silence; but it is not easy to set up a rule that generates a phoneme /|/ at the end of just those terminal strings which are subsequently going to be used as source strings in transformations of the type shown above. (It can be done, of course, but at the moment I consider it an unnecessary complication of the grammar.)

(11) $T_{emphatic}$ SD.   X, Y, $\left\{\begin{matrix} Intrg \\ Disc \\ Cont \end{matrix}\right\}$, JP

SC.   1, 2, 3, 4 $\Rightarrow$ 1, 3, 2, 4
Condition: X is not A, Af, Wh-

The result of this transformation is to move the center of the intonation contour, to place the middle pitch and the phrase stress freely by shifting it back from the end. It does this, however, by moving the whole element C. Thus it will generate *I went* TO *the movies, I* WENT *to the movies*, etc. It is mutually exclusive with the affirmation transformation.

The transformations briefly discussed under (9), (10), and (11), it must be emphasized, are tentative and illustrative only. I believe they show that intonation patterns can be integrated with some ease into a generative grammar, and that both the grammar and the analysis of intonation may be sharpened by such a step.

Part III

LINGUISTIC GEOGRAPHY

INTRODUCTION

IN THE PAST THREE-QUARTERS of a century one field of applied linguistics, that called linguistic or dialect geography, or sometimes area linguistics, has yielded a rich harvest in the understanding of relationships between language forms and the places where language forms are used.

Linguistic geography, the study of the regional distribution of language forms and their variants, has attained maturity in Europe, where for some time there have been in existence completed studies of the dialect speech of Germany, France, Belgium, Holland, Switzerland, Italy, and some other areas. Indeed, one great pioneering project, the *Atlas linguistique de la France* (1902–1910), has been finished for so long that a second survey is now proceeding, since such a study desirably should be repeated every fifty years.

In the United States a projected Linguistic Atlas of the United States and Canada began with a pilot investigation in New England, the results of which were published as *The Linguistic Atlas of New England* (1939–1943). Since then, other regional projects have been organized but as yet no other complete atlases have been published. The vocabulary, pronunciation, and verb forms of the Middle Atlantic and South Atlantic atlas projects have been treated in three volumes by Hans Kurath, Kurath and Raven McDavid, and E. Bagby Atwood. Data from field records in other projects are available for most of the northern United States. Colorado, New Mexico, and the Pacific Coast, with some additional materials from Tennessee, Louisiana, and Texas. These data have been used already for the preparation of a number of doctoral dissertations and various articles in scholarly journals.

This Part begins and ends with the work of Hans Kurath, director of the Linguistic Atlas of New England and also of the atlases of the Atlantic states. Marckwardt and Allen join him in discussing some of the values and implications of the evidence provided by dialect research, especially with reference to the greater accuracy of language description which it makes possible.

The next two articles, also by Marckwardt and Allen, are included because they are at present the only available comprehensive mapped material in addition to the books named above. These articles and books may be supplemented by the excellent chapter on American dialect written by McDavid for W. Nelson Francis's *The Structure of American English* (Ronald, 1958). Such information is increasingly relevant in the background of the teacher of English as more and more attention is being given to varieties of American speech in the secondary curriculum.

Atwood then supplies the exemplary case study of *greasy* with its relatively sharp line of demarcation between two main dialect regions. A number of similar studies have been published in the *Publication of the American Dialect Society, American Speech, Language,* and the *Journal of the Canadian Linguistic Association,* as well as in *Orbis,* the international journal of dialectology.

Insight into the often unsuspected relationship between speech forms and social status is given by McDavid, who elsewhere has written further about this use of dialect information.

In conclusion, Kurath turns the section back to the general field of linguistics by indicating the value of dialect evidence in the historical study of language.

20

Area Linguistics and the Teacher of English

HANS KURATH

IT SHOULD BE OBVIOUS that the teacher of English in grade school, high school, or college should know the usage of the area in which he does his teaching before he undertakes to 'mend' the speechways of his pupils. If there is a class cleavage in usage within the area, he should be aware of it, so that for the good of his students he can set 'better' or 'cultivated' usage over against socially less desirable practices. If several regional dialects are current within the area (as for instance in Detroit, with its large groups of recent immigrants, black or white, from south of the Ohio), he should be familiar with them in order to deal sensibly with his wards.

How does the teacher of English get the information he needs to do a good job? Can he rely upon the ordinary textbooks, the desk dictionaries, Kenyon and Knott's *Pronouncing Dictionary,* Craigie and Hulbert's *Dictionary of American English?*

Yes, to some extent. However, the *DAE* deals with American vocabulary without identifying regional usage or the social standing of the expressions, though a check of the quotations often permits an inference; Kenyon-Knott is adequate for Northern pronunciation, including Eastern New England's, but fails to deal satisfactorily with usage in Metropolitan New York and the South; the desk dictionaries, though registering some variant cultivated pronunciations, give no indication of their habitat; the ordinary textbook is tailored for the national market and is apt to gloss over regional differences, even if the author knows better.

Reprinted by permission from *Language Learning,* Special Issue 2, March, 1961, pp. 9–14. The author is Professor Emeritus of English at the University of Michigan, former editor of the Middle English Dictionary, and director of the Linguistic Atlas of New England.
The examples are taken from: Hans Kurath, *A Word Geography of the Eastern United States,* (University of Michigan Press, 1949); Hans Kurath and Raven I. McDavid, Jr., *The Pronunciation of English in the Atlantic States,* (University of Michigan Press, 1960); Bagby Atwood, *A Survey of Verb Forms in the Eastern United States,* (University of Michigan Press, 1953).

Two recent textbooks on AE (Hill and Francis) practically obliterate regional differences current in cultivated use by imposing Trager's 'over-all' nine-vowel system. Only 'incidental' differences are admitted, and rather effectively concealed by the transcription at that.

Clearly, the teacher of English must be given better information than he now has at his disposal. What can area linguistics, the study of regional and social dialects, do to help him? I shall try to show, by dealing with differences in pronunciation current in the Eastern States, how a useful body of information can be made available, and how this sort of information can be instrumental in developing a scholarly, and therefore salutary, point of view.

Some sections of the Eastern States (all of the South and the South Midland) have a /j/ after the initial alveolar consonant (as in *tube, due, new*) on all social levels, others not (as Pa and eNE). Should a teacher in Boston or Philadelphia make his students adopt the /j/? In other sections usage is divided, as in MNY: should the teacher insist upon one or the other of these pronunciations in such a community?

In eNE, MNY, Va, and SC postvocalic /r/, as in *ear, care, four, poor,* is not pronounced as such by a considerable majority. Should the minority be urged to 'drop the /r/,' i.e., substitute unsyllabic /ə/, in this position when no social stigma attaches to pronouncing the /r/? What should be done when /r/ is an index of rusticity, as in most of eNC and parts of SC and Ga?

In the greater part of the South and the South Midland the diphthongal vowel in *down, owl, crowd* begins like the vowel of *man* on all social levels, whereas in NEngland and elsewhere this pronunciation is confined to folk speech. How should a teacher behave under such diverse circumstances? What should he do in Michigan, where [æu] is uncommon, except among recent immigrants from south of the Ohio?

Eastern NEngl and wPa have the same vowel in *law, caught, salt* and in *lot, cot, rod,* whereas all other sections of the Eastern States have contrasting vowels in these two sets. If a Michigan student lacks the contrast, as many do, should he be taught to distinguish *caught* from *cot, taught* from *tot*?

On the Atlantic seaboard, the vowel in *care, chair, stairs* ranges regionally all the way from the /æ/ of *cat* to the /ɛ/ of *get* and the /e/ of *gate* without social implications. Should one insist upon one of these pronunciations in view of the fact that, except for parts of SC and Ga, no regional dialect has more than one vowel phoneme between high and low before historical /r/, pronounced regionally as /r/ or unsyllabic /ə̯/?

Hoarse and *horse, mourning* and *morning* are homophonous in an area extending from the Potomac northward to MNY and westward throughout Pa, but not elsewhere in the Eastern States. For the sake of a few homonyms, or for some other reason, should one undertake to teach contrasting vowels in *four* and *forty* in the schools of Michigan, if usage is divided among the student body?

If a student pronounces *Mary* like *merry* and *fairy* like *ferry*, or rimes *story* with *sorry*, should he be urged to differentiate them, as Southerners, New Yorkers, and most New Englanders do? Or is Pennsylvanian usage good enough?

When a Michigan student says *he et* (=*ate*) *it, he dove* (=*dived*) *right in*, and *he hadn't ought to* (=*ought not to*) *talk so much*, like his Yankee forebears, should the teacher 'correct' him or merely point out to him that others say *ate, dived*, and *ought not to?* If his own usage is in line with that of well educated New Englanders, why should he change his ways? On the other hand, if he says *he eat it all up, he clumb a tree, he driv in the nail*, he should be told to avoid these past tense forms if he wants to appear to advantage, since they are strictly folk forms, though they are of venerable vintage, being derived by normal phonemic change from standard forms of earlier English.

These examples and queries have probably suggested to you the drift of my thinking in this matter. Unless a variant is clearly marked as 'low class' or 'rustic' within the area in which one teaches, it should be tolerated. To fight it is not only a waste of time, but an insult to students coming from well educated families or from other sections of the country. It breeds confusion, if not resentment, in the student body. On the other hand, a teacher who can say: 'Your family must come from New England' or 'Did you grow up in New York City?' or 'That's the way they say it in Virginia,' will command the respect of his class. In any event, he will stimulate the interest of his better students in our language, if he can tell them that well educated New Englanders, New Yorkers, Pennsylvanians, and Virginians don't talk exactly alike (although they understand each other quite easily), and point out some of the salient differences.

To put the teacher of English into a position to make pertinent comments on usage, we need better textbooks; and before we can produce better textbooks we must have more adequate information on regional and social differences in usage than we now possess. We are making progress in that direction, but we still have a long way to go.

We must realize that the linguistic situation in this country is rather different from that in England and France, and even from that in Germany. The former have *one* unquestionably dominant social dialect, and German-speaking Europe has at least the *Bühnenaussprache* (stage pronunciation) as a guide, though Bavarians, Austrians, and Swiss don't hew exactly to the line. On the other hand, we have rather well marked regional types of cultivated speech, and there is no reason for assuming that in matters of pronunciation Virginians will bow to New Yorkers, or Detroiters to Bostonians, within the foreseeable future. It is equally unlikely that the Ohio Valley will conform in usage to the Greak Lakes Basin. Though postvocalic /r/ is fairly regularly used in both of these major areas, there are many differences in the incidence of the vowels and in their phonic character, as Professor Marckwardt can tell you, the common fiction of a 'General American' type notwithstanding.

DISCUSSION

Question: If we base acceptable pronunciation of American English on what would be used by educated speakers in a given area, what should the teacher of English in a foreign country do?

Answer: That is a practical question, and a very important one. I should say that in Europe Standard British English will continue to be taught, and for good reasons. If any type of American English is also to be taught, I would suggest using one in which post-vocalic /r/ is preserved, either that of the Great Lakes Basin or that of the Ohio Valley. These differ the most from British English and are spoken over wide areas. However, if your teacher is a cultured New Yorker or Virginian, let him have his way. All varieties of cultivated American English are mutually intelligible.

Question: I wish to ask about the English used in our mass media, radio and television. Might this be considered standard pronunciation?

Answer: What we hear on the radio are all the varieties of more or less cultivated American English, and some British English. Even if the announcers were all trained in one and the same dialect, they would have little influence on our youth, who are much more fascinated by cowboy talk and the lingo of the jokesmith. The chief contribution of the radio is to familiarize the listeners with a great variety of regional and social dialects.

Question: Is there any way of knowing how quickly people who move from one area to another acquire the local dialect?

Answer: This is a problem that needs investigation. Detroit would be a wonderful place for making such a study. How long do the Negroes from south of the Ohio retain their dialects in that city? Do Negroes born in Detroit talk two dialects, one in their homes and another in school? How about the second Detroit-born generation? I have had some experience with the Irish in New England. They adapt their speech completely to the local Yankee types in the first New England-born generation, though they remember some of the Irishisms of their parents.

Comment: You were speaking of the Negro boy as speaking two dialects. I teach quite a few Negro children and I notice that not only do they talk differently at home, but the minute they are out of the school building and are walking along the street with their playmates they immediately begin to talk the way they had first learned to talk.

Question: I wonder if you've ever speculated on the causes of these regional distinctions.

Answer: Well, yes, and in my *Word Geography* I have suggested some things, partly by implication. Of course, the Atlantic seaboard is much more highly subdivided than areas farther west. There are various factors involved. First of all, the early colonies, strung out along the Atlantic seaboard, had little contact with each other. Their contact was with back home, with England. Even in New England it took nearly a century and a half before the Massachusetts Bay settlement expanded far enough to the west to meet the settlements on the lower Connecticut River. In three or four generations different dialects, more or less uniform, had developed in the Boston area on the one hand and in the Hartford area on the other; and to this day eastern and western New England have noticeably different dialects. Other dialects came into being in the several Middle and Southern Colonies before the Revolution and were carried westward in the nineteenth century. It is a complicated and fascinating story. Will anyone predict that one day Richmond will bow to New York or Boston to Chicago?

21

Linguistic Geography and Freshman English

ALBERT H. MARCKWARDT

EVERY AUTUMN approximately half a million students enter the colleges and universities of the country. Virtually all of them are required to take a course in freshman English. Over a ten-year period their number mounts to a total of five or six million. Year in and year out several thousand instructors in English devote most of their time to teaching these students.

In one sense this is a thumbnail sketch of the most amazing linguistic enterprise in the history of the civilized world. Varied as are the aims and outlines of freshman English the country over, the hundreds of courses which fall into this category have one element in common: they seek to give the individual student a mastery of standard American English as a medium of communication. Never before has any educational system committed itself to the teaching of a national standard, that is to say a prestige dialect, on so vast a scale.

This common aim poses certain problems. First, it is still true that many high school and college students come from homes where standard English is not habitually spoken or written. For these, this phase of the English program of school and college means that the individual student must be trained to forego his habitual use of certain language features characteristic of the regional and social dialects of English and to substitute for these, features of that prestige dialect which we call Standard English.

At the same time we must recognize that this so-called Standard English is not absolutely identical the country over, although most college handbooks and rhetorics are blandly written upon the assumption that it is. To select just a single instance, the use of *for* in "I would like for you to write

Originally a talk made at the Rocky Mountain Modern Language Association conference, Boulder, Colorado, October, 1951, this paper is here reprinted by permission of the author and The College English Association, Copyright ©, *The CEA Critic,* 14.1 (January, 1952). Professor Marckwardt, for many years at the University of Michigan and now at Princeton University, is Director of the Linguistic Atlas of the North Central States.

me a letter," is characteristic of cultivated speech and writing over large parts of the South and totally absent from most other sections of the country, yet college textbooks often quite unreasonably legislate against this particular construction. I recall very vividly my own bewilderment when, as an undergraduate, I read in the textbook we used in those days that the use of *taken* as an active past-tense form—*I taken it*—was one of the worst errors that anyone could make. As I learned much later, this statement undoubtedly made a great deal of sense to students in some parts of the country, but to my classmates and me, with our particular regional linguistic background, it was wholly meaningless. We simply couldn't imagine anyone's doing it.

The situation is similar, if not even more aggravated, in the speech field with respect to matters of pronunciation. I say more aggravated because a good many manuals of speech are written from a more rigid, authoritarian point of view than are the best hand-books of composition. For example, when even a usually careful and competent phonetician applies the label "substandard" to the voiced *t* in better, the diphthongal pronunciation of the vowel in *bird,* the *w* of *somewhat,* and the voiceless initial fricative of *thither,* one feels the need of a body of objective fact to put these impressionistic judgments to the test. We have only to remember that even today, all candidates for teaching positions in New York City must demonstrate by examination that they have mastered the south-eastern British—so-called Received Standard—pronunciations recorded in Daniel Jones's *Pronouncing Dictionary of the English Language,* for which the editor claims no validity whatsoever outside of the particular area from which they were gathered.

The problem then becomes one of securing authoritative data about standard American English, as it exists in various parts of the country. One source of such data is to be found in the materials which have been collected for the Linguistic Atlas of the United States and Canada. At present this consists of the published *Linguistic Atlas of New England,* the completely collected field records of the Linguistic Atlas of the South Atlantic States and of the Linguistic Atlas of the Middle Atlantic States, together with the fragmentary materials of at least four other linguistic atlas projects in various stages of completion throughout the country.

There is no question that these materials, even in their present incomplete state, present a more complete body of carefully gathered information concerning pronunciation than the most authoritative dictionaries are based on today. The second edition—still the current one—of *Webster's New International Dictionary* employed 104 consultants on pronunciation, and subsequent analysis showed these to be very unevenly distributed throughout the country. The cultured informants represented in the three coastal atlases alone comprise more than half again that number. When the country is completely covered, there will undoubtedly be from two to three times as many. Moreover, the atlas will contain affirmative evidence of substandard speech in quantity. That is to say, the evidence will be there and will not have to be guessed at negatively in terms of whatever does not happen to be known to, or habitually used by, the author or lexicographer. Finally, the wide variety of pronunciation characteristic of the cultured informants should serve to check some of the excessive dogmatism found in speech classes.

With respect to problems of vocabulary, morphology, and syntax the situation is much the same. Any examination of a dozen or more college textbooks in composition will demonstrate that in large measure the authors of these books have copied one another as assiduously as have the lexicographers. Or even if they have gone to the current factual sources of the language on many moot points, what help can they expect to get? A dictionary label of "colloquial" or a classification of "popular English" in a standard work on syntax is, after all, just another man's subjective judgment, often based upon somewhat meager evidence. It is reasonable to maintain that the selective sampling technique employed by the atlases and the sheer mass of evidence they have collected impart a greater validity to their findings than most collections of fact relative to current use of the language.

Early in 1951 a minor furore was created in one of the pedagogical journals when someone insisted that the apparent relaxation of standards in English grammars and handbooks over the past quarter-century could be accounted for by the fact that the linguistic habits of the freshmen were influencing, and indeed overcoming, those of the instructors. This somewhat startling conclusion was purportedly based upon a comparison covering twenty points of form and syntax between the 1949 Norman Lewis survey of the language of college professors, editors, lexicographers, authors, etc., and a presumably similar survey of the usage of a group of freshmen.

What the author of the article overlooked, and what so far few of his critics have pointed out, was that the instructions given to the two groups differed so radically that the results of the surveys simply did not admit of a valid comparison. To make his point, the author might much more profitably have consulted the atlas materials for the normal usage of the cultured informants. Had he done so, however, his point might well have vanished, for a spot check of one or two items considered in the study shows the cultured informants closer to the reported usage of the freshmen than to the so-called authorities consulted by Mr. Lewis.

There is still another way in which atlas findings can be of considerable service. In our attempt to assure our students, on the secondary as well as the college level, of a habitual command of standard English equal to the demands of any situation in which their abilities may place them, we must operate with a high degree of efficiency. Language habits are formed only by dint of constant repetition. Even in the twelve or sixteen years of schooling through the high school and college levels, the number of new habits which can be formed and of the old ones which may be eradicated is not too great. This calls for a highly judicious selection of the particular language features to be attacked and replaced by new habits. It demands careful curriculum planning.

We know now that it can no longer be assumed that all substandard forms and syntactical patterns are alike the country over. Professor E. Bagby Atwood, of the University of Texas, in analyzing the field records of the three coastal atlases, has found sharp lines of demarcation in the inflectional forms of folk speech. The same is also true with such syntactical matters as the choice of preposition in "sick (to) (at) or (in) one's stomach." If it is decided that there is enough prejudice against, or social stigma connected with *sick to his stomach* to make the substitution of *at* a justifiable item somewhere in the language curriculum, in those areas where *sick at his stomach* is the characteristic folk form, this item may be safely omitted. It does not constitute a problem. The same conclusion will apply to *all the farther, dog-bit* as a past participle, or *taken* as a past-tense form. Atlas results merit the attention of those who are charged with framing courses of English instruction at virtually all levels of schooling.

There are, of course, many broader implications of the splendid work that has been done and that which is now under way in determining the regional features of American English. My only purpose here is to suggest that since so many of us are concerned with the teaching of the English language on a practical level, the work of the linguistic geographer is by no means merely a remote endeavor, presenting a few research scholars with an opportunity to demonstrate their virtuosity, but rather an activity than can touch intimately and affect profoundly our everyday classrooom practices.

22

The Linguistic Atlases: Our New Resource

Harold B. Allen

A FEW YEARS AGO a teacher in South Carolina was pushing her less than enthusiastic pupils through a grammar drill book, painfully but relentlessly. The class struggled on to an exercise intended to teach the correct use of the negative of *ought*. Here the students found sentences with the approved construction *ought not*. But they found also some sentences with a construction they were supposed to cross out, *hadn't ought*. This the pupils had never seen or heard before, and they were delighted with it. True, the book said it was wrong, and teacher, as always, agreed with the book. But there it was—in the book—as plain as anything could be; and somehow it seemed marvelously sensible. *He hadn't intended to do it: He hadn't ought to do it. I hadn't wanted to go: I hadn't ought to go.* Why not? So within a week or two the puzzled teacher began to find more and more of her pupils using *hadn't ought,* pupils who up until then had used *ought not* with unconscious ease.

Such an incident can not happen in the future if teachers and textbook writers know and use the new data now becoming accessible to them. This is the body of facts about American English coming from the great research projects collectively designated the Linguistic Atlas of the United States and Canada.

Of course, this is not the first mass of information about American usage available to teachers of English. During the past forty years an increasing number of studies have effectively demonstrated the unreliability of much that had been accepted as truth. The NCTE itself has led in the publication of the significant and familiar studies by Sterling Andrus Leonard, Albert H. Marckwardt and Fred Walcott, and Charles C. Fries. Dozens

Reprinted by permission from *The English Journal*, 45.188–94 (April, 1956). This article is adapted from a paper read at the convention of the National Council of Teachers of English, New York, November, 1955. It has been slightly revised since its appearance in the First Edition. The author is Professor of English at the University of Minnesota and Director of the Linguistic Atlas of the Upper Midwest.

of articles on specific items of usage have appeared in our own Council publications as well as in *Language, American Speech,* and a few other periodicals. Also there have been published the increasingly reliable commercial dictionaries and our first pronouncing lexicon, Kenyon and Knott's *Pronouncing Dictionary of American English.*

Now all this weight of evidence has had its clearly perceptible effects upon the handbooks and the school grammars. A comparison of those published in 1920 and those appearing since 1950 reveals a much higher proportion of sweet reasonableness, of honest recognition of the facts of linguistic life. But influential as this evidence has been, it generally has had one important limitation. On the whole, these studies and investigations of usage have assumed the validity of the criterion of national use, a criterion enunciated by the Scottish rhetorician Alexander Campbell in the late eighteenth century. Campbell insisted that national use must be one of the determinants of what is good usage. Following him, these studies assume that what is true in the determination of usage in a smaller country like England or France, with one cultural capital, is equally true for the vast United States with its cultural diversification and many cultural centers.

A second limitation of these studies is that generally they ignore the lexical and grammatical usage of the normal everyday, informal speech of cultivated people (though Leonard did record opinions classifying forms as "colloquial"). Part of this limitation, of course, is also the fact that these studies generally have not treated matters of pronunciation in informal speech. An exception, again, is Kenyon and Knott's dictionary, which did record conversational pronunciations reported by independent mail surveys.

These limitations are reflected naturally enough in the contents of the textbooks. The laudable improvement in the general treatment of usage is accompanied by conspicuous inadequacy in the treatment of any language matters having variations which correlate with geographical distribution. This improvement, furthermore, is offset also by the persistence of considerable misapprehension concerning various matters of pronunciation whether regional or not.

But any textbook or reference book with these inadequacies will soon be obsolete. Already valuable evidence about regional usage in words and grammar and pronunciation is beginning to emerge from the tremendous research activity within the framework of the Linguistic Atlas of the United States. Already enough evidence from this source is available so that textbook-makers will shirk responsibility if they do not take these new facts into account.

DATA ON PRONUNCIATION

What is the Linguistic Atlas of the United States? It is not a single project; it is a number of regional research projects using similar procedures and collecting the same kinds of evidence, hence producing results that can be added together and compared.

Essentially this evidence is gathered like this. Using a tested selective sampling technique, linguistically trained fieldworkers interview native residents representing three groups, older and uneducated speakers, middle-aged secondary school graduates, and younger college graduates. From each of these persons information is sought about more than 800 language items (in the first project there were 1200). Each response is recorded in a finely graded phonetic transcription, so that all responses have value as pronunciation evidence. Some items are included for that reason only; others are included for their lexical or grammatical or syntactic significance. The basic list of items in the questionnaire is usually modified slightly in each area through the dropping of some which are irrelevant there and the adding of others significant there. (It is pointless to ask a North Dakota farmer what he calls the Atlantic round clam, a /kwáhɑg/, /kwɔhɔ́g/, or /kwəhɔ́g/. He never heard of it by any name!) But this basic list is essentially the same countrywide, so that national comparative studies will be possible when the fieldwork is finished.

At present, organizations to gather this evidence have been effected in eight different areas: New England, Middle Atlantic States, South Atlantic States, North Central States, Upper Midwest, Rocky Mountain States, Pacific Coast, and Louisiana. The New England Atlas has been completed and published. From it and the unpublished materials of the other eastern surveys has come the evidence presented by Hans Kurath in 1949 in his *Word Geography of the Eastern United States,* by E. B. Atwood in 1953 in his *Verb Forms of the Eastern United States* and by Kurath & McDavid in 1960 in *The Pronunciation of English in the Atlantic States.* Derivative articles by Raven I. McDavid, Jr., Atwood, Alva Davis, Walter Avis, Thomas Pearce, David Reed, Marjorie Kimmerle, and others have made public additional usage evidence in *American Speech, College English* and *The English Journal, Orbis, Language,* and *Language Learning.* Virginia McDavid has completed her dissertation on the verb forms of the North Central and Upper Midwest regions, and Jean Malmstrom has finished her dissertation on the support provided by dialect evidence for the usage statements made in school and college textbooks. [See pp. 316–24.] These publications, together with the Atlas files, constitute a vast accumulation of data for the use of teachers and textbook writers.

When we look at the information now available about regional usage we find that probably the most important single fact is the reconstruction of the picture of American language areas. It has been assumed for years that we have Eastern, Southern, and Northern (sometimes called General American) dialect divisions in this country. But evidence from the Atlantic field records presented by Kurath has led to the recognition of a quite different structure consisting of Eastern New England, Northern, Midland. and Southern, with various subdivisions in each region and, of course, with some overlapping of regions. Midland is the speech of the Pennsylvania-Delaware settlement area and of its derivative areas in central Ohio, northern Indiana, central Illinois, southern Iowa, and so on. It exists also in the variety called South Midland, which extends south along the Appalachians as "Mountain English" and into southern Illinois, Missouri, Arkansas, eastern Oklahoma, and eastern Texas.

For significant matters of pronunciation I would suggest reference to McDavid's excellent article, "Some Social Differences in Pronunciation," in *Language Learning* in 1953.[1] McDavid's thesis here is that, although certain pronunciations may lack recognition or distribution nationally, they can enjoy high prestige in a given region through the influence of such a focal center as Boston, New York, Philadelphia, Richmond, or Charleston. Differences in pronunciation, in other words, are not merely a matter of social and educational background; they may also be related to geographical differences.

For example, despite the tendency of the schools toward spelling-pronunciation, the unaspirated forms /wɪp/ "whip," /wilbæro/ "wheelbarrow," and /wɔrf/ "wharf" are in common cultured use in the Midland area and, as a matter of fact, occur sporadically elsewhere among cultured speakers. A few years ago a teacher in Utica, N.Y., yielding to the probably normal impulse to consider one's own speech or that of a textbook as the proper one, wrote to *College English* that she had never observed a person of true culture who lacked the /hw/ cluster in such words. Yet, as McDavid has observed, this teacher would have had to go only a few miles south to central Pennsylvania to observe thousands of cultivated speakers who say /wɪp/ and /wilbæro/; indeed, even in her own community the Atlas's cultivated informant is recorded as having /w/ and not /hw/ in these words. In the function words, of course, the customary lack of stress has resulted in the loss of aspiration everywhere, not just in certain areas; yet in my own state of Minnesota the new guide for instruction in the language arts enjoins the teacher to insist upon distinguishing /wɪč/ "witch" and /hwɪč/ "which" and /wɛðər/ "weather" and /hwɛðer/ "whether."

Similarly, the /hy/ consonant cluster in *humor* reveals primary geographical distribution. This cluster commonly occurs in Northern speech, but elsewhere in the nation the usual form among all speakers is simply /yumər/.

In Northern American English and in South Carolina, probably in some other sections, a restressing of the second vowel in *because* has led to the form /bɪkɔ́z/ as usual among cultivated speakers. Yet many teachers, likely

[1] IV, 102–16. [It is reprinted in this edition, **pp. 251–61**.]

influenced by spelling and lacking the information forthcoming from the Atlas studies, insist punctiliously upon /bɪkɔz/.

The sounds represented by the letter *o* in *orange, horrid,* and *forest* also vary according to region. In much of New York state and in eastern Pennsylvania, for example, an unround /ɑ/ appears instead of the more common /ɔ/. Not long ago a teacher came to Minnesota from New York state and promptly began insisting that her pupils say only /ɑrɪnj/ and /fɑrɪst/; and recently a textbook came out with the same injunction, that the only correct form is /ɑrɪnj/.

The diphthong /ɪu/, mistakenly called "long *u*," offers another case in point. In the South, as in British English, a strongly consonantal /y/ beginning is heard in this diphthong in post-alveolar contexts, as in *newspaper, tube,* and *due* or *dew.* But in the North this beginning is quite weak, often almost imperceptible, and it is gone completely in northeastern New England and in Midland. Yet many teachers in the Middle West diligently drill their pupils in the pronunciation /nyuz/ instead of their normal /nuz/. More than half of my own students each year report that this was their high school experience, although on only a few of them did the attempted inoculation "take." (To prevent misunderstanding, it should be clear that there can of course be no objection to the form /nyuz/ where it is the normal prestige form. What is objectionable is well-meaning but unenlightened tampering with acceptable speech.)

The same kind of thing, but with a much more complicated geographical picture, occurs with the pronunciation of a group of words spelled with *oo.* I should be surprised if many of the readers of this article, or of the original audience hearing it read, would have for all of these words the same pronunciation which I, a native of southern Michigan, have: /rʊf, rʊt, hʊf, hʊp, hʊpɪŋ kɔf, kup, rum, brum, fud, spuk/ (with /ʊ/ as in *put* and /u/ as in *moon*). But I should also be surprised if you have not sometime been in a situation—on either the giving or the receiving end—where someone was being instructed to pronounce *root* and *roof,* perhaps even *soot,* with /u/ rather than /ʊ/. The Atlas files reveal a complicated distribution of these forms, each word having its own distinctive regional pattern; and nothing in this information supports the familiar injunctions.

Another vowel dilemma with historical roots in Middle English is that offered by *creek.* Many Northern teachers, probably swayed by the double *ee* spelling, for years have insisted upon their pupils' learning the Southern standard pronunciation /krik/ despite the fact, which should be obvious to an objective listener in a Northern community and which is fully attested by the Atlas records, that the basic Northern form is /krɪk/. Even in Battle Creek, Michigan, I am informed, there is this attempt to lift at least the school population to the cultural heaven, Southern division, where /krik/ is the shibboleth.

There are numerous other moot matters of pronunciation upon which Atlas research now can provide information making possible an enlightened approach. I think, for instance, of such *loci critici* as /hɑg/ and /hɔg/, /rɑzbɛriz/ and /ræzbɛriz/, /grisi/ and /grizi/, /iðər/ and /ɑiðər/, /kɑfi/ and /kɔfi/, /kɑnt/ and /kænt/ and /kent/ "can't," /ves/ and /vɑz/, /kɛč/ and /kæč/, /wɑtər/ and /wɔtər/, /tord/ and /təwɔrd/, /sɝˑəp/ and /sɪrəp/, /təmetoz/ and /təmɑtoz/, /rædɪš/ and /rɛdɪs/, and /dɪfθɪryə/ and /dɪpθɪryə/—for information about which the Atlas sources are invaluable.

DATA ON GRAMMAR AND IDIOM

Then the category of grammar and idiom is another in which Atlas materials contribute to our knowledge about usage. As with pronunciation we quite humanly yield to the notion that what is standard or customary for us either is, or ought to be, standard for others. A recent rhetoric textbook for the college freshman course was written by two authors of southern background. They say, *"Bucket is more likely to be the ordinary word, pail . . . a little more old-fashioned and endowed with more 'poetic' suggestions."* Any freshman speaking Northern English who finds this statement on page 372 must find it rather puzzling, for to him *bucket* refers to some unfamiliar wooden vessel in a well and is a word invariably preceded by *old oaken.* The Atlas files provide evidence for a much more objective statement about the relationship between *bucket* and *pail.*

Again, more than one textbook writer has condemned *sick to one's stomach* in favor of *sick at one's stomach,* but the Atlas findings reveal *sick to* as the usual Northern locution and *sick at* as a Midland variant, along with *sick from* and *sick with* and *sick in.*

Even those who have confidently relied upon the data in the 1932 Leonard report will now need to revise their statements in the light of what Atlas evidence tells them about *depot* (∼railroad station), *in back of* (∼behind), *mad* (∼angry), *off of* (∼from), and *like* (∼as if)—all of them rated as disputable usages by Leonard—as well as about the expressions *the dog wants in* and *all the further,* both of which actually are rated there as illiterate.

Now such matters of pronunciation and of vocabulary may readily be accepted by the teacher as likely to be clarified by research in regional language. We are accustomed to thinking of dialect as consisting of differences in sounds and words. Actually, regional linguistic studies may also considerably illumine certain other matters of high importance to the teacher, those in the field of grammar.

At least seven of the grammatical items that Leonard's monograph listed as disputable were included in the Atlas worksheets. These are *dived∼ dove, I'll∼I shall, eat∼et, aren't I?∼ain't I?∼am I not?, it (he) don't*

~*doesn't, these kind*~*those kind,* and *sang*~*sung.* At least eight more Atlas items appeared in the group classified by Leonard as illiterate: *have*
drank~*have drunk, began*~*begun, lay down*~*lie down, a orange*~*an*
orange, hadn't you ought~*ought not you, run*~*ran, set down*~*sit down,*
and *you was*~*you were.*

The Atlas records offer data, some of it surprising, about these items. For
instance, the frequently found textbook admonition about the preterit *dove*
implies that this is non-standard in contrast with the historical form *dived.*
But the records show plainly that *dove* is the usual form among speakers of
Northern English and *dived* is Midland and Southern. In other words, the
present-day distinction is regional and not social.

But beside these items the Atlas files include comprehensive information about the social and regional distribution of many others that have
been in controversy, such as the preterit forms *give* and *gave, did* and *done,*
dreamed and *dremt, swam* and *swum, fitted* and *fit, shrank* and *shrunk,*
saw and *seen, kneeled* and *knelt, taught* and *learned;* the participial forms
worn out and *wore out, have taken* and *have took, I been thinking* and *I've*
been thinking, spoiled and *spoilt, was bitten* and *was bit, have drove* and
have driven; together with *you* and *you-all* and *it wasn't me* and *it wasn't I.*

APPLICATION OF THE DATA

For teachers of English, clearly the immediate application of this new
source of information about our language is in the revision of previous
statements about usage. In the simple interest of accuracy this revision is
demanded. Those of us who have anything to do with the training of future
teachers have the responsibility of using such revision in attention paid to
usage items in our language and methods classes. The class room teacher
has the special responsibility of using the new information in class drills,
in class discussion, and in the evaluation of student oral and written language. As the experience of the South Carolina teacher with *hadn't ought*
indicates, the teaching of standard forms must be done in full awareness
of frequency and distribution of the contrasting non-standard forms.

But the teacher's application ordinarily must result from revision of
usage statements in books of reference and in textbooks. Those who pre-
pare texts, workbooks, drill exercises, and the like cannot in all conscience
ignore the findings of the Atlases. Such revision is normal, of course, in the
editing procedure of the main dictionaries, which constantly note the new
evidence in published research. Full use of Atlas evidence was made, for
example, by the editors of Webster's *Third.*

But we may look forward to a second kind of application of Atlas materials in the classroom. It is high time to recognize the validity of some regional
speech in the scope of standard American English. There *are* standard
forms which are regional and not national. The label *dial.* in a dictionary

does not necessarily consign a linguistic form to either the linguistic slums or the linguistic backwoods. If you want to refer to the strip of grass between the sidewalk and the street, you are driven to awkward circumlocution unless you use a dialect word; there simply is no national word for it. But the cultivated speakers who in various parts of the country call this strip of grass the *boulevard, berm, tree-lawn, curb, parking, terrace, curb strip, sidewalk plot,* or any of several other names would be surprised, if not disgruntled, to be told that they were not speaking standard English.

Recognizing the validity of our own regional speech as standard means also that we recognize the validity of the standard speech of other regions. The time is surely long past when we need to take seriously such an unenlightened statement as this which appeared in a speech textbook several years ago: "There is perhaps no deviation from standard English that sounds as provincial and uncultivated as [the retroflex or inverted r-sound]. ... Inverted sounds are not used in standard English pronunciation. They will do more to make one's speech sound uncultivated than any other one thing."

Students can be helped toward recognition of this regional validity through various kinds of inductive exercises, especially in the vocabulary. Through such an exercise students for the first time approach objectively the language of their family, their neighbors, the community leaders, and speakers of other areas whom they hear. This particular investigative activity, it may be observed, fits naturally also into a language arts program that seeks to draw upon community resources.[2]

Then, finally, a further utilization of the Atlas data, possible in both college and secondary school, would be for the aim of developing awareness that language is a complex, changing, and always relative structure, not a set of absolutes. The use of regional language information can help our students attain a desirable degree of objectivity in their observation of language matters, can help them see that language is essentially a system of habits related at every point to non-language habits of behavior. And this kind of awareness, this kind of objectivity, is at the heart of a disciplined and informed ability to use language effectively for the communication of meaning.

[2] [EDIT. NOTE. Such content and exercises are now available for classroom use in Jean Malmstrom's *Dialects: U.S.A.,* published in September, 1963, by the National Council of Teachers of English as the first publication of its Commission on the English Language.]

23

Principal and Subsidiary Dialect Areas in the North-Central States

ALBERT H. MARCKWARDT

WITH THE PUBLICATION OF Kurath's *Word Geography of the Eastern United States*,[1] students of American English were provided for the first time with a sound and solidly based concept of the dialect areas to be recognized in this country. There is no need to go into details of his study. It will suffice to say that Kurath disposed once and for all of such negatively conceived catch-all categories as General American. On the positive side he must be credited with the concept of Midland as a specific speech area and type, and with recognizing the essential unity of Northern. This is brief, but it establishes a basis for the present discussion.

It will be recalled that each of Kurath's major dialect regions is divided into a number of sub-areas. Those which are significant for the present purpose are shown on Map 1. The largest single subdivision in the Northern speech area is Kurath's Number 4, consisting of upstate New York and western Vermont. It leads directly into the Western Reserve of Ohio and into the portion of Ontario which is included in the territory covered by the Linguistic Atlas of the North-Central States. The three sub-divisions of the Midland area adjacent to the territory included in the North-Central atlas are numbered 10, 11, and 12 by Kurath. He calls these areas the Upper Ohio Valley, Northern West Virginia, and Southern West Virginia respectively. In general the boundary between areas 10 and 11 follows the northern watershed of the Monongahela; that between areas 11 and 12 is the line of the Kanawha Valley.

Except for a few scattered places in Kentucky and Indiana, the field records of the Linguistic Atlas of the North-Central States have been completed. They are approximately 350 in number, representing some 175

Reprinted, by permission of the American Dialect Society, from *Publication of the American Dialect Society*, No. 27, 3–15 (April, 1957). Professor Marckwardt's accompanying maps originally were for only the North Central area. For greater significance to the reader the editor of the Readings has taken the liberty of extending the coverage by extending the isoglosses into the Upper Midwest region.
[1] Hans Kurath, *A Word Geography of the Eastern United States* (Ann Arbor, 1949).

communities in the six states and the portion of Ontario indicated on Map 2 and those which follow. Preliminary chartings made soon after the beginning of the project indicated that in general the principal boundary between the Northern and Midland speech types would continue westward in such a way that most of Indiana would be included within the Midland area, but that the upper third of Ohio and Illinois would be Northern.[2] All subsequent studies, notably those by Davis[3] and Potter,[4] and numerous incidental observations by McDavid have confirmed this early prognostication.

Now, with virtually all the material necessary for the atlas in hand, it is time to subject this early conclusion to a somewhat more detailed scrutiny and to begin to outline the minor or subsidiary dialect areas on the basis of more complete evidence than Davis had at his disposal. Since the boundaries which Kurath drew between his areas 10 and 11, and between 11 and 12, as they are presented on Map 1, lead directly into the North-Central region, this naturally raises the question as to how they are to be projected. The present study is at least a beginning of an examination of these questions.

Maps 2 and 3 serve to reaffirm the major boundary between the Northern and Midland areas. Map 2 in particular reflects the kind of isogloss that has generally been employed to establish this line: namely, the northernmost extension of typical Midland features. The isoglosses of the four items here represented all have several common characteristics. Three of the four go around the Western Reserve, and even the fourth, though penetrating the Reserve proper, dips below the adjacent Fire Lands. All four cut across the northwestern corner of Ohio, the transition area studied in detail by Potter. Most of Indiana falls below these isoglosses; in one instance, virtually all of it. In three of the four cases, the Illinois boundary terminates in Henderson County, just across the Mississippi River from Burlington, Iowa.

Less frequently have the southern limits of distinctly Northern terms been employed to establish the Northern-Midland boundary. Four of these are indicated on Map 3. It will readily be observed that some of these are somewhat to the south of those items charted on Map 2, the net effect being to create a transition belt, varying in its width but particularly broad in Indiana and the adjacent portions of Illinois and Ohio. In one instance, that of *stone boat,* there is an additional speech island along the Mississippi, opposite St. Louis.

[2] Hans Kurath, "Dialect Areas, Settlement Areas. and Culture Areas in the United States," in *The Cultural Approach to History,* ed. Caroline F. Ware (New York, 1940).
[3] Alva L. Davis, "A word atlas of the Great Lakes region," unpubl. diss. (University of Michigan, 1948).
[4] Edward E. Potter, "The dialect of northwestern Ohio: a study of a transition area," unpubl. diss. (University of Michigan, 1955).

Map 1. SPEECH AREAS OF THE EASTERN UNITED STATES
(According to Kurath)

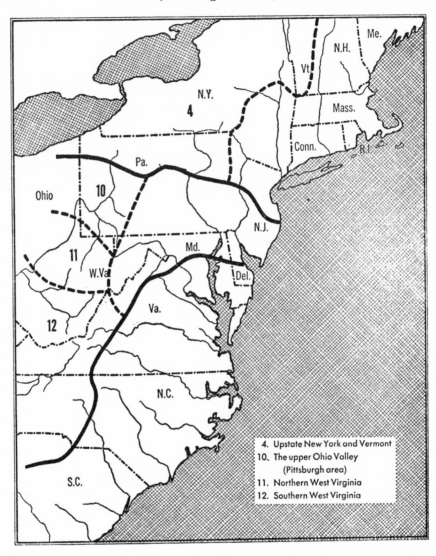

4. Upstate New York and Vermont
10. The upper Ohio Valley
    (Pittsburgh area)
11. Northern West Virginia
12. Southern West Virginia

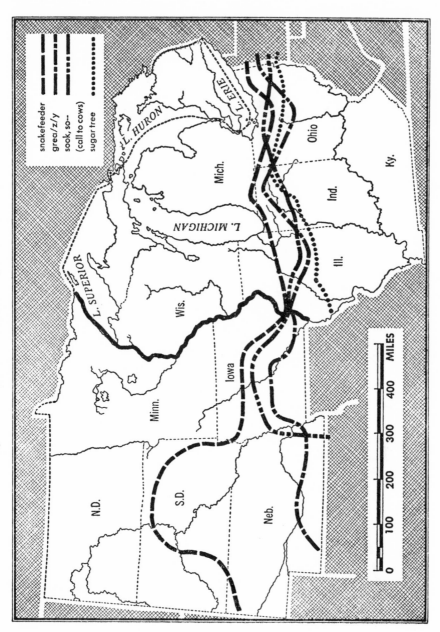

Map 2. MIDLAND TERMS—NORTHERN LIMIT

Map 3. NORTHERN TERMS—SOUTHERN LIMIT

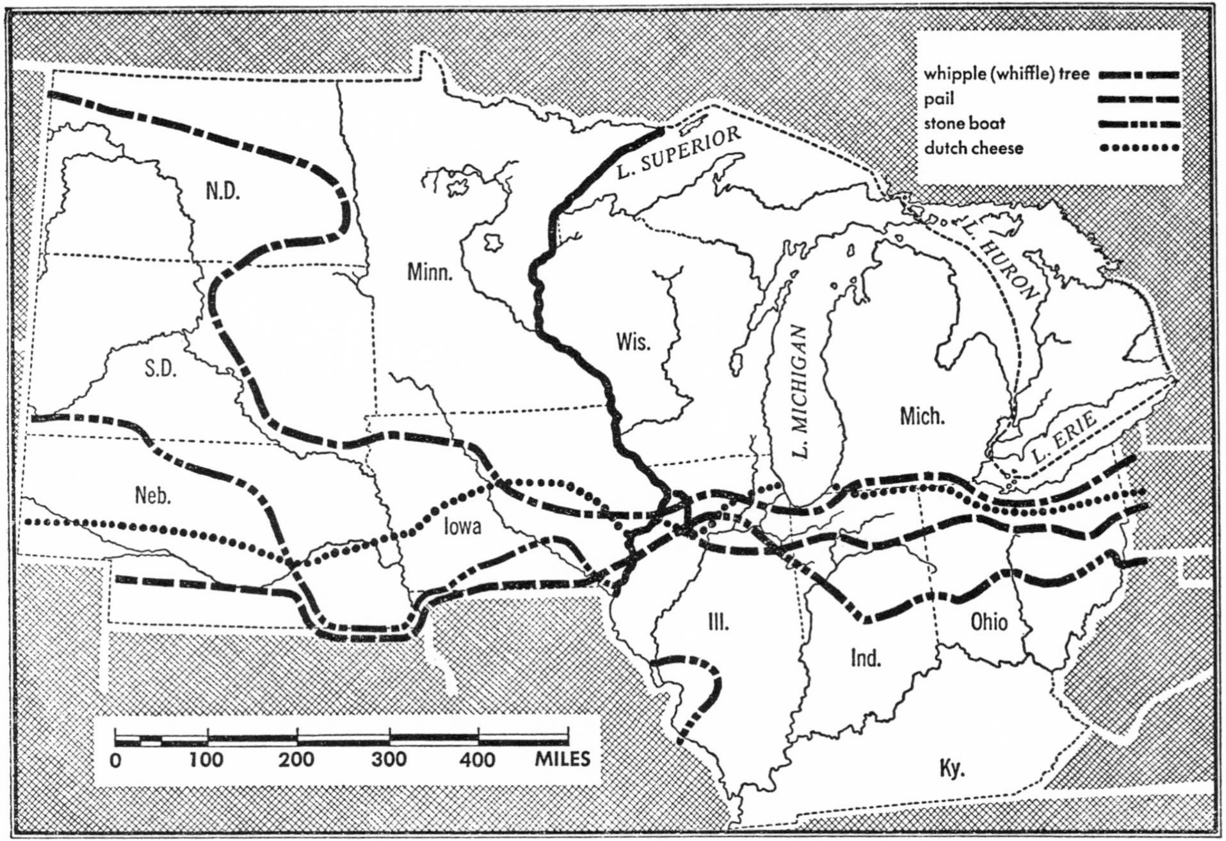

whipple (whiffle) tree
pail
stone boat
dutch cheese

L. HURON

L. ERIE

Ohio

Ky.

Mich.

Ind.

L. MICHIGAN

L. SUPERIOR

Ill.

Wis.

Minn.

Iowa

N.D.

S.D.

Neb.

MILES

0   100   200   300   400

What we see indicated here is symptomatic of the overlapping spread in the North-Central territory of a number of individual items which maintain a well-defined regional distribution to the east. For example, Kurath's *Word Geography* shows a clear-cut line of demarcation between *sweet corn* and *roasting ear*, following the general direction of the isoglosses separating the North and the Midland.[5] In the North-Central territory, *sweet corn*, though concentrated in the North, is found throughout the area. No state is without an instance of it, and even as far south as Kentucky there were seven occurrences. *Roasting ear* has a complementary distribution, heavy in the south but thinning out as one goes northward. It was not recorded in Ontario, only twice in Wisconsin and once in the Upper Peninsula of Michigan, but it turned up no less than thirteen times in the Michigan Lower Peninsula. Although space does not permit the presentation of additional examples, we now know that many items, between which the line of cleavage was sharp in the East, have invaded each other's territories in the North-Central states, resulting in broad belts of multiple usage. The nature of these items, their general cultural patterning, the extent to which they may have developed distinctions in meaning, are all matters for future investigation.

We shall find it convenient to consider next certain of the features whose boundaries in the Eastern United States generally follow the line separating the eleventh and twelfth of Kurath's divisions. Map 4 shows four of these; one is the southern limit of a Northern and North Midland term, *hay mow*. The remaining three isoglosses represent the northern limits of South Midland features. In general the lines follow the Ohio River. On occasion they veer upward, but rarely do they penetrate north of the line of the Old National Road, which connected Wheeling, Columbus, Indianapolis, Vandalia, and St. Louis.

Judging from the general configuration of these isoglosses, we are led to the conclusion that the New England speech island consisting of the area around Marietta, namely the Ohio Company lands, offered an initial obstacle to the introduction of South Midland features. The dips in two of the isoglosses reflect this, and in them there are no significant bulges to the north until they cross Indiana and Illinois. The remaining two items apparently did gain acceptance in the Marietta area, but their spread north of that was prevented by the prior establishment of terms current in Pennsylvania. Nevertheless, they did spread north as far as the line of the Old National Road. At all events, these extensions of the boundary between what Kurath calls the Northern and Southern West Virginia areas do present a fairly clear-cut picture, one which is repeated in other items which have not been charted here.

Much less predictable is the behavior of the features which constitute

[5] Kurath, *Word Geography*, Figure 41.

the boundary between the tenth and eleventh of Kurath's subdivisions. A glance at Map 5 will indicate that their behavior is not such as to warrant any general conclusion. The isogloss of *nicker,* though entering Ohio just a little north of Wheeling, quickly rises toward the Western Reserve and follows generally the major boundary between the Northern and Midland speech areas. In addition, we find the term current in the Galena Lead Region, which though mixed in settlement history was originally developed by a Kentuckian. The northern limit of *gutters* follows the Old National Road in Ohio, but upon reaching Indiana again jumps northward almost to the principal Northern-Midland boundary. *Dogbit* as a participial form behaves in a decidedly different fashion. Though not charted by Kurath, this item does appear in Atwood's analysis of verb forms in the Eastern United States.[6] He shows it to be current throughout all of West Virginia and extending into Pennsylvania up to the Monongahela. This isogloss, after following the Old National Road two-thirds of the way across Ohio, suddenly dips toward the Ohio River, and in fact veers considerably below it over a large part of Kentucky.

This raises a question. How are we to account for the erratic behavior of these items? Any explanation undoubtedly can be little more than conjectural, but up to the present there is little ground even for conjecture. It is true, of course, that between the Old National Road and the principal dialect boundary separating the Northern and Midland areas there were no natural barriers, no important pathways of communication and travel, nor patterns of settlement which might have helped to create a second east-west line continuing the division between the tenth and eleventh of Kurath's areas. Moreover, a glance at the last map in the series will suggest that whatever items current in the area between the Monongahela and the Kanawha might have entered Ohio at this point, they would have been in competition with the northern features of the Western Reserve and the Ohio Company lands and also with the Southern or extreme South-Midland features of the Virginia Military District. Consequently, a deflection of these isoglosses either upward or downward is not too surprising.

More important still, perhaps, is the fact that features of the language spreading westward from the West Virginia panhandle and along the Monongahela were thrown into competition with others current throughout Pennsylvania, which were also penetrating the Ohio territory. The general path of this penetration is shown on Map 6. *Spouting,* as the term for gutters or eavestroughs, is now found in a band running all the way across central Ohio, crossing slightly into Indiana. *Run,* as the term for a small stream tributary, covers somewhat more territory, with one point heading into southeastern Michigan as well. Serenade, as an alternate for *belling, horning,* or *chivaree,* has an even larger radius; it does not go quite as far

---

[6] E. Bagby Atwood, *A Survey of Verb Forms in the Eastern United States* (Ann Arbor, 1953), Figure 3.

Map 4. **EXTENSION OF BOUNDARIES BETWEEN AREAS 11 AND 12**

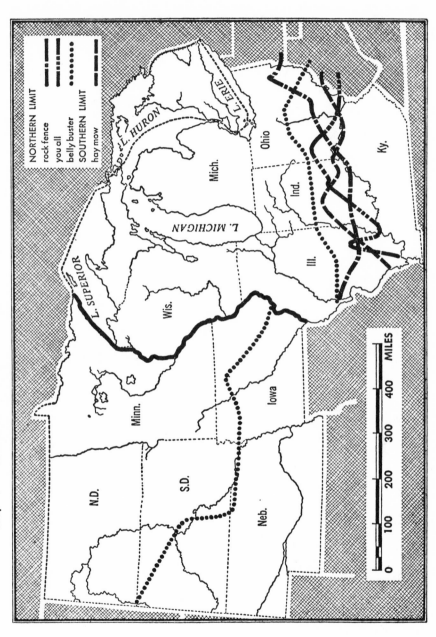

Map 5. EXTENSION OF BOUNDARIES BETWEEN AREAS 10 AND 11

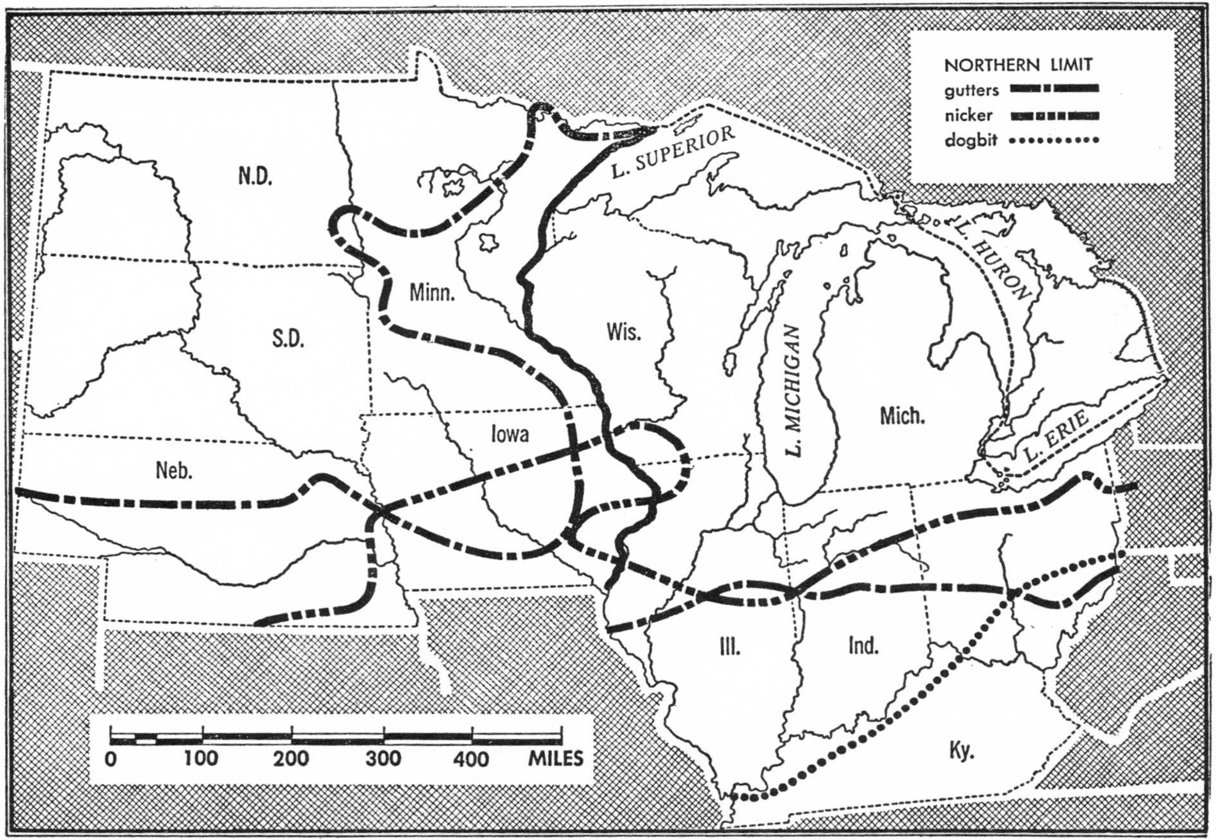

Map 6. **WESTWARD EXPANSION FROM PENNSYLVANIA AND WEST VIRGINIA**

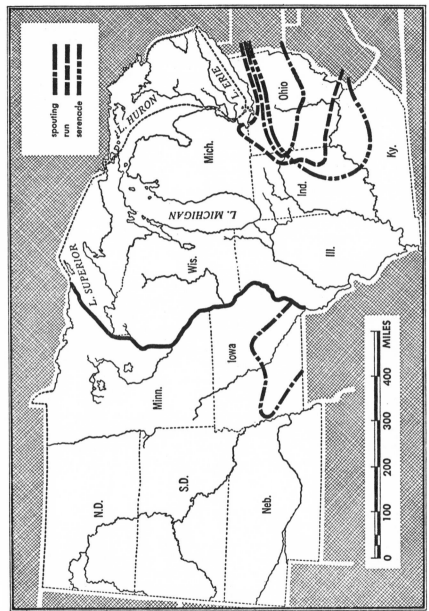

north as the others but includes the Kentucky bluegrass and part of the hill country. *Fishing worm,* not shown on the map, is more extensive in its coverage than any of those charted.

This points to the fact that in the North-Central area we must reckon with three major population movements and corresponding transmissions of speech features. Heretofore much of our thinking has been primarily in terms of two: the migration from New York and New England into the northern part of the territory, and that from Virginia and the Carolinas into Kentucky and then northward across the Ohio River into southern Ohio and Illinois and most of Indiana. In fact, the census figures for 1870 do explain very satisfactorily the predominance of Northern items in Michigan and Wisconsin, of Midland terms in Indiana, and the division between Northern and Midland in Ohio and Illinois. Convincing and helpful as all of this is, as far as explaining the Hoosier apex is concerned, it does not take into account the migration from Pennsylvania as a third factor, which suggests an historical reason for what may be called an Ohio wedge.

This brief account does not exhaust the possibilities of subsidiary dialect areas which a further examination of our records will enable us to chart. The Northern items entering the area were not all of one piece, and we may confidently expect to find belts or islands in which coastal New England terms are current. We have seen that with respect to at least one feature, the Galena Lead Region constitutes a distinct island. There are others as well, and indeed I am confident that we shall find the movement of settlers up and down the Mississippi River reflected in the distribution of a number of items.

Thus far our analyses do seem to verify the existence of a bundle of isoglosses cutting through our three central states in an apical line, thus constituting the principal dialect boundary between Northern and Midland speech. In general these isoglosses form a relatively broad band, and in many instances they must be interpreted as representing the limits of areas of concentration rather than of actual occurrence. For many terms there is considerable spreading throughout much of the area.

Another band, bounded on the north by the Old National Road and on the south by the Ohio River, constitutes a second transition belt, north of which Southern and South-Midland features fail to penetrate. A third group of South-Midland items, entering the area slightly to the north have failed to establish a well-defined boundary of their own but have either spread as far as the Northern-Midland boundary or have been squeezed behind the subsidiary belt to the south. Finally, a wedge-like intrusion of Pennsylvania terms into and across Ohio has immensely complicated the dialect picture in the latter state.

At this point it is clear that we are dealing with a challenging and highly complex dialect situation: one which will require our drawing upon every available facet of cultural and settlement history to give it meaning and to make it understandable.

24

The Primary Dialect Areas of the Upper Midwest

HAROLD B. ALLEN

IN 1949 HANS KURATH, drawing upon the materials of the three Atlantic coast atlases for his *Word Geography of the Eastern United States*, made obsolete the traditional tripartite division of American English into Eastern, Southern, and General American. Four years later his overwhelming lexical evidence for the existence of what is now called the Midland dialect between the Northern and the Southern areas was supplemented by E. Bagby Atwood's *Verb Forms of the Eastern United States* with its showing that many non-standard forms are distributed according to the dialect divisions outlined in Kurath's study.

By implication both works raised the question: How far do the principal Atlantic coast dialect boundaries extend west of the Appalachians? For the immediately contiguous area in the northern part of the country an answer has now appeared in a preliminary review of the data collected under the direction of Albert H. Marckwardt for the Linguistic Atlas of the North Central States [See pp. 220–30]. These data suggest that the principal dialect areas in the North Central states are reflexes of the Midland—Northern areas along the Atlantic coast. The major bundle of Midland—Northern isoglosses stretches west to the Mississippi so that roughly the northern third of Ohio, the northern fourth of Indiana, and the northern third of Illinois lie north of the bundle, that is, in a territory settled largely by people who had moved westward from the Northern speech areas of northern Pennsylvania, New York state, and western New England. South of the bundle lies derivative Midland and South Midland speech territory.

The recent completion of fieldwork for the Linguistic Atlas of the Upper Midwest now makes possible for the first time a definitive demonstration of the Midland-Northern relationship in the region immediately west of the North Central states. It is the function of this paper to delineate that rela-

Reprinted, by permission of the English Language Institute of the University of Michigan, from the Festschrift for Charles C. Fries due for publication in 1963.

tionship rather than to establish a correlation between dialect patterns and population history, but a brief covering statement may provide a framework for the language information.

Settlement in the five states designated as the Upper Midwest—Minnesota, Iowa, North and South Dakota, and Nebraska[1]—began with the first inrush of English-speaking families shortly before the Civil War. Into northern Iowa and southeastern Minnesota came settlers from western New England and New York state and from their secondary settlements in Ohio, Michigan and northern Illinois, and even Wisconsin. Into central and southern Iowa—but with a large overflow into Minnesota—came settlers from the mid-Atlantic area, principally Pennsylvania, and from the derivative settlements in Ohio, Indiana, and Illinois. And also into southern Iowa came a third group, smaller but distinctive, with its source in the earlier movement westward through the Cumberland gap into Kentucky and thence into southern Indiana and southern Illinois. Gradually, though with waves roughly corresponding to economic cycles, population spread after the Civil War into western and northern Minnesota, the Dakotas, and Nebraska, reaching some parts of the extreme western sections as late as 1910[2]. This later spreading was caused by an influx of newcomers having the same three origins, by a second westward move on the part of families who already had settled in Minnesota or Iowa, and to a very large measure by the massive advent of thousands of immigrants directly from non-English-speaking countries in western and, later, in eastern Europe. For all these except the last, the following delineation of the principal Upper Midwest dialect divisions will permit reasonable inferences about the population distribution even though fully detailed treatment of the settlement history must await the future publication of the Upper Midwest Atlas. That in this area such inferences can be drawn safely without regard for any influence of the non-English-speaking immigrants has already been ascertained.[3]

Evidence for the dialect divisions described here is almost entirely that provided in the field records of 206 informants interviewed by fieldworkers between 1947 and 1956. Of this number, 102 are classed as Type I (older and uneducated or old-fashioned), 88 as Type II (middle-aged with high school education), and 16 as Type III (younger with college education). Except for about twenty-five additions the questionnaire used is essentially that of the short worksheets of the New England Atlas and of the worksheets of the North Central Atlas. The additions were of some general items

---

[1] These states have an area of 365,297 square miles and, in the 1950 census, a population of 7,931,298.

[2] The region adjacent to the extreme western boundary between the Dakotas had no significant permanent settlement, for example, until the Milwaukee railroad extended its line west to the Pacific coast in the late 1900's. Previously, of course, a sparse handful of cattle ranchers had occupied the region for three or four decades.

[3] Support for this statement was offered by the writer in a paper, "The validity of the use of informants with non-English-speaking parentage," read before the Linguistic Society of America in Chicago, December 29, 1955.

thought to be productive, such as *slick* and *boulevard,* and of other items intended to probe lexical differences in the vocabulary of the cattle-country west of the Missouri river. Besides the general body of data there is available a supplementary resource in the marking of 136 lexical items on checklists returned by 1064 mail informants in the five states. For these particular 136 items, therefore, there actually is evidence from 1270 informants. Although it is statistically unsound to add the returns from the two groups together in light of the lower validity of the mailed responses, the latter often turn out to have a strong confirming value.

Even though full analysis of the data is only now under way, the preliminary analysis of replies to more than 125 items in the full questionnaire offers clear evidence for the establishment of the primary isogloss patterns shown on the accompanying map. Replies to some two dozen others indicate a gradual dialect variation corresponding to these primary divisions, one so gradual that it can more effectively be shown by percentage comparisons. By "primary" is meant "reflecting Midland-Northern differentiation as carried west by population movement." Secondary patterns, those reflecting ecological, commercial, or other influences peculiar to the Upper Midwest, will be treated in another article for publication elsewhere.

Of the primary patterns revealing Midland-Northern differentiation the major isogloss bundle is shown on the map by the 1 - 1 line, with certain deviations represented by the a - 1 line. (All references to the symbols on the map will read from right to left in conformity with population movement).

The 1 - 1 boundary represents generally the northern limit of the following lexical items: *rick, scum* (of ice), *fire dogs, bucket* (of metal), *slop* (-*pail* or -*bucket*), *coal oil, nicker, piece* (a distance), *piece* (a lunch), (*died*) *with, slick* (of a pavement), and *taw* of *taw-line.* Of these items *fire dogs, bucket, slop-, coal oil, nicker, piece* (distance), and *piece* (lunch) are shown in the *Word Geography (WG)* as typical Midland or South Midland forms. Inferentially, the other items may be considered as having at least a typical Midland distribution pattern in the Upper Midwest, although *slick* cannot be checked with materials of the other atlases since it is one of the added items.

Phonological matters occurring largely in this Midland area are |mɪnɪz| *minnows,* [ɛ] in *since,* and [k] in *spigot.*

The a - 1 boundary, which presumably indicates the presence of a strong Northern population element in the Iowa triangle set off by Davenport, Cedar Rapids, and Dubuque, is the northern limit for Midland *draw* 'shallow valley,' *light bread, snake feeder,* and *belly-buster,* as well as for the non-standard morphological item *clum,* the preterit of *climb.* Of these *light bread, snake-feeder,* and *belly-buster* are attested as Midland in the *WG;* and *clum* is similarly classified by Atwood.

The 1 - 1 boundary is also the southern limit in the Upper Midwest for the common slough [slu] 'swamp,' *griddle cake,* and the infrequent *quite* (*cold*), and for the phonological items [ɑn] *on* stressed, [ɛ] in *scarce,* [ɔ] in *caught,* [hj] in *humor,* and [ɑ] in *nothing.* Of these *griddle cake* is dominantly Northern in the *WG,* and [ɑ] for *o* is revealed as Northern (though not eastern New England) in the Linguistic Atlas of New England and in an unpublished summary by Atwood.

The a - 1 boundary appears as the southern limit of Northern lexical features such as *devil's darning-needle* 'dragonfly' and *belly-flop,* but of no phonological items. Both of these are of frequent occurrence despite competition with a considerable number of other Northern regionalisms.

Study of the lesser areas within the principal Midland zone reveals at least three isogloss bundles which may represent successive waves of Northern and Midland population, although the first bundle may well indicate also the extension of South Midland features into this area.

The Midland lesser area included within a - 1 - b or 1 - b, southern Iowa, is marked by the occurrence of *spouting* 'eavestrough,' *branch* 'stream,' *dogbit, pullybone* 'wishbone,' *sook!* 'call to cows,' *corn*)*pone, sick in* and *sick on* (*one's stomach, drying cloth, -towel,* or *-rag* 'dishtowel,' *french harp* 'harmonica,' and *rack* 'sawbuck,' within the lexical evidence, and by fronted beginning of the [au] diphthong as in [kæu] *cow* and by the [e] in *Mary,* within the phonological evidence. South Midland origins are likely for the infrequent *dogbit* and *pullybone;* the others presumably are Midland.

The second Midland lesser area includes southern Iowa and the eastern half of Nebraska below the isogloss line 1 - c. Like the first lesser area, it is marked by the appearance of exclusively Midland forms, although the boundary marks also the southern extension of two Northern pronunciation features. Lexical inclusions are *weather-boarding, barn*)*lot, plumb across, fice*(*t* 'small dog,' [pui] and [hoi] as calls to pigs,*chickie!, clabber cheese* and *smearcase, barn owl, polecat,* and *babycab.* Phonological matters include [rɛnts] for *rinse,* [kæg] *keg, tushes* for *tusks.* [ʌ] in *rather,* and [u] in *Cooper.* At the same time the 1 - c bundle includes one isophone and one isomorph limiting two expanding Northern forms, [æ] in *married* and *dove* as the preterit of *dive. Dove,* incidentally, is significantly dominant with all types of speakers despite repeated pedagogical injunctions against it.

The third Midland lesser area, 1 - d, includes the southern two-thirds of Iowa and all of Nebraska. Its main lexical features are *till* (in time expressions), *blinds, dust up* (a room), *comfort* 'bedcovering,' *pallet, paving* 'rural concrete highway,' *dip* 'sauce for pudding,' *hull* (of a walnut), *butter beans, snake-feeder,* and *sick at* (*one's stomach*). *Sick at,* which competes with two other Midland regionalisms, interestingly enough is often listed in textbooks as standard in contrast to the dominant Northern form *sick to.* A conspicuous non-standard phonological characteristic in this area is the excrescent [-t] on *trough* and *eavestrough.*

At the same time the 1 - d bundle serves to set off a fourth area between 1 - d and 1 - 1, southwestern South Dakota, in which is found the maximum extension of a few Northern forms, *parlor match, haycock,* and *tarvy* or *tarvia* for a macadamized road. Of these only *parlor match* was reported as used in Iowa. The *tarvy* item may require further study, as its incidence could be related to variables not related to population distribution.

Although detailed investigation of the Type distribution of each of the terms in these three lesser areas would be needed before accurate classification of each as expanding or receding, a reasonable inference would seem to be that, in general, Midland forms limited to these areas are receding or at least checked and that Northern forms found here are expanding.

The converse, then, may with equal reason be inferred with respect to the Midland and Northern forms whose distribution is marked by the isogloss bundles setting off the lesser areas north of the main dialect boundary, 1 - 1. There appear to be four such lesser isogloss bundles, 1 - e, 1 - f, 1 - g, and 1 - h, designating the limits of expanding Midland or checked or receding Northern forms.

Isogloss bundle 1 - e, for example, clearly represents the northern limits of the Midland *armload* and seed (as in both *cherry-seed* and *peach-seed)*, which are found in nearly all of South Dakota. They compete with Northern *armful* and *stone.* On the other hand, it appears to represent also the limit of the rather infrequent Northern expression *pothole.* This last term was not recorded in Minnesota or Iowa during fieldwork, but checklist returns show a spotty frequency in Minnesota in addition to the recorded uses in North Dakota.

Similarly, the boundary 1 - f is chiefly comprised of isoglosses showing the northern expansion of Midland terms. Here in northwestern South Dakota and western North Dakota the Midland *hayshock* and *haydoodle* have successfully competed with the receding Northern *haycock.* Midland *mouth harp* likewise is found here as far north as the Canadian border; so are Midland *bottoms* or *bottomland, roasting-ears, firebug* (firefly), and the locution *want off/in.* Only one apparently Northern word has so far been found to be limited by 1 - f, *boulevard.* This term was not included in any eastern atlas study, so that no comparative data are available except some isolated occurrences reported in private correspondence from northern and central Ohio. However, in the sense 'strip of grass between sidewalk and street,' this term patterns exactly like a typical Northern word, and strong confirmation of this patterning is found in the responses on the checklists.

Although the line 1 - e,g, setting off the eastern Dakotas, does indicate the full northern expansion of several Midland terms, it largely denotes the limited western extension of Northern forms which probably are receding or checked. Midland forms which have spread widely, if sparsely, as far as Canada are: *evening* 'time before supper,' *cling peach, took sick, come back* and *come back again,* and *the baby) crawls.* Northern words rarely found beyond this boundary are *the wind) is calming (down* (mostly in Minnesota), *curtains* (on rollers), *red up* and *rid up, whipple-* or *whiffletree, cluck(hen* 'brooding hen,' *fried cakes* 'doughnuts,' and *skip school.* Even in the North Central states the Midland *singletree* was unaccountably well on its way to supplant *whippletree* before the advent of the tractor. The Northern term now appears on the road to obsolescence. In addition several Northern pronunciation items are seldom recorded beyond this boundary: [ɑ] in *fog* and *foggy,* [gul] *goal,* [draut] 'drouth,' [sut] *soot,* and [bɑrəl] *'barrel.'* The last three of these apparently are old-fashioned, used almost exclusively by Type I speakers. The receding and infrequent Northern [klɪm], non-standard preterit of *climb,* also occurs only within this lesser area. [ɑ] in *fog,* it is curious, is obviously receding while the [ɑ] in stressed *on,* contrariwise, is expanding with vigor.

Boundary 1 - e,h, enclosing principally northern Iowa and southern Minnesota with a small margin of South Dakota, chiefly sets off the extreme extension of receding Northern forms. Among them appear to be *spider* 'frying pan,' *fills* or *thills, brook* 'fishing stream' (only in Minnesota), *feeding time,* [ho] 'call to a horse,' [kə'de] 'call to sheep,' *lobbered milk,* and *sugar bush.* Also apparently receding Northern forms are the pronunciations with [θs] or [ðs] in *troughs* and *eavestroughs* and [e] in *dairy,* and the morphological feature *see* as the preterit of *see.* This limited area also represents a last-ditch stand against at least two Midland forms which have spread throughout the rest of the Upper Midwest, possibly because of reinforcement by Midland population influx through Duluth. One is *rock,* as in *He threw a rock at the dog;* the other is *bawl,* to describe the noise made by a cow.

The regional patterns which have been outlined above are slightly complicated by the presence of at least one enclave and perhaps another. The area marked X on the map contains a number of Northern forms not reported generally in southern Iowa or elsewhere in Nebraska. Its existence probably is to be correlated with the migration of a number of New York and Ohio families into the eastern Platte river valley after the Civil War. Within or marginal to this enclave, for example, both parents of each of two informants came from New York and the mother of another was born there. One informant reported both parents born in Ohio; another reported his mother's birthplace in that state. Besides, one informant's father came from Illinois and both parents of another came from Wisconsin. All other informants are of foreign-born parentage. Among the hence presumably Northern forms which appear in the Platte river valley are *parlor match, haycock,* [ho], [kə'de], *fried cake, boulevard,* and *quite (cold),* in addition to the pronunciations [ɑ] in *fog* and *foggy,* [ɔ] in *caught,* and [hj] in *humor.*

The putative second enclave is designated by Y on the map. It includes Duluth, Minnesota, and the communities along the Mesabi iron range. Considerable investigation is called for by the appearance in this area of a number of Midland forms. Although no one informant has consistent Midland speech (not one of them has a Midland background), the frequency with which Midland items occur points to a possible Midland influence because of the contacts between Duluth, a major port, and the Lake Erie ports of Sandusky, Cleveland, and Erie, which are not far from the Midland territory of southern Ohio and Pennsylvania. Lexical items with usual Midland distribution which turn up in this enclave are *cling* (*peach, blinds, lot, bucket* (of metal), *spigot* 'faucet,' *bag* (of cloth), *armload, coalbucket, bawl, chickie!, dip* 'sauce,' *hull* (of walnut), *butter bean, come back again, died with,* and *took sick.* Phonological forms recorded here include [e] in *chair* and *Mary,* [u] in *spoons,* [ɔ] in *on,* [u] in Cooper, and [wo] 'call to horse.'

But the description of the Midland-Northern differentiation in the Upper Midwest is by no means complete in terms of isogloss boundaries. As the existence of the various "lesser areas" reveals, a number of Northern terms have been recorded in various parts of that principal Midland-speaking territory which is set off by the main isogloss bundle 1 - 1; and, correspondingly, a number of Midland terms have been recorded north of that bundle. Clearly the Midland-Northern distinction becomes less sharp as the dialect boundary is followed westward. The distinction is clearest in Iowa; it has so far broken down in South Dakota that that state might as well be designated a transition area. Actually the degree of the breakdown is much greater than the map would suggest, for the diffusion of many a dialect feature is so gradual that an isogloss can not be drawn for it. Rather, recourse must be had to percentage of frequency.

For nearly all forms already cited the distribution patterns are so clear that isoglosses may be drawn with some certainty. For example, a quick glance at a map bearing symbols marking the occurrence of *comfort, comforter,* and *comfortable* is adequate for one to be able to draw the isogloss of *comfort,* which is clearly limited to the Midland 1 - d area. To establish its distribution pattern there is no need to resort to a study of the percentages. The statistics merely confirm the obvious. How percentages are related to a clear pattern may be seen in the figures for *comfort:*

$$
\begin{array}{cc}
0 & 2 \\
0 & \\
25 & 35
\end{array}
$$

This table, in which the figures are arranged so as to correspond spatially with the relative positions of the Upper Midwest states, is to be read like this: Two percent of the Minnesota field informants replying to this particular question use the lexical variant *comfort,* thirty-five percent of those in Iowa, none in either of the two Dakotas, and twenty-five per cent of those in Nebraska.

Such a table should now be compared with the following, which shows the percentage of frequency of occurrence of *poison* in the locution "Some berries are poison" (in which it contrasts with *poisonous*):

31	29.5
50	
54	39

Reference to a map bearing symbols for the occurrences of *poison* would indicate no possibility of drawing an isogloss. Even the slight differences in percentage at first appear to be insignificant, easily due to the variables that operate when informants are interviewed by different fieldworkers. But when a corresponding differential appears with item after item, and when each variation correlates consistently with the Midland -Northern contrast, then the gradation must be recognized as significant and not accidental. Examination of numerous tabulations now makes clear that, regularly, some attested Midland forms not susceptible of delimitation by isoglosses occur with greatest frequency in Iowa and Nebraska, less in South Dakota, still less in Minnesota, and, usually, least in North Dakota. Conversely, some attested Northern forms appear regularly with highest percentages in Minnesota and North Dakota, less in Iowa and South Dakota, and least in Nebraska. Since the percentages have been calculated on the artificial basis of the political boundaries, actually the figures are more significant than at first sight, for the Midland percentage for Iowa would be still higher if the informants in the Northern-speech territory of the two upper tiers of counties had been counted in Minnesota rather than in Iowa. The reverse, of course, would hold true for a Northern form, which would have a lower frequency in Iowa if the northern third had been counted in with Minnesota.

Now even though the spread in the percentages for *poison* is not great—between 29.5 and 54, the spread clearly indicates a higher rate of occurrence in Midland territory. Similar spread appears in the percentages ascertained for these words:

the sun)	*came up*	*skillet*		*paper)*	*sack*
11.5	10.5	27	49.5	70	55
27		65		85	
40.5	22	81	90	81	73

Of these, *skillet* is shown in the *WG* to be the dominant Midland term, with only a scattered handful of instances reported along Long Island sound. It would seem to be expanding with some vigor in the Upper Midwest, and the checklist replies confirm this expansion. The figure for *sack* may be questioned, but they conversely match those for *paper bag,* which appears to have a slight Northern dominance.

With the phonological items recourse to percentage analysis is particularly productive, for matters of pronunciation seem much less likely than vocabulary items to be characterized by fairly distinct regional patterns. Yet regional variation on a graduated scale appears when the statistics are examined for such as these:

[sʌt] *soot*		[æ] in razor-strap		[ɑ] in wheelbarrow	
19	25	46	37	10	22
24		48		8	
30	31	47	49	22	39

[-o] final in *wheelbarrow*		[-wain] in *genuine*		[θ] in *with milk*	
19	22	56	66	36	34
27		59		42	
30	50	62	73	41	52

[u] in root	
38	23
25	
40	46

A Midland emphasis appears also in the distribution of a few morphological items which do not have sharp isoglossal patterning. With each of these items the variation is heard from only Type I and Type II informants:

bushel (pl. after numeral)		*who-all?*		*begun* (pret.)		*drownded*	
36	40	51	57	0	6	19	19
52		57		0		43	
50	72	78	66	11	19.4	14	35

At least two lexical items exhibit Northern weighting in their distribution:

paper) bag		*warmed up*	
73	74	62.5	62.5
56		61.5	
40	58	38	28

Phonological responses revealing Northern emphasis are:

[bɑb] *wire*		[ɑ] in *harrow*		[ɪŋ] in ppls. & gerunds	
23	16	16	33	59	82
19		7		47	
11	10	6	12	48	46

Two morphological items may have Northern weighting also, the nonstandard adverbial genitive *anywheres* (contrasting with *anywhere* and *anyplace*) and the preterit *fitted:*

anywheres		*fitted*	
23	19	28.5	22
16		17	
13	11.7	8	14

Although certainly most of the Upper Midwest worksheet items classed in the eastern atlases as either Midland or Northern reveal, to some extent at least, the same correlation, there are a few for which the evidence is puzzling and will require some special investigation if not supplementary collecting. *Clean across,* for instance, is reported in the *WG* as a "regional phrase" current along the South Atlantic coast; but in the Upper Midwest it turns up only twice in Midland Iowa and Nebraska, four times in South Dakota, and five times in North Dakota. *Mosquito hawk* 'dragonfly' is reported in the *WG* only along the South Atlantic coast from southern New Jersey to South Carolina (although Raven I. McDavid, Jr., has additionally recorded a few scattered occurrences in upper New York); in the Upper Midwest this variant shows distinct Northern distribution with its seven occurrences in Minnesota and four in North Dakota but none in either Iowa or Nebraska. *Buttery,* according to Kurath, "is unknown in the Hudson Valley and in the entire Midland and South." Yet as a relic term it appears not only in Minnesota but also in the Midland speech area of Iowa and Nebraska. *Lead-horse,* according to the *WG,* is limited to Midland and South Midland areas; as a relic in the Upper Midwest it has fairly even distribution in the five states. *Fishworm* was recorded frequently in both New England and New York as well as in South Midland territory; in the Upper Midwest it is exclusively Midland. Both the field records and the checklists show that *angleworm* is the overwhelmingly dominant form in the Northern speech regions of the Upper Midwest. *Firebug* is reported in the *WG* as Pennsylvania vocabulary variant for *firefly,* with only a solitary instance in New York. But in the Upper Midwest the percentage distribution surely is not Midland:

15.4	9.5
16	
2.7	1

Furthermore, the checklist responses number 45 in Minnesota and North Dakota with only ten in Iowa and nine in Nebraska. *Raised* in "The sun raised at six o'clock" Atwood calls Middle Atlantic, but in the Upper Midwest it occurs as a rare non-standard form seven times north of the 1 - 1 boundary and only four times in Midland territory south of it.

In summary:

1. The primary Midland-Northern dialect contrast of the Atlantic coast states is maintained in the Upper Midwest.

2. The distinction is particularly clear in the eastern half of the Upper

Midwest, that is, between the lower two-thirds of Iowa and the upper third of Iowa.

3. The distinction is less clear in the western half, that is, west of the Missouri river, where splitting of the major isogloss bundle reveals several lesser dialect areas delimiting expanding or receding forms.

4. In general, Northern speech forms seem to be yielding to Midland.

    a. The principal isoglosses bend northward, even to the point of indicating a complete blocking of some Northern terms.

    b. Most of the expanding forms are Midland; most of the receding forms are Northern.

    c. Diffusion appears to be more intensive for Midland forms in Northern territory, especially in Minnesota, than for Northern forms in Midland territory, especially southern Iowa.

5. One Northern enclave occurs in Midland territory; a probable Midland enclave occurs in Northern territory.

UPPER MIDWEST MAIN DIALECT PATTERNS

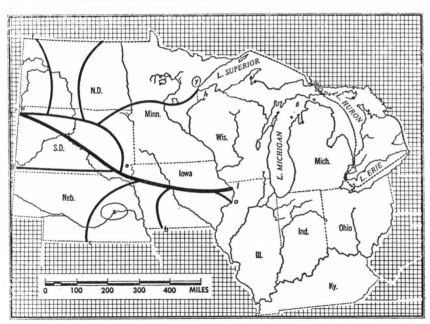

25

Grease and Greasy: A Study of Geographical Variation

E. Bagby Atwood

THE FACT THAT the verb *to grease* and the adjective *greasy* are pronounced by some Americans with [s] and by others with [z] has long been well known even to amateur observers of speech.[1] It has also been pretty well accepted that the incidence of [s] or [z] in the words in question is primarily dependent on the geographical location of the speaker rather than on his social or educational level—that [s] is, in general, "Northern," [z] "Southern."

As early as 1896, George Hempl published a study[2] of these two words, based on a rather widely circulated written questionnaire. His returns enabled him to divide the country into four major areas, according to the percentages of [s] in *to grease* and *greasy* respectively. The "North"[3]—ex-

Reprinted with permission from the University of Texas *Studies in English,* 29.249–260 (1950). Before his death in October, 1963, the author was Professor of English at the University of Texas and head of the Texas dialect project.

[1] Webster's *New International Dictionary* states that [z] in *grease* is found "esp. Brit. and Southern U.S."; [z] in *greasy* is "perhaps more general in England and the southern U.S. than in the North and East." Kenyon and Knott, *Pronouncing Dictionary* (Springfield, Mass., 1944), give [s] and [z] for the country as a whole, only [z] for the South. *The Century, Funk and Wagnalls New Standard,* and the *American College Dictionary* merely give [s] or [z] for both words. Kenyon and Knott state that "['grizɪ] and [tə griz] are phonetically normal; ['grisɪ] and [tə gris] imitate the noun *grease* [gris]." Certainly many verbs since Middle English times have been distinguished from the corresponding nouns by voicing the final fricative; cf. *house: to house, proof: to prove, wreath: to wreathe, abuse: to abuse*—and with vowel change) *bath: to bathe, breath: to breathe, grass: to graze,* etc. This paper will not be concerned with the origin or history of the feature.
The pronunciation of the vowels is of no significance in our study. For convenience I am using the symbol [i] for both the stressed and the unstressed vowels in *greasy.*

[2] *"Grease* and *Greasy," Dialect Notes,* I (1896), 438–44.

[3] In addition to New England, this area includes New Brunswick, Quebec, Ontario, New York, Michigan, Wisconsin, North Dakota, South Dakota, Minnesota, and the northern portions of Pennsylvania, Ohio, Indiana, Illinois, and Iowa.

tending from New England to the Dakotas—showed 88 and 82 per cent of [s] pronunciations; the "Midland," comprising a fairly narrow strip extending from New York City to St. Louis,[4] 42 and 34 per cent; the "South,"[5] 12 and 12 per cent; and the "West"—an ever-widening area extending westward from St. Louis—56 and 47 per cent. The material which Hempl was able to collect was admittedly "insufficient";[6] moreover, he had no means of selecting strictly representative informants;[7] and the answers may not always have been correct, since, it seems to me, an understanding of the questions would have required a certain degree of linguistic sophistication.[8] Still, in spite of these handicaps, Hempl's study has not been greatly improved upon by later writers. Most authorities content themselves by stating that [z] in *to grease* and *greasy* is predominantly Southern, and that either [s] or [z] may occur elsewhere.[9] Few investigators have gathered material that would enable them to draw clearer lines between [s] and [z] than Hempl was able to do.[10]

The field records that have been gathered for the *Linguistic Atlas of the*

[4] This includes New York City, New Jersey, Delaware, the District of Columbia, southern Pennsylvania, southern Ohio, northern West Virginia, middle Indiana, middle Illinois, and St. Louis, Missouri.

[5] This includes everything to the south of the Midland, as far west as Texas.

[6] *Op. cit.,* p. 438.

[7] For example, he urged his colleagues, especially "teachers of English in colleges, normal schools, and young ladies' seminaries" to use the questions as an exercise in English. (*Ibid.,* p. 444.)

[8] Question 45 reads: "In which (if any) of the following does *s* have the sound of *z: 'the grease,' 'to grease,' 'greasy'?*" (Hempl, "American Speech Maps," *Dialect Notes,* I [1896], 317.) Judging from my experience in teaching phonetic transcription to college seniors and graduate students, a considerable proportion of a class would simply not know whether [s] or [z] was used in such words; certainly many students unhesitatingly write [s] in words like *rose* and *has* simply because the *letter s* is used in standard spelling.

[9] See footnote I. It is sometimes pointed out that the same speaker may use both ['grisi] and ['grizi] with a distinction in meaning. This point will be discussed below.

[10] A. H. Marckwardt was able to draw a fairly clear line through Ohio, Indiana, and Illinois, though on the basis of relatively little data. See "Folk Speech in Indiana and Adjacent States," *Indiana History Bulletin,* XVII (1940), 120–140. Henry L. Smith has long been using the word *greasy* as a test word in his demonstrations of regional variation and to determine the origins of speakers, though he has not published his material. I presume that Dr. Smith's observations are the source of Mario Pei's statement: " 'greazy' . . . would place the speaker south of Philadelphia, while "greassy" would place him north of Trenton." (*The Story of Language* [Philadelphia and New York, 1949], p. 51.) C. K. Thomas considers the word *greasy* in his survey of the regional speech types, but comes to the strange conclusion that "the choice between [s] and [z] in words like *discern, desolate, absorb, absurd,* and *greasy* seems to be more personal than regional." (*An Introduction to the Phonetics of American English* [New York, 1947], p. 154.) G. P. Krapp is likewise at fault when he states that, in *greasy,* "popular usage and, in general, standard speech have only the form with [z]." (*The Pronunciation of Standard English in America* [New York, 1919], p. 119.)

United States and Canada[11] provide us with an excellent basis for delimiting the geographical and social spread of speech forms in the eastern United States. A number of features of the *Atlas* methodology[12] are conducive to an accurate picture of native and normal speech. The informants, though relatively few,[13] were carefully chosen, each being both native to and representative of his community. The answers to questions were elicited, so far as possible, in a conversational atmosphere, and thus the occurrence of ungenuine forms was minimized. Finally, the forms were recorded by trained phoneticians, who would be very unlikely to make such errors as to write [s] when the informant actually uttered [z].

A few words should be said regarding the cartographical representation of linguistic atlas data. In such works as the *Atlas Linguistique de la France*,[14] in which each community, or "point" on the map, is represented by a single speaker, it is usually possible to draw lines, or *isoglosses,* separating those communities where a form occurs from those where it does not occur. Often these isoglosses set off a large block of "points," forming a solid area—as, for example, the southern French territory marked by initial [k] in the word *chandelle.*[15] A more complex presentation is sometimes required, as in the case of the northern French occurrences of [k] in this same word: after setting off our solid area we find outside it a number of scattered communities where the feature in question occurs; these must be indicated by additional lines encircling the "points" where the form is found.[16] In still other cases, the communities where a given speech form occurs (for example, *conin* for 'rabbit') are so scattered that it is impossible to connect them; in such cases our isoglosses must consist merely of scattered circles here and there on the map.[17] When this situation obtains we would probably do better to assign a symbol (say, a cross, a dot, or a triangle) to the scattered form in question, lest the labyrinth of lines becomes too much for the reader to cope with.

Now, in presenting data from the American *Atlas,* we are faced with all

[11] The New England materials have been published as the *Linguistic Atlas of New England,* ed. Hans Kurath and Bernard Bloch, 3 vols. (Providence, R.I., 1939–43). Field records for most of the Middle Atlantic and South Atlantic states were gathered by the late Guy S. Lowman; recently (summer, 1949) Dr. Raven I. McDavid, Jr., completed the work for the eastern seaboard. The records, in an unedited but usable state, are filed at the University of Michigan, where they were made available to me through the courtesy of Professor Kurath.

[12] See *Handbook of the Linguistic Geography of New England,* ed. H. Kurath and others (Providence, R.I., 1939), for a complete account of the *Atlas* methodology.

[13] Something like 1600 informants have been interviewed, representing communities from New Brunswick to northern Florida, approximately as far west as Lake Erie.

[14] Ed. J. Gilliéron and E. Edmont, 7 vols. (Paris, 1902–1910).

[15] See Karl Jaberg, "Sprachgeographie," *Siebenunddreissigstes Jahresheft des Vereins Schweiz. Gymnasiallehrer* (Aarau, 1908), pp. 16–42; also Plate III.

[16] *Ibid.,* Plate III.

[17] *Ibid.,* Plate X.

these complications, plus others arising from the fact that more than one informant was chosen to represent each community. That is, at nearly every "point" the American field workers recorded the usage of one elderly, poorly educated informant and one younger, more modern informant. In certain key communities, a third type was included—a well educated, or "cultured," speaker who presumably represented the cultivated usage of the area. Thus, at the same point on the map we often find such variants as *sot down* (preterite), representing rustic usage, *set* or *sit down*, representing more modern popular usage, and *sat down*, representing cultivated usage.[18] It is obviously impossible to draw isoglosses separating *sot* from *set* or *sat;* it is even impractical to set off the *sot* areas, since the form occurs in about every other community through considerable areas. In other cases, of course, it is quite easy to mark off an area where a certain form is current. *Holp* (for *helped*), for example, occupies a very clear-cut area south of the Potomac.[19] Yet a line marking off this area would by no means constitute a dividing line between *holp* and *helped,* since most of the younger informants within the *holp* area use the standard form *helped.* My point is that an isogloss based on American *Atlas* materials *should in all cases be regarded as an outer limit, not as a dividing line between two speech forms.*

The examples hitherto adduced have, of course, illustrated the incidence of "non-standard" as against "standard" speech forms. What of those instances of two forms which are equally "standard," each within its area? Kurath's map of *pail* and *bucket* provides an example.[20] Here too we must follow the same principle: we must first draw the outer limit of one form, then that of the other. The two lines will lap over each other at some points, enclosing certain communities of mixed usage.[21] Thus, *a dividing line is a double isogloss,* each line being the outer limit of one of the two speech forms in question. The areas of overlapping between the two lines may be wide or narrow, depending on many social, geographical, and historical considerations.

Let us return to *grease* and *greazy.* The variation between [s] and [z] in these words furnishes an almost ideal example of geographical (as against social) distribution. Consider first the verb *grease.* It is unneces-

---

[18] In addition, the same informant often uses more than one form; all of these are of course entered at that point on the map. On at least one occasion McDavid picked up from the same informant, as the preterite of *see, I seen, I seed, I see,* and *I saw.*

[19] This verb, as well as the others mentioned, is treated in my *Survey of Verb Forms in the Eastern United States.* [Ann Arbor, Mich., 1953]

[20] *A Word Geography of the Eastern United States* (Ann Arbor, Mich., 1949), Figure 66.

[21] Even after drawing the lines we would find a good many scattered, or "stray," occurrences of *pail* within the *bucket* area and vice versa. Kurath's lines, which are all outer limits, do not attempt to indicate the presence of stray forms or small patches which occur outside the main area; however, since he also publishes maps on which each occurrence of each word is recorded by a symbol, the reader can easily check and interpret his isoglosses.

sary to describe in detail the incidence of [s] and [z], since the accompany-ing map tells its own story. The northern line of the [z]-form, it may be observed, takes in the southwestern corner of Connecticut (west of the Housatonic); from there it passes westward just to the north of New Jersey; then it dips sharply southward to Philadelphia, to the west of which it again rises gradually northward to the northwestern corner of Pennsyl-vania. The transition area (where both [s] and [z] are used), is relatively narrow to the west of Philadelphia; to the northeast, however, it widens considerably so as to include most of northern New Jersey, as well as New York City and eastern Long Island.

Outside our pair of isoglosses there is a surprisingly small number of "stray" forms. All together, there are only six occurrences of [z] in the [s] area and only six of [s] in the [z] area.[22] (It will be observed, of course, that there is a second area, or island, of [s] along the Ohio River extending northeastward from the vicinity of Marietta, Ohio.) There is no sign what-ever of social variation within the solid [s] and [z] areas; cultivated usage is in strict agreement with popular usage.[23] Within the areas of overlapping there is naturally some variation between older and more modern inform-ants—yet the general trend is not at all clear. In the communities of divided usage to the west of Philadelphia the more modern informant uses [s] in six out of eight instances; in such communities to the northeast of Philadelphia the modern preference is for [s] in six instances, for [z] in six others. As for cultured informants within the areas of overlapping, ten use [griz], five use [gris], and one offers both [s] and [z] forms. One might state, very tentatively, that cultivated usage has tended to favor [griz], particularly in New York City and northern New Jersey.

For the adjective *greasy,* the pronunciations [grisi] and [grizi] show almost precisely the same isoglosses as those for [gris] and [griz]. The northern limit of [z] pushes further northward at three points in Pennsyl-vania;[24] correspondingly, the southern limit of [s] retreats northward at one point in Ohio, three in Pennsylvania, and two in northern New Jersey.[25] Within the [s] area, there are ten stray forms with [z], scattered through New England and the Hudson Valley; six of these occur in the cultured type of informant. Within the [z] area, we again find six stray occurrences of [s]; and precisely the same island of [s] occurs along the Ohio River. In short, a few more eastern informants use [z] in *greasy* than in *grease,*

[22] This amounts to less than one per cent of the informants. Most of the informants who show exceptional usage also give the "normal" form; that is, they use both [s] and [z] forms.

[23] Although the preterite form of the verb was not called for in the work sheets, Lowman picked up some five instances of *grez* [grɛz] in the [z] area; and a number of other informants reported having heard this form.

[24] Lehigh, Columbia, and Lancaster counties.

[25] Columbia, Armstrong, Blair, Cumberland, Hunterdon, and Morris counties.

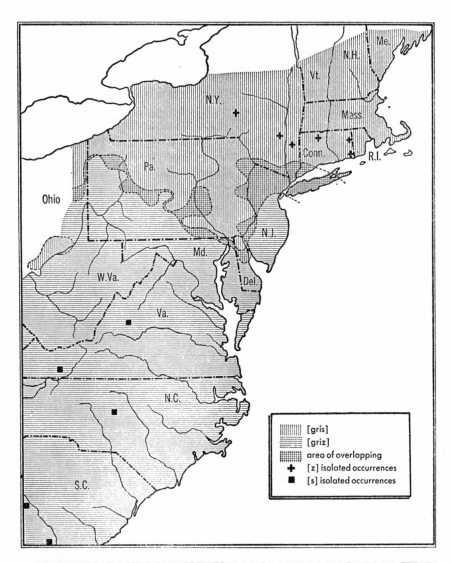

MAP SHOWING THE DISTRIBUTION OF [s] AND [z] IN GREASE (VERB)

Northern Maine and Eastern Georgia (not shown on the map) show the same usage as the adjoining areas. At the time of this study, no field records were available for Northern New York.

though the difference is not great. Within the areas of overlapping we find almost exactly the same social distribution as in the case of *grease*. Cultured informants prefer [grizi] by eleven to four; this fact, together with the six "stray" northern uses of [z] in the cultured type, inclines us to believe that [z] in *greasy* has penetrated into northeastern cultivated speech a little more palpably than in the case of *grease*—though still to a very slight extent.

After describing the incidence of the speech forms in question, we are still faced with a number of questions, to which our data can provide only partial answers.

What becomes of our isoglosses in the areas west of Pennsylvania? The materials being gathered for the Great Lakes atlas (under the direction of Professor A. H. Marckwardt) will undoubtedly provide an answer. I have not been able to examine the latest of these materials; but judging from preliminary information, as well as from a map already published by Professor Marckwardt,[26] the northern limit of [z] in *greasy* passes through central Ohio, then swings northward so as to take in almost the whole of Indiana, then bends southward through central Illinois in the direction of St. Louis. Whether the areas of transition are wide or narrow we can probably not determine with accuracy, since, in general, only one social type (the elderly, or rustic) is included in the Great Lakes survey.

Why should the isoglosses run where they do? The answer, in part, is relatively simple. Of the two sets of variants, the [s] forms were evidently generalized in the New England colonies, the [z] forms in the Middle and South Atlantic colonies. The westward migrations and settlements of the New Englanders covered New York (State), northern Pennsylvania, Michigan, Wisconsin, and the northern portions of Ohio, Indiana, and Illinois.[27] Many speech features mark off this Northern area from the "Midland"— the area occupied primarily by Pennsylvania.[28] Most of the northern lines,

[26] "Folk Speech of Indiana and Adjacent States," *op. cit.*, p. 128. [EDITOR'S NOTE: for a later statement based upon the completed study involving all three types of informants see A. H. Marckwardt: "Principal and Subsidiary Dialect Areas in the North-Central States," *Publication of the American Dialect Society*, No. 27 (April, 1957), reprinted in this edition pp. 220–230.]

[27] Kurath, *Word Geography*, pp. 1–7; see also Lois K. M. Rosenberry, *The Expansion of New England* (Boston and New York, 1909). Even the island of [s] forms around Marietta, Ohio, is to be explained on the basis of early settlement; this area was first settled by New Englanders as early as the 1780's. See Rosenberry, pp. 175ff.

[28] Examples of Northern words (from Kurath) are *whiffletree, pail, darning needle* ('dragonfly'), and *co, boss!* (cow call). Verb forms which I have found to have similar distributions are *hadn't ought* ('oughtn't'), *how be you?*, *clim* ('climbed'), and *see* as a preterite of *to see*. Note that Kurath's definition of "Midland" does not coincide with that of Hempl; the area, according to the former, extends much farther to the southwestward of Pennsylvania than Hempl indicated. (See *Word Geography*, pp. 27–37). [EDITOR'S NOTE: see also Atwood's own later study, *A Survey of Verb Forms in the Eastern United States* (University of Michigan Press, Ann Arbor, 1953).]

to be sure, pass further to the north in Pennsylvania than do those of the [s] in *grease* and *greasy*. Yet the penetration of northern forms to the area of Philadelphia is occasionally to be observed in other instances; for example, the line of Northern *clapboards* (as against Midland and Southern *weatherboards*) dips sharply southward so as to take in Philadelphia and northern Delaware. Another explanation for the prevalence of [gris] and ['grisi] in east central Pennsylvania might be the fact that much of the area was occupied in the early 18th century by Palatine Germans, whose native dialect had no [z] phoneme at all[29] and who may, for this reason, have favored [s] in any English words where variation between [s] and [z] occurred.

What is the British practice with regard to the pronunciation of *grease* and *greasy?* No complete survey has been made; but there seems no doubt that London usage, as well as "Received Standard" usage throughout southern England, is mixed.[30] The questionnaires which Hempl circulated in England (for his study cited above) showed that in London only 25 and 33 per cent of the informants used [s] in *grease* and *greasy;* but that in England exclusive of London the percentages of [s] were 84 and 74.[31] We have no ground, even yet, for rejecting these figures; but it should be pointed out that folk speech in England, just as in the United States, shows its isoglosses. A survey of the linguistic atlas type conducted by Guy S. Lowman in 1934[32] shows that the [z] in *grease* (I have no information on *greasy*) occupies East Anglia and a small adjoining area; that [s] is universal in the remainder of southern England (we are speaking strictly of the rustic type of speaker). Since the line passes through (or very near) London, it is easy to see why the metropolitan area should show a mixture of usage.

Is there any evidence of a differentiation in meaning between ['grisi] and ['grizi]? The *Atlas* provides no answer to this question, since, in the interest of obtaining comparable data, the words were always called for in the same context ("grease the car, axle, etc." and "my hands are greasy"). In general, such differentiations in meaning are characteristics of areas of mixed usage, not of those where one pronunciation or another is definitely established. The distinction usually given in dictionaries is that ['grisi] may mean literally 'covered with grease,' while ['grizi] may be used with less

[29] See Carroll E. Reed, *The Pennsylvania German Dialect Spoken in the Counties of Lehigh and Berks: Phonology and Morphology* (Seattle, Wash., 1949), pp. 20 and 29.

[30] See Daniel Jones, *An English Pronouncing Dictionary,* 9th ed. (London, 1948).

[31] Hempl, *op. cit.,* pp. 442–43.

[32] Lowman's British field records are filed in an unedited state at the University of Michigan.

literal, and sometimes unpleasant, connotations.[33] What we can say with confidence is that speakers to the south of our isoglosses do not follow thi.; practice: ['grizi] is universal with the meaning 'covered with grease'; whether or not speakers in the area of overlapping, and to the north of it, would have used ['grizi] had the context between different we are unable to determine.

How should we evaluate the *Atlas* data as a picture of reality? What is most important to realize is that the *Atlas* makes no attempt whatever to record the usage of non-native speakers, or even of those natives who have resided for long periods outside their home communities. Such speakers are rather uncommon in some communities, fairly numerous in others; in a few of the latter, the *Atlas* may even reflect the usage of a minority of old-timers. In view of this, we might be inclined to wonder whether the percentage method might not give a truer picture of prevalent usage than the isogloss method. The proportion of non-native speech forms in a community would, of course, roughly correspond to the proportion of non-native residents; such data would certainly be valuable, though to collect it on a large enough scale (say, 100 or so informants from each county) would be so difficult as to be practically impossible. Few investigators are qualified to make extensive phonetic observations, and those few must take their informants from such captive groups as college classes whose usage may or may not be spontaneous or representative. Another feature of the *Atlas* that must be considered is the preponderance of rather old informants. Since the interviews were conducted several years ago, many of the forms shown to be current among the aged may now be rare or even obsolete; moreover, the *Atlas* records would not reflect the most recent trends, fads, and innovations—some of which are extremely rapid, others extremely slow. It seems unlikely to me that the lines on *grease* and *greasy* have shifted radically in the last few years, yet I have no doubt that usage may have shifted in certain individual communities.[34]All things considered, the *Linguistic Atlas* offers the most reliable body of data as yet assembled, or likely to be assembled in the

---

[33] Daniel Jones, *English Pronouncing Dictionary:* "Some speakers use the forms . . . with a difference of meaning, ['gri:si] having reference merely to the presence of grease and ['gri:zi] having reference to the slipperiness caused by grease." *Webster's NID* states: ". . . many people in all sections use ['grisi] in some connotations and ['grizi] in others, the first esp. in the literal sense, covered with grease." Cf. Kenyon and Knott: "Some distinguish ['grisi] 'covered with grease' from ['grizi] 'slimy' " (*op. cit.*). G. P. Krapp states: "A distinction is sometimes made in the meaning of ['gri:si] and ['gri:zi], the latter being regarded as a word of unpleasant connotation" (*op. cit.*, p. 119). Webster's implies that this distinction is fairly general throughout the country—a very dubious proposition. T. Larsen and F. C. Walker simply prescribe [s] for the meaning 'sticky' and [z] for the meaning 'slippery'—as though this feature were standard and universal. (See *Pronunciation,* Oxford Press, 1931, p. 92.)

[34] Dr. Smith expresses the opinion that the younger generation in New York City has gone over almost entirely to the [s] in *greasy.*

near future, on American speech; isoglosses based on it reflect the usage of a highly important segment of our population, and they are, moreover, of the highest value in a study of our cultural and settlement history.

26

Some Social Differences in Pronunciation

RAVEN I. McDAVID, JR.

WHEN WE COMPARE varieties of American English, we generally assume that differences in grammar reflect social differences, and that differences in vocabulary or pronunciation reflect regional differences. Yet we must often modify this useful practical rule. The word *bastard* occurs everywhere, but everywhere it seems to be a cruder term than *illegitimate child*. In all regions where *jacket* and *vest* are synonymous, *jacket* is apparently more rustic and old-fashioned. Conversely, Atwood's monograph[1] shows that the differences in status between the preterites *dove* and *dived, woke up* and *waked up, sweat* and *sweated,* are more regional than social. Moreover, though /klɪm, kləm, klom, klæm, klam, klum/ all have less prestige as preterites than *climbed,* at least three of these forms occur in definite regional patterns: /klɪm/ in the North and South, /kləm/ in the Midland, /klom/ in eastern Virginia.[2] Even /ɛt/ as the preterite of *eat*—a social

Reprinted by permission from *Language Learning,* 4.102–116 (1952–1953). This paper was originally presented at the meeting of the Michigan Linguistic Society, December 8, 1951. Professor McDavid is a member of the Department of English at the University of Chicago and is associate director of the Linguistic Atlas of the North Central States.

[1] E. B. Atwood, *The Verb Forms of the Eastern United States* (Ann Arbor: University of Michigan Press, 1953).

[2] The regional designations are those found in H. Kurath, *A Word Geography of the Eastern United States* (Ann Arbor: University of Michigan Press, 1949), and in articles by Kurath, E. B. Atwood, Raven McDavid, and A. L. Davis. Linguistically the North includes New England, the Hudson Valley (including New York City) and derivative settlements in upstate New York, Pennsylvania, and further west. The Inland North is the northern area exclusive of the Hudson Valley and eastern New England. The Midland includes most of New Jersey and Pennsylvania, with derivative settlements to the west and south. The North Midland includes most of New Jersey and Pennsylvania, plus northern West Virginia. The South Midland includes the Shenandoah Valley, southern West Virginia, southwest Virginia, and the mountain and upper Piedmont areas of the Carolinas and Georgia. The South includes the older plantation areas of eastern Virginia and the coastal plain and lower Piedmont of the Carolinas and Georgia. The boundaries between these sections are much less sharp west of the Appalachians than along the Atlantic Seaboard.

shibboleth to many speakers—turns out to be the socially elegant form in Charleston, South Carolina, where the use of /ɛ/ (and of *ain't* in informal speech) sets off those who belong to the best Charlestonian society from those who would like to belong but don't.

We should therefore not be surprised if some pronunciations carry connotations of social prestige or lack of it. We can discuss a few of these pronunciations by examining the evidence collected for the Linguistic Atlas of the United States and Canada. This evidence has been collected in the field by trained investigators using a finely graded phonetic alphabet and a questionnaire of selected items dealing with everyday experience. The persons interviewed are strongly rooted natives of their communities, typical of various age or social groups. Usually there is one person, as unsophisticated as possible, from the oldest generation, and another either younger or more sophisticated or both. Besides, there are enough cultured informants to indicate the local or regional standards. For the Atlantic seaboard states alone, the field workers for the Atlas interview over 150 cultured informants—a greater number of cultured informants than even the largest standard dictionary has utilized for the entire United States.

Besides the relative status of informants in their own communities (indicated by the field worker after he has completed the interviews), one must evaluate communities, or groups of communities, against the whole body of American English. Previous work in linguistic geography, especially Kurath's *Word Geography of the Eastern United States,* enables us to judge pronunciations by the type of dialect areas in which they occur.

Focal areas are those areas whose economic, social, or cultural prestige has led to the spread of their linguistic forms into other areas. Examples are eastern New England (Boston), eastern Pennsylvania (Philadelphia), the Hudson Valley (New York City), the Virginia Piedmont (Richmond), and the South Carolina Low-Country (Charleston). Pronunciations characteristic of focal areas are likely to have prestige, especially when used by the younger and more sophisticated speakers.

Relic areas, on the other hand, are those whose geographical or cultural isolation, and relative lack of prestige, has caused the retention of older forms or prevented the spread of forms characteristic of these areas. Examples are northeastern New England, the eastern shore of Chesapeake Bay, and eastern North Carolina. Pronunciations characteristic of relic areas are likely to lack prestige, especially if they are chiefly used by the older and less sophisticated speakers.

A third problem we must consider is the attitude of speakers towards particular pronunciations—whether we call them "secondary responses" with Bloomfield or "metalinguistic details" with Trager. Here, incidental comments of the informants are of great value. For instance, the American *vase* /ves/ is a /vaz/ in Southern British Received Pronunciation. We might expect /vaz/ to have prestige in the United States, especially in those areas of New England and the Old South where British customs are admired and British speech forms are often adopted into local cultured speech. However, not only is /vaz/ rare as a spontaneous pronunciation, but the frequent comments of informants that "if it costs over $2.98 it's a /vaz/" suggest that many people who say /vaz/ are judged as parvenus who have acquired the pronunciation during a recent exposure to culture and who wish to use it to impress their neighbors. Judgments that pronunciations are characteristic of less privileged social groups—Negroes, unsuccessful farmers, recent immigrants—indicate for such pronunciations a lack of prestige in the community, regardless of their status elsewhere or their occurrence in the informant's unguarded conversation.

Finally, some informants may deliberately stick to pronunciations they know are considered old-fashioned, unprivileged, or simply peculiar. New Yorkers generally consider it substandard to pronounce a curl of hair and a coil of rope the same way, yet I know at least one prosperous and well-educated New Yorker of colonial stock who does not distinguish such pairs. The most sophisticated informant interviewed in Charleston proclaimed that she personally said /tə'mætəz/, though she knew other people said /tə'metəz/ or /tə'matəz/—"because Grandmother H—— always said /tə'mætəz/, and what Grandmother H—— said is good enough for me." One cultured informant near Galt, Ontario, consistently says /bul, pul/ for *bull, pull,* instead of /bül, pül/ because these pronunciations have come down in his Scotch-Canadian family. Such examples of "rugged individualism," family pride, or personal stubbornness do not give us patterns of prestige, but they warn us to go slow in condemning what we do not say ourselves.

As Kurath has often pointed out, there are three types of differences in pronunciation:

(1) Differences in the pronunciation of the individual phonemes.
(2) Differences in the occurrence of the individual phonemes.
(3) Differences in the system of phonemes.[3]

---

[3] The particular type of analysis one favors will often determine the category to which he assigns these differences. The analysis here used is basically that of *The Pronunciation of the Eastern United States* as adapted to the system of transcription generally used in *Language Learning.* Phonetic symbols are enclosed in brackets; phonemic symbols in slanting lines. Phonemic equivalents are as follows:

Vowels:

/i/	as in *beet*
/ɪ/	as in *bit*
/e/	as in *bait*
/ɛ/	as in *bet*
/æ/	as in *bat*
/a/	as in *hot, father*

Footnote continued on next page

Differences in the pronunciation of the individual phonemes are hardest to detect and evaluate. Some of these pronunciations are fairly striking, and do denote social status:

1. The ingliding diphthongal pronunciation of *date* and *boat*, as [deət] and [boət] is generally confined to the Charleston area.

2. The fronted [u] in *two, boot* is very common in the Midland and the South.

3. The monophthongal or near monophthongal variety of /ai/ occurring finally and before voiced consonants in *high, hide*. This type of pronunciation is chiefly found in Southern and South Midland dialects. Though sometimes ridiculed by speakers from other regions, it is rarely considered an unprivileged form in the areas where it occurs—and then only if the speaker does not differentiate *high* from *hah, blind* from *blond, hide* from *hod* or *hard*.

4. The fronted beginning of /au/ ([æu, ɛu]) in such words as *cow* is found in northern New England and the New England settlement area, and in the South and South Midland. In the North they are generally considered old-fashioned or rustic, and are disappearing. They are very common in the Richmond area and seem to be spreading nearly everywhere in the South except in South Carolina.

5. The centralized beginning of /ai, au/ ([əɪ, əu]) in *rite, ride, lout, loud*. Sometimes this occurs only when the diphthong is followed by a voiceless consonant, sometimes in all positions. In the inland North the centralized beginning may occur regardless of the consonant following the diphthong, but in this region the centralized beginning is often considered somewhat old-fashioned and rustic, though it is used by many cultured informants. The centralized beginning when the diphthong is followed by a voiceless consonant, but not otherwise, is characteristic of the speech of three well-defined areas: Canada (especially Ontario), the Virginia Piedmont, and the Atlantic Tidewater area from Georgetown, South Carolina,

---

/ɔ/	as in *bought*
/o/	as in *boat*
/ô/	the New England "short o" as in *coat, road, home*
/ʊ/	as in *put*
/u/	as in *boot*

Diphthongs:

/ai/	as in *write*
/au/	as in *rout*
/ɔi/	as in *oil*
/æi/	as in the common Southern and South Midland *bag, half*
/ɔu/	as in the common Southern and South Midland *law, hog*. This diphthong also occurs in New Hampshire.
/iu/	as in the common New England *beautiful, music*. This diphthong also occurs along the south Atlantic coast.
/ˈ/	primary stress
/ˌ/	secondary stress

to St. Augustine, Florida. In view of the social prestige of the Richmond and Charleston areas, the pronunciations of *light* and *lout* as [lɔɪt, lɔut) probably have privileged status.

6. An ingliding vowel with a rather high beginning sometimes occurs for /æ/ in such words as *calf, bad* [æ̂ə, ɛə] or for /ɔ/ in *law* [ɔ̂ə, ɔ̂ə]. These pronunciations are most common in such cities as New York, Philadelphia, and Baltimore. They are especially common in families with a central or eastern European background, and the more extreme varieties are often considered substandard.[4]

There are relatively few differences in the system of phonemes that all students would agree upon.

1. For some speakers the "New England short *o*," /ŏ/, occurs alongside /o/ in such words as *coat, road, home, whole*. It probably is found everywhere in the New England settlement area since it has been recorded as far west as Montana. On the other hand, even in New England it is losing ground, since it is found chiefly in smaller and relatively isolated communities and in the speech of the older and less sophisticated informants.

2. A falling diphthong /iu/ occurs alongside /yu/ (or /u/) in such words as *puke, beautiful, music, tube, due, new, suit, sumach, grew, blew*. It is found chiefly in the New England settlement area, but also occurs along Chesapeake Bay and the Carolina and Georgia coast. It is slightly old-fashioned, especially in the North (it occurs most frequently in *puke*, which does not have a "schoolroom pronunciation"); yet it still occurs in cultured speech.

3. In the Pittsburgh area the vowel /a/ occurs only before /-r/, with both *cot* and *caught, collar* and *caller* having /ɔ/. This feature also seems to occur frequently in western Canada and in the Minneapolis area. If anything, it seems to be spreading among younger and better educated speakers.

Differences in the occurrence of individual phonemes are most common and easiest to evaluate. They may be grouped according to several social types, though we must remember that these groupings are only tentative ones.

1. Some differences are purely regional:

In such words as *whip, wharf,* and *whoa,* some speakers have /hw-/ others /w-/.[5]

For *humor,* the pronunciation /hyumər/ occurs sporadically and chiefly in the Northern area, though elsewhere there are indications it is being sponsored by the schools as a spelling pronunciation. /yumər) is far more

---

[4] These differences in the pronunciation of the individual phonemes are sometimes analyzed as phonemic or systematic differences. See George L. Trager and Henry Lee Smith, Jr., *An Outline of English Structure* (Norman, Oklahoma: Battenburg Press, 1951).

[5] Raven I. McDavid, Jr. and Virginia Glenn McDavid, "h before semi vowels in Eastern United States." *Language,* Vol. 28, 1952, pp. 41–62.

common, at all levels of usage. For other words of this group, however, (though the evidence is less adequate) the forms with /yu-/ seem to be less widespread and somewhat lacking in prestige.

For *without,* the middle consonant may be either /θ/ or /ð/ at any social level. In the North and eastern North Carolina /ð/ is overwhelmingly predominant; in Canada, the Midland area, eastern Virginia, South Carolina, and Georgia /θ/ is very frequent.

Ewe is /yo/ in most of the country where people have knowledge of sheep. Since this pronunciation is never heard from those who have not lived where sheep were raised, it may be considered an occupational pronunciation among sheep herders.

Bleat, the cry of a calf, is prevailingly /blæt/ in the North and /blet/ in the south, being replaced by *bawl* in the Midland; /blit/ is almost exclusively a city pronunciation.

Because is frequently pronounced /bɪ'kəz) in the North and in South Carolina, but rarely in other regions. Where this pronunciation occurs it is used by speakers of all degrees of sophistication.

The unstressed vowel of *without* is always /ɪ/ in the North and the South, but usually /ə/ in the Midland.

Beside the usual /ču-/, Massa*chu*setts is often /ju-/ in New England, but /tyu-/ or /tu-/ in the South and south Midland.

Instead of /wɔnt/ (or the common Southern (wɔunt/) *want* is very often /want/ in Massachusetts and Vermont, /wənt/ in New Jersey and Western Pennsylvania. Both of these pronunciations occur sporadically in western areas settled ultimately from New England.

Words such as *orange, Florida, borrow,* and *tomorrow* may have either /a/ or /ɔ/ before /-r-/. In the Atlantic seaboard states /ɔ/ is most likely to occur in these words in northern New England, western Pennsylvania, and the Charleston area. For such words as *Florida* and *oranges,* /ɔ/ is practically universal in the North Central States and westward, but in these same areas /a/ or /ɔ/ may occur in *borrow* and *tomorrow.*

For *bulge, bulk,* and *budget,* both /u/ and /ə/ occur: /ə/ in the North and North Midland, /u/ in the South Midland, eastern Virginia, and the Piedmont of the Carolinas and Georgia, /ə/ again along the southern coast south of Chesapeake Bay.

For *won't,* /wont/ occurs everywhere. In addition there are four forms with regional distribution: (1) /wənt/ in the North, outside of the Hudson Valley; (2) /wɔnt) in North Carolina; () /wunt, wʊnt/ in Canada, New York City, the Hudson Valley, Chesapeake Bay, eastern North Carolina, and the Charleston area. All of these forms occur in cultured speech.

For many of the words derived from Middle English /o:/—and some borrowings that have fallen into the pattern—both /u/ and /ʊ/ occur, without social distinction but with sharply differing regional patterns. This is true of *coop, cooper, hoop, goobers, room, broom, root, cooter, food, hoof, roof, spooks,* and probably others. For instance, I—a native of upper South Carolina—normally have /u/ in *root, cooter, food, roof, spooks,* and *goober,* /ʊ/ in *coop, cooper, hoop,* and either /u/ or /ʊ/ in *room, broom, hoof.*

For such words as *tube, dew, new,* we find /iu/ in the North and occasionally along the southern coast, although it is somewhat old-fashioned in both areas. In the South and South Midland, /yu/ is predominant. It occurs as a prestige form in some communities in the North and North Midland. In northeastern New England, the Hudson Valley, and the North Midland, /u/ is almost universal and is spreading in other parts of the North.

Such pairs as *horse* and *hoarse, morning* and *mourning, border* and *boarder* are usually distinguished in the North, the South, and the South Midland, but not in the North Midland. In many parts of the Inland North and in Canada the distinction is disappearing.

2. A few pronunciations seem to lack prestige everywhere. *Italian* as /'ai 'tælyən/ is generally looked down upon; /dif/ (instead of /dɛf/) for *deaf* and /'waundɪd/ (instead of /'wundɪd/) for wounded are generally considered old-fashioned.

3. Other pronunciations lack prestige, but occur in limited regions.

Along Chesapeake Bay, *fog* and *hog* occasionally have /o/.

Rinse is rarely /rɪnč, rɛnč/ in the North, but these pronunciations are common in the Midland and the South. They are slightly old-fashioned, but not uncommon in cultured speech. The hyper-form /rɪnz/ is less common, limited to the same areas, and chiefly found in the speech of the half educated.

Coop occurs with /-b/ on Delaware Bay and along the southern coast south of Chesapeake Bay. This pronunciation is not common in cities, is slightly old-fashioned, but is used by many cultured speakers.

In parts of the South Midland and the South (but not in the Virginia Piedmont) *took, roof,* and *hoof* frequently have /ə/ in uneducated speech.

In much of the South and South Midland, the less educated speakers have /ə/ in *put,* to rime with *cut.*

For *loam* and *gums,* the pronunciations with /u,ʊ/ are confined to the New England settlement area, with /ʊ/ more common in Maine and New Hampshire than elsewhere. Although generally lacking in prestige, /gʊmz/ and /lʊm/ sometimes occur in cultured speech in Maine and New Hampshire. In other areas cultured speakers occasionally say /gumz/ and /lum/.

Two pronunciations of *can't*—/kent/ and /kæɪnt/—occur chiefly in parts of the South and South Midland. Although both pronunciations seem to have spread from the Virginia Piedmont, /kent/ seems to be the older and /kæɪnt/ the more recent form. Consequently, although both forms occur in the speech of all types of informants, /kent/ is often considered just a little more old-fashioned.

4. Several pronunciations may lack prestige in one region but be acceptable in another:

In the South and South Midland the pronunciation of *creek* as /krɪk/ is usually considered very quaint and lacking in prestige, since it is largely confined to the uneducated Negroes of the Carolina and Georgia coast. Even in the South, however, /krɪk/ may occur in the speech of cultured Charlestonians. In the North both /krik/ and /krɪk/ occur, with some pressure from the public schools to enforce /krik/ as a spelling pronunciation. However, /krɪk/ is very common in northern cultured speech. In the North Midland, especially in Pennsylvania, /krɪk/ is practically universal.

In the Atlantic seaboard states, *farm* and *form* are rarely homonymous, and where this homonymy occurs, as occasionally in South Carolina and Georgia, it is only in uneducated speech, and consequently frowned upon. In parts of Louisiana and Texas, however, this homonymy is normal among all classes of speakers.

Soot is most frequently pronounced as /sət/, except in Pennsylvania. In many parts of the country /sət/ is looked upon as old-fashioned, rustic, or uneducated. In the South, however, it is the pronunciation used by a majority of cultured speakers.

Many scholars, even C. C. Fries,[6] have labeled the pronunciation of *catch* with /ɛ/ as lacking in prestige. However, /kɛč/ is overwhelmingly the normal pronunciation, for the nation as a whole and for all regions except southern New England, the Hudson Valley, Pennsylvania, and the city of Charleston, where /kæč/ is the majority usage. In the areas where /kæč/ is the usual pronunciation, it is naturally preferred by educated speakers. In Virginia, and to some extent in North Carolina, /kæč/ is a prestige pronunciation, used by a majority of the culture informants but by few others. In other parts of the country, however, a majority of the cultured informants say /kɛč/.

5. For some words, one pronunciation may have prestige in one region and another pronunciation have prestige somewhere else.

For *raspberries*, the "broad *a*" pronunciation with /a/ seems to have some prestige in eastern New England, and to a lesser extent in New York City and eastern Virginia. In other parts of the country, however,—particularly in the Inland North—the pronunciation with /æ/ is socially preferred, and the /a/ pronunciation considered old-fashioned or rustic.

For such words, as *hog* and *fog*, pronunciations with /a,ɔ,ɔu/ have been recorded from speakers on all social levels. The /a/ pronunciations seem to have social prestige in Boston, New York City, Philadelphia, Charleston, Richmond (but not in smaller communities in the Virginia Piedmont), western North Carolina, northwestern South Carolina, and northern

[6] Charles C. Fries, *American English Grammar* (New York and London: Appleton-Century-Crofts, 1940), p. 10.

Georgia. In other southern communities the cultured informants have /ɔ,ɔʊ/. It is probable that /ɔʊ/ is an older prestige pronunciation that has spread from the Virginia Piedmont, with /a/ replacing it in cultured Richmond speech and in the cultured speech of other metropolitan centers.

Almost everyone knows that the two pronunciations of *greasy* sharply divide the eastern United States, with /-s-/ more common in the North and North Midland but /-z-/ usual in the South and South Midland. In some areas where both pronunciations occur, they are associated with different social levels or social contexts. Trager has frequently pointed out that among his boyhood playmates in Newark the /-z-/ pronunciation was confined to such derogatory phrases as a *greasy grind*. In South Carolina and Georgia the /-s-/ pronunciation is regular among the Gullah Negroes but almost never occurs in the speech of whites.

6. Occasionally a pronunciation may have social prestige in one area but elsewhere be only one of several acceptable pronunciations. For instance, *office* with /a/ has social prestige in eastern Pennsylvania and eastern Virginia; in other areas /a/ or /ɔ/ or ɔʊ/ may occur without any implication of social distinction.

7. Some pronunciations have prestige in the limited areas in which they occur.

The pronunciation of *can't* with /a/ is the socially preferred form in eastern New England, and to a lesser extent in New York City, Philadelphia, and eastern Virginia. Elsewhere it is extremely rare.

The pronunciation of *soot* as /sut/ is largely confined to the northern areas. Wherever it occurs, it is likely to be found in the speech of the moderately or better educated.

The lack of constriction of post-vocalic /-r/ (the so-called "loss of /r/") in *burn, barn, beard* occurs mostly in eastern New England, New York City, and the South Atlantic States. In the areas where it occurs, it is most likely to appear in the speech of the younger and better educated informants. In some communities in the South Atlantic States the rustic and uneducated white speakers preserve the constriction of /-r/, while Negroes and the more sophisticated whites lack constriction. In such communities visitors from the Inland North or the North Central States, where the constriction of /-r/ occurs in the speech of all classes, are likely to be at a social disadvantage. Conversely, in some Inland Northern communities, the only residents who lack constriction of /-r/ are the Negroes who have come from the South in the last generation. In these communities, Southern students have had difficulty securing rooms. In telephone conversations, landladies may identify the lack of consideration of /-r/ as a Negro characteristic and announce that no rooms are available.

8. A few pronunciations are always somewhat prestigious since they occur most frequently in cities and in the speech of the younger and

better educated informants. However, if the group of informants using such a pronunciation is very small, the prestige of the pronunciation may be lost since the pronunciation will be interpreted as a mark of conscious snobbery.

The pronunciation of *soot* as /sʊt/ always has social prestige, not only in Pennsylvania where /sʊt/ is the usual pronunciation but in the North where /sut/ is a common pronunciation among educated speakers and in the South where /sət/ is the usual pronunciation among speakers of all classes.

The pronunciation of *vase* as /vez/, (less frequently /vaz/) and of *nephew* as /'nɛvyə,-yu/ (much less commonly /'nɛvi/) are largely confined to cultured informants—chiefly in Southern Ontario, Boston, New York City, Philadelphia, Richmond and Charleston, where British speech forms are likely to have prestige. Inland informants who say /vez/ or /'nɛvyə/ usually have strong family or cultural ties to one of those centers.

The pronunciation of *sumach* with /su-/ instead of the more common /šu-/ is also largely confined to the larger coastal cities and to a relatively few inland cultured informants.

Such words as *suit, blew, threw* are normally pronounced with /u/. Although the pronunciations with /yu/ have social prestige in England they are extremely rare in this country, occurring almost exclusively in the North. Most Americans consider them unnatural and affected.

9. Sometimes the pronunciation of a word may involve a number of intricately related cultural, historical, and political facts. One of the most complex of these is *Negro,* where the pronunciations involve not only the status and the attitudes of those who use them, but the reactions of those the pronunciations designate. The historical pronunciation /'nɪgər/ is by far the most common, and in many communities it is the normal pronunciation used by speakers of both races. However, since it is used by many people as a term of contempt, it is actively resented by Negro spokesmen —regardless of the intent behind it. The spelling pronunciation /'nigro/ is comparatively new, but it has been actively sponsored as a polite pronunciation and is so used by most cultured speakers of the North and North Midland. However, /'nigro/ is very rare south of the Mason-Dixon line, partly because it is recognized as a Northern pronunciation of a word about which most Southerners have strong prejudices, partly because it violates the normal Southern tendency to have /ə/ in unstressed syllables. The pronunciation /'nɪgro/ is also a common polite form in the North and North Midland, but relatively uncommon in the South. The normal polite form in the South (and occasionally in other sections) is /nɪgrə/. Most cultured informants in the South do not use /'nɪgər/, which they feel is both derogatory to the Negro and characteristic of poor white speech. The difference in status and implication of /'nɪgrə/ and /'nɪgər/ is very sharply

maintained in the South, though frequently outsiders do not understand the distinction and wonder why the Southerner does not say /'nigro/, which to the Southerner seems unnatural.

Even such a limited approach to the problem of social differences in pronunciation indicates that it is very complex and that the person who attempts to label the status of a pronunciation must have information about such social forces as trading areas, educational practices, and community structure. Nor will it be a simple matter for teachers to apply the knowledge gained from studies such as this. Yet one may suggest certain procedures.

Those who teach English in the public schools should be fully aware of the socially preferred pronunciations in the communities in which they are teaching. They should not waste time and energy attempting to force exotic pronunciations upon their students, regardless of how desirable or elegant such pronunciations seem. They should also be aware that other types of pronunciation may be acceptable in other communities. Such awareness will not only make it easier for teachers to deal with the student who has moved to the community from another region, it will also make it easier for them to teach in communities outside their own dialect area.

Teachers of English to foreign students must also recognize this problem. In universities with a cosmopolitan student body, the instructors and drillmasters may speak any one of several varieties of American English. Even if it is possible to choose instructors and drillmasters from one dialect area, or require them to use something like a uniform dialect in their classes, as soon as the foreign student goes into his regular classes he will hear other types of pronunciation from the professors and his fellow students. The problem would be less difficult at smaller colleges where the faculty and the student body are predominantly from one region. Even here, however, the students will occasionally encounter other varieties of English. The longer they are in the United States and the broader their contacts—by travel, movies, radio, or television—the more frequently they will hear other pronunciations than those they have learned. How much attention the teacher should pay to variant pronunciations is a matter of practical pedagogy, depending on circumstances—it is much more important for the student to master one American pronunciation of *can't* than to learn a little about several pronunciations—but certainly the advanced students should know that speakers may differ markedly in the details of their pronunciation, and yet all speak socially acceptable American English.

27

Phonemics and Phonics in Historical Phonology

HANS KURATH

MY PURPOSE IN THIS ARTICLE is to discuss the interplay of phonemic and phonic data in historical phonology, and to demonstrate by examples chosen from the collections of the Linguistic Atlas the importance of giving adequate attention to phonic data not only in historical phonology but also in synchronic linguistics.

To achieve my purpose, I must first outline my view of the field of linguistics, even at the risk of making the tail wag the dog. As I see it, linguistics has two major fields: pure linguistics, whether synchronic, diachronic, areal, or social, which deals with usage without reference to the history of the speaker or the speech community; and historical linguistics, which undertakes to account for usage, or change in usage, by correlating purely linguistic data with the character and the history of the speaker or the speech community.

Pure synchronic linguistics (glottotechnics) proceeds on the assumption that in a given society, at a given time, the sounds of the current language constitute a system. Operating on this theory, the descriptivist establishes the functional units of sound (the phonemes) and formulates the system of sounds of the language in question. Focusing his attention upon systematics, he stands the best chance of finding all the systematic features peculiar to it. In this pursuit he sets aside, quite properly, all historical considerations and the culture of the community in which the language is used. The feasibility of abstracting from historical and social realities is, indeed, one of the crowning features of this method of dealing with language.

To say that language is essentially systematic at any given time, and therefore amenable to the descriptive technique, is not to admit that it is ever wholly systematic. The findings of diachronic and of area linguistics sharply contradict any such assumption. Relics of older usage that no longer fit into the current system and piecemeal innovations not yet systematized are ever

Reprinted by permission from *American Speech,* 36.93–100 (May, 1961).

present. Moreover, the descriptivist cannot ignore the patent fact that systems do change, and that a change in the system of a language is not conceivable without a temporary breakdown of certain structural features.

The proper procedure in synchronic linguistics is, therefore: (1) to identify all the systematic features; and (2) to isolate those features that are no longer, or not yet, systematized. To invent ingenious formulas in order to make irregularities look regular is a futile exercise, to say the least, since it is based upon a misconception of the nature of language, which is a historically created system of communication.

Pure diachronic linguistics employs essentially two techniques in its efforts to trace the changes in a language, to determine the genetic relationship between languages, and to reconstruct a prehistoric parent language of a linguistic stock.

Proceeding on the theory that changes in the phonemes of any language occur with regularity, the diachronist undertakes to establish the historically corresponding phonemes of two or more chronological stages of one language, or of two or more related languages. In reconstructing a prehistoric parent language, he utilizes the corresponding phonemic units thus established as a basis of inference. All such operations can be performed without reference to the peoples who speak, or spoke, these languages.

The theory of the regularity of phonemic change thus serves the purpose of identifying all regularities and of sorting out apparent irregularities. It is a heuristic device of diachronic linguistics parallel to that of the theory of essential systematization in pure synchronic linguistics; and, like the latter, it need not take account of the culture and the history of the speech community. It can be applied abstractly.

Just as pure synchronic and diachronic linguistics have methods of dealing with language without reference to the speaker or the speech community, so does pure areal and social linguistics—an aspect of linguistic research more widely known as linguistic geography or dialectology.

Using a sampling technique, the linguistic geographer undertakes to establish the regional and social dissemination of heteroglosses—differences in pronunciation, morphology, syntax, and vocabulary—within an area. He maps separately the variants of each feature investigated, making separate entries for each speaker. If the regional dissemination of heteroglosses warrants it, he draws isoglossic lines setting off the heteroglosses within the area; if the heteroglosses exhibit a social dissemination, he tabulates them in some way. After handling each item in this manner, he compares the regional dissemination patterns as exhibited by the heteroglossic lines, and finds that the heteroglosses (lexical, morphological, and phonetic) form bundles of various sizes in some sections of the area investigated but not in others. These bundles he takes to be indicative of the existence of major and minor dialect boundaries within the total area, and hence also of the existence of major dialect areas and their subdivisions.

All these operations and inferences are purely linguistic. They do not, and should not, take into account the history of the speech communities at this stage of the investigation. The historical interpretation of the dialect areas in terms of settlement areas, political and economic subareas, dominant cultural centers, and so forth, is an independent subsequent enterprise.

To summarize: the techniques of pure synchronic linguistics, pure diachronic linguistics, and pure area linguistics are effective scientific devices applicable to language without reference to the culture and the history of the speech community.

However, the synchronist must be aware of the fact that language is a historical product shaped by complicated cultural and social processes, and therefore it cannot be wholly systematic at any time. The diachronist will want to relate the changes in language to the history of the speakers whenever possible; and the linguistic geographer should not stop short of interpreting heteroglosses, dialect boundaries, and speech areas in terms of demographic areas and forces of one kind or another.

Pure linguistics achieves its immediate ends without reference to the culture or the history of the speech community. Thus the system of phonemes and the distribution of the units can be described, in the abstract, for any given time. Changes in the system of a language can be established and described simply by comparing two or more chronological cross sections. A parent language can be reconstructed by comparing the phonemic systems of two or more genetically related languages and the incidence of the phonemes in the shared vocabulary (etymology), even though the history of the peoples speaking these languages may not be known. Speech areas can be delineated and subdivided on the basis of heteroglosses without reference to settlement history, population centers, or lines of communication. For certain purposes this is enough, and under certain circumstances this is all that can be achieved.

But historians of language, comparativists, and dialectologists understandably want to relate their purely linguistic findings to the culture and the history of the peoples who use, or have used, the language, and in matters of pronunciation to known facts concerning habits of articulation. They want to know how phonemes split or merge, how allophones of one phoneme come to be subsumed under another phoneme, how native phonemes are replaced by foreign phonemes, how foreign phonemes are adapted to the native system, and under what conditions foreign phonemes are adopted.

For all these problems the phonemic point of view is essential. But for most of them a careful consideration of the phonic character and range of the several phonemes is of crucial importance. In dialectology (areal and social linguistics), positional and prosodic allophones are directly observable. In diachronic linguistics they must be inferred from phonemic splits and mergers, for which dialectology and instrumental phonetics furnish the clues.

Relying upon the findings of the Linguistic Atlas of the Atlantic States, one can illustrate the way in which new phonemes arise or are lost, how the incidence of phonemes in the vocabulary changes, and how the phonic character of phonemes is modified. In some instances, the immediate drive for a change can be safely inferred from the regional and/or social dissemination of the variants; in others, a probable source of the change can be pointed out by considering demographic factors such as settlement, migration, population and cultural centers, the British background, and so on.

My illustrations are necessarily brief and simplified. A fuller account will be found in *The Pronunciation of English in the Atlantic States*,[1] to be published this spring. The unitary phonemicization of diphthongal vowels I use is fully described in that publication.

To make my points, I have introduced a number of clear examples from earlier English and from Primitive Germanic.

THE ADDITION OF PHONEMES

New phonemes arise, or are introduced, in various ways:

1. The PGc back vowels have fronted allophones before the high-front vowels /īi/ and the palatal semivowel /j/ in WGc. With the loss of these position markers, rounded front vowels become separate phonemes, as in OE *mȳs* (pl.) vs. *mūs* (sg.), *fǣt* (pl.) vs. *fót* (sg.). This process has been well described by W. Freeman Twaddell.[2]

2. OE had only one set of short fricatives, /f þ s h/, voiceless in all positions except between voiced sounds. In intervocalic position, short /f þ s/, pronounced as voiced [v ð z], contrasted with long /ff þþ ss/, pronounced without voice. Through the loss of phonemic length in the consonant system (*c*. 1200 in the North Midland, *c*. 1400 in the South Midland), the intervocalic voiced allophones [v ð z] were raised to phonemic status, contrasting henceforth with voiceless /f þ s/ in this position, as in /bāðən, rīzən/vs./ wraþe, kisen/. In initial position, voiced /v z/ became established in ME through the adoption of words from OF and L.

In an earlier article, I have described the development of contrastive voiced and voiceless fricatives in ME.[3] They came into being partly as a native development, partly through borrowing from OF.

3. In several subareas on the Atlantic coast, the postvocalic /r/ of *ear, care, four, poor,* and so on, articulated as a constricted [ɝ] elsewhere, developed into an unconstricted mid-central semivowel [ə]. Since this phone has nothing in common with the prevocalic /r/ of *read, road,* and so on, in articulation or acoustic quality, it must in my opinion be taken as a separate

[1] Hans Kurath and Raven I. McDavid, Jr., *The Pronunciation of English in the Atlantic States* (Ann Arbor, 1961).

[2] 'A Note on Old High German Umlaut' (1938) in *Readings in Linguistics*, ed. Martin Joos (Washington, D. C., 1957), pp. 85–87.

[3] 'The Loss of Long Consonants and the Rise of Voiced Fricatives in ME,' *Language*, XXXII (1956), 435–45.

phoneme. If the incidence of this semivowel /ə/ is restricted to certain positions, the same is true of the consonants /ŋ z/ of *sing, pleasure;* and the semivowels /j w/ of *yes, well* are restricted to prevocalic position, if one treats diphthongal vowels as units, as I do.

The gradual phonic shift from fully constricted [ɝ] to unconstricted [ə̣] is well documented on the periphery of the areas that now have the semivowel /ə/ in *ear, four,* and so on. Other speakers, of course, simply replace post-vocalic /r/ by /ə/, as in the lower Hudson Valley, under the influence of metropolitan New York.

4. In the areas on the Atlantic seaboard that have the semivowel /ə̣/ after high and midvowels, as in *ear, care,* and so on, this /ə̣/ has merged with the low checked vowel /ɑ/ of *hot* to create a new free vowel, as in *car, far, garden* /kɒ, fɒ, gɒdən/. Here *hard, barb* and *hod, bob* have contrastive vowels, which differ in quality but not in length. However, some speakers on the periphery of these areas, in adopting that distinction, substitute for the free vowel a prolonged variant of the checked vowel /ɑ/ of *hod, bob.* This usage is clearly in transition.

THE LOSS OF PHONEMES

The loss of phonemes by merging is too well known to need extensive illustration. Thus the three IE vowels /o ɒ ə/ coalesce in PGc /ɒ/, IE /ō ā/ in PGc /ō/; OE *ēa* and *ǣ* (<PGc ai/j) are merged in ME /ɛ̄/, ME *ai* and *ā* in MnE /e/; and so on.

Two examples from American English will serve to show how complicated this type of process can be.

1. In eastern New England some words that had a long open /o/ in ME have a checked vowel /ɵ /, e.g., *stone, coat, road.* This phoneme is most common in rural areas (especially from Maine to the upper Connecticut Valley) and more common in rustic words than in other expressions. It is relatively rare in cultivated urban speech, though some cultured speakers take pride in retaining it in *the whole thing* and *wholly.* Relics of / ɵ / survive in the New England settlements along the Great Lakes.

The areal and social dissemination of this phoneme, and its peculiar incidence in the vocabulary, provides valuable insight into the complicated gradual recession of a unique regional phoneme in American English. Though the social forces behind the replacement of this checked / ɵ / by the free /o/ of *know* are complex, it is nevertheless clear that New England is in this instance bowing to national usage.

Walter S. Avis has described this process in great detail.[4] It is perhaps not inappropriate to point out that one of the nine vowels in the Trager-Smith 'over-all' system hangs by this frail thread.

---

[4] 'The Mid-back Vowels in the English of the Eastern United States: a Detailed Investigation of Regional and Social Differences in Phonic Characteristics and in Phonemic Organization' (University of Michigan dissertation, 1955).

2. The merging of the free vowel /ɔ/ of *law* with the checked vowel /ɑ/ of *lot* in a free vowel /ɒ/ in eastern New England and in western Pennsylvania is treated by Thomas H. Wetmore in his University of Michigan dissertation.[5] The British background of this phenomenon is so complex, and the situation in the Eastern states so fluid, that it would be foolish to attempt a description of the process before the English dialect atlas is published.[6]

It is clear, however, that the merger has taken place in the two areas mentioned above and, at least in part, in the Great Lakes area and the Pacific Northwest.

CHANGES IN INCIDENCE

1. In America, *mood, good,* and *food* now regularly have three different vowel phonemes, all derived from the same ME vowel /ō/ in one and the same position, that is, before /d/. In other words, these three derivatives of ME /ō/ occur in varying regional dissemination: (*a*) *broom* and *room* often have the checked /u/ of *full* in eastern New England, eastern Virginia, and the Low Country of South Carolina, the free /u/ of *fool* elsewhere; (*b*) *coop* has the vowel of *full* in the South and the South Midland, that of *fool* in the North Midland and the North; (*c*) *roof* as /ruf/ is common in New England, on Delaware Bay, and in northern West Virginia, /ruf/ predominating everywhere else; (*d*) *soot* as /sut/ predominates on all social levels in the North and in much of Pennsylvania, whereas in the South it is largely confined to cultivated speech. The variant /sʌt/ is regular in Southern folk speech and in middle-class speech but is uncommon farther north. The variant /sut/ occurs in the New England settlement area, rarely elsewhere, and has the earmarks of a prestige pronunciation.

This chaotic regional and social incidence of the three derivatives of ME /ō/ defies formulation in phonetic rules. However, from the social dissemination of the variants in the several focal dialect areas present trends in usage can be inferred; and on the margin of these areas phones can be observed that cannot be definitely assigned to one phoneme rather than another, as in the case of *room* and *broom*. Such 'compromise' pronunciations (unsystematized phones) are a reality, and must be reckoned with in synchronic and diachronic linguistics.

The situation in Standard British English is no less confused than in American English. Blending of regional derivatives of ME /ọ/ in England appears to be at the root of the matter. At any rate, the incidence of /u/, /ʊ/, and /ʌ/ in *room, roof, soot, root,* and *hoop* varies just as much in English folk speech as in American English.

2. In the greater part of the Eastern states Early Modern English short /o/ and long /ō/ before an /r/ of the same syllable have remained distinct.

[5] *The Low-central and Low-back Vowels in the English of the Eastern United States,* Publication of the American Dialect Society, No. 32 (University, Ala., 1959).

[6] Harold Orton, director of the English atlas, tells me that the fieldwork has been completed. [ED. NOTE. The Handbook and first volume appeared in 1962.]

But in a wide belt extending from the lower Hudson Valley westward through New Jersey and Pennsylvania and southward to the Potomac, the two phonemes have coalesced in this position. In this belt *four* and *forty, hoarse* and *horse* have the same vowel phoneme (as also in Standard British English). The lowering effect of postvocalic /r/ upon high and midvowels is well known. Thus the old long midvowels of *poor* and *ear* fail to be raised in some regional dialects of American English (which have /po₃, e₃/), the high vowel of *pure* is lowered to /o/ in the South and in northeastern New England, and the midvowel of *care* is lowered to the /æ/ of *cat* in parts of the South and of New England. The merging of the vowel of *four* with that of *forty* must therefore be attributed to the same cause.

The history of the vowels before an /r/ of the same syllable points up the importance of dealing with subphonemic (phonic) features adequately. In diachronic linguistics we usually have no *direct* evidence of the phonic range of phonemes, that is, of their positional and prosodic allophones. We infer their existence and their approximate phonic character from mergers and splits in the phonemes as evidenced by changes in the spelling, by rhymes, and so forth. In dialectology, phonic recording of living speech gives us direct evidence of the phonic range of the phonemes (their positional and prosodic allophones), evidence that leads to a realistic treatment of phonemic mergers and splits.

3. In Virginia, North Carolina, and the upcountry of South Carolina, the vowel in *aunt, half,* and *ashes* is extensively articulated as an upgliding [æɪ] This regional allophone of /æ/ is especially common in *can't,* which is so frequently heavily stressed. In some sections of this extensive area, notably in North Carolina and in the Appalachians south of the Kanawha, *can't* has the vowel of *cane.* Though avoided by the cultured, /kent/ is here common among the middle class and all but universal among the folk.

Since /kent/ is confined to the area in which the vowel of *aunt, half,* and *ashes* is articulated as an upgliding [æɪ], the origin of /e/ in *can't* is quite clear: as an upgliding vowel, articulated with raised tongue position under heavy stress, it fell in with the normally upgliding /e/ of *cane.*

In similar fashion the upgliding positional allophone of checked /ɛ/ in *egg* is often phonemicized as the free /e/ of *plague* in folk and common speech of the South and the southern Appalachians, and of eastern New England.[7]

Changes of all these types are documented in areal and social linguistics, based upon the observation of living speech. When the areal and social dissemination of features of pronunciation is established by systematic sampling, the manner in which changes occur in a given regional or social dialect

[7] The terms *North, Midland, South Midland, South,* and so forth, refer to the speech areas of the Atlantic seaboard as defined in Hans Kurath, *A Word Geography of the Eastern States* (Ann Arbor, 1949).

can often be pointed out with a high degree of probability.

Areal and social linguistics, therefore, make a substantial contribution to our understanding of historical processes in phonology—not that such discoveries are entirely new or revolutionary. Traditional historical phonology has for more than a century undertaken to account for changes by distinguishing indigenous changes from borrowed features, by adducing positional variation in the articulation of the phonemes in dealing with splits and mergers, and by pointing out parallel phonemic developments (as in the development of the long high and midvowels of ME in Early MnE).

However, while the historical interpretation of phonological events in diachronic linguistics is achieved by inference from the events, the processes themselves are directly observable in areal and social linguistics. Having fuller and more precise data at his disposal, the dialectologist is often in a position to pinpoint changes and to document the complexity of changes that ultimately lead, or may lead, to uniform results in a given dialect. Knowing not only the phonemic data—the only data directly accessible in diachronic linguistics—but also the phonic range of the several phonemes in the system, he can observe directly how phonemic splits and mergers, whether partial or comprehensive, come about. The dialectologist will therefore attach great importance to an exact phonic record of the speech of his informants.

He has no reason to fear that the phonic record will prevent him from setting up the phonemic system for each speaker, always provided that the record is ample. He will be skeptical of facile schemes that fail to make allowance for unsystematized items and fluctuations in idiolects and dialects. He will not accept an 'over-all' phonemic scheme for all varieties of American English as a scientific statement. Whether it has some pedagogical value or not is another question.

Part IV

LINGUISTICS AND USAGE

INTRODUCTION

As a sometimes ironic platform from which to view the subject of usage this Part offers first the article by the distinguished linguist, the late Leonard Bloomfield, who found himself vastly entertained—and yet deeply concerned—by the phenomena of popular reactions to certain language matters and especially by popular reaction to linguists' statements about language matters.

McMillan and Hill then tackle in their respective articles the rather difficult assignment of making persuasively clear some important distinctions. McMillan seeks to clarify the distinction between grammar and usage by treating usage as a function of rhetoric, quite another discipline. Hill, moved by a previous article by Morton W. Bloomfield advocating a certain degree of dogmatism in the teaching of style and usage, would clear the air of misunderstandings by avoiding a direct clash and trying to find common ground in the purpose of teaching.

Pedagogical recognition of actual usage as the basis of statements about English pronunciation, grammar, and syntax is really quite recent. Neither of the articles by McMillan and Hill could have been written thirty-five years ago, and neither would make so much sense to a teacher of English today had the Sterling Andrus Leonard NCTE monograph, *Current English Usage,* not appeared in 1934, nor Fries's *American English Grammar* in 1940. These studies, along with the first "liberal" handbook, Perrin's *Index to*

English (1939), helped to popularize the concept of levels of usage. But that this concept itself is inherently fallacious is the tenor of the article by Kenyon, in my opinion the most significant single statement about English usage yet published. Kenyon finds that while it is possible to recognize "levels," each level must then in turn be recognized as including a wide range of usage from formal to informal. He calls attention to the easily attested but previously unaffirmed existence of nonstandard formal usage alongside formal nonstandard. J. J. Lamberts has recently added an interesting additional level, "hyperstandard," to the Kenyon series (*College English*, 24.141–43, November, 1962), and the extraordinary complexity of usage relationships has been treated by Martin Joos in his monograph, *The Five Clocks* (Publication Twenty-two of the Indiana University Research Center in Anthropology, Folklore, and Linguistics, 1962).

The next two articles also inject modifications into the theory of usage. The excerpt from a longer article by Hill introduces a sharpening of the concept of "colloquial" by recognition of a "koine" which includes a spoken mode. Baker, taking off from Robert Hall's *Linguistics and Your Language* (1960), and disagreeing with McMillan, wishes to make prominent the fact of attitude, emotional or other, toward various linguistic forms as a fact which actually prevents such a semantic equation as Hall would set up.

At this point I should like to abuse an editor's prerogative by drawing upon a short paper that I read at the Miami Beach convention of the National Council of Teachers of English in November, 1962, titled, "Three Hats and Five Dimensions." I want to draw upon it because it seems to me that it can be useful to the teacher confronted with the task of clarifying—at the risk of oversimplification—this extraordinarily complex matter of usage.

The three hats are worn by persons who have three different jobs—or, theoretically, at different times by the same person doing the different jobs. The first hat is worn by the linguist, the person whose job is to study and describe the system of a language. Any such description, accurate or inaccurate, is a grammar. The second hat is worn by such a person as a dialect geographer, a research scholar, a dictionary editor, or perhaps even a social anthropologist. His job is to study the correlation of linguistic forms with the nonlinguistic environment, that is, to study usage. The third hat is worn by the teacher, by the person who takes one set of the correlations between grammar and usage and assumes the responsibility of helping students to gain control over that set, the Standard set.

I said in that paper: "Grammar is the description of what goes on inside a language. That is one thing. Usage is the relationship between what goes on inside a language and the context of speaker, audience, time, place, and occasion in which it occurs. That is another thing. As professionals we must insist that grammar and usage are not synonyms. They simply do not mean the same thing."

The five dimensions I spoke of clearly have their origin in Kenyon's thesis. They constitute an over-simplification, but it is a practical and not inaccurate over-simplification. The term dimension is used deliberately to suggest the idea of a continuum between two extremes, a multi-valued rather than a two-valued orientation. The term is useful also because it permits easy visual demonstration before a class.

For the first dimension one may simply take a stick, a piece of doweling perhaps a foot or eighteen inches long. It will represent the range between the two extremes of speech and writing. Any language matter can be placed somewhere along that range. For the second dimension one may make a square with four sticks, such as the kind often used in children's construction toys. This dimension, this continuum, is that between formality and informality. Any language form can be stated as occurring at any point within this two-dimensional area. It may be informal spoken, informal written, formal spoken, or formal written.

But we know that language occurs in the behavior of people with little or no schooling and with limited social contacts and also in the behavior of people with a great deal of education and with wide social contacts. These two extremes are familiar to us, and also the long range between them. Language characteristic of the first group we can call non-standard; that of the second group, standard. Many forms, of course, are in the middle. Further, the situation is complicated by the existence of slang, cant, jargon, technical nomenclature, and the like, each having its own range along the central core, so that temporarily we can change the figure and think of our stick as something like a telephone cable with many parallel strands. But since we are adding this dimension to the two other dimensions we now need more sticks in order to produce a cube. And, again, we can identify any language form as occurring somewhere within the three-dimensional space of the cube, so that we can have formal spoken standard and formal spoken nonstandard, informal written standard and informal written nonstandard, through all the possible combinations.

But there are two additional dimensions. If one picks up the cube and moves it quickly from one place to another on a desk or table he is visually representing the continuum from here to there, the dimension of space. This, of course, is the dimension treated in the articles about linguistic geography in Part III of this book. Any language item may undergo a change in its relative position in the cube as the cube is moved from one place to another. For example, *Any more he comes to see us* would be informal spoken standard in much of the south; it certainly is not standard in the north.

The fifth dimension one demonstrates by moving the cube very slowly from one place to another. Obviously this suggests the dimension of time, for with the passage of time the relationships of language forms also manifest change. The change may be slow, as with syntactic forms; it may be more rapid, as with the acceptance of the progressive *-ing* phrase of the verb in the eighteenth century; it may be almost overnight as with the adoption of the term *sputnik*. Any statement about usage, therefore, needs to be made with a superior date [1963] or [1850] or [1375].

A case study of one specific correlation between a language form and the social context is provided in this section by Fischer, a sociologist. Mrs. Malmstrom then draws upon linguistic atlas findings to demonstrate that textbook statements about language often ignore the context in which language occurs and hence are suspect as statements of fact. Her recognition of the facts of language life in time and situation and social class is followed by the article by Pooley, who, wearing the third hat, specifies why the schools must operate with an enlightened prescriptivism. Miss Higgins then tells how in her own school context she applies this principle in actual teaching. But that the country could use many more Miss Higginses is finally indicated by Womack's survey with its clear indication of the strong persistence of linguistically uninformed authoritarianism among all too many teachers who are supposed to be teaching high school students the facts of language life.

28

Secondary and Tertiary Responses to Language

Leonard Bloomfield

Utterances about language may be called secondary responses to language. For us, the most important are those which are made in the systematic study of language—the utterances, above all, which, recorded in books and essays, embody the past results of linguistic science. They will not concern us here; to the extent that we succeed in working scientifically, the verbal phase of our work takes on the general characteristics of scientific utterance.

Reprinted by permission from *Language*, 20.45–55 (April–June, 1944). Only the portion to the top of page 51 appears here. The author was Professor of Linguistics at Yale University.

On other than a scientific level, our culture maintains a loosely organized but fairly uniform system of pronouncements about language. Deviant speech forms in dialects other than the standard dialect are described as corruptions of the standard forms ('mistakes,' 'bad grammar') or branded as entirely out of bounds, on a par with the solecisms of a foreign speaker ('not English'). The forms of the standard dialect are justified on grounds of 'logic.' Either on the strength of logical consistency or in pursuance of largely conventional authoritative rules, which constitute a minor tradition within the main one (for instance, the rules about *shall* and *will*), certain forms are theoretically prescribed for the standard dialect. When it is noticed that speakers of the standard dialect do not use these forms or use others beside them, these deviations are again branded as 'mistakes' or, less often, attributed to 'usage,' which appears here only as a special and limited factor, mentioned doubtfully as interfering with more legitimate controls.

Traditional lore of this kind is occasionally put into literary form and developed in detail, as in the well-known treatise of Richard Grant White, *Words and Their Uses, Past and Present: A Study of the English Language* (New York, 1870).[1]

The speaker is able to discourse also upon more remote topics. In spite of the degenerative character of dialects other than the standard one, some distant local dialects are said to maintain pure Elizabethan English.[2] As a dim reflex of statements concerning linguistic relationships, one hears that the Finnish and Hungarian (or the Bengali and Lithuanian, or the Basque and Malayalam) languages are mutually intelligible. Some ignorant people and some savage tribes are said to have a vocabulary of only a few hundred words. This may be attributed to illiteracy, for 'spoken language' fleetingly renders the forms which have their basic and permanent existence in the 'written language.' The latter 'fixes' and 'preserves' linguistic tradition. Operations upon the system of writing immediately affect a language. The following press releases embody various other phases of popular linguistics, but are especially illuminating on the matter of language and writing.

From the *Tulsa Daily World* of February 27, 1941:

[1] Contemporary with Whitney's *Language and the Study of Language* (1867) and *Life and Growth of Language* (1874). Our undergraduate instructors advised us to read Richard Grant White; Whitney was not mentioned.

[2] An Associated Press dispatch (*New York Times,* November 26, 1939) is headed 'Fishermen speak in Middle English'. Part of the wording is as follows: 'A touch of Elizabethan England still flourishes on the "outer banks," a serpentine strand off North Carolina's coast ... one hears on the "outer banks" words and phrases so similar to the language of Queen Elizabeth's day that philologists and historians see a distinct connection.'

For this and most of the following citations, as well as for much kind help and criticism, I am indebted to Bernard Bloch.

TULSAN WANTS SEQUOYAH'S ALPHABET TAUGHT IN PUBLIC

Sequoyah's alphabet should become a part of the standard equipment in Oklahoma schools, a Tulsan declared Tuesday as he mailed letters to officials at the state capitol proposing that the Cherokee language be made a part of the regular curriculum in all state high schools.

"It's the only native tongue conceived and taught as a language in America," Dr. C. Sterling Cooley, 415 South Guthrie, wrote A. L. Crable, Oklahoma superintendent of public instruction. Copies were sent to Senator Henry Timmons and Representative W. H. Langley of the state legislature which is now in session at Oklahoma City. . . .

Possibility that Sequoyah's languages could fool the Germans again, however, was just a minor point in the doctor's contention the Cherokee tongue should be taught in school like English, French or Latin.

"Oklahoma schools have taught a lot of subjects a lot more useless," Doctor Cooley said. . . .

Doctor Cooley said the 86 characters of Sequoyah's famous alphabet were memorized by some Cherokees in as little time as three days.

"One-semester course should be sufficient for Oklahoma students to learn the subject," he said.

Doctor Cooley's letter to Superintendent Crable follows:

"Dear Sir:

"To perpetuate a beautiful language that would prove uniquely useful in time of war; to preserve the only native tongue conceived and taught as a language in America; to offer something better than the "trial of tears" as a memory of our treatment of them and to honor a great leader of an historic people I believe Oklahoma ought to make it possible for its citizens to choose the syllabus of Sequoyah as an elective study in the curriculum of any public school where languages in addition to English are taught.

"I propose this to you because you are logically the one who can best open the door of opportunity to any and all who wish to learn the tongue of the Cherokees, the language of Indians everywhere, and I shall be grateful to you if you will advise how others and myself may help to make it possible for our schools to perpetuate a language that is solely American in origin."

Doctor Cooley said he sent a copy of the letter to Representative Langley because, to his knowledge, he is the nearest full-blood Cherokee Indian in the legislature and might be interested in furthering the proposal.

From the *Tulsa Daily World* of April 2, 1941:

CRABLE INDORSES SEQUOYAH'S LANGUAGE AS COLLEGE COURSE

Indorsement of a proposal for teaching Sequoyah's alphabet in public schools, coupled with a recommendation as to where the subject might be experimented with was received here Tuesday from A. L. Crable, state superintendent of public instruction.

In a letter to Dr. C. Sterling Cooley, originator of the proposal which has grown, more or less, into a movement, Crable said, "I am in thorough sympathy with your interest in the syllabary of Sequoyah," and suggest that the State Teachers College in Tahlequah would be the school in which the course should be instituted as an elective study.

"Probably all the colleges of the state would be interested in the effort to perpetuate the great work of Sequoyah, in the way you suggest," the state superintendent's letter to Doctor Cooley read. However, the education executive specifically recommended that the Tulsan take the matter to the president of Northeastern State College in Tahlequah, capital of the Cherokee Nation. This Doctor Cooley indicated he would do.

The movement to perpetuate Sequoyah's alphabet and tongue has reached into states other than Oklahoma. Doctor Cooley pointed out after receiving a letter Tuesday from a Mrs. F. P. Arthurs who wrote in behalf of the department of modern languages at Western State College of Colorado at Gunnison. Mrs. Arthurs, who Doctor Cooley believes to be officially connected with the college, asked for references on the life of Sequoyah and inquired about the progress of the Sequoyah movement in Oklahoma.

"I shall write her," said the Tulsan, "that the movement has plenty of encouragement, but no official action—as yet."

Turning back pages of history to 1917, at which time the unveiling of Sequoyah's statue took place in the national capitol's hall of fame, Doctor Cooley found the kind of praise for the Cherokee Indian he has been looking for.

"Sequoyah invented the only sensible alphabet in the world," the Tulsan quoted the late Speaker Chomp Clark [3] of Missouri as saying at the unveiling ceremonies. "It has one letter for each and every sound the human throat can make," the speaker added in praising phonetics of the language. "If he (Sequoyah) had lived 2,000 years ago, one-fifth of the usual time of life could be saved." Here Clark said that it took years of schooling to acquire even a fair command of the English language, while the Sequoyah alphabet could be learned in only a few days.

On the same occasion, the late Senator Owen of Oklahoma said: "It is a strange thing that no alphabet in all the world reaches the dignity, the simplicity, and the value of the Cherogee [3] alphabet, the Cherokee could learn to spell in one day."

For release September 3, 1941:

Tulsa, Oklahoma:—Bookkeeping, Typing, Shorthand and kindred subjects for business people, will move over slightly, to make room for a subject never before taught the white man. An Indian language, the tongue of the Cherokees, from the syllabus of Sequoyah, is to be offered as a special course with real Indian full-bloods as teachers.

To preserve the only native tongue in America before it is too late, Leon E. Crawford, President of the American Business College here, announced today he had made arrangements to bring an octogenarian from out of the hills of eastern Oklahoma, the only Indian alive who can set Cherokee type, to Tulsa to

[3] So spelled in our reprint of the release.

start work on grammars and dictionaries, necessary for classroom instruction. Crawford explained ordinary adults can learn the tongue in a couple of semesters of easy lessons, which he plans to give at night, to scores of business and professional men and women, who have expressed a desire to study Cherokee, in an endeavor to perpetuate it.

Levi Gritts, last elected Chief of the Cherokees, and his wife, together with J. B. Shumatonna, Chief of the Otoe tribe, all Oklahoma Indians, will supervise the classroom attempt to have Indians teach the white man how to speak and write the only printable language indigenous to North America.

In more abstruse matters our tradition gives the speaker some freedom of improvisation, but even here the pattern is fairly uniform. Theories about the origin of language and suggestions for research on this problem run along certain well-fixed lines.[4] The speaker has the right to improvise etymologies; these, however, adhere to a rather simple scheme.[5] This phase of popular lore also is capable of development in literary hands.[6]

The speaker who discourses about language sometimes adds that he himself has not a perfect command of his native language—the reasons differ with biographic details—but is aware of his weakness and tries to overcome it; he alludes patronizingly to other speakers who do not know enough to make a similar effort. In fact, it soon appears that the speaker possesses a fairly extensive stock of authoritative knowledge which enables

[4] The following, from a reader's letter to the *New York Times,* dated August 6, 1937, is quite characteristic.

'Some years ago a scientist lived in a land of monkeys to learn their language. I suggest that the study of language begin there with the primitive sounds of animals, followed by a survey of what is known of the speech of savages. After this might come a review of the most ancient fragments of recorded tongues, tracing them down into the developed languages of Egypt, Mesopotamia, Persia, India, China and elsewhere. Some idea of a dispersal of tongues from a common Asiatic center might thus be had and the earliest roots of our commonest words be learned. A brief survey, in translation, of the recorded literature of these dispersal tongues would bring us down through the ancient classics in all lands to the Greek and Roman cultures, where we should learn not merely a few pages of Xenophon and Homer; of Caesar, Cicero, Virgil and Horace, but, in translations, the whole glorious range of Greek and Latin literary, poetic, scientific and philosophic accomplishment, and the bearing of it all on our modern thought.'

[5] A letter to the *New York Times,* dated Caracas, Venezuela, November 18, 1939, contains the following characteristic passage: 'But from what root did the word "Reich" grow up? Certainly not from the same as the world "realm." I rather believe that "Reich" has something to do with the German word "reichen" (i.e., reach). On this basis I think I have a more satisfactory explanation of the designation of "Deutsches Reich" and "Frankreich," as those countries or lands that "reach" (or embrace within their respective boundaries, present or former) the Germans, respectively the French (or Franks, originally).... a long time ago, probably after the division of Charlemagne's Holy Roman Empire, the western part (chiefly present-day France) came to be designated by the German word Frankreich (although probably spelled in the then prevailing German), i.e., the realm, or rather the land within which "reached" the Franks, from which word afterward a new word, France, resulted.'

Cf. the discussion of a similar instance by R. G. Kent, *JAOS,* 55.115–9 (1935).

[6] Thus, a fairly elaborate theory is built up by Burton Rascoe, *Titans of Literature: From Homer to the Present,* pp. 48 ff. (New York, 1932).

him to condemn many forms that are used by other speakers.

Several peculiarities of these secondary responses deserve further study. The speaker, when making the secondary response, shows alertness. His eyes are bright, and he seems to be enjoying himself. No matter how closely his statement adheres to tradition, it proffers it as something new, often as his own observation or as that of some acquaintance, and he is likely to describe it as interesting. If he knows that he is talking to a professional student of language, he first alleges ignorance and alludes modestly to the status of his own speech, but then advances the traditional lore in a fully authoritative tone. The whole process is, as we say, pleasurable.[7]

The linguist's cue in this situation is to observe, but if, giving in to a natural impulse (or else, by way of experiment), he tries to enlighten the speaker, he encounters a TERTIARY RESPONSE to language. The tertiary response occurs almost inevitably when the conventional secondary response is subjected to question. The tertiary response is hostile; the speaker grows contemptuous or angry. He will impatiently reaffirm the secondary response, or, more often, he will resort to one of a few well-fixed formulas of confutation.

Invariably, in my experience, the linguist's counter-statements are treated as eccentric personal notions—even by speakers who otherwise are aware of the cumulative character of science.[8] The knowledge that the linguist has in person investigated the topic under discussion does not alter this response.[9] Statements about the relation of standard and non-standard forms are likely to be interpreted as 'defense' or 'advocacy' of the latter.[10] Especially, linguistic statements about the relation of writing to language conflict so violently with self-evident truth that they can be interpreted

[7] Undefined popular terms, such as *pleasure* or *anger*, are here used because there is not (or I have not) enough physiology and sociology to redefine them. See, for the rest, A. P. Weiss, *A Theoretical Basis of Human Behavior*, revised edition 419 ff. (Columbus, 1929). Similarly, I use terms like *mechanist* or *non-mentalist:* in a community where nearly everyone believed that the moon is made of green cheese, students who constructed nautical almanacs without reference to cheese, would have to be designated by some special term, such as *non-cheesists.*

[8] After I had outlined the relation of writing to speech, with explicit reference to the history of our science, before a group of educationists who were interested in elementary reading instruction, I was finally refuted by the statement that 'you'll have to SHOW the modern educationist'.

[9] A physician, of good general background and education, who had been hunting in the north woods, told me that the Chippewa language contains only a few hundred words. Upon question, he said that he got this information from his guide, a Chippewa Indian. When I tried to state the diagnostic setting, the physician, our host, briefly and with signs of displeasure repeated his statement and then turned his back to me. A third person, observing this discourtesy, explained that I had some experience of the language in question. This information had no effect.

[10] 'You surely don't expect me (You wouldn't want your children) to go around saying things like *I seen it* or *I done it.*' A college administrator expressed his wonder at the very 'liberal' attitude of linguists in matters of 'grammar.'

only as a perverse refusal to consider certain facts.[11] A cultured speaker, in confuting the linguist's statements, is likely to appeal, without making clear the connection, to the existence of great writers in his language.[12]

A literary instance of the irate tertiary response is the controversy between George Washington Moon and Dean Alford. Neither contestant had any knowledge of the subject, but one had questioned the other's secondary response.[13]

The ordinary speaker makes a response of the tertiary type only when some secondary response of his is questioned or contradicted; but, on a higher and semi-learned plane, a tertiary response may be aroused in a speaker who merely hears or reads linguistic statements and possesses enough sophistication to see that they conflict with his habitual secondary responses. Thus, Oscar Cargill, *Intellectual America,* p. 521 (New York, 1941), writes:

> One cannot ignore the weight of Freeman's essay, "Race and Language" (1885), upon the efforts of these pure scholars. His praise of philosophy and his use of it as a test of nationality tickled the egos of these new scientists who fancied that their researchers would be of the utmost consequences to society. Further and further back into German forests, up Scandinavian fjords, and over Icelandic barriers they pushed their quests for the origin of words. Now, while it is true that the commonest words in English speech

[11] Having read a few sentences about the difference between language and writing, a philosopher concludes that the linguistic author refuses to talk about writing. This conclusion is not shaken by a following fairly wordy passage about the use of graphic signs. To say that writing is not the central and basic form of language is simply to ignore writing altogether. See *Journal of Philosophy,* 36.613 (1939).

Naïve invention of phonetic alphabets is not uncommon. The inventor usually believes that he has made an important discovery. Usually, also, he views this discovery as capable of immediately affecting language—removing language barriers or the like. Thus, Senator Robert L. Owen of Oklahoma invented a 'global alphabet' (78th Congress, 1st Session; Senate Document No. 49, Government Printing Office, 1943). The *New York Times* (July 29, 1943) quotes Senator Owen as follows: 'Through it I can teach any reasonably intelligent man Chinese in two months,' he asserted. 'It is a means by which we can teach the English language to all the world at high speed and negligible cost. It will pay its own way.'

[12] A Russian savant was shocked, in the classical manner described by Jespersen, *Grundfragen der Phonetik,* p. 56 (Leipzig, 1904), at the sight of the transcriptions used in an elementary Russian course for American students, transcriptions which deviate from the conventional orthography, such as /trúpka/ for graphic *trubka,* /sát/ for graphic *sad,* /búdjit/ for graphic *budget.* In his complaint to an administrative officer he alluded at some length to 'the written and spoken language . . . of Turgeniev, Tolstoy and Chekhov', and to the circumstance that one of his schoolmates later became well-known as a poet.

[13] Henry Alford, *The Queen's English* (London, 1864 [1863]); George Washington Moon, *A Defence of the Queen's English* (London, 1863); *The Dean's English* (London, 1864). These books went into several editions, taking the shape of a polemic; see the entries in A. G. Kennedy. *A Bibliography of Writings on the English Language* (New York, 1927). Alford and Moon develop the art of finding 'errors' in English to a point where probably no utterance could escape censure. On Alford, see W. D. Whitney, *Oriental and Linguistic Studies,* 2.166 (New York, 1874).

have Anglo-Saxon originals and these in turn have Gothic counterparts, not one of these scholars has demonstrated that the ideational content of these limited Northern vocabularies was a heavy burden for the intellect of a moron. Words like *the, is have, sleep, drink* and *eat* represent the profundity of Anglo-Saxon thought. Pundits, of whom the revered Walter W. Skeat, Litt.D., LL.D., D.C.L., Ph.D., F.B.A., of the University of Cambridge, is typical, have laboriously traced *Ha* (interj. E.) back to Old Friesic *haha* to denote laughter!) and to German *he;* but it is said that Caligula quite unethically uttered a similar sound when he ordered Pomposo, the philologist, thrown to the lions. In all the northern vocabularies there are no equivalents for such words as *democracy, politics, morals, aesthetics,* and—horror of horrors—*scholarship!* The wolfish pursuit of moronic vocabularies and the ghoulish unearthing of the kennings and pennings of the Northern barbarians diverted young students from the true historical fount of wisdom—the Greek and Roman classics, which fell into the greatest disuse in Western history. There was treachery, alas, among the teachers of classics themselves; for under the leadership of Basil Gildersleeve (educated at Berlin, Bonn, and Göttingen, though a graduate of Princeton), who was appointed Professor of Greek at Hopkins in 1876 and editor of *The American Journal of Philology* in 1880, American classical scholars are turned away from the teaching of concepts to the venal study of syntax and word origins. Before long there were no classical scholars in the old sense in America but only philologists, papyri readers, and robbers of tombs. On every front save that of history the triumph of *Kultur* over culture was complete.

The following remarks are briefer, but perhaps diagnostically even more significant:[14]

The study of language today is not the learning to speak and write or even read: it is a technical subject, excessively dry, largely wrong, and thoroughly repellent. Yet an appreciation of language and its uses may be about as enlightening as any discipline we have. Enlightenment, however, is not a matter of accidence, morphology, and other technical aspects so dear to the German-trained and inspired. We give pretty much the same course in "English" from the grades through a couple of years of college—and yet we insist that we enlighten our students. Truly, we are fatuous as well as conceited!

It is only in recent years that I have learned to observe these secondary and tertiary responses in anything like a systematic manner, and I confess that I cannot explain them—that is, correlate them with anything else. The explanation will doubtless be a matter of psychology and sociology.

[14] S. A. Nock of the Kansas State College of Agriculture and Mechanic Arts, in the Bulletin of the American Association of University Professors, 29.202 (1943).

29

A Philosophy of Language

JAMES B. MCMILLAN

DURING THE LAST FIFTY YEARS the discipline which we call "linguistic science" has developed a considerable body of knowledge and a trustworthy methodology; likewise the study of aesthetics has made productive use of comparative and historical facts and the findings of relevant sciences. Yet the study of the English language in our schools (which one would naïvely suppose to be based on linguistics and aesthetics as biology is based on chemistry, physics, and genetics) has gone its own way, changing, it is true, but never aligning itself with the kindred disciplines. In fact, a remarkable dichotomy has occurred, with the specialists in language operating almost completely outside the sphere of the teachers and textbook writers in grammar, composition, and rhetoric.

In spite of this anomaly, the kinship of the matters discussed in the various kinds of English language classes suggests that an integrated philosophy of language (grammar, composition, rhetoric) can be formulated; such a formulation is the purpose of this paper. Since it is a philosophy for use and not for ornament, it will be called *a* philosophy, not *the* philosophy. Just as people who want to measure a rug do not argue the fundamental validity of the meter or the foot but agree to use meters or feet and proceed with their measuring, so I propose to state certain basic postulates and proceed to derive from them several useful sequiturs and implications. And just as use of the foot requires the measurer to use feet and inches throughout his job, and to divide feet into inches, not centimeters, so the use of particular postulates requires the writer to limit his derivations to those legitimately entailed by the postulates. The basic premises will not be defended. The dissenter is welcome to reject them and choose others or to choose none at all. Eclecticism is practiced, sometimes knowingly, by many people.

The first premise is the assumption that the job of the student or teacher of grammar, composition, or rhetoric is to make statements about language.

Reprinted by permission from *College English,* 9.385–390 (April, 1948). Professor McMillan is chairman of the Department of English at the University of Alabama.

The second premise is that we expect such statements to be true, according to the speaker's definition of truth. And the final premise is that there are recognized in this context two kinds of truth: (1) objective truth and (2) subjective truth.

Two factors determine the speaker's choice of one or the other kind of truth: (a) the purpose of the speaker and (b) the nature of the matter discussed. If the speaker wishes to make his statements verifiable by other competent observers, he uses objective truth. His statements are thus independent of his personal authority; they stand or fall as they are observationally verified. Being hypotheses, they are subject to revision, and they claim no finality. If, however, the speaker wishes to base his statements on private authority, he uses subjective truth. He validates his asseverations by his personal prestige, eloquence, high motives, conformity to a selected tradition, or superior desk-pounding. Being descriptive of his private attitudes, such statements pertain in whole or in part to the speaker's interior bodily activities and to his history, not to the subjects mentioned in his sentences.

But a desire for objectivity does not alone make statements objective. The data discussed must have tangible, sensory reality. Only matters which can be quantitatively measured or described in physical terms can be the subject of objectively true statements. Metaphysics is thus ruled out, as is poetry,[1] theology, and ethics.

Now back to the grammarian. If he proposes to write literature, if to him grammar is a species of poetry or fiction, he is welcome to utilize subjective statements. There is no law against it. But he should be fair to his readers and announce that he depends for truth primarily on his private impulses. He is not operating within a learned discipline, and he should no more condescend to debate his assertions than should a poet or a prophet. In the very nature of his activity he can do nothing but assert his views and reinforce them by some sort of external authority. The reader cannot test the validity of a subjective statement; he can only test his willingness to be bound by the authority of the speaker or the extent of his accidental agreement with the speaker. This condition is true in grammar no less than in aesthetics.

If we make the arbitrary assumption that the grammarian wants to use objective truth wherever he can, we turn to his data to find when and where he can be a scientist. We discover that the facts pertaining to language fall into two groups, one made up of measurable data, and the other made up of imponderables. The first we shall call "grammar"; it can be a science. The second we shall call "rhetoric"; limited by present knowledge, it is an

---

[1] This does not mean that literature is all lies; it means that the writer of literature, in order to discuss some subjects, may go beyond the bounds of sensible reality, giving up objective verifiability but counting it no loss.

art. This division is not arbitrary, it is made automatically by the objectivity or subjectivity of the relevant data. The division does not bind the grammarian who does not desire objectivity.

The province of the grammarian qua scientist is twofold, because the facts with which he operates fall into two categories: (1) linguistic and (2) sociological. The linguistic facts concern the phonology, morphology, syntax, and lexicon of the language. The sociological facts concern the attitudes toward locutions held by people in various societal situations. Each of these two categories has two subdivisions: (a) present-day facts and (b) historical facts.

Linguistic facts are statements severely limited to description of the forms of the language and are derived from actual observation of speech and writing. The objective of the grammarian qua linguist in this subprovince is the objective of any scientist: the collection, classification, and analysis of all relevant data and the formulation of "laws" (descriptive hypotheses). His goal is "understanding" language. Sociological facts concern the folklore of language, the beliefs of people about specific words and constructions. Such facts are usually records of the situations in which certain locutions are disfavored and the situations in which locutions are used without disfavor. The objective of the scientific grammarian in this field is to label language forms according to their usage and so to provide a useful information service which helps citizens "win friends and influence people" by using the "right" locutions.

If the grammarian as student of the language proposes to state what should be rather than what is in the language, he leaves the confines of objective verifiable truth; this course is perfectly all right, provided he knows that he is making unverifiable statements. If the grammarian as student of language etiquette proposes to define what should be called "bad English" rather than to say what expressions are actually treated as "bad English," he likewise becomes a subjective moralist. Moralizing instead of describing is, of course, legitimate, but the honest moralizer labels his statements personal assertions, and he renounces any claim to verifiability.

This insistence that moralizing statements in grammar be clearly recognized as personal assertions is not a pedantic vagary; it is a necessary implication of comparataive and historical language study. There is not a single philologist, living or dead, who has been able to adduce a single iota of objective factual evidence for saying that *are not* is more legitimately English than *ain't*. Philologists can, however, find evidence that people in some social contexts punish the user of *ain't*. The reason for such punishment is nonlinguistic. If the language habits of one group of people are respected or disliked by other people, the respect or dislike is a matter of social psychology, not of grammar. In language "whatever is, is right" simply because there is no discovered source of knowledge about language except language itself. And, in sociology, that which a group of people consider right is, to that group, right. From his objective study the grammarian knows that there is nothing ambiguous or inefficient about the common double negative; but, if some people taboo the construction and others want to emulate those who taboo it, the job of the grammarian is, perforce, to record the taboo.

The grammarian (linguist) in his function of "understanding" language as an intellectual discipline records the plain facts that *It's me* and *It's I* are alternative forms in present-day English, just as *can't* and *cannot* are alternative forms. The grammarian in his function as an Emily Post of language records the treatment accorded *It's me* and *It's I* by various social groups.

Textbook writers are frequently betrayed into confusing linguistic and sociological provinces because the nomenclature of the two fields is the same, because "laws" of etiquette are phrased exactly as are "laws" of language, and because certain social prejudices have been traditionally stated as grammatical laws. For instance, the linguist finds English-speaking people saying *It's me* and *It's I,* but not *It's my.* He proceeds to state the law that the case of a pronoun which is a complement after *is* is nominative or objective, not possessive. He knows that any case can follow *is* which actually follows it, and he states his role as a description of what he finds. The usage student may find *It's me* taboo in formal written English, along with *It's her, It's them,* etc., and may state the generalized rule that the nominative is required after *is.* But his statement applies only to formal written English, and it is a rule only as long as it is true to the observed facts. It is not true of the English language that *is* must be followed by a nominative; it will be true of formal written English only as long as such is the practice, and the law will apply only to the societal situations in which it actually obtains. Formal written English is not the language, it is merely one type of English. Its rules are pertinent only to people studying or writing formal written English; other types of English have their own rules.

It is the duty of the grammarian to announce publicly which of his functions he is performing, just as it is his duty to announce what kind of truth he is using. (The confusion of grammar and language etiquette is epidemic in conventional handbooks, where there is a superstition that analysis of the language has something to do with "speaking and writing correctly.")

The rhetorician has likewise two provinces: (1) the useful art of communication and (2) the fine art of speaking and writing beautifully. Our present ignorance of biosociology makes it impossible for the rhetorician to be a scientist.

In the practical art of communication, the rhetorician can be objective only as far as semantics is a science. In practice most rhetoricians use the lexicographer's common-knowledge and synonymy tests to determine whether an expression serves as an efficient means of communication, and so operate with a good deal of practical objectivity. (This statement does not apply to the grammarians and rhetoricians who talk about the "essential" meaning of a word; they are moralists.) In this field the rhetorician may choose to use the statements of the grammarian, but he is not a grammarian, because he does not deal solely with language forms.

In the fine art of composition the rhetorician is an aesthetician and is thus obliged to set up and use aesthetic standards. Such standards are necessarily at bottom subjective, as the history of aesthetics so insistently shows. The rhetorician may hold as one of his tenets that artistic composition must be in idiomatic English, and he may therefore make use of grammar; he *may* hold that in certain contexts the language of certain social groups is desirable, and in such cases may use the statements of usage students; he *may* be concerned with efficiency of communication as a factor in art and, if so, may make use of the statements of practical rhetoric. But, in addition, the rhetorician legitimately talks about the desirability or undesirability of words and constructions without being concerned with idiom, usage, or denotation. For example, he may prefer the word *carmine* to the word *red* in a particular sentence because his taste dictates *carmine*. No objective standard for such preferences can be required of the rhetorician, since "beauty" in language is not a simple tangible entity or quality. It may be any quality liked or approved by any person. The presence of beauty cannot be demonstrated; it can only be asserted. Competent aestheticians, like competent critics, poets, spiritualists, and theologians, can be flatly contradicted without suffering any disadvantage.

The important point for our analysis is this: a grammarian who is ostensibly discussing grammar cannot legitimately drag in rhetorical criteria and values. When he sets out to describe objectively the language or the etiquette of the language, he is expected to do just what he proposes; if he covertly slips in aesthetic statements, he misrepresents the facts he is supposed to be presenting. This is no disparagement of rhetoric; I am merely insisting that, because it is by nature subjective, its practitioners should carefully avoid being mistaken for grammarians and that grammarians should carefully leave rhetoric out of grammar.

It is obvious that the textbook and instructor in discussing the English language must at times make evaluative statements. It is useful to recognize two sharply distinct kinds of value: (1) instrumental and (2) terminal. Anything having instrumental value is useful as a means to an end. Anything having terminal value is good as an end in itself. It is not possible to debate questions of value. If a discussion concerns an instrumental value, the disagreement cannot be settled by logical argument but must be settled by getting the requisite information. That is, one simply finds out, by observation, whether the thing actually serves as a means and accomplishes its end. If a discussion concerns a terminal value, there can be no debate because there is no way to settle such a dispute. No objective moot question is raised. What is "bad" to one person (for instance, homely idioms or precious writing) may be "good" to another. Is peppermint or cinnamon a "better" flavor? Since terminal evaluations are descriptive of the speaker's taste, they cannot be debated as if they were objective; they can only be asserted.

When the grammarian is a scientist speaking in his function as an understander of the language, he makes no evaluative statements whatsoever (although he accepts the basic social premise of all the sciences that "understanding" is valuable); he merely describes the language as he finds it. Like any scientist, he is interested in what is, not in what ought to be.

In his function as a student of language etiquette, the grammarian must use evaluations, but he cannot make them. This fact is obscured by the grammarian's habit of using the terms "good" and "bad" in labeling expressions. When one of these adjectives is applied to a language form by a scientific grammarian, it is not in reality an evaluative term; it is a shorthand label meaning something like "This locution is favored (or disfavored) by so-and-so people in such-and-such contexts." When we translate "good English" and "bad English" into these meanings, it is clear that the phrases are not judgments of value, as they appear to be, but are simple descriptive statements. Since they merely record the presence or absence of specific locutions in specific contexts (the existence of taboo or disfavor being presumed when a popular expression is regularly avoided in a given context), the labels are completely objective and can be verified by anybody who can read or head.

The evaluations used (not made) by the grammarian in this province are made by society. The social groups whose language is considered "right" in certain contexts are selected by nonlinguistic criteria. The avoidance of expressions which are disliked by a "superior" group may be a good-in-itself or it may be a means to an end. The grammarian is not concerned with the basis of the evaluation, since it is not a linguistic matter; he simply uses it, confining himself to facts about the usage. Because professional writers of belles-lettres use words as their stock-in-trade, they have been commonly supposed to have some mysterious genius-knowledge of language, and conformity to their grammatical habits has come to be for some people a terminal value. In the same way, grammarians (rhetoricians) have in the past acquired a spurious reputation of knowing what is "good" in grammar, and people have attached a terminal value to speaking and writing according to certain dogmatic rules. But values in language etiquette are usually instrumental; most people want to talk and write like the socially and economically successful as a means of identifying themselves with the "upper classes." Likewise they want to avoid resemblance to the socially unsuccessful, the "illiterate." Such evaluations are made precisely as are evaluations in dress and manners.

The scientific student of usage is a servant of society. He can describe the usage of any group that interests his audience, or he can describe the usage of all groups; but he cannot arrogate linguistic "superiority" to any particular group.

The rhetorician also deals with evaluations. In the useful art of writing and speaking, communication is assumed to be valuable, and whatever further instrumental values are necessary to effect communication are legitimate. In the fine art of literature, the rhetorician must set up terminal values according to aesthetic criteria, and objective instrumental values may be derived from the terminal values.

It is sufficient for our purposes to note that rhetorical values are proper and legitimate as long as they are labeled rhetorical values. The grammarian cannot be a scientist and assume that an aesthetic "good" is an objective reality pertinent to grammar. Church windows are frequently much admired, but they are not the sole standard for judging residence and museum windows.

If the three basic postulates of this exposition are acceptable and valid, the following conclusions appear to be justifiable:

First, it is possible for the English teacher to hold an integrated, consistent philosophy of grammar and rhetoric which is based on and makes use of the relevant underlying disciplines, and which allows him as much practical objectivity as most of the learned disciplines permit. It seems to be true that most of our colleagues in other fields have renounced authoritarianism and are encouraging students to demand reasons which they can verify instead of dogmas which they must swallow; it is not likely that the English teacher can long claim exemption from this tendency, and it is likely that he will be much happier when he can be as objective as a psychologist or a sociologist.

Second, if the English instructor chooses to use scientific methodology, then he will have to divorce the study and teaching of "correct" usage from the study and teaching of grammar. This means that in usage he must follow the general principles of modern scientific language study. If the study of grammar as an intellectual discipline is to be included in a curriculum (and the curriculum-maker must decide whether it is or not), then the course must be different from what passes for grammar today. Conventional formal grammar, which is an eclectic application of certain rules of Latin grammar to arbitrarily selected segments of English morphology and syntax, must give way to a thorough-going inductive study of the English language. The traditional superstitious identification of the "rules" of English grammar with the "rules" of a mythical "good English" must go.

Third, the present dichotomy between the specialists and the teachers (including the textbook writers) appears to have little excuse for existence and little hope for survival. It cannot be long that English teachers who hold scholarly research in literature in high regard will persist in ignoring scholarly research in language. If the literature teachers were scornful of objectivity generally, then the objective study of language could hardly hope to attract them; but factual knowledge in literary history has become indispensable, and factual knowledge in language must surely become equally indispensable.

30

Prescriptivism and Linguistics in English Teaching

ARCHIBALD A. HILL

IN A RECENT ARTICLE in *College English*[1] Morton W. Bloomfield presents a cogent, informed, and admirably good-natured account of the problem involved in teaching English to native speakers of the language, now that linguistic scientists (a notably prickly group of men) have begun to question many traditional attitudes and even to deny vehemently, not always wisely but sometimes certainly with good evidence, some of the things we all learned in the classroom as gospel truth. Professor Bloomfield comes to the conclusion that what is taught in an English class must be some form of wise and moderate prescriptivism, checked by the limits of fact as established by linguistics. The reason for his position is that the teaching of English involves questions of value, which characteristically are not settled merely by the accumulation of facts.

It is probably natural that Bloomfield, as a man primarily interested in the discipline of English, though aware of linguistics, should lean in the direction of value, just as it is natural that a linguist, even though he be

Reprinted by permission from *College English,* 15.395–399 (April, 1954).
[1] October, 1953.

a practicing teacher of English, should lean in the direction of fact. I do not wish to question Bloomfield's central thesis or to add fuel to an already unfortunate blaze. Rather it seems to me possible, if a linguist states some modifications of what Bloomfield seems to believe the linguists' position to be, that the area of mutual understanding may be increased, with benefit to all.

Bloomfield defends prescriptivism first because it has social utility. That is, the public judges, and will continue to judge, our students by the language they use. Therefore, he says, the honest teacher must neither hinder nor hurry change but teach realities; an unwise liberalism will expose students to censure. With this position the majority of responsible linguists would agree. We are to blame for not having made ourselves clear on the point, though my own experience in the failure of serious attempts at explanation leads me to believe that perhaps not all the blame lies with the linguists. No intelligent linguist would think of denying that the use of a given linguistic form will have inevitable social consequences for the user —the position that language patterns are a part of larger patterns of social behavior and that each reacts on the other is central to linguistics. In my own classes, as an example of social consequences from language use, I often tell a story told me by an old Charlestonian. She had brought a beau home for family inspection, and her father was proudly displaying his collection of art. "Now this," he said, "is called 'The Broken Pitcher.' "

"Yes," said the young man, "I see the corner's damaged." The suitor was never invited to the house again. The form "pitcher" cannot be ugly in itself—we use it as a perfectly good word. Nor can the confusion of two words, as the result of natural tendencies of change, be a very heinous sin. Millions probably confuse them, just as even more millions confuse *affect* and *effect*. The point, however, is not that it would be easy to defend the young man's misunderstanding. It is rather that the consequences of it were very real for him and presumably unpleasant. The nonlinguist often argues violently that there is something inherently wrong, ugly, or illogical in such a form as "pitcher" and equates any denial of the inherent "wrongness" of the form with a denial of the social consequences of using it.

The linguist maintains merely that in itself a form, say *golpet,* is as good as another form, say *thaltep;* the difference between them is merely one of attitudes, not of inherent qualities. I have chosen nonsense illustrations deliberately, in an effort to find forms to which the reader has not already learned to respond with conditioned attitudes of value. It seems to me that a linguist is performing a service in attempting to separate such conditioned value reactions from the inherent qualities of the stimulus and that we have a right to complain when our attempts to do so are received as further illustrations of the blindness of men who are supposed to believe that "anything goes."

Bloomfield's second reason for teaching a prescriptive grammar and usage is that it is an aid in understanding the past. Again a linguist cannot quarrel, at least with the aim. Yet it is to be doubted whether prescriptive grammar is always conservative. For instance, one of Bloomfield's examples of vulgate (the language of the majority) which he would rightly resist in classroom use is "I ain't got no dough." Two of the three objectionable forms in this sentence, *ain't* and the double negative, are older than the prescriptivist objection to them and are therefore more in line with past usage than are the modern condemnations. A linguist would hope to accomplish Bloomfield's aim of understanding past language structures not by reliance on prescriptivism but by knowing the structures of the present, with adequate recognition of the fact that different forms and structures are in use in the English-speaking community, in different places, on different social levels, and for different purposes. With such a background a student would, we hope, be ready to deal with the language of the past not as a primitive jargon less perfect than his own speech but as a structure to be respected and understood—a structure different from others, as all language structures are, and, by virtue of difference, capable of artistic effects as good as any open to Hemingway or Housman.

Bloomfield's third and fourth reasons for rejecting vulgate in favor of a prescriptive norm are that vulgate is deficient in all artistic qualities except vigor and is likewise deficient in intellectual breadth and depth. The two statements are closely related and should be discussed together. In a measure, a linguist can agree. If we listen to talk heard on street corners or in grocery stores, it is true that we hear little that is memorable for beauty or intellectual penetration. Language use is an art, and all can agree that great practitioners of any art are few in number. Similarly it is a truism that intellectual leaders are anything but numerous—otherwise they would not be leaders. Yet many linguists would feel that, when Bloomfield says that vulgate is deficient in beauty and intellectual qualities, he is confusing the language with its use. We can agree with him heartily that good models of language use should be given to our students, but we would maintain that the nature of an instrument is different from its employment.

Language structure, with which linguists are primarily concerned, remains relatively constant, and in all important ways is shared by all members of the community, both those who use the language well and those who use it ill. For instance, though it is not universally agreed to by all linguists, many would now say that English has four degrees of stress. If so, this is an example of an important structural feature shared by normal English contemporary speech on all levels and in all localities. Even if we grant that such structural characteristics can only be created by the habitual usage of the community and are further changed only as these habits change, the striking facts about such structural features is how slowly and how little they change. If English has four stresses, it has acquired the fourth at some time since the Norman Conquest; otherwise the stress system has apparently remained unchanged for approximately two thousand years. If there should be only three significant stresses in Modern English, there has been no change at all. If such structural features can remain so little changed in the face of all the social upheavals and linguistic rivalries of two millenniums, it would seem that we should not worry too much over such details as where a student stresses a word like *justifiable*. At most the choice can affect the student and this particular word; the system of stress distinctions will remain the same. It should be emphasized that structure in language is something more, and more important, than a collection of items. A change in the number or type of stress distinctions would be vastly more important (for good or ill) than the introduction or the loss of vocabulary items. I am aware, for instance, that confusion of *disinterested* and *uninterested* destroys a useful vocabulary item and one which I would have been glad to see preserved, even though nowadays I cannot talk of "disinterested judges" for fear of being misunderstood. But, though vocabulary items can be lost, others can be gained, and somehow we manage to carry on our necessary business with the vocabulary we have at any one time. Therefore, it seems to me that we need not fear that the whole of our language will be damaged by those who would say "bored, disinterested judges." For the individual and the community, structure is a broad, pervasive pattern, already determined, and capable of very little change. As such it is relatively neutral and colorless. Indeed, in large measure, it is something which escapes the user's conscious attention. The use he makes of his structure and the items within it is something different. Language use is important to the individual; he is highly conscious of it and rightly seeks advice and help in improving it.

For the reasons which I have tried to outline, when Bloomfield goes on to say that to accept the use made of our language by the majority would be to destroy the beauties of the language itself, I think it is necessary to disagree. He is here assuming that poor use is essentially the same thing as poor structure. I should rather say that the use of language is an area in which value judgments must indeed be made, and is an area in which English teachers should increase both their vigilance and their research, but that structure is different and is not subject to the same kind of criticism we would bring to bear in order to evaluate a paragraph by Winston Churchill or a sonnet by Shelley. Bloomfield goes so far as to say that one who does not recognize the beauty of "Forever wilt thou love and she be fair" is unfit to teach English. But the example belongs to art and is beautiful because it is a part of a literary work the totality of whose beauty we all admire. It is difficult to argue that the forms contained in the line—considered either as separate items or as a special dialect—are in themselves any better or more beautiful than the forms of vulgate. For instance, if *wilt* is more beautiful than *will,* does that lead us to the conclusion that the sequence *-lt* is beautiful, so that *kilt* is better than *killed?* Of if a dialect employing a distinction betwen singular and plural in second-person pronouns is better and more logical than one which does not, are we to defend the metropolitan low-class distinction between *you* singular, and *youse* plural? I wish, however, to be as clear as possible and therefore to say as emphatically as I can that I agree that anyone who cannot appreciate the beauty of the Keats poem is unfit to teach English. And I should add further that, if there is any student who has drawn from linguistics the idea that the poem is in a strange and inferior dialect because its vocabulary and forms differ from contemporary everyday usage, he holds a horrifying and absurd conclusion. If linguistics leads to such beliefs, it earns nothing but opposition. May I hope, however, should any student of literature be led into the equally horrifying and absurd idea that the dialect employed by Keats is better than vulgate in all social and even in all artistic situations, that Bloomfield would join me in giving such a fallacious conclusion as vigorous opposition as I am sure he would give the other?

Much the same sort of objection applies to Bloomfield's fear that too much liberalism would destroy intellectual activity. It is usual in our culture to write about intellectual matters in a very formal kind of English, which it is all too easy to identify with the intellectual activity itself. The same thing is true of other cultures, yet elsewhere in the world the disappearance or replacement of a special intellectual language or dialect has not meant the disappearance of intellectual activity. Such replacements have almost always been by the form of a language originally regarded as an unintellectual vulgate. Yet, when the replacement takes place, the old vulgate quickly becomes the new intellectual language. For instance, no one would maintain that the body of intellectual writing in the vernacular tongues is inferior to that in Latin or that intellectual vigor has been circumscribed by the disuse of the scholar's language. For once, therefore, I think I am safe in denying one of Bloomfield's theses. If, by vulgate, Bloomfield means the language structure used by the majority, then I should oppose him with this statement: Good style, whether artistic or intellectual, is possible in any language structure. Mark Twain, in *Huckleberry Finn,* employed the vulgate structure of rural America in his day, yet Huck's description of a village funeral and of a backwoods front parlor are among the classics of our literature. It seems to me that as teachers of English, whether with or without linguistic training, we should strive for clarity. If we assume that style and structure need no differentiation, we are in danger of obscuring both.

I have tried to equal Bloomfield's urbanity and his grasp of first things first. I may have failed, but I hope I may permit myself to believe that he as English teacher, I as linguist, might agree that all who teach the native language have a solemn duty in understanding language, its structure, its social implications, and the use, beautiful or otherwise, which men have put to it. Further, since literature is necessarily a part of language, all that a linguist can discover about his subject should not merely limit what the English teacher can say but is of positive though potential value to him in all his work.

31

Cultural Levels and Functional Varieties of English

JOHN S. KENYON

THE WORD *level,* when used to indicate different styles of language, is a metaphor, suggesting higher or lower position and, like the terms *higher* and *lower,* figuratively implies 'better' or 'worse,' 'more desirable' or 'less desirable,' and similar comparative degrees of excellence or inferiority in language.

The application of the term *level* to those different styles of language that are not properly distinguished as better or worse, desirable or undesirable, creates a false impression. I confess myself guilty of this error along with some other writers. What are frequently grouped together in one class as different levels of language are often in reality false combinations of two distinct and incommensurable categories, namely, *cultural levels* and *functional varieties.*

Among *cultural levels* may be included, on the lower levels, illiterate speech, narrowly local dialect, ungrammatical speech and writing, excessive and unskilful slang, slovenly and careless vocabulary and construction, exceptional pronunciation, and, on the higher level, language used generally by the cultivated, clear, grammatical writing, and pronunciations used

This paper was read before the College English Group of Northeastern Ohio (Modern Language Association) at its annual meeting at Oberlin College, October 25, 1947. Reprinted by permission from *College English,* 10.31–36 (October, 1948). The author was Professor of English at Hiram College.

by the cultivated over wide areas. The different cultural levels may be summarized in the two general classes *substandard* and *standard*.

Among *functional varieties* not depending on cultural levels may be mentioned colloquial language, itself existing in different degrees of familiarity or formality, as, for example, familiar conversation, private correspondence, formal conversation, familiar public address; formal platform or pulpit speech, public reading, public worship; legal, scientific, and other expository writing; prose and poetic belles-lettres. The different functional varieties may roughly be grouped together in the two classes *familiar* and *formal* writing or speaking.

The term *level,* then, does not properly belong at all to functional varieties of speech—colloquial, familiar, formal, scientific, literary language. They are equally "good" for their respective functions, and as classifications do not depend on the cultural status of the users.

The two groupings *cultural levels* and *functional varieties* are not mutually exclusive categories. They are based on entirely separate principles of classification: *culture* and *function.* Although we are here principally concerned with the functional varieties of standard English (the highest cultural level), yet substandard English likewise has its functional varieties for its different occasions and purposes. Thus the functional variety colloquial English may occur on a substandard cultural level, but the term *colloquial* does not itself indicate a cultural level. So the functional variety formal writing or speaking may occur on a lower or on a higher cultural level according to the social status of writer or speaker, and sometimes of reader or audience. It follows, for instance, that the colloquial language of cultivated people is on a higher cultural level than the formal speech of the semiliterate or than some inept literary writing.

Semiliterate formal speech is sometimes heard from radio speakers. I recently heard one such speaker solemnly announce, "Sun day will be Mother's Day." Because the speaker, in his ignorance of good English, thought he was making himself plainer by using the distorted pronunciation *sun day* instead of the standard pronunciation *sundy,* he actually was misunderstood by some listeners to be saying, "Some day will be Mother's Day." About forty years ago the great English phonetician Henry Sweet used this very example to show that "we cannot make words more distinct by disguising them."[1] He was referring to the use, in this instance, of the full sound of vowels in unaccented syllables where standard English has obscure vowels. On the same page Sweet gives another example of the same blunder: "Thus in the sentence *I shall be at home from one to three* the substitution of **tuw** for **tə** [ə = the last sound in *sofa*] at once suggests a confusion between the preposition and the numeral." This was also verified on the radio. Not long ago I heard a radio speaker announce carefully, "This program will be heard

[1] Henry Sweet, *The Sounds of English* (Oxford, 1910), p. 78.

again tomorrow from one two three." I have also recorded (among many others) the following such substandard forms from the radio: *presidEnt* for the standard form *presidǝnt*, the days of the week ending in the full word *day* instead of the standard English syllable *-dy*, *ay man*, for the correct *man*, *cahnsider* for *cǝnsider*, *tooday* for *tǝday*, *too go* for *tǝ go*, *Coalumbia* for *Cǝlumbia*, etc. This is merely one sort among many of substandard features in the formal speech of the semi-literate.[2]

To begin my strictures at home, in *American Pronunciation* (9th ed., 4th printing, p. 17), I use the page heading "Levels of Speech." This should be "Functional Varieties of Standard Speech," for the reference is solely to the different uses of speech on the one cultivated level. Similarly, in the Kenyon-Knott *Pronouncing Dictionary of American English* (p. xvi, §2), I carelessly speak of "levels of the colloquial" where I mean "styles of the colloquial," as three lines above. For though there are different cultural levels of colloquial English, the reference here is only to standard colloquial.

S. A. Leonard and H. Y. Moffett, in their study, "Current Definition of Levels in English Usage,"[3] say (p. 348): "The levels of English usage have been most clearly described in Dr. Murray's Preface ["General Explanations," p. xvii] to the *New English Dictionary*. I have varied his diagram a little in order to illustrate better the overlapping between the categories." It appears to me that Leonard and Moffett have so varied the diagram as to obscure Murray's intention. For he is not here primarily exhibiting levels of speech but is showing the 'Anglicity,' or limits of the English vocabulary for the purposes of his dictionary.[4] The only topical divisions of his diagram that imply a cultural level are "slang" and "dialectal," and the only statement in his explanation of the diagram that could imply it is, "Slang words ascend through colloquial use." This may imply that slang is on a lower cultural level than "colloquial, literary, technical, scientific, foreign." We may also safely infer that Murray would place "Dialectal" on a lower level than colloquial and literary if he were here concerned with cultural levels. Murray's diagram rests consistently on the same basis of classification throughout ('Anglicity'), and he emphasizes that "there is absolutely no defining line in any direction [from the central nucleus of colloquial and literary]." Moreover, Murray's exposition here concerns only vocabulary, with no consideration of the other features that enter so largely into "levels" of language—grammatical form and structure, pronunciation, spelling, and meaning—of styles, in short, only so far as they are affected by vocabulary. These he treats of elsewhere but without reference to levels.

[2] See further *American Speech*, VI, No. 5 (June, 1931), 368–72.
[3] *English Journal*, XVI, No. 5 (May, 1927), 345–59.
[4] The word *Anglicity* is a coinage of the *Oxford Dictionary*. They define it as 'English quality, as of speech of style; English idiom.'

It is not quite clear just how far Leonard and Moffett intend their grouping "literary English," "standard, cultivated, colloquial English," and "naïf, popular, or uncultivated English" to be identical with what they call Murray's "levels," his description of which they commend. But it is clear that they call their own grouping "three levels of usage" (p. 357) and classify them together as a single descending scale (cf. "the low end of the scale," p. 358). The inevitable impression that the average reader receives from such an arrangement of the scale is: Highest level, literary English; next lower level, colloquial English; lowest level, illiterate English; whereas, in fact, the first two "levels" are functional varieties of the one cultural level standard English, while the third ("illiterate or uncultivated," p. 358) is a cultural level.

Krapp has a chapter on "The Levels of English Speech,"[5] in which he reveals some awareness of the confusion of cultural levels with functional varieties. He says:

> Among those who pay any heed at all to convention in social relationships, a difference of degree is implicit in all use of English. This difference of degree is usually thought of in terms of higher and lower, of upper levels of speech appropriate to certain occasions of more formal character, of lower levels existing, if not necessarily appropriate, among less elevated circumstances. These popular distinctions of level may be accepted without weighting them too heavily with significance in respect of good, better, and best in speech. A disputatious person might very well raise the question whether literary English, ordinarily regarded as being on a high level, is really any better than the spoken word, is really as good as the spoken word, warm with the breath of the living moment.

At the risk of having to own the hard impeachment of being disputatious, I must express the fear that the logical fallacy in treating of levels, which Krapp rather lightly waves aside, is having a serious effect on general ideas of speech levels, and especially of the significance of colloquial English in good usage. Krapp's grouping, frankly on a scale of "levels" throughout, constitutes a descending scale from the highest, "Literary English," through "Formal Colloquial," "General Colloquial," "Popular English," to the lowest, "Vulgar English." Here the fallacy is obvious: Literary English, Formal Colloquial, and General Colloquial are not cultural levels but only functional varieties of English all on the one cultural level of standard English. The last two, Popular English and Vulgar English, belong in a different order of classification, cultural levels, without regard to function.

So in his succeeding discussion *level* sometimes means the one, sometimes the other; now a functional variety of standard English, and now a cultural level of substandard or of standard English. It is functional on page 58 ("a choice between two levels") and on page 60 ("level of general

---

[5] George Philip Krapp, *The Knowledge of English* (New York, 1927), pp. 55–76.

colloquial"), cultural on page 62 ("popular level" and "cultivated level") and on pages 63-64 ("popular level," "level of popular speech"), functional on page 64 ("general colloquial level"), cultural again on the same page ("popular level," "still lower level"), cultural on page 67 ("vulgar . . . level of speech," "applying the term 'vulgar' to it at certain levels"), cultural on page 68 ("its own [popular] level"), cultural and functional in the same phrase on page 68 ("speakers from the popular and the general colloquial level meet and mix"), and so on most confusingly to page 75.

The same kind of mixture of cultural levels and functional varieties is thrown into one apparently continuous scale by Kennedy: "There is the formal and dignified language of the scholarly or scientific address or paper. . . . The precision and stateliness of this uppermost level . . . is a necessary accompaniment of thinking on a high plane."[6] Next in order he mentions colloquial speech, which he refers to as "the second level, . . . generally acceptable to people of education and refinement." Clearly this is not a cultural level but a functional variety of standard English, like the "uppermost level." The third level is, however, a cultural one: "the latest slang," workmen's "technical slang and colloquialisms which other persons cannot comprehend," "grammatical solecisms." "The speech of this third level can fairly be ranked as lower in the social scale." His fourth level is also cultural: "At the bottom of the scale is the lingo, or cant, of criminals, hobos, and others of the lowest social level."

Finally, Kennedy fixes the false mental image of a continuous and logically consistent descent from "the cold and lonely heights of formal and highly specialized scientific and scholarly language" to "the stupid and slovenly level of grammatical abuses and inane slang." In reality there is no cultural descent until we reach his third "level," since "formal and dignified language" and "colloquial speech" are only functional varieties of English on the one cultural level of standard English.

In Perrin's excellent and useful *Index*,[7] under the heading "Levels of Usage," he names "three principal levels": "Formal English (likened to formal dress), "Informal English" (described as "the typical language of an educated person going about his everyday affairs"), and "Vulgate English." From his descriptions it appears clearly that Formal and Informal English are functional varieties of standard English, while Vulgate is a substandard cultural level. A similar classification appears in his table on page 365.

On page 19 Perrin uses level apparently in the sense of functional variety, not of cultural level: "Fundamentally, good English is speaking or writing in the level of English that is appropriate to the particular situation that faces the speaker or writer. It means making a right choice among the levels

---

[6] Arthur G. Kennedy, *Current English* (Boston, 1935), pp. 15–17: "Speech Levels."
[7] Porter G. Perrin, *An Index to English* (Chicago, 1939), pp. 364–65.

of usage." His advice, however, involves two choices: (1) choice of a standard cultural level and (2) choice of the appropriate functional variety of that level.

A clear instance of the inconsistent use of the term *level* is found in Robert C. Pooley's *Teaching English Usage* (New York, 1946), chapter iii, "Levels in English Usage." He names five levels: (1) the illiterate level; (2) the homely level; (3) standard English, informal level; (4) standard English, formal level; and (5) the literary level. In (1) and (2) *level* has an altogether different meaning from that in (3), (4), and (5). In the first two *level* plainly means 'cultural level'; in the last three it just as plainly means 'functional variety of standard English,' all three varieties being therefore on the one cultural level of standard English. So *level* in the two groups belongs to different orders of classification. All misunderstanding and wrong implication would be removed from this otherwise excellent treatment of levels if the last three groups were labeled "Standard English Level, Informal Variety"; "Standard English Level, Formal Variety"; and "Standard English Level, Literary Variety." Pooley's groups contain three cultural levels (illiterate, homely, standard) and three functional varieties of the standard cultural level (informal, formal, literary).

The misapplication to colloquial English of the term *level,* metaphorically appropriate only to cultural gradations, is especially misleading. We often read of English that is "on the colloquial level." For example, Krapp writes: "*Who do you mean?* . . . has passed into current spoken use and may be accepted on the colloquial level."[8] This implies that colloquial English is on a different cultural level from formal English (literary, scientific, etc.), and a too frequent assumption, owing to this and other misuses of the term *colloquial,* is that its cultural level is below that of formal English. This supposition, tacit or explicit, that colloquial style is inferior to formal or literary style, leads inescapably to the absurd conclusion that, whenever scientists or literary artists turn from their formal writing to familiar conversation with their friends, they thereby degrade themselves to a lower social status.

This misuse of *level* encourages the fallacy frequently met with of contrasting colloquial with standard English, logically as fallacious as contrasting white men with tall men. For instance, Mencken writes: "I have no doubt *but* that' . . . seems to be very firmly lodged in colloquial American, and even to have respectable standing in the standard speech."[9] This contrast, not always specifically stated, is often implied. For example, Kennedy writes: "Colloquial English is, properly defined, the language of conversation, and especially of familiar conversation. As such it may approximate the standard speech of the better class of English speakers, or it may drop

[8] *A Comprehensive Guide to Good English* (New York, 1927), p. 641.
[9] H. L. Mencken, *The American Language* (4th ed.; New York, 1936), p. 203.

to the level of the illiterate and careless speaker."[10] *May approximate* should be replaced by *may be on the level of.*

Similarly, on page 440: "Some measure words [are] still used colloquially without any ending in the plural . . . ; but most of these are given the *s* ending in standard English usage." Here *standard* is confused with *formal.*

Kennedy (pp. 534, 616) several times contrasts colloquial English with "standard literary English." This implies that colloquial English is not standard, while literary English is. If he means to contrast standard colloquial with standard literary, well and good; but I fear that most readers would understand the contrast to be of colloquial with standard.[11]

The term *colloquial* cannot properly designate a substandard cultural level of English. It designates a functional variety—that used chiefly in conversation—and in itself says nothing as to its cultural level, though this discussion, and the dictionary definitions, are chiefly concerned with cultivated colloquial, a functional variety of standard English. When writers of such standing as those I have mentioned slip into expressions that imply lower cultural status of colloquial English, it is not surprising that colloquialisms should not be represented as standard American speech. But the context of the statement indicated that its author was using *colloquialism* in the sense of 'localism.' I could hardly believe how frequent this gross error is, until I heard it from a well-known American broadcaster.[12]

The best dictionaries, at least in their definitions, give no warrant for the various misuses of *colloquial, colloquially, colloquialism, colloquiality.* I urge the reader to study carefully the definitions in the *Oxford English Dictionary* with its many apt examples from standard writers, and in *Webster's New International Dictionary, Second Edition,* with its quotations from George Lyman Kittredge. Kittredge's views on the standing of colloquial English are well known. It is said that somebody once asked him about the meaning of the label "Colloq." in dictionaries. He is reported to have replied, "I myself speak 'colloke' and often write it." I cannot verify the story, but it sounds authentic.

It seem to me inevitable that the frequent grouping of so-called "levels" such as "Literary, Colloquial, Illiterate," and the like, will lead the reader to suppose that just as Illiterate is culturally below Colloquial, so Collo-

---

[10] Kennedy, *op. cit.,* p. 26.

[11] Greenough and Kittredge in *Words and Their Ways in English Speech* (New York, 1909), Chap. VII, only apparently treat literary English as the sole standard form: "What is the origin of standard or literary English?" (p. 80). They use *standard* in a special sense for their particular purpose, calling it "the common property of all but the absolutely illiterate," "the language which all educated users of English speak and write" (therefore including colloquial). For the usual current meaning, see the definitions of *standard* quoted in *American Pronunciation* (6th and subsequent eds.), pp. 14–15.

[12] Leonard and Moffett also mention the frequency of this blunder (*op. cit.,* p. 351, n. 5).

quial is culturally below Literary. While I can scarcely hope that my humble remonstrance will reform all future writing on "levels of English," I believe that writers who confuse the meaning of the term *level* must accept some part of the responsibility for the popular misunderstanding of the true status of colloquial English; for I cannot avoid the belief that the popular idea of colloquial English as something to be looked down upon with disfavor is due in part to the failure of writers on the subject to distinguish between *cultural levels of English* and *functional varieties of standard English.*

32

Institutional Linguistics

TREVOR HILL

IN A TONGUE such as modern Standard English, it is usual to distinguish two important styles, a *colloquial* and a *formal* (the latter is often called *literary,* but in the contexts in which we wish to operate this term would be ambiguous). Other styles—those of official writing, of liturgy, of military commands, etc. etc.—may be enumerated, but can be excluded from the present general discussion. The colloquial and formal styles differ in sentence structure—each admitting constructions not usual in the other. Specifically colloquial constructions in English are, for instance, the following; *Me do that? I should have liked to have met him; It's not everybody would agree to that.* Formal examples, on the other hand, are: *This once decided, we may . . . ; The persons with whom I discussed it . . . ; In no way can he be said to have succeeded.* In many koines [Hill defined *koine,* p. 443, as "any tongue, distinct from his own vernacular, that a person shares with the speakers of some other vernaculars"] there may be differences of morphology, as northern Germ. coll. *die Jungs,* formal *die Jungen;* Swedish coll. *vi gick,* formal *vi gingo.* Colloquial and formal styles also differ in a large number of lexical items, as English *start/commence, funny/strange.* Synchronically, the distinction between the members of such a pair is arbitrary, and maintained solely by the practice of using them in mutually exclusive

Reprinted by permission from *Orbis,* 7.448–49 (1958). The author is director of The Linguistic Survey of Scotland, University of Edinburgh.

contexts. Ordinarily, we will expect to find that a dialect has a colloquial style, but no formal one; a koine may have a formal style only, or (if it is also a vernacular) both.

Another set of categories, cutting across the foregoing as another dimension, may be called *genres*: of which we will select *conversation, poetry* and *prose*. The precise limitation of these requires to be worked out in more detail than in the present paper; we should however note that, M. Jourdain notwithstanding, prose is *not* identical with conversation, but a complex medium that only emerges at a fairly late stage in cultural development. By coupling these categories with those of style, we can make such statements as: standard English has a complete range of styles and genres, whereas the Scots of literature, from Ramsay through Burns to the present day, has only a colloquial poetry and a colloquial prose (the latter mainly comic); Older Scots, on the other hand, had like Standard English a complete battery of styles and genres, and the modern literary vehicle known as Lallans (distinct from the literary Scots just mentioned, and regarded by its users as being rather a continuation of literary Older Scots) exists principally as a formal poetic tongue. . . .

Distinct from both the above types of classification is that into spoken and written modes. Koines tend in general to exist in both, in distinction to dialects which are mostly only spoken.[1] Diachronically, it is true that certain of the styles and genres mentioned above are associated with the development of writing (formal style, prose genre). Even so, in synchronic description it is useful to provide for the two modes as distinct categories, adding a third dimension to those already given. Latin as used by Newton and Leibniz, for instance, was a koine existing only in a formal prose style and in a written mode. On the other hand, the vernacular of educated modern Egyptians (studied by English-speaking persons under the name 'Colloquial Egyptian Arabic') is a koine existing in a spoken mode only; its place in newspapers, serious books etc. (formal prose, written), university lecturing (formal prose, spoken), private letters (colloquial prose, written) and various other linguistic situations is taken by a pan-Arab koine known as "Classical Arabic".[2]

---

[1] "Dialect literature" does of course exist: but normally in an orthography derived from that of the koine, so conventionalised that one cannot attribute a production to a specific local dialect in our definition—thus a "Lancashire poem" written at Rochdale cannot be distinguished from one written at Stalybridge. In any case, the great majority of the world's dialects have not so far produced "dialect literature" even in this sense.

[2] The ability to use this in its pure form varies widely, in fact, between individuals, and perhaps it is better as one element in a bipolar system.

33

The "Linguistic" Theory of Usage

R. J. BAKER

THE BATTLE between the new grammarians or linguists and the school grammarians has been won decisively by the linguists. In academic journals defenses of notional grammar are rare and new work based on notional categories almost non-existent. The struggle continues in pedagogical journals and in the schools, but there are signs that the new grammar is gaining ground. No such comments can be made about the battle over the various doctrines of usage. Since what is taken to be the "linguists'" view of usage frequently hinders the acceptance of their grammar, no harm will be done by re-examining a "linguistic" theory of usage.

So many straw men have been patiently made to be burnt in the battles over what is "good" usage that I prefer to avoid any abstraction such as *linguist* and shall restrict my comments to one man and one book: Robert A. Hall, Jr. and his *Linguistics and Your Language* (Anchor, 1960), the second, revised edition of *Leave Your Language Alone!* Professor Hall is typical of many linguists, however, and his book has been enthusiastically reviewed in linguistic journals.

In his preface he pays his respects to many of the most eminent linguists in North America, "Colleagues and friends," he says, "who have read all or part of the book at various stages of its development, and from whose suggestions I have profited greatly, not hesitating even to 'lift' at times whole phrases or sentences from their comments." His list includes Bernard Bloch, Archibald A. Hill, Charles F. Hockett, Henry M. Hoenigswald, Harry Hoijer, Kemp Malone, Raven McDavid, William G. Moulton, Kenneth L. Pike, Ernst Pulgram, Henry Lee Smith, Jr., C. K. Thomas, and W. Freeman Twaddell, as powerful a battalion as one could muster. We dare not assume that they would all agree with every detail in Hall's book, but it is reasonable to assume that Professor Hall speaks for many modern linguists.

Reprinted by permission from the *Journal of the Canadian Linguistic Association,* 6.209–212 (Spring, 1961). Professor Baker is a member of the English department of the University of British Columbia.

First, let us not misrepresent Hall. He does not maintain, as many hostile critics imply, that "anything goes." He recognizes social disapproval of certain forms, and he says, "If my child is likely to run into trouble later on for saying *I done it* or *hisn,* I will try to keep him from getting into the habit of using those forms which are actually not acceptable socially and which may cause others to react unfavorably towards him. But, if I am sensible about it, I will realize that the reason I want him to avoid these 'incorrect' forms is not any inherent badness or evil character that they may have, but a purely practical consideration of their social acceptability" (13-14).

Second, let me make a few debating points just to get them out of the way as irrelevant to the main issue. In spite of all he says about accepting current usage, he wants to redefine words like *grammatical, ungrammatical, language, correct* and *incorrect* as applied to language, *uneducated,* and *ignorant.* He says "From time to time we shall redefine familiar terms and use them with special meanings, often rather different from those they popularly have" (74). All studies try to refine their terms, and if Hall can make the general public accept the specialized vocabulary of our science, I am only too happy to ignore the inconsistency it introduces into his book. Furthermore, like many reformers, he is inclined to make some of his equal terms more equal. In general, he rejects words involving value judgments about language, but he can still say "One might even argue that the 'incorrect' form is actually somewhat preferable from the point of view of clarity and simplicity" (12). And the tone, in a book that makes so much of "scientific objectivity", is frequently objectionable. Hall himself calls the book "to a certain extent, a tract . . . " (vii), and it suffers from the faults of many tracts—emotional pleas aimed at our better democratic instincts, appeals to the authority of the goddess science, and so on.

Those are all insignificant points, however, compared with what I take to be an inconsistency in the theory of meaning implicit in the book, the theory which must underlie the doctrine of usage advanced. Essentially, I believe that Hall uses two mutually exclusive theories of meaning, one for most utterances, the other for those utterances that are socially unacceptable. Both theories are well known. The first, commonly called contextual, maintains that the meaning of an utterance can be derived from the context in which it is used. The meaning of *apple* in a particular context is shown by what you get when you make the noise *apple* together with other noises that indicate that you are asking for something. This theory implies that words may have quite different meanings in different contexts. Hall himself says:

> . . . the meaning of the word *pie,* like that of every other word, differs for each situation in which it occurs—depending on the state of mind, attitude, and so on, of the speaker and the hearer—and no two situations are ever

alike; the term *pie*, for instance, may cause me pleasure or disgust, or leave me indifferent, according to how I am feeling, how hungry I am, the previous experiences I may have had with pie, and so forth. Emotional factors such as these last are usually left out of dictionary definitions (it would be hard to include them), but they are very real factors in the total meaning of any linguistic signal in each specific situation in which it is used (123).

I quite agree with that statement. And if I apply it to a situation which involves speakers from different dialects, let us say an *ain't* - dialect and an *isn't* - dialect, the feelings of distaste aroused in the *isn't* speaker when he hears *ain't* are "very real factors in the total meaning" of the utterance. (And, although far less often than Hall implies, *isn't* may similarly affect an *ain't* speaker.)[1] The feelings may be quite illogical, just as one may illogically shudder at the sound of *eel pie* even though one has never tasted an eel. In other words, the distaste, hostility, snobbery, etc., aroused by *ain't* are part of the meaning of *ain't,* just as disgust may be part of the meaning of the word *pie*.

The fact that the hostility to *ain't* is arbitrary is as irrelevant as the fact that it is socially induced. *All* meanings are arbitrary and socially induced. As Hall says in a passage immediately following that quoted above:

> But the meaning of any specific linguistic form is purely arbitrary. There is no underlying connection, no inherent and inescapable relationship, between any linguistic form and what it signifies (123-124).

> It is wholly a matter of social convention; the meaning of words is something determined by the usage of the speakers of a language [for a dialect, regional or social, I would add], not by some divine fiat. . . (124).

When it comes to words that arouse social disapproval, Hall suddenly abandons his contextual theory of meaning and switches to a theory that is based partly on translation and partly upon reference to the extra-linguistic events. The meaning of *ain't,* he implies, is the same as the meaning of *isn't, haven't,* etc. He thus gives a translation meaning in another dialect. The terms *sexual reproduction* and *elimination of bodily waste* are "equivalent" to the taboo words (20). But if the reactions are different in some situations and for some speakers for *ain't* and *isn't* and for *sexual reproduction* and —,[2] why should we say, on the earlier theory of meaning, that their meanings are the same?

---

[1] He quotes the story of a friend who could not work harmoniously with a group of shipyard workers until he changed his "those things" to "them things". That may be so in the United States, but a received British speaker who tried to change a few lexical items while working with Cockney dockers would be asking for a black eye for being condescending and "taking the mickey out of us".

[2] Without claiming undue innocence or ignorance, I must confess I cannot find an unacceptable "equivalent" for *sexual reproduction*. None of the derivatives of the two famous four letter words is an equivalent, even in Hall's sense, for me.

Obviously they are not; people react differently to them. Hall has switched his theory of meaning at a key point in his argument. He has forgotten what he said early in the book: "Words do not have any 'real' meaning as opposed to other, 'false' meanings. Any meaning people give to a word is automatically its *real* meaning under those circumstances" (6). And when a speaker uses a word that produces an effect quite different from the one he intended, we are quite entitled to say that he has used the "wrong" word. Had Richard cried "My kingdom for a cow" when he wanted to escape, we should say that his mind had been affected by his misfortune so that he used the wrong word. The attempt to split off "social" meanings as extra-linguistic makes all linguistic phenomena extra-linguistic.[3] It makes sense only within a theory that accepts "real" meaning, something Hall has explicitly, repeatedly, and rightly, rejected.

To argue as I do is not to reject the possibility of objective statements about acceptable or unacceptable usage. If the linguist can give the lexical meaning of any pejorative utterance, there is no reason why he cannot record objectively that such and such a word arouses hostility in such and such a group of people. But he cannot go on from his objective recording to say that the specific word means the same thing as another word that does not give rise to hostility. Nor does my argument imply that I have anything but sympathy for Hall's attack on snobbery. But linguistics as a science is neither democratic nor aristocratic. It simply describes bits of language. It could record the language of snobbery quite objectively, as A.S.C. Ross has shown. When a particular political view leads to inconsistency in what purports to be an objective study, however, we must take care to eradicate the inconsistency. Sad though it may be, the hostility to *ain't* is part of the linguistic meaning of the word. And Professor Hall himself says, "Good language is language which gets the desired effect with the least friction and difficulty for its user" (27), a conclusion not so different in practice from that held by many people who would say, perhaps more economically and with closer conformity with popular usage: Good language is the use of the right words.

[3] James B. McMillan does a similar thing when he tries to maintain a difference between *linguistic* and *sociological* facts in language. "A Philosophy of Language", *College English*, 9.385–390 (April, 1948). He there says, "The sociological facts concern the attitudes toward locutions held by people in various societal situations". This makes all statements about language sociological. If I correct a foreigner's pronunciation of English, I am merely revealing my attitude toward English phonology.

34

Social Influences on the Choice of a Linguistic Variant

JOHN L. FISCHER

DURING THE YEAR 1954-55 my wife and I were engaged in a study of child-rearing in a semi-rural New England village.[1] In the course of the study I had occasion to record two or more interviews on Audograph discs or tapes, with each of the 24 children of our sample. Previously certain inconsistencies in the children's speech had attracted my attention, especially the variation between *-in* and *-ing* for the present participle ending.[2] Accordingly, in transcribing the discs and tapes, I decided to note the choice of these two variants, and this paper is intended to summarize and discuss this information.

To begin with, all of the 24 children, except three, used both forms to some extent at least. The three exceptions used only the *-ing* form, and since they were less loquacious than most of the other children, it is possible that a larger sample of their speech would have revealed the use of the other variant as well. This may then be regarded as a case of so-called free variation of two linguistic forms within a local speech community, and within the speech of most individual members of our sample community. In general, the choice of one or the other of the variants would not affect the denotation of acts, states, or events by the word.

"Free variation" is of course a label, not an explanation. It does not tell us where the variants came from nor why the speakers use them in differing proportions, but is rather a way of excluding such questions from

Reprinted by permission from *Word,* 14.47–56 (1958). Professor Fischer is a member of the Department of Sociology and Anthropology at Tulane University.

[1] This study was part of a larger cross-cultural study of socialization financed by the Ford Foundation and under the general direction of John Whiting of the Harvard Graduate School of Education and others.

[2] The variation in this dialect between *-in* and *-ing* in the participle ending does not extend to words with a final *-in* in an unstressed syllable in standard speech. This variation is therefore probably best viewed as a case of free alternation of two allomorphs which happen to differ in respect to one phoneme, rather than as a case of phonological free variation.

the scope of immediate inquiry. Historically, I presume that one could investigate the spread of one of these variants into the territory of another through contact and migration, and this would constitute one useful sort of explanation. However, another sort of explanation is possible in terms of current factors which lead a given child in given circumstances to produce one of the variants rather than another, and it is this which I wish to discuss here.

Before discussing the determinants of selection of the variants it will be helpful to understand a little of the general background of the data. The 24 children in our sample consisted of an equal number of boys and girls, both divided into two equal age groups, ages 3-6 and 7-10. By the time the recordings were made my wife and I had been observing the children periodically for eight to ten months and most of the children were fairly well acquainted with us. Most of the children were interviewed in an office in our house, which was located in the middle of the village. Most of the children had visited our house before, some a number of times. Four younger children who had not were interviewed in their own homes. Three general types of text were obtained:

(1) Protocols for all children for a verbal thematic apperception test (TAT) in which the children were asked to make up stories starting out from short sentences given by the investigator.

(2) For older children only, answers to a formal questionnaire.

(3) For a few of the older children, informal interviews asking them to recount their recent activities.

I shall present first some counts of variants in the TAT protocols, since this test was administered to all the children. As is shown in Table I, a markedly greater number of girls used -ing more frequently, while more boys used more -in.

Table I. Number of children favoring -ing and -in variant suffixes in TAT protocols according to sex.

	-ing>-in	-ing<-in	
Boys	5	7	Chi square: 2.84; 05<P<.1 (by
Girls	10	2	two-tailed test)

This suggests that in this community (and probably others where the choice exists) -ing is regarded as symbolizing female speakers and -in as symbolizing males.

Within each sex, differences in personality are associated with the proportion of frequency of -ing to -in as illustrated in Table II.

Table II: Frequency of use of -ing and -in in TAT protocols of two boys.

	-ing	-in
"Model" boy	38	1
"Typical" boy	10	12

Chi square: 19.67;P<.001

The first boy was regarded by his teacher and others as a "model" boy. He did his school work well, was popular among his peers, reputed to be thoughtful and considerate. The second boy was generally regarded as a "typical" boy—physically strong, dominating, full of mischief, but disarmingly frank about his transgressions. The "model" boy used almost exclusively the -ing ending here, while the "typical" boy used the -in ending more than half the time, as shown above.

In Table III below, one may also note a slight tendency for the -ing variant to be associated with higher socio-economic status, although this is not statistically significant with a sample of this size. The community studied is fairly small and does not have strong class lines, which is probably why more marked results did not appear.[3]

Table III. Number of children favoring -ing and -in endings according to family status.

Family Status	-ing>-in	-ing⩽-in
Above Median	8	4
Below Median	7	5

Chi square (corrected): 0;P>.9

Besides asking *who* uses which variant and how much, we may also ask whether there are situational differences in *when* a single speaker uses these variants. One variant in the situation may be described as degree of formality: in the children's terms I would think of this as degree of similarity to a formal classroom recitation. The best child to examine for this variable is the "model" boy of Table II since he was interviewed in all three situations mentioned above and was obligingly talkative in each. As Table IV shows, the frequency of choice of variants changed from an almost exclusive use of -ing in the TAT situation to a predominance of -in in the informal interviews.

[3] Most previous studies of sociological factors connected with linguistic variants have been concerned with linguistic indices of class, caste, or occupational groups. Group boundaries have been regarded, implicitly or explicitly, as barriers to communication analogous to political boundaries, geographical distance, etc. The emphasis in this paper is rather on variations within a face-to-face community whose members are in frequent free communication: variations between social categories of speakers and between individual speakers, and situational variations in the speech of individual speakers, as noted below.

TAT	Formal Interview	Informal Interview

Table IV: Frequency of *-ing* and *-in* in a ten-year old boy's speech in three situations in order of increasing informality.

-ing	38	33	24	Chi square: 37.07
-in	1	35	41	P<. 001

Of course, these three situations should not be regarded as exhaustive of the frequency range of these variants in this boy's speech. In the interviews I myself used the *-ing* variant consistently and this probably influenced the informant's speech somewhat. Probably in casual conversation with his peers the *-in/-ing* ratio is even higher than in the informal interview.

Another measure similar in implication to the frequency of variants by type of interview would be differences in frequency between the beginning and later parts of a single interview. Especially in the TAT protocols, which are the most formal texts, I noticed for a number of children that the *-ing* frequency was higher in the beginning of the interview and later dropped off, presumably as the child became more relaxed and accustomed to the situation. In only one child was the reverse trend noted, and there are reasons to believe that this particular child may have become more tense during the administration of the test.

A linguist might ask whether there is any association betwen the suffix variants and specific verbs. The corpus is not large enough to establish stable frequency indices for the suffixes of individual words, but there is certainly a trend for markedly "formal" verbs to have the *-ing* suffix and markedly "informal" verbs to have the *-in* suffix. The first boy in Table II above, for instance, used *-ing* in *criticizing, correcting, reading, visiting, interesting,* and used *-in* in *punchin, flubbin, swimmin, chewin, hittin.* For some common verbs, however, such as *play, go* and *do* he used both alternatively. Probably only a few verbs are formal or informal enough in their connotations so that the same variant would always be used with them. Of course, the choice of verb vocabulary is itself related to personality and situational factors.

In brief, then, the choice between the *-ing* and the *-in* variants appear to be related to sex, class, personality (aggressive/cooperative), and mood (tense/relaxed) of the speaker,[4] to the formality of the conversation and to the specific verb spoken. While these are "free variants" in the standard type of description of languages in which only grammatical facts and differences in none but "denotative" meaning are taken into account, if we widen our scope of study to include the meaning of these variants to the

---

[4] And doubtless of the person spoken to, although this was not investigated.

conversants we might call them "socially conditioned variants," or "socio-symbolic variants," on the grounds that they serve to symbolize things about the relative status of the conversants and their attitudes toward each other, rather than denoting any difference in the universe of primary discourse (the "outer world").[5]

What are the wider implications for linguistics of such an analysis of social factors influencing choice of linguistic variants? For one thing, many linguists have recognized that "free" variation is a logically necessary stage in most or all linguistic change.[6] Less widely appreciated but also recognized by some is another fact: Although the mechanisms of psychic economy are becoming better understood in diachronic phonemics, they are not always sufficient to explain fully the progressive adaption of variant forms, and that people adopt a variant primarily not because it is easier to pronounce (which it most frequently is, but not always), or because it facilitates some important distinction in denotational meaning, but because it expresses how they feel about their relative status versus other conversants.

The clearest and most comprehensive statement of social factors in linguistic change which I have encountered is found in an article by Martin Joos dealing with medieval sibilants.[7] He speaks of "the phonetic drift,

[5] Uriel Weinreich has suggested to me the term "symptomatic signs," after Karl Bühler, as an alternative for "socio-symbolic variant" which already has a basis in established usage. However, it seems to me that "symptomatic signs" might be in one sense too broad and in another too narrow: too broad in the sense that it might be interpreted to refer to "non-linguistic" features of speech such as general pitch, loudness, timbre, rate, etc., and too narrow in the sense that Bühler appears to regard the symptomatic function as, ideally, purely expressive of the speaker, while I am looking for a broader term which would cover this function but also include expression of the dyadic relationship between the conversants. This cannot simply be taken care of by adding in Bühler's "signal" function which deals with the "appeal" to the listener, since at least some aspects of the relationship do not exist primarily either in speaker or listener but rather *between* them, e.g. relative age, relative rank. See Karl Bühler, *Sprachtheorie*, Jena (1934), esp. p. 28 — Whether I should here introduce a term incorporating "symbol" is a further question which I acknowledge but do not discuss here, as it is complex and is not directly relevant to the main argument of the paper.

[6] I find in checking over the literature that this statement seems to be based more on my impressions of conversations with linguists than on published statements. One clear statement of this principle, however, is to be found on p. 367 of Hans Vogt's paper on "Language Contacts," *Word* 10.365-74 (1954). A more general statement applying to any type of cultural element, and by implication linguistic elements, can be found in Ralph Linton's *The Study of Man*, p. 280, N. Y., (1936).

[7] Martin Joos, "The Medieval Sibilants," *Language* 28.222–31 (1952); reprinted in M. Joos (ed.), *Readings in Linguistics*, Washington (1957), pp. 377-8. Others have separately recognized the importance of fashion in linguistic change, especially in the spread of standard dialects, and to a lesser degree have recognized the complementary process of using distinctive linguistic features to emphasize social exclusiveness. J. O. Hertzler in "Toward a Sociology of Language," *Social Forces* 32.109-19 (1953), gives a bibliography including studies of both sorts. Joos's statement however appears to me to be unique in his recognition that the two processes combine to constitute a self-perpetuating cycle. Since Joos is noted for his rigorous definition of the scope of linguistics proper it is perhaps all the more interesting that he should throw in this "sociological" aside.

which was kept going in the usual way: that is, the dialects and idiolects of higher prestige were more advanced in this direction, and their speakers carried the drift further along so as to maintain the prestige-marking difference against their pursuers. The vanity factor is needed to explain why phonetic drifts tend to continue in the same direction; the 'inertia' sometimes invoked is a label and not an argument." This protracted pursuit of an elite by an envious mass and consequent "flight" of the elite is in my opinion the most important mechanism in linguistic drift, not only in the phonetic drift which Joos discusses, but in syntactic and lexical drift as well.[8]

The study of social factors in linguistic drift is in the field of the sociology of language rather than linguistics proper. However, this study can not reach ultimate fruition without certain linguistic studies by competent linguists. I refer here to studies of individual variations in linguistic forms in small, face-to-face speech communities, and of variations in these forms in the speech of single individuals in a range of social situations. Studies of this sort constitute tasks of respectable magnitude which have, in the main, been neglected.[9]

A student of social factors in the choice of linguistic variants would wish to know for a fairly large stratified sample of a speech community how often members of a given sub-group used a sizable sample of series of socially significant variants, and for at least some of the sub-groups one would want to know how these frequencies of choice of variants changed under different situations and in the presence of conversants of different social status and personal relationships. A linguist as such would not wish to analyze these social factors in great detail. But it would be well within the scope of linguistics to identify individual informants in a unitary speech community by name or code number and group them according to their similarity or dissimilarity in the use of variants in some standard situation, say, in conversation with the linguist. The psychologist and sociologist could then take these groups and see what sense they made in their terms. In

---

[8] Incidentally, this flight-pursuit mechanism might be regarded as an explanation of the constant rate of decay of basic "non-cultural" vocabulary postulated by Morris Swadesh's theory of glottochronology. To make it suffice one would also need to assume that all societies possess some form of elite group—if only the "ideal conformist" in some societies—and that mass envy of the elite and ambition to join them are everywhere the same. These assumptions may seem radical and against common sense, but they are not as easy to refute as one might think. Needless to say, one would not assume that the elite is always a property or authority elite. In politically and economically undifferentiated societies, the most important criterion might be technical skill and productivity in consumer goods, admired personality traits, etc.

[9] The classic study in this field is Louis Gauchat's "L'Unité phonétique dans le patois d'une commune", *Aus romanischen Sprachen und Literatur*, Halle, 1905, pp. 124. Other references are cited by W. von Wartburg. *Problémes et méthodes de la linguistique*, Paris, 1946, p. 33 (footnote). Modern techniques, of course, open entirely new perspectives for research.

practice, of course, such a rigorous separation between linguistics and the more general social sciences is not required since linguists and other lay-men are presumably capable of making a number of distinctions of con-siderable sociological interest, such as male versus female, etc.

A word about the relation of the proposed study to dialectology is ap-propriate here. It has generally been the aim of dialectologists to describe linguistic variations between groups which are separated by some com-munications barrier, especially geography or social class. What I am ad-vocating here is the study of linguistic variations within small groups where there is free and relatively intense communication, so that as far as possible the lack of contact between speakers is not a reason for failure to use the same forms. Of course in a large society such as ours, small closed groups are rare, and some of the variation among the individuals of any group picked for study will be due to the fact that they have different contacts outside the group. But this empirical fact does not reduce the importance of studying variation within the face-to-face community, although it sug-gests that the best place to study such variation would be on a remote Pacific atoll with a small, long-established population.

What I am proposing might be called comparative idiolectology rather than dialectology. Ideally, a thorough description of a single dialect would be based on the study of a sizable sample of the idiolects in a local speech community, in the same way that a thorough description of a language would be based on the study of a sizable sample of its dialects. In compara-tive idiolectology one might, as a device of fieldwork, still concentrate on a single informant, but one would want to follow him around with a portable recording machine and note changes in his speech in different settings and situations and with different conversants. Moreover, since phenomenol-ogically language is as much listening as speaking one would be led to analyze what was said comprehensibly to him by others as well as what he said himself.

The untrained listener will not, of course, generally be able to reproduce or identify the differences in the speech of others whom he encounters, unless he is an accomplished mimic. But he does react to these differences by making interpretations about the social situation on the basis of them and will be able to tell when a speaker is talking like a woman, like an upper class person, like a relaxed person, etc., even though he cannot specify all the variant forms on which he bases his judgment.[10] (This is not to deny the presence or importance of other "non-linguistic" features of speech as well as things entirely unconnected with speech such as dress,

---

[10] The "tape experiment" described by Putnam and O'Hern investigates language and social status in this manner, although the speakers were not members of a single face-to-face community, so the complication of barriers to communication is introduced. See G. N. Putnam and E. M. O'Hern, "The Status Significance of an Isolated Urban Dialect," *Language* 31, Supplement, Language Dissertation, No. 53 (1955).

physical appearance, gestures, etc., which also serve as cues for judgments of the conversational situation.)

In analyzing socio-symbolic variants there will obviously be a certain amount of association between variant series. In many of the series at least one variant could be distinguished as "formal," and another as "informal." But it is a question for empirical investigation whether this distinction applies to all variant series, and, if so, with how much force. I have suggested above a number of factors which influence the -in/-ing distinction. Conceivably they all bear on formality, that is, compliance, tenseness, femaleness, and high class all make for formal behavior. But even if this is true for these factors in American culture, are they a unitary complex in all cultures, and may there not be other social factors affecting socio-symbolic variants which are independent of the formality complex? Are variants associated with being female always associated as well with formality? In three languages with which I am acquainted, English, Japanese, and Ponapean, I can think of a number of instances where this link is found, but there also appear to be exceptions. In Ponapean, for instance, a minority of women have an unusual allophone for the r phoneme, but this seems to have no relation to the degree of formality. Lisping in English is regarded as feminine, but would indicate little about degree of formality.

Even where the same factor determines the choice of alternants in several series of variants, the breaking point for each series will probably be different. For instance, in the TAT texts discussed above, three of the children used the pronunciation [ey] for the indefinite article a. This pronunciation can be regarded as formal to the point of being artificial and is much more restricted for speakers in this community than the -ing variant of the present participle ending, yet the direction of social symbolism is the same, though not the intensity. In other words, [ey] in itself is more a sign of formality than -ing though both are signs of formality. The "formality" index of a given text would be determined by the variant chosen in several series of socio-symbolic variants, each of which would have a different socio-symbolic level with respect to formality. Presumably these series could be ordered in terms of increasingly greater thresholds of formality required to bring about the shift from the informal to the formal form.

I have been stressing here the synchronic implications of socio-symbolic variants. The diachronic implications are at least equally interesting. Obviously the threshold for a given variant does not *necessarily* remain the same, generation after generation. If a particular variant has for whatever reason greater prestige, it will gradually be adopted in more situations by more people: its threshold will be lowered. But as its threshold is lowered and approaches universality in the speech community, its socio-symbolic load is reduced and eventually vanishes. One could hardly convey much of an air of informality, for example, by saying [ə] for the indefinite article, though saying [ey] would be quite stilted. But presumably new series of variants keep arising to replace those which achieve uniformity in this way.

Now what is meant by "variants of greater prestige"? One could determine which of a pair of variants had the greater prestige by noting which tended to "spread" when two conversants who in other situations differed in their choice came together. But the grounds of prestige clearly vary according to individuals and societies. A variant which one man uses because he wants to seem dignified another man would reject because he did not want to seem stiff. Societies likewise have characteristic average value preferences. Using the variable of formality, it is quite possible that one society would show a tendency, at least in some situations, to show a preference for adoption of formal forms of speech, and another in analagous situations show a preference for informal forms. These preferences could in turn be related by persons so inclined to social structure. One would end up with a statement not simply of the direction of linguistic drift, but what this drift meant psychologically and what social changes might check it. It would be very interesting, for instance, to find and examine cognate variants from some related societies with differing descent practices, and see whether the current drift is in the direction of femininization or masculinization. Such data would not only illuminate the mechanism of linguistic drift, but would provide students of social structure with extremely valuable indices of the distribution of envy and cross-segmental identification in the communities speaking the language studied.

35

Linguistic Atlas Findings versus Textbook Pronouncements on Current American Usage

JEAN MALMSTROM

A LINGUISTIC atlas is one tangible result of applying the principles and methods of descriptive linguistics to the language behavior of a specific geographic area. A linguistic atlas usually consists of maps that show graphically the dialects of the region being studied. A linguist engaged in the preparation of a linguistic atlas is called a linguistic geographer, or a dialect geographer, or a dialectologist. In his vocabulary, the word "dialect" has no connotations of slovenliness or ignorance. "Dialect" means simply "a variety of a language, regional or social, set off (more or less sharply) from other varieties by (more or less clear) features of pronunciation, grammar or vocabulary."[1] The word "dialect" is thus a neutral, precise, convenient, and scientific term used to describe a particular kind of language.

Linguistic geography is founded upon the key principles of descriptive linguistics. These are:

1. A language is a structural system, a set of behavioral habits by which the inhabitants of a particular community interact; as such it is an integral part of this community's total cultural pattern of behavior.

2. The facts of a language, like those of other behavior, can be objectively observed and described, and then scientifically analyzed to yield a consistent and complete theory by which the observed facts can be classified, and the non-observed facts can be predicted.

Reprinted by permission from *The English Journal*, 48.191–8 (April, 1959). This article, based on an address given at the 1958 convention of the NCTE, reports the findings of a University of Minnesota doctoral study which compared information from the Linguistic Atlas of the United States with that from current textbooks about certain items of usage. The author is an associate professor of English at Western Michigan University.

[1] Raven I. McDavid, Jr.'s definition in "The Dialects of American English," in W. Nelson Francis' *The Structure of American English* (New York: Ronald Press, 1958), p. 480.

3. Speech is primary in the approach to the study of a language; in the development of the child and of the race, speech precedes writing. Writing is secondary; it represents speech by graphic symbols, and does so imperfectly. That is, writing cannot indicate completely and precisely the language's intricate patterns of pitch, stress, and juncture; it cannot reveal gesture or facial expression, nor other communicative elements inherent in the primary speech situation.

Information for a linguistic atlas is usually collected by means of face-to-face interviews between trained fieldworkers and representative natives of communities within the area being studied. These communities are chosen to give a fine-meshed cross-section of the area's composition—historical, cultural, economic, and geographic. The individual informants are selected to represent the community's different classes—in terms of age, education, and social and economic status. Interviews are permissive and open-ended, running anywhere from four to twenty hours. The fieldworker has a questionnaire containing specific usages that will reveal the characteristic pronunciation, grammar, and vocabulary of the region, but he listens to catch many of these forms in the normal flow of conversation rather than by direct questions, hoping thus to avoid any self-conscious or artificial usage. Each informant's responses are recorded on separate sets of worksheets, in a finely graded phonetic alphabet, and when all the interviews are finished, the linguistic geographer possesses a body of firsthand facts about the language which he can present on maps to make a linguistic atlas.

OUR LINGUISTIC ATLAS

The Linguistic Atlas of the United States and Canada was originally a project of the American Council of Learned Societies, and is historically connected with the National Council of Teachers of English. Between 1911 and 1917, the Council sponsored studies which revealed that memorizing conjugations and declensions or reciting "rules of grammar" did not improve students' ability to read, write, and speak their language. The profession was deeply concerned about improving English teaching. In the 1920's the great tradition of European linguistic geography spurred American linguists to give serious consideration to a Linguistic Atlas of the United States. In 1929, the National Council of Teachers of English bore the expense of a meeting in Cleveland at which the definite proposal for the Atlas was formulated. The Council deemed the Atlas project on present-day American English closely relevant to its concern with the improvement of English teaching.

Field work for the Atlas began in New England in 1931. It has been subsequently carried on by correlated but independent regional atlases in the eastern and northern parts of the country and on the Pacific Coast.

Records are complete for the Atlantic Seaboard from the northeastern boundary of Maine to the northeastern tip of Florida, and also in the North Central States of Wisconsin, Michigan, Illinois, Indiana, Kentucky, and Ohio, and in the Upper Midwest States of Minnesota, Iowa, North and South Dakota, and Nebraska. Analysis of these completed records has revealed three major dialect areas—Northern, Midland, and Southern—extending from east to west across at least the eastern half of the United States. The informants whose speech is reported in these completed records represent more than half of the total population of our country. Geographically, their residence covers one-third of the continental area of the United States. They represent discretely the highest, the middle, and the lowest levels of education within their respective communities. These levels may be thought of as corresponding roughly to a college education, a high-school education, and a common-school education or less. Usually these educational levels correlate fairly closely with social levels.

The Atlas therefore contrasts sharply with two other important and more familiar sources of information on usage: Leonard's *Current English Usage* and Fries's *American English Grammar*. Leonard gives opinions—expert opinions, it is true, but still only opinions—about current usage. Fries, on the other hand, deals solely with written materials in his grammar. These two sources are valuable indeed, but quite distinct from the Atlas in both purpose and result.

Like Leonard and Fries, the Atlas dialectologists did not attempt the impossible task of investigating all the items of current American usage. But for the items which are included in the Atlas, the information on the usage of the language is definitive. I have recently finished spending five years studying fifty-seven of these items to find out how this definitive Atlas information matches the statements which English teachers find in their textbooks. To cut the investigation to reasonable size, one representative grade was selected from each major level of English teaching for exhaustive analysis—grade 3 to represent lower elementary instruction, grade 6 for upper elementary, grade 8 for junior high school, grade 11 for senior high school, and grade 13 for college freshman instruction. For each of these grades I scanned the latest edition of all English language arts textbooks published between 1940 and 1955. There were more than two thousand of them, and of this group 312 were relevant to the study. That is, they contained statements concerning at least one of the fifty-seven selected usages. All these statements were copied, classified, and analyzed. The results throw new light on old controversy about usage.

From the evidence certain facts are immediately obvious. First, no textbook discusses all the fifty-seven items. Second, the lower the grade-level of the text, the greater the number of items omitted. Third, no two textbooks discuss identical sets of items. Fourth, the distinction between speech and writing is not strictly and consistently maintained in the textbooks. Fifth, textbook writers do not agree with each other on the meanings of the terms "colloquial," "standard," "nonstandard," "formal," "informal," and "vulgate."

ATLAS FINDINGS VS. TEXTBOOK STATEMENTS

A detailed comparison of the body of textbook statements with the Atlas findings reveals six fairly consistent patterns of divergence and congruence between them. These six patterns, in general, reflect (1) agreement between Atlas and textbooks on usages that agree with the received standard, and (2) great variety of disagreement on usages for which the Atlas shows divided usage, or educational, regional, or temporal variants. A few examples can illustrate each pattern.

Typical Pattern 1

In the first place, the Atlas reveals that cultured informants regularly use *sit* in a sentence like "Sit down." The linguistic geographer therefore terms this usage "standard." This finding agrees with the received standard regularly supported by the textbooks. But the Atlas shows also that, in large areas of the Atlantic Seaboard, *set* predominates in the speech of the high school graduates, and occurs with some frequency in the speech of the college graduates too. This same educational spread is only slightly less evident in the midwestern areas. The dialectologist terms such usage "popular," or characteristic of the middle level of education. This statement is an objective description of the facts of usage. In contrast, the 170 textbooks which discuss *sit* versus *set* express nine different viewpoints. Their usual procedure is to bracket *sit* and *set* together and call them a "troublesome," or "confusing," or "bothersome" pair of verbs. Students are then told that, in order to use these verbs "correctly," they must learn and compare their principal parts, their meanings, and their uses, and must know also that *sit* is intransitive while *set* is transitive. Strangely however, one of these textbooks, while insisting on the transitive nature of *set,* illustrates the principle with examples that contradict it, namely: "The lamp sets on the table" and "The vases set there too." Thirteen texts state that while *sit* is usually intransitive and *set* is usually transitive, certain "exceptions" or "idioms" that reverse this "rule" are acceptable. Examples of transitive *sit* are, for instance, "Sit the baby in a chair," "Sit yourself down," or "Sit a horse." Intransitive uses of *set* are, for instance, "Set out on a journey," or "The sun sets," as do concrete, jelly, plaster, and hens. Six other texts, however, state that, poultrymen to the contrary notwithstanding, the hen cannot set; she is a sitting hen. This kind of agreement on the received standard and disagreement on the popular usage is the mark of the first typical pattern of divergence and congruence between the Atlas and the textbooks.

Typical Pattern 2

Then we may consider *dove,* as alternate past tense for *dived,* in a sentence like "He dived in." The Atlas shows that cultured speakers in Northern dialect areas, from New England to North Dakota, strongly prefer *dove.* In southern and western Pennsylvania, through the other regions of the Middle Atlantic States, and in the South Atlantic States to the Peedee River, cultured speakers strongly prefer *dived.* In north central and eastern Pennsylvania and in South Carolina and Georgia south of the Peedee, *dived* and *dove* both occur, with *dove* preferred by the more modern, younger, more educated speakers. Similar distribution is found in the North Central States where *dived* is used by a majority of only the most uneducated speakers in the more southern regions. These findings show that *dove* is a standard Northern form expanding southward. No textbook, however, mentions this regional distribution of *dove* in educated speech, although about one-third of the books discuss *dived* versus *dove.* Well over half of these books do not admit that *dove* is ever acceptable, and only a very small minority say without qualification that both *dived* and *dove* are standard. All this small minority are high school and college texts; elementary and junior high students find only *dived* judged acceptable in their textbooks. One of these offers the undocumented pronouncement that "expert swimmers usually say *dived.*" In all, seventeen percent of the textbooks express twelve different opinions. These statements reflect the second pattern of divergence and congruence between the Atlas and the textbooks. It occurs typically when the Atlas shows an expanding usage which conflicts with the received standard.

Typical Pattern 3

A third pattern is observable with items like *he don't,* which also shows regional variations but which, unlike *dove,* is not expanding into neighboring regions. The Atlas shows that about seventy-five percent of the cultured informants in the Middle Atlantic States and about fifty percent of the same type in the South Atlantic States regularly say *he don't.* Only rarely in these areas do we find *he doesn't* along with *he don't* in educated speech. But in New England, the North Central States, and the Upper Midwest, where again many college graduates say *he don't,* we find *he doesn't* more often as a companion form. In fact, in these areas *he doesn't* becomes more frequent in ratio to better education and greater socio-economic advantages. Thus, in the light of the Atlas, *he don't* is standard in Midland and Southern Atlantic Seaboard speech but not expanding northward or westward, since it is popular rather than standard in New England, the North Central States, and the Upper Midwest. More than half of the textbooks discuss *he don't.* Eighty-five percent of them say that since *don't* is a contraction *for do not,* it cannot be used for *doesn't,* which is a contraction for *does not.* Such statements assume obviously that the traditional "rules of agreement" have eternal verity; the Atlas denies this assumption. Further, they assume that language is logical; the Atlas disproves this assumption too. Smaller groups of textbooks assert variously that *he don't* is "nonstandard," or "vulgate," or "illiterate," or a "vulgarism," or "a common mistake of the older generations," or "as careless as going to a party with a soiled blouse or a dirty neck." Thus the textbook writers agree generally with each other but disagree with the Atlas.

When Fries examined the three thousand letters on which he based his *American English Grammar,* he found that no educated writer used *he don't.* This fact does not contradict the facts revealed by the Atlas. On the contrary, it serves to emphasize an intrinsic difference between speech and writing. The textbooks' comments on *he don't* show how easily their authors lose sight of this difference.

Typical Pattern 4

When we consider a usage like "It's me," we discover another typical pattern of divergence and congruence between the Atlas and the textbooks. The Atlas shows that an overwhelming majority of all informants in all areas say *it's me.* Moreover, an almost equally overwhelming majority are consistent in their use of the objective case in the third person, singular and plural. About sixty-six percent of the textbooks, 205 in all, comment on *it's me.* Their statements divide into five groups. The largest group—112 or about eighty-eight percent of the total—is the most prescriptive in tone and the farthest away from the Atlas facts, while the smallest group—six texts or about three percent of the 205—agrees precisely with the Atlas. In other words, the largest group states without qualification that the nominative case must follow the verb *to be,* while the smallest group states that *it's me* is established American English usage. This kind of inverse correlation marks the fourth typical pattern. Since Fries found only one use of the predicative personal pronoun in his three thousand letters, we may conclude that *it's me* and *it's him, it's her,* or *it's them* occur almost always in speech not writing, and that consequently the Atlas evidence is completely authoritative. Again we can see that the textbooks do not keep speech and writing clearly separated.

Typical Pattern 5

Another pattern appears when the textbooks discuss an item on which the Atlas shows that standard usage is divided between different forms. For instance, in a sentence like "The broom is behind the door," the Atlas shows that both *back of* and *in back of* are standard alternates for the received standard *behind.* In other words, we have a case of divided usage. The textbooks, however, unanimously support the use of *behind* while about a fourth of them, adding comments about *back of* and *in back of,* express thirteen different points of view. For instance, twenty-five texts approve *back of* along with *behind;* ten condemn *back of* along with *in back of;* seven separate the three forms and call *behind* "formal," *back of* "informal," and *in back of* "vulgate"; one text states that *in back of* is "colloquial," while *behind* and *back of* are "formal." Here we can see vividly how loosely terms are used and how unpredictably they vary from textbook to textbook.

Typical Pattern 6

The sixth and last pattern appears when the Atlas shows that standard usage agrees with the received standard, which the textbooks unanimously support, but that several nonstandard variants are common also. For instance, Atlas and textbooks agree that *climbed* is the standard past participle of *climb*. When the textbooks warn their readers against nonstandard forms, however, they present a picture of uneducated usage that is inaccurate and incomplete in the light of the Atlas evidence. The only strong forms that the textbooks prohibit are *clum*—often spelled *c-l-u-m-b*—and *clom*—always spelled *c-l-o-m-b*. (The inclusion of that unpronounced *b* shows again the confusion between writing and speech.) The Atlas reveals, however, that *clim* is a much more common nonstandard variant in certain Northern dialect areas than either of the forms which the textbooks regularly mention.

In the light of all these facts, we reach the conclusion that, since the textbook writers as a group approach current American usage normatively, their statements are based on a premise that some arbitrary standard of "correctness" exists, that it can be discovered, and that it should be taught. This premise is usually unstated and often specifically denied, but nonetheless clearly evidenced by this study. We have already noted many examples of subjective and undocumented proscription. Very few textbooks published between 1940 and 1955 are entirely free from statements like "Never say *he don't*" or "Avoid *it's me,*" for example. They are especially common in elementary and junior high texts. Of course, some textbook writers cite evidence to support their statements, but usually do so unscientifically. For instance, we often find published studies of usage excerpted without due regard for their total context or their original purposes. The work of Leonard, Marckwardt and Walcott, Pooley, and Fries, as well as the Atlas itself, all receive this kind of treatment. In like fashion, dictionaries are cited prescriptively with little or no recognition of the descriptive nature of lexicography or of the different definitions to be found in different dictionaries. We also find statements that "authorities agree" that certain controversial usages are "correct," but since these "authorities" are usually unspecified, too often we suspect that they are other textbook writers. My evidence shows that agreement among textbook writers on controversial usages is rare indeed.

Therefore, since the textbook writers as a group do not succeed in defining any consistent standard of "correctness" for the fifty-seven items herein discussed, their basic premise that such a standard exists comes into question. If it is an indefinable abstraction, it is of little practical value in teaching. Indeed, as we have seen, it can all too easily lead to contradictions and confusions.

IMPLICATIONS FOR TEACHING

Descriptive linguistics, as exampled by the Atlas, suggests that we need a five-dimensional model for evaluating current American usage. The necessary five dimensions are social, situational, methodological, temporal, and regional. That is, we must keep in mind that either standard or nonstandard forms may be used in either formal or informal situations, transmitted by either speech or writing used by either young or old persons in either isolated rural areas or urban centers of culture, in the Northern, or the Midland, or the Southern dialect areas. Such evaluation is not simple.

While on the one hand, however, the Atlas cautions us to be careful and precise, on the other it comforts us. It shows that, whatever differences may distinguish dialects, likenesses far outnumber differences in current American English. Indeed, controversial usages demand attention mainly because they do not follow this normal tendency. In other words, typical intonation patterns, customary subject-verb-object word order, the inflectional -s which signals plural number or third person singular of the present tense, and the vast majority of vocabulary items belong without distinction to all dialects of American English. Consequently no functional block in communication normally obtrudes between native users of American English. If a teacher creates a psychological block by overemphasizing differences and underemphasizing likenesses, his pedagogical philosophy needs re-examination.

Thus from descriptive linguistics, as applied in the Atlas, we can learn not only specific facts about certain controversial usages, but much more importantly, an attitude toward the teaching of our language. From our Puritan forefathers we Americans have inherited the idea that things are either *right* or *wrong,* and as teachers we tend to see ourselves as the guardians of the right. The Atlas, however, by displaying the marvelous diversity of current American English, frees us from moral obligation to any one of the many American dialects. It suggests that we observe and discuss language behavior with the same objective interest that we use in talking about the other cultural mores of America. By giving more than lip-service to the concept of individual differences, we will expect and accept individual differences in language with the clear realization that each child speaks the dialect which he has heard spoken, and that he has heard much more speech outside the classroom than in it. Our function is not to make him ashamed of the dialect he has learned from his parents and his friends, but to add to it the standard dialect in order to increase his social and intellectual mobility. We do this job first, by teaching him to read and write the symbols by which language is recorded in books, and the spelling system by which they are arranged; and second, by encouraging him to use his new powers of reading and writing, along with his powers of speaking and listening, which he learned long before he entered our classrooms, to gather, consider, and express ideas that are important and new to him.

36

Dare Schools Set a Standard in English Usage?

ROBERT C. POOLEY

THE TOPIC assigned to me is "Dare the School Set a Standard in English Usage?" I shall answer this question Yankee-fashion with another question: Do we dare *not* to set a standard? To this there seems to me to be but one answer: We should not and cannot fail to set a standard. To do so is to abandon the very core of our obligation to the youth we are employed to teach. We are committed by duty and conscience to bring every student as close as possible to the attainment of a decent standard of English usage by every means at our command. But what is this decent standard and by what terms do we describe it?

One of the commonest misunderstandings of the point of view of the linguistic scholar with regard to English grammar and English usage is that when he observes and reports changes which take place in the English language, he thereby weakens the position of the English teacher and lowers standards. It is extremely important to us all to correct this misapprehension and to recognize why the objective study of our language properly interpreted results in a strengthening of standards rather than in laxity. To do so we shall need to examine more closely what is meant by a standard. It may well be that a misconception of the nature of a language standard is at the root of the misunderstanding.

Reprinted by permission from *The English Journal,* 49.176-81 (March, 1960). Professor Pooley is Chairman of the Department of Integrated and Liberal Studies at the University of Wisconsin.

RANGE OF LATITUDE IN STANDARDS

In all matters concerned with human behavior to which standards may be applied, it will be found that such standards, far from being fixed and unchangeable, are actually only approximations within a fairly wide range of latitude and tolerance. A standard, in human conduct, is a sort of gentleman's agreement as to the norm reasonably expected, but behavior superior to this norm and behavior inferior to it are tolerated to a fairly wide degree. When the behavior exceeds the limit of tolerance to the point of becoming noticeable, amusing, embarrassing, or annoying, the standard is violated. But when deviate behavior remains within the range of normally accepted tolerance, the standard may be said to be maintained.

To cite some instances: a gentleman when seated is expected to rise when a lady enters the room. This is the standard. What are the degrees of tolerance? Behavior may and often does range from a ceremonial rising with a bow and offering of a chair to a half-hearted semi-squat movement as a sort of grudging recognition of the standard. The latter behavior is on the edge of tolerance; if it becomes habitual and noticeable the offender may be considered a boor. On the other hand, excessive politeness and ceremonial attached to this simple standard becomes amusing or annoying, and thus violates the standard of behavior. But within the range between these extremes, the standard is considered to be met. Yet within this tolerable range there are troublesome variations. Does a male guest rise when an eight-year-old daughter of the house is introduced? Does a husband rise every time his wife enters the room? At what point in a daughter's age does a father rise for her entrance? Is he a boor if he does not rise when she is fourteen, sixteen, or eighteen? I do not need to elaborate further to illustrate that a standard of behavior such as this has considerable latitude.

Another example may be observed in the so-called "bread and butter" note—the note of thanks sent to one's hostess when one has been a dinner guest or a house guest. Punctilious meeting of this standard requires a note to be written within three days. A formal note sent the day after the engagement may have a tone of rigidity and coldness, as though one were getting a disagreeable task out of the way; failure to respond within a month is a laxity beyond tolerance within the standard. With considerable variation between these extremes is the friendly note of thanks and acknowledgment of courtesies, differing in degree of formality in proportion to the degree of acquaintanceship of the correspondents. It is almost impossible to write exact rules to cover the variety of situations within which this standard must function. Nevertheless, it is a standard whose performance one neglects only at his social peril. Parental instruction, experience, and general good taste determine the readiness to meet this standard; but the standard must be met if one is to remain within the ranks of the socially acceptable.

I have spoken of the two examples above as if they were unchangeable with time. But we are still aware that behavior patterns change with time and that the norms of expected behavior, in other words the standards, shift from one period to another. When I was a young man a formal dinner required a black dinner coat with formal trousers, a black vest, a black tie, and a starched white shirt with jewelled studs and cuff links. I recently attended the Captain's dinner (which was announced as formal) on board a cruise ship of the Norwegian-American line. The passengers were from the ranks of those Americans who may be called the privileged class. Less than a third of the gentlemen were arrayed in the dinner costume of my youth. The black vest has almost disappeared. In its place a cummerbund is worn. Nor need this be black. A number of guests wore dark maroon, deep blue, or plaid cummerbunds, with ties to match. The starched shirt has almost disappeared; soft shirts with studs and links are rare; soft shirts with ordinary buttons are common. Moreover, there were dinner jackets not black, but deep blue, dark maroon, and a few in resplendent plaid. Does this variety and differentiation mean that gentlemen no longer dress for dinner; that anything goes? Not at all; the standard is perfectly clear, but a range of deviation within the standard is now acceptable which a few years back was not.

In contrast, I would remind you that before the turn of the century every hotel, restaurant, and public parlor in which gentlemen gathered was adorned with cuspidors, and most private homes possessed them, even if discreetly concealed. A pattern of behavior once tolerated or taken for granted is today outside the pale; a hostess would be shocked to be asked to produce a cuspidor.

In the realm of social behavior most of us accept the two principles governing standards which I have illustrated; namely, range of tolerance within the standard at any one period of time, and change in the description of the standard from one period to the next. Any wise parent knows that to insist upon the details of a standard as observed a generation before is to breed rebellion at home and ridicule abroad; the essence is to teach the standard as it is observed today by persons of taste, refinement, and social experience. And as part of the teaching the latitude which exists in the performance of any standard should be included. Our aim for our children and ourselves is neither heel-clicking regimentation, nor loutish laxity. Between these undesirable extremes lies a range, not a point, of tolerated behavior within the standard.

Now we return to language, a form of human behavior, to observe that standards of language, unlike those of other behavior, are considered by many to be rigid and fixed with no range of tolerance, and no change of pattern from one period to another. But because language is a form of human behavior, such fixity of standard is an untrue fiction. It cannot be, it never has been, it never will be. At no time in the history of English can the most intolerant investigator find a time or a place where all the polite, educated elite employed exactly the same usages. On the contrary, the investigator finds volume after volume of writings criticizing the "errors" of the great authors and men of distinction of the previous generation. Apparently, to the neutral historical scholar, the only ones who ever spoke purely correct English were the authors of the books condemning their predecessors and contemporaries for gross errors, and of course, no two of them agreed with each other!

Let us face the facts in all seriousness. What we call "good English" is a gentleman's agreement covering a range of acceptable behavior, exactly parallel with the observance of standards in other types of human behavior. This range can be described, it can furnish a pattern of behavior, it can set a standard of the sort that an intelligent scholar of English can accept and use.

STANDARDS FOR CLASSES

It remains to define and describe the standard of English usage we may properly set for our classes, and are indeed obliged by our duty to maintain so far as we are able. I would like to define this standard first in general, universal terms to lay the foundation for particulars. To this end I quote a definition I wrote nearly thirty years ago, which has been adopted by the Council in its curriculum volumes: "Good English is that form of speech which is appropriate to the purpose of the speaker, true to the language as it is, and comfortable to speaker and listener. It is the product of custom, neither cramped by rule nor freed from all restraint; it is never fixed, but changes with the organic life of the language."[1] You will note that this definition allows for a range of latitude within tolerable limits, and provides for the changes which are inevitable in a spoken language. But a definition so broad leaves the classroom teacher with a great many specific decisions to make, and it is to clarify these decisions that the following specific matters are presented.

In proceeding from the most elementary details to the more complex, I do not intend to imply a grade level distribution, for some usage items are easily overcome and others tend to persist into adult life. The order of presentation is roughly that in which the usage matters become significant in the student's command of his language.

The standard we can rightfully set for ourselves, our colleagues in other departments, and our students, for public and private use, contains at present these particulars:

1. The elimination of all baby-talk and "cute" expressions.

[1] Robert C. Pooley, *Grammar and Usage in Textbooks on English, Bureau of Educational Research Bulletin,* No. 14, University of Wisconsin, August 1933, p. 155.

2. The correct uses in speech and writing of *I, me, he, him, she, her, they, them.* (Exception, *it's me.*)
3. The correct uses of *is, are, was, were* with respect to number and tense.
4. Correct past tenses of common irregular verbs such as *saw, gave, took, brought, bought, stuck.*
5. Correct use of past participles of the same verbs and similar verbs after auxiliaries.
6. Elimination of the double negative: we don't have no apples, etc.
7. Elimination of analogical forms: *ain't, hisn, hern, ourn, theirselves,* etc.
8. Correct use of possessive pronouns: *my, mine, his, hers, theirs, ours.*
9. Mastery of the distinction between *its,* possessive pronoun, and *it's, it is.*
10. Placement of *have* or its phonetic reduction to *v* between *I* and a past participle.
11. Elimination of *them* as a demonstrative pronoun.
12. Elimination of *this here* and *that there.*
13. Mastery of use of *a* and *an* as articles.
14. Correct use of personal pronouns in compound constructions: as subject (Mary and I), as object (Mary and me), as object of preposition (to Mary and me).
15. The use of *we* before an appositional noun when subject; *us* when object.
16. Correct number agreement with the phrases *there is, there are, there was, there were.*
17. Elimination of *he don't, she don't, it don't.*
18. Elimination of *learn* for *teach, leave* for *let.*
19. Elimination of pleonastic subjects: *my brother he; my mother she; that fellow he.*
20. Proper agreement in number with antecedent pronouns *one* and *anyone, everyone, each, no one.* With *everybody* and *none* some tolerance of number seems acceptable now.
21. The use of *who* and *whom* as reference to persons. (But note, *Who did he give it to?* is tolerated in all but very formal situations. In the latter, *To whom did he give it* is preferable.)
22. Accurate use of *said* in reporting the words of a speaker in the past.
23. Correction of *lay down* to *lie down.*
24. The distinction between *good* as adjective, as *well* as adverb, e.g., He spoke *well.*
25. Elimination of *can't hardly, all the farther* (for *as far as*) and Where is he (she, it) *at?*

This list of twenty-five kinds of corrections to make constitutes a very specific standard of current English usage for today and the next few years. Some elements in it may require modification within ten years; some possibly earlier. Conspicuous by their absence are these items which were on the usage lists by which many of us were taught and which survive today in the less enlightened textbooks.

1. Any distinction between *shall* and *will.*

2. Any reference to the split infinitive.
3. Elimination of *like* as a conjunction.
4. Objection to the phrase "different than."
5. Objection to He is one of those boys who *is*.
6. Objection to the reason . . . is because. . . .
7. Objection to *myself* as a polite substitute for *I* as in "I understand you will meet Mrs. Jones and myself at the station."
8. Insistence upon the possessive case standing before a gerund.

These items and many others like them will still remain cautionary matters left to the teacher's discretion. In evaluating the writing of a superior student I would certainly call these distinctions to his attention and point out to him the value of observing them. But this is a very different matter from setting a basic usage standard to be maintained. I think it is fair to say that the items I have listed in the basic table lie outside the tolerable limits of acceptable, current, informal usage; those I have omitted from the base table are tolerated at least, and in some instances are in very general use.

I would like to conclude with a very useful distinction in usage made by one of the distinguished members of our profession, Louis Zahner of Groton School. In the *Atlantic Monthly* for November 1959, he points out the difference between "inventive language," that is, language created to produce a desirable effect, as for example, *to pussyfoot,* or, a *lounge lizard;* and "preventive language," words which defeat meaning by abandoning it: "Isn't it a terrific day:" "He was terrific:" etc. The teacher who loves English will do well to recognize and on occasion praise an unorthodox expression which is creatively effective; but he will condemn with all his force the substitution of meaningless cant for meaningful words.

Let Geoffrey Chaucer have the last word on standards in English:

Ye knowe ek, that in forme of speche is chaunge
Withinne a thousand yeer, and wordes tho
That hadden pris, now wonder nice and straunge
Us thinketh hem; and yit they spake hem so,
And spedde as wel in love as men now do.

37

Approaching Usage in the Classroom

V. LOUISE HIGGINS

IN SEPTEMBER of this year, a revised course of study for the Westport system was made public, and you need to know of it to see how our approach to usage is part of that plan. We have included the following statement in our syllabus: "We support the linguistic approach to grammar"—a disarmingly simple statement that is, in essence, a necessary amendment to our original charter. Two years ago at the Council meeting in Minneapolis, I reported that I was using linguistic grammar and that one other teacher had started to use this method in a junior high school. As of this September, all our teachers started to work on this method. To implement the transition, an in-service course in linguistics is being given during the year. Concurrently, the foreign language departments have started to shift over to the structural approach. Throughout this entire re-organization, we know we can count on an alert administration to assist and encourage us as it has in the past. If Valley Forge is to come, it is always a comfort to know that Washington plans to attend.

Deluged by newspaper and magazine articles on the subject of usage, it is often hard to keep its minor role in mind. Yet, perspective is essential in this instance and one must constantly be aware that an approach to usage stems from the major approach to language. In dealing with usage, we operate from two premises. Number one: the teacher, specifically, the English teacher usually, is the arbiter of usage for all practical purposes. Number two: usage is psychologically based and the varieties of usage constitute varying degrees of social acceptance.

Before I take up these premises, I want to stress one point. Since no two communities are exactly alike, you will have to devise your own methods for implementing the two premises. I suggest that you carefully assess the language situation in your community, take it as you find it, and tailor your methods to fit it. We are all outposts in the sense that our solutions have

Reprinted by permission from *The English Journal,* 49.181-6 (March, 1960). Miss Higgins is a member of the English department of Staples High School, Westport, Connecticut.

to be derived from the specifics of our situations. Some here may be plagued by Indians; in Westport, we may have a surfeit of Tories. But we both share the same problem, and the premises, I think, are our common ground.

THE TEACHER AS ARBITER OF USAGE

The teacher of English is the arbiter of usage. Who else? After all, it is the English teacher who receives the daily questions about usage from students, other faculty members, and the general public. I suggest that a large portion of our difficulties in handling usage questions comes not from unduly restrictive rules or the lack of reliable references, but from our failure to man our posts properly. Our fatal reluctance may stem from two unhappy, past experiences. On the one hand, we have been accused of being pedantic reactionaries who are completely out of touch with real language; on the other, of being footloose radicals who promote general language laxity. A lot depends on which magazine article you read or which meeting you go to—but whichever it is, the teacher always turns out to be the Benedict Arnold of the case. Neither camp is a happy one, so we might as well assume our proper role, even if this includes upsetting some of the prevalent "togetherness" policies.

If the teacher is to be arbiter, then he must be equipped with a thorough knowledge of language. This means not just acquaintance with the traditional rules, but it means a knowledge of descriptive linguistics. The teacher has to take all the expert advice and tailor the conclusions to meet her own school situation. To be able to do some "community customizing," the instructor must have broad training and that means a firm foundation in both the prescriptive and descriptive fields of language.

At the moment there seems to be a deficiency in linguistic training among teachers. Thurston Womack, in an article entitled "Teachers' Attitudes toward Current Usage" (*The English Journal,* April 1959), reports, "the survey revealed . . . that comparatively few teachers had taken course work in linguistic science. . . ." He also states that "The teacher . . most likely to reject items of debatable usage is the high school teacher. . . ." Apparently, a lot of teachers are engaged in arbitration already. The important point is that Mr. Womack's report reveals that as arbiters most of these teachers are inadequately trained, their basis for rejection of usage too narrow. Obviously then, the first job is to broaden the base, and as I indicated earlier, we have this additional training under way in the Westport system. Make no mistake about one thing—we are broadening the base, not substituting one base for another. Description and prescription must go hand in hand.

Besides specific linguistic training, the broader base means that an instructor must have a genuine proficiency in the use of language. The teacher has to develop a wide understanding of usage levels so that she can identify, explain, and illustrate various usage gradations to her students. It is not enough that she be identifiable in the thick of battle by her clarion call, "It is I"; neither is it enough that she have a mere armory of Beatnik terms and all that jazz. We are not interested in the reactionary teacher who does little but polish the subjunctive for the dress parade; we are not interested in the radical who purports that language only lives when it is doing syntactical somersaults. We want teachers who can handle all the levels.

In addition to sound training and genuine proficiency in language, the teacher-arbiter must have a realistic grasp of the present language situation. While the volume of language has increased with mass communication, the general public is still woefully ignorant as to the nature and function of language. For the time, we must assume that our students are linguistically naive and that until we can get a measure of linguistic understanding, the development of usage competence is going to be a slow process. During these transition years, there will inevitably be controversy and confusion. To be able to survive these years, the teacher needs a comprehensive base on which she can stand firmly, but at ease.

Now that I have profiled the arbiter as one who has thorough training, proficiency on the various usage levels, and an understanding of the milieu in which she works, we can proceed to the classroom. I shall take some four examples from my own experience.

USAGE IN THE CLASSROOM

First, knowing that I am dealing with the linguistically innocent, I am careful not to make statements that, however true, could be misunderstood by my pupil audience and my unseen but formidable public audience. From the beginning, I work on developing the concept of usage levels, using a myriad of examples from all forms of communication—good, bad, and appalling. I constantly call the attention of my students to the difference between written and spoken English. Aware of the "Is it right or wrong?" set of mind common to our American culture, knowing that usage will not fit this artificial duality, I try to get my students to stop asking, "Is this correct?" and to start asking, "What level of usage is this?" I try not to be caught in that familiar trap of having to give a fast "yes" or "no" answer on questions of usage, but I insist on time for full explanation. In language problems, a little explaining is not only dangerous, it can also be fatal.

Second, in taking up levels of usage, the first big distinction I make is that between public and private utterance. This clears the ground of dear old Dad and all the other parental ghosts, or don't your students ever say, "Well, my father says that at home all the time!" The hallmarks of private utterance are that it is definitely limited and that the emphasis is on content, not form. It is language in most pragmatic form and we all use it with our families, our friends, in our notes to the milkman. Public communication differs in that it is meant for a wider audience and that both form and content are considered. In our classrooms, we are dealing primarily with usage as it pertains to public utterances. May I remark here that although I seem to infer that private communication is an unholy mess of grammatical barbarism, unworthy of any consideration at all, such is not my intent, and I ignore the private merely because it is not our main concern. Public language is our main concern. In such utterances, we need to pay attention to grammatical prescriptions because the intent of standardization is to make ideas clear to large groups, and we are held accountable for this clarity. A brief consideration of slang offers an example of the difference between public and private language. On the one hand, I do not deny that slang constitutes a form of communication and that it is a form that is widely used. On the other hand, I maintain that its limitations, the fact that you have "to be with it" to understand it, places it in the category of private language. It may be and is used in public communication as a stylistic device, but not as the primary medium of communication. Since class assignments are public writings, I do not allow slang to be used in them. I shall take up the problem of stylistic slang in a moment.

From the vantage point of public language, I make other subdivisions. There are obviously legal, business, journalistic, scientific levels of usage, to name a few. Within these levels, I place formal and informal expression, for these two divisions depend primarily on the material under consideration. Formal English, I see as essentially ritualistic. It has an elegance to it and is suitable for material of high seriousness. Proclamations from the President, the Bible, the Constitution are written in formal English and their ritualistic nature is seen very quickly in the heavy use of archaic verb tenses. Informal English is used in the bulk of our public utterances. One small example will point up the difference between the formal and informal operating within the same usage level. A legal document such as a will, a bill of divorcement, is written in formal English; a letter from your lawyer is written in informal English. In the letter, the lawyer does not throw grammatical rules to the wind, for this is a public letter between lawyer and client, not a private communication. This is informal, public language. Where do I place the colloquial, the regional? Why, in the realm of private utterance, because such utterances are strictly limited in nature. Although we all use them, we know they will not serve all situations. In Denver, I would ask, "Where is the shoe repair shop?" At home, I ask, "Where is the cobbler's?"

Third, in dealing with usage, I have found that the primary need of the language neophyte is some kind of order. My plan of order is the approach by levels. To hold my students to this, I have to be especially cautious in the twilight zone known as "creative writing," for it is in this area that the linguistically inept strays the farthest. The student, believing that anything goes as long he gives vent to genuine feelings or that all is acceptable if he can cite a passage from Kerouac or Hemingway to substantiate a usage, usually displays serious usage errors when he writes a short story or a so-called "personal essay." In most cases, usage errors occur because artistic usage is employed on unartistic material. Style is too quickly defined as "the way the author writes." Most students do not interpret this fully to mean that this is the way the author writes, given these circumstances, this point of view, this artistic intent. The student does not make usage errors because he writes *like* Kerouac or Hemingway, but because he does not write with the same purpose, the same understanding, the same artistry. I often think our failure to make the student defend his usage as artistic in his context rather than in Hemingway's turns much of our creative writing into an orgy of literary extravagance rather than the literary experience it should be. I handle stylistic slang in this fashion. The student must show me that it is stylistic, apt, and effective, that it does stem from stylistic vigor not vacuous vocabulary. So, with creative writing, I am perhaps more demanding than I am with ordinary, expository prose.

Fourth, I make frequent use of reference books, but I try to make my selection eclectic. *The Dictionary of Contemporary American Usage* is next to the *O.E.D.* Fries is next to Fowler. The multi-reference system, which must include recent publications, helps not only in settling disputes, but also in removing a usage from the area of dispute. It is possible to waste time correcting "errors" which are in fact no longer "errors" at all. Let me cite one example. In the two-volume *New Century Dictionary* (I use the 1952 edition), the past participle of "prove" is listed as "proved"; "proven" is given as legal phraseology. But in the *Dictionary of Contemporary American Usage,* "proven" is listed as acceptable American usage, and "proved" as the form used most often in Great Britain. Result—I accept either form. Besides specific references, a teacher has to make use of what I can only term "common sense" observation of language. A reference on business usage is fine, but perhaps it is just as well to review some business letters, some stockholder's reports, if we want to have a current view. No matter how eclectic her references, the teacher-arbiter can become unduly restrictive if she does not keep in mind that her important job is not corrective but constructive. She needs to be interested in language, not just academically, but personally, for she is not just an instructor in language, she is a user of language. I cannot pretend to have a scholarly approach, although I hope I use what scholarship is available; I cannot pretend that I *always* proceed from statistically substantiated facts. On an outpost, one has a tendency to walk up to language, grab it, and use it. I cannot apologize for this, for while the scholar may walk with measured tread, on an outpost, I do believe one has to step lively.

In any event, a teacher can arbitrate if she accepts a few realities about language and arms herself with proper training. She can avoid being cut down in the rather senseless crossfire of the Indians who maintain that a few filtered smoke signals cover any and all communication situations and of the Tories who insist that only Bacon uses English correctly. Whether you are hit by an arrow or a bullet, you are just as dead, and the teacher's first job as an arbiter is to stay alive.

USAGE AND SOCIAL ACCEPTANCE

Usage is psychologically based and the varieties of usage constitute varying degrees of social acceptance. I list this as a separate premise because in this case the teacher is not so much an arbiter as a referee. The degree of status seeking varies from area to area, but vary as it will, it is a factor in our society, and as teachers, we might as well take advantage of the situation. No need for us to be like Clym Yeobright. If you remember, in *Return of the Native*. Clym's school was a resounding failure. His failure was not the result of his poor eyesight or of Eustacia's notable lack of enthusiasm, but of his own inability to understand a fundamental aspect of human nature. Hardy says, "In passing from the bucolic to the intellectual life the intermediate stages are usually two at least, frequently many more; and one of these stages is almost surely to be worldly advance." Indeed, one does not always hurtle from the McGuffey to Milton; one often has to go via the paycheck. We are doomed to becoming mere purveyors of status in its worst sense without a thorough knowledge of language.

In implementing premise number Two in my classes, I take the candid approach because it fits my teaching situation. My students understand very well what social status means, so I simply tell them, "If you speak this way, you go in the back door; if you speak *this* way, you go in the front door." I make it very clear that I neither built the house nor did I designate the doors. In this case, I am merely an agent showing off the real estate. I have the key to the front door, and once the student has the concept of usage levels I have given him the key. The back door is always ajar.

In the event that I am faced with students who feel this whole situation is un-American and surely must have been foisted on us by subversive elements, I try to get the students to see themselves as "society," and to see that they too evolve usage fashions. I need only go to student jargon to illustrate how a particular student body imposes its language on a group. In the fall, our sophomores arrive with a bagful of left-over junior high terminology. By the end of the first quarter, most of them have exchanged it for the high school brand. A "composition" becomes a "paper"; the "wheels" (elite of the school) are now "hi si" (meaning high society). Sophomores soon call Building 7 where science is taught A.R.P. (short for Atomic Research Pile). Where possible, I try to use language about me to explain concepts. The varying degrees of social acceptance that are reflected in usage can be seen very clearly in the microcosm of my own school. I feel no need to go barrelling off into an academic study of usage in the Tennessee hills.

Now remains the question of whether schools are to be nothing more than status mills, whether different usage levels have not some value other than the most commercial. I think we can agree that our goal cannot be to produce a nation of glib confidence men, that implicit in our whole teaching of language is the premise that people have something of value to communicate and that those things of value enhance rather than degrade the human spirit. If I profess these ideals, you may wonder why I take the status situation so calmly and deal with it so summarily. The reason is very simple—usage is a product of society, not a cause of it. To replace affluence with wisdom as a status mark will take a major battle. It is a battle in which I intend to participate, but it is not the point at issue this morning. Usage is only a symptom and we should treat it as such. We can refuse to be intimidated by status speech; we can use vigorous, clear, effective language ourselves. There is no point in wasting ammunition in random shots until one is ready to have them heard around the world.

38

Teachers' Attitudes toward Current Usage

Thurston Womack

THERE IS SOME FEELING among teachers of English that the battle of usage has been won, and that the current fracas concerns structural linguistics. There is a feeling too among some of us that discussions about moot or debatable usages are somehow old hat—that everybody knows nowadays that to object to the split infinitive is, as Robert C. Pooley put it in *Teaching English Usage,* "little more than pedantic rubbish."

We now generate the same emotion and fever about teaching—or not teaching—structural linguistics in the classroom that we did about teaching the relativity of correctness a number of years back. The books we now find

Reprinted by permission from *The English Journal,* 48.186-90 (February, 1959). Professor Womack is in the Division of Language Arts, San Francisco State College.

our attention turning to are books like Fries's *Structure of English,* Warfel and Lloyd's *American English in Its Cultural Setting,* Paul Roberts' *Patterns of English,* and Nelson Francis' *The Structure of American English* instead of S. A. Leonard's *Current English Usage,* Marckwardt and Walcott's *Facts About Current English Usage,* Pooley's *Teaching English Usage,* and the "liberal" handbooks, Perrin's *Writer's Guide and Index to English* being the most notable. But Perrin seems dated, Pooley seems a little conservative—and all of these latter books seem concerned with something that has now been taken care of—like the social problems depicted in Upton Sinclair's early novels.

And it is undoubtedly true that the doctrine of usage has become widely disseminated, mainly through the efforts of the NCTE and its publications. But a study of teachers' attitudes toward fifty debatable items of usage, which I completed this past year, reveals that perhaps the battle of usage has not been entirely won and that the study of usage and the dissemination of information about usage to teachers must be continuous and persistent.

I undertook to show that teachers' attitudes toward debatable items of English usage are affected by two kinds of experience: academic as revealed by background of course work and familiarity with important publications in language study, and environmental and social, including size of community in which the teacher teaches, years of teaching experience and level at which the teacher teaches. It is necssary to point out that the survey makes no attempt to establish what the facts of usage actually are. The survey sought teachers' attitudes and opinions toward the usages and reveals the discrepancy between the facts of usage and opinions about what usage should be.

DESIGN OF THE STUDY

The teachers included in the survey were all members of the NCTE[1] and included elementary, secondary, and college teachers. The fifty debatable items of usage were selected from the "disputable" items of S. A. Leonard's survey, *Current English Usage,* from the occurrence of certain items in the "Current English Forum" in *The English Journal* and *College English,* from suggestions made in Pooley's *Teaching English Usage,* and from glossaries of usage in English handbooks. The usages are listed here as economically as possible, either by the familiar grammatical label, by a truncated example, or by description, whichever way seems clearest.

The split infinitive; the case of the noun or pronoun before the gerund; seven items of agreement between subject and verb and pronoun and antecedent; *one . . . he; . . . is when . . . ; these kind . . . ; data is . . . ;* preposition

---

[1] The Executive Office of the NCTE provided a random sample of its membership. Nine hundred questionnaires were sent out. Thirty-eight percent or 339 were returned from forty-five states and the District of Columbia.

at end of a sentence; *either* of three; *shortest* of two; dangling participle (not an absurd one); *myself* used in the nominative; between you and *I; who* are you waiting for?; drive *slow;* as if he *was;* it is *me;* aren't I . . . ; Jones was younger than *him; building's* roof; after discussing the heroine, most of the young women expressed no desire to be *her;* it looks *like* it will rain; the boy felt *badly; can* in the sense of permission; very *nice* people; *fixed* in the sense of repaired; *different than; awful* colds; New York is *further* east than Chicago; try *and* finish; *due to* in the sense of because of; has *proven; raised* instead of *reared;* Americans *have got* to make democracy work; some students do not know *if* they can . . . ; divided *between* three; the *reason . . .* was *because . . .* ; the students *enthused* about . . . ; The state *hung* the murderers; the old man *laid* down on his bed . . . ; . . . *cannot help but . . . ;* the swimmers *dove* into the pool; the soldiers fulfilled the *dying wish* of the commander.

The questionnaire used in the survey asked the teacher to judge each item with regard to acceptability in formal or informal speech and formal or informal writing, thus allowing a choice of four variables in each of the two categories, speech and writing. No questionnaire, of course, can cover all the variables of any given language situation. The questionnaire used, however, put emphasis upon the difference between speech and writing and upon formality and informality within speech and writing, an emphasis which did not exist in the questionnaires used in previous studies. The fifty items were offered as being usages which sometimes occur in the language of students. The teacher was asked what the teacher's attitude should be toward the items.

Published information which would seem to be readily accessible to all English teachers was collected for each usage in Leonard's *Current English Usage,* Marckwardt and Walcott's *Facts About Current English Usage,* "Current English Forum" in *The English Journal* or *College English,* Pooley's *Teaching English Usage,* Perrin's *Writer's Guide and Index to English,* Roberts' *Understanding Grammar,* and two dictionaries, the *American College Dictionary* and *Webster's New Collegiate Dictionary.* Some of the usages are not discussed in some of the publications, and in one instance the usage is not discussed in any of the publications (the soldier fulfilled the *dying wish* of the commander).

TEACHER VIEWS VS. PUBLISHED INFORMATION

A comparison item by item of the teachers' views with the published information reveals that in general the majority of the teachers still reject most usages that published information tends to support as acceptable. Teachers' comments often clarify their reasons for not accepting the items, and are often more revealing than the statistics. Many teachers in the survey felt that English teachers are obligated to hold a conservative view toward language change and should acknowledge changes in usage only after such changes are reported in journals, textbooks, and dictionaries. One college teacher who rejected most of the items on the questionnaire claims familiarity with the history of the English language, with Fries, Marckwardt, and Bloomfield, yet maintains his position on the basis of personal preference for the so-called correct usages.

Other teachers succinctly label the items as "incorrect grammar." Some comment that the line must be held or "these errors . . . will continue to exist." The "rules of grammar" are often cited, and frequent misuse, it is claimed, is no justification for grammatical errors. One teacher asserts that the American people have become "grammar lazy," that it is the English teacher's responsibility to uphold standards in language. There is also the view expressed that such words as *enthused* and *proven* "do not literally exist." Some teachers feel that teaching that more than one usage is acceptable further confuses an already confused student. Other teachers claim to be "old-fashioned" and to be influenced by extensive training in Latin as reasons for rejecting most of the usages. At least one college teacher blames poor instruction in language for the ignorance of high school and elementary school teachers, and in turn, criticizes the poor education they receive in teacher-training institutions.

The foregoing characterizes roughly a prescriptive, or "right" or "wrong" view toward usage. Among the written-in comments on the questionnaires were many which reveal a descriptive view toward usage. The descriptive view observes levels of usage, sees acceptable usage not as being "right" or "wrong," but as being relative to the social situation in which language is used. The descriptive view of usage is the position held by such scholars and students of usage as Fries, Marckwardt and Walcott, Pooley, Bryant, and others.

Among those voicing a descriptive approach to usage study and teaching are many who feel that insistence upon usages which teachers themselves do not observe is not only ludicrous but a waste of time. Many teachers state that the usage they try to get their students to observe and imitate is the usage of the educated people of the community in which they live, regardless of whether or not that usage violates the rules of the grammar books.

Published information clearly supports all but two of the usages (between you and *I* and intransitive *laid*), though Pooley and Perrin offer some evidence in support of these. One must conclude that teachers either do not heed the evidence in their teaching or are not informed about it.

The great majority of all teachers in the survey admit variation in usage between speech and writing, and within speech and writing. The standard for writing, of course, does not admit as many usages as does that for speech.

OTHER FINDINGS

The questionnaire provided statistical data for demonstrating the possible relationship between scores on the usage items and the variables (1) grade level at which teacher teaches, (2) size of community in which teacher teaches, (3) years of teaching experience, and (4) highest academic degree held by the teacher. Significant relationships were demonstrated by chi-square analysis. Earlier studies suggested that high school teachers in small towns tended to reject items of debatable usage. The present survey confirms this tendency and adds two other variables, experience and degree held. The teacher, then, most likely to reject items of debatable usage is the high school teacher with more than ten years of teaching experience living in a small town, who holds either an A.B. or an M.A. degree. On the other hand, the teacher most likely to accept items of debatable usage is the college teacher in a city of more than 50,000 people with less than ten years of teaching experience and a doctor's degree. The fact that the elementary teacher generally falls between these two furnishes interesting material for conjecture. One might safely infer in the case of the college teacher that a tendency to approve items of debatable usage is directly related to linguistic sophistication. Logically, then, one might conclude that elementary teachers are in general more sophisticated linguistically than high school teachers, although this conclusion should be made only tentatively, since the position of elementary teachers toward the usage items might be explained on the basis of their *not* being specialists in language and of *not* being linguistically sophisticated enough to identify"wrong" usages. There is, however, some information in the survey which indicates that the elementary teachers can hardly be considered benighted about linguistic matters.

The teachers participating in the survey were members of the NCTE. What observations might be made in light of this fact? In the first place, to what extent do NCTE members reflect the views of the English teachers of the country at large? It seems safe to suggest that NCTE members are probably better informed than English teachers generally. It is also important to consider the probable characteristics of the teachers who returned questionnaires. It is likely that these teachers would be among those having the greatest sense of professional responsibility, since they took the time and trouble to return the questionnaire. Teachers returning questionnaires, then, would be likely to be those best informed about professional concerns, particularly linguistic matters, although it would be difficult to assess accurately the characteristics of these concerns. Questionnaire studies have revealed that potential respondents are likely to complete questionnaires which appeal directly to their interests, not those which do not.

If it can be assumed that the bias of the results of the survey is in the direction of having a preponderance of teachers particularly alert to linguistic concerns, then it can be assumed also that those teachers not represented in the survey, NCTE members as well as English teachers in general, would have less acquaintance with usage information and other linguistic studies, and would, consequently, have a narrower, more pre-scriptive view of usage matters.

The survey revealed, further, that comparatively few teachers had taken course work in linguistic science or were familiar with the works of Leonard Bloomfield and Edward Sapir. Less than half were acquainted with the work of Jespersen, Fries, Marckwardt and Walcott, and Perrin.

The present survey provides at least tentative and partial answers to the following two questions:

1. To what extent has the evidence of scientific language study affected the linguistic views of teachers?
2. To what extent has the official view of the NCTE, as stated in its journals and its volumes on the English curriculum and as reflected in its sponsorship of linguistic study, affected the views of teachers?

One thing seems clear: the usage battle has not been won, though prog-ress has been made. Two recommendations seem in order: (1) regardless of teaching level, there should be included in the preparation of teachers of English a sound orientation in the views and methodology of modern scientific language study; (2) the NCTE should continue its program of support to committees on current English usage and its publication of books and articles dealing with the usage of American English.

Part V

LINGUISTICS AND THE TEACHING OF GRAMMAR AND COMPOSITION

INTRODUCTION

ALTHOUGH several earlier articles in this book have touched upon problems of teaching, those problems are the focus of the material in this Part, where both linguists and classroom teachers of English consider the relevance of linguistic information to the teaching of grammar and composition.

Two opening articles, by Hackett and Mrs. Norris, provide a kind of prolegomenon for the section. Hackett insists that language must be recognized as part of the general culture in which the student lives and to the changes in which he must adjust. He reflects the points of view of Whorf and of the sociologist, George Herbert Meade. In the excerpt here reprinted Mrs. Norris likewise draws upon both linguistics and anthropology to arrive at essentially the same position.

Smith, one of the nation's leading linguists, next indicates what seems to him the essential language information the teacher ought to command. Another linguistic anthropologist, McQuown, then applies linguistic theory to the practical problem of teaching English in the elementary grades, and Ives describes the linguistic basis of teaching composition in the secondary school and college. Hunt proceeds with the further specific application of the structural approach to the improvement of sentences. Burnet extends the structural application to the inter-relationship of sentences in the paragraph. Hill then focuses structural application upon the whole problem of style.

Roberts would de-emphasize stress upon the remedial value of linguistics in straightening out students who have composition troubles and instead would insist that the study of the language for its own sake is a legitimate function in the English classroom. Here he joins many linguists who for some time have been saying precisely this, Fries, for one, as early as 1925. That point of view, of course, underlies this very collection.

In his own book, *English Sentences* (Harcourt, Brace, 1962) Roberts has been faithful to this principle by being the first to attempt to bring into the high school classroom some content knowledge of that recent development in linguistics, transformation grammar. Thomas here reduces some of the forbidding aspects of Chomsky's formulas to such simplified form as renders them acceptable in secondary teaching. Sledd then introduces some very cogent criticism of over-readiness in attempting, as Roberts does, a working classroom synthesis of structural grammar and transformation grammar. Myers concludes the section with a further note of caution.

39

Some Assumptions . . . To Be Examined

HERBERT HACKETT

I WOULD LIKE to state some assumptions, drawn from a variety of fields, about the nature and function of language, assumptions which I think are defensible on the evidence but all of which need further study.

1. Language is behavior and must be taught on behavioral principles.

2. Language is first of all a functioning tool of interaction and only relatively rarely a means of reflective thought; as such it has no meaning apart from the total context of situation; meaning is context.

3. Language operates within a cultural context and is limited by it.

4. Language is not only dependent on its culture, but in turn structures

This letter to the editor is reprinted in part by permission from *College English,* 16.452-453 (April, 1955). Professor Hackett is at the State University of New York at Buffalo.

reality for this culture. The individual cannot operate outside the limits set by this language, nor see the world except as it is given structure by his language. This structure will vary from culture to culture.

5. As behavior, language is measured by effectiveness in terms of purpose; it must adapt to the situation, the user, the audience, the subject matter.

6. As behavior it must be studied in terms of group norms, the expectations of the group as to usage, content and purpose. These expectations must be found by observation, they cannot be prescribed on the authority of historical or theoretical considerations.

7. Language cannot be taught prescriptively, since the prescription may fail to keep up with the actual practice of the culture; rather, the student must be taught to observe and to fit his communication to accepted good usage.

8. The unit of language is not the part—the word, sentence or paragraph —but is the total perception to be transmitted, to which the parts are bound. Thus, the approach to teaching communication skills is the teaching of a total perception.

9. The end of language is not language but content, leading to better perception by the audience. The teaching of skills, then, will be concerned with what is said, in its context; how it is said will develop from this.

10. Language as social behavior has social responsibility, including proper recognition of bias, accurate use of data, and a positive acceptance of the opinion of others and of the relativity of knowledge.[1]

These are a few of the assumptions about language and the process of communication which many of us make, with or without consciously phrasing them. None of these has been sufficiently examined by teachers of skills, although a substantial body of data in other disciplines supports them. Some are over-simplifications, *all are to be doubted.*

And yet these assumptions and many related to them indicate the direction in which our thinking about the teaching of skills must go. They are not the final formulations of a discipline but must be reexamined, restated, framed into hypotheses, observed, tested, rehypothesized. . . . Only then may we sit in the circle of language scientists and from them learn, because we will know what they are talking about.

[1] Some of the wording and emphasis of the above assumptions is borrowed from Frederic Reeve, "Toward a Philosophy of Communication," *Education* 72:445-455 (March, 1952).

40

Linguistic Science and Its Classroom Reflections

Mary Jane M. Norris

THIS PAPER is an attempt to bring together the various assumptions, statements, findings, or other contributions generally included within the scope of linguistic science that have a bearing on language teaching, and to show to some extent how they are reflected in the language classroom. These elements of linguistic science can be divided into the following five points:

1. The realization of the nature of language.
   a. Language is vocal.
   b. Language symbols are arbitrary.
   c. Language has system.
   d. Language is for communication.
   e. Language is made up of habits.
   f. There is a relation between a language and the culture in which it is used.
   g. Languages change.
   h. No two languages have the same set of patterns of pronunciation, words, and syntax.[1]
2. The realization (assumption) that patterns of one's native language interfere with learning later the patterns of another language.
3. Methods of analyzing and describing languages.
4. Descriptions of some languages.
5. Techniques for comparison of two languages.

These points with their reflections, or potential reflections, in the classroom follow.

Excerpted and reprinted, by permission of the University of Michigan Research Club in Language Learning, from *Language Learning,* 10.55-59 (1960). The late Mrs. Norris taught in the English Language Institute at the University of Michigan.
[1] Redundancy might be added as a feature of language, a concept which has come to the fore through the work of Claude L. Shannon and W. Weaver, *The Mathematical Theory of Communication,* Urbana: University of Illinois Press, 1949. Waldo E. Sweet in "The Carrot on the Stick," editorial, *Language Learning,* 9.1-2, 1959, mentions a use of redundancy, as fill-the-space exercises, in the language classroom.

THE REALIZATION OF THE NATURE OF LANGUAGE

Language is Vocal

The vocal nature of language makes us view the written language as secondary. It brings the primary attention upon oral-aural work in the classroom. Henry Sweet in *The Practical Study of Languages,* 1899, advocated beginning with the spoken language. Leonard Bloomfield in *An Introduction to the Study of Language,* 1914, p. 293, said that "not one in a thousand [foreign language students in the USA] ever learns to carry on a conversation in the foreign language," and he stressed, among other things, pronunciation drill. The same emphasis is made by Harold E. Palmer in *The Oral Method of Teaching Languages,* 1923. Charles C. Fries in *Teaching and Learning English as a Foreign Language,* 1945, presents the "oral approach," with the aim of learning to speak a language and to understand it when it is spoken—this does not mean, he points out, that reading and writing cannot be used, but that reading and writing are not the aim of the first stage of learning a language. The English Language Institute of the University of Michigan follows the oral approach in its Intensive Course in English, which began in 1941. From 1942 to 1945, the Intensive Language Program of the American Council of Learned Societies (ACLS) got under way to teach the spoken language. Linguists conducted the classes, using speakers of the language as informants and models. In the classes, mimicry and memorization (known as Mim-Mem) played a great part. In 1943-44 the Army Specialized Training Program (ASTP) at various American universities also emphasized the spoken language and followed techniques of the ACLS program. These techniques are stated later by William E. Welmers in *Spoken English as a Foreign Language,* 1953, Instructor's Manual, ACLS Program in English as a Foreign Language.

Language Symbols Are Arbitrary

There are no true or correct symbols or sets of symbols except with reference to the language and dialect of which they are a part. What "lift" is a symbol for in London is symbolized by "elevator" in Ann Arbor and by "ascensor" in Buenos Aires. No one of these is a truer symbol of the object than any of the others. This arbitrariness of language symbols is significant in deciding upon the dialect to be taught—it is not a matter of one dialect being more correct than another, but a matter of which dialect the

[2] Linguistic geographers have been determining language and dialect areas. For a description of the dialect areas of the eastern U. S. see: Kurath, Hans, with Marcus L. Hansen, Julia Bloch, and Bernard Bloch. *Handbook of the Linguistic Geography of New England.* Washington, D.C.: American Council of Learned Societies, 1939. See also: Kurath, Hans. *A Word Geography of the Eastern United States.* Ann Arbor: University of Michigan Press, 1949.

student will encounter most or have most use for. The basis for dialect decision is brought out by Fries (1945, p. 4), and also by David W. Reed in "Choice of Dialect," editorial, *Language Learning,* 1.4, 1948.[2]

Language Has System

Edward Sapir in "Sound Patterns in Language," *Language,* 1.2, 1925, p. 40, says ". . . a complex psychology of association and pattern is implicit in the utterance of the simplest consonant or vowel." On all levels of language, not only pronunciation, system is manifested, with language forms falling into patterns. With this view of language, it is the system, instead of lists of unrelated items, that is presented in the classroom—the patterns of pronunciation, words, and syntax. The language teacher's subject can now be better defined, for the patterns of a language are limited.

Language Is for Communication

Human beings communicate, that is, convey meaning to one another, through language. One implication of this aspect of language is that the vocabulary selection (selection of the lexical units) for a class will depend on the kind of communication situations the students will be in. Various word-lists have been compiled to help the teacher or textbook writer select a useful vocabulary.[3] Some considerations of vocabulary selection are discussed by Robert Lado in "Patterns of Difficulty in Vocabulary," *Language Learning* 6.1-2, 1955, and by Michael West, "A Plateau Vocabulary for Speech," *Language Learning,* 7.1-2, 1956-1957. The vocabulary selection of Michigan's Intensive English Course textbooks is determined by the "areas of living" of the learners.[4]

Another implication of this communicative feature of the nature of language comes in the presenting and practicing of the teaching points. The teacher sets up situations, or contexts, verbally and through the use of visual aids to teach a particular point. Thus, instead of emphasis on recitation of conjugations, declensions, terminology, and vocabulary lists, conversations and other utterances that communicate play a great role in the language classroom.

Language Is Made Up of Habits

The patterns of a language are habits for speakers of the language. Practice is usually necessary to form language habits. In the words of the

[3] For a survey of English word-lists see: Fries, Charles C., and A. Aileen Traver [Kitchen]. *English Word Lists: A study of Their Adaptability for Instruction.* Washington, D. C.: American Council on Education, 1940. For notes on more recent publications on vocabulary selection see: Lado, Robert. *Annotated Bibliography for Teachers of English as a Foreign Language.* (U. S. Department of Health, Education, and Welfare Bulletin 1955, No. 3) Washington, D. C.: U. S. Government Printing Office, 1955.
[4] Fries (1945), pp. 50-51.

Canadian neurosurgeon, Wilder Penfield,[5] language habits as developing in a child "are more than motor skills of tongue and lip; they are units of sound and units of thought established in a physical form within the brain. He uses these units over and over again while he is constructing the nerve cell basis of each new word, and he deposits these word patterns in special areas of the cerebral cortex." For second-language learning, Bloomfield (1914) recommended at least eight hours a week of constant drill in the first year or two. The ASTP called for many class hours and small classes. Pattern practice is an integral part of the Intensive Course in English of the English Language Institute, University of Michigan. Language laboratories[6] have been established for additional practice opportunities, with tape recorders, phonographs, and other electronic devices.[7] (John B. Carroll in *The Study of Language,* 1953, questions whether much drill is necessary for habit information and says that psychologists must give the answer.)

There is a Relation Between a Language and the Culture in Which It Is Used

The extent of the relationship between language and culture, discussed in *Language in Culture,* Harry Hoijer, editor, 1954, remains in question. Statements made by Edward Sapir and Benjamin L. Whorf on this relationship are known as the Sapir-Whorf hypothesis. Sapir, in *Selected Writings of Edward Sapir,* D. G. Mandelbaum, editor, 1949, p. 162, said, "We see and hear and otherwise experience very largely as we do because the language habits of our community predispose certain choices of interpretation." Whorf, in *Collected Papers on Metalinguistics,* 1952, p. 36, wrote of "fashions of speaking" within a language which largely make up the speaker's "thought world' . . . the microcosm that each man carries about within himself, by which he measures and understands what he can of the macrocosm." It would seem, then, by knowing the patterns of a language we would learn something of the culture in which the language is used. But on the other hand, culture, the total situations in which a language is used, gives meaning to the utterances of a language (see 1.d above). The implication for the classroom is that the situation, the pattern of a culture, in which an utterance is made must be understood in order to understand a particular utterance. (We should not infer from this aspect of language that a language is limited to a particular culture. English, Spanish, French, and Arabic, for example, are being used in various cultures throughout the world.)

[5] Penfield, Wilder. "The Human Brain and the Learning of Secondary Languages," Radio Broadcast, mimeographed, New Delhi: February, 1957.

[6] For a survey of language laboratories see: Johnston, Marjorie C., and Catharine C. Seerley. *Foreign Language Laboratories in Schools and Colleges.* (U. S. Department of Health, Education, and Welfare Bulletin 1959, No. 3) Washington, D. C.: U. S. Government Printing Office, 1958.

[7] The possibility of "teaching machines" to replace, not merely to supplement, the language teacher is being explored.

Languages Change

English today is different from the English at the time of Shakespeare and still more different from that of King Alfred's time. The fact that languages change, and the fact that language symbols are arbitrary (1.b), have led to movements to get rid of prescriptiveness in grammar books and to have descriptions instead. As evidence for these movements we have, for English, Fries' "What is Good English," 1928, reprinted in *Teaching of English,* 1949, and *Facts about Current English Usage,* Albert H. Marckwardt and Fred G. Walcott, 1938.

No Two Languages Have the Same Set of Patterns of Pronunciation, Words, and Syntax

What is true of one language system is not necessarily true of another; we cannot impose grammar rules from one language to another. That Latin has infinitives that are not split does not mean that English has or should have infinitives that are not split. Consideration of this uniqueness of each language system makes most word-for-word translations invalid, and suggests that translation is not a good teaching device. . . . .

41

Language-Learning from an Anthropological Point of View

Norman A. McQuown

Language, most broadly conceived, may be said to include all the ways of behaving which serve to communicate with other persons and to reaffirm an individual's own integrity. Among these ways of behaving are stance, bodily movement, facial expression, vocal movement, and speech. Of especial interest are the effects of these on objects in the world about us—the products of the manual arts, the products of the vocal arts, and the products of speech. The most important of the latter are writing and written records.

Reprinted by permission from *The Elementary School Journal,* 54.402-8 (March, 1954). The author is Professor of Anthropology at the University of Chicago.

Of all the modes of communication, that which involves talk and that which involves frozen talk, or writing, are undoubtedly the most generally influential.

Language, more narrowly conceived, is limited to speech and to writing. This article is concerned with certain aspects of speech and of writing and of their interrelations. Of interest will be the process whereby spoken language is learned and the spoken language arts are taught. Likewise of concern will be the process whereby a child, already in command of a goodly amount of spoken language, learns how to transfer what he says to paper and how to get from paper what other speakers have said there.

We are interested in the whole process of the acquisition and transmission, via language, of the ways of feeling and acting appropriate to the role which an individual plays in a community. We are interested in language from beginning to end, from literacy to literature, or, for that matter, from lap to literature! We are concerned not merely with the acquisition and utilization of the mother-tongue: we are likewise, in the modern world, increasingly interested in the acquisition and utilization of another tongue. We are interested in reading and in writing—and in our own community, in spelling—in the art of plain talk and clear writing, as well as in the appreciation and encouragement of the more rhetorical and literary aspects of fine speech and good writing. We are interested in the inculcation of the ability to read critically and with discrimination, as well as the capacity to absorb efficiently and handle competently the content of our formal and informal education which we get from books. We are interested in the acquisition of skill in foreign languages and in the broadening of understanding of other peoples which ideally results from such skill. I shall here briefly discuss only certain limited aspects of these general problems: learning to read and write and learning grammar.

UNDERLYING POINT OF VIEW

Before embarking upon this discussion, however, it may be helpful to clarify the point of view which lies behind these remarks. Anthropologists, somewhat self-importantly, call it the "anthropological" point of view. In essence, this point of view simply says: "Life is real. Life is earnest. Life is complex. No man alone is adequate to its problems. Obtaining a sympathetic understanding of, and appreciation for, other people's answers to life's problems is good sense and may turn out to be enlightened self-interest."

By "other people's answers" we do not merely mean those of our immediate family, our next-door neighbors, or even our fellow-countrymen. No human group, of whatever color or creed, has any vested interest in the right answers. There is no line between the man we face and the man on the other side of the globe. What one learns about how the game of life is played there may shed surprising light on how the game is played at home. As a guide in the solution of particular problems, anthropologists have arrived at certain generalizations about the nature of human beings and their behavior. The generalizations which have to do with language behavior[1] will be of particular interest here.

THE YOUNG CHILD'S KNOWLEDGE OF LANGUAGE

A linguist of my acquaintance has made the following somewhat drastic statement: "Everyone who is not deaf or idiotic has fully mastered his native language by the end of his fifth year."[2] If this statement were to be taken literally, it would seem that teachers of the language arts would have little to do in the years that followed! In order to understand what my friend meant by this statement, we need to fill in some of the background.

A language is not a mere conglomerate of incoherent parts haphazardly put together. It consists of a limited number of discrete parts arranged in complex patterns—patterns that are distinguished by its speakers and discoverable by students of language. Among these parts are those which tradition has taught us to call "words" and which we separate by spaces when we string them together in writing. Words are made up of sound which we represent in writing by letters. The orders in which words are put together, both in speech and in writing, follow a few basic patterns, as does the ordering of the sounds which make up these words.

Thus, what my linguist friend meant by his statement was more or less the following: "By the age of five, a child has learned to pronounce very much in the manner of the people around him all the individual sounds that make up particular words, has mastered most of the combinations of sounds to be found in words in the language, and has acquired a command of the conventional ways of arranging these words in the few most basic patterns to be found in the language." A child of this age does not have to be taught to "pronounce" words with which he is already familiar, nor does he need any instruction in the principal ways of putting these words together. He will do both of these things precisely as do the people around him from whom he has learned to speak.

If the kind of speech with which he comes ready equipped to the school is acceptable to his teacher, the teacher's only task, at the earliest stage, will be to teach him to represent with letters on paper, and to recognize in print, the things which he already says. If, however, the kind of speech with which the child comes ready equipped is unacceptable to the teacher, that fact renders the task considerably more difficult, because he must then teach the child to speak in a way acceptable to him before he can effectively teach the child to read and write in this new kind of speech.

[1] Edward Sapir, "Language," *Encyclopedia of the Social Sciences,* IX, 155-69. New York: Macmillan Co., 1933.

[2] Bernard Bloch and George L. Trager, *Outline of Linguistic Analysis,* p. 7. Baltimore: Linguistic Society of America, 1942.

TEACHING WRITING TO THE CHILD WITH "ACCEPTABLE" SPEECH

Teaching the child to write is complicated by nature of English spelling.—
Let us take the simpler of the two situations. The first stage—teaching the
child to represent by letters on paper what he says—is greatly complicated, in
English, by the fact that there is no general, one-to-one correspondence between the sounds which the child already carefully distinguishes and the
conventional choice of letters with which they are represented. We do not,
unfortunately, write as we speak. "Spelling" takes up a considerable proportion of our time during far too many years of elementary school. Some of us
never learn to spell. Some of us go so far as to make a virtue out of necessity.

So long, however, as completely conventional literacy is valued by our
society, we cannot operate by the slogan, "Every man his own speller,"
attractive as that course might seem; we must continue to spend a sizable
amount of time learning to spell. That this requirement derives not from
our language but rather from our outmoded traditional spelling is evidenced
by the fact that, if a language has a good alphabet, its speakers can become
completely literate in a very short time. This fact has been observed in
numerous cases of languages only recently provided with alphabets. In the
author's personal experience, Tarascan Indians[3] in Mexico became literate
in their own language in about three months of evening classes, in a total
of well under a hundred hours of classroom attendance. If English were
spelled as it is pronounced, it should be possible to make children completely literate in about their first half-year of schooling. Since, however,
this is not the case, one must be prepared to compromise.

Overcoming difficulties caused by spelling.—Bad as English spelling is,
there are within it, nonetheless, many regular ways of representing the
sounds of the language. If the most general and the most internally consistent of these ways could be presented first, and the irregular and less
widely found ways could be grouped in smaller systems and equated to
those of more general application, it should be possible to devise a rational
procedure[4] for progressively presenting the difficulties of our spelling. We
could build on the speech habits already well grounded in the children by
providing them, in the first stages, with instruction in the rational and
regular core of our spelling, until the habit of tying particular sound with
particular letter, and particular letter with particular sound, was well established. In the later stages we could present the complicating other spellings
for particular sounds, in small and easily absorbed doses.

The gain in confidence in the first stages, when the child would be laboring under the happy delusion that he could spell anything he could say,

[3] Norman A. McQuown, "Linguistics Contributes to Native Education," *International
Science,* I (May, 1941), 2-6.
[4] Leonard Bloomfield, "Linguistics and Reading," *Elementary English Review,* XIX
(April and May, 1942), 125-30, 183-86.

would more than compensate for the subsequent whittling-down of this confidence as he was introduced to multiple other spellings. The automaticity of reaction to the printed forms with regular spelling would give the child such a head start in reading that he could take subsequent irregularities, gradually introduced, in his stride.

Prerequisites for this teaching method.—In order to be able to institute such a system, however, certain preliminary requirements, both for teacher and for textbook writer, need to be mentioned. Before we can properly select the "regular" English spellings, that is, those in which every sound is represented by only one spelling, we need to know what the *sounds* of the language are. Although there is a considerable amount of local variation in pronunciation, and although some words have different sounds from place to place, there is sufficient uniformity in the over-all system and in the number of distinct sounds recognized by the language to make possible a single list of English sounds. Specialists[5] in the English language can supply the pedagogue with such a list. The teacher must know what the sounds are in such a list and must also be aware of the commonest local variations in particular words. He should be prepared not only for the child who says "hog" but also for the child who says "hawg." The teacher must also know what the most common and most regular English spellings are and must be prepared to separate the various classes of irregular spellings. The textbook writer needs to know all this and, furthermore, to be prepared to subject the raw material to his artistry, so as to make it both intelligible and palatable to the five- and six-year-olds.

GRAMMAR FOR THE CHILD WITH "ACCEPTABLE" SPEECH

The child at the age of five has mastered all the sounds of his native language and, if given matching letters, could write them with ease. He has likewise mastered the main features of the grammar of his language, and, unless he must first acquire a new variety of language in order that his speech may be acceptable to his teacher, needs no new instruction in how to manipulate these main features. If the kind of speech with which the child comes ready equipped is unacceptable to the teacher, that fact will complicate the situation, since the teacher must, in this case, teach the child to speak in a new way, in a way acceptable to him.

But let us again consider first the simpler of the two situations: that in which the child needs no instruction in what ordinarily passes for "grammar," being already in command of the chief features and, in this respect, speaking like the adults around him. The teacher is then free to concentrate on more important matters, such as clarity of presentation, succinctness of statement, and amenity of style. He can polish vocabulary and

---

[5] George L. Trager and Henry L. Smith, Jr., *An Outline of English Structure.* Norman, Oklahoma: Battenburg Press, 1951.

encourage appropriate use of forms which are coming within the child's ken for the first time. He can encourage the more gifted children, who even at a tender age may show literary talent, to make good use of this gift. In short, the teacher can do all those things which make for a more facile, a more adequate, and a more pleasing handling of the language as a medium of communication.

Undoubtedly, many children would feel more secure, and would develop a greater feeling of confidence in themselves and in their effectiveness in the world around them, if they were relieved of the frustrating experience of feeling that they could not speak "correctly" and of the often traumatic experience of being unable to apply rules of grammar which, by their very nature, are inapplicable. In the situation where, in their basic essentials, pupil and teacher speak the same language, the child will quite unconsciously follow the model set for him, since his speech is already in microcosm what his teacher's is in macrocosm. Here again, the saving of time would be considerable, and the psychological gain for the child incalculable.

I have suggested (1) a rational presentation of the intricacies of English spelling (taking off from a skill already in the child's possession, namely, that of pronouncing all the sounds in the language as he hears them from those around him) and (2) a de-emphasis of traditional grammar combined with an earlier and more effective training in the niceties of style (again taking off from a skill already commanded by the child, namely, that of speaking his language with all its essential features substantially like those around him). Such a program would result in a considerable saving of time in the educational process and a not inconsiderable psychological gain for the child.

TEACHING THE CHILD WITH "UNACCEPTABLE" SPEECH

Let us now consider the difficult case. Suppose the child does not speak in a fashion acceptable to the teacher, either with respect to pronunciation of the sounds or with respect to his use of the forms of the language. We are in a situation which does not differ in its essentials from that involved in learning a foreign language. There is no fundamental dividing line between the dialect which is strange to the child and the "foreign" language which is strange to him. Indeed, in some parts of the world (and even in some parts of our own country) the child, when he reaches school age, is faced with the task of learning a different tongue. Foremost among the problems[6] which arise in such a task is that of motivation. In such a situation, if the child were approaching adulthood, the teacher might take him aside and say to him: "Look, son! The circles in which you're going to be moving during the next few years speak a different lingo. If you want to be an effective operator in those circles, you'll have to learn their talk, distasteful though it may be to

[6] Leonard Bloomfield, *Outline Guide for the Practical Study of Foreign Languages.* Baltimore: Linguistic Society of America, 1942.

you. So if you think it's worth your while, why don't you try so and so . . . ?"
This might be called the hard-boiled approach, and it should carry weight,
if suitably rephrased, with the realistic small child as well. The teacher would
then proceed to outline for the child the steps toward acquisition of the
new language. What would some of those steps be?

To begin with, the teacher should know what the similarities are between
the child's speech and the speech of those he would imitate. The teacher
will waste no time on those. He should try to pinpoint the differences, contrast what the child does with what the speakers of the new language do,
and drill the pupil on those points. Of course, if the teacher does not speak
the new language, either as a native or with a native-like command, he will
be of little help to his pupil as a model. If the teacher is not thoroughly
familiar with every detail of pronunciation and grammar, both of his pupil's
mother-tongue and of the language he is trying to teach the child, he will not
operate efficiently. If the teacher is not equipped, furthermore, to take full
advantage of every pedagogical trick of the trade, a great deal of time will
be wasted.

Finally, and most important of all, if the teacher does not present the
new task in such a way as to instil in the pupil the desire to learn the new
language as an accomplishment of which he is to be proud, maintaining all
the while a carefully objective and respectful attitude toward the way of
speaking with which the child comes ready equipped to the school, the
teacher will run the risk of doing the child irreparable psychological harm.
Whatever status or lack of status a child's speech may seem to have to the
teacher, it does constitute for the child a precious link with those closest
to him. Any lack of respect for the child's ways of talking will reflect on
those for whom he has respect and will be damaging to his self-esteem.
From the purely practical point of view, the presence in the child of a
feeling that the speech of his family is not acceptable will materially hinder
his acquisition of the new skill and so defeat the teacher's purposes. A
knowledgeable, skilful, and respectful approach to the problem of language-
learning on this simplest level will pay off in the end.

IMPLICATIONS FOR EDUCATORS

The implications of these considerations with respect to language-learning
might be spelled out as follows. In the initial stages, new training operations
are required. Summer workshops, in-service training, seminars, and additions to the regular curriculums of schools of education are needed. Such
training operations would be devoted to the study of the general nature of
language, to the relation of spoken to written language, and to the acquisition of the basic essentials with respect to the makeup, both in sound and in
form, of the mother-tongue. The goal of this training would be not only
theoretical understanding but also practical mastery and conscious control

of the patterns of the student's own speech and those of closely related varieties of it. Such new training would be appropriate for teachers, curriculum designers, textbook writers, and trainers of teachers-to-be.

A survey of contemporary spellers and readers, of textbooks in English grammar, and of handbooks of rhetoric and composition gives no hint that a great many new facts on their subject matter are now available. It is high time that these new facts be evaluated and their implications for language-learning assessed. It is essential that this new knowledge be made generally available, that it be used in our educational programs, and that new tools deriving from it be placed in the hands of our educators.

42

Linguistics in the Classroom

SUMNER IVES

ANYONE WHO has been reading periodicals for English teachers or who has been attending conventions of English teachers must be aware of the controversy over linguistics and its relevance to the teaching of composition. As one whose research is primarily in descriptive linguistics, but whose teaching includes at least one composition class each semester, I have a personal interest in the interaction of linguistics and the practical use of language. I am somewhat disturbed by what appears to be a conflict between linguists and teachers of writing when I can detect no valid reason for such a conflict.

I suspect, both from reading the exchanges and from listening to the discussions, that much of the disagreement comes from misunderstanding. I observe arguments which promote linguistics without showing an exact appreciation of the significance of its findings; I notice defences of positions which linguistics, properly understood, does not attack. Moreover, although many composition teachers have come to believe that traditional grammar is a very poor description of English structure, some of the more judicious have complained, rightly, that the arguments of the linguists have been largely negative, that they have given little to replace that which they have attacked. This, then, is the situation with which this paper deals.

Reprinted by permission from *College English,* 17.165-172 (December, 1955). Professor Ives is a member of the Department of English at Syracuse University.

In order to accomplish its purpose, the discussion must be both general and specific, for the usefulness of linguistics is two-fold. One contribution is a valid and useful theory of what language is and how it works. The other is a description of the specific forms and constructions which are used in a particular language for the expression of meaning.

In general academic usage, the term linguist includes those who teach the language courses in an English or other modern language department. However, the criticisms of traditional grammar have come chiefly from those who have made particular study of descriptive or structural linguistics, and the counterattacks have been made against this group. In this discussion, therefore, linguistics means descriptive linguistics, and linguists are those who work in this branch of language study. In his study of language, the linguist uses the standard methods of observation and classification common to all systematic studies of human behavior and the natural world. In describing the structure of a language, he is guided by the forms of words and their characteristic patterns of use. His criteria of definition and classification are therefore very much the same as those of the anthropologist or the chemist.

The major aims of the linguist are the discovery of the principles true of all living languages and the accumulation of detailed and systematic descriptions of the phonology and the grammar of these languages. Both these major goals have relevance to promoting facility in the native language and to teaching the use of a second language. Hence, as a methodology of investigation, linguistics is one of the social sciences, but the nature of its subject matter and the application of its results give it primary association with the humanities. The study of the forms of language is a science; the proper and effective use of language is an art.

The difficulty which many persons trained in the humanities seem to have with linguistics is due primarily to our intellectual climate. Most of the notions which underlie our common vocabulary for talking about language are survivals from a pre-objective period of language study. The words in our vocabulary reflect an orientation on language matters which is very different from that which is derived through direct observation of individual languages. When a non-linguist reads what a linguist has written about language, there is often a break-down in the communication, even when familiar terms are used, for the non-linguist is often interpreting the discussion in a frame of reference which differs from that in which it was written. This difficulty is compounded when the linguist uses terms from the technical jargon of his field. Yet such a technical vocabulary is necessary and is no more exotic than those in other fields. Physicians, for example, no longer use such terms as "humorous" and "sanguine" in their medieval sense, for these terms reflect a theory of disease which they no longer hold.

The consequences of this misunderstanding, which is often greater than either party realizes, are most easily observed in the extrapolations from linguistics which persons without training in its methods attempt to make. Any statement in any field is only a partial expression; it must be interpreted within the restrictions imposed by the nature of what is talked about, by the context, and by all the assumptions, postulates, and qualifications which are part of the accumulated knowledge in the field. This does not mean that linguists talk only with each other, though they are as prone to this as anyone, but it does mean that the statements of linguists should be accepted and applied only to the extent that they are explicit, that conclusions should be drawn only within the limits of the primary statements and only about that aspect of the subject concerning which they are made. When, for example, a linguist uses stretches of actual speech as material for grammatical analysis, his purpose does not include the establishment of a standard dialect, and his results apply only to his sample.

Aside from this difficulty, which is concomitant to every major advance in fundamental knowledge, linguistics is not a hard subject. Its subject matter is all around us. Ordinary people have mastered and use quite easily all the forms, constructions, and sound patterns it deals with. Its results, whenever a particular language is described, can be checked by any native speaker who will believe what he observes and not what he has been taught to expect. And any native speaker who has the necessary perseverance and mental discipline can learn and use its methods to extend his conscious understanding of the form and constructions of his own language.

But at the present time, direct provision for the development of an adequate theory of language and for the accumulation of knowledge about the actual constructions of English is seldom made in the training of English teachers. Virtually all their upper division and graduate courses are in literature. When language courses are required, and they are seldom taken unless required, they generally consist of reading more literature, this time in a stage of the language which is no longer current, or they consist primarily of tracing individual sound changes, with some attention to resulting changes in morphology, and some checking on etymologies. This language program undoubtedly has cultural value, but it has little direct bearing on the teaching of composition. It is possible for a student to go through such a program with excellent marks and yet remain basically ignorant of the nature of language as a socially directed activity, unaware of the difference yet interaction between a language and its written symbolization, blind to the operation of its grammatical devices, and unprepared even to read many of the basic publications which describe the current characteristics of his own language or to analyze that language for himself.

This has not been said in any spirit of superiority or condemnation. It is the simple truth. Any blame is general. It is up to linguists to relate their findings to the larger aims of education. But they have the same right to attention and trust as the zoologist, the political-scientist, or the specialist in the pastoral elegy. The problem is the familiar one of cultural lag. A solution will come only with time, careful explanations, and a decent regard for human feelings and fallibility on all sides.

Much of the misunderstanding about what the linguist does and says comes from his insistence on two of his basic principles and their corollaries. One of these is the primacy of speech as the language, with writing as a secondary and derivative manifestation of speech. The other is the dynamic, changing nature of language, with its corollaries about stability and standardization. Both principles are derived from studying languages as physically observable structures; neither is a threat to the basic aims of the composition course—namely, to teach students to write their own language as clearly and effectively as they can, and with full regard for the conventions of usage observable in the products of recognized masters.

In explaining his attention to speech, the linguist points out that all systems of writing are based on the prior existence of speech, that all alphabetic systems depend ultimately on the sound system of the language, even though, as in English, the correspondence between sound and spelling is very complex and difficult to describe. The linguist realizes that the writing system, even with its marks of punctuation, never quite symbolizes all the components which contribute to meaning in speech. He comes to see the teaching that English has five vowels as nonsense and the mother of error, and the designation of long and short vowels in English as little better. And he learns to dismiss such questions as whether English is a phonetic language as meaningless. These lessons may not have direct bearing on the teaching of good composition, but they are vital if one is to understand the relationship of writing to the language, of spelling to pronunciation, or of reading to speaking.

On the other hand, distinct from the alphabetic representation of words on paper, speaking and writing are different but interacting activities. They are not the same, do not follow all of the same conventions, and are not done for the same list of purposes. Neither is finally and fully determinative for the other. No competent linguist would suggest that the teacher of written English should accept in student writing all of the conventions and the same characteristics of style as are customary in speech, even that of the most cultivated. The notion that linguists make speech determinative for writing is one of the false extrapolations made by people who interpret the findings of linguistics without knowing what they mean. They are failing to distinguish between writing as a graphic representation of a linguistic expression (which is secondary to speech) and writing as a special kind of communicative activity (which differs in style and purpose from speech).

The fundamental reason why the linguist gives his primary attention to speech is the fact that only in speech does he find all the signals which convey information. For example, the two phrases, "a stone wall" and "a race horse," are not spoken with the same patterns of stress. In the first phrase, "stone" is functionally an adjective, just as "high" would be in the same place. In the second, "race" is functionally a part of a compound noun, in spite of the orthography, like "black-" in "blackberry." It is the difference in the patterns of stress which makes the grammar clear. With the grammatical importance of stress in mind, read the following sentences aloud and then parse "drinking" and "water" in all of them. (1) Our drinking water fortunately remained fresh. (2) Drinking water from our canteens rather than from open streams kept us from getting dysentery. (3) Drinking water rather than wine made the boys healthy.

Another practical result of investigation into these "supra-segmental" characteristics of speech is the recognition of the relationship between pitch patterns and structural unity. In ordinary prose, the ends of statements and of most questions are marked by a quick rise in pitch, followed by a quick drop to a level below that of the bulk of the sentence. A sentence which has the word order of a statement can be made into a question by a quick rise of pitch at the end. When there is a quick rise and then a drop back to the basic level, a shift in constructions within a sentence is marked. These pitch signals mark the places where punctuation decisions are to be made if the speech is set down in writing. A student can often clarify his constructions and rectify his punctuation simply by reading his themes aloud, for he will generally find that an unEnglish construction cannot be read with the English supra-segmental patterns—what are popularly called intonation patterns—and he has used these since childhood.

For these reasons, any analysis of English grammar which is not based ultimately on the signals of speech is necessarily incomplete. The other basic principle which is sometimes misunderstood is corollary to the fact that language is a social institution with the same counteracting tendencies towards stability and adaptability as other social institutions.

A typical expression of the linguist's view is found on page 177 of W. D. Whitney's *Language and the Study of Languages,* published as long ago as 1867. "Language is an institution founded in man's social nature, wrought out for the satisfaction of his social wants; and hence, while individuals are ultimate agents in the formation and modification of every word and every meaning of a word, it is still the community that makes and changes its language."

The relevance which this principle has for the composition teacher is its bearing on the formation and continuity of the conventions which he should teach as part of the standard language. That dialect of English which we now call edited written English is the product of changes resulting from the interaction of individuals as agents of the community. The dialect whose modern development we teach originally had no discernible virtues as a language which made it superior to other local forms of English. Its selection for cultivation was almost surely the result of socio-economic factors. Nonetheless its fortuitous origin does not invalidate its claim to superiority today. But these claims rest in part on the growth and refinement of special vocabularies, in part on the great store of literature which is written in it, in part to the social prestige which is granted to those who use it, and in part to the size and importance of the territory over which it is spread. These reasons are fully adequate to demand that it be taught as a school subject.

Yet, this standard English cannot be exactly defined, nor does it remain constantly the same, in spite of the factors which give it stability. No complete, definitive, and final dictionary of English usage can be made so long as English is in active use, although the list of disputed usages is never large at any one time. A teacher of writing simply has to maintain the same kind of contact with changes in his basic material as that maintained by doctors and lawyers.

A special problem in dealing with usage is the presence of shibboleths. So long as overt marks of social and educational status are considered useful by society, some of these will be linguistic. For example, the adequacy of one's education is often judged by his ability to spell, or by whether he splits infinitives, or by whether he says "eyether" or "eether." It is in the area of shibboleths that the purist feels most authority, for he is usually their custodian. To the linguist, however, most of these have the status of myth, as the term is used in sociology. Nevertheless, a rather large part of one's acceptance in society is his adjustment to myths of this type. Hence, it is, I think, the duty of the school teacher to point out the current shibboleths, for they change, and to advise how much they are observed and by which people.

Language is thus a social institution. It has the same kind of stability and adaptability as other social institutions, from table manners to democratic government, and its conventions are just as obligatory while they last. The scholar should remember that the major purpose of language is not to preserve for the future, but to serve the exigencies of now. To ask for a static language makes just as much sense, and no more, as to ask for a static society. There are, of course, people who do this. To put the language in the hands of a self-appointed few is just as reasonable, and no more, as to put the regulation of government in the hands of a similarly appointed group. There are people who want to do this too.

These principles constitute the major elements in a theory of language which is valid and which should assist the composition teacher to deal more intelligently with his basic subject matter. The major tool which linguists can give to the teachers of composition is a true and adequate description of the forms and constructions which are used in English for the expression of grammatical meaning, in short, an English grammar. Such a grammar will retain some of the categories and their terms which are in traditional grammar, but its methods of classification and definition will be fundamentally different.

When we attempt to relate the terminology, with its implied classification, of traditional grammar to the actual forms of English and their behavior, at least four major defects appear. Some terms, e.g., grammar, have more than one referent; some terms, e.g., passive voice and tense, have referents which are not, by their very nature, susceptible to sharp definition in English; some terms, e.g., adverb and pronoun, are in use without a genuine referent (the supposed referents of these terms lack identity as single classes or categories of items); finally, some terms, e.g., noun and verb, are identified, not by definitions, but by statements which may well be true, but which do not name the particularizing characteristics of the classes which the terms refer to.

In traditional grammar, an adverb is defined as a word which modifiies a verb, adjective, or other adverb. However, the "adverbs" *quite* and *very* simply do not obey the same rules of syntax as the "adverbs" *usually* and *soon,* for *quite* and *very* do not modify verbs. Another false classification is that which includes *he* and *few* in the same category, for one is inflected and the other is not, one can be modified by *very* and the other cannot, and one has a noun antecedent and the other does not. It is true that both can act as subjects, but then, so can adjectives. The concept of tense in traditional grammar is complicated by the fact that verb phrases made with *will* are called a future tense, yet these phrases have the same formal characteristics as those made with *must* and other modal auxiliaries

I am, admittedly, judging a grammatical description according to criteria of form and usefulness. To be valuable in teaching a language or in promoting facility in its use, a description of its grammar should isolate those classes about which statements need to be made. These statements may be rules for word order, for the formation of phrases, for derivational change, for functional change, for inflectional concord, and so on. There is obviously very little which one can say about word order which will be true of both *very* and *soon,* of both *he* and *few.*

A classification must select out and associate in identity a group of items which, so far as the purpose of the classification is concerned, are equivalent. These items must be, within the purpose for which the class is isolated, freely substitutable for each other. In defining this class, a property must be named which is tangible, which is present in all members of the class, and which is absent from all items not in the class. If this definition is part of a taxonomy, it must be one of a set. The definitions in a set must contrast with each other and must conjointly exhaust all items in the same division and level of analysis. These sets must each have a common factor which excludes members of other sets, and so on until the entire classification is complete. A properly developed taxonomy, therefore, has the outward design of a genetic tree.

In framing definitions, one must enumerate a list of attributes generally agreed upon, or one must name one or more characteristics whose presence or absence can be verified by direct observation. Many of the terms in literary criticism, e.g., "romanticism," rest upon agreement to associate the term with a list of attributes. Other terms, such as those in the taxonomy of botany, are defined by direct appeal to nature. Anyone who has good eyesight and the proper instruments can count the cotyledons in a seed. One may have more trouble with "hirsute" and "pubescent," but the degree of fuzziness which they denote can be easily distinguished after a little experience. Since Linnaeus, the botanists have had a way to bring order to the apparently limitless variety of nature; they had a classification system for what is, to the layman, infinite discreteness. The objective of the descriptive grammarian is to do for the forms of individual languages what the botanist has done for plant life.

In popular usage, grammar is often considered to be a crystallization of human logic, a set of concepts and distinctions in terms of which all languages should be described, a set of formal characteristics and correspondences to which all languages should conform. In this view, which is that implied in some recent articles and found in most older books on language, the most convenient expression of grammar is one based on Latin. When it was shown that a knowledge of traditional grammar had little correlation with an ability to use English correctly and effectively, the result was a belief that grammar need not be studied as a prerequisite to training in composition. This view, is, I think, wrong. I think that, on the contrary, an adequate knowledge of the forms of English and of the rules for their use should be a very valuable pre-requisite to instruction in composition. Arguments based on current experience are irrelevant, for the grammar has not been English grammar.

Now the linguist studies a language by analyzing, in turn, its levels of complexity. These correspond only roughly to the levels indicated by the common terms phonology, morphology, and syntax. In this division into levels, that which deals with the combination of the smallest meaningful units into the largest self-sufficient and independent constructions is grammar. These smallest meaningful units are called morphemes. They may be affixes like -ness, -ed, and non-; they may be words like kind, his and the; they may be stress patterns like those which make a word like subject into a noun or into a verb. Every utterance consists of segmental morphemes, like words, stems, and affixes, and of supra-segmental morphemes, which include what the layman means by intonation. Grammar classifies these morphemes into groups according to similarities of form and grammatical meaning. It includes the rules by which morphemes are combined into constructions and the rules governing the formation of still larger constructions until the ultimate limit of strict structural relationship has been reached. The units at the limit of strict structural relationship are sentences.

Grammar as conformity to the conventions of the standard dialect becomes a matter of comparative grammar. The dialects of English which comprise vulgate English all have grammars, as the term is defined in the preceding paragraph, but the rules and forms of these grammars differ in some ways from those of the standard dialect. The teaching problem is the correlation of equivalent expressions and the substitutions of standard for nonstandard forms and constructions. The only inherent source of confusion is the presentation by the teacher of conventions which differ from those which the student observes in his academic reading.

A more serious cause for confusion is a failure to distinguish between grammar and style. The rules which govern the combination of morphemes into sentences are imposed on the individual; the words and constructions which he uses, out of those which conform to the rules, are matters of choice. This area of language choice is style, or rhetoric. For example, after "individual," just above, I could have used a period or a semicolon, for both show the boundary between structurally complete units. But I could not have used either mark before that word, for it is grammatically related to those which immediately precede. Such matters as the selection of words and constructions, the length of sentences and their complexity, and the organization of the total expression are matters of style. Such matters as consistency in parallel structure, reference of pronouns, and agreement of subject and verb are matters of grammar. These matters of grammar are finite, they can be discovered and described.

An example of confusion arising from a failure to make this distinction clear is the trouble students have with "sentence recognition." The customary definition of the sentence as the verbal expression of a complete thought does not, by itself, separate the sentence from the paragraph or from larger sections which are supposed to have unity. As the term is applied in most handbook discussions of punctuation, it designates a unit in style but not necessarily in grammar. The crucial information—that there is an identifiable unit in grammar, that, in connected prose, the juxtapositions of these units must be marked, and that one of the ways to make these juxtapositions is with a period—does not follow from the traditional definition.

In English structure, the sentence, the independent unit in connected discourse, has the following characteristics: (1) it must contain at least one finite verb or verb phrase; (2) all words must be structurally related; (3) it must not, as a unit, have a grammatical function in a larger construction. There are three types of such units in English. In the statement, the subject normally precedes the verb, unless it begins with a word of the class of "never." In the question, the subject is normally inserted inside the verb phrase. (If the verb is not a phrase, it is made into one with a form of "do".) In the request, there is no subject. The verb may come first, or it may be preceded by a word to get attention or to show courtesy.

There are two other types of constructions which are marked by end punctuation or intonation. One is the response; the other is the exclamation. Both of these constructions get their "incompleteness" from something which has been said or is physically close enough to be pointed out by a gesture. Thus, we can use a construction which is structurally not a sentence when we reply to a question, stated or implied, or when we react to an automobile accident, or when we point to something and comment on it.

The most common error in student themes is the failure to mark the juxtapositions of structurally complete units, or the habit of marking as sentences groups of words which are not structurally units. But difficulty with "sentence recognition" can be virtually eliminated by teaching what is in the preceding paragraphs, listing the devices for marking the juxtapositions, and giving the following suggestions. At the beginning of a sentence, structural relationship points forward; at the end it points backward. If the student reads what he has written, aloud and phrase by phrase, he can detect the point where there is a break, where the shift from backward to forward relationship occurs. "Sentence fragments" ordinarily result from one of two causes. One is the insertion of an end sign where no structural end exists; the other is the failure to keep the structural patterns clear enough so that a structural unit can be isolated. In this case, a break in communication will almost be noticed. It has been my experience that native speakers of English can determine the presence or absence of grammatical relationship even when they cannot give a name to the type which exists.

In so far as their academic functions are concerned, linguists and composition teachers are related in somewhat the same way as botanists and gardeners are related in raising plants. Their duties do not confict; they complement. The botanist identifies plants, groups them in families, analyzes their physiology, and observes the ecological factors which promote or retard growth. The gardener uses such information and adds to it his knowledge of the virtues of different fertilizers and methods of cultivation. If he has good soil and healthy stock, he may get good results regardless of how little he knows. But if his soil is not good, his stock is poor, or his experience is little, there is much he can learn from the botanist, although the botanist cannot teach him all he needs to know. There is, of course, nothing to prevent the botanist from becoming a gardener or to keep the gardener from gaining through experience a great deal of useful but un-coordinated knowledge.

What this means is that the students whose environment has provided them with habitual use of good English are likely to do well whether their teachers knows much about language or not. On the other hand, in so far as the students do not have these habits, the teacher will find useful what the linguist has to say. Even if he does not have this preparation for formal and systematic teaching, he may still get acceptable results with some students by requiring practice, making corrections, and insisting on revision, provided he is himself a reasonably competent craftsman.

I should confess, nay insist, that linguistics simply gives the teacher additional or more effective tools and a better understanding of what he is working with. Any improvement he makes in his knowledge of language, any details he learns about the actual forms and constructions of English, will make him a more expert instructor. But at the present time, although linguists know and can teach information which is more accurate than the traditional notions, they still have to learn much about the details of English, and some of what they have learned is not ready for publication. Moreover, the field itself does not cover all the things that the composition teacher needs to know. There is still no royal road to good writing, no magic method that will turn out skilled writers, and neither linguistics nor any other field is likely to provide one.

43

The Teacher and the World of Language

Henry Lee Smith, Jr.

Today, more than ever before, vistas are opening that show us again the supreme importance of language. From one point of view it can be seen as man's first and greatest invention. Without it, human culture and human societies as we know them would be impossible; through it human beings have created their own unique adaptations. In short, language is truly the

First read as a paper at the NCTE convention in Minneapolis, November, 1957, this article is here reprinted by permission from *College English,* 20.172-78 (January, 1959). The author is Professor of Linguistics and English and Chairman of the Department of Linguistics and Anthropology at the University of Buffalo.

mark of our very humanity, for man is human by virtue of the kind of interaction that goes on through *human* communication systems, of which language is the queen. The very survival of the individual as well as the survival of the species is dependent upon language, and perhaps even more important, language *in* culture provides for the possibility of the development of individual consciousness and awareness of self, for the formulation of concepts, and for the creation and transmission of man's spiritual values, his art, and his literature.

Though I am primarily a linguist and an anthropologist, I speak as one who has "English" as well as "Linguistics" in his academic title, and though I will be reporting in some respect on "research in progress," I am equally interested—and have been for over twenty years—in the application of the results of linguistic research to the teaching of the mother tongue from "literacy to literature." My experience has convinced me that a knowledge of the structure and the functioning of language and the other human communication systems is the essential basis for all really successful pedagogy in the area that has come to be called the "language arts." But even more important, I feel that to understand language and the human communication process is in a very real sense to understand the essence of our humanity. Like other animals, man communicates through touch, taste, and smell; but only man can talk. Like other animals, man communicates his species membership and his position within his species by the very *set* and *quality* of his voice and bodily motions; but only man can talk.

Language is the most minutely structured, patterned, configured of all man's cultural systems, but there is system, order and pattern in other communication systems than language. More and more clearly, we are seeing the importance of these other learned and patterned systems. More and more obvious does it appear that speech does not take place in a vacuum but is surrounded, as it were, by patterned bodily motions—the *kinesic* system—and by systematically analyzable vocalizations, or *paralanguage*. Here we include the *vocal qualifiers,* consisting of such phenomena as perceptibly measurable degrees of overloudness and oversoftness; degres of drawl and "clipping" of portions of utterance; and degrees of increased or decreased height of pitch over the base-line established in the language itself. Paralanguage also includes laughing and crying "through" speech, the breaking of the voice, and the whole gamut of "tuts," clicks, sniffs, snorts, "uh's," "uh-uh's," and "uh-huh's," these latter termed the *vocal segregates*.

Kinesic and paralinguistic phenomena constitute separate patterned systems, which differ in their structure from culture to culture. However, of more real importance is the fact that in all cultures no one "just talks," but communication goes on only when there is a symphony of interplay of each system with each. As language is more than words, communication is more than language. Each system provides a means of *commenting* on the portions of the message that is being carried by the other systems, and for considerable stretches we may not talk at all but carry on our end of the interaction entirely through the other systems. And when we talk, we are reinforcing, emphasizing—maybe even negating—what we are saying by *how* we are saying it. Simultaneously, throughout the entire process, we are sending additional messages as to how we feel, who we think we are, and how we evaluate the person or persons with whom we are interacting. Communication is interaction, and the whole can be seen as a multi-leveled, complex, integrated package of interrelated and systematized phenomena. The more *congruently* the package is assembled, the more effective the interaction, and hence communications, will be.

Communication, then, is more than language, and language is far more than words on a printed page. Both the creator and the interpreter of literature and the plain writer and reader have only the letters of the alphabet and a sprinkling of punctuation conventions with which to represent this wonderfully complex symphony we have been describing. The artist has only the written language through which to transmit his understanding, his experiences, his emotions, his reactions, his ideas. The reader, if he has learned the same language and is a member of the same culture, can be moved to supply and even to recreate the artist's world, his beliefs, and his intentions.

But even so marvelous an invention as writing is always *incomplete* and *inconsistent* in relation to the language that it symbolizes. It is a derived system, and speech is always prior, even though spoken language is frequently influenced by written language. Granted that the written language in the hands of a skillful artificer can be made to carry much more than just a recording of linguistic events, writing as a system remains a sort of shorthand reminder to the native speaker of something that has been said or could be *said* in the language. As we all know, however, the written language is more immediately accessible than the spoken language; the written language has a permanence in contrast to the ephemeral character of speech; the written language is always more rigidly structured, more insistent on precision and clarity by the very virtue of the fact that it must stand alone. For these reasons, if for no others, it should be studied, understood, and mastered.

With a real understanding of the difference between the spoken and written language, it should be obvious that we should never allow our students to write "just the way they talk" any more than we should try to teach them to talk the way they *have* to learn to write. The failure to see and to understand the distinction between standard colloquial speech and the literary language, and the failure to understand the relationship between speech and writing have been, I am convinced, the chief obstacle in imparting to our students both real literacy and a confident competence in speaking. Traditional grammar has been based, understandably enough, on the literary language, but far too often the prescriptive rules which must be followed if we are to *write* acceptably have been used as a basis for how we should *talk*. The result, I'm afraid, has been to inject into our population a sort of mild schizophrenia which has produced many afraid to talk and totally unable to write.

In trying to alleviate the situation, "traditionalists" and "structuralists" often almost come to blows over the term "usage." To those who link the term with grammar, it means *prescription;* to the linguist it means linguistic events which are to be *described* on all levels and in all contexts. Contrary to the belief of many, the linguist does not say that "anything goes," or that any way of talking or writing is "just as good" as any other. He simply states that for him as a student of human behavior, *all* of language and speech, *every* linguistic event, constitutes data to be described and analyzed. As an anthropologist he is just as much concerned with the contexts in which "them things" occurs, as he is interested to find out when "those things" occurs. He is well aware that there are correlations between the *status* of individuals and their use of language; he notes dispassionately and with every means at his disposal which usages seem to be most *congruent* with which culturally defined situations. He knows that in all cultures certain persons or classes of persons are highly regarded while others are merely tolerated. The language of those with the status of "educated"—however the culture may understand this term—are those who by definition will be trustworthy informants as to acceptable and effective usage. Thus if our students are to be educated people, and they come to us unable to speak standard colloquial English, our educational system must teach them this level of language; if our students have little acquaintance with the literary language, every effort must be made to give them control of it as both readers and writers. By doing any less, we fail as educators and unless we accomplish this minimum successfully, we have no chance as *teachers* of *English* to instill an appreciation and understanding of the language and of the great things that have been thought and said in it.

As a structural linguist whose main interest over the years has been English, I have been greatly concerned about how little is really known about our most priceless possession. I have been even more concerned when I have seen the extent to which much that is taught about it is irrelevant, and more confusing than elucidating. I have been much interested and professionally preoccupied with the application of the results of linguistic research to the teaching of English throughout our educational system and to the problem of teaching Americans foreign languages and foreigners our language. My experience has convinced me that at the basis of all really successful pedagogy in these areas is a knowledge of linguistic *structure*. But the application of linguistics is not the sole purpose for study-

ing the structure of languages or of language; it is a conviction of mine
that the educated person should be aware of how his language really works
as a matter of interest, concern, and value in and of itself.

If a knowledge of structure is essential, how are we to go about acquiring
it? One thing the linguist has learned is that language—and I think this is
true of all cultural systems—must be analyzed and described in and of
itself, in terms of its own unique components—its sounds, forms, and constructions. Language is language; the kinship system is the kinship system;
the technological system is the technological system, and so on. Granted,
language uniquely reflects and transmits the other systems of culture, but
to try to get at the structure of language through other cultural systems only
obscures the structure of all the systems. What I am saying here is that if
we want to really understand how language relates to other systems of
culture—the usual term for this is "meaning"—we first must know how
language itself structures. I am also saying that we can get at meaning *only*
through structure, and that we cannot get at *structure* through meaning.

Oftentimes statements like those I have just made are interpreted to the
effect that the structuralist isn't interested in meaning; that he allows no
room for all of the important values that language study really should carry.
Nothing could be further from the truth. It is just because the linguist *is*
interested in meaning that he is content to absent himself from felicity awhile.
Quite true, he does object to meaning-based or philosophy-based attempts
to define parts of the language, such as, "A noun is the name of a person,
place, or thing." Such a definition tells us nothing we didn't know, but a
structurally based definition like, "A noun is a class of words that can be
inflected for plural and possessive" *does* tell us something, particularly if
we define our other word classes with similar criteria.

Since the linguist is aware that to understand the written language he must
first understand the structure of the spoken language, and since he knows
that traditional grammar is based on the literary language recorded in an
incomplete and inconsistent writing system, he must first concern himself
with completeness of description and consistency of description of the
spoken language. This means he must know all the significant classes of
sounds *(phonemes)* of the language and how these group themselves into
words, constructions, and sentences. Failure to see all the significant entities
at any level obscures the understanding of the structuring of each succeeding level. Rigorously, step by step, level by level, the linguist must advance,
going to the next higher level for unanalyzed data to be treated systematically on the level that concerns him. Thus if we are concerned with phonemes, we go to words for our data, knowing that only when we have all
our phonemes can we understand the structure of our words. To study our
word-classes or parts of speech, we get our data from unanalyzed groups of
words, knowing that only when we know how our words are classified can

we attempt an analysis of occurrences of more than one word. To understand the patterning of constructions and sentences, we go to unanalyzed *discourse* for our data, building each set of statements on those that have gone before.

Throughout this technical and laborious process, the linguist classifies and arranges the data step by step, level by level, operating on the principle that certain events are the same as others and certain are different. Thus the word *pin* is determined as not the same as the word *bin* by virtue of the contrast between the initial phonemes *p* and *b*—not because one means a shiny, pointed metal object and the other a place to put coal or grain. By this procedure, the first sound in *pin* and the second sound in *spin,* even though they differ in quite a few respects, are classified as members of the same *p* phoneme, since all *p*'s *automatically* sound like the *p* in *spin* when an *s* precedes. And as a further check, the linguist finds that *k*'s and *t*'s pattern or behave in the same way.

Through the application of the criteria for establishing the phoneme classes, the linguist finally arrives at an inventory for English which includes twenty-one consonants, nine short vowels, three semi-vowels (*y, w, h*), four significant degrees of loudness or *stress,* four significant levels of *pitch,* three *terminal junctures,* or ways to end stretches of utterance, and an *internal* or *plus* juncture, which is an open transition between vowel and/or consonant phonemes and contrasts with a normal or smooth transition.

Of the forty-five phonemes in the over-all pattern of English, I have space to exemplify only the stresses and the internal juncture and to examine how these phonological structure-points enter into patterns on the higher levels of the linguistic structure. The functioning of these patterns has only recently been understood but at long last we have the basis for a truly systematic statement of many aspects of English grammar.

The four stresses are generally designated *primary* (′), *secondary* (ˆ), *tertiary* (`), and weak (˘). All four can be distinguished in the following examples:

(1) Líght + hoùse + keêper: keeper of a lighthouse.
(2) Lìght + hoúse + keèper: one who does light house-keeping.
(3) Lîght + hoúse + keèper: a house-keeper light in weight.
(4) A nêw + Yórker / is not a Nèw + Yórker.
(5) Lòng + Íslánd / is a lông + ísland.

The internal or plus juncture—versus the normal transition, can be heard in the following set of items, with normal transition exemplified first:

nítràte; níght + ràte; dye + tràde

Now the combinations of patterns of these stresses and transitions are, as I have mentioned, the very blood and bone of English grammar. The way in which words are coupled, so to speak, in terms of the stresses they bear on either side of the juncture between them is the basis of how we can tell "what goes with what." But first we must draw the distinction between one word and more than one word. A single *word* in English is defined as having only one *base,* though it may have a *prebase*—usually called a "prefix"—and a number of *postbases,* or "stem-forming suffixes." These postbases then may be followed by *grammatical* or *inflectional* suffixes—the "endings" of nouns, verbs, and pronouns. Then each word, to be complete, must have a *stress pattern* or *word superfix.* Thus *boyishness* is one word, consisting of the base *boy*—combined with the postbases *-ish-* and *-ness-,* terminated by the plural "ending" *-es* and completed by the stress pattern of primary stress followed by these weak stresses. But an item like *Whíte + Hoùse,* though it refers to a single, easily identified object in the culture outside the language, is not one word but two, since it combines two bases. *Whíte + Hoùse, whìte + hoúse, sêldom + rúns, rûns + séldom, sét + ùp, sèt + ùp, sêt + úp, úp + sèt, ùp + sét, ă + bóy; táke 'im* are all *phrases,* and the composition of phrases is in the province of *syntax.*

Before he can study phrases, the linguist must first have gotten out his *word classes,* or "parts of speech," which are determined in a language like English on the basis of which words can take inflectional suffixes. Only three such classes can be so set up for English nouns, verbs, and pronouns; all other words are classified as *uninflectible.* It is in the classification of the uninflectible words that a complete phonology·can be of the greatest help to us, and such a phonology—one that includes stresses and junctures—also gives us the clue to the way in which all these words—inflected and uninflectible alike—pair with each other. For the *key* to the phrase is that it always includes two parts; it is a binary arrangement. The *clue* to the phrase is the *phrase superfix,* a combination of *one* primary stress, one internal juncture or a normal transition, and another stress, not a primary. In other words, the word superfix may give up its primary stress when it enters into a phrase. Thus the word *whíte* combined with the word *hoúse* (each with primary stresses) when put together under the phrase superfix of the shape + results in the phrase *Whíte + Hoùse.*

There are two kinds of phrases, the *constructs* and the *constructions.* The constructions are formed by phrase superfixes that have a *secondary* stress with their primary stress, and the constructs *never* have a secondary stress. Thus *gôod + bóy, Jôhn + rán, rûns + fást, sêt + úp* are all constructions: *úp + sèt, ùp + sét, sèt + úp, sét + úp, ă + bóy, táke 'im* are all *constructs.* Constructs may include constructions and vice versa. Thus the construction *gôod + bóy* can be combined with the word *a* under the construct superfix *˘ +′* to result in the construct *a + (gôod + bóy).* Further layerings of constructs and constructions can be exemplified by the utterance fraction *ă + nêw + áir + ràid + wàrden + pôst.* Here the procedure is to go first to the *internal* construct and follow the principle of binary composition throughout, always going to the end of the composition first. Thus *aír + ràid* is a construct under *'+'*, and the word *warden* is then combined with the construct *aír + ràid* under the construct superfix *'+'* to give the construct (*aír + ràid*) *+ wàrden*. Then the construct (*aír + ràid*) *+ wàrden* is put together with the word *post* under the construction superfix *'+^* to give the nominal construction, [(*aír + ràid*) *+ wàrden*] *+ pôst*. Then going to the front of the composition, the word *new* is now combined with the construction [(*aír + ràid*) *+ wàrden*] *+ pôst* under the construction superfix *^+'* with the result *nêw +* [(*aír + ràid*) *+ wàrden*] *+ pôst*.) Finally the combination of constructs and constructions is combined with the word *a* under the construct superfix *+* and we have the construct *ă +* [*nêw +* [(*aír + ràid*) *+ wàrden*] *+ pôst*.)] You will note the procedure has been purely mechanical; the *immediate constituents* of the utterance fraction have been established in a definite order and relationship and every phonological juncture and stress has been assigned a syntactic role. No recourse to referential meaning has been resorted to, no pure "hunches" as to "what goes with what" have been followed.

As I mentioned earlier, the phrase superfix provides us with a means of classifying uninflectible words. For example, *of, in, out, up, to, our, down,* etc., have been classed both as "prepositions" and "adverbs" in such ways that only confusion has resulted. To "define" these words is extremely difficult; to *identify* them is extremely simple. If one of these uninflectible words enters into a construction it is an *adverbial* ("adverb," if you will). If it appears in a construct, it is a *prepositional*. Thus in *sét + ùp, sèt + úp, úp + sèt* and *ùp + stáirs, up* is a prepositional. In the constructional *wênt + úp, up* is an adverbial.

By further examination we find that nouns and verbs enter ultimately into constructions—the *subject-verb* construction or the *verb-object* construction (*Jôhn + rán, hît + Bíll*). Words that have been traditionally called adjectives and adverbs also appear only in constructions—prenominal, preverbal; adnominal and adverbal (e.g., *gôod + bóy, sêldom + rúns; trîp + abróad, rân + fást*). Pronouns in subject, object, or possessive cases appear almost without exception in constructs, as does the verb *be*. Articles and conjunctions are other uninflectible words which also appear, only in constructs. The so-called relatives, interrogatives, and demonstratives form an interesting class of words (and constructs) which appear both under construct and contruction superfixes.

I wish time and space permitted my going into the function of the intonation patterns—pitches and terminal junctures. I can only say that these give us the phonological basis for another syntactic pattern—the *arrangement,* and here we can handle perfectly mechanically such old bug-bears as the "dangling participle" and the "restrictive" and "non-restrictive" clauses. Suffice it to say in conclusion that syntax is dependent on phonology; or—to put it another way—just in so far as our phonology is incompletely understood, analyzed, and inventoried, so will our understanding of the composition of words, phrases, constructions, and sentences be incomplete. Not only will it be incomplete, but we will be forced to use criteria from *discourse* to make statements on the level of syntax. Much that is unsatisfactory in both traditional grammar and in recent linguistically oriented "positional grammar" or "pattern grammar" lies in the fact that a clear level distinction between syntax and discourse analysis has not been made. For instance, such terms as "modification," "question sentence," "intransitive," "transitive," "direct object," "indirect object," "object complement," "statement," and so on are not matters of syntax but of the *distributional patterns* that are the concern of discourse. For example, *syntactically,* "John made Bill money," and "John made Bill captain" are identical, but on the level of discourse, the terms "indirect object," "direct object," and "object complement" are useful in making distinctions between *distributional* occurrences both within the sentence and between sentences in the discourse under analysis. To sum up, *syntax* stops with the syntactic analysis of the syntactic sentence or sentence fractions; *discourse analysis* concerns itself with further classification of relationships within the sentence and with distributional patterns of sentences and sentence fractions in actual discourse, spoken or written. From this last vantage point perhaps we can really tackle *meaning!*

Improving Sentence Structure

Kellogg W. Hunt

Last summer, as I was driving from Tallahassee to Iowa, I missed my turn in downtown Dothan, Alabama, and drove several miles out of town headed west instead of north. When I finally realized that I was headed the wrong way, I turned around and went back to Dothan. I discovered the place where I had missed my turn. There was the turn-marker almost hidden by

Reprinted by permission from *The English Journal,* 47.206-11 (April, 1958). The author is Professor of English and Director of the Program in Written Communication at the Florida State University.

a branch of a tree. Cursing the Alabama Highway Department, I made the right turn and got on my way toward my destination.

I fancy that the same thing has happened to most people at one time or another when they were making a car trip. But I am sure that a similar kind of thing happens to every composition teacher every few minutes while he is reading student themes. He will be reading along the sentence, perhaps even interested in what is being said, when all of a sudden he runs smack into a road block. He can't get through the rest of the sentence on the interpretation he is using. He has to turn around and go back to an earlier spot in the sentence. There he discovers the place where he missed his turn. This time, when he sees the sign, he reads it differently; he takes off in a different direction, and now proceeds successfully through the rest of the sentence. But he curses the Highway Department for not making its signs clearer. Next day in class he says, "Students, it is not enough that a sentence be capable of being understood. A good sentence must be incapable of being misunderstood even on a first reading."

The special kind of misunderstanding I have in mind is the kind that arises under either of two circumstances: stated abstrusely, either the lexical meaning of certain words is at odds with the structural signals established by the rest of the sentence; or the structural signals, at a given stage in the sentence, are ambiguous and liable to be misinterpreted. The purpose of this discussion is to present a dozen examples of the error, and to suggest a teaching device that seems to help students to spot and correct the difficulty.

In a theme last week I came across a sentence which was bad because the words that appeared in two places were the wrong kind to put in those places. Next day in class I put the sentence on the board, leaving blanks where the wrong words appeared. *We talked from ———— to ————.* The students were asked to suggest words to go into the blanks. They suggested, *We talked from nine to eleven. We talked from evening to morning.* All the pairs of words they suggested designated times. They saw clearly what kinds of lexical meanings had to go into those blanks to fit the structure of the rest of the sentence. When I wrote into the blanks the words used on the paper I had been grading, the students rejected them immediately with the same click of amusement and annoyance I had felt. They rejected: *We talked from religion to politics.*

SHOWING FAULTS CLEARLY

Using blanks helped. If the faulty sentence in its entirety had appeared on the board to start with, the students would not have spotted the error so clearly. They would have got the writer's meaning in spite of his structure. He meant that *We talked about everything from religion to politics,* and the students would have gotten that meaning even though that is not what the author wrote. The sentence, though faulty, would have communicated.

It is a fact established by communication research—especially research investigating garbled messages sent by telephone and radio during wartime —that a somewhat garbled message still has a chance of being properly interpreted. When we teachers find fault, as we must, with sentences which are garbled though not unintelligible, we must be prepared for a slightly resentful reaction from our students. If the message gets through to the student-reader we can expect the author of the message to feel, "Well, they knew what I meant. The teacher just didn't like the way I said it. I never was any good in English anyway." At this point the technique of using blanks comes to the teacher's rescue. Not knowing the meaning content the author intended, the student-readers and the student-author are forced to look at the structure first and to declare the kind of content they expect. Once committed in this way, they recognize along with the teacher the little outrage committed when the wrong lexical meaning is jammed into a slot which it won't fit. That is the psychological advantage of the blanks.

Another time the following words go on the board: *He will blow loudly on his horn and whistle . . . .* When a student is asked to read this aloud, his pitch and juncture indicate clearly that he groups the last three words together. If I ask him whether this sentence is complete he will answer, yes, it can be. If I ask him to add more words, he can do that too. Now if I add the words *as shrilly as he can,* so that the sentence in its entirety reads *He will blow loudly on his horn and whistle as shrilly as he can,* the student will experience a slight shock. The student who read it aloud before will read it differently now, grouping the word *whistle* with the words that follow, instead of with those that precede.

Again the blanks help. By seeing only the first part of the sentence to begin with, the student is made to formulate the structural grammatical interpretation he will naturally make at first reading. Then when the remaining words are added, the word *shrilly* becomes a road block. Any reader must turn around and go back. He will re-interpret the grammatical significance of the word *whistle.* If the reader happens to be an English professor, he may possibly say to himself, *"Whistle* must be considered a verb instead of a noun. It is parallel with the verb *blow,* not the noun *horn.* The coordinating conjunction *and* joins two predicates instead of two ob-- jects of a preposition. I was misled at first." No one but an English professor talks like that. Any other reader would simply change his word grouping or his silent intonation, and group *whistle* with the words that follow. That done, he can speed right past *shrilly* and out through the rest of the sentence. Though less articulate than the English professor, even the ordinary reader will know that something was wrong with the sentence at first reading.

Students can spot the difficulty in this sentence without needing to know any grammatical nomenclature, either the traditional nomenclature of nouns and verbs or of "form classes" 1 and 2. All readers respond to structural signs even when they cannot name them. Our job as composition teachers is to improve students' sentences, using the most economical devices. If our students know grammatical nomenclature we can use those terms, but if they do not, we need to be able to communicate to them anyway.

The coordinating conjunctions very frequently cause structural difficulty because of the fact that the reader is uncertain at first whether the conjunction joins the preceding and following words or the preceding and following clauses. Many first clauses end with nouns, and many second clauses begin with nouns. Thus *To be a freshman means to wear a rat cap and a green look* can be followed either with *for a year,* or *is to be expected.* The latter group of words requires us to go back and readjust our structural interpretation of *a green look* if no comma appears to warn us, for in one case we group *a green look* with *a rat cap,* while in the other case we separate those two.

Here is another. *But this period didn't seem long for the first day . . . .* That can stand by itself, and consequently the reader is troubled if he finds it followed by the words *ended with a freshman picnic.* At first reading, the words *for the first day* are thought to be a modifier of the beginning clause, but then it becomes clear that they are needed to provide a subject for the verb which follows. The words cannot do both jobs. An oral reading will show the difference between *But this period didn't seem long for the first day* and *But this period didn't seem long for the first day ended with a freshman picnic.* We can tell a student he has ignored a rule for the comma, but he will learn much more if we let him discover the misreading which occurs when the comma is omitted.

Using blanks is also helpful when the grammatical relationships are spread out over several places in the sentence. *Dating in America is a routine followed by each teen-ager that seems to be . . . .* When students are asked to complete the sentence they suggest *normal* or *interested in the other sex* or *able to afford it.* Students suggest only those expressions that describe the teen-ager who dates. When the teacher supplies the words which appeared in the original faulty sentence, the class will not accept the substitute. Students are baffled by the sentence when it reads, *Dating in America is a routine followed by each teen-ager that seems to be a good idea.* The last three words cannot fit into this structural context, even if they are intended to go with *routine.*

Another short one: *She was very strict in grading tests, especially . . . .* Student accept *when she was cross* or *final exams,* but will not accept *mechanical errors* in this position.

USING NONSENSE WORDS

Sometimes instead of using blanks, it is more effective to supply nonsense syllables which carry the marks of the nouns or verbs or adjectives or adverbs which the nonsense syllables replace. We cannot replace other kinds of words with nonsense syllables, for the structure or function words plus the word order are needed to provide the structure. The parts of speech that can be replaced by nonsense syllables are only the nouns, verbs, adjectives, and adverbs. Under certain circumstances students can see structure more clearly when all lexical meaning has been removed from an expression.

At least sentence fragments are more amusing this way. *In years later after the foons womped it* can stand as the answer to a question or the beginning of a statement, but students quickly see that it is only a fragment. Whether or not it is a complete thought, it is an incomplete structure. The student's original was, *In years later when the Italians conquered it.*

I can give them this: *Puffing and panting, the womble was woobled at last.* In place of the first nonsense word, students will substitute words for people, for animals, for a number of things that can puff and pant. But when I substitute what the student wrote, they reject it with a laugh. I write on the blackboard, *Puffing and panting, the top of the hill was reached at last.* They see that tops of hills don't really puff and pant even when they are being reached. They see this far more clearly when I substitute nonsense syllables than when I lecture to them on dangling modifiers.

If nonsense syllables are used, punctuation problems become more novel. *No one said that they were beekish fortunately the bol serped upon the woofing gup of the bok then I woked it out.* As students struggle with this structure, they will immediately sense a couple of difficulties that only punctuation can clear up. For instance, does *fortunately* go with the preceding or the following words? Being what Whitehall calls a movable modifier, it can either end one sentence or begin the next. Until punctuation is supplied we cannot tell whether to read *they were beekish fortunately* or *fortunately the bol serped upon the woofing gup.*

A student can read this aloud with such an intonation as to place *fortunately* with the preceding words, or he can provide the intonation which will place it with the following words. A similar kind of difficulty may arise with *then,* though most students will feel it must go with the following group.

Another kind of problem also is noticeable in this sentence. Were the *They who were beekish* the same people who "didn't say," or were they different people? This is real pronoun-antecedent trouble. How we interpret this one structural sign will determine the meaning of the first third of the sentence. Some students will feel that "no one" can take a plural substitute word, and some will feel it requires a singular. In this circumstance our concern over agreement in number is not fussiness: it makes a real difference in meaning.

Once the structural pattern with nonsense syllables has been analyzed, the difficulties in the original sentence in the original theme are seen clearly. *No one said that they were afraid fortunately the car stopped upon the crumbling edge of the bank then I backed it out.*

Blanks or nonsense syllables also help to show a writer's difficulties in positioning modifiers. The writer needs to discover that all readers try to attach modifiers to the most nearly adjacent head-word. Single-word modifiers, with certain exceptions, are attached to a following head-word; word-group or word-cluster modifiers attach to the preceding head-word. The writer needs to know this, not because all handbooks say so, but because all readers *do* so. If the lexical meaning of the writer's modifier conflicts with this structural tendency, then the reader will have to go back and re-read the sentence.

Here are two examples. *The prize will be announced by the committee to be ———ed next week. Named* or *elected* will fit the blank because a committee can be named or elected. But the student who wrote *to be awarded* intended that expression to attach way back to the head-word *prize*. Such lexical meaning does not fit into this place in this structural pattern, so the reader must correct the writers' work for him.

Another similar sentence begins, *He put the typewriter on the table which . . . .* Word order dictates that words following *which* will be understood to apply to *table*. The student who wrote *He put the typewriter on the table which made the blackest carbon* allowed his structural signals to contradict his lexical meaning.

TOTAL MEANING

Looked at conventionally, the faults which have appeared in these sentences cover a wide range. They include fragments, fused sentences, misplaced modifiers, squinting constructions, omitted words, dangling modifiers, problems in agreement. Looked at more freshly, they involve not several problems but one. Only rather recently have we begun to appreciate that the total meaning of a sentence is the sum of its lexical meaning plus its separate structural meaning. The total meaning cannot be clear until the grammatical structure is clear. The faults in these sentences have nearly all involved the grammatical structure. Either the lexical meaning has been at odds with the structural meaning, or the structural signals have themselves been ambiguous so that a reader would be misled at first, and would have to go back and revise his interpretation of the grammatical structure before he could make any sense at all out of the whole sentence.

The teaching problem is complicated by the fact that nearly all of these sentences can be understood on second reading. The proper use of pitch and juncture would make most of them clear even at a first oral reading. Here lies the crux of the teacher's problem. The students who write these sentences give them the correct interpretation at first reading, and consequently are inclined to feel that the teacher who finds fault with them does so from deliberate ill-will or school-marmish finicality. To counteract this resistance to the learning process the teacher may be wise to rely on the class, as a group of normal readers, to report its interpretation of the structure in the doubtful sentence. The student-author's peers are less likely than the teacher to appear over-finical.

When the teacher is confronted by a sentence which is clear on a second but not a first reading, he must be able to isolate the structural difficulty. Only then can he devise a test frame so sharp and critical that his jury of students will be able to give a decisive "Yes" or "No," "Will fit" or "Won't fit" to the doubtful item.

The students will not be able to define the structural difficulty in abstruse terms. The teacher's label for a part of speech or a form or a function word may be meaningless to them. Surely immediate constituents, which are the heart of structural problems, will be unknown; talk about lexical and structural meaning may at first seem so much jargon. But even though students cannot define a structure abstrusely, they do react to it concretely. They can differentiate between those structures which will, and those which will not, fit into a larger structural context. These students may be unconscious as to which stimuli produce a given response in them, but nonetheless they respond almost infallibly. According to Henry Lee Smith, "these systems are thoroughly learned and internalized by all psychologically normal human beings in all cultures at about five and a half years of age!"[1]

Under these circumstances much of the writing teacher's job is to make each student-author conscious of how his writing will be read.

[1] *Linguistic Science and the Teaching of English* (Harvard University Press, 1956), p. 8.

45

Structural Syntax on the Blackboard

MacCurdy Burnet

THE GRAMMARS of Charles C. Fries—especially his *Structure of English*[1]—have been used in composition courses at Maryland State Teachers College for the past several years.[2] The approach and techniques suggested have paid off in several ways: Better writing results, less time is taken up with grammar, and more grown-up attitudes toward language are adopted. More is learned in less time—more skills, more knowledge, more insight. This adds up to a phenomenally efficient way of talking about writing—and having more time to talk about other things.

I'm going to break an important rule in telling about the approach used: I'm going to use old fashioned terminology.

The first of these techniques, which involves "tracking structures" through stretches of prose longer than the sentence, can be presented on the black-board in some such fashion as this:

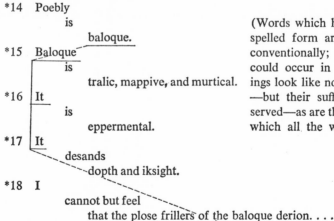

(Words which have only one spelled form are reproduced conventionally; words which could occur in several spellings look like nonsense words—but their suffixes are preserved—as are the positions in which all the words occur.)

Reprinted with permission from *College English*, 16.38–43 (October, 1954). This article is adapted from a talk made to the Michigan Linguistic Society in Detroit, spring, 1954. Professor Burnet is at Maryland State Teachers College.

In spite of the oddity of this material, we can, as readers of English, make certain statements about "baloque;" it includes "Poebly," whatever that is; it's tralic, mappive and murtical, and desands dopth and iksight, and there's a derion which is baloque, according to the writer. Although this little passage refers to nothing known on heaven or earth, it does have certain built-in signals of meaning, we feel.

The "step-format" is queer-looking, too, but that's beside the point at the moment.

And another parenthetical point can be made here, one that's really important in a composition course: Recurring similar words like "baloque" occur in just about nineteen out of twenty adjacent printed sentences. And so it seems practical in the classroom to assume that their recurrences constitute "links" of a sort, between sentences. Now more of these links occur between subject-areas in printed materials than in student papers; the ratio is approximately eight subject-links in print to three subject-links in passages from freshman themes.

The fact that these figures confirm what teachers of rhetoric have known for untold years is neither surprising nor important. What is important in a course in freshman composition is this: *Good-naturedly forcing students to look at the signs built into real language as a system of signals of meaning.*

This involves a firm yet merry tactfulness in distinguishing between "conventional grammar" and what we may choose to call "structural analysis," which, in turn, makes necessary a fresh set of names for parts of sentences —during the first class meeting perhaps "this area," "this word," "premodifier," "postmodifier," supplemented with gestures. Later, "nounform," "verbform," "complement," "punctuation unit," and "sequence signal" can be introduced, together with "adverbform" and adjectiveform." It is useful in a survey, I think, to avoid definition as such entirely—and postpone classificatory techniques until several students are both interested and puzzled. Then the time is ripe for saying, "We'll call this word an "adjectiveform'; what other words could occur in the same position?" Finally, a more generally useful test sentence with a hole or two in it can be provided —e.g., where the same word could plug up both spaces in the frame sentence: The *hot* thing's *hot*.

But showing the forms and positions which signal differences in meaning is of secondary importance. The most important thing is to present, and

¹ *The Structure of English* (Harcourt Brace, 1952) and *American English Grammar* (Appleton-Century-Crofts, 1940).

² Special thanks are due to Dr. J. D. Blackwell, President of Maryland State Teachers College and to Dr. Howard E. Bosley, Dean of Instruction; and to Warner G. Rice, Chairman of the Department of English and John Weimer, Chairman of the Committee for Freshman English, University of Michigan. To men like these, teachers who are attempting to infuse aspects of linguistic method into classroom teaching owe a great deal.

have students collect and examine real language—the materials not ordinarily brought to the classroom for analysis, like prose in periodicals or books of readings—genuine language in printed form which will both interest students and furnish some sort of a model for the writing the instructor wants them to submit in college.

Presenting sentences in some such form as the "step format" we looked at in the "baloque" passage has several advantages: It shows the positional relations of "blocks of structures" which occur over and over again in printed sentences. It exposes modificational patterns, too—and it helps to hammer home the notion that sentences consist of "blocks of structure" within which words are relatively incidental. The format, if a teacher chooses to use it, need not be taught as such; students find that after blackboard demonstration they can transcribe nearly every sentence they encounter. I'd like to illustrate some of the commoner format patterns into which nearly all printed sentences fall: First, let's take the utterance made famous by Dr. Fries and put it through its paces on the page as if we had found it in printed form. Conventionally, it would look like this:

> 1a   The uggle wogs a diggle.

In the "step format," it would look like this:

> 1b   The uggle
>   wogs
>   a diggle.

We have cut it into three strips and placed them on the page so that one line includes the subject, the next line the verb, with the complement trailing after. The format consists of nothing more or less than an eye-guide for amateur grammarians.

Most sentences, though, come in longer strips. Let's add some modifiers:

> 1c   The uggle to the norp
>   uffly wogs
>   a seckly diggle of nerbal facks.

Here, we have indented the format so that the first words in the subject structure, the verb structure, and the complement occur at different distances from the left margin. By asking students what words or groups of words could be erased with a minimum of damage to whatever this sentence means, we can draw arrows showing the direction of modification:

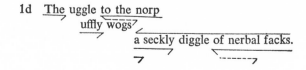

Now we can take the sentence away and leave the arrows:

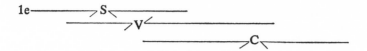

What's left over is one of the most frequent modificational patterns of the English sentence, with the different "layers of modification" chalked on the blackboard. (The fact that students rather enjoy playing with a topological gimmick like this is again incidental. I believe the primary value of this exercise is that it tricks students into looking at real material analytically— and teaches aspects of "structure" unconsciously.)

The above sentence-form is the most popular one in English—where a form of "be" does not occur in the verb structure. The three other most frequent ones all have the "be" form:

> 2 A diggle
>   is wogged
>   by the uggle.
>   (Note the "ed" form)
> 3 The uggle
>   is
>   a vemp.
>   (Note the "a" and lack of suffix)
> 4 The uggle
>   is
>   vemper.
>   (Note the lack of "a" and suffix.)

The meanings of the above four sentences, in terms of their contrasts in form, are "that which performs, (1); undergoes, (2); is identified, (3); is described, (4)" respectively.

But about a fifth of the sentences which appear in print don't begin with subjects but with "opener modifiers" which connect them somehow to something that came before the sentence in question. If these structures don't fit the patterns of subject premodifiers, the chances are that they serve as "whole-sentence modifiers" and stand outside the sentence. Usually, they have the same kind of general meaning that "thus," "then," and "there" have; usually they occur as prepositional phrases, single-word adverbs which may have modifiers, subordinate clauses, or participial phrases —or any of these forms in combination. They can be identified by form almost invariably and parked, as far as format is concerned, over in the left margin:

Into tenk and meckle and
at the melk
5   the uggle and
    his breep
        weg and
        fleb
            a diggle and
            a larg. . . .

Sentence 5 also illustrates a format treatment of several items within the same block of structure. Words like "and" and "but" usually separate exchangeable structures; when they occur between blocks of structure, we can place them at the end of a format-line; when they occur within blocks of structure, they can be buried in the interior of a line of text (It is useful, I think, to consider them, with adjacent punctuation, as punctuation units in the form of words.)

Verbs are worrisome, too, when two forms occur separated by another word of structure:

6 The uggle
      wogs
          a diggle
      up.

(This is what happens to a prepositional adverb preceded by a complement.)

7   How
      can
  a diggle
      wog
        an uggle?

(Many questions can be treated like this.)

More than thirteen out of fourteen printed sentences can be dissected as shown in sentences 1-7. Others, usually where the subject structure is "longer" in relation to the complement, are these:

8 It   ("that . . . diggle" can occur in the
    is   same position as "It." See sentence 4.)
      vemper
that the uggle wogs a diggle.

9 It   ("to . . . uffly" can be substituted for
    is   "It" See sentence 3. Subject structures
      a vemp   in sentences like 8 and 9 can assume
to wog a diggle so uffly.   any substantive form.)

10 There   (If "There" is not a "gesture-word,"
     is   "is" has the range of meaning of "ex-
the uggle which wogs a diggle. ist.")

11   Into tenk   (When a form which may be a whole-
        wogs   sentence-modifier stands first but is fol-
    an uggle with a diggle.   lowed by a verb before its subject, the
                                       "modifier" is part of the complement.)

This takes us past two points of procedure which I have wanted to stress:
First, the forms and positions of words in real material must be examined
by students. Second, the form of transcription they use must illustrate
rather than obscure the arrangements of blocks of structure which characterize English prose. If you feel that this format serves that purpose, I
hope you'll experiment with it.

It's useful especially for laying out sentences which are to be examined
in relation to each other. Here is the English of the "baloque" passage:

For
12p   to write good prose
            is
    i   an affair of good manners.
13   It
            is, unlike verse,
    i   a civil art.
14   Poetry
            is
                baroque.
15   Baroque
            is
    d   tragic, massive, and mystical.
16   It
            is
    d   elemental.
17   It
        demands
    p   depth and insight.
18   I
        cannot but feel
    p   that the prose writers of the baroque period, the authors of
                    King James Bible, Sir Thomas Browne, Glanville, were
                    poets who had lost their way.
19   Prose
            is
    i   a rococo art.
20   It
        needs
    p   taste rather than power, decorum rather than inspiration and
                    vigour rather than grandeur.[3]
        etc.

[3] These sentences are quoted from W. Somerset Maugham's *The Summing Up*
(Doubleday Doran, 1938), p. 37.

Here, the nounforms or structures which could be shifted from one sentence to an adjacent one are underlined, and the underlined "sames" connected by lines. When these connecting lines cross lines separating sentences, we call the connecting lines hypothetical links between sentences.

Other "sames" in adjacent sentences may be of interest: Sentence 12p, as indicated by the "p," occurs as the opening sentence in a paragraph. It is the only sentence in the extract which begins with a whole-sentence-modifier. And several adjacent sentences have the "same" general structural meaning: 12-13, "Identified;" 14-16, "Described;" 17-18, "Performer." In addition, sentences 12-16 have the same verbform. Sentences 15-16 end with the same two letters.

Similarities like these, since they occur frequently in adjacent sentences, probably constitute a kind of rhetorical "glue" which binds sentences together. If so, they furnish a suggestive starting point for a grammar which goes beyond the borders of the sentence—a descriptive rhetoric which might help students in composition courses to write papers that more people want to read.

From methods of classroom approach like the ones discussed here, students gain at least a subjective sense of what happens from one sentence to the next. They also gain a command of the forms in which the English sentence appears. They add to their vocabularies a set of terms which refer to language rather than to language superstition; this command of terms shortens the time spent both in conference and in class—and in correcting papers. And they gradually adopt a point of view toward language which makes it possible for them to grow in their freedom to use it more effectively. No teacher can ask for more.

Shortly after the two-week structural survey, the incidence of "graphic errors"[4] in themes—of the sort that instructors note with their red pencils—is reduced to a small and dwindling fraction. "Structural trouble,"[5] statable in technical terms, all but disappears from student writing. The practical result of an approach which fixes linguistic attention on real language can be summed up in one word: Efficiency. This means that more time in the composition course can be devoted to matters which are more important than the marks made on a sheet of paper.

[4] For example, misspellings and typographical slips.

[5] These are matters like agreement, case, coherence, coordination, emphasis, fragment, misrelated modifier, parallelism, principal parts, reference, subordination, tense and word order.

46

Correctness and Style in English Composition

Archibald A. Hill

THE TEACHER OF ENGLISH is often accused by students of language of being unable to modify his teachings in accord with facts of usage no matter how well proved, and the linguist in turn seems to those of us who have to struggle with freshmen to be a wild libertarian who would accept the most shapeless writing on the ground that all linguistic forms are equally good. Perhaps, as with other disputes, some of the differences may be resolved if the basic terms are more clearly defined.

I shall begin with correctness, giving a few well-worn statements of what it is not.

Correctness is not logic, since all languages are largely illogical. English says, "I see him," as if sight were a positive act of will comparable to that in "I hit him." Yet all of us know enough optics to realize that, if there is any action involved, it starts with *him* and reaches and affects *me*. Languages which happen, like Eskimo, to avoid this particular illogicality fall into others as great.

The basis of correctness is not beauty inherent in the forms used. Beauty in linguistic forms is due to the associations they arouse. Such a form as "goil" is ugly only if the hearer happens to dislike Brooklyn. To realize the truth of this statement, one has only to consider variants where we have no such associations. If a child in the New Mexican pueblo of Santa Clara puts the sentence, "I am going to town," in the form *bupiyeummang,* the "ugly" pronounciation is immediately corrected to *bupijeummang.* The Tewa parents are not being merely arbitrary; they are objecting to an unacceptable dialect. I doubt if any English speaker can seriously maintain that he finds one Tewa form more beautiful than the other.

The basis of correctness is not history; such a belief would contradict the results of linguistic science. Further, the belief that older forms are better than newer can readily be reduced to an absurdity. If only old forms

Reprinted by permission from *College English,* 12.280–285 (February, 1951).

are right, then we do not speak English but bad Old English—or bad Indo-Hittite.

Equally certainly correctness is not the result of an authoritative ruling by an individual or a book. A neat example of this last view is the statement of a columnist who once said that 98 per cent of Americans mispronounced a given word, since they failed to follow dictionary recommendations. Actually such a statement demonstrates that 2 per cent of America mispronounces the word or that the dictionaries had better catch up on usage.

A final view once widely held is that anything which is impossible in Latin is incorrect in English. The view hardly needs denial, baleful as its lingering influence may be on the analysis of English grammar. At least, no one would now seriously maintain that "Oh, father!" is a vocative case, incapable of being split into two words.

I can start my positive exposition with a quotation which puts clearly the idea that the composition teacher has a double task. Most of what will follow will be merely an attempt to sharpen the distinction set up in the quotation.

> Competence . . . has to do with the organization of ideas . . . with putting words together . . . in such a way as to convey meaning easily and clearly. Decency may be regarded as the manners of discourse, and bears the same relation to speaking and writing that good table manners have to eating. The schoolboy who declares, "We ain't goin' to have no baseball team this year" is using language with competence, for his meaning is perfectly clear, but he is not using it with decency.[1]

For these terms I should like to substitute "correctness" and "style." Any form is correct if it is current in the dialect—to be defined, of course, beforehand—that the writer is using. A form is incorrect only if it has no such currency. It follows that it is possible to be incorrect in the use of other dialects than the rather vaguely defined Standard Written English with which teachers concern themselves. Professor Thorpe's schoolboy was using language incorrectly if he was speaking in the formal atmosphere of the schoolroom; but, if he was speaking to playmates across the tracks, he was speaking correctly enough. A more serious illustration is that the English department of one of our leading universities was recently taken to task because its training did not equip graduates to communicate with workmen. The point was well taken: it is as serious an error to use the forms of Standard English where they are socially out of place as it is to use Gullah in the pages of a learned article. Incorrectness can result also, not merely from the use of a dialect in an inappropriate situation, but as well from the mixture of dialects or the improper imitation of a dialect. Readers of Galsworthy may remember that he sometimes makes an American

---

[1] Clarence D. Thorpe (ed.), *Preparation for College English* (Ann Arbor: University of Michigan Press, 1945), p. 12 n.

character say sentences like, "If you've gotten a sense of humor, you've gotten it jolly well hidden up." Such sentences are grossly un-American at the same time that they are un-British; they are therefore incorrect.

The second term was "style." If forms A and B both occur in a given dialect, it is impossible to say that either is incorrect in that dialect. It may, however, be possible to show that A is better than B in the particular context in which it occurs. Such an evaluation will be based on the positive qualities of the passage under criticism; that is, A is better than B if it is clearer, more in accord with artistic conventions, or fits better with the structure of the utterance in which it falls. It should be stated emphatically that good and bad style are both possible in any dialect—Professor Thorpe's schoolboy was speaking with excellent style, since his statement left no doubt of the vigor of his denial. It should also be pointed out that, if a stylist variant is condemned in one passage, it is by no means implied that it should be condemned elsewhere.

A third form of variant also exists. These are the different variants. If A and B both exist, and no stylistic reason can be found for preferring one over the other, the variation is indifferent. The existence of indifferent variants is of some importance, since somehow the idea has gotten abroad that, if there are two ways of saying a thing, one must always be better than the other. English teachers are all too often called on to adjudicate between six and a half-dozen, though to devote effort to such decisions can only falsify what we so much need to tell our students.

From these rather generalized examples we can pass to discussion of variants such as actually appear in student themes. We will begin with variants which involve correctness, the first group of them springing from insufficient knowledge of the way in which writing represents the forms of speech. It is characteristic of these forms that, if read aloud with normal pronunciation, they immediately become acceptable Spoken English.

He couldn't *of* had a worse introduction.

Sentences like this have a sort of currency in dialect writing but have no currency in Standard Written English. The mistake consists in selecting the wrong spelling for a weak form which is homonymous for *have* and *of*. It is odd that the reverse mistake as in "a pair *have* shoes" seems never to occur.

Rooms for *Tourist*.

This is a type of form which is common in much of the South. What is back of it is an assimilation of *-sts* to *-ss* or simply to *-s*. It occurs at all levels of regional speech, and even teachers of English use it quite unconsciously. The mistake can be explained to students by giving the conditions under which the assimilation occurs and by pointing out that written forms do not recognize the change.

The next group of variants are incorrect because they employ local or social dialect forms not found in the Standard language.

Youse had better not do it.

This sentence will be recognized as belonging to uncultured New York City speech. Its badness, however, is altogether the result of its lack of currency in standard dialects of any type—it cannot be condemned as illogical or out of keeping with the structure of the language, since it makes a contrast between singular and plural just as other pronouns do, and since it is parallel to the southern *you all*.

I want this *doing* immediately.

This sentence is not likely to occur in compositions by American students, but it is nonetheless instructive, since we are likely to think of anything British as all right. The form is northern British local dialect, which finds its way into occasional printed books, among them those of Hall Caine. It is certainly not correct in this country. Another local sentence type is the southern "I *might could* do it," which is common enough in colloquial speech, but which I have never seen in print. The sentence should be rejected in compositions, acceptable as it may be in less formal situations.

The next group of incorrect variants arises from an unsuccessful attempt to use the forms or vocabulary of a standard dialect and is thus comparable to the mistakes made by foreigners.

This phone broken. Do not *uses*.

This sentence appeared on a sign put up by a colored janitor in a government building. The writer presumably used a type of dialect in which the present forms of verbs are without variation. Knowing that an -*s* appears in many forms where he would not use it, he corrected a little too much.

Modern culture is *sadistic*. Its music, painting, and literature are all sad.

In these sentences from a doctoral examination it is amusing to watch what starts out to be a provocative statement evaporate into a merely unfortunate attempt at elegance. The mistake is parallel to the student habit of describing modern poetry as "mystic" under the belief that this word is a critical term meaning "hard to understand."

A final type of incorrect variation is of rather common occurrence in student themes. This is contamination of one construction by another, with consequent production of variants lacking currency. A convenient if somewhat mentalistic explanation is to say that the writer intended one construction and then shifted his intention to another. Readers can readily supply other examples than the one which follows.

> There are *a points* which I can make. . . .

The author of this phrase has mixed *are a few points* with *are points,* producing a mistake which at first sight seems quite improbable for a native speaker.

> John met Jack, and *his* wife spoke to *him*.

In English, as in many languages, we have no way of distinguishing the reference of pronouns when there are two nouns of the same class, so that ambiguity often results. The sentence above must be condemned as bad style, though similar sentences can be found by the hundreds in all sorts of writing.

> Record the pronunciation on the lists in capital letters.

This sentence is drawn from a set of directions made up by a professor of English, who will, I hope, pardon my use of it. The sentence seems clear enough, but unfortunately the intended meaning was: "Record the pronunciation of only those words which appear in capital letters on the lists." Such ambiguities pursue us all.

> This factory is two miles beyond Lynchburg, going south.

This sentence is the only really bad example of our friend the dangling participle which I collected in two sessions of theme-reading. You will note that I have called it bad style, not an example of incorrectness. First, it produces ambiguity, not perhaps of a sort dangerous to real understanding, but sufficient to give a comic effect. Thus the sentence has positive badness. Second, dangling participles are surprisingly common in Standard Written English, though the handbooks do not admit it. Generally, no matter what our rationalizations we do not notice danglers unless the stylistic effect is bad.

The next sentence may strike the reader as wildly improbable, though it comes from an actual composition.

> Mrs. Jackson devoted many years of endeavor to establishing and supporting a home where unfortunate women who had made mistakes (which they often regretted) could go to have their bastards.

The stylistic fault is obvious, since the final word comes with a distinct shock, the stronger for the vaguely elegant verbiage which precedes it.

The next variants are some which seem to me indifferent, though occasionally a particularly puristic handbook condemns one or more of them.

> He *dove,* OR He *dived.*
> It's *me,* OR It's *I.*
> We carried it in a *burlap* bag (OR *croker sack,* OR *gunny sack*).
> Let him do it if he dares (OR *dare*).

The first three of these are regional variants or are regional variants sometimes crossed with social variation. Yet since both forms appear in Standard writing, no matter what the origin, none of them can be condemned as incorrect. The second set is perhaps the most interesting, since *It's I* seems to occur as the natural form around Boston, though elsewhere it is a school-mastered product not to be recommended. Shelley's line, "Be thou me, impetuous one!" is a helpful quotation in dealing with the overmeticulous, since, though it may be a trick, it is always possible to point out that no one would wish the line changed to "Be thou I." The last set shows variation between an older and a newer form, both of which occur in formal writing.

There follow some forms of wide currency, which seem to me also defensible stylistically, though they are nonetheless often condemned.

> The mail is all delivered by plane, *which* is not only remarkably efficient, but is the chief weekly excitement.

This sentence violates the frequently expressed rule that *which* must have a definite antecedent. Yet vague antecedents are common in modern writing and have been common at all periods of the language. There is no ambiguity in the sentence above, and *which* seems a convenient device for avoiding a clumsily exact rephrasing. The sentence comes from the *Saturday Evening Post*.

> We might assume that Standard Oil is going to sponsor a news program. *They* will select a commentator with political views which coincide with *their* own.

This example comes from a student theme discussed by a panel of English teachers, a majority of whom regarded the indefinite *they* as incorrect. The sentence is of a type similar to the one above, has wide currency, and is certainly convenient. The stylistic effect of *it* would be quite different in this passage, and some such periphrasis as "the board of directors of Standard Oil" would be awkward. In the opinion of one person at least, illogical suppleness has always been one of the beauties of English.

I hope that I have by now given enough examples to make it clear that skepticism toward handbook rules does not mean undue libertarianism. To sum up, that part of a composition teacher's activity which concerns itself with correctness is grammar—normative grammar if he is telling students what to use; descriptive grammar if he is himself finding out what forms are current. That part of his activity which concerns the excellence of forms is a part of literary criticism. Both activities are difficult, and both important. On the one hand, it requires investigation rather than mere acceptance of authority to determine whether a given form is right or wrong. For instance, I recently wanted to know whether students should be graded down for writing "the table's leg" or "the story's climax." I went to a national periodical and found there about a hundred examples of both the -s *genitive* and the *of* phrase, about equally divided between living beings and inanimate objects. The handbook rule is clearly false, and students should not be corrected for genitives which break it. As for stylistics, on the other hand, it is not my task to try to cover the subject, though it is obvious that we must bring to the reading of themes the same sort of detailed analysis which we give to understanding the literature we teach. I am aware that teachers are overworked and that it is perhaps too much to expect them to devote even an hour a week to investigating usage, or that they criticize their themes in the same spirit in which they analyze a paragraph of Swift or Arnold. There is only one answer to such an objection, arrogant as the answer may sound. It is surely better, and in the long run easier, to find the facts and teach them than to rely on a merely convenient myth.

47

The Relation of Linguistics to the Teaching of English

PAUL ROBERTS

IT IS PROBABLY FAIR to say that linguistics is the hottest topic on the English teacher's agenda at the present time. It is the one topic almost certain to be on the program wherever English teachers come together, and articles on the subject claim an increasing share of the space in our professional journals. Linguistics is hot also in the sense that it gives off heat. Views tend to be extreme and to be extremely held. From one side we gather that linguistics is about to clear away all the problems of teaching English, to show us delightfully simple ways of bestowing literacy on the illiterate; from the other it is that linguists are satanically in alliance with progressive educationists bent on the destruction of humanism and the corrup-

Reprinted by permission from *College English,* 22.1–9 (October, 1960). The author, for a number of years Professor of English at San Jose State College, currently is Director of the Cornell University Linguistics Program in Italy.

tion of the youth. Whichever side you are on, it is perfectly clear to you that holders of opposing views are willful idiots and probably venal to boot.

The worst possible position to occupy in this struggle is that of the wise moderate, skillfully mediating between the extremists. Such a person is certain to get clubbed mercilessly from all directions and is likely to end screaming louder than anybody. I have no intention of falling into this snare. Forsaking, if necessary, any claims to either wisdom or moderation, I must ally myself with the linguists and say that I think they have much the better of the argument—that, indeed, I can see no real argument against them. But I take this position at some cost. I have no natural bent for controversy and take no pleasure in being the object of attack either in school board meetings or in the pages of *College English*. I could wish for a cooling off, based on a greater measure of understanding than has so far been obtained.

Whether any great measure of understanding is actually obtainable seems sometimes doubtful. It may be that ultimately the differences are temperamental rather than rational, that those whose major professional commitment is esthetic can find no common ground with those whose commitment is scientific. Perhaps what is required for a lying down together of traditionalists and linguists is nothing less than the long-sought rapprochement of the humanities and the sciences, and this may be altogether beyond our powers. Still I cannot give up hope of persuading my colleagues in the humanities that linguists, though working in a different direction, may yet be friends to their ground and liegemen to the Dane.

It seems to me that the major points at issue may be indicated in a series of three questions:

1. What essentially are the differences between linguistic grammar (or whatever you call it) and traditional grammar (or whatever you call *that*)?

2. What is the linguistic view on correctness?

3. What exactly is the application of linguistics, supposing its views to prevail, to the teaching of English?

It is easy to exaggerate the weakness of traditional grammar and the superiority of linguistic grammar, as it is easy to exaggerate the differences between them. They are similar in the important sense that they come out with by and large similar answers. A traditionalist can tell an English verb or an indefinite relative clause when he sees one just as well as a linguist can. They may have different names for these categories, but surely we can agree that differences in terminology are trivial differences.

What is not trivial, however, is the framework in which the concepts are described and discussed. It has been traditional practice to describe such concepts as *noun, verb, subject, sentence* with what are called notional definitions—i.e., definitions based on the supposed meaning of the classes. These definitions have certain weaknesses. For one thing, they are invulnerable statements: one can never conclude an argument about their truth or falsity, and arguers must end by simply stamping their feet. It may be true that sentences are groups of words expressing complete thoughts, as it may be true that angels are incorporeal beings, but such statements can be pursued only to tautology: what is a complete thought?—that which a sentence expresses; what is an incorporeal being?—an angel.

What can, I think, be demonstrated is that such definitions are altogether unusable and that in fact nobody ever uses them. No one can learn the definition "a sentence is a group of words expressing a complete thought" and then use that as a criterion to sort out sentences from non-sentences in some particular language. Anyone who tried to apply it seriously would find himself instantly in serious perplexity. For instance, in what sense is the first sentence of this paragraph a complete thought? It would certainly not stand alone, since the word *such* necessarily implies a preceding statement. If we were to take this definition seriously, we would have to conclude that the sentences of a paragraph have no relation to one another and that there is no connection between paragraphs.

Similarly, no one can actually apply such a definition as "a verb is a word that expresses action." If he did, he would have to list as verbs such English words as *arrival, operation, action*. There must be some sense in which the word *action* expresses action. We do not count these words as verbs, not because they do not express action, but because they do not occur in what we recognize (somehow or other) as verb structures: we do not say "He will arrival," "I actioned."

Such traditional definitions as are not notional are relational, and these lead to another difficulty, that of mixing hierarchies in the analysis. *Adjective* and *adverb,* for example, are defined relationally, in terms of what is modified: an adjective is a word that modifies a noun. This leads us to conclude that "dirty sink" and "kitchen sink" are identical structures, each consisting of a noun modified by an adjective. But our intuition tells us that they are in some way different, that *dirty* is somehow a different kind of word from *kitchen*. If we were given a third structure, say "empty sink," we would I suppose not hesitate to say it is more like "dirty sink" than like kitchen sink." The traditional definition of adjective—anything that modifies a noun—simply buries and conceals a large and important part of English expression, throwing together such quite different structures as "our sink," "dirty sink," "kitchen sink," "leaking sink," "scrubbing sink," "repaired sink," "sink upstairs." All are different, and the difference is that in each case the modifying word belongs to a different class or subclass. I am aware that traditional grammarians can perceive and express such differences, using such terms as "limiting adjective," "descriptive adjective," "participle," "gerund," but they can do so only clumsily and with clear contradiction of earlier statements.

The basic fallacy here is a mixing of levels of description. English structures can be analyzed on the word-class level into such categories as *noun, verb, adjective*. They can also be analyzed on a relation level into such categories as *modifier* of *a noun, modifier* of *a verb, subject, object*. Both classifications are logical and both are necessary to a description of English syntax. But to mix them is like sorting the students of a college into the categories *men, women,* and *commuters*. To ask, in the traditional framework, whether *kitchen* in "kitchen sink" is a noun or an adjective is like asking whether John Jones is a man or a commuter.

To point out the weakness of traditional definitions is to invite the question—with what do you propose to replace them? The answer to this is—nothing. We must, I think, give up hope of finding definitions for such concepts as *noun, adjective, subject, sentence* which are both short and operable, which can actually be used to sort out the members of the categories. It is not hard to frame rational definitions for these concepts. A modern dictionary, for example, will give for *sentence* some such definition as this: "A structure in a language which is not shown by some grammatical feature to be a part of a larger structure." But this of course is not applicable as a criterion until we outline the grammatical features which do or do not make a structure part of another structure. To make the definition operable, we should have to describe such features as subject and predicate, modification, subordination, conjunction, transformation. In other words, we cannot really define the concept "sentence in English" short of describing English grammar.

Linguists have not, I fear, always been clear on this point. We have sometimes talked as if we had, or were on the point of getting, short and usable tests for determining whether items belong to one category or another. Thus we say "a noun is a word that can fill the blank in 'The ——————— was interesting.'" Or "a noun is a word that forms a plural." But as definitions such statements fail in both directions. It is true that any item, any noise, that occurs in the blank in "The ——————— was interesting" will be construed as a noun. But there may be nouns that do not occur there (some things may not be interesting) and there are many other positions in which nouns occur.

Definitions based on morphology—inflectional endings and the like—seem to me to lead to error. If *noun* is defined as "any word that forms a plural," then *chaos* cannot count as a noun. This would appear to go contrary to our intuition as speakers of English. Adjectives have sometimes been defined as words that add the endings /-er/ and /-est/, as *small, smaller, smallest*. This also fails in both directions. It has been pointed out that if we were to apply it literally we would have to take *tear* as an adjective: *tear, terror, terraced*. Even worse, it requires us to put *beautiful, courageous, hopeful,* in a different class from *pretty, old, sad,* which, again, is contrary to our intuition.

What is true, it seems to me, is that in a real language it is only rarely that word classes or other structures are signaled by some simple and unique signal. If we were making up a language, creating an artificial language, we might wish to order things differently. We might, for example, make a rule that all nouns end in -*a* and that no other words end in this sound. Then we could always tell by the occurrence or nonoccurrence of -*a* whether a word was a noun or not.

But no real language has such a simple structure. In English, we must always know whether a word is a noun or not; otherwise we shall not be able to understand the sentence. But the signals which sort out nouns from the other classes with which they might be confused—verbs and adjectives, particularly—are multiple. The signal might be an inflectional ending, like the plural or the possessive; it might be a derivational ending, like -*ness or -ation;* it might be position; it might be the fact that our only previous experience with the word is in noun uses, so that we take it as a noun even when it occurs in a position in which other classes occur. Thus *Jones* in "It was Jones" is clearly a noun. But *Green* in "It was Green" could be taken, in speech, as an adjective. For any particular unambiguous sentence we could specify exactly how we know that a word is a noun and not an adjective or a verb, but there is no short and simple way of saying how we know in all sentences.

Similar remarks can be made about the concept *sentence*. One can imagine an artificial language in which sentences are marked in a simple way. Suppose that we had the custom, in English, of beginning every sentence with the expression *eek* and concluding it with the expression *awk*: "Eek, I ran into Sam Jones today, awk. Eek, he's been visiting his mother in Plainsville, awk. Eek, that's not far from Toledo, awk." Then we could easily define *sentence*: a structure that begins with *eek* and ends with *awk*. Students would memorize this definition at the age of six and never thereafter write comma faults or fragments.

Unfortunately, no real language has a simple and unique signal marking the sentence unit, either in the intonation or in the segmental structure. There is such a thing as "sentence in English," but it is marked as such in multiple fashion. "I have some" is a sentence; "if I have some" is not; "I have some--" (with the pitch staying level) is not; "I have some money" is; "Have some" is; "Is home" is not. There is simply no way of comprehending the concept "sentence in English" short of learning English grammar, either unconsciously as a child learns it, or through explicit instruction. Certainly nobody learns or teaches through steady repetition of the incantation "a sentence is a group of words expressing a complete thought."

Traditional teachers do teach the concept "sentence in English," as they teach such other concepts as *noun, verb, adjective, subject.* Some of their students at least, come to recognize these structures and to be able to identify them in a more or less uniform way. A linguist should recognize this success. But he must point out that it is achieved not because of the definitional apparatus but in spite of it. The traditional teacher has the students learn the definitions, but must then take care that they never apply them. The learning comes not from definition and discussion of the concepts but from illustration, correction of mistakes, and the like. The whole burden of generalization is placed on the student, who must work through the examples to an understanding of what the teacher means when he says "a sentence is a group of words expressing a complete thought," "a verb is a word that expresses action, being, or state of being."

People nowadays frequently make remarks like "Linguistics may be all right but we had better not give up traditional grammar until we are provided with something to take its place." This is reasonable enough, unless by "something" is meant something similar, a comparable battery of short definitions. But neither linguistics nor anything else can ever provide such an apparatus. The classes English noun and English sentence are exactly as complicated as they are, and linguistics has no way of making them simpler. What linguistics does suggest is that the complexities be directly faced, not obscured in a fallacious philosophy. What a grammarian is— or ought to be—interested in is not meaning directly but the structure through which meaning is expressed, the mechanism by which meanings are distinguished. Every teacher of grammar must deal with structure, and is therefore in some sense a structural linguist. But it is clear that the study could proceed much more efficiently, and infinitely more interestingly, if we could get through the philosophical fog and focus on the actual signals of the language.

The debate about correctness has been with us much longer than the debate about structure, but it seems no nearer conclusion. The difficulty seems to be at least partly a matter of misunderstanding, for which linguists are no doubt at least partly to blame. For one thing, linguists use the terms "correct" and "incorrect," but their usage departs considerably from the common one. By "incorrect English" a linguist is likely to mean such a mistake as might be made by a foreigner or a child learning the language. Thus both "I it bought" and "I buyed it" are incorrect sentences. But a linguist, as a linguist, would not say that "I done it" or "I brung it" are incorrect sentences. They are correct in relation to the dialects in which they occur, and the question of whether the dialects are admired in the nation as a whole is a sociological, not a linguistic, question.

Linguistics simply has to work in this way or it cannot operate as a science. To ask it to condemn "I done it" is like asking botany to condemn weeds. This is not to say that schools should not correct students who say "I done it." Those who go into college or into business saying "I done it" are clearly headed for difficulties which ought to be pointed out to them. There is a correlation, though not a perfect one, between the achievement of material success and the avoidance of expressions like "I done it," and therefore there is a strogne sense in which "I done it" is incorrect. But the reason is purely sociological. The best people—so defined by wealth or education or some other criterion—don't say it, and that is all there is to it.

What more might be supposed to be to it, I simply can't figure out. We are not concerned here with "good" and "bad" sentences. If we are talking about good and bad, we can bring in such criteria as clarity, grace, euphony, economy, discrimination. But if we are talking about correctness, there is simply no criterion but somebody's usage. If a student asks me whether an expression is correct or not, I have no resource but to reflect on whether I use it or whether I hear it in the conversation of my friends, a small but select group of professors of English. If my answer does not satisfy, and it often does not, I am quite at a loss. There is no other principle I can invoke. Certainly not an historical one—I cannot suppose it proper that everyone speak Elizabethan English. Not an analogical one— if I insist on *bring/ brought* on the analogy of *think/thought,* I should also, I suppose, have to campaign for *cling/clought* and *sting/stought.* So I answer according to the only principle I know—the usage of the best people, i.e., my friends and me. If the student persists—"I don't care what you and your friends say; what I want to know is which is *correct"*—I can only suppose him to be asking what God says.

If we knew what kind of English God speaks, we would have no problem, but we don't, and so we are reduced to figuring out who the best people are and reporting their English and persuading our students to emulate it. This is difficult, and perhaps linguistics will again be accused of destruction without replacement. But how is it a loss to be without what one never had? There has never been any criterion of correctness but somebody's usage. Linguistics does not create this complication; it merely points it out. Surely the first step in solving a problem is to discover the nature of the problem.

The problem is no doubt more complicated in the United States than it is —or at least than it has been—in England and on the continent of Europe. In countries with an aristocracy, it is relatively simple to define correct language: it is the language of the aristocracy, which is partly synonymous with the educated class. But in the United States, which has no visible aristocracy and where the tides of anti-intellectualism sometimes run strong, the situation is quite different. To decide what correct English is, we must in some sense decide who the best people are. I think this is what makes the subject explosive. Professors of English probably sometimes feel that linguists are somehow traitors to their class, pandering to the masses. I should like to point out that such a position is no necessary consequence of linguistics. It is possible to be both a linguist and (in some sense) a purist. I myself am in no doubt about who the best people are. They are the intellectuals, like Jacques Barzun and my friends and me.

It should be noticed that the problem of correctness becomes much simpler when we are careful to discriminate between speech and writing. Usage governs both, but in quite different ways. We must be forever in disagreement among ourselves and with our fellow citizens on what is correct in speech. It depends on who and what and where we are and on who and what and where we want to be. But in writing, and particularly in certain aspects of writing, we can achieve very considerable agreement. Nowhere are items more clearly right or wrong than in spelling. With a very few exceptions, all English words are correctly spelled in only one way. Like correctness in pronunciation, correctness in English spelling has no logical basis, but unlike pronunciation, spelling is uniform, and the agreed on system is knowable. The same is true, though to a lesser extent, of punctuation, word forms, sentence structures that occur in writing.

Yet in writing as in speech it is usage that controls, the difference being that in writing it is the usage of a relatively small and easily discernible group—the publishing industry largely—that matters. The question "Is this correct written English" can be more specifically phrased: "Would a copy editor pass this?" "Does this accord with the style books of the publishing houses?" One cannot change speech or retard its development by taking thought about it. It is doubtful that all the not inconsiderable efforts of mass education have had very much effect on the speech of the population as a whole. But the writing system is very largely controllable. It changes, but it changes very slowly, compared to speech. If we wanted to change it radically—e.g., if we wanted to reform our spelling—we could do that.

The last of the three questions posed was, what exactly is the application of linguistics, supposing its views to prevail, to the teaching of English? First of all, it must be said that this is a question that no linguist, as a linguist, can answer, just as no mathematician, as a mathematician, can say what the applications of mathematics should be. The application is a question for the teacher of English, and I speak from here on as a teacher of English and not as a linguist.

I think that the effect of linguistics on the teaching of English may be profound but that it will not be the sort of effect commonly expected. There seems to be a widespread hope that the teaching of grammar according to linguistic principles will lead directly to a great improvement in writing, a falling off in comma faults, fragments, dangling modifiers, and such errors. I think that linguistics might make some contribution in this direction, but I doubt that it will be substantial. Certainly I know of no way in which punctuation can be taught or in which "sentence sense" can be communicated to those who haven't got it, except through some kind of teaching of the grammar; and it is reasonable to suppose that a good grammar will serve better here than a confusing one. But we must ask more fundamental questions. How much does the classroom teaching of any grammar contribute to improvement of writing? More generally, what are the processes through which people learn to write?

These questions must here be answered impressionistically, since the subject, oddly, has been very little studied. It is curious that it has not been, for the problem, though extremely complex, does not seem to be beyond the reach of ingenuity plus foundation money. It is nevertheless true that for the teaching of literacy we have built an elaborate and expensive educational system without really knowing whether it does much good or not. It is certainly true that millions of people in every generation learn to write passably well. What we do not know is whether this success is achieved because of English classes or in spite of them or irrelevantly to them.

One thing that is perfectly clear is that only in the first years of school can we see the teacher making obvious and consistent progress. We must all envy the first-grade teacher. She takes children who cannot shape the letters and shows them how. She receives in September youngsters who are largely illiterate and dismisses them largely literate in June. In the second, third, and fourth grade, similar progress is made, and we can see a clear connection between the instruction and the improvement.

In later grades, in high school, and in college, the connection is much harder to make out. The students— or some of them—continue to improve, but we don't really know whether to ascribe their improvement to reading habits, to correction, to practice in writing, to imitation of favorite authors, to interest, to growing older—or, perhaps, to instruction in grammar and the principles of composition. I myself am inclined to doubt that there is much connection between being able to analyze a sentence and being able to write one. I am a grammarian and I suppose more conscious of sentence structures than most people; yet when I write, I very rarely choose structures deliberately, very rarely say to myself, "I think a subordinate clause might serve my turn here rather better than a participial phrase," I do consider structure in punctuating. Probably punctuation can be taught only through some reference to structure, but there is a question to what extent it can be taught at all to those who are unable to learn it in some other way— e.g., through reading.

What has been said about grammar goes more than triply for rhetoric. Grammar is hard to teach and hard to learn because the sentence is so very complex; yet it is absurdly simple compared to the paragraph. When we say that a paragraph ought to be unified and coherent and meaty, we have said about all there is to say. The means of achieving unity, coherence, and meatiness are infinite beyond description. It seems to me perfectly obvious that nobody ever pauses in the heat of writing to think about Topic Sentences or Methods of Paragraph Development. Nobody, unless he is doing an exercise for a composition class, ever asks himself, "Now what would be a good topic sentence for this one?" or ever reflects, "I organized the last paragraph inductively, so I think I had better try a comparison-and-contrast this time." I would not say that exercises in these matters are useless. Probably they are effective now and then in impressing on the students the need for order and logic. But I think that their effectiveness is limited and that returns diminish rather soon. It does not seem reasonable to spend a large part of each year, from the seventh grade through the first year of college, pondering the mysteries of the topic sentence, methods of paragraph development, and figurative language.

The dilemma that faces us as English teachers is that a great many students write quite badly and that the populace has the feeling that there is something we can do about it. We are to some extent to blame for the difficulty. In assuming responsibility for the improvement of writing, we have implied that we can improve it. And of course we can improve it, and we do, but only within rather severe limits. Given the situation—the necessity of educating all the children, dull as well as bright—given a nation not especially oriented toward reading and writing, not especially fond of intellectuals or intellect—given television and the other diversions that compete so successfully with the book—given a school system in which writing is done almost entirely in English classes and in which other teachers criticize English teachers because students mispell words on their objective tests—given these circumstances, we must realize, and make other people realize, that there is a point beyond which we cannot improve writing, no matter how many papers we assign, or how thoroughly we correct them, no matter how small our classes, no matter how powerful our methods.

I think that the only salvation for teachers of freshman English or of high school English is to find a subject matter, and I think that the great contribution of linguistics is that it provides one. It give us something that is teachable, interesting, and pertinent, and this is what most distinguishes it from traditional grammar. The chief trouble with classes in English composition (insofar as that means classes in rhetoric and traditional grammar) is that for interest they must depend entirely on the personality of the teacher; the subject contributes nothing. The traditional point of view is that grammar is useful but dull, and virtually no one has ever pretended to discern intrinsic interest in the topic sentence. The linguist has an entirely different notion. He is not at all certain that his grammar is useful, but he is dead sure that it is interesting, and he doesn't have much trouble in persuading students to the same opinion. There is nothing closer to us than our native language, nothing more important to us, more a part of us, and I see no reason why it is illegitimate to devote school time to studying it, objectively and dispassionately, and for its own sake.

I am well aware that such remarks as these are not likely to find favor with school boards or PTA's or with high school or college administrators. The layman is alarmed by the truly alarming illiteracy in the land, and he responds by wanting to put in more anti-illiteracy courses, by redoubling the effort in the teaching of writing. But this is a naive view, stemming from a misunderstanding of the problem. We might, by doubling the effort, get some improvement in writing, say five or ten percent. But it would be expensive. The most practical way of redoubling the effort would be to cut in half the student-teacher ratio, but this would cost millions of dollars annually in a large school system, hundreds of thousands in a large university. It is doubtful that many laymen are as alarmed about illiteracy as all that.

In suggesting that English classes shift their emphasis from composition to subject matter—and particularly to language and literature— I am not suggesting that they suspend their efforts to improve writing. I would have students in English classes write just as much as they do now, and I would have their papers as rigorously corrected. But I would have them write mostly on topics in the field of English—that is, on English literature and the English language. And I would hope that instructors in other departments would be giving similar care to writing in their fields. If a teacher in history or health education complained to me, "My students can't write," I should reply sympathetically, "I'm having trouble with mine too. What are you doing about yours?"

48

Generative Grammar: Toward Unification and Simplification

Owen Thomas

THE GRAMMATICAL theories of Noam Chomsky, Morris Halle, and their followers are widely discussed but only rarely, if at all, are they applied to the teaching of English grammar in secondary schools. The reasons for this lack of application are many, varied, and complex, and even the primary reasons make an almost overwhelming list:

Reprinted by permission from *The English Journal,* 51.94–99 (February, 1962). The author is a member of the Department of English at Indiana University.

1. Chomsky, the generally acknowledged leader of the group, published the original statement of the theory less than ten years ago and, consequently, the development of the theory is still in its early stages.

2. The explications of his theory have been directed more toward linguists, psychologists, and mathematicians than toward teachers of English grammar.[1]

3. The criticisms of his theory by other linguists have generated more heat than light, and most secondary school teachers—who, after all, neither are nor need be linguists—have prudently rejected the opportunity to be burned.

4. The secondary school teacher, even if he should be curious, has no effective way of satisfying his curiosity since, almost without exception (according to the two-score catalogues I checked), departments of English offer no courses in comparative grammar.

Unfortunately, these reasons (and I have idealistically ignored the inertia of school boards and the conservatism of traditionally trained parents) have caused many teachers of English to assume that generative grammar—though perhaps "correct" in some mathematical sense—is pedagogically unadaptable to the needs of a secondary school curriculum.[2] Such an assumption, I feel, is false.

This personal feeling is based largely upon the response to a course, "English Grammar for Teachers," that I conducted in the summer of 1961 at Indiana University. The thirty students in the class were of widely varying backgrounds and experience. Some had just completed their second year of college work; others had been teaching for more than twenty years. All of them, however, although they didn't know it until the end of the eight-week session, were subjects in an experiment that the liberal administration of Indiana University permitted me to conduct. Briefly, and this is something of an over-simplification, we hoped to answer one question: what do secondary school teachers—not professional linguists—think of generative grammar?

The answer proved the validity of the question. Without exception, the students were convinced that certain deductions from the theories of Chomsky could be applied systematically to the teaching of grammar, not only in the secondary school but with equal effectiveness in the elementary school.

[1] Chomsky's pertinent publications include the following: "Systems of Syntactic Analysis," *J. of Symbolic Logic* (18.242-56, 1953); *Transformational Analysis*, Ph.D. Dissertation, U. of Penna. (1955); "Three Models for the Description of Language," *I.R.E. Transactions on Information Theory*, v. IT-2 (Sept., 1956); *Syntactic Structures* ('S-Gravenhage, 1957); and a review of B. F. Skinner, *Verbal Behavior*, in *Language* (35.26-58, 1959).

[2] The terms "transformational grammar" and "generative grammar" are sometimes used interchangeably. The latter term, however, seems to be supplanting the former. This trend was particularly noticeable at the recent (summer 1961) meeting of the Commission on English which debated some of the questions considered in this article.

Because of the unanimity of class opinion, it seems worthwhile to examine the structure of the course. Purposely, no text was assigned for general use during the first four weeks. Purposely also, the initial lectures were devoted to the history of the language and to the development of grammatical studies during the eighteenth and nineteenth centuries. The course, in short, was made to appear as non-controversial as possible. As a supplement to the lectures, the students were given daily assignments: "memorize the eight parts of speech, the four kinds of sentences, the six kinds of pronouns, and the four kinds of adjectives; diagram ten sentences; conjugate three verbs." Every Friday was given over to an informal clinic where we discussed the work of the preceding week. For the students, the initial clinic was a nearly shattering experience. Controversy forced its way into the syllabus.

TRADITIONAL GRAMMAR EXAMINED

Since no single text was assigned, the students had necessarily sought their definitions and diagraming rules in different books; without exception, these books were "traditional." The marked lack of agreement among these books (many of which were texts currently being used in various school systems) was surprising and, for most students, disconcerting. Some texts defined eight parts of speech; others admitted only seven (dismissing or ignoring the interjection). Some presented purely semantic definitions ("A noun is the name of a person, place, or thing"); others made a half-hearted blow toward structural definitions ("A noun is a word that names something"); and still others tried to combine the two types ("A noun is a word used to name a person, place, or thing"). Some listed four kinds of pronouns; others, six; and one, bravely, twelve. Some diagraming rules (which a few texts quietly ignored) called for left-slanting lines, some for right-slanting lines, some for perpendicular lines, and some for dashed lines. The students soon concluded that the traditionalists were not united, even on basic definitions, that—in fact—there was no single traditional grammar.

The second two weeks of the course were spent in determining why this lack of agreement existed. The lectures continued to be historical, although somewhat more controversial, and emphasized the contributions of Otto Jespersen, Holger Pedersen, Edward Sapir, and Leonard Bloomfield.[3] Meanwhile, the students were consulting the initial chapters (those generally devoted to debunking the traditionalists) in works by structural lin-

[3] Jespersen, *Language: Its Nature, Development and Origin* (1923); Pedersen, *Linguistic Science in the Nineteenth Century* (trans. by Spargo, 1931); Sapir, *Language* (1921); Bloomfield, *Language* (1933). For an introductory discussion on the contributions of these authors, see C. C. Fries, "Advances in Linguistics," *College English,* vol. 23, no. 1 (Oct., 1961). pp. 30-37. [ED. NOTE. See pp. 36–45 in this edition of *Readings*.]

guists such as Charles C. Fries, James Sledd, and Harold Whitehall.[4] These analyses, particularly Sledd's concise discussion, convinced the students that the inconsistencies of traditional grammar were fundamental. But curiously, the Friday clinic revealed that their initial dissatisfaction with the traditionalists was somewhat tempered, and they agreed (with Sledd) that traditional grammar—although Latinate and essentially inadequate to describe English—provides at least a useful terminology.

Probably the most important conclusion reached by the class during this period was that "form underlies meaning."[5]

At this point, and building on this axiom, we began a detailed study of Fries's method, which we supplemented from time to time with definitions taken from Sledd. The class was eager and excited; they expected to find, as they later revealed, a simple, self-consistent system to replace traditional grammar. They had no difficulty in accepting the essentials of Sledd's definitions since they were not aware that "mixing levels" is supposedly the unpardonable sin among structuralists. (They balked slightly, however, when Sledd introduced pitch and stress levels into some of his definitions.) They admitted, in theory, that Fries was right in emphasizing patterns and functions, but they rebelled, in fact, when we came to a sentence analysis such as the following:[6]

$$D \quad 3 \quad 3 \quad 1^a \quad f \quad D \quad 1^b \quad 4 \quad 2 \quad D \quad 3 \quad 1^c \quad f \quad D \quad 1^d \quad f \quad 2 \quad f \quad 1^e$$
$$- \; F \qquad - \qquad - \qquad\qquad - \; F \; + \; J \; + \; F-$$
$$\text{it} \qquad\qquad \text{it} \qquad\qquad \text{it} \qquad\quad \text{he he} \qquad \text{it}$$

As one student said at a Friday clinic, "The high school pupil who understands *that* doesn't have to study grammar." They felt, in brief, that the cure was worse than the disease.

Thus halfway through the course, the students were wandering through two worlds, "powerless to be born." While in this uncomfortable state, they investigated—during the third two-weeks—the pertinent literature in *College English, Educational Forum,* the *English Journal,* and the *NEA Journal.* They found the attacks, counter-attacks, and counter-counter-attacks of the traditionalists and the structuralists. (They found very little on Chomsky.) These investigations convinced them that they were not alone

---

[4] Fries, *Structure of English* (1952); Sledd, *A Short Introduction to English Grammar* (1959); Whitehall, *Structural Essentials of English* (1951).

[5] This is one of the major points of disagreement between the structuralists and the traditionalists and probably stems (as Fries notes in *The Structure of English,* p. 7) from Jespersen: "But in syntax meaning is everything." Curiously, no traditionalist has noted that William Cobbett—as staunch a traditionalist as ever conjugated a verb—anticipated the structuralists in "Letter XII" of his *Grammar of the English Language* (originally published in 1818 and reprinted by Ward, Lock, & Bowden, Limited, London, n.d.) when he said: "the sense in which a word is used . . . determines what is the part of speech to which it belongs."

[6] Fries, *Structure of English,* p. 268.

in their confusion and that the structuralists were as divided as the traditionalists, perhaps even more so.

At this point, then, most of the class felt that they could not conscientiously teach traditional grammar: the inconsistencies were too widespread and too basic. But they also felt that structural grammar—even assuming that the disagreements could be resolved—was far too complex to be readily adapted to the needs of secondary school pupils. Furthermore, they were antagonistic toward the emphasis by the structuralists on stress, pitch, and juncture, particularly as incorporated in "immediate constituent analysis" which splits the sentence, as one student said, "into a hodge of podges." They were, in short, ready for any theory that would justify traditional grammar or simplify structural grammar, particularly (in the latter case) if the theory redirected the emphasis toward the sentence as the most significant part of grammar.

With this attitude, they began their study of generative grammar, using the same text for the first time in the course: Chomsky's *Syntactic Structures*. Within one week they were agreed that his theory provided the necessary simplification of structural grammar (or rather, that his theory was simpler to understand than that of the structuralists) and that the resultant grammar could be adapted readily to the needs of secondary school students. During the final week of the course, the class experimented—both in and out of class—with applications of Chomsky's theory.

What, then, is the theory? And how can his theory be applied to the teaching of grammar? Before answering these questions, we must consider his definition of grammar: a grammar is a device for generating the sentences of a language. Thus (to belabor the point), if a student understands the grammar of a language, he can construct grammatically correct sentences in that language. No grammar, however, can tell a student which of two grammatically correct sentences is *stylistically* better. Such judgments are outside the realm of grammar; they are solely matters of taste and must be taught accordingly.

"KERNEL" SENTENCES

After having defined the limits of his theory, Chomsky introduces a basic concept: that of a group of "kernel" sentences. A kernel sentence is "simple, active, declarative," and Chomsky feels that "all other sentences" are derived from kernel sentences by means of "transformations." Roughly, a "transformation" is a rule that either introduces new elements into kernel sentences (e.g., adjectives, negatives), or rearranges the elements of a kernel sentence (e.g., to produce an interrogative sentence), or both (e.g., to produce a passive sentence). Chomsky implies, therefore, that passive, interrogative, and negative sentences, and sentences containing, for example, adjectives, adverbs, and conjunctions, are all more complex or "sophisticated" than kernel sentences.

Not surprisingly, Chomsky's "kernel sentence" bears a strong resemblance to the simple "subject-verb-complement" sentence of traditional grammar. He states that a kernel sentence is composed of a "noun phrase plus a verb phrase." A "noun phrase" (symbol: NP) consists simply of an article (T) plus a noun (N), and the presence of the article is optional.[7] A "verb phrase" (VP) consists of an auxiliary (Aux) plus a main verb (V) plus a noun phrase (and this last "noun phrase" is, of course, similar to the traditional "complement"); the noun phrase contained within the verb phrase is also optional. This may seem confusing at first reading, but the symbolic representation is straightforward and easy to understand:[8]

Sentence → NP + VP (where the arrow means "rewrite," i.e.,
$\qquad$ "rewrite Sentence as NP plus VP")
NP → T + N
VP → Aux + V + NP

Thus, the following are "noun phrases":

John, the boy, a dog, the men

And the following are "verb phrases":

reads, eats the apple, may bury a bone, have bought the farm

Therefore, the following are "kernel sentences":

John reads.
The boy eats the apple.
A dog may bury a bone.
The men have bought the farm.

Chomsky thus simplifies the descriptions of English (such as that from Fries, quoted above) by limiting these descriptions to a relatively small number of simple sentences. All other sentences are "generated from' (i.e., built upon) these kernel sentences by applying certain constant and *invariable* transformations, and the constancy of the transformation is, for most teachers of English, a major feature of Chomsky's theory.

Thus, given a kernel sentence (e.g., "The men have bought the farm"), we may generate a passive sentence ("The farm has been bought by the men'), a negative sentence ("The men haven't bought the farm"), a "yes-or-no" interrogative sentence ("Have the men bought the farm?"), two

---

[7] More properly, I feel, the "article" should be called a "determiner" according to a definition such as that of Sledd in *A Short Introduction to English Grammar*, p. 207.

[8] This is the simplest possible presentation. Copyright laws being what they are, we cannot duplicate the presentation, and it must suffice to say that those rules, for example, pertaining to "noun phrase singular" (NP^s) are equally explicit, self-consistent, and easy to understand.

"wh?" interrogative sentences ("What have the men bought?" and "Who has bought the farm?"), and even combinations of these sentences (e.g., a negative-passive: "The farm hasn't been bought by the men"). Furthermore, with still other transformations we may introduce adverbs, adjectives, and prepositional phrases into any or all of these sentences ("Who has finally bought the old farm on the hill?").[9]

These transformations, it is worth repeating, are invariable. Given a kernel sentence of a particular form (and Chomsky defines the required form precisely), then any and all related non-kernel sentences can be generated by applying the appropriate (and quite simple) transformation. One specific example will serve to illustrate these remarks. The "passive transformation" may be given in the following form:

To derive a passive sentence, we first need a kernel "string," containing the following elements: a noun phrase (NP), an auxiliary (Aux), a verb (V), and a second noun phrase (NP). These might be represented as follows:

$$[NP_1] + [Aux] + [V] + [NP_2]$$

To transform this string into a "passive string," the four basic elements are rearranged and three other elements are (invariably) added, as follows:

$$[NP_2] + [Aux] + be + en + [V] + by + [NP_1]$$

(The "en" which is added is the so-called "past participle morpheme.")

Finally, the resultant string is converted into an English sentence by inserting appropriate parts of speech into the string.

Thus, given the kernel sentence:

$$[The\ man] + [has] + [eaten] + [the\ apple]$$

we may apply the transformation to produce:

$$[The\ apple] + [has] + be + en + [eaten] + by + [the\ man]$$

This, of course, reduces to: "The apple has been eaten by the man."[10]

Such is the nature of Chomsky's major contribution toward the simplification of grammar. In addition, he makes another, quite important contribu-

---

[9] There is quite obviously a relationship between Chomsky's kernel sentences and simple traditional diagraming, and even between those transformations which add adjectives and phrases to the kernel and those diagrams which indicate the subordinate position of adjectives and phrases. Transformations, however, indicate the exact nature of subordination; more importantly, they indicate the exact nature of the relationship between a kernel sentence and the associated passive, negative, and interrogative sentences.

[10] For purposes of illustration, the transformation, as given, is somewhat simplified as the reader may see for himself by substituting, for example, a plural subject or object into the kernel. Such refinements, however, are easily and systematically handled through certain so-called "obligatory" transformations. The principle, at any rate, is invariable.

tion: he divides all of grammar into three parts. The first part presents those rules that pertain to kernel sentences ("phrase structure"), and here his theory will certainly draw upon the work of the structuralists. The second part presents rules that generate non-kernel sentences ("transformational structure"). And the third part presents the rules that are necessary to account for such irregular forms as "child, children" and "buy, bought" ("morphological structure"), and this part of his theory will probably draw upon the work of the historical grammarians (e.g., Jespersen).

The theory, then, is not too difficult for an adult to understand. And most persons acquainted with Chomsky's work, including the members of my class, feel that his theories provide the only logical explanation currently available for the intuitive sense which most native speakers have of a relationship between active and passive, or positive and negative, or declarative and interrogative sentences. But we may legitimately ask whether transformations can be taught to secondary school pupils. This is essentially the same question we asked above: "How can Chomsky's theory be applied to the teaching of grammar?" To answer this question completely would be to write a text, or at least a syllabus, for a course on methods of teaching grammar. Obviously, nothing of that sort is being attempted here. But during the final meetings of my class, we reached agreement on a number of points that will probably be included in any text that is written.

APPLICATION TO SENTENCE STRUCTURE

We agreed, for example, that the study of grammar has one primary function: to enable a student to construct grammatically correct sentences. The most significant advance that an understanding of Chomsky's theory permits is the organization of this study according to increasing ("graduated") levels of sophistication in sentence construction. Thus, we should first teach the use of the kernel sentence (terminology is unimportant and should be subordinate to an understanding of the kernel form, i.e., to an understanding of a sentence that is "simple, declarative, active, with no complex verb or noun phrases"). The following sentences are typical kernel sentences:

1. The boy hit the ball.
2. The girl bought the dress.
3. The teacher ate the apple.
4. John loves Mary.

Conversely, the following sentences are *not* kernel sentences:

5. The ball was hit by the boy.
6. The girl didn't buy the dress.
7. Did the teacher eat an apple?
8. Who loves Mary?

Secondary school pupils, the class agreed, could construct kernel sentences of their own. Next they could be taught to construct passive sentences from their kernels; then, negative sentences, "yes-or-no" interrogative sentence, and "wh-" interrogative sentences. At each step, the teacher can point out the recurring elements of the resultant sentences (i.e., the underlying form). The repetition would familiarize the student—unconsciously, perhaps, but nonetheless effectively—with the basic form, and the ordering of the exercises—in gradually increasing levels of complexity—would enable the student to build his confidence systematically.

Students may then combine their sentences, for example the passive and the negative (and the teacher may note that the passive is formed before the negative is added). After (and sometimes during) exercises of this type, the teacher may introduce adjectives, adverbs, and prepositional phrases, noting that any of these may appear in any sentence form.[11]

Of course, in any presentation, certain definitions are required, but the definitions should be introduced only when they are necessary, that is, only when a student needs a "label" to discuss the elements he is, in fact, using. Thus, "noun" and "verb" should be defined when the students are being taught the form of the kernel sentence. (I feel Sledd's definitions are quite appropriate.) In this way, those parts of speech that are simplest to define (and for the student to understand) are taught first, and the hard-to-define (and to understand) parts of speech, such as the "preposition" and the "conjunction," are postponed until the student has developed familiarity and confidence with the simpler and more important forms.

There are still other benefits to be derived from an understanding of Chomsky's theories. Transformations *per se,* as we have noted, probably cannot be taught to pre-college students; but from *any* transformation a teacher can deduce several invariable rules. For example, from the passive transformation we can deduce such rules as the following (and the list is by no means exhaustive):

1. There can be no passive voice unless a kernel sentence contains a subject and its object.
2. There can be no passive voice without an auxiliary verb or verbs. (If there is only one auxiliary, it must be a form of *to be.*)
3. The subject of the kernel sentence invariably follows the verb in the related passive sentence and is invariably introduced with the word "by."
4. The main verb in a passive sentence is invariably in the past participial form.

Similar rules, it is worth repeating, can be derived from any transformation, and the form of the transformation guarantees that there are no exceptions to these rules.

In brief, then, Chomsky's theories are not difficult to understand. They

---

[11] A method such as that advocated by D. M. Wolfe ("Grammatical Autobiography," *English Journal,* XLIX, 1 (January 1960), pp. 16-21) would be quite suitable for this kind of study.

are, in fact, a means of systematizing the almost countless "rules" of both traditional and structural grammarians. And most importantly, an understanding of Chomsky's theories permits a teacher to select and arrange grammatical elements in the most logical order and to build effectively upon preceding material. As teachers, we can hardly ask more of any theory.

49

Syntactic Strictures

JAMES SLEDD

I

IN 1954, Professor Paul Roberts published *Understanding Grammar,* in which he tried to clarify the basic assumptions of the schoolroom tradition and "to explain the conventional grammatical terminology." He did not then attempt a marriage of the "modern science" of language and the "old tradition," and two of the three grammarians to whom he acknowledged a special debt were Curme and Jespersen, whose great scholarly books are so different from the usual work of structural linguists that today they too are sometimes called "traditional" and thus wrongly classified with the common textbooks of the schools.

By 1956, Professor Roberts had "turned entirely away from the tradition." In that year he published *Patterns of English,* which he described as "the first serious effort" to provide the secondary schools with "a method of teaching the English language according to the principles of linguistic science." His principal sources were two incomplete but apparently complementary American structural grammars: Fries's *Structure of English,* for the syntax, and the Trager-Smith *Outline of English Structure,* for the phonology. In *Understanding English,* a textbook for college freshmen which appeared in 1958, Roberts included a wider range of rather miscellaneous material for the composition course but did not materially alter the structural analysis of the language which he had offered in *Patterns.*

The first weeks of 1962 have seen the appearance of still a fourth book

Reprinted, by permission of the New England Association of Teachers of English, from *The English Leaflet,* 61.14–23, 54 (Midwinter, 1961). The author is Professor of English at Northwestern University.

by the man who at the least might claim to be the best popularizer of American linguistics. In 1956, Roberts could comfortably assert "that where all the experts agree, one has no recourse but to agree with the experts." Not all the experts did agree, to be sure; but one could say they did without obvious absurdity. It would be riskier to say so now. Already in 1957, Professor Noam Chomsky of M. I. T. published his *Syntactic Structures* as "part of an attempt to construct a formalized general theory of linguistic structure" and to apply that theory in the description of a number of languages, including English; and further publications by Chomsky and his colleagues and followers have since totally destroyed the possibility of complacent acceptance of unmodified American structuralism. Again Roberts has changed his position, not at all discreditably, with the changing times. His latest book, *English Sentences,* introduces high school teachers and their students to some parts of Chomsky's theory of transformational or generative grammar and to a partial grammar of English based partially on that theory. The book differs in a number of ways from Roberts' earlier publications.

In Roberts' opinion, however, the nature and extent of those differences and of the underlying differences between structural linguists like Fries on the one hand and transformationalists like Chomsky on the other do not create a radical discontinuity between *English Sentences* and *Patterns of English*. Roberts thinks instead Chomsky's work "goes a long way toward reconciling highly divergent views about English teaching—the linguistic and the traditional," that Fries's *Structure of English* was "really in large measure a transformational grammar," and that therefore *English Sentences* "contradicts very little of what is said" in *Patterns* but will "seem much more familiar than that book did to teachers and students. . . ." In this view, *English Sentences* is a happy synthesis of elements from the three or four grammatical traditions which have shaped Roberts' work and is therefore an excellent choice to follow *Patterns of English* as the second book in a program of English grammar for high school students. Some well-known linguists and teachers have already proposed such a combination.

As a pedagogue on the fringes of linguistics, I should like to question that proposal. Doubtless some thoroughly competent teachers will accept it; for whatever the ultimate judgment of *English Sentences* may be, the book is certainly not a failure. Written with the engaging clarity that distinguishes all of Roberts' work, it will introduce its readers painlessly to new methods and results in the study of the English language, and its very existence is a tribute to the intellectual vitality of its author. Yet *English Sentences* does not satisfy, for every reader, the high expectations which news of its coming appearance raised. Roberts may have underestimated the differences and overestimated the similarities between structuralists and transformationalists; since his book is eclectic, its distinctive merits are not those of the systems from which its elements are drawn in itself the book describes only a fragment of the English language; and it raises both theoretical and practical problems which will baffle more teachers than one. Generative grammars of English are still fragmentary, still subject to rapid revision. Their relations to grammars of other kinds are still disputed, and for teaching them few English departments are prepared either by training, by long experience, or by the possession of tested pedagogical materials. In these circumstances, imprudent haste can mean disaster.

II

Nothing is more intriguing in *English Sentences* than the statement in the bibliography of the teachers' guide that Fries's *Structure of English* "is really in large measure a transformational grammar." The innocent observer would never have thought so after listening to Fries, after hearing eminent transformationalists dismiss structural linguistics as misguided, or after watching acrimonious debates in which communication seems to fail completely; and a comparison of Fries's book with Chomsky's *Syntactic Structures* makes it quite plain that Fries has taken many of the positions which Chomsky refuses or condemns. Fries sets out, for example, to describe a definite corpus of English sentences, not to construct a grammar which will generate all and only the grammatical sentences of the language; Fries seems to assume the familiar division of a grammar into phonology, morphology, and syntax, not Chomsky's three sets of phrase structure rules, transformational rules and morphophonemic rules. Fries talks a good deal about his procedures in constructing his grammar from his raw data, but Chomsky doubts that discovery procedures can be formulated "in any interesting way", Fries insists that the investigator must always know or be able to determine whether any two forms are identical or different "in a particular aspect of meaning," but Chomsky rejects all such proposals "for the use of semantic information in constructing . . . grammars"; Chomsky believes that attempts like Fries's "to assign 'structural meanings' to grammatical . . . constructions" are of "very questionable validity"; Roberts himself points out that there is no place in transformational analysis for efforts like Fries's to provide a brief definition of the sentence; Fries accepts the dogma of binary constituents and gives elaborate rules for stating the constituents within subjects and predicates, but Chomsky finds much binary analysis unrevealing and therefore restricts its application much more narrowly than Fries has done; and so forth and so on.

Beside these obvious differences, the similarities which Roberts cites are so very general that his description of Fries's grammar as "in large measure . . . transformational" seems to strip that word of its distinctive meaning. Many grammars of many kinds distinguish and subdivide "four large word classes in English," show the patterns in which the members of those classes typically appear, describe various types of basic sentences, describe or suggest "the mechanism for expanding the basic sentences," and "share with transformational analysis the same kind of interest in speech, in form and function, in language as a signaling system." Excessive emphasis on such similarities may lead to an undistinguished and even inconsistent eclecticism.

III

That Roberts has not totally avoided this danger in *English Sentences* appears most notably in his treatment of immediate constituents and in his acceptance of the Trager-Smith phonemic system, which has no place in a generative grammar such as Chomsky's.

The rules for constituent-analysis in *Patterns of English* came from Fries. Assuming that English sentences consist of a series of levels on each of which there are two parts, Roberts first split off any "sentence modifiers" and then divided each sentence into its subject and its "verb or verb cluster." Within the "noun clusters" which he assumed as typical subjects, he cut off post-modifiers from right to left and pre-modifiers from left to right; within verb clusters, he reversed that procedure, cut off elements before the main verb from left to right, and finished the dissection by removing elements after the main verb from right to left. The "pattern parts of S-groups" were taken to be "the subordinator as one part and the sentence pattern as the rest," and the "pattern parts of P-groups" were "the preposition as one part and the rest as the other." These rules were applied, with some appearance of success but with little comment on their obvious inadequacies, to fairly complicated but carefully chosen sentences.

English Sentences marks a withdrawal from this Friesian position on constituent-analysis, but a watchful reader may conclude that even in his modified statement Roberts has not achieved consistency either with himself or with his new mentor Chomsky. For both reasons, teachers and students of *Patterns* are likely now to be somewhat distressed. They need not, of course, be bothered by differences in terminology. *Immediate constituents* is a better term than *pattern parts, prepositional phrase* than *P-group, subordinate clause* than *S-group;* and the removal of the unmotivated ban on the term *predicate* is undoubtedly wise. That the majority of Roberts's substantive changes are equally wise may not, however, alleviate the reader's discomfort when he sees a confidently stated position so quickly abandoned. Students must forget what they have learned in *Patterns* about the left-to-right dissection of noun phrases like *the little boy* and about the binary analysis of verbal phrases, and they must no longer attempt to isolate the constituents of relative clauses like *whom he saw*, statements like *There was a man in the room*, or questions like *Didn't he see you?* Confidence in books and teachers may be shaken by such retractions, and teachers themselves may not be able to vindicate the internal consistency of the new text. At least the basic sentences, Roberts still insists (p. 121), are binary in their construction and may therefore be analyzed by successive dichotomy down to the level of the single words; but the analysis (pp. 54, 222 f.) seems to the innocent to show four immediate constituents, and the analysis of the whole verb phrase in the teachers' guide (pp. 26, 27, 34) seems to show three. Has the effort to preserve the binary dogma led to contradiction?

Teachers' problems about constituents will not end here. What are we to make of the seeming discrepancy between the diagram on p. 9 of the guide, which divides the phrase *the little girls* into *the* and *little girls,* and the statement on p. 36 of the guide that "if we must speak of the immediate constituents of *the small boy,* they would have to be *the . . . boy* as one and *small* as the other"? What are we to think when Chomsky in *Syntactic Structures* apparently assigns three immediate constituents to noun phrases like *the boy* or *the boys,* whereas Roberts finds only two? Whom are we to believe when Chomsky suggests one constituent-analysis for verb phrases like *considers John incompetent* or *brought the criminal in* (*Syntactic Structures,* pp. 75 f.), while Roberts holds to the quite different Friesian rule of removing elements after the main verb in succession from right to left?

Roberts ought surely to have remarked on such problems, even if they turn out to be imaginary, and just as surely he should have clarified the notions of head and modifier on which so much constituent-analysis has rested. The difficulties with both notions are multiple. Thus Roberts defines the headword as that part of a structure of modification "which has a function in relation to another part of the sentence"; but the definition would seem to make *his* and *is* into headwords in *John ate his own father* and *Mary is screaming*—a consequence which would be clearly inconsistent with other parts of Roberts' analysis. Similarly, his extremely broad concept of the sentence modifier will produce ungrammatical "dangling" constructions if the passive transformation is separately applicable to the main clause in a sentence like *Scanning the horizon, the captain sighted the ship;* and to say (p. 123) that the meaning of an initial sentence modifier "applies to the whole sentence pattern that follows" makes an oddity of the statement (p. 154) that an initial appositive to a following subject is a sentence modifier itself. Consistency is hard to preserve in talk about modification.

Some uncertainty seems to exist in Roberts' own mind concerning his continued use of the Trager-Smith phonemic system, for his teachers' guide is not so confident as his text. The text presents the Trager-Smith analysis in a fairly straightforward way: four pitches, four stresses, four junctures, nine vowels, and twenty-four consonants. Some of the statements are qualified ("It is generally believed . . . ," "English is usually described . . ."), but others are not ("English has a total of forty-five sound units called *phonemes*"); and though the presentation is so sketchy that the student will hardly master its details, he will certainly get the impression that this description of English pronunciation is factually accurate, theoretically solid, and generally accepted. The teacher, on the other hand, will learn from the guide that not all linguists accept the Trager-Smith analysis and that at least some parts of it may shortly be replaced by new descriptions.

The explanation of Roberts' uncertainty is simple, though the problems involved are complicated. As a basis for teaching spelling and punctuation, he wants to give some account of the sounds of English, and five years ago an arguable choice would have been the account by Trager and Smith. Today that choice is much harder to justify, particularly in a transformational grammar; for many linguists, such as Kurath, have never accepted the Trager-Smith phonology, and Chomsky and his colleague Morris Halle are now at work on a totally different analysis based on totally different assumptions. In their system, the phonemes of Trager and Smith do not exist. Roberts' practical purposes have thus compelled him to repeat statements which presumably he himself would no longer defend except by the argument that a less vulnerable description is not yet available and that in *English Sentences* the phonological chapters are of no great importance. Perhaps such compromises are necessary in popularizing a rapidly changing science.

IV

Everyone who has tried to write a grammar knows the painful truth of the saying that "all grammars leak": any grammarian can be certain that his successors will find much to complain of in his work, and if he studies his predecessors attentively, he may discover that from them also he still can learn. The great collections of English grammatical data are still the books of scholarly nonstructuralists like Sweet, Jespersen, Poutsma, Kruisinga, Curme, Palmer, Zandvoort, and most recently Ralph Long. It is one of the merits of the transformationalists that they have directed attention once again to these standard grammars.

English Sentences would therefore be a better and a more attractive book if Roberts' polite prefatory bow to the scholarly tradition were a more convincing gesture. The author of *Understanding Grammar* now mentions in his bibliography none of the names recorded in the preceding paragraph, and his condescending remarks about "prescientific" studies are as distressing to a conservative mind as his offhand dismissal of twenty centuries of rhetoric. A case in point is his statement that "traditional grammar has not formally distinguished all of the subclasses of verbs," of which Roberts suggests that there may be "twelve or fourteen or sixteen." A glance, however, at a "prescientific" book like *The Advanced Learner's Dictionary* reveals a subdivision of verbs into some twenty-five types, and a reader who follows the trail from that dictionary to Harold Palmer's *Grammar of Spoken English* will find that Palmer was elaborately subclassifying the parts of speech on a largely formal basis twenty years before that useful undertaking became fashionable as a part of generative work. Compared to the standard grammars, the transformational descriptions are only fragments.

Just how fragmentary they inevitably are in this early stage of their development might not at once appear from *English Sentences,* where material from structural grammars is used to fill out the description; but the reader may form a clearer notion of their present incompleteness by examining Roberts' discussion of the definitions of the sentence and the parts of speech. Earlier attempts at definitions, he says, were all unsatisfactory, but transformational analysis "avoids the problem altogether by beginning with the largest, most abstract level—sentence—and working down to the concrete items." In such a grammar, the parts of speech "are defined, as we arrive at the concrete level, by showing the words ... that occur" in the different classes. So when we follow the rule which allows us to rewrite the symbol *V* (for verb) as *Vs* (a verb like *seems*) plus *Adj*, we encounter for the first time the adjectival class, whose members will later be listed as "a set of words in a complex, a piece in the pattern that goes to make up grammatical English sentences"; and "there is never any need to frame a definition of *sentence,* because the whole grammar is a definition of sentence." "Classroom experience shows that when word classes are approached in this direction, the problem of definition largely vanishes. It just isn't there any more."

For present purposes, the fact may be ignored that classroom teachers will still find practical uses for the older, brief "definitions" of grammatical terms, however indefensible they may be in theory; but one should not forget that the "whole grammar" of which Roberts speaks has not yet been written. Its first component alone, the phrase structure rules, will eventually be much bigger than Roberts' entire book. In the phrase structure the parts of speech will have as he says to be elaborately subdivided, the members of the subclasses of lowest level will have to be enumerated, and numerous and often minute restrictions on their co-occurrence will have to be stated. A lexicon (without definitions) will be one part of a transformational grammar.

Some of Roberts' examples give further indications of the complexity of the lexicon. One subclass of English nouns, he says, will be datable nouns like *game, appointment,* or *rehearsal,* which appear in frames like *The——was on Saturday.* If datable nouns are necessary, then presumably the number of similar subclasses will be very large indeed, for one thinks at once of nouns of length (*ten——long*), nouns of time (*a——ago*), nouns of weight (*it weighs ten——*), etc. The rules for co-occurrence of the different classes will also be most complex. For instance, Roberts cites the two phrases *the chair in the room in which she usually sat* and *the chair on the porch in which she usually sat.* If only the first phrase is ambiguous, it is because we say *in* with *chair* and *room* but not with *porch,* which calls for *on.* Other examples of the narrow limits of co-occurrence are the mistakes in predication which we teachers too often dismiss simply as "awkward" or "illogical." One which Roberts cites is the sentence *The plans for Homecoming Day were done by the Student Affairs Committee,* where *plans* is not a grammatical subject for the passive *were done* because it is not a grammatical object of the active *did.* Rules which will not allow the generation of mistaken predications such as this will have to be both numerous and detailed.

The intent of these remarks is neither to question the validity of Chomsky's admirable theory nor to criticize Roberts for not doing the work of a lifetime in two years; but the raising of questions must not be confused with the answering of them. It is not unfair to insist on the obvious fact that *English Sentences* is only a piece of a grammar, though a useful piece; and perhaps Roberts himself has not realized how big a book a "whole grammar" would really be. If he had, he might not have repeated the familiar saying that a child has mastered the structure of his language by the age of six. English teachers as a group have not been quick to accept that saying, and the complexity of the phrase structure rules in a generative grammar may justify their scepticism.

V

Common opinion among linguists is of course against the sceptical teacher, whose questionings are treated with clinical condescension as "resistance"; but by using Chomsky's theory the teacher can quite simply demonstrate the literal falsehood of statements that "even the dullest child is a walking grammar and a virtually complete one." Such statements presuppose a very special definition of grammar, by which, for one thing, grammar and vocabulary are sharply distinguished. In Chomsky's theory, however, the old grammar-lexicon distinction is radically shifted. It now becomes a fact of grammar, for example, that there is a word *averse* which is used only postpositively and predicatively and is followed by the prepositions *to* or *from;* for words will have to be listed and their basic distributions and patterns of co-occurrence stated in any phrase structure rules whose aim is to generate all and only the grammatical sentences of the language. Hence the child who does not know the word *averse* at all has not learned his grammar in its entirety; and when one considers all the limitations on the child's vocabulary, this single but plain demonstration of literal falsehood becomes much more than a quibble. The acceptance, that is, of a new grammatical theory will force the re-examination of all statements based on the old rejected theory.

What then should a teacher do if Johnny insists that he does not know as much grammar as his textbook says he does? A snow job would be easy, but a serious answer difficult. And *English Sentences* raises many other unresolved theoretical and practical problems. Two of them will trouble the teacher who seriously examines Roberts' statements concerning the passive transformation or his assertion that parts of speech cannot be defined semantically; for the passive transformation will produce thousands of ungrammatical sentences unless Roberts' Pattern 4 is more narrowly defined, and generative grammarians have re-baptised as formal and have re-introduced into their grammars much that structural linguists banished as semantic. The appearance of familiarity in *English Sentences* may be deceptive.

But all these problems may seem as remote to classroom teachers as the "well-developed idea of grammaticality" which so many people have had such difficulty in understanding. The teaching of punctuation is closer to our practical concerns, and Roberts' treatment of that subject is the weakest part of *English Sentences*. Its weakness stems from his beliefs that English intonation is much simpler and more uniform from dialect to dialect than it actually is and that the correspondences between grammatical constructions and intonation patterns are more nearly one-to-one than they actually are. On p. 176 he writes, for example, that "junctures occurring within a sentence are usually either rising or level junctures. Rising junctures are usually symbolized in writing by a comma. Level junctures are usually not indicated by any punctuation mark." At least in the speech and writing that I know best, that statement is false, and if I myself should follow Roberts' rules for punctuating by intonation, I would simply have no commas at all in the forty sentences of his Exercise 45. Teachers of large and varied classes can almost certainly expect comparable difficulties.

So much for one teacher's estimate of some of the difficulties in using *English Sentences* as a high school text to follow *Patterns of English*. Those difficulties, however, should not prevent the serious consideration of both books. *English Sentences* in particular would be valuable if it did nothing but introduce its readers to Chomsky's remarkable analysis of verbal phrases. It does that, of course, and a good deal besides; and Roberts' view of the book as a happy synthesis must be weighed against the arguments offered here. Should his view prove correct, he will have established a claim to a much more distinguished status than that of an accomplished popularizer, and my strictures will be forgotten in the general applause.

50

Two Approaches to Languages

L. M. MYERS

WE ALL KNOW that *linguist* has lately become a magic word. Men who used to be merely English or Spanish professors find that when they are called by this term they are welcomed almost as equals by ecologists and astrophysicists; and scientifically trained administrators on public platforms, anxious to show the breadth of their interests but not feeling quite up to coming out in favor of poetry, are happy to be able to bow in the direction of departments that once seemed hopeless. For the first time within living memory there is even a good deal of money and patronage available for language students—as long as they are labeled linguists.

It would take a wretch lost to all proper feeling to rock a boat as lovely as this, and I am none such. I enjoy being a linguist, if only because fewer people now start looking for an exit when introduced to me. But if our serene voyage is to continue much longer there are a few precautions we ought to take. There is an old saying about how many people you can fool for how long. If we don't want the tide of opinion to become uncomfortably choppy, we had better start talking a little less complacently about the state of our discipline.

We might begin by outlawing the rather pathetic slogan that "linguistics is a rigorous science," since its obvious inaccuracy alienates many competent observers at once. Then we can consider the implications of Gleason's more moderate estimate of the situation: " . . . in some places, linguistics has achieved an appreciable measure of scientific rigor and has the foundations for further development in this regard."[1] He does not here specify the places, but he provides a useful clue:

> Descriptive linguistics is concerned with two very different but intimately related tasks. The first is to describe individual languages or dialects in terms

Reprinted by permission from *Publication of the Modern Language Association,* Vol. 77, No. 4, Part 2, pp. 6-10. Professor Myers is a member of the Division of Languages and Literature at Arizona State University.

[1] H. A. Gleason, *An Introduction to Descriptive Linguistics,* rev. ed. (New York, 1961), p. 12.

of their own characteristic structure. For each of the numerous speech forms this is a separate task; the structure of no other language is directly relevant.

The second task of descriptive linguistics is to develop a general theory of language structure—that is, to set up a conceptual framework within which an investigator can work as he seeks to understand a specific language. This theory must be sufficiently general and flexible to provide for any type of language structure that may be encountered, but also sufficiently precise and systematic to give real help.[2]

It seems to me that Gleason exaggerates the intimacy of the relation between these two tasks. Something over fifty years ago Saussure made an illuminating (though not precisely demonstrable) division of speech into langue and parole. Langue is a social institution, a set of conventions that each speaker must (more or less) master; parole is actual speaking. Any act of parole would be utterly meaningless if it were not a reflection of an underlying langue, but it can only be a reflection, and may involve a very considerable distortion. American linguists, following Bloomfield,[3] have usually approached through parole and concentrated on Gleason's first task. Most European linguists have followed Saussure, who declared that linguistics is properly concerned with langue alone.[4] The typical American position, certainly influenced by the availability of hitherto undescribed Indian languages to direct observation, will here be called anthropological; and the European one, with its emphasis on underlying abstract relations, mathematical. There are linguists on both sides who dislike this terminology, since they prefer to call their own approach simply scientific, and the opposite one worthless.

The anthropological linguists, studying each language on its own merits and in its own time, feel that the investigator should make his description directly from the immediate evidence. Resemblance to any other language should be regarded as no more than a coincidence, and any theory of historical development should at least be postponed until there is an ample supply of synchronic descriptions. Linguists using this approach may be careful, methodical, able, and generally admirable; but they can't very well be rigorous, because their job is not of a kind in which rigor is possible.

The mathematical linguists are basically interested in abstract relations and only secondarily concerned with physical phenomena of any sort. They do not regard the parole of native informants as the inviolable raw data

[2] Ibid., p. 440.

[3] "The only useful generalizations about language are inductive generalizations. Features which we think ought to be universal may be absent from the very next language that becomes accessible." Leonard Bloomfield, *Language* (New York, 1933), p. 20.

[4] Ferdinand de Saussure, *Cours de Linguistique Générale* (Paris, 1916), p. 40. The book was not actually written by Saussure, but compiled, from notes on his lectures, by two of his students, Charles Bally and Albert Sechehaye. It has been translated into English by Wade Baskin as *Course in General Linguistics* (New York, 1959).

from which inductive generalizations must be drawn, but rather as a sort of haze they must see through in order to get at the real organization of the underlying langue. Starting with postulates and proceeding by deduction, they want to work out the basic general laws of linguistic structure in such a comprehensive way that the structure of any given language will appear as a special case. In such work rigor is perfectly possible, but of course it applies only to the internal consistency of the theoretical system. The question of how accurately this system describes the actual phenomena of human communication is quite another matter.

To summarize the differences, anthropological linguists are concerned with the practical task of making useful descriptions of such languages as they encounter, while mathematical linguists are concerned with investigating the underlying structure of "language itself." It is of course possible for a man to be (at different times) both a geometer and a practical surveyor. But the two tasks remain fundamentally different; and though the findings of each may prove helpful to the other, we cannot simply add them together without getting most peculiar results. The second paragraph quoted from Gleason provides an example. If each language must be examined for itself, and the structure of no other language is directly relevant (anthropological), a general theory of language structure (mathematical) seems quite as likely to be an obstacle as an aid to accurate investigation. When this idea first occurred to them the anthropological linguists threw out (quite noisily) the old concept of universal grammar. To reintroduce the concept one level higher under the guise of universal analysis seems dubious progress.

It would certainly be convenient to find a general theory both sufficiently flexible to apply to any language and sufficiently precise and systematic to give real help in analyzing each one; but no evidence has yet been produced to indicate that any such theory is possible. We simply do not know that, either by common origin or by coincidence, all languages have enough in common to permit any one linguistic theory to provide for grammars that will usefully describe them all. It is of course clear that *some* languages have enough in common to be susceptible to compatible, though not identical, treatments, and that there would be decided advantages in having adequate grammars of these languages based on a common linguistic theory. But what is clearly true of some is not necessarily true of all, and the search for a universal theory may turn out to be as hopeless as the search for the Northwest Passage. Meanwhile it is using up a lot of valuable time, for many problems that could be handled quite simply by special theories are being complicated considerably in the hope that their treatment will fit in with the universal picture when it finally emerges.

Perhaps the best way to illustrate this point is to consider certain aspects of, and reactions to, Chomsky's *Syntactic Structures,* which for the past few years has been causing both excitement and confusion in linguistic circles.

This is by our definition a completely mathematical treatment, though Chomsky prefers to call it Saussurean. As such it seems to me extremely interesting and definitely valuable. I am not surprised that it has converted some linguists from the anthropological to the mathematical approach. What does surprise me is that a good many linguists who continue to proclaim the anthropological faith seem to be rather placidly trying to fit Chomsky into it, with no awareness of the fundamental conflict.

Chomsky not only avoids phonetics but barely touches on phonemics. He says specifically that his monograph forms part of an attempt to construct a formalized theory of linguistic structure in which the descriptive devices utilized in particular grammars are presented and studied abstractly, with no specific references to particular languages. His investigations convince him that grammars have a naturally tripartite arrangement. Specifically:

> A grammar has a sequence of rules from which phrase structure can be reconstructed and a sequence of morphophonemic rules that convert strings of morphemes into strings of phonemes. Connecting these sequences, there is a sequence of transformational rules that carry strings with a phrase structure into new strings to which the morphophonemic rules apply.[5]

As an illustration he develops a tentative and partial grammar of English containing eleven rules of phrase structure, two morphophonemic rules (with a few others suggested), and sixteen transformational rules. It is clear that he has limited the sections on phrase structure and morphophonemics (which would be extremely large in a full grammar of this type) to the minimum required to provide him with material for developing the section on transformations, which is the really new and interesting part of the work.

The phrase-structure section is a kind of constituent analysis with such rules as *"Sentence→NP+VP," "NP→T+N,"* and *"N→man, ball,* etc." [Here *NP* stands for *noun phrase, VP* for *verb phrase, T* for *the,* and *N* for *noun.*] Each rule of the form *"X→Y"* is to be interpreted as "rewrite *X* as *Y*." And each *Y* is either an analysis of the corresponding X into smaller parts or the substitution of a specific example for the symbol of a type. The morphophonemic section has rules of a similar form, such as *"walk→ /wɔk/"* and *"take+past→/tuk/."* Obviously in a full grammar of this type each of these sections must include the whole lexicon—the phrase-structure section by listing all the members of each of the categories (which will apparently be considerably more numerous than the traditional parts of speech), and the morphophonemic section as a sort of pronouncing dictionary (though I am sure Chomsky would never call it that).

Chomsky says that a grammar of English could conceivably consist of these parts alone; but:

[5] Noam Chomsky, *Syntactic Structures* (The Hague, 1957), p. 107.

We can greatly simplify the description of English and gain new and important insight into its formal structure if we limit the direct description in terms
of phrase structure to a kernel of basic sentences (simple, declarative, active,
with no complex verb or noun phrases), deriving all other sentences from
these (more properly, from the strings that underlie them) by transformation,
possibly repeated. (pp. 106-107)

The "strings that underlie them" are the sequences of symbols that represent
the order of morphemic elements in legitimate English sentences.

When Chomsky says that we can "greatly simplify the description" by the
use of transformations he is speaking from the somewhat specialized view-
point of a mathematical linguist. I know English students, and even instructors, who would not regard the following rule as a particularly simple way
of indicating where to put *not* or *n't* into a sentence to make it negative:

T_{not}—optional:

Structural analysis: $\begin{cases} NP-C-V \ldots \\ NP-C+M— \ldots \\ NP-C+have— \ldots \\ NP-C+be— \ldots \end{cases}$

Structural change: $X_1-X_2-X_3 \rightarrow X_1-X_2+n't-X_3$ (p. 112)

They might even be upset to find that many of the sentences derived by
application of this transformation would be utterly impossible until they
were corrected by another transformation of which this one contains no hint.

I do not wish to imply that the transformational theory is silly. On the
contrary, it is extremely illuminating, particularly as it shows that certain
aspects of English structure that have hitherto appeared anomalous are
perfectly regular if we dig deep enough for the underlying pattern. There
is no doubt whatever that *Syntactic Structures* makes some important contributions to our knowledge of English.

It does not, however, show much promise of leading to a comprehensive
description of the ways that people, with all their inconsistencies, actually
talk; rather it is a step in the development of a program by means of which
machines (probably electronic, though a few flesh-and-blood ones might
qualify) may some day be able to communicate. Though it is based on habits
that happen to have developed, it in effect prescribes these habits (or rather
a systematic selection from them) for future use, and demands that they be
followed with a rigidity of which no considerable speech community has yet
proved capable. For example, failure to make a verb-form agree with a
remote subject is not merely a slip, but "the result will simply not be a sentence" (p. 45). In fact, except for the recognition that *not* may appear as *n't,*
there is scarcely a mention of any possible human variation—nothing on
dialects, only a very little on intonation (and that little very tentative) and
nothing about the interaction of sounds as they occur in the flow of speech.
Instead the whole analysis is of rigid, unvarying elements.

This is of course natural—in fact, inevitable—in a formal and rigorous system. We cannot reliably make even such a simple transformation as x—y—z into x—z—y if the elements blend with and influence each other; if significant contrasts are only relative; or if one man's x is another man's y, as it often is in ordinary speech. But when such a system completely ignores irregularities that are well known to exist it follows that there are some limitations to the ways in which it can be usefully applied.

Consider, for instance, the passive transformation:

> *Passive*—optional:
> Structural analysis: NP—Aux—V—NP
> Structural change: X_1—X_2—X_3—X_4
> $\rightarrow X_4$—X_2—$+be+en$—X_3—$by+X_1$ (p. 112)

This says in effect that if any utterance of the form "The dog bit the boy" is a grammatical sentence, then "The boy was bitten by the dog," derived by applying the transformation, is also a grammatical sentence.

At first glance this may seem like a mouse from a laboring mountain. We all know that most active sentences can be shifted into the passive, and can say so in a way that seems simpler than this. But our first reaction is unfair. Chomsky's mathematical statement is both more precise and more compatible with statements about other transformations than any that we should be likely to make, so that it will work out better in really complicated situations. Moreover, unlike ours, it has no exceptions whatever. To clarify this point I wrote him to ask what he would do about such sentences as "This room seats thirty people," "The dress becomes Mary," and "The climate suits his health." He answered: "As to rule (34), the examples that you mentioned, and similar ones, I think can best be regarded as showing that *becomes, seats, suits, weighs,* etc. are not transitive verbs, in line with the reasoning on pp. 83, 84."

Here once again we must be careful of our reactions. It is natural enough to think: "That's ridiculous. In the sentence given, *becomes* is exactly parallel to *adorns,* and everybody knows that *adorns* is a transitive verb, so of course *becomes* is too." But *becomes* is not parallel to *adorns* in its re-action to this particular transformation, and Chomsky has the mathematician's right to refine his definition in order to avoid a contradiction. He is in quite a different position from an experimental scientist, who has no right whatever to disregard a piece of physical evidence because it happens to conflict with his theory.

It seems probable that Chomsky's work will be of considerable importance in machine translation and in such other machine communication as may be developed. Here the reordering of the elements in many of the formulas, which would be very difficult for most people to grasp, will cause no trouble; nor will the proper sequence in the application of the various transformations, which would put an intolerable burden on most human memories. And of course machine translation positively demands that the grammars of the languages involved in any one operation be based on the same underlying linguistic theory. This theory need not, however, be universal.

It might well prove better to have two quite different machine grammars of English, one compatible with Russian and another compatible with Chinese. Such grammars may be complete in the sense that they will do all that is required of them, but it seems likely that the lexicon will be reduced to a manageable figure and that the rules of phrase structure and transformation will somewhat limit the range of stylistic variation. It is now possible to envision the routine electronic translation of scientific papers and other factual discourse, but hardly of poetry or some other kinds of imaginative work.

Chomsky himself, however, tells me that he has no interest at all in machine translation or any other machine use of language. What does interest him is "a precise description of a set of abilities possessed by humans" which play a role in speaking and perceiving of sentences. The representation of this set of abilities is, he says, the grammar of the language. If the description is really precise it can be regarded as a set of instructions for an abstract machine, but he considers it a matter of no importance whether such a machine, or computer program, is actually constructed.[6]

The phrase "a precise description of a set of abilities possessed by humans" seems to imply that humans are a good deal more regular—more machinelike—in their linguistic reactions than my own experience would indicate. It would be silly for me to attempt a public argument with Chomsky on this point, since neither one of us claims any special competence in psychology or neurology; but it does seem to me that anyone who has spent much time trying to weed out some of the more conspicuous irregularities that crop up in a batch of themes would be likely to take my side. Altogether I am considerably puzzled to find that some of my friends who used to call themselves anthopological linguists now (a) don't seem to notice that this grammar is completely prescriptive, and (b) do seem to think that *these* prescriptions can be developed and applied, to the great benefit of all concerned. I do not, myself, regard *prescriptive* as a nasty word in all contexts; but, like most of us, I feel that any set of prescriptions for people who want to use standard English should be based on a very careful and accurate description of the habits of people who already use it, with no gross oversimplification of the very considerable variety that such people exhibit.

For this reason the expansion of Chomsky's sketch into a fairly complete description of human habits in the use of standard English appears

---

[6] I sent Chomsky a draft of this paper, got a rather extensive criticism in reply, and have made some modifications as a result, though not as many as he suggested.

impracticable. With no arbitrary limit on either the lexicon or the variety permissible in the syntax it seems likely that both the size and the complexity of the product would put it beyond the range of human usefulness. Moreover, it would necessarily depart so far from the simplicity and elegance that attract Chomsky that it is hard to see how anybody capable of compiling it would be interested in doing so.

I do not of course mean that there can be no further interesting developments. There have already been a number, by Chomsky himself and others, which we needn't go into here, and there are bound to be more. But quite aside from the prohibitive size of a complete grammar of this sort, I simply cannot find out what it is to be about. Chomsky says: "The grammar of L [a given language] will thus be a device that generates all of the grammatical sequences of L and none of the ungrammatical ones" (p. 13). I can see, if rather dimly, how this might work out in a machine; and I think I can see quite well how it could work out in an elementary language class, with a carefully selected list of words and a limited number of rules for arranging them. But when I think of the language at large the phrase "all the grammatical sequences of L" becomes completely unreal. I am forced to conclude that Chomsky has taken a very illuminating, but dangerous, remark of Saussure's as the literal truth.

Saussure says: "La langue existe dans la collectivité sous la forme d'une somme d'empreintes déposées dans chaque cerveau, a peu près comme un dictionnaire dont tous les exemplaires, identiques, seraient répartis entre les individus" (p. 39). Of course it might be objected that what we all have in our heads that makes it possible for us to talk to each other is more like a grammar than a dictionary, but that is quibbling. The real flaw is that the word *identiques,* placed so emphatically between commas, is false. Our copies are not from a single press run; in spite of all our attempts to make them uniform, they are much more like individual manuscripts—and anybody who doesn't know how much they can vary is invited to examine a page or so of the six-text edition of Chaucer. To collate a few million copies would be a task of some magnitude, though of course it would only be a preliminary step in devising a grammar that would generate all the grammatical sequences of a language, and only those.

There remains the possibility that particular developments of Chomsky's may be incorporated in grammars of a very different kind. Certainly his discussion of transformations is too illuminating to be disregarded, particularly that part of it which is based on section (37), since he proves an underlying regularity in such apparently different types of sentences as yes-or-no questions, negations, stressed statements, and statements after *so,* as well as some apparent anomalies in the use of *have* and *be.* His demonstration here is as fascinating and unexpected as Grimm's Law. However, like Grimm's Law, it is neither comprehensible nor useful to everybody, and it may not prove to be particularly important in grammars designed for general instruction.

Two other aspects of his work may well turn out to be of more significance in the development of improved English grammars. One is his rather casual demonstration that the theory of unmixable levels is unsound. The other is the unintentionally convincing evidence that a rigorous treatment of a language must be both selective and prescriptive. It may therefore be appropriate as a grammar of a rather artificial dialect of written English designed to meet specific editorial standards, but it cannot be an accurate description of speech as it happens. Thus an anthropological linguist who wishes to attempt a purely descriptive grammar can stop bothering about either mathematical rigor or final truth, and concentrate on making an analysis that is reasonably consistent and understandable from a given point of view.

Part VI

LINGUISTICS AND THE DICTIONARY

INTRODUCTION

NOT SINCE the famous "Battle of the Dictionaries" in the mid-nineteenth century has lexicography attracted such public attention as was aroused by the publication of Webster's *Third New International* (G. and C. Merriam, 1961). A great many editorial writers, publicists of various sorts, language popularizers, and periodical literary critics rushed vehemently into print—into *Time* and *The New York Times,* into *The New Yorker* and *The Atlantic Monthly* and even *The Wall Street Journal*—with a massive and shameless display of ignorance of simple linguistic facts and of long-established lexicographical principles.

This amazing performance has been so excellently recorded in James Sledd's symposium, *Dictionaries and* That *Dictionary* (Scott, Foresman, 1962), that there is no point in trying here to duplicate his work on even a small scale. Instead, this Part aims at providing the reader with some understanding of dictionary values and some insight into the complicated problems of dictionary editing. With this understanding and this insight he should be able to draw upon his information about usage (Part IV) to become an intelligent and informed user and critic of his own dictionary.

Mathews, who opens the section, is himself a distinguished scholarly lexicographer trained by Sir William Craigie, final editor of the great *Oxford*

English Dictionary. He describes how the dictionary has deeper values for the student than the immediate satisfactions of ascertaining correct spelling or preferred pronunciation. Hill supplements this article with his informed advice on how a dictionary may be used in language teaching, both in classes for native speakers of English and also in classes in English as a second language.

Warfel, a biographer of Noah Webster, here offers a background for appreciation of the relationship between linguistic theory and practical dictionary production. Cook, a former member of the G. and C. Merriam editorial staff, pinpoints this relationship with his case study of the lexicographical treatment of the word *chicken*.

The next article, by Barnhart, frankly would not have been included in this collection had not the controversy over Webster's *Third* occurred. It is the longest selection in this book, and it is minutely detailed. But its value in dispelling ignorance about dictionary fundamentals amply justifies its filling so much space. Barnhart, one of the country's leading lexicographers as first editor of the *American College Dictionary* and then of his own series of dictionaries, draws cogently upon a lifetime of experience in sharply outlining and explicating the problems found within the frame of reference of preparing a commercial dictionary.

But since Webster's controversial *Third* could not be quite ignored, the Part includes as its final article a dispassionate and able critical comment by Marckwardt, a linguistic scholar.

51

The Freshman and His Dictionary

Mitford M. Mathews

WHEN I WAS A SMALL BOY a carpenter once said in my presence that few workmen, even among master mechanics, knew more than a fraction of the uses of an ordinary steel square. The remark amazed me, as at that early age I thought a carpenter's square was a very simple tool. It certainly ap-

Address at the annual luncheon, CCCC Spring Meeting, March 24–26, 1955, Chicago, Illinois. Reprinted by permission from *College Composition and Communication*, 6.187–190 (December, 1955). Dr. Mathews edited *The Dictionary of Americanisms* for the University of Chicago Press.

peared so to me,—nothing more than two flat pieces of metal forming a right angle, and useful in marking a plank that one wished to saw in two in something like a workmanlike manner. True, the instrument has numerous markings and numbers on it, but I had never seen anyone making the slightest use of these, so I had concluded they might be ignored.

When I became older and found that large books have been written on the uses of the steel square, I changed my mind about the simplicity of the tool and the limited range of its usefulness. For many years as I have observed the use made of dictionaries by even good students, I have been reminded of that remark by the carpenter about steel squares.

Dictionaries are tools, and they are much more complicated, and capable of many more uses than students suspect. All of us know students need encouragement and guidance in the use of dictionaries, and perhaps there are few teachers of freshman composition but that devote a part of their program to an effort to help students form the habit of consulting dictionaries. Composition books for freshmen point out the need for instruction of this kind.

Despite what is being done, however, the fact is easily observable that few students are able to use their dictionaries with anything like efficiency. Certainly there must be very few of those who come up through the grades these days who are not familiar with the details of looking up words in dictionaries, but it is one thing to find a word in a dictionary and quite another to understand fully the information there given about it. It seems to me that college freshmen are fully prepared for and could profit by a well-planned introduction to the larger of the English dictionaries, and an acquaintance with what they contain. Such a program might well include material of the following kinds.

1. Students should know something about the large, unabridged dictionaries to which they have ready access in college. They might well be given brief sketches of the *Oxford English Dictionary,* the *English Dialect Dictionary,* by Joseph Wright, the old *Century Dictionary* (12 volumes), and the modern unabridged *Webster.* These may be called the "Big Four" in the dictionary field, and while it is certainly not anticipated that the freshman will ever provide himself with all of them, it is a cultural experience for him to become acquainted with the circumstances under which each of them was produced, and with the special excellencies each exhibits.

An acquaintance with these larger works will not only make the student aware of what kind of information about words is available in them, but it will leave him much better prepared to make efficient use of the desk-size dictionary with which he has some familiarity.

Many years ago a graduate student inconvenienced himself greatly to come a long distance to see me to ask if I could help him secure some information about the term "poll tax." He was preparing a doctor's thesis, he told me, and needed to know how long this term had been in the language, what its basic meaning was, and what other meanings it may have had in the course of its use in English. He was most surprised when I opened the *OED* to the appropriate place and showed him that all he needed to know about this term had been available within a few feet of his desk in the school where he was studying. It is not at all likely that any but the exceptional student will ever need all the information about words that the larger dictionaries afford, but it is well worth the while of every student to become acquainted with the fact that such information is available for those who at any time need to make use of it.

It is to be hoped that in such general instruction as may be given about the different dictionaries, some emphasis will be placed on the fact that modern dictionaries do their utmost to *record* usage, not to *prescribe* it. The tendency to regard the lexicographer as a linguistic legislator is so deep-seated that it will probably never be entirely overcome. The habit of thought that is back of such expressions as "the dictionary now permits us to pronounce it thus," has been with us for a long time, and will continue. But every student should have the wholesome experience of being taught that dictionaries attempt to give commonly accepted usage, and that correctness in the use of language varies sometimes according to time and place.

2. Along with some information about the origin and scope of the large dictionaries mentioned, there should be given some elementary information about the history of the English language and the place it occupies with reference to the others of the Indo-European group. I am certainly not foolish enough to suggest that all teachers of freshman composition become instructors in Germanic philology. What I have in mind is nothing more detailed than could be easily covered in one, or at most two, class sessions, the over-all relationships of the languages being presented briefly, with a few well chosen examples to indicate the relationship of a few of them.

The desirability of this elementary acquaintance with the linguistic position occupied by English is brought out quite clearly by Professor Pei in his *Story of Language:*

> Many years ago, I was requested to tutor in French a young girl who had to take College Entrance Examinations. Knowing that she had had four years of Latin as well as three years of French, I spared no occasion in the course of the tutoring to remind her that certain French words which she had difficulty in remembering came from Latin words which she knew. For a time she took it patiently, though with a somewhat bewildered air. But one day she finally blurted out: "Do you mean to tell me that there is a *connection* between Latin and French?" In the course of four years of one language and

three of the other, it had never occurred to any of her Latin teachers to inform her that Latin had descendants, or to her French teacher to tell her that French had a progenitor!

3. The attention usually devoted to instruction in the use of the dictionary apparently stresses spellings, meanings, and pronunciations somewhat in the order here given. Certainly these are conspicuous features of any dictionary, and it is altogether desirable for students to be encouraged to turn to these works when they are confronted with a problem of the kind indicated.

The impression, however, inevitably conveyed by instruction restricted altogether to employing the dictionary as a problem-solver, is that such a book is of no particular use unless there is a problem requiring immediate attention. Students are sorely tempted to so manipulate things as to avoid encountering problems that drive them to a dictionary. It is to be feared that, for many of them, the dictionary is a form of medicine to be resorted to only in time of unavoidable need. They associate it perhaps with castor oil or some other undesirable, dynamic type of cathartic. It is a most helpful thing for the student to learn that dictionaries are filled with interesting information from which one can derive much pleasure and instruction, even though he may not be confronted with an urgent problem of any kind.

Students should be encouraged to develop a wholesome curiosity about words that present no particular problem in spelling, pronunciation, or meaning. As a rule, the words we know well do not rise to the surface of our consciousness. It is only rarely that some common, everyday term forces itself upon our attention so urgently that for the first time we turn to the dictionary to see what lies back of it.

This use of the dictionary when there is no immediate, pressing need to do so, this giving attention to words we have known for a long time but have never grown curious about, is most rewarding. This kind of use of the dictionary we may think of as the labor of free men; the forced use is more properly likened to that of slaves.

On every hand there are words of fascinating backgrounds about which the dictionary has much to teach us. Certainly the name *Jesus,* that of the founder of Christianity, is well known to all those with whom you and I come in contact. Perhaps few of us have ever felt impelled to look the word up in a dictionary, or even realized that dictionaries contain it. An examination of the dictionary, however, reveals that the name his parents gave the Saviour was Joshua, and it was by this thoroughly Jewish name that He was known by those He lived among.

The first accounts of His life were written in Greek, and in these writings *Joshua* was transliterated into *Jesus,* a name that is certainly not Jewish in its present dress and at the same time appears odd as a Greek name.

Not even a grade-school pupil is likely to be baffled by *ostrich,* but one who is allergic to words may well become curious about it. Allow it to become the focus of your attention for a moment and see how odd the word appears. Make a guess as to where you think it might have come from, and then check up on yourself by turning to the dictionary. You may be surprised, as I was, to find the word is made up of two, one from Latin and one from Greek, which have so blended as to obscure altogether the fact that the expression signifies "bird-bird" or "bird-sparrow." It is a good term to bear in mind and use upon those of our brethren who insist that only "pure English" should be used, and profess to be pained by such obvious hybrids as *cablegram* and *electrocute.*

There may be few teachers who have discovered how rewarding it is to look curiously at the scientific terms used in dictionaries in the definitions of plants and animals. These expressions are usually hurried over by most of us as being the exclusive property of scientists and of very little interest for others.

It is surprisingly interesting to linger over such terms. It is a gratifying experience to discover one that yields its significance somewhat readily. Our common mocking bird, for instance, is *Mimus polyglottos.* The ingenuity needed for deciphering this expression is possessed by all of us. *Mimic* and *polyglot* are all we need to see that our expression means "the many-tongued mimic," a fitting description of the bird in question.

In the spring when the snow has melted, and the earth is warming up from its long cold sleep, the cheerful piping notes of a very small frog begin to be heard in the woods and marshes. People call this little creature a *spring peeper* because of the season when his little peeping notes are first heard, but scientists dub him *Hyla crucifer.* As we puzzle over this name we are likely to give up on *Hyla* for there is no other word in the English language with which we can, perhaps, associate it profitably. It has descendants among us, but we are not likely to be acquainted with them.

Crucifer though is easier. Even if we do not know that a *crucifer* is one who carries a cross, especially in a church procession, we can reason out the two elements in the word and see that it must have the meaning of one who carries a cross. Our ability to reason out this much of the scientific expression may increase our curiosity about the first element *Hyla.* Here is a helpful hint. As we all know, these scientific genus names are often from Greek. So we are reasoning sensibly when we suppose *Hyla* is Greek.

The fact is elementary that when we are confronted with a Greek word which begins with an *h,* i.e. with a rough breathing, it behooves us as cautious scouts to cast about in our minds for a possible Latin cognate beginning with an *s.* Substituting an *s* in *hyla* we come up with *syla.* Let us study *syla* a bit. It is almost a word. If we might be so bold as to insert a -v- and make it *sylva* we have a word that is in our dictionary, and one we met in a slightly different form, *silva,* when we studied first-year Latin.

The little detail of why this -v- is necessary need not bother us in the slightest at this point, because we are just having fun with no idea of becoming linguisticians. And this is it. *Hyla* and *sylva* go together and they both mean wood or forest. Now we can interpret this *Hyla crucifer* "the (little) fellow who lives in the woods and carries a cross," and when we find that this spring peeper has a dark marking on his back shaped like a cross, we are indeed gratified that now light is shining where previously all was darkness.

A teacher who is fortunate enough to have an assiduously cultivated curiosity about words will over and over again bring to a class gleanings of unexpected sorts from dictionaries. Such sharing of treasures will do more than anything else to bring home to students the fact that dictionaries are not dull, enlarged spelling books. They are filled with such a number of things that we can never exhaust their treasures but we can all be as happy as kings as we come time after time upon interesting nuggets of the kind just mentioned.

52

The Use of Dictionaries in Language Teaching

ARCHIBALD A. HILL

THE RECENT PUBLICATION of the *American College Dictionary*[1] has given us the best short dictionary the English language has ever had. It would be pure pleasure to praise its many improvements, as doubtless reviewers are now doing. Instead I intend to discuss certain ways in which the *ACD* and other dictionaries fall short of the ideal reference work which we will never achieve, but which each new attempt ought to bring appreciably closer. Before I do so, however, I want to make it as clear as I can that I am not criticizing the *ACD,* for which no student of English can have anything but respect.

Reprinted by permission from *Language Learning,* 1.9–13 (October, 1948).
[1] *The American College Dictionary* edited by Clarence L. Barnhart with the assistance of 355 authorities and specialists (Random House, New York). First printing, November, 1947; second printing, February, 1948. (Reviewed in *Language Learning,* Vol. I, No. 3, July, 1948.)

The practical necessities of dictionary making demand, first of all, that every dictionary give as much information as possible in three related but separate fields: the descriptive, the comparative, and the historical. Each dictionary places its emphasis differently within these three; the *New English Dictionary*[2] is mainly historical, dialect dictionaries are mainly comparative, while the *ACD* is mainly descriptive. However necessary such triple aims may be, they nonetheless make it inevitable that no one aim will be perfectly achieved. Accordingly I shall simplify the task of discussion by assuming a situation in which only one goal is striven for, the descriptive. I am envisaging a monolingual dictionary, whose usefulness would be limited to those who had a considerable, but still imperfect knowledge of English. In other words, the users would be foreign learners of English, or native children.

*   *   *

We should expect these five kinds of information about words from the ideal dictionary. They are in ascending order of complexity: the phonemic structure of the word,[3] its morphemic structure,[4] the grammatical modifications it undergoes, its syntactic habits, and its meanings. It is worth while to review, with varying degrees of attention, how well dictionaries fulfill their share in giving information of these several types. I shall, however, omit consideration of meanings, since the problem of giving all the meanings of even one word is certainly impossible of ideal solution, and such a dictionary as the *ACD* does as well with solving the unsolvable as anyone has any right to expect. As to the first type of information, the phonemic structure, there is also nothing which I have to contribute, except to praise the *ACD* for being the first college level dictionary which gives a workable phonemic[5] transcription of American English.

As for the second type of information, morphemic structure, no dictionary gives more than incidental information on the morphemes of which words are made up, nor does the public demand that a dictionary should give more. It is true that if one looks at a series of words such as *con-struct, construc-tive*, the divisions given in the dictionaries will give a very rough idea of the morphemes. But such divisions are, of course, intended to tell

[2] Murray, James A. H., Bradley, Henry; Craigie, W. A.; Onions, C. T. *Oxford English Dictionary*, corrected re-issue (Clarendon Press, Oxford, 1933). 12 vols. and supplement. (Originally issued as *A New English Dictionary on Historical Principles*, 1884–1928, 10 vols.)

[3] The phonemes of a word are minimum contrastive sound units usually represented by single letters, accents, or other marks in phonemically spelled languages.

[4] The morphemes of a word are minimum meaningful elements, either a word, as *paint*, or part of a word, as *-er* in *painter*.

[5] Considered strictly, the pronunciation system of the *ACD* is not phonemic, but is rather a system of key words designed to reconcile dialect differences. Within the framework I have chosen, that is, an assumption that there are no dialect differences, such a system becomes phonemic.

the reader how to divide the letters when the written form runs over the end of a line, and only accidentally coincide with morphemes. For instance, the second form must surely end in a morpheme *-ive* rather than *-tive*. It may be objected that the practical user of a dictionary has no need for a morphemic analysis of words, but though he may not now demand such an analysis, it ought to be obvious that such information would be useful. We have assumed that the user of the dictionary is one who is imperfectly acquainted with English—typically a foreigner at a moderately advanced stage of learning. A morphemic analysis of a new word to such a reader, would immediately relate the new word to familiar words which contain the same morphemes. Further, a morphemic analysis would often clear up points which are now confused. Thus at least a part of the confusion which learners experience in handling the *-ics* words like acoustics (of which more later) is caused by the fact that no dictionary makes clear that the final *-s* in these words, no matter what its origin, is not identical with the familiar plural morpheme of nouns which happens to be homonymous with it. In short, it seems to me that a requirement for dictionaries ought some day to be that as well as the rewriting of the word in a phonemic notation, there should be a second rewriting which would show the morphemes it contains and point out their boundaries. Such a notation should at least remove the disguises morphemes undergo in automatic variation, though the description of the rules governing such alternation properly belongs in the grammar. Unfortunately such morphemic analysis must also await the growth of substantial agreement among morphologists.

The remaining two types of information about words, their inflectional and syntactic habits, can most easily be treated together. The handling of this information presupposes a thorough grammar which describes first the inflectional classes and subclasses of English words, and next the syntactic classes. The dictionary, as I have said earlier, would confine itself to showing to which classes words belong. Further, the method by which this designation of class can be given is not any longer new. There are already in existence various schemes of description and enumeration which can indicate conveniently and completely, by the use of symbols, the class to which a given word belongs.

It is not my purpose to go into details about how to construct such systems, but rather to point out certain conditions which must be fulfilled before any system can be safely applied in the pages of a dictionary. English inflectional classes must be described separately, and each word given a designation assigning it to its inflectional class and to its syntactic class separately. In present dictionary practice this is not done. If a foreign speaker goes to the *ACD* to look up *so,* he will find that it is classed as a pronoun, among other parts of speech. The reasons why *so* is called a pronoun must be either syntactic or semantic since *so* shares none of the inflectional characteristics which appear in pronouns. The reader is nowhere given this information, so that it seems to me that there is a real danger that he will construct some monstrous paradigm as *so* * *sor* * *sors* * *som,*[6] assuming that it has the inflectional characteristics of *they.* What is called for, then, in a completely adequate entry for such a word as *so,* is a statement that it belongs to an inflectional class which undergoes no modification, but a syntactic class sharing some of the characteristics of pronouns.

If such non-existent paradigms as that given above can be dismissed as somewhat unlikely dangers, there are other pitfalls in our dictionaries which are troublesomely real. The most important type of danger results, it seems to me, from an insufficiently rigid distinction between individual properties of words, which belong in the dictionary entry, and class properties, which do not. Among the individual properties of words are the forms which a given word may lack, and words lacking one or more of the normal paradigmatic set are spoken of as defective. The statement that defectiveness is an individual word property may not seem important in English nouns where the inflectional forms are few, and it would be relatively easy and economical to group together all defective nouns in classes in the grammar. But in any paradigm where the forms are numerous there will have to be a separate class for every word lacking a special form, and a separate class for every new combination of missing forms. It is obvious that the result would be unwieldy description, and that defectiveness is therefore best handled as a property of the individual word. Another not quite obvious distinction is that between words whose forms can be shown by their syntax to be constructed with a zero modification,[7] and words which are genuinely defective. A simple illustration is that *sheep* has a plural in zero, whereas *ethics* is defective in the plural. The importance of the distinction here is that forms having zero modifications are subclasses of the major form classes to which they belong, so that description of these subclasses belongs in the grammar, while I have suggested that defectiveness forms a part of the lexicon.

The *ACD,* in common with other dictionaries, follows the practice of making no entries for words which are considered regular in their paradigms, listing the forms only for words which have some peculiarity. Now unfortunately the *ACD* also omits, in many instances, information as to defectiveness. The result is very real confusion, unless the reader already knows about the paradigm. The learner can only assume that if an entry makes no comment on the grammatical forms of a word, that word has

[6] A star before a word indicates that the form is nonexistent in the language, or if existent, it does not appear in the given context.

[7] A hypothetical affix: "The Hindus hit upon the apparently artificial but in practice eminently serviceable device of speaking of a *zero element:* in *sheep: sheep* the plural-suffix is replaced by *zero*—that is, by nothing at all." Bloomfield, Leonard, *Language* (Henry Holt and Co., New York, 1933), p. 209.

a full and normal paradigm. If one looks up such a word as *spaghetti,* he will find that there is nothing in the entry which indicates that such a sentence as "Please put some *spaghettis on my plate," is not possible in English. Even more confusing is the fact that in some uses the word has a normal paradigm, though it is usually defective. Thus though we cannot use the sentence I have given above, the sentence "The spaghettis made by Brown and Jones are equally good," is certainly acceptable. Indeed, if our user of the dictionary is really unwary, or has an Italian background, he may make a further mistake. A good deal of reading is necessary before he can infer that the general practice in the *ACD* is to assume that a noun is singular unless otherwise stated. In the entry for *spaghetti* the word is described as being derived from an Italian plural, and its final could easily suggest such plural forms as *banditti.* Thus it seems not unlikely that our foreigner might construct such phrases as "a *spaghet is" and "the spaghetti *are."

Some measure of the importance of this sort of difficulty is given by the fact that in the letter *A* alone I have counted no less than eighty nouns which for one reason or another left room for doubt as to whether their paradigms were full and normal, whether they had irregular forms, or whether they were defective in one or more forms. The *-ics* words like *ethics* are a typical class which will illustrate the whole group. The entry for *acoustics* is one of the fullest and clearest since it is stated that when the word is constructed as a singular it means the science of sound, when construed as a plural it means acoustic properties. This is certainly true, but it suggests to the reader that he may form a plural *acoustics* for one meaning, and a singular *acoustic* for the other. You will remember that I said earlier that the *-s* of these words was not the plural morpheme. It is true that some of the difficulty with words of this sort might be removed if it were stated that this particular morpheme is a derivational element. Yet not even this would cure the difficulty since only the further statement that both forms of the word are defective, and making clear what forms each lacks, would completely clear up the trouble . . .

53

Dictionaries and Linguistics

Harry R. Warfel

Ever since 1928, when Noah Webster published the world's first dictionary based upon scientific principles, American dictionaries have kept abreast of the theories and researches in linguistics. Like monuments stand the old Century and the superseded volumes of the Merriam-Webster unabridged dictionary. They never can be discarded. We return to them to interpret the literature of their day. Yet always we greet the latest work with confidence, knowing that both unabridged and desk dictionaries will reflect the ultimate in scholarship. One of the glories of American intellectual achievement, one that is too seldom given recognition, is the patient, painstaking, dedicated toil that provides us with these admirable handbooks to language, the instrument that makes us human.

Lying behind each of these great dictionaries is a philosophy of language that determines a great many decisions. Partly because Clarence Barnhart and Edward Artin have presented fascinating discussions of linguistic problems and practical solutions, I should like to raise a few questions about fundamental presuppositions. I realize that metaphysics is not a popular subject nowadays. Yet it is only by examining our unprovable assumptions that somehow we make progress. What we are and what we do are more rigidly regulated by these beliefs than we realize.

I

Samuel Johnson apparently had no scholarly interest in the problem of the origin of language. In his Preface, Introduction, and Definitions he did not allude to, and I assume that he took for granted, the traditional Christian view of the supernatural grant of language. Noah Webster was made of different stuff. He accepted nothing without rigorous examination. Conversion to Congregationalist Calvinism led him to a dynamic faith in the literal veracity of the Bible. He believed, as told in Genesis, that God spoke to Adam and thus gave Adam "language as well as the faculty of

Reprinted by permission from *College English*, 22.473–78 (April, 1961). The author is Professor of English at the University of Florida.

speech" as an "immediate gift." After the Fall "Adam and Eve both replied to their Maker, and excused their disobedience." Their possession of language was undoubted; as the parents of mankind they transmitted this language to their descendants. The dispersion of the human family after the Flood led to the formation of the several families of languages; these developed differently as a result of the great changes incident to the increase of knowledge and to men's different social circumstances. The inescapable conclusions, Webster thought, were that there was one original language and that from this original descended into all others "many of the primitive radical words." It was his belief, therefore, that Saxon, Danish, and Welsh words—the basic rootstock of English—"are of equal antiquity with the Chaldee and Syriac." The tracing of kinship, therefore, served as a means of proving the survival of Adam's words.

This belief supplied the motive power that led Noah Webster to invent the science of etymology. To combat the notions of the Deists and others who denied the literal truth of the Bible, Webster set out to trace the history of words through twenty languages. If he could demonstrate the persistence of Adamic words in modern languages, to that extent he would refute the notions of the unbelievers. In fulfilling his purpose Webster created the formula which has been adopted by all succeeding etymologists. Whereas Dr. Johnson traced the preposition *by* only to Saxon *bi* and *big,* Webster brought together "Saxon *be* or *big;* Swedish and Danish *be;* Dutch *by*; German *bei*; all contracted from *big.*" He added that "The Swedish and Danish *paa,* and Russian *po,* may be from a different root, although they are nearly allied in signification, and may be the same word differently written. This preposition occurs as a prefix in all Shemitic languages, contracted indeed into *beth.*"

Dr. Johnson gave the etymology of *father as* the Saxon *faether.* He added: "This word is likewise found in the Persian language." Webster traced the word in Saxon, German, Dutch, Icelandic, Danish, Greek, Latin, Spanish, Italian, Portuguese, French, Persian, Russian, Sanskrit, Bali, Zend, and Syrian. With perceptiveness he added, "The Gothic *atta,* Irish *aithir* or *athair,* Basque *aita,* must be from a different root, unless the first letter has been lost."

The point I stress is that Webster's etymologizing had a purpose that has been lost today. Twentieth-century dictionaries reject Webster's thesis. In *Webster's New International Dictionary,* Second Edition (1934), the etymologies are justified as "a record of the origin and development that is of value and interest for its own sake as well as necessary to a full understanding of the word itself" (xiii). Kemp Malone, etymology editor of *The American College Dictionary,* states: "In sum, the etymologies here set down present, in succinct form, the fruits of scholarly research, old and new, on the origins of English words" (xxiii). *Webster's New World Dic·*

tionary states that "Dr. Whitehall and Dr. Umbach, who were in charge of the etymological research for this dictionary, have related the etymologies to the definitions in such a way that the 'semantic flow' of the word—its evolution from earlier forms and its sense development—as well as its kinship to other words in English and related languages, is immediately made clear."

It is obvious that there is a wholly different attitude in these three books from that taken by Webster. The *New International* views etymology as disinterested yet useful knowledge. *ACD* considers etymology a scientific enterprise. NWD makes etymology a basis for understanding the changes in meaning which many words have undergone. The key thought in all seems to be that language must be viewed objectively, dispassionately in line with a positivist philosophy.

The question I now raise is whether the editors of our dictionaries must not discover a different principle upon which to formulate and present etymological knowledge. Facts are inert, especially when they are presented solely as facts. Principles, as Webster demonstrated, are dynamic. My own feeling is that the *New World Dictionary* made a breakthrough toward a satisfactory approach. The editors were right in placing the needs of the reader first. The suspicion lingers that etymology has been a fenced-off scholarly playground inaccessible to the common reader. Possibly the unabridged dictionaries should continue to present detailed etymologies. But I question the utility of etymologies in desk dictionaries that do not make these entries of value in giving the reader a grasp of the primary sense of a word and in helping him to understand the meanings that radiate therefrom. Or to state the problem differently, if Noah Webster's reason for linking English words with all other languages has no validity, a new theory of etymology and a new mode of presentation must be found that is tenable for our generation.

II

A presupposition of Dr. Johnson seems to remain unquestioned in some recent dictionaries. It is that vocabulary and language are synonymous. He wrote: "Our language, for almost a century, has . . . been departing from its original *Teutonick* character, and deviating towards a *Gallic* structure and phraseology, from which it ought to be our endeavour to recall it." The fact is that the system of English has been so powerful that the addition of many thousands of foreign words has not affected the structure of the language at all. Every foreign verb, adjective, and adverb operates on the English plan. Only a few dozen foreign nouns retain their original plurals. A parallel to this tenacity in syntax is the tenacity of pronunciation in this country. Despite the arrival of millions of immigrants to the United States between 1890 and 1924, the children and grandchildren of those immigrants today speak the same brand of English as do their neighbors whose original arrival in this country from England may date from 1620 or 1700 or 1800. Vocabulary is like the players in a football game. No matter how many different players temporarily enter the game, the rules of the game remain the same. Vocabulary happens to be, like the stars in a football game, more newsworthy than the system, but the system is dominant.

Professor Kittredge in *The New International* (1934; p. lxxxvi) glimpsed this fact but did not know what to do with it. As a consequence he made a distinction between foreign and native words. He wrote: "The words which belong more to the grammar than to the lexicon . . . are almost wholly native . . . . The substantial elements of the proposition, nouns, adjectives, verbs, may all be obtained from abroad, but the connecting links, which must unite them in the framework of sentences, can be found only at home." The same inability to escape from word origins doubtless led Porter Perrin to assert that the Latin derivative *prior to* is heavier than the native *before*. I do not know the kind of scale which Perrin used, but apparently it was the same one employed by Dr. Johnson. Certainly such a distinction, arising from one of the major dogmas of usage study, is unscientific and indefensible. The truth is that all words adopted into English have the same weight as native words; the test is not one of origin but of utility. All that we know about usage study, therefore, requires us to place the system ahead of the vocabulary.

The new science of communication theory discriminates the terms channel, code, and message. In speech the channel is the speech tract, the code is the system of sounds and patterns produced by the channel, and the message is the set of ideas transmitted by employing vocabulary in the code. The limited nature of the channel is apparent when we use speech in a dark room. Facial expression and gestures are thus eliminated. The basic code of vocal signals can now be analyzed. Quickly it is discovered that vocabulary is subordinate to the code. The sound signals, intonational patterns, and syntax—operating together—form the code. The derived code of writing can use a typewriter with as few as thirty keys to transcribe every message that can be devised in the English language. As soon as we realize that language is a system containing a small number of items, the code and the structure of that code take precedence in our thinking over the message, over the vocabulary.

III

A corollary to the philosophical view that the system is more important than the vocabulary is the idea that the basic explanation of language must come at the structural level. In the past decade it has been discovered that in English there are fourteen basic statement-sentence patterns and four or five minor patterns. All question and command patterns and all clause patterns are modifications of these. These sentence patterns have their origin in fixed positional arrangements of the four major word-classes. By the mathematical principle of functionality every position in basic sentences can be filled by members of the other word-classes and by word-groups. A word-class supplies the constant in a position, and the other word-classes and word-groups supply the variables. What has hitherto seemed to be very complicated is now quite as simple as first-year high-school algebra, as Donald J. Lloyd and I demonstrated in *American English in Its Cultural Setting* (1956). The old and very narrow concept of functional change must now be superseded by the overriding concept of functionality. Basic sentences are not sequences of members of word-classes but of functions.

As soon as the concept of functionality is accepted, it will become apparent that the old principles of word-order must be reorganized to embrace the notions of fixity in word-groups and of relative variability in the order of the functions. A noun-group like "the boy" and a prepositional phrase like "at dinner" must always have this sequence. Any number of additional words can be inserted between *the* and *boy* or between *at* and *dinner*. The permuted nature of these groups is absolute in standard English. When these groups are put into a sentence like "The boy is at dinner," it becomes obvious that the sentence can be stated "At dinner is the boy" and "The boy at dinner is." No matter how long the sequence in any function, inverted order requires the shifting of the group. It becomes immediately apparent that attempts to explain English word-order in contrast with Latin word-order must seem wrong unless the mathematical principle in English order is explained.

The recent discoveries in language operation make clear the conclusion that all languages operate on the same principles. All have a small number of phonemes that combine systematically to form morphemes, words, and sentences. All languages have a small number of basic sentence patterns with their own intonational patterns. All languages have the principles of modification, word order, apposition, and compounding. The extent to which languages have inflection and/or composition as devices to show number, case, person, tense, mode, voice, aspect, and other grammatical ideas may vary, but that every language has harmonious systematic manipulations is quite evident. Every language apparently employs the mathematical principles of permutations, combinations, and functionality. No language, therefore, is a unique manifestation. A kinship in the systematic operation of the codes seems an inescapable philosophical conclusion. A new dictionary, it seems to me, will be well advised to orient its presentation to this concept of structure.

IV

Another problem which the lexicographer must face is that of the extent to which his dictionary can go in giving an up-to-date description of the structure of language. Dr. Samuel Johnson devoted about 125 words to five rules of syntax, because he thought that "our language has so little inflection, or variety of terminations, that its construction neither requires nor admits many rules." Still with us is the fallacy of Johnson that inflection is the chief key to language operation. In a context of a denunciation of an English grammar that is based upon Latin, in a chapter on "The Modern View of Grammar and Linguistics" in *The English Language Arts* (1952), Robert C. Pooley asserted that "To insist that a certain fixed arrangement of *shall* and *will* constitute [*sic*] the future tense in English is to perpetuate an error originally derived from Latin influences." The assumption of Johnson and Pooley was that inflection is a determining factor in tense creation. Tenses in many languages are formed both by inflection and composition. Pooley made the further mistake of asserting that "English expressed the idea of future by the use of the present tense (*I go tomorrow*), by the present progressive form (*am going tomorrow*), and by a large number of various phrases, including *I shall go, I will go, I hope to go, I plan to go,* and so forth." It must be obvious that *tomorrow* expresses the concept of future in *I go tomorrow* and *I am going tomorrow*. Tense in English must always operate in relationship to a non-verb statement of specific time. Tense and specific time are not at all identical ideas in English.

By contrast with Dr. Johnson, Noah Webster inserted into his *An American Dictionary* (1828) his *A Philosophical and Practical Grammar* in which position was given prominence as a structuring essential. In about 10,000 words of explanation he presented forty-five rules of syntax. Webster was on the right track. He gave new names to the parts of speech. He accepted current usage and explained many of the structure-words in a more modern way than most grammars widely used today.

Recent dictionaries have uniformly limited grammatical information to the entries and have not ventured to devote a section to the structure of English or to the grammar of current English. Some of them give grammatical material in a history of English, but in general there has been no adequate presentation of the systematic organization of English. The distribution of words into classes can be accomplished only on the basis of the positions taken by words in sentences. As a consequence the lexicographer must have a firm grasp upon syntax and upon the principles of functionality in language operation.

V

I have posed problems in the metaphysics of language as they relate primarily to lexicography. Were I to offer a single solution to all problems and thus to suggest a new metaphysical principle, I would say that the formulation of an answer would come through a comparative study of representative languages in all families. Structural linguistics has provided a sound basis for a philosophy and psychology of language. In this brief paper I have been able to mention only four major generalizations. These are of significance to the grammarian and the formulator of teaching theory and practice, as well as to the lexicographer. Language is a system whose structure is more important than vocabulary, and the etymological and operating analyses, as well as the teaching procedures in language, must move in harmony with these new discoveries. As the handbook to language, a dictionary will show its modernity by adopting these or other scientifically based concepts.

54

A Point of Lexicographical Method

Daniel Cook

IN JANUARY OF 1913 in Hagerstown, Maryland, there occurred an act of faith that pleasingly illustrates certain central problems of the dictionary user and of the dictionary maker. The event was described in the New York *World* of January 19:

> ### DICTIONARY SAVES HIM WHEN ARRAIGNED FOR 'FOWLLY' GREETING GIRL
>
> *Hagerstown, Md., Jan. 18*—. . . Starner was arrested on complaint of a young woman who charged that he had accosted her with: 'Hello, chicken.'
>
> 'Your Honor,' said Starner when arraigned, 'I don't see that I did anything wrong. I called the young woman "chicken, "a perfectly proper term. Just look in Webster's dictionary and you will find that I have transgressed no laws.'
>
> Magistrate Moore rummaged through his desk until he found an antiquated copy of Webster and turning to the word in dispute found:
>
> 'Chicken—The young of various birds, a child, a young woman.'
>
> Magistrate Moore discharged the prisoner.

Although it may seem rather a pity to inquire more closely into this event, a look at the then current 1909 edition of *Webster's New International Dictionary* is rewarding: 'chicken, *n*. . . . 4. A young or youthful and in-

Reprinted by permission from *American Speech*, 34.20–25 (February, 1959). Professor Cook is a member of the English Department at Southern Illinois University.

experienced person; a child; also, a timid person. "Stella is no chicken" (i.e., no longer young). Swift.' It is now perhaps clearer, from the quotation from Swift, how Magistrate Moore's severely abridged Webster could coolly equate *chicken* and 'young woman.' One is also entitled to wonder, however, whether such an unqualified equation is entirely valid. It may be noted that *damsel, girl, maid, maiden,* are also variously defined in current dictionaries as 'young woman,' 'young unmarried woman,' and the like. Is there, then, an implied equation, *chicken=damsel,* for example? The question answers itself, of course, but in doing so it makes explicit a chief point of this paper: the widespread and long-standing inadequacy in the lexical treatment of terms that are actually available only for an extremely limited range of contexts.

Before examining this problem at greater length, however, it may be useful to note the degree to which public failure to comprehend the real nature of the dictionary makes desirable the inclusion of contextual guides in the definition of such terms. A case in point is Magistrate Moore's unquestioning faith in the authority and accuracy of his dictionary. This, of course, should be no surprise to us. Very few indeed are the users of dictionaries who have learned to look at a definition as an interpretation or generalization of a certain specific group of citations. The issue of the incident provides further illustration of the failing. I have seen eleven newspaper accounts of the episode. It is not, of course, remarkable that such good copy was picked up by many papers. What is interesting is that so many saw in it the opportunity for editorial reflection on the dictionary and the language. The nature of these reflections provides excellent illustration of the folkways of Americans with their dictionaries.

The Springfield (Mass.) *Republican* of January 16 pays honor to the prophet even in his home town: 'Is it slang or is it not to speak of a young woman as a "chicken"? Strictly it is not, for Webster's dictionary admits the definition.' We note incidentally and with respect the *Republican's* apparent view that when Webster's admits the definition of a word, it is henceforth not slang. Further illumination of the dictionary's role in the language process is provided by the Kansas City *Post* of January 26: "Since it has been discovered that it was our old friend Noah Webster who applied the term "chicken" to young women, we would like to know upon whom we may place the blame for designating them as "ponies," "squabs," and "broilers." ' Here the assumption seems to be that since the dictionary makes up the words, it is only right that it should determine what its creations shall mean. This is in some ways a convenient position: if the dictionary 'applies the terms' and stands authority for them, of course no question of accuracy arises. But, unfortunately, questions of taste and judgment remain and have in fact been asked. An editorial writer in the New York *Herald* of April 9, 1893, gives earlier evidence of this concept of the dictionary as creator and judge, while he lambasts the same authority for, among other things, admitting useless lumber to clutter up the language:

> Our pure and good old Saxon word 'sweat' was good enough for our fore-fathers through many a generation and down the centuries from the time of Adam, but some of our dilettanti lexicographers whose ideas of taste and euphony had run away with them declared it vulgar and now we have at least three words in our dictionary to express the idea of water passing through the pores of the skin to the surface—namely, perspire, transpire, and sweat.

It is evident from these passages that Magistrate Moore's view of the dictionary is the usual one. The question of accuracy simply never arises. Criticisms of policy may be made, but a definition, no matter how general or how inclusive, is rarely questioned.

This state of affairs is of course no news to lexicographers. Unfortunately, however, in too many instances they have for various reasons done little to accommodate their practice to it. An analysis of the nature and history of the lexical treatment of *chicken* provides an excellent illustration. First of all, the locution objected to by the young ladies of Hagerstown will probably be recognized by most of us as a familiar though now somewhat archaic usage of the word in question. It is equally certain that this is not the usage employed by Swift and, presumably, recorded in the magistrate's desk dictionary. If, then, there are two senses, it will be useful to see exactly what evidence for them exists. Available citations for Swift's sense are, in historical order:

1711 Richard Steele, *Spectator,* No. 216. 'You ought to consider you are now past a *Chicken;* this Humour, which was well enough in a Girl, is insufferable in one of your Motherly Character.'

1720-21 Jonathan Swift, *Stella's Birthday,* in *Poems,* ed. Harold Williams, II (1937), 735.

> Pursue thy Trade of Scandall picking,
> Thy Hints that Stella is no *Chicken* . . .

1738 Jonathan Swift, *Polite Conversation,* ed. Herbert Davis (1957), p. 145. 'I swear she's no *Chicken;* she's on the wrong Side of thirty, if she be a Day.'

1809 *Cobbett's Political Register,* XV, No. 12, col. 421 (March 25). 'An infant at law? a mere *chicken?*'

1877 E. Walford, *Great Families* I, 170. 'He must have been well forward in years—or at all events, as they say, no *chicken.*'

1880 Spencer Walpole, *History of England,* III, xii, 43. '[Taylor] calling himself on one occasion "a mere *chicken* in the law," he was ever afterward known as "Chicken Taylor." '

It is always difficult to decide just when a figure of speech has become sufficiently detached from the original comparison to be recognized as a lexically admissible sense. The dictionaries are probably right in recognizing a new sense of *chicken* here. It is obviously not, however, to be rendered simply as 'a young woman' or 'a young person.' Some indication must be made that the term is available almost exclusively for the mildly derisive context 'no chicken' and that the central reference is to youth—or its absence.

Citations for the Hagerstown sense are, in historical order:

1788 *New Hampshire Spy*, June 10, 'The Married Man's Litany.'
 From visiting bagnios, those seats of dispair,
 Where *chickens* will carry you my duck and my dear
 In hopes that your purse may fall to their share,
 Deliver Me.

1860 G. D. Prentice, *Prenticiana*, p. 97. 'Call a lady "a *chicken*" and ten to one she is angry. Tell her she is "no chicken," and twenty to one she is still angrier.'

1923 G. H. McKnight, *English Words and Their Background*, p. 61 '(. . .) a girl is a . . . *chicken* [glossed as current student slang].'

1929 Sinclair Lewis, *Dodsworth*, p. 284. ' "I'll show you a good noisy dance place tonight," said Sam. "You'll see all the pretty *chickens* you want . . ." '

1934 John Collier, *Defy the Foul Fiend* (Penguin Books, 1948), p. 111. 'A huge and flashy fellow, with something the look of a prosperous heavy-weight boxer . . . saw Louise. "Hullo, *Chicken!*" said he. . . . "why didn't you wait inside, Baby?" '

This is clearly distinct from the Swiftian sense. The central reference here is to femaleness rather than youth. The specific denotation is not necessarily, I would judge, sexual looseness, but the context often suggests something less than respect for the person so termed. The term appears to be pretty much the equivalent of the current *chick*.

We may now examine the dictionaries for traces of these senses. We should at the same time notice and evaluate any devices designed to define the contexts to which the terms are appropriate or to identify the senses more precisely than by a simple equation with 'young woman' or 'young person.'

The earliest notice that I have seen is in Dr. Johnson's dictionary of 1755: '3. A term for a young girl. [followed by the quotation given above from *Stella's Birthday*].' Here the accompanying quotation may be interpreted as limiting the usage, though reliance upon that alone is surely placing too much of a burden on a reader's sophistication. John Walker's *A Critical Pronouncing Dictionary* (Philadelphia, 1818), repeats Johnson's definition, 'a term for a young girl,' but omits the quotation. R. G. Latham's 1878 revision of Johnson combines the entry with that for *chick* and reads only

⟨in that part of the definition which is applicable) 'Young person.' His only illustrative quotation is for *chick*. Both of these entries are, then, to say the least, misleading. Robert Hunter's *Encyclopaedic Dictionary* (London, 1879), again combines the entry with that for *chick* and defines as follows, most of the quoted definition probably being applicable to *chick* in such expressions as 'neither chick nor child': 'II Figuratively: . . . 2. An infant, a young or helpless person. (Colloquial) *No Chicken* = a person well advanced in years. [with the quotation from *Stella's Birthday*].' In so far as this specifically defines the 'no chicken' locution, it is an improvement in clarity, though the first part of the definition introduces some ambiguity, as it pretty clearly refers to other senses recorded and discriminated in the *Oxford English Dictionary*: '2. *transf.* of human offspring: A child [quotations follow],' and '3*b*. Applied to one who is as timorous or defenceless as a chicken [quotations follow].'

In John Ogilvie's *Imperial Dictionary of the English Language* (London, 1883), widely recognized as an excellently edited dictionary, we see the first really adequate job of limiting one of the senses: '2. A person of tender years: generally used of females and as in the following quotation. "Stella is no chicken." *Swift*.' The well-known *Century Dictionary* (New York, 1889) improves even upon this, completely orienting and explaining the usage in question: '5. A person of tender years; a child: sometimes used as a term of endearment, or with a negative (no chicken), in satirical implication of mature years. "Why now you are my *chicken* and my dear." Fletcher . . . "Stella is no chicken." Swift.' Here the explanation of the two usages quoted is complete and unambiguous. It should not be overlooked, however, that the generalized definition, variously expressed in the initial phrases of these and subsequent definitions as 'a person of tender years, a child, etc.,' refers to other senses cited above from the *OED*.

The next authority to be noted is the *OED*, which, relying upon the warning note '*fig.*' and upon its quoted illustrations to clarify and limit the usage, defines only '3. *fig.* A youthful person; one young and inexperienced. (*To be*) *no chicken:* no longer young [the quotations that follow are those cited above at the dates 1711, 1720, 1809, 1877, 1880].' Following this is the first edition (1909) of *Webster's NID*, quoted at the beginning of this article. This definition, as will be seen, reverts in its lack of orientation to pre-*Imperial* standards. And without the breadth of illustration provided by the *OED*, this lack is of course fatal. The third edition of the *Webster's Collegiate Dictionary* (1916), deriving from the *NID*, abridges it: '4. A young or inexperienced person; a child.' Lacking the special point of view advanced in this paper, this abridgment is logical enough. Unfortunately, however, this, like most abridgments, saves space at the expense of vital orientation of the scope of the usage. Literally, it could be interpreted as recording a natural context somewhat as follows: 'Are you married now?' 'Oh yes, and we have three chickens.' This interpretation of the entry is hardly less reasonable than that of Magistrate Moore, and both are made possible by the same shortcomings of abridgment.

With the next dictionary we reach consideration of popular reference works currently in print and in widespread use. Here in the second edition (1934) of *Webster's NID,* we have what is clearly the best oriented and most thorough report of the range of usage:

4.a A young person; a child; esp., derisively in the phrase *she is no chicken,* a woman no longer youthful. 'Stella is no *chicken.' Swift. b.* A young or youthful and inexperienced person; often applied to a timid person. 5. *Slang.* A young woman of easy familiarity.

Several points may be noted. In 4*a* the sense 'young person' is specifically directed by the 'esp.' to the locution most commonly recorded in the citations above. In 4*b* there is properly separated the sense recorded in *OED,* 2 and 3*b,* and found in such contexts as 'don't be a *chicken;* there's nothing to be afraid of.' And finally, of course, sense 5, properly discriminated, is the first dictionary notice of the Hagerstown sense documented above.

Unfortunately, the record does not end here. The other principal large or 'unabridged' American dictionary, the *Funk and Wagnalls New Standard Dictionary* (1952) has distinctly less thorough coverage, resulting in considerable ambiguity of the type already observed in its predecessors: '3. A child, or a young, helpless, or inexperienced person: often used satirically, with a negative. "She's *no chicken;* she's on the wrong side of thirty, if she be a day." Swift.' In addition to this, all of the most commonly used desk dictionaries fall into the same errors of omission previously observed in abridgments. The *American College Dictionary* has '4. *Colloq.* A young person, esp. a young girl.' The *Webster's New World Dictionary* has '5. a young or inexperienced person.' The *Webster's New Collegiate Dictionary* has '4. A young, youthful, or inexperienced person.' The *Thorndike-Barnhart Comprehensive Desk Dictionary* has '*U.S. Slang.* young or immature woman; young person.' The *New College Standard Dictionary* published by Funk and Wagnalls has '3. A child, or an inexperienced person.' On the other hand, two somewhat less well-known dictionaries do rather better. *Swan's Anglo-American Dictionary* (New York, 1952) has in the relevant sense 'a young person; *Amer. sl.,* a girl (familiarly or disparagingly), a prostitute,' and *Cassell's New English Dictionary* (15th edition; London, 1949), has '(fig.) a person of tender years. no chicken: older than he appears or makes out.'

Clearly, if any of these abridgments, with the possible exception of *Swan's,* had replaced Magistrate Moore's 'antiquated copy of Webster,' we could expect no improvement in his understanding of the usage. We have seen much improvement in lexicographic method reflected in the gradual clarification of this entry since Johnson, but in this instance (and in many similar ones) it has not carried over to our desk dictionaries.

One qualification of this judgment should be made. In view of the pressing problem of space in making a desk dictionary, we can hardly expect that there will be room for archaic slang. It is likely, therefore, that the Hagerstown sense will be missing even from an ideal abridgment. Yet this fact does not justify an entry for the Swiftian sense (which must, of course, be retained) that is capable of being extended in a hit-or-miss fashion over an indeterminate area of meaning. We have a right to expect clarity and precision even when we cannot have completeness. If neither is to be found in our desk dictionaries, we must hope for increased magisterial reliance on the unabridged.

A third alternative will commend itself to many: to cultivate a healthy intransigence in the often too easily cowed user. An early and hopeful sign of this mood can be observed in the literature of the Hagerstown incident. This single voice of dissent was heard from Parkersburg, West Virginia, where the *State Journal* concluded an editorial on the subject with the words, 'In fact Dean Swift was not a particularly elevating and virtuous writer himself, and we do not see how anyone could contend that the use of the word chicken as applied to the women sex could be considered dignified, elegant or a compliment or tribute.' While this may miss the point a bit, the attitude of independence has far-reaching possibilities. And possibility becomes actuality forty lears later in a ruling of a New York City license commissioner. The New York *Herald Tribune* of April 21, 1955, carries the story:

> Ruling that 'burlesque' means what the public thinks it does and not what Webster's Unabridged Dictionary says it does, License Commissioner Edward T. McCaffrey yesterday reaffirmed his refusal to license a burlesque show in Brooklyn . . .
>
> Webster's defines a burlesque show as [the definition that was offered in evidence by the applicant] 'a type of theatrical entertainment . . . characterized by broad humor and slapstick presentation . . . short turns, as songs, ballet dancing and caricatures of well-known actors or plays.'
>
> Declaring that 'to the mind of most citizens the current meaning of the word, burlesque, is synonymous with the strip and the tease, the bump and the grind and the dialogue of double meaning or unvarnished salaciousness,' he denied a license . . . [for] a burlesque show at the Orpheum Theater.

55

Problems in Editing Commercial Monolingual Dictionaries

C. L. BARNHART

This paper deals with some of the editorial problems in the production of commercial English = English dictionaries. Such dictionaries out of necessity are of a popular nature because they must depend for their existence upon widespread acceptance by the general public. The publisher usually determines the audience for which he wishes to make a book. His determination of the market he would like to reach depends upon the type of his previous publications. His salesmen are probably trained to reach only one type of market, and ability to sell in that particular market conditions to a great extent the type of dictionary to be made. A publisher of schoolbooks will probably start with a school dictionary; a publisher of trade books with a college dictionary.

It is the function of a popular dictionary to answer the questions that the user of the dictionary asks, and dictionaries on the commercial market will be successful in proportion to the extent to which they answer these questions of the buyer. This is the basis on which the editor must determine the type of information to include. The editor's very first concern, therefore, must be to determine the probable buyer of a particular book. The amount of information that the editor can give is limited by the price that the buyer will pay for a dictionary in a particular market; his editorial judgment is always limited by the space available. All of these factors must be considered in order for the commercial editor to produce a single dictionary or a series of dictionaries that will enable him to stay in business.

To what extent, then, can the editor answer the questions of any buyer about any word of the English language? This depends to some extent upon

Reprinted by permission from Fred W. Householder and Sol Saporta, Eds., *Problems in Lexicography*, Publication Twenty-one of the Indiana University Research Center in Anthropology, Folklore, and Linguistics, 161-181 (Bloomington, 1962). The author is head of *Reference Books* and editor of the various Barnhart dictionaries. The reader should note that *WU* in the text refers to the Second Edition of the *New International*, not to the recent *Third*.

the number of words in actual use in the literature (reading matter) of today and in the literature of the past that is widely read and studied today. For the popular dictionary tends to be a dictionary of the standard language and is concerned with slang and various specialized vocabularies only so far as they may appear in current newspapers, magazines, and books.

Some years ago Professor Robert L. Ramsay of the University of Missouri estimated the size of the working vocabulary of the English language —the words which any literate person may encounter and about which he may have questions dealing with spelling, pronunciation, meaning, idiomatic use, synonyms, levels of usage, and origin—to be around 250,000 active words.

The usual desk dictionary of educated people in the United States is a college dictionary containing 120,000 to 150,000 of these words. Unabridged dictionaries may contain as many as 500,000 words and one-volume or two-volume dictionaries may contain 200,000 or 250,000 words but they are priced so high that there is little bookstore market for them. The ordinary college dictionary will contain somewhere between 14,000,000 and 17,000,000 characters. Since there are five-and-a-half characters to the average word, a college dictionary will contain some three million running words. If the editor attempted to include the complete active vocabulary, he would have to use 500,000 or more words simply to list the entries and the pronunciations. He would have only ten words to define the entry, provide illustrative sentences and phrases, give the etymology, and list synonyms and antonyms. Since there are approximately twice as many meanings as entries put in college dictionaries, this would reduce the amount of space for each definition to about four words a definition and leave only two words for illustrative phrases, etymologies, synonym studies, and so forth. This is obviously an impossible situation. The editors of all college dictionaries are forced, then, to make a selection of the terms which they put in their dictionaries.

Which 125,000-150,000 words should be entered and how should they be treated? This selection of material to be included depends upon the judgment of the editor as to the type of user of his book and the kind and level of information that the user will want. One important market for the college dictionary is the freshman composition market. In 1955 I circulated 108 questionnaires in 99 colleges in 27 states (5 eastern, 8 southern, and 14 western) reporting on the use of the dictionary by some 56,000 students. The teachers were asked to rate six types of information commonly given in college dictionaries according to their importance to the college freshman. Their replies indicate that the college freshman uses his dictionary most frequently for meaning and almost as frequently for spelling. Pronunciation is third with synonym studies and lists, usage notes, and etymologies far behind.

The selection of the 125,000-150,000 terms to be included depends to some extent upon the importance the editor assigns to the six types of information given. An editor of a college dictionary who emphasizes the importance of meaning may consider the omission of all or part of the meanings of such "easy" words as *good* or *bad* or *with*. An editor interested in spelling may give more irregular inflected forms. One interested in usage may omit spellings of irregular inflected forms and undefined run-on entries such as *absolutely* or *badness*. A college dictionary editor interested in pronunciation may give more variant pronunciations than one primarily interested in meaning. The selection of material to be included should depend upon the interests and needs of the buyer and not upon the specialized interest of the editor. For example, it is possibly an editorial mistake to include rare Scottisms as William Allen Neilson did in the last Webster's Unabridged, for they take up at least some of the space of the 70,000 compounds Tom Knott crossed out.

If the interest of the buyer is a primary consideration, certainly spelling would require major consideration, for spelling is one of the principal problems of the users of dictionaries and one of the principal reasons for buying dictionaries. What are the spelling difficulties that most people encounter? Where the difficulty in spelling is in the middle or end of a root word it is easy to verify the spelling in almost any dictionary. The distinction in spelling between *capital* and *Capitol* or between *principal* and *principle* is easy to find. Treatment of inflected forms *(antagonize, antagonized, antagonizing; travel, traveled* or *travelled, traveling* or *travelling)* in which the inflected form is not a simple root + a suffix is handled differently by different dictionaries. If the editor feels that the average buyer of the dictionary knows the rules for dropping *e* or doubling of the consonant when *-ed* and *-ing* is added he will not list these inflected forms.

One of the principal spelling difficulties with derivative or run-on entries is the recognition of the root form. Derivative words in which the root form is clearly recognized (such as *absolutely* or *resolutely*) might well be run-ons unless there is a meaning or pronunciation problem as there is for *absolutely*. Of the four major college dictionaries on the market, one omits the entry entirely, two others enter it as a run-on with pronunciation, and the fourth enters, pronounces, and defines it. *Resolutely* is not entered in one, is spelled out in full as a run-on after *resolute* in two, and entered as a *-ly* run-on in the fourth. Those derivative entries that have some change in the root (e.g., *arbitrarily, atomization, archaistic*) often throwing them out of alphabetical order or making it hard to recognize the root must either be put in the alphabetical list in the proper place or run-on. To do this, however, takes a certain amount of space that cannot be used in defining some rare and difficult word. In this conflict between the user of the dictionary for spelling and the one who uses it for the meaning of hard words, the editor must make a choice unless he has enough space to include both types of information. His first problem, then, is to choose whether he will give more importance to information about spelling or about meaning. Since meaning difficulty outranks all other uses of the dictionary in importance so far as college freshmen are concerned, the editor usually compromises and enters derivatives without meaning difficulty but with simple spelling or pronunciation difficulty as run-ons instead of as main entries. *Arbitrarily* is a main entry in one of the four college dictionaries and a run-on in the other three; *atomization* is omitted in two of the college dictionaries and given as a run-on in the other two; *archaistic* is run-on in two of the college dictionaries and defined in the other two. If you are making a dictionary for college freshmen or for secretaries, the dictionary that enters most forms in their proper alphabetical place would be most useful to the buyer.

Having made a fundamental decision whether to define all entries or to have run-ons, the editor is in a position to select the 125,000-150,000 entries to be included in his dictionary. Nearly all college dictionaries agree close to 90 per cent of the time upon the choice of words to be entered and differ largely in the number of abbreviations, geographical names and biographical names to be included. All include all types of entries but differ markedly in the treatment of the basic vocabulary, the inclusion of idioms, the fullness of the definitions of scientific and technical terms, the illustrative sentences, phrases, and quotations used, the type of etymology given, and so forth. In spite of the fact that the real difference of most dictionaries lies in the description of the words entered, there are a few important differences that each editor must face in the selection of entries.

The agreement among the editors of college dictionaries on a basic, common vocabulary of 100,000 terms is due to the fact that we have such a rich storehouse of material from which to choose. The history of English words and meanings is probably fuller than that in any other language. The commercial dictionary editor can turn to the big *Oxford English Dictionary,* to the ten-volume *Century Dictionary,* to the *Dictionary of American English,* and to the *Dictionary of Americanisms* for scholarly information. Quotations for each important sense are abundantly supplied in these dictionaries. When I was corresponding with the compiler of the Hungarian-English dictionary, Professor Ladislás Orszagh, he stated that they had nothing comparable to the OED on which to draw. He had to collect quotations in order to proceed with his book; there was no historical dictionary of the Hungarian language. All dictionary makers owe a great debt to the OED and they owe a similar debt to the big ten-volume *Century* prepared by one of the great linguists of the nineteenth century, William Dwight Whitney, who produced a superb descriptive dictionary of the English language and was the first to give adequate treatment to scientific terminology.

Probably no proper survey of the thousands of pages in the OED and the

Century (there are over 8,000 pages in three columns in this book alone) has ever been made. These mines of information can be read and studied again and again. On my first high-school dictionary a staff of ten editors spent over five years combing the OED. Out of this mass of material we selected the meanings that were to be included in our high-school dictionary. We were aided in this task with a semantic count which Dr. E. L. Thorndike had made of current standard literature that assigned meanings to some 5,000,000 words in running context. In this fashion, we could determine the order in which the meanings of words were used in the current English language in material ranging from children's books to the *Britannica* and through technical literature. This count was of enormous importance in verifying editorial judgment in collecting definitions. In Table I, I have given the semantic count for the word *create* as a sample of the usefulness of this count. Many semantic counts should be made but evidence, such as a typical quotation for each meaning, should also be provided. Counts are one criterion for selecting meanings (and entries) but more data is needed.

Commercial dictionary editing, however, that depends only upon scholarly dictionaries is out-of-date because the language recorded is out-of-date. The record of English from 1900 to the present should be sampled. In Table II is a sample of the books in a long-time reading project of standard literature to remedy this lack of a modern record. In order to meet the needs of modern users of the college dictionary it is necessary to sample the reading of the public to which you address your book. If a word or meaning occurs in several different sources over a wide range of magazines and books during a considerable period of time, such a word or meaning may be worth considering for inclusion in a current, college dictionary. Obviously, we must get a wide enough sampling to help the editor decide which words and meanings are important enough to include in a college dictionary. In reading for this purpose, we read for words and meanings normally in an unabridged dictionary but not in current college dictionaries, as well as for new words and meanings making their way into the language. Our selection of new words and meanings depends upon the extent and accuracy of our sampling. Too large a sampling is expensive and serves no purpose if it duplicates information already existing in the OED, the *Old Century,* the *Dictionary of Americanisms,* and the *Dictionary of American English.* Our problem is to add to that material which has been compiled before us. With the commercial resources that we have at hand we need to sample newspapers, popular magazines, literary magazines, and technical magazines, and to keep at this sampling systematically over a period of years. This is expensive. Every quotation that reaches my files costs approximately 30c. When one considers the vast amount of printed matter probably no sampling would be adequate with fewer than 50,000 quotations a year; 100,000 quotations would be a more adequate sampling. Perhaps reading of such

Table I

CREATE   524

             29

create,   ppl. a.
         1. ppl. a. created. no occ.
008   2. as adj. arch.
---
2   1477. Norton *Ord. Alch.* v. in Ashm. (1652)62.
                 A create perfection.

create, v.
055   3. *trans.* Said of the divine agent: To bring into being, etc.

11

006   3b. with complemental extension.

3

574   4a. *gen.* To make, form, constitute, or bring into legal existence, etc.

24

011   4b. absol.
---
4   1775 Sheridan *Rivals* Pref., The imagination. . .
                 becomes suspicious of its offspring, etc.

004   4c. Of an actor: To be the first to represent (a part or role), etc.

2

078   5. To constitute (a personage of rank or dignity), etc.

6

256   6. To cause, occasion, produce, give rise to (a condition, or set of
---
24   circumstances).

created,   ppl. a.
002   7. Brought into being by an agent or cause. esp. a. Made or formed by
---
1   the divine power.

002   b. constituted of a certain dignity or rank.

1

creating,   vbl. sb.
002   8. The action of the verb create.

1

creating,   ppl. a.
002   9. That creates.

1

The count is to be read as follows: *create* occurred 524 times in 29 different types of reading. Eight thousandths of these occurrences in two different types of material were for the second meaning of *create, ppl. a.;* fifty-five thousandths in eleven different types of material were for the third meaning of *create, v.* Ability to select important meanings as indicated by a semantic count makes it possible for a commercial publisher to use the OED in making a dictionary.

scientific magazines as the *Scientific American, Science News Letter,* the *New Scientist,* and such newspapers as the *Wall Street Journal,* the *Manchester Guardian,* and the *New York Times,* and such general magazines as *Harper's,* the *Atlantic Monthly,* the *Saturday Review,* and the *Listener* will give a fairly good picture of the magazine and newspaper reading of educated people. Reading various annuals and yearbooks as well as a number of important current novels and books will give an adequate basis for the selection of new definitions and entries. In all reading it is important to sample both British and American usage. See Table II for a partial sample of the standard literature that could be read to bring the record of standard English up-to-date.

Table II

Code: essential ***
desirable **
possible *

	Author	*Title*	*Date*	*Type*	*Nation*
54.	Edman, Irwin	Philosopher's Holiday **	1938	Essay	Amer.
55.	Eliot, T. S.	For Lancelot Andrewes ***	1928	Essay	Amer.
		The Sacred Wood ***	1920	Essay	Amer.
56.	Faulkner, Wm.	The Hamlet ***	1940	Novel	Amer.
		Sanctuary **	1931	Novel	Amer.
57.	Fisher, Vardis	No Villain Need Be *	1936	Novel	Amer.
58.	Fitzgerald, F. S. K.	Tender is the Night **	1934	Novel	Amer.
		The Crack-up **	1945	Misc.	Amer.
59.	Ford Madox Ford	No More Parades ***	1925	Novel	Brit.
60.	Forster, E. M.	Howard's End ***	1910	Novel	Brit.
		Abinger Harvest **	1936	Essay	Brit.
61.	Frank, Waldo	City Block *	1922	Novel	Amer.
62.	Galsworthy, J.	The Man of Property *	1906	Novel	Brit.
63.	Garland, Hamlin	A Son of the Middle Border **	1917	Novel	Amer.
64.	Gerould, Katherine F.	Conquistador **	1923	Novel	Amer.
65.	Glasgow, Ellen	They Stooped to Folly	1929	Novel	Amer.
66.	Greene, Graham	The Labyrinthine Ways **	1940	Novel	Brit.
		The Heart of the Matter ***	1948	Novel	Brit.
67.	Hammett, Dashiell	The Maltese Falcon *	1930	Novel	Amer.
68.	Hand, Learned	The Spirit of Liberty **	——	Essay	Amer.
69.	Hemingway, Ernest	Green Hills of Africa **	1935	Essay	Amer.
		Death in the Afternoon **	1932	Essay	Amer.

Adequate sampling, then, is one of the editor's major considerations, and he can accomplish this with a continuing group of readers who are aware of what is already in the file. A balanced quotation file of perhaps half a million modern quotations that supplements the file of the *Oxford,* the *Century* and the *Dictionary of Americanisms* would be adequate to give authority to the selection of new material. See Table III for a sampling of new words and meanings which results from such a reading.

Table III

	New Word or New Meaning	*No. of Quotes*
	ABATTOIR, *n.*	
Not added WU o	2. (figuratively) a place of physical punishment, as of a boxing or wrestling ring, bull-fighting arena, etc: *two heavyweights in an abattoir.*	2
	ABC or ABC WEAPONS,	
WU o	atomic, bacteriological, or chemical devices or substances, as instrument of war	3
	ABEGGING, *adv.*	
Not added WU o	in an unwanted or overlooked condition: *Used books often go abegging.*	1
	ABELL / COMET,	
Not added WU o	a new comet sighted (1953) in the range of the pole star (named after its discoverer, George Abell).	1
	ABENLENS, *n.*	
Not added WU o	a race of pygmies of the Philippines.	2
	ABLARE, *adj.*	
WU +	noisy; raucous. —adv. full of noise.	0
	ABLATIVE, *adj.*	
WU o	2. *Especially British.* of, having to do with, or designating a material that will accomplish or permit ablation.	1

Table III (*cont.*)

New Word or New Meaning	*No. of Quotes*

ABLATION, *n.*

WU o 3. *Aerospace.* A. the removal or carrying away   3
of heat by melting or vaporization. B. the removal of the nose cone of a ballistic missile by
burning and falling away when the missile re-
enters the atmosphere.

AB / NATURA,   1

WU o *Latin.* unnatural.   1

ABOARD, *adj.*

WU o 5. *Baseball.* on base: *to hit a double with three*   2
runners aboard.

A-BOILER, *n.*

WU o a boiler for which the heat is generated by an   1
atomic reactor.

ABOUT-TOWNER, *n.*

WU o a man or woman who frequents the fashionable   1
night clubs, the theaters, etc., of the city.

ACCESSION / NUMBER,

WU + the number given to a book, periodical, etc.,   0
when it is entered in an accession book.

ACCESS / TIME

WU o the time required for an electronic computer to   5
respond to a request for stored data.

ACCIDENTAL, *n.*

Not   2. THE ACCIDENTAL, that which occurs by acci-   1
added   dent or is developed without plan or design:
WU +   *The freedom of science is so important. . . be-*
cause it allows the accidental to occur (Bulletin
of the Atomic Scientists, 1955).

ACCIDENT-TOUT, *n.*

Not   *British Slang. . . . an ambulance-chaser is an*   1
added   *accident-tout* (London Journal, 1952).
WU o

Table III (*cont.*)

	New Word or New Meaning	*No. of Quotes*
	ACCORDIONIZE, *v.t.*	
WU o	*U.S. Informal.* to compress; condense.	2
	ACE, *n.*	
WU o	7. ACES (or ACES-HIGH) *with, U.S. Slang.* highly regarded by: *He's aces with me.*	1
	ACE, *v.t.*	
WU o	*U.S.* 2. *Informal.* to achieve a high mark in: *He aced the examination.*	1
	ACHHUT, *n.*	
Not added WU o	(in India) an untouchable.	1
	ACHY, *adj.*	
WU +	Informal, full of aches.	1
	ACNEFORM, *adj.*	
WU +	resembling acne.	0
	ACRYLIC / FIBER,	
WU o	any of various synthetic textile fibers produced from acrylonitrile, as Acrilan, Dynel, and Orlon.	8
	ACT, *n.*	
WU o	GET INTO THE ACT, *Informal,* to do what is currently fashionable, expedient, etc., to do.	3
	ACTUAL, *n.*	
WU o	a motion picture, radio, or television program based upon real events; documentary.	2
	ADD-ON, *n., adj.*	
WU o	—*n.* an added sum, quantity, item, etc.	1
	—*adj.* that may be added; accessory.	1
	ADLESS, adj.	
WU o	*U.S. Informal.* without advertising.	2

Table III (*cont.*)

	New Word or New Meaning	*No. of Quotes*
	ADOLESCE, *v.i.*	
WU +	1. to be or become adolescent. 2. to behave like an adolescent.	1
	ADORAL, *adj., n.*	
WU + WU adj. 2 o	*Anatomy.* .—*adj.* 1. near or adjacent to the mouth: *adoral cilia.* 2. having a mouth: *an adoral organ.* —*n.* an adoral part or function.	1
	ADULTLY, *adv.*	
WU o	in the manner of an adult; maturely: . . . *two small, adultly dressed boys. . .* (New Yorker, 1957).	1
	ADVISEE, *n.*	
WU +	1. a person who is advised. 2. *Education, especially U. S.* a student assigned to an adviser.	1
	ADWOMAN, *n.*	
WU o	*U. S. Informal.* a woman engaged in the business of advertising.	2
	AELUROPHILE, *n.*	
WU o	a person who likes cats.	1
	AELUROPHOBIA, *n.*	
WU +	a morbid fear or hatred of cats.	1
	AEROBEE, *n.*	
WU o	any of several rockets used for exploring the upper atmosphere, of which an advanced version is able to attain an altitude of 300 miles.	11
	AEROPHILATELY, *n.*	
WU + Run-on WU +	the branch of philately that specializes in airmail stamps.—*aerophilatelist, n.*	1 1 (Runon)
	AFFINAL, *adj., n.*	
WU o	1. having a common origin or source. 2. related by marriage. —*n.* a relative by marriage; kinsman.	1 adj. 1 n.

Table III (*cont.*)

	New Word or New Meaning	*No. of Quotes*
	AFFRONTED, *adj.*	
WU +	offended; slighted; insulted.	1
	AFRIKA / KORPS,	
WU o	a specially trained and equipped unit of the German army in World War II that served in northern Africa under Field Marshal Erwin Rommel.	4
	A / FROID,	
WU o	*French.* without prejudice or passion; calmly and coldly: . . . *examined à froid, the thing appears to make a lot of sense* (New Yorker, 1955).	1
	AFTERHOURS, *adj.*	
WU o	that takes place or is in effect after the usual time: *afterhours conferences, afterhours recreation.* ..—*adv.* after the appointed time: *We do not serve afterhours.*	21 adj. 3 adv.

To select 125,000-150,000 terms to include in a college dictionary means combing the standard scholarly sources such as the *Oxford, Century,* and the two American dictionaries, the using of the counts, and accumulating a modern quotation file which will supplement and amplify the information that has been collected in the past. This work can only be done by a well-trained staff over a period of years.

However, an editor with this trained staff, a modern quotation file, and the backing of a publisher who seeks a particular market, must make numerous policy decisions involving a great many areas of linguistic knowledge. No single editor can have the necessary knowledge to formulate the policy in matters of pronunciation, etymology, definition, and levels of usage, but one way of acquiring trustworthy advice is to form an editorial advisory committee. The function of a committee is to supplement the experience, training, and information of the editor; it does not do the work of special editors or supervise or direct the work that is done. Such a committee should have members who represent various points of view, and more than one scholar should represent any particular field such as etymology, pronunciation, or usage. Curiously enough, specialists in one particular field often give very useful suggestions in nonrelated fields. A large committee, representing many points of view, is one of the most useful adjuncts to an editor in framing policies. Otherwise policies are very likely to be decided in the seeming commercial interest of the publisher or limited by the narrowness of the editor. Such a committee, however, cannot function by majority vote. To vote democratically about matters of information is not the way to settle an intellectual problem. Some one person, in this case, the editor, must have the power of final decision and this power of final decision should be made on the side of the agreed-upon knowledge of the experts. The function of a general reference book is to make available to the general public in understandable language the knowledge upon which scholars and specialists are agreed. It is the function of the editorial advisory committee to remind the editor of this agreed-upon knowledge. The editor must be able to evaluate his committee and to know when to take the advice of a particular scholar and when not to. The editorial advisory committee makes it possible for the editor to set policies which are in accordance with the advances in knowledge of the day.

What are some of the important policies that an editorial advisory committee, the editor, and his staff must consider? One of the most pressing of these and one that occupies a great deal of time and attention is pronunciation. Opinions on pronunciations are likely to vary violently according to the experience and background of the person who holds them. Two great scholars, Leonard Bloomfield and Harry Morgan Ayres, said that the pronunciation key was of no importance whatsoever; they felt that any key that used symbols consistently was adequate. Other scholars, such as the late Miles Hanley, feel that the only key to be used is the International Phonetic Alphabet or some adaptation of it. Others now hold out for a Smith-Trager key as the only defensible key from a theoretical point of view. Is there one key suitable for all types of transcription—for the scholar, for the worker on a linguistic atlas, for the teacher of speech, for the student of linguistics, for a newspaper reader, for the high-school graduate, for the fourth grade child? There are four possible keys—a textbook key using diacritics on letters of the alphabet, the IPA key using few diacritics and based on continental speech habits, a Smith-Trager key that analyzes the make-up of sounds, and a newspaper key that uses familiar letters of the alphabet to respell a word. See Table IV below for the equivalent symbols for the vowels in these keys. Which of these different kinds of keys are suitable for a college dictionary? This central problem of a key must be faced; and it is more difficult when there is a series of dictionaries involved than when there is only one dictionary.

By what standards should we select a key? Should it fit the speech habits of the largest body of users of the dictionary? Must the symbols be easily written and easily read? Should there be only one symbol for each sound? Since the letters of the alphabet are directions to say sounds, which of various letters of the alphabet can be used and which should be modified either by substituting some other letter from some other alphabet or by

Table IV

Example Word	Textbook Key	A "K + K" System	A "S − T" System	Newspaper Key
hat	(a)	[æ]	/æ/	a
age	(ā)	[e]	/ey/	ay as in day
				aCe as in date
care	(ãr)	[ɛr]	/ehr/	are as in care
				air as in air, fair
father	(ä)	[ɑ]	/ah/	ah as in calm
let	(e)	[ɛ]	/e/	e
equal	(e)	[i]	/iy/	ee as in bee, meet
term				
(stressed)	(ėr)	[ɝ·]	/ə r/	ur as in fur
other				
(unstressed)	(ə r)	[ɚ]	/ə r/	er
it	(i)	[ɪ]	/i/	i
ice	(ī)	[aɪ]	/ay/	igh as in sigh, sight
				ie as in tie
				iCe as in mine
				y as in my
				ye as in dye
hot	(o)	[ɑ]	/a/	o
open	(o)	[o]	/ow/	o as in go
				oe as in toe
				oh as in oh
				oCe as in poke
				oa as in boat
order	(ô)	[ɔ]	/oh/	o as in for
				aw as in law
oil	(oi)	[ɔɪ]	/oy/	oi
house	(ou)	[aʊ]	/aw/	ou as in out
				ow as in now
cup	(u)	[ʌ]	/ə/	u
full	(u)	[ʊ]	/u/	oo as in book
rule	(ü)	[u]	/uw/	oo as in food
use	(u)	[ju]	/yuw/	ew as in few, pew, mew
about	(ə)	[ə]	/ə/ or /ɨ/	u in unstressed closed syllables
taken (unstressed)				
pencil				uh in unstressed open syllables
lemon				
circus				

using some kind of diacritic or special symbol? If some form of IPA is to be used, what form—that by Daniel Jones or that used by Kenyon and Knott? Is the key to be phonetic or phonemic? The choice of a pronunciation key is of no great importance in a scholarly dictionary since scholars are trained to read many keys but a commercial man bets his economic life on ideas that are advanced by linguists. The editor has to have some assurance that the principles on which he bases his key are going to stay alive. The editor must further believe that the pronunciation key chosen permits an accurate statement of the pronunciations given and is, once learned, simple to use.

Another important problem the editorial committee must consider is the order of definitions. Should the historical order be followed, or should the dictionary be a descriptive dictionary of the current English language and start with the central or core meaning today? If we decide upon the historical method, how are we going to determine the dates of each meaning? Must we rely upon the OED and the *Dictionary of American English* or do we have additional information that we can turn to in our own files to verify dates? What attempt will be made to change the order of the definitions as dates in the OED and the *Dictionary of American English* are corrected by new information? If we have the central or core meaning as the basis of organization, how are we to determine the central or core meaning? Are there any semantic counts that would show what is commonest today? (See Table I showing the frequency of the meanings of *create*.) Would the frequency of the modern quotations give some clue?

Are the definitions to be written on the same level or is the editor to make some effort to determine what type of person will look up a particular word or meaning and then frame definitions in language suitable for the person looking them up?

What is to be done with scientific entries, particularly the names of plants and animals? Is the technical name to be given or is it to be excluded as useless and the space devoted to other more important matters? What is to be the differentiation in the treatment of words like *get, with,* and so forth, as over against a word like *aristocracy?* When are illustrative sentences to be used? To what degree are idioms to be covered? See Table V showing the distribution of 30 possible idioms in three college-level dictionaries priced around three dollars. Should illustrative sentences be made up, should they be from modern sources, or should they always be quotations of some author? If the latter is given, should chapter and verse be cited in a book for general reference? How much space should be devoted to illustrative sentences? College dictionaries devoted from 54 to 61 per cent of their space to definitions and from .7 to 1.3 per cent to illustrative sentences and phrases. Should more space be devoted to illustrative sentences and less to definitions?

How are various levels of usage to be labeled? Should the spoken vocabu-

Table V

Below are 30 idiomatic expressions (e.g., *taken aback*, *abide by*, etc.) in a combined list from seven different dictionaries ranging from college dictionaries at $5 or $6 to desk dictionaries. These idiomatic expressions are phrases or expressions that cannot be understood from the meanings of the words which combine to form them; they deserve special attention in a dictionary.

		Coll. 1	Coll. 2	Coll. 3	Desk 1	Desk 2	Desk 3	Desk 4
1.	from *A* to Z	+	−	−	−	−	−	−
2.	taken *aback*	+	+	+	+	+	+	+
3.	in *abeyance*	+	+	−	+	−	+	−
4.	*abide* by	+	+	+	+	+	+	−
5.	all *aboard*	−	−	−	+	−	−	−
6.	*abreast* of or with	+	−	−	+	−	+	−
7.	in the *abstract*	+	+	+	+	−	−	−
8.	*accessible* to	+	+	+	+	−	−	−
9.	of one's own *accord*	+	+	+	+	+	+	−
10.	with one *accord*	−	−	−	+	−	−	−
11.	*according* to	+	+	+	+	+	+	+
12.	*according* as	+	+	+	+	+	+	−
13.	call to *account*	−	−	−	+	−	−	−
14.	on *account*	−	−	−	+	−	−	−
15.	on *account* of	+	+	−	+	+	−	−
16.	take *account* of	−	−	−	+	−	−	−
17.	take into *account*	+	−	−	+	−	−	−
18.	turn to *account*	−	−	−	−	−	+	−
19.	*account* for	+	+	+	+	+	−	−
20.	*accredit* with	+	−	−	+	+	−	−
21.	within an *ace*	+	−	+	−	+	+	−
22.	be *acquainted* with	+	+	−	+	+	−	−
23.	*acquit* oneself	+	+	+	+	+	+	−
24.	come *across*	+	−	+	+	−	−	−
25.	*act* on or upon	+	+	−	+	−	−	−
26.	*act* as	−	+	−	+	−	−	−
27.	*act* for	+	−	−	+	+	+	−
28.	*act* up	−	−	−	+	−	−	−
29.	take *action*	+	−	−	+	−	−	−
30.	in *addition* to	+	−	−	+	−	+	−
	TOTALS	22	14	11	27	12	12	2

lary be labeled *Colloq.?* Should the formal vocabulary be labeled *Literary?* How can the uniqueness of a spoken word and a formal written word be established? How should we distinguish between informal spoken and informal written? Or should the distinction be between *formal* and *informal?*

Should the current dialects of English be recorded and to what extent? Should we include only those dialectic words that occur in newspapers, magazines, and novels? To what extent should we include South African, Anglo-Indian, and Australian words? What words in different parts of the United States should be included? What about Briticisms? Is Briticism a good restrictive label or should we say "in England"? So also should we use "in India" instead of "Anglo-Indian"?

When is a word or meaning archaic and when is it obsolete? Is a word archaic when it is used only to give an old-fashioned flavor to writing? Can we define *obsolete* as a word that is not used at all? What happens if an obsolete word is revived, say, by Spenser, Scott, or Robert Graves, and becomes current for a while among literary people? Is it then an obsolete word or an archaic word? The same problem, incidentally, arises in dialect words. Of what value is the label *poetic?* Does a poetic language exist?

I have listed some of the policy problems of pronunciation, meaning, and levels of usage so that you may have some idea of the problems that could be submitted to an advisory committee. The process of submitting problems to the committee is illustrated by a questionnaire on derogatory words. Several questions are asked about a list of words which are often used to convey an unfriendly attitude toward or opinion of some person, class, or group of persons. The words included are:

Canuck	limey
Chinaman	mammy
Chink	mick
dago	nigger
frog	polack
greaser	Shylock
guinea	spik
hunky	wop
Jap	yid
kike	

The advisors are first asked to indicate their judgment on the present status of the words under one of three headings: "Always unfriendly, a 'fighting' word"; "Likely to be unfriendly"; or "Relatively Innocuous".

The second question concerns the exclusion of derogatory words ("Always unfriendly") and words which may be derogatory ("Likely to be unfriendly") from school dictionaries at different levels, i.e., whether they should be excluded from all school dictionaries, or whether they should be excluded only from those used up to the sixth grade, in junior high school, or in high school. Those advisors who suggest exclusion of any words at the school level are asked to check the words they would exclude from college-level dictionaries.

For terms which they think should be included, the advisors are asked to suggest a qualifying or restrictive label. A list of typical restrictions used in dictionaries is attached to the questionnaire for help in framing the labels:

A. Linguistic Labels:

1. Pop. (= popular usage)
2. Colloq.
3. Slang.
4. Loosely.

5. Local
6. In the S United States.
7. Americanism, Southern.
8. Esp. in Southern States

B. Social Labels:

1. Unfriendly use.
2. Used in an unfriendly way.
3. In discourteous use.
4. An objectionable usage.
5. Offensive.
6. An offensive usage.
7. Originally a corrupted form of speech; now generally coarse, always offensive.
8. Opprobrious use.
9. A derogatory term.
10. Derogatory.
11. Derogatory use.
12. Usually derogatory.
13. Used chiefly in contempt.
14. Often used familiarly, now chiefly contemptuous.

15. Hostile and contemptuous term.
16. A hostile and contemptuous te.m.
17. A shortened-form often expressing contempt, hostility, etc.
18. A term of contempt or derision.
19. Vulgar term of prejudice and contempt.
20. Now a vulgar usage.
21. A vulgar, offensive term of contempt, as used by Negrophobes.
22. Vulgar term indicating a contemptuous or patronizing attitude.
23. Vulgar, offensive term of hostility and contempt, as used by anti-Semites.

When the questionnaires are returned, the opinions are collected, sifted, analyzed, collated, and often returned to the members of the committee to be reviewed a second time. Finally, a decision is made by the editor.

Once the editor and his committee have settled on the policies for the dictionary, the editor then has the problem of combing the vast amounts of information available to him, selecting it, arranging it, and preparing it for publication. Usually, an office staff prepares the copy for the dictionary in order that everything included may be adjusted to the space that we have and a proper balance between the various types of information presented may be maintained. This involves people who are highly skilled in the art of abstracting, careful and judicious in their judgments, and capable of writing good clear English. Even etymologies and pronunciations are best prepared by a staff.

Assuming that the staff has looked carefully through secondary sources and followed the policies of the editorial advisory committee as set by the editor, there is the problem of checking the accuracy of the facts given in the dictionary. No dictionary should be content to merely abstract secondary sources. There are a great many fields of knowledge. It is very hard to conceive of a dictionary for general use being prepared by a staff inside an office without any special checks of accuracy made by an outside staff. Nowhere is this principle of outside checking more important than in the handling of scientific material. The names of plants and animals, the terms in chemistry, physics, aeronautics, electronics, and so forth should be checked by at least one specialist in each field. Is one specialist enough? Is it better to have both a British and an American critic if we are to have a representative dictionary of the English language?

I have gone into some of the various editorial problems from the standpoint of a statement of policies, the work of the staff, and the work of the special editors. The work of all editors must be coordinated by the general editor and put into a book which the publisher promotes on the general market. The editor has combined the thinking of all of these people and balanced one interest against the other in order to furnish a book which will be acceptable to all the parties concerned, as well as to the general public. He is the interpreter of the linguist to the publisher, the publisher to the linguist, the definer or staff member to the etymologist in the conflicts for space. The editor has given from 54 to 61 per cent of space to definitions, .7 to 1.3 per cent to illustrative phrases, from 5 to 8.5 per cent to etymologies, from 2.1 to 4.4 per cent to synonym studies and lists, and around 28 per cent to entries, pronunciations, parts of speech, inflected forms, usage notes and other material.

I hope from these general observations and from the specific problems that I have listed that you will get at least some idea of the special editorial problems that the editor of a commercial dictionary has. Many of these problems are the same as those of the scholarly dictionary. For any dictionary—commercial or scholarly—is more valuable when it gives the agreed-upon knowledge of the experts, carefully labels opinions as such, and balances the types of information given to meet the needs of its public.

56

The New Webster Dictionary:
A Critical Appraisal

ALBERT H. MARCKWARDT

A COMPLETE REVISION of our largest commercially produced dictionary of the English language has become a regularly recurring event in American life. Upon occasion the time table has varied a bit, but the following listing reveals an astonishing degree of regularity over the past century:

An American Dictionary of the English Language (Royal Quarto Edition, Unabridged)	1864
Webster's International Dictionary	1890
Webster's New International Dictionary	1909
Webster's New International Dictionary (Second edition)	1934
Webster's Third New International Dictionary	1961

Of the five Webster editions listed above, probably none has called forth such extremes of critical comment as the recent Webster Third. It has been characterized as "a very great calamity." Its general tone has been described as "a dismaying assortment of the questionable, the perverse, the unworthy, the downright outrageous." At the same time, other reviewers speak of the work as "an intellectual achievement of the very highest order," and "a reference work which worthily carries on a tradition of great reference works."

These extremes of praise and blame are reminiscent of the reception of the 1828 edition of *An American Dictionary of the English Language,* compiled by Webster himself and the real parent of the long line of dictionaries which bear his name. At that time a reviewer in *The Southern Literary Messenger* denounced the treatment of pronunciation as horrible and the orthography as abominable. The English *Quarterly Review* judged it "a decided failure, conducted on perverse and erroneous principles," and, in

Originally read at a meeting of the Michigan Linguistic Society, this paper is printed here by permission of the author, Professor of English at Princeton University.

much the same vein as some of the critics of the Webster Third, complained that "we do not recollect ever to have witnessed in the same compass a greater number of crudities and errors, or more pains taken to so little purpose." But Webster's 1828 work had its admirers as well, particularly among the Germans, who praised the profound learning that it reflected.

The disparate comments on Webster's early work are of interest today only as a historical phenomenon, but those which have been applied to the Webster Third have given rise to considerable confusion. It is scarcely possible for both the critics and the admirers to be right in all that they say, and one may reasonably ask what a more dispassionate evaluation might be.

In approaching such an appraisal, we must understand first of all that the American lexicographer in his concern with current English faces something of a dilemma. He is the inheritor of two traditions clearly in conflict, both of which have their roots in England.

The earlier tradition is that of Samuel Johnson, the compiler of the 1755 *Dictionary of the English Language,* who lent the first touch of sheer genius to English lexicography. In the preface of this great work, he pointed out that "every language has its improprieties and absurdities, which it is the duty of the lexicographer to correct or proscribe." According to him, the function of a dictionary was one, "by which the pronunciation of our language may be fixed and its attainment facilitated; by which its purity may be preserved, its use ascertained, and its duration lengthened." That Johnson was expressing the spirit of his age is shown by comments such as that of Lord Chesterfield, who wrote, "We must have resource to the old Roman expedient in times of confusion and choose a Dictator. Upon this principle I give my vote for Mr. Johnson to fill that great and arduous post."

This concept of the lexicographer as linguistic legislator or arbiter, if not absolute dictator, is still strong in the United States. It is frequently reflected, and indeed encouraged, by the slogans which dictionary publishers—not the editors, let me hasten to say—choose to advertise their wares. The very phrase, "Supreme Authority," which the G. and C. Merriam Company used to employ, supported this view of the dictionary; whether intentionally or not is open to conjecture.

The slightly later and opposed tradition is that of the lexicographer as the objective recorder of the language. For the English-speaking nations this concept was first realized on a substantial scale in what is now known as *The Oxford English Dictionary* but originally entitled *A New English Dictionary on Historical Principles.* Here the purpose is stated as follows:

> The aim of this dictionary is to present in alphabetical series the words which have formed the English vocabulary from the time of the earliest records down to the present day, with all the relevant facts concerning their form,

sense-history, pronunciation, and etymology. It embraces not only the standard language of literature and conversation, whether current at the moment or obsolete, or archaic, but also the main technical vocabulary, and a large measure of dialetical usage and slang.

Note that this statement contains not one word about fixing the language, about proscription or prescription of any kind. Operating on this basis, the lexicographer contents himself with setting down the record, leaving its interpretation to the reader. Needless to say, the prestige of the *Oxford English Dictionary* is enormous; it is generally conceded to be superior to the corresponding major dictionaries for the other western European languages. The principles on which it is based were formulated as early as 1859.

The conflict of principle which has been pointed out need not necessarily be troublesome. If the language involved is confined as to number of speakers and is the vehicle of a static and stabilized society, there is virtually no problem. But this is not the case with English, which is spoken natively by some two hundred and seventy millions, spread over five continents of the globe. In the United States, at least, the language is that of a highly mobile society, both geographically and up and down the social scale. Under such circumstances, the linguistic reporter and the legislator are more likely to seem to be working at cross purposes.

Nevertheless, it is clearly evident that as the various editions of Webster march down the century, the statements of principle which are to be found in them move steadily away from the Johnsonian or prescriptive concept toward the descriptive position of the Oxford editors. The following excerpt from the front matter of the 1934 edition (p. xxvi) refers specifically to pronunciation, but it is a fair representation of the attitude of its editors toward all language matters:

> The function of a pronouncing dictionary is to record as far as possible the pronunciations prevailing in the best present usage, rather than to attempt to dictate what that usage should be. In so far as a dictionary may be known and acknowledged as a faithful recorder and interpreter of such usage, so far and no farther may it be appealed to as an authority.

> In the case of diverse usages of extensive prevalence, the dictionary must recognize each of them.

A somewhat broader treatment of the editorial function is to be found in the Introduction (p. xi) to the 1934 Webster:

> Both Samuel Johnson and Noah Webster conceived it to be a duty of the dictionary editor to maintain the purity of the standard language. However, with the growth in literacy of the past century, and the increase in fiction and drama, in radio and motion picture, of the use of dialect, slang, and colloquial speech, it has become necessary for a general dictionary to record

and interpret the vocabularies of geographical and occupational dialects, and of the livelier levels of the speech of the educated.

It would be difficult to imagine a more cogent or forthright exposition of the descriptive function of the dictionary than these two statements of editorial policy. The first of them apparently satisfied the editors of the Webster Third, for they repeat it in their Introduction (p. 6a) with only one minor expansion: "best present usage" of the earlier edition now reads, "general cultivated conversational usage, both formal and informal." This offers additional support for the conclusion that with respect to the conflict between opposing lexicographical concepts, the descriptive had been accepted, the prescriptive rejected, as early as 1934. Whatever differences there may be between the 1934 and 1962 editions, they are not matters of policy or principle. They are instead differences in the way in which a principle common to both dictionaries has been realized.

Lexicographical policy is not ordinarily a matter of absorbing interest, but it has been necessary to deal with it at some length because the Webster Third has been criticized on occasion for repudiating, even sabotaging the principles of the second edition. Such charges serve only to reveal a total lack of awareness on the part of the critic as to what these principles were, as well as an inability to distinguish between principle and practice.

The extremes of public reaction to the new Webster must therefore be understood in terms of editorial decisions on a practical rather than a theoretical level. Such an understanding may best be attained by considering certain of the practical questions which confronted the editors, what the decisions on them were, and what the reasons for them may have been.

At the very outset of their preparations, the editors apparently felt an obligation to increase considerably the amount of evidence upon which the new dictionary was to be based. Dictionary evidence normally exists in the form of citation slips, the products of an extensive reading program. The citations are filed under their appropriate headwords, and in the editing process they constitute the raw material for the definitions and in fact for most of the word treatment.

At the time of the compilation of the second edition, the files in the Springfield offices held some 1,615,000 citation slips. In the years intervening between the two editions, as the result of what must have been a tremendous effort, this figure was nearly quadrupled. Just under 4,500,000 citations were added, resulting in a total of 6,000,000, a number approximately equalling the collection for the *Oxford English Dictionary*, but far more heavily concentrated on the language of the present day. In addition, the *Dictionary of American English* and the *Dictionary of Americanisms* had both been completed in the years 1944 and 1951 respectively, constituting a further increase in the size of the corpus available to the editors of the Webster Third. As a result, they found themselves with approximately 50,000 new words, that is, words not entered in the Webster Second, and 50,000 new meanings for words already entered.

At this point physical and financial factors enter into consideration. For a number of reasons, undoubtedly based upon a century of business experience, the publishers are firmly committed to a single-volume dictionary. They had made the Webster Second as large, that is to say thick, as any one volume could possibly get and still assure a back that might withstand the rigors of long and constant use, particularly in schools and libraries. Thus it was manifestly impossible to increase the number of pages by the ten or fifteen percent necessary to accommodate the new entries. If these were to be included, something had to come out. The kind of material that was removed forms the basis of some of the criticisms of the present edition.

The first excision consisted of the materials which, in earlier editions, had been placed below the horizontal line running across the page. These included archaisms, dialect forms, variant spellings, and proper names. To quote the editors, "Many obsolete and comparatively useless or obscure words have been omitted. These include, in general, words that had become obsolete before 1755 unless found in well-known major works of a few major writers." Incidentally, the significance of the date 1755 can scarcely escape one's attention. In the first place it was the publication year of Dr. Johnson's dictionary. Moreover, as a deadline for obsolescence, it marks an advance of two centuries and a half over the corresponding date of 1500 for the Webster Second. Thus, in word selection as well as in other matters, the emphasis is clearly placed upon the current state of the language.

Getting rid of the obsolete and the obscure did not in itself solve the space problem. Still other things had to go, and these taken together constitute the parts essential to a peripheral function of the dictionary long cherished by Americans—the encyclopedic function. In the process of elimination, the editors removed among other things:

1. The gazeteer section.
2. The biological section.
3. Titles of written works and works of art.
4. Names of characters in fiction, folklore, and mythology.
5. Names of battles, wars, organizations, cities, and states.
6. Mottoes and other familiar sayings.

There have been further excisions as well. Color plates and illustrations are reduced in a proportion somewhere between one-fourth and one-third. Even the number of pages has gone down from 3210 to 2720.

This elimination of encyclopedic material has caused anguish. "Think, if you can," complains Wilson Follett, "of an unabridged dictionary from which you cannot learn who Mark Twain was, or what were the names of the apostles, or that the Virgin was Mary, the mother of Jesus of Nazareth, or what and where the District of Columbia is." Actually, this is not at all difficult. The great Oxford comes immediately to mind, as does Henry Cecil Wyld's *Universal Dictionary of the English Language,* or any of the great academy dictionaries of such languages as French or Spanish.

Nevertheless, Follett's reaction will be shared by many Americans. In the past, dictionaries published in this country have cheerfully served an encyclopedic as well as a lexicographic function, and ironically enough it was Noah Webster himself who was primarily responsible. His first dictionary, published in 1806 included tables of the moneys of most of the commercial nations in the world, tables of weights and measures, ancient and modern, the divisions of time among the Jews, Greeks, and Romans, and an official list of the post-offices in the United States, to mention only a few of the extra features. Although the editors of the current volume have broken with their progenitor in cutting out these impedimenta, they have not at all departed from the essential principles of lexicography in so doing.

Undoubtedly they felt that the considerable increase in the number of illustrative citations would readily compensate for the loss of the peripheral material. Such citations do constitute the core of the reportorial dictionary. For instance, there were no citations for the adjective *oratorical* in the second edition; the Third has three. The second edition gave three identified citations for *chase,* verb. In the Third, there are four identified and seven unidentified citations.

According to the Preface of the current edition, "More than 14,000 different authors are quoted for their use of words or for the structural pattern of their words . . ." Many of these are contemporary. The reader is also informed that the verbal illustrations (citations apparently unidentified as to author) are "mostly from the twentieth century."

This innovation has met with something less than universal approval, a reaction not so much attributable to the editorial policy itself as to some of the advertising antics of the business office. The original brochure, announcing this edition as "one of the most remarkable literary achievements of all time," included among the list of authors cited such names as Billy Rose, Fulton Lewis, Jr., Art Linkletter, Dinah Shore, Ted Williams, and Ethel Merman. In addition there were Harry Truman, Dwight D. Eisenhower, John F. Kennedy, and Richard Nixon, whose names were undoubtedly signed to reams of material which they did not compose. To the sympathetic this signalled a conscious attempt to include a wide range of current authors. To the critical it betokened a lack of discrimination and responsibility. Actually, the citations from such sources are few in number and small in proportion.

A point which must be taken into account here is that which was made at the very outset of this essay, namely that the life of a Webster edition is roughly calculated at twenty-five years. Thus, the overriding concern of the dictionary is quite appropriately the language in its current state. It is on these grounds that the editors may logically justify the preponderance of citations from current authors, irrespective of lasting literary merit. It may be assumed that in the 1986 edition many of them will be discarded, to be replaced by others from the 1970's and early 1980's. In this respect the Webster practice will differ sharply from that of the *Oxford English Dictionary,* for which no new edition was contemplated, although certainly only a small proportion of the authors cited in that work are literary giants of lasting reputation.

Another departure in the Webster Third from the practice of earlier editions, which has given rise to considerable criticism, is the treatment of what are called *status labels.* Here again some of the disapproval has its source in misunderstanding. Basically, the editors have developed a terminology which is at once semantically neutral and more precise than that which has been employed in the past. The label *illiterate* has been discontinued. It has become a term of censure rather than a dispassionate indication of the inability to read and write. The current replacements, *substandard* and *nonstandard* are matter-of-fact rather than pejorative and permit a gradation of acceptability, the latter indicating a wider range of occurrence than the former, although it is applied to a smaller number of words and expressions. American dialect ascriptions represent a great advance in precision over those of the second edition in that they reflect an adaptation of the terminology for the various dialect areas developed by Professor Hans Kurath, editor of the Linguistic Atlas and the most eminent linguistic geographer in the country. It was unfortunate, however, that the editors chose not to indicate those words current in all regions of the United States but not in England or other parts of the English-speaking world.

Another innovation in the Webster Third is the elimination of the label *colloquial.* There are two conceivable reasons for this: In the first place the term is ambivalent, signifying informality on the one hand and the spoken rather than the written medium on the other. It is customary now among students of the language to be somewhat more precise, recognizing not only *colloquial* but *casual* and *intimate* as further gradations of the spoken variety of the language, any of which not only may be but are regularly employed by speakers of unquestioned cultivation.

An even greater objection to the label *colloquial* is the persistence with which an unfavorable connotation has adhered to it. Dictionary users never interpreted the term in the way in which dictionary editors intended. It was not meant as a condemnation either in the Webster Second or in the various abridged dictionaries based upon it. The editors took great pains to say so, both in the prefatory material and in the definition of the word itself, but this went quite unheeded. So for the present edition the staff was faced with the alternative of finding an acceptable substitute less liable to misinterpretation, or of eliminating the label altogether. It chose the latter, partly perhaps because of the unsatisfactory experience of other dictionaries which had experimented with a substitute.

In general the changes in the choice and ascription of labels reflect an endeavor to achieve greater precision and objectivity. The attempt at precision undoubtedly finds some adherents, although there will be disagreements over the application of the labels in specific instances. The attempt at objectivity has, understandably enough, resulted in the disappearance of the censorious tone which, for many, seemed to be part of the proper function of the labels *colloquial* and *illiterate*. To such persons, the lack of censure will be understood as a lowering of standards.

In dealing with pronunciation, the editors of the Webster Third had to contend with two factors which had not faced their predecessors. One was a new electronic development, namely voice amplification. The other was a new concept in the analysis of language, that of the phoneme or meaningful unit of sound.

Voice amplification affected the kind of pronunciation which the dictionary undertook to record. In preloud-speaker days, the second edition of Webster recorded what it called "formal platform speech," the speech of cultivated users of English, speaking formally with a view to being completely understood by their hearers. That there were other types of pronunciation wholly appropriate to less formal situations was readily conceded by the editors, but they evidently felt that their editorial responsibility could be discharged with the greatest amount of effectiveness and least confusion by indicating just the one.

The microphone has changed all this. Certain devices of articulation necessary for clarity when the speaker was forced to depend on lung power to make himself audible to the last row of a large auditorium are no longer necessary. Nor are they often employed today. They have gone, along with the orotund periods of the old-time spellbinder.

This change led the Webster editors into a complete revision of the manner in which evidence on pronunciation was collected. Where Webster Second had attempted a sampling, by means of written questionnaires, of the pronunciation of persons who did a considerable amount of public speaking, the Webster Third staff turned its attention directly to the language itself rather than to opinion about it. They listened to radio, television, and recordings; to speech in all parts of the country and in all types of situations. Again, as with the citations for word occurrences, forms and meanings, the body of evidence was tremendously increased in range and scope, but certainly less skewed toward a single type of pronunciation.

In any English dictionary, and particularly one designed for use in the United States, a decision upon the particular system, or respelling, to indicate pronunciation always poses a problem. For a number of reasons, the American public has been unwilling to accept the International Phonetic Alphabet; nor is this a particularly economical device when a number of variants must be shown. The Webster Second continued with few changes the system of its predecessors, which was cumbersome in that a single sound was indicated by more than one transcription, and confusing in that a single character sometimes covered far more latitude than the user was likely to realize.

The editors of the current edition have attempted to take advantage of a concept basic to present-day linguistic science, that of the phoneme. A cogent discussion of this concept and its impact upon the way in which pronunciations are indicated may be found under the rubric *phonemicity* in the Webster Third *Guide to Pronunciation*. The general result has been the disappearance of a rash of diacritics which made the earlier dictionaries difficult to read and to interpret. Some useful characters have been taken over from the phonetic alphabet, notably the elongated *n* to indicate the usual sound of *ng,* and most important, the inverted *e* or schwa for the neutral vowel used in weakly stressed syllables. The latter, it must be confessed, is an innovation in which Webster followed some of its competitors. At all events, the public will no longer be misled into believing that the final vowel of *caucus* is somehow different from that of *fracas.*

Unfortunately the necessity of economizing on space has led to the excision of the authoritative treatments of the individual sounds of English which lent scholarly distinction to the second edition though perhaps read by only a few. Also, certain innovations of the Webster Third will cause annoyance until the public becomes accustomed to them. One of these may well be the indication of stress by a mark preceding rather than following the syllable. The removal of the pronunciation key from the bottom of the page is another. The use of a modified *d* character to indicate what the editors call, "the usual American pronunciation of *latter,*" will seem to the critical like countenancing the slipshod, and it is possible that a *t* with a diacritic might have served quite as well without outraging quite so many sensibilities.

With pronunciation as with countless other features of the dictionary, the editors have attempted to present the facts of the language as they saw them. It is an honest presentation, maintaining the principles and the concept of the dictionary characteristic of previous editions, but carrying them out with greater consistency and basing them upon far more evidence. There have been errors of judgment, more often perhaps with respect to manner of presentation than in the interpretation of the facts which are reported, but this is inevitable in an undertaking of such magnitude.

My comments so far should have suggested, to a degree at least, the reasons for some of the changes which are to be found in the Webster

Third. They have not yet given an answer to the question which was initially posed: why the extremes of praise and blame. The encomiums are easy to account for. They represent the approval of those who accept the descriptive principle and find in the current product a generally conscientious and more thorough implementation of it than is otherwise available.

The chorus of protest is somewhat more complex in origin. It is in part the expression of a desire for linguistic authoritarianism, an attitude which can be explained only in terms of a number of complex and interrelated factors in American cultural history. Added to this is the mistaken notion that the Webster Third represents a change in lexicographical principle, an error which is fostered by the more complete coverage and greater accuracy of the edition. The excision of certain kinds of non-essential material represented a sudden departure from a time-honored practice. Finally, there is, as always, a tendency toward careless reading and inept comparison. Upon occasion a judgment objected to in the third edition was already present in the second, and there is the amusing instance of the critic, writing in a semi-sophisticated weekly, who was outraged by what seemed to him to be undue permissiveness. But some of the matters about which he complained were already present in the 1909 edition.

In the light of all this, one can only say that by a more literal acceptance of its declared function, and by running counter more obviously to what people want or think they want in a dictionary and to what they think they have been getting, the Webster Third represents a calculated risk of $3,500,-000. Depending on one's point of view, it is either a courageous or a foolhardy venture into the latter half of the twentieth century. For the staff, who in the face of the public clamor must wonder if it has been at all worthwhile, there is only the dubious comfort in Macaulay's words, "The best lexicographer may well be content if his productions are received by the world in cold esteem."

Part VII

LINGUISTICS AND THE STUDY OF LITERATURE

INTRODUCTION

BECAUSE so many users of the First Edition welcomed the Part dealing with the controversial area of linguistic applications in literary criticism and the study of literature, the section has been retained, with some changes occasioned by recent publications. It is certainly still true that no methodology has been accepted; yet an increasing number of teachers of literature seem to be finding that valuable supplementary insights are obtainable through various linguistic approaches.

Applying linguistics to the study of poetry has so far been an activity of only a bare handful of scholars oriented to both linguistics and literature. A focal point of this activity appears in the synoptic report by Whitehall and Hill of the language and literature seminar at Indiana University during the summer of 1953. Since then, application to poetry has taken at least two directions. One is that followed by Hill himself in the structural analysis of a poem as a whole. The First Edition offered one such example, Hill's analysis of Browning's "Pippa Passes." The other direction is illustrated by the article by Chatman with his use of structural findings, including the use of suprasegmental phonemes of pitch and stress, in clarifying poetic meaning and removing ambiguities.

Sutherland, whose article here precedes Chatman's, deals with only part of Chatman's larger concern, the use of the suprasegmentals. Although reluctant to deny practical and traditional values in established prosodic analysis, Sutherland affirms that linguistics does have a positive, though, small, contribution to make in the field of metrics. An excellent related article is that by George B. Pace, "Meter and Rhythm," *PMLA*, 76.413-19 (September, 1961).

Hill then undertakes to demonstrate that a close study of semantic parallels, a study perhaps metalinguistic rather than linguistic, opens doors to deeper meanings than are readily perceptible. Francis finds that linguistic analysis of syntax, in more precise terms than traditional grammar makes available, also opens doors to clearer understanding of a literary work.

Finally a quite different application of linguistics in the study of literature is demonstrated by Ives with his investigation of the use of dialect by Joel Chandler Harris to individualize his characters.

57

A Report on the Language-Literature Seminar

Harold Whitehall and Archibald A. Hill

We started with what we believe to be a necessary series of assumptions for any objective study of literature, even though we are aware that these assumptions are necessarily limited, and may even be objected to by several schools of literary criticism. We believe, however, that quarrel over the assumptions given below is unnecessary and unfortunate, since these assumptions merely constitute the necessary rules for a certain kind of game—a very serious game, however, in which the only prize is increase of human knowledge and understanding. In other games—again we use a word which we do not wish to have understood in any flippant sense—the rules would be different.

Reprinted by the permission of the authors from the original mimeographed report. Professor Whitehall is a member of the Department of English at Indiana University; Professor Hill is at the University of Texas.

Our first assumption is that a work of literature, whether a full length novel, or merely a triolet, is an utterance fully contained in the utterances which make up human language. A piece of literature is therefore a language act, like other language acts, but differentiated from them by characteristics of its own. As a further assumption, which in part necessarily follows from the first, we believe that a work of literature can be behavioristically investigated as a language act having reality in the outside world like other language acts. It can not, contrariwise, be usefully investigated if we make the assumption that it exists only in the mind of the author, the mind of the reader, or in a sort of union of the two. In making this assumption, you will note, that we are not denying the reality of what goes on in the mind of author and reader, but merely stating that we can not usefully study it. Once the behaviorist assumption outlined above is made, it then becomes possible to study the structure of a work of literature, secure in the belief that our study is throwing light on the object of investigation, and that we are not merely describing our own subjective reactions to it.

If then, literature is a type of language act, we believe that it follows that it can not be studied with the fullest fruitfulness unless the student is deeply versed in scientific linguistics, and is prepared to focus this knowledge on both the external and internal characteristics of literature, in hope of finding, eventually, those particularly significant characteristics which define, in each culture, the difference between literature and mere everyday use of language. There is no phase of literature where there is a more intimate relation between the structure of language and the structure of the literary work than in metrics. As a result, the Seminar this summer set itself the primary task of re-examining English metrics in the light of phonemic theory. The results of this re-examination follow.

English, being a language in which stress differences are a basic and significant structural device—in contrast to many languages where stress differences may exist but are not significant—builds all its metrical patterns on stress differences. No matter whether the metre is that of Beowulf, Pope, or T. S. Eliot, there is always a pattern of alternating stronger and weaker stress. The metrics of such a language as Hungarian, on the other hand, makes no such fundamental use of stress, since there the pattern is often a merely symmetrical arrangement of syllables. The stress phonemes of English are four, though it is probable that there were only three in Old English. Metrical stress, however, recognizes only two stresses, a stronger and a weaker. It therefore follows, as we think we have been able to demonstrate, that there is a permissible range of stress variation within which variety is felt as one of the conventional ornaments of English, though variation beyond these limits is a blemish. The two extreme stresses, primary or weak, are poetically fixed, the first being necessarily always a poetic strong, the second always a poetic weak. The two middle stresses, secondary and tertiary, may be poetic strongs, or poetic weaks. The principle of poetic stress is that a syllable is strong if it is stronger than those which surround it, so that as indicated above, a tertiary stress followed by a weak may count as a poetic strong, while if followed by a secondary or primary stress, it may count as a poetic weak. Those English poets who are generally admired as metrists make use of these differences to produce variety, and we have tested enough poetry of all periods and types so that we are sure of this statement. It will be noted that this formulation, simple though it may be, is at least useful in imposing a theoretical limit on variation, and explains why some poets can make use of metrical variation without offending the reader, while others invariably produce the effect of lack of skill by stress conflicts.

Next, English has three phonemes of the type called terminal junctures. These are essentially pitch shapes which occur at the ends of (phonological) clauses and sentences. Two of them can be readily heard by pronouncing the sequence "one, two, three." After the first two numbers there is a slight rise, and after the third, a fall. These are the two junctures known as double bar, and double cross (//, and #). A third type, single bar (/), functions in much the same way as double bar, but does not have the rise of double bar. Instead it seems to have a continuation of the pitch level of the preceding material, whatever that level may be. It is important to note that these juncture phenomena are not pauses, since though pause may accompany them, it is not a necessary accompaniment. In all English poetry these junctures are made use of. In relatively unskilful and unvaried poetry there is a juncture placed at the end of each line, as a heavy reinforcement of the rhyme. In more skilful poetry, the juncture pattern is extremely varied in relation to the rhyme words. There is no better poet for the study of the subtle variations in juncture than Pope, who takes a rigid basic structure, and varies it continually with junctures within the line, and with junctures absent at the ends of lines. It is worth noting in passing that criticism has concerned itself a good deal with the "caesura" in Pope, believing it possible to explain his verse in terms of a relatively mechanically placed pause in the middle of each line. This form of statement now turns out to be largely irrelevant.

The third characteristic of English which is strikingly used in metre is a feature which is not a part of the significant structure, but is nonetheless a basic phonetic characteristic of the language. We owe knowledge of this feature to the phonetician Kenneth Pike of Michigan. This feature of English is the fact that the amount of time between two primary stresses tends to be the same, irrespective of the amount of material between them. This feature can be called isochronism, and it is intimately related to juncture, since isochronism is often secured by increasing or decreasing the pause which always may accompany a terminal juncture. In contrast to English, such a language as Spanish tends to make all syllables occupy the same amount of time, thus producing the effect that we have called isosyllabism. For those wishing to test the English characteristic of which we speak, the Pike drill sentences

> Énglish / is éasy#
> Énglish / is very éasy#
> The Énglish lesson / is very éasy#

will demonstrate what is meant.

We believe that a language having characteristics like English will almost necessarily create a metrical form in which what is counted is the number of strong stresses, and in which the number of weak stressed syllables is irrelevant. The whole of the material will be further arranged into the time units of the same length, marked off, not into feet, but into juncture units. It is just this type of verse which represents the native English tradition, beginning with the verse of Beowulf, continuing through ballads and proverbs, and nowadays once more practiced by selfconscious and highly sophisticated poets. This type of verse we call isochronous verse, and believe that it is to be identified with the type of verse imperfectly described but brilliantly practiced by the 19th century poets Hopkins, Bridges, and Patmore. The name given by this group to poetry of this sort is "dipodic verse" which we believe to be a name less useful, because less accurately descriptive, than "isochronic verse." Two useful examples of isochronic verse may make these statements clearer.

> A stitch in tíme // saves níne.#
> Fát // bláck // búcks# (in a winebarrel room . . .)

It will be noted that the first is popular, the second literary. In each, the material between junctures is clearly isochronous.

Beside the pattern of isochronous verse there exists also a borrowed form which appears for the first time in the verse of Chaucer, which is isosyllabic or syllable-counting. The theory of English metre has always recognized this type, and unfortunately all too often seems to assume that it is the only type. We do not attempt to judge between the two types, but could content ourselves with pointing out that Pope and Dryden belong to this school, and that the usage of Milton seems to be a blend of this school with isochronism. We believe further, that these two types exhaust the forms practiced in English. The attempts, at several different periods, to introduce quantitative classical metres are necessarily doomed to failure, since though differences in quantity exist in English, they are not phonemic.

A word about metrical theory can conclude this portion of the report. English metrical theory has generally been of two schools, a relatively mechanical school which has taken over the terminology of classical metrics, even to such terms as "long and short," which counts syllables, and breaks verse up into units of various kinds of feet. This is usually the metrics of school handbooks. It works reasonably well with isosyllabic verse, but breaks down almost completely with isochronic verse. A second school, largely founded by Lanier, insists that poetry is a kind of music, and records isochronic verse with considerable success in musical notation. Both schools, however, are pre-phonemic, and both attempt to explain English verse by extraneous material—the structure of Latin verse in one school, the structure of music in the other. We believe, then that our conscious linguistic analysis of English verse can make use of stress units, juncture units, and time units, in such a way as to give a coherent theory of verse structure broad enough to take into account any form of English verse. Neither of the two previously practiced types of analysis can do this.

58

Structural Linguistics and English Prosody

RONALD SUTHERLAND

IT SEEMS LIKELY that future generations will look upon the present age as one which witnessed not only the birth of the guided missile, but also the death of the misguided grammarian. The science of linguistics has completely revamped our notions of the English language. Former grammarians, who attempted to ram this language into the alien patterns of Latin and Greek, were in error; for it has been proven that English has a structure uniquely its own, requiring unique grammatical description. But what of the field of literary criticism? Can the findings of linguistic scientists affect that field in any way? To date, although many suggestions have been made, a conclusive answer has not been supplied.

Various theorists, including John C. McGalliard, have generalized on the matter, lamenting that structural linguists tend to be cultural philistines and

Reprinted by permission from *College English*, 20.12–17 (October, 1958). Professor Sutherland is a member of the Department of English in the Faculté des Arts of the Université de Sherbrooke, Québec.

calling for a liaison between them and the literary critics.[1] René Wellek and Austin Warren, however, attempted to pinpoint the situation and made the following prophetic statement: "Phonemics seems indispensable for comparative metrics and a proper analysis of sound patterns."[2] The purpose of this inquiry will be to ascertain exactly what the science of linguistics can contribute to English prosody.

In the summer 1956 *Kenyon Review,* a series of papers dealt with this very subject. Harold Whitehall and Seymour Chatman, both structural linguists, argued for linguistics-based metrical analysis, while John Crowe Ransom and Arnold Stein supported conventional prosody. Although several important ideas were forwarded (to be referred to later), after digesting all these papers one concluded that the linguists were taking a wrong approach. Of course their system permits highly accurate representation of any particular recitation, but the purpose of metrical analysis, most critics will agree, is not to discover the idiosyncrasies of particular readings of a poem, but to examine in broad terms how the meaning and effect of a poem are reinforced. In other words, the ideal is to get as far away as possible from the relative and as near as possible to the standard; structural linguistics, it would seem, would only reverse this process. Moreover, in the eyes of many literary men that science encourages the cardinal sin of separating words from meaning.

Accordingly, if the science of linguistics is going to bestow anything on English prosody, a new approach is needed. In Brooks and Warren's *Understanding Poetry,* which has become a sort of bible in many of our schools, one finds:

> This is not to say that any system of indicating scansion, certainly not the rather rudimentary system suggested in this book, will render the enormous subtlety, the complication and shading, of rhythm and texture in language when it is well used. We must depend upon the tact and discrimination of our ear to do that. But the use of a system will help us. It will give us a sort of standard, however crude, to which we can refer the actual language. And it is to the actual language that we always want to come back. That is where poetry exists.[3]

Now the "rather rudimentary" system employed by Brooks and Warren probably represents the peak of development in conventional metrics. Although it is unlikely and unnecessary that any system "render the enormous subtlety, the complication and shading, of rhythm and texture in language" —and we have already observed that such a system could never be universally meaningful—there is every probability that the present system can

---

[1] Norman Foerster, et al., *Literary Scholarship, Its Aims and Methods* (1941), p. 35.
[2] René Wellek and Austin Warren, *Theory of Literature* (1949), p. 179.
[3] Cleanth Brooks and Robert Penn Warren, *Understanding Poetry* (1950), pp. 124-125.

be relieved of some of its crudity to become a more polished "sort of standard." If this can be done, then the most salient key to its accomplishment is Whitehall's suggestion in the *Kenyon Review* that linguistics information about pitch and juncture should be part of the prosodist's equipment. To substantiate this point, I shall examine closely one of the most complete and rewarding analyses in *Understanding Poetry*. But first, a brief statement of the pertinent linguistics information must be made.[4]

There are four degrees of stress: primary ('), secondary (^), tertiary ('), and weak (ᵛ). Corresponding to these are four pitches: low (1), mid (2), high (3), and extra high (4). Since hardly anything, and especially not poetry, is spoken in a level monotone, the voice goes higher and lower in the course of an utterance, and this is known as change in pitch. When a person speaks more loudly than normally, the greater amount of air employed causes an increase in the vibrations of the vocal apparatus, often resulting in a rise of pitch; although loudness can also be combined with low pitch, as in the case of bass drums and bassoons. Also, when a person puts emphasis on a certain word, it is usually by means of a correlative increase in stress and pitch; for assisted by junctures these two factors condition every word, producing, as Whitehall so aptly puts it, chords rather than notes—the essence of what has been known to many men as "verbal music." Closely connected with the idea of pitch are the differing junctures between words and syllables. In the normal flow of a phrase, the various sounds run into one another; yet there is something between most words which allows us to distinguish them as separate. This slight pause, as it were, is called the "transitional juncture" (+). But there are three other junctures indicating greater divisions. The end of a statement is usually accompanied by a lowering of pitch and a fading of the voice into silence, and the resulting hiatus is described as a "fading juncture" (↓). To the conventional prosodists, this type of juncture is known as the "caesura"; without being able to explain why, the conventional prosodists also know that such a juncture causes unusual emphasis to be placed on the initial following syllable, and their knowledge is happily corroborated by linguists' research. Since the voice fades into silence, the next sound to be heard is a fresh mark on a clean slate, like the first note of a solo violinist after the orchestra has hushed. When, as in the case of a good many questions, a group of words ends with a rise in pitch, we have a "rising juncture" (↑). This type of pause ordinarily creates an expectancy of more to come; its precise explanation in terms of linguistic data clarifies the prosodist's general notion of "secondary pauses." Sometimes the gap between two units of language is characterized by a sustention of pitch, like

---

[4] With certain modifications, this information is based upon H. A. Gleason's *An Introduction to Descriptive Linguistics* (1955). Mr. Gleason lists three clause terminals (↓ ↑ →) and one open transition (+); these are all called junctures above.

a taut clothesline between two poles, causing the syllable before the gap to be "prolongated." Most noticeable when the pitch is high, this type of pause is known as the "sustentional juncture" (→).

With the above information in mind, we shall now turn to the analysis of William Butler Yeats's "After Long Silence" in *Understanding Poetry* (pp. 116-121). The poem:

> Speech after long silence; it is right,
> All other lovers being estranged or dead,
> Unfriendly lamplight hid under its shade,
> The curtains drawn upon unfriendly night,
> That we descant and yet again descant
> Upon the supreme theme or Art and Song:
> Bodily decrepitude is wisdom; young
> We loved each other and were ignorant.

Now the first line of this poem is scanned by Brooks and Warren as follows:

Λ Spéech|ăftĕr lóng|sílence;| ʌ ĭt|ĭs ríght,

With the information we have acquired above, we might modify this scansion to:[5]

Λ ²Spéech+àftĕr+lóng² ↑ ³sílence;¹ ↓ ²ĭt+ĭs+ríght,³ ↑

Brooks and Warren go on to say that "the fact that the reader must hurry over the two unaccented syllables of *after* before he can rest on the accent of *long* makes the emphasis on *long* greater than it would otherwise be; and this heavy emphasis on *long* fortifies the meaning of the word." To this we can add that the rising juncture after *long,* causing the sound volume of that word to be sustained as the pitch rises, is another reason for the emphasis. The study continues: "This emphasis is further increased by the fact that the accented syllable *si*—of the trochiac foot *silence* follows the accented *long* without an intervening unaccented syllable. But when two accented syllables are thrust together in this way, the reader is forced to take a slight pause between them. The effect of such a condition is to increase the emphasis on the accented syllables, because the reader has lingered at that point in the verse." The "slight pause," of course, is a rising juncture; and since the stressed initial syllable *si* has a pitch of (3), we can explain further that the increased emphasis upon it is due to a harmonic of stress and pitch.

Brooks and Warren go on to say that "The heavy pause after *silence*

---

[5] Only changes in pitch and the pitches before and after a juncture need be marked. Tertiary and secondary stresses are indicated here as a means of suggesting slightly less than a primary stress and slightly more than a weak. Since this is a more or less subjective distinction, there is no interference with the conventional notions of feet and meter.

(a pause dictated by rhetorical construction) gives the effect of the speaker's meditating a moment . . . . The word *it* receives, by reason of the weak syllable (the second syllable of *silence*) and the pause which precede it, more than its ordinary emphasis. This emphasis, again, is dramatically right . . . ." In other words, *silence* is followed by silence; the "heavy pause" is a fading juncture, giving the word *it* all the emphatic quality of an initial note which breaks a silence.

". . . For the word *it,* usually a fairly unimportant word and lightly stressed, in this context is important. When the word occurs we do not yet know what the *it* refers to and what it does refer to—what the speaker says is 'right'—constitutes the basic statement of the poem. Explaining the *it* gives us the body of the poem." Furthermore, the word-group *it is right* ends with a rising juncture, instilling, as is usually the case with such junctures, a sense of expectancy concordant with the dramatic pattern of the poem.[6]

Of the second line in the poem, not much needs to be said. Brooks and Warren point out the emphasis on *estranged;* we might add that the line ends with a fading juncture, which observation will be of some use later.

The conventional and modified scansions of the third line are as follows:

Ŭnfriénd|ly lámp|light hid|ŭndĕr|ĭts sháde, ²Ŭnfriéndly+lámp+lîght²→²híd +ûnder+ĭts+sháde,¹↑

"The third line," reads the analysis, "offers two slight variations from the norm. There is a strong *secondary accent* on the syllable *-light,* for in the compound word *lamplight,* as is true of most such compounds (*midnight, bookcase*), there is a marked secondary accent . . . . The result is to give the accent in the foot *-light hid* a hovering effect rather than that of a decisive fixing on one of the two syllables." Here we have a most interesting phenomenon. Brooks and Warren describe the foot *-light hid* as having a "hovering effect"; one look at our modified scansion tells us exactly what they mean and how the situation is brought about. Between *-light* and *hid* is a sustentional juncture, which, it will be recalled, causes the prolongation of the first syllable as the pitch is sustained. It should also be observed that this line, like the second, ends with a fading juncture.

Now the analysis has nothing to say about the metrical patterns of lines four and five, they being regular iambic pentameter; however, I believe they contain a point of some interest. Unlike lines two and three, ending with low-pitched words and fading junctures, line four ends with a high

---

[6] It is interesting to note that in Paul Roberts's *Understanding Grammar* (1954), p. 251, the word *it* as used in this poem is classified as "Situation It." Mr. Roberts, who based much of his work on linguistics research, points out that "When we use this *it,* we withhold for a moment the name and nature of the substantive we want to mention; consequently we introduce a bit of suspense and make the substantive more emphatic when it comes."

pitch on the word *night* followed by a rising juncture. If the fourth line be interchanged with lines two or three, the meaning of the poem will remain perfectly intact; yet, an attempt to read the work with these three lines arranged other than they are will swiftly convince one that something is thereby lost. The fact of the matter is that the rising juncture at the end of line four at once recalls the similar ending of line one (*it is right* ↑) and waves the reader on to the beginning of line five, consummating the construction (*It is right that we descant*). Neither line two nor line three, since each ends with the kind of juncture that does not create a sense of expectancy, could do this so well. We might also note incidentally that line five ends with a transitional juncture, carrying, as grammatical structure would lead one to expect, that line into the next.

Brooks and Warren next center the attention on the sixth line:

Ŭpón| thĕ supréme|théme|ŏf Árt|ănd Sóng:

It is interesting that they add in a note: "Some students may prefer to scan the line as follows:

Ŭpón|thĕ sú|preme theme|ŏf Árt|ănd Sóng:

though this alternate scansion is somewhat arbitrary in that it gives a primary accent to *su-* and thus suggests that it is on something of the same stress level as *-preme,* a syllable actually much more heavily accented." Here we have these two gentlemen admitting a troublesome kind of inadequacy in their system, to a certain extent illustrating what they meant by "rather rudimentary." They know that *-preme* has a heavier accent than *su-,* yet they are not completely happy about giving *su-* either a weak or a strong stress. The whole problem might be solved by the following scansion:

²Ŭpôn+thĕ+sùpréme²→²théme+ŏf+Árt+ănd+Sóng:²→

Although, as was intimated earlier, the meticulous marking of four stresses will likely only cause a system of metrics to become less a significant norm and more a subjective evaluation, there are bound to be situations like the above when the prosodist will welcome four defined stresses at his disposal, when, ironically, their use will enable him to establish a more significant norm. It will be noticed that our modified scansion labels the accent on *su-* as midway between the weak stress and the less-than-primary stress indicated by Brooks and Warren's alternate scansions.

The analysis has more to say about line six: "The second foot, *the supreme,* is anapaestic; this means that the syllable *-preme* receives a more than normally emphatic pronunciation. The next foot is imperfect, containing only the syllable *theme;* a lingering on the syllable *-preme* and a pause compensate for the missing syllable in the next foot. This situation, as we have already seen from line 1, gives unusual emphasis." Here again, we are in a position to explain what has been observed. A sustentional juncture constitutes the "pause" between -*preme* and *theme,* and this combined with two high pitches accounts for the "lingering on the syllable -*preme.*" Harmonics of high pitch and primary stress on both *theme* and -*preme* magnify their accents so that the emphasis upon them is indeed unusual. Unlike any of the others, this line ends with a sustentional juncture, and this observation should be kept in mind as we move on to the seventh line, the conventional and modified scansions for which are:

$$\text{Bódĭly}|\text{dĕcré}|\text{pĭtúde}|\text{ĭs wís}|\text{dŏm; yoúng}$$
$$^2\text{Bódĭlý}+\text{dĕcrêpĭtûde}+\text{ĭs}+{}^3\text{wísdom;}^1 \downarrow {}^2\text{yoúng}^2 \uparrow$$

Brooks and Warren mention that because of the three unaccented syllables, "The reader is forced, as it were, to accelerate the pace to reach the second accent." Another factor contributing to this acceleration is the sustentional juncture at the end of line six. Since the pitch is sustained, the reader does not have to start at the bottom of the hill again; he simply coasts on.

They go on to say that "After the pause, therefore, the reader is forced to stress, and linger on, the syllable *young,* for only by this accent does the line achieve any metrical system .... *Young,* is, obviously, a very important word here .... The unusual emphasis forced on it by the metrical arrangement of the line fortifies the whole meaning of the word in the poem." Our scansion shows the word *young* to be strategically situated between two junctures: it is the initial word after a fading juncture, and although the body of the word is not high-pitched, there is no drop-off in volume and a sharp rise in pitch before its sound has disappeared. All this adds up to a unique kind of accentuation, and the rising juncture acts as an invitation to the concluding line of the poem. There does not seem to be anything we can add to the description of the regular, iambic pentameter last line.

Before I go on to seek conclusions from the examination just conducted, one more thing must be said. I have no doubt that a linguistic scientist could manipulate his descriptive devices with much more precision than I have demonstrated. Moreover, he could apply much more complicated notions, such as voice qualifiers, differentiators and all the recent discoveries of metalinguistics and microlinguistics, provided—and this is the important point—provided he were dealing with a particular reading of a poem. But as I have mentioned, the purpose of prosody is to seek a norm, a standard from which individual interpretations can move. Now that years of detailed research lie behind the science of linguistics, only a fool would question the ability of a qualified structural linguist to analyze particular speech performances, but he is equally foolish who thinks that the exact description of such a performance would constitute what literary scholars call "a metrical analysis." It follows, then, that much of the information accumulated by this new science is inconsequential to English prosody.

Prior to examining "After Long Silence," we made a selection from available linguistics information. Armed with a general understanding of pitch, junctures, and two extra stresses, we proceeded to experiment with a long-standing metrical analysis made by two reputable conventional prosodists. We were not able, except in one minor case, to arrive at a *greater* understanding of how the language pattern of the poem reinforced its effect and meaning; however, I venture to say that we did achieve a *clearer* understanding. In many instances, when Brooks and Warren seemed to be groping for appropriate words ("hovering effect," "slight pause," "heavy pause," "unusual emphasis"), we had precise descriptions ready. We did not transcend the norm established by Messrs. Brooks and Warren, but within the limits they defined, we were operating more efficiently. In effect, we illustrated how the application of linguistics principles does not have to interfere with the purposes, general methodology, or conclusions of the prosodist, but can help fulfill his purposes, clarify his methodology and fortify his conclusions.

Our conclusion, therefore, seems obvious. The science of linguistics does have something to offer to English prosody, and thus to English literary criticism. The adoption of certain selected descriptive devices will hardly revolutionize the old system of metrics, nor even provide for greater insight into poetry. The analysis found in *Understanding Poetry* is striking evidence that the old system works; there is no necessity for an overhaul, yet the addition of a few linguistics-manufactured accessories will expedite the achievement of its end. The prosodist who realizes this can still travel on the same road, enjoy the same scenery, reach the same destination—only in a slightly more efficient machine.

59

Linguistics and Teaching Introductory Literature

Seymour B. Chatman

I assume that the purpose of introductory courses in English literature is to teach students how to read it. Yet many college students, in spite of the best intentions, never *do* learn to read the masterpieces of our language with even elementary comprehension. One reason for their failure is that the basic skill of interpretation is all too easily assumed by the instructor, whose anxiety is to prove the value of literature or whose scholarly interests may insulate him from the beginner's major problems. The kind of English which we want our students to learn to read differs strikingly from the kind they are used to. For the first time, they must try to make plain sense out of a dialect which is infinitely more subtle in lexical distinction and more complex in structure than any they have ever known; and there is no use in minimizing the size and dangers of the linguistic gap that yawns before them.

The central problem in the teaching of literature is to bridge the gap: to show students how to expand and refine their disturbingly narrow grasp of potential structures, to develop a whole new syntactic and lexical musculature for dealing with the complexities of Milton, Shakespeare, and Pope. One way to accomplish this is to treat the text almost as if it were a foreign language (for it is at least a foreign dialect), to be parsed and worked over until pattern and meaning are learned and overlearned. All the devices that linguistics has developed for teaching foreign languages might be tried: substitution within a frame, imitative oral drill (with particular attention to stress, pitch, and juncture), restructuring for analysis, expansion, and omission, etc. Furthermore, the instructor must be aware at every moment of the specific linguistic complexities of the piece he is teaching in relation to the level of his class. This is as important to his immediate job

Reprinted by permission from *Language Learning*, 7.3–10 (1956-1957). Professor Chatman is a member of the Department of Speech at the University of California, Berkeley.

as a knowledge of mythic patterns in the Modern English novel or what nasty fellows Elizabethan printers were. He must attempt—and it is a painful job—to uncover the multifoliate layers of his own literary sophistication and put himself in the students' position. He must realize that students are unable to move with the linguistic facility that he has developed in himself, that they are not alert to the lexical and structural possibilities of language and are quickly reduced to helplessness if the first meaning which comes to mind proves untenable. Nor are they willing to pore over a passage until it makes sense, because they know that more than poring will be needed to help *them*.

Let us consider the three areas where linguistics might be helpful.

I. *Lexicon.* We must be careful not to shrug our shoulders over the lexical problem and say, 'It's all in the dictionary.' First of all, the facts of American college life are such that we cannot count on a student to *buy* a decent dictionary, let alone use one. This bit of student pathology, of course, is not our problem. What *is* disturbing is that even where a student shows a willingness to use the dictionary, it is all too clear that he often doesn't know *when*. Most students dutifully look up words that they don't 'know'; that is, *words that they've never seen before*. But it isn't the unusual word that causes the trouble. Even lazy students can be expected to look up 'incarnadine' and 'multitudinous' if threatened with quizzes. The real danger lies with relatively simple words that are known in one—but the wrong—definition. Not only doesn't the student understand the word, but far worse, he doesn't even *know* that he doesn't understand it. And the astonishment and disbelief in his eyes when you tell him that words *often* have more than one meaning! Here are a few rather obvious instances that have troubled my students:

> I only hear
> Its melancholy, long, withdrawn roar.
> Retreating, to the breath
> Of the night wind, down the vast edges drear
> And naked *shingles* of the world.   (small beach stones)

> From this descent
> Celestial *virtues* rising will appear
> More glorious than from no fall.   (angelic host)

> . . . leaving the tumultuous throng,
> To cut across the *reflex* of a star
> That fled, and flying still before me, gleamed
> Upon the glassy plain . . .   (reflection)

> Love's not Time's fool, though rosy lips and cheeks
> Within his bending sickle's *compass* come.   (range)

> I sigh the lack of many a thing I sought
> And with old woes new wail my *dear* time's waste.   (precious)

Becoming *aware* of a lexical difficulty is far more than half the battle, for it is precisely the skill of recognition that students lack so desperately. And it is obviously the teacher's affair, for even the most heavily glossed text-book will not help students whose real problem is that they refuse to admit that they do not 'know' rather simple words. The teacher must demonstrate with semantic exercises the perniciousness of taking the first meaning that comes to mind if his students are ever to become competent and self-dependent readers. Those students who have successfully studied foreign languages will be the first to believe him; anyone who has had to look up *facio* or *affair* or *Bestimmung* a dozen times for a dozen different contexts will readily accept the principle of semantic diversity in English. It is the monolithic monolingual who will be hardest to convince, just as he is the hardest to teach to write decent compositions. This is basically a problem in sensitizing students to a higher degree of semantic awareness than they have ever known, and they may offer fierce resistance. The whole drift of their lives in the culture which nurtured them may go against recognizing the possibility of finely wrought discrimination of meaning. But it is a vital job of pedagogy and worthy of more scientific interest among linguists than it has so far aroused.

II. *Form-class identification.* Separate from the lexical problem (which is self-evident and a little removed from my major concerns) is the difficulty the beginner frequently encounters in identifying a word's part-of-speech. Students are accustomed to taking the path of least resistance: they only know how to identify a word's structure in terms of its most frequent assignment, and are reluctant to analyze the specific syntactic demands which the environment makes upon it. For example:

> The Sea of Faith
> Was once, too, at the full, and *round* earth's shore
> Lay like the folds of a bright girdle furled.

I have had all eighteen students in a class of eighteen tell me that 'round' is an adjective modifying 'shore.' The reason is obviously quantitative: 'round' occurs more frequently in their idiolects as an adjective than as a preposition, and its occurrence immediately before 'earth' seems to have utterly incapacited these readers from making any other form-class identification. ('Full,' too, is easier for them to take as an adjective modifying 'earth' than as a nominal, the axis of 'at the . . . ' .)

But we are more competent to handle this problem than the lexical problem, for we have the signals to help us. Rather than *tell* the student that 'round' should be taken as a preposition, we can make him *hear* his mistake. After convincing him that his reading is meaningless ('What then is the subject of "lay"?'), we contrast his superfixes with our own.

His:

The Sea of Faith
Was once, too | ²at the ²fûll and rôund êarth's shóre²
Lay like the folds of a bright girdle furled.

Ours:

The Sea of Faith
Was once, too| ²at the ²fúll¹#² and rôund êarth's ³shóre²
Lay like the folds of a bright girdle furled.

The insertion of # between 'full' and 'round' and the substitution of tertiary for secondary on 'round' will be enough for three out of four students, simply because the signals are stronger than any abstract grammatical explanation could be. (And, of course, if Smith's new syntactic views are correct, the phonological *is* the grammatical explanation. The less astute fourth student will not understand the difference, but for non-linguistic reasons; either because he has never heard the expression 'at the full' before, or 'round' used as a preposition, but *not* because he is unprepared to interpret the comma as # and the tertiary on 'round' as the signal of a preposition.

Another example:

Me though just right, and the fixed laws of heaven,
Did first create your leader, next free choice . . .

Most students take 'just right' to modify "me," thus tertiary on 'just' (and in some idiolects /jɨst/ instead of /jəst/), and secondary on 'right':

³Mé though jùst rîght²

But if forced to imitate another reading, many grasp the structure immediately:

³Mé¹ | ²thòugh ²jûst ríght² | ²and the ²fîxed lâws of héaven²

('Although righteousness and heaven's laws first created me your leader . . .') Here are some other lines from the same passage:

from this descent
Celestial virtues rising will appear
More glorious than from no fall.

Several students, after learning that 'virtues' refers to the fallen host, took 'celestial virtues' as a vocative, and 'rising' as a gerund, rather than as a post-positional participial modifier (with 'from this descent' as adverbial object):

²from thìs de²scént³|
²Celêstial vir²tues || ²rising¹| ²will appêar
Mòre ²glórious¹ | ²than from ²nó fâll¹#
(and trust themselves to fear no second fate.)

('From this descent, o ye virtues, your rising will appear more glorious than from no fall.') But this reading is only superficially possible, for 'trust,' then, has no subject. We ask them to imitate the following:

from ³thìs descént²|

²Ce³lêstial vírtues || rîsing² ²will ap³péar³ |

³Môre glórious² |²than from³ nó fâll²|

('Celestial virtues, rising from this descent, will appear more glorious than from no fall and will trust themselves to fear no second fate.')

A final example: one student, reading it this way

O bright-eyed Hope, ²my ³môrbid fâncy chéer¹#

wondered how Hope could be at the same time 'bright-eyed,' 'fancy,' and 'morbid.' Her embarrassment knew no bounds when she heard the following reading and immediately saw her error:

O bright-eyed Hope, my ²mòrbid ³fáncy¹ | ¹chéer¹#

('O hope, please cheer up my morbid fancy.')

III. *Word Order*. Word order is so vital in Modern English structure that inversions[1] offer perhaps the most difficult syntactic adjustment that a student has to make. What he needs is basically a re-education in signalling potential. There is no use saying that this comes with reading experience, because all too often even graduate students appear unable to parse locutions like Johnson's

Behold surrounding kings their pow'r combine,

And one capitulate and one resign;

or Milton's

to consult how we may best

With what may be devis'd of honours new

Receive him coming to receive from us

Knee-tribute yet unpaid, prostration vile,

Too much to one, but double how endur'd

To one and to his image now proclaim'd?

Since inversions are easily analyzed and catalogued,[2] it is strange that no one has ever compiled a primer or drill-book to develop among novice readers the essential skill of interpreting them. It would seem that the very act of going through several examples of the same type would prove

---

[1] I use the term in the broad sense to mean any order of words not usual in normal spoken English.

[2] The job has been done excellently by Mats Redin, *Word Order in English Verse from Pope to Sassoon* (Uppsala: Universiteits Arsskrift, II, 1925), from whom most of my examples are taken. I am grateful to Professor Josephine Miles for calling this study to my attention.

eminently useful as 'pattern practice.' An example is the difficult inversion of Object-Imperative (for Imperative-Object), which the tremendous pressures of the *usual* meaning of the NV pattern often lead students to interpret as Subject-Predicate, particularly where signals of potential subject-predicate agreement are lacking: 'Then, pilgrim, turn; thy cares forego' or 'Here subterranean works and cities see,' or 'Round my true heart thine arms entwine.' The student must be taught to search for *other* clues than he could normally count on; for example, in the Object-Imperative pattern, he could use previous straightforward imperatives as a hint ('turn,' in 'in . . . turn'). The important thing, however, as in all pattern practice, would be to set the model and then to fill it with numerous confirmatory examples.

Here are some of the kinds of poetic inversions that cause students trouble[3]:

SOV   Bright Thames the brightest beauties yield
Prep SOV   With hairy springes we the birds betray
OSV   What though no credit doubting wits may give
OVS   Among the Shepherd-grooms no mate / Hath he
SAuxOV   Gums and pomatums shall his flight restrain
SprepV   Not fierce Othello in so loud a strain
            Roared for the handkerchief that caused his pain
SVprepO   The God who darts around the world his rays
OConjSV   But fortune's gifts if each alike possessed
AdvSV   Unless aside thy purple had been thrown
AdvPrepVS   Swift on his sooty pinions flits the gnome
SAuxPrepV   There all the Learn'd shall at the labour stand
PrepImp   Hope humbly then; with trembling pinion soar
PrepP   A vile conceit in pompous words expressed
PrepInf   What moved my mind with youthful lords to roam
SPredNV   Some figures monstrous and mis-shaped appear.
            For I thy own dear mother am.
ObjCompOSV   Modes of Self-love the passions we may call
PrepN   O thou! Of Bus'ness the directing Soul.
NAdj   Not tyrants fierce that unrepenting die
AxisPrep   She talked and sung the words among.
            I went my work about.

The teacher has no business assuming that his beginning students have either the initiative or the ability to learn how to interpret poetic inversions on their own. What they need is the same kind of intensive drill that has proven so effective in foreign language instruction—drill within the pattern, in this case with instances drawn from all periods of English poetry. The alternative is a continuing incapacity to handle any other structure

---

[3] S = subject, O = object, V = verb, Prep = prepositional phrase, Conj. = conjunction, Adv = adverb, P = participle, Inf = infinitive, PredN = predicate noun.

than SVO or its standard variations—in short, incompetence as a reader of poetry.

It would be fatuous to suggest that all the problems of teaching introductory literature can be solved by linguistics, for the obvious reason that literature can never be defined in terms of language alone. Obviously our methods do nothing to develop the vital poetic prerequisites of emotional maturity, esthetic sensitivity, and general culture. Yet, as important as these qualities are, they do not even *become* problems until the student has succeeded in piecing together the plain syntactic sense of a poem. Let us not evade our linguistic responsibilities. Let us try to solve linguistic problems with linguistic methods, and let the other things take care of themselves.

60

Principles Governing Semantic Parallels

ARCHIBALD A. HILL

SOME YEARS AGO I found myself in a discussion of the meaning of two passages in Frost's poem "Bereft." The passages were:

> Where had I heard this wind before
> Change like this to a deeper roar?

and

> Leaves got up in a coil and hissed
> Blindly struck at my knee and missed.

The questions were whether *roar* in the first passage involved a reference to a lion, and whether the several verbs in the second were a reference to a snake. My opponent maintained that reference to a lion enriched the imagery of the poem. My own position was that there was indeed a snake, but that the lion was unnecessary. What follows is an attempt at a justification of this position, together with an exploitation of its theoretical consequences.

First for *roar*. The notion that it must refer to a lion is certainly not required, since, though we use it in connection with the noise of animals,

Reprinted by permission from *Texas Studies in Literature and Language* (Austin, Texas), 1.356–65 (Autumn, 1959). The author is Professor of English at the University of Texas.

we also use it for the noise of wind. The Joos law, the first law in semantics, states that in seeking a translation or paraphrase for a given item, that meaning is best which adds least to the total meaning of the context.[1] Under these conditions, it seems clear that a paraphrase "noise of wind" adds far less to the context (wind is specifically mentioned) than does "noise of lion." In spite of possible loss of a certain amount of Empson-type richness, the Joos law would seem to dispose of the lion quite effectively.

The snake is different. In the first passage one could argue that at most there was a transfer of a single lexical item, *roar,* from a discourse about lions to a discourse about wind. In the second passage there are four items, all appropriate to snakes, which are applied to leaves. They are "got up in a coil," "hissed," "struck," and "missed."

A rough kind of calculation can be resorted to, which quickly establishes the fact that it is far more likely that a snake reference is a part of the design than was the lion possibility. If we take any one of these items alone, such as *hiss,* we can say that it either refers to a snake or does not. The chance of snake reference by pure chance is then one out of two. I am of course perfectly aware that an accurate weighting would be very difficult, probably impossible.[2] One way of trying to weight probabilities would be to tabulate all the non-linguistic items to which the form *hiss* might be applied, all the way from escaping steam to an angry theatrical audience. The chance that *hiss* referred to a snake would then be one out of this whole list of possibilities. Such a count would contain a large number of objects, but would not be reliable no matter how exhaustively done. The nature of language is such that we continually apply old symbols to new situations, and indeed must do so if we are to talk at all. As a result, any list of items to which *hiss* might refer is necessarily open-ended and subject to growth.

But while there is a reason to suppose that the probabilities involved in deciding whether a single item does or does not refer to a snake are one out of a very large number, there is contradictory evidence which points towards the assumption that they are one out of a very small number. Figurative language is often repeated. Thus whoever first referred to using

[1] Martin Joos, "Towards a First Theorem In Semantics," a paper delivered before the Linguistic Society of America, 29 December, 1953. See also Joos, review of Eric Hamp, *A Glossary of American Technical Linguistic Usage, LANGUAGE,* XXXIV (1958), 286. "The guiding principle here, in the lexicographical tradition, is the one which I appear to have been the first to formulate in public, [that] the best meaning is the LEAST meaning, or in other words, the proper definition is the one which makes the term MAXIMALLY REDUNDANT in the group of citations. This sounds queer, almost as if it were a counsel of despair; but it is in fact the principle which governs all good lexicography even though the expert workers may not have verbalized it."

[2] I am indebted to my colleague Professor R. E. Greenwood for enlightening discussion of the mathematical difficulties involved in an accurate rather than merely approximate measure of probabilities of this sort.

money to start a money-making operation as "pump-priming," very probably had in mind the image of an old-fashioned hand pump. Nowadays, however, *pump-priming* is used by many individuals who never saw, much less operated, a pump handle. Thus if we are considering *hiss* alone, we could say that we would be reasonably sure that it involved reference to a snake only if we had the unlikely assurance that this instance was the first time that *hiss* had ever been used in connection with leaves. It is the fact that repetition involves loss of reference in figurative language which enables us to apply the Joos law in rejecting reference to a lion in the use of *roar*.

In the discussion which follows, I shall assume that the possibilities involved in *hiss* as a reference to a snake are one out of two. Such a figure may be arbitrary, but it will serve our purposes none the less. The test which is of most importance to us is not whether an individual reference is likely or unlikely, but rather whether as references are repeated, they move towards greater or less likelihood of interpretation. The arbitrary figure of one out of two is adequate for discovering the direction of movement in probabilities. Let us suppose that the lines in which we were hunting for a lion reference had been

> Where had this wind shaken its mane and roared?

Roared we have decided, has a ½ chance of occurrence "by chance," that is, without reference to a lion as a part of the design of the poem. The same figure applies, of course, to *shaken its mane* considered alone. But the probability of the two items occurring together "by chance" is only ¼. When two such items occur, then, the probability that reference to a lion is significant is considerably increased. If there are three possible lion items, the possibility that they are meaningless is ⅛; if four items, the chance is 1/16. Chances of lion reference being significant go up, therefore, as the number of items increases.

If we now turn to the possible snake reference, we see that there are four "snake items." Considering these items merely as a cluster in which the only principle of ordering is that they occur together without interruption by any "non-snake items," the chances that the passage represents a meaningful reference are 15/16, or the reverse of the statement that there is 1/16 possibility that all these items are here "by chance." This calculation is quite sufficient to establish the conclusion that it is reasonable to believe that the reference to a snake is genuine. Yet there is a second principle which we have not yet considered. Three of the items, *coil, strike, miss,* occur not merely in a cluster, but in the order in which they would be found if they were applied to a snake. They are in a specific order, significant because it is that of the reference we are endeavoring to test. The number of orders is a factorial of the number of items; the number of possible orders with three items is six, or $3 \times 2 \times 1$. Order, in short, adds a significant dimension as soon as the number of items reaches three, which is simply another way of saying that it takes three trees to make a row. In our snake reference, 1/16 must now be multiplied by 1/6, giving us a final statement that, measured as we have been doing it, there is 1/96 possibility of the snake sequence occurring "by chance."[3]

We can now, I believe, state two general principles governing possible semantic parallels. First, the likelihood of the parallel being significant is approximately doubled with each additional item which is added to form or extend a cluster. Second, when there is a parallel involving the order of items, the likelihood of significance is further multiplied by a number which is the factorial of the number of items in the parallel. It is these two principles which were used to establish the reasonableness of the conclusion that Frost was referring to a snake as well as to leaves; the Joos law was used to reject the possibility that he was referring to a lion as well as to wind.

We can now go on to work out some of the implications of these principles. First, no single item of figurative language, no matter how strikingly picturesque, can be assumed to contain a parallel, even when it is possible to express the parallel in an exact analogical structure. For instance, suppose that I say "I looked at the eyes of the house." It is easy to see here an analogy; *eyes* are to *face* as *windows* are to *house*. Yet since any such figurative transference may be borrowed rather than original with the speaker, the analogical statement is merely an etymological observation, not a necessary analysis of the semantic content of the utterance before us. Here there is a sharp and significant difference between metaphor and simile. When Poe speaks of the "vacant, eye-like windows" of the House of Usher, there is an overt statement of comparison, and the analogy becomes an accurate analysis of the semantic relationships Poe is using.

These facts have a bearing on lexicography. Since it would seem to be the duty of the lexicographer to collect all examples of occurrence of words which define their possible meanings, context by context, it would seem that instances like Frost's *roar,* and the possible utterance "eyes of the house," should be collected, and used to define *roar* as noise of wind, and *eyes* as windows—though in these contexts only. It does not seem that it is the duty of the lexicographer to collect all instances of genuine figures of speech, that is, those instances in which there is a significant semantic parallel with consequent figurative transfer. Thus a lexicographer would not need to collect the Poe quotation, unless he were in need of a quotation which might explain the origin of a later metaphorical use. Similarly, a lexicographer would not need the Frost lines which refer both to leaves and to a snake. An explicator of the poem, on the other hand, would be

[3] The number of items here is four; but one *(hiss)* can occur in any position in the series.

under a direct obligation to point out and establish the snake reference.

The Joos law and the importance of support in judging possible parallels add up to a unified tool of great utility in both lexicography and annotation of texts. A principle which says that any unsupported figurative or transferred occurrence of a single item is to be read with maximum redundancy can (and should) be easily expanded to read that if there is conflict between two possible figurative uses, the one with the greatest amount of support is chosen, that with the least amount of support rejected by being read as maximally redundant.

Thus the Joos law alone—without reference to support elsewhere—disposes of the much discussed crux in Hamlet

> or to take arms against a sea of troubles
> and by opposing end them.

The maximum redundancy for the unsupported *a sea of* is *a lot of*. Commentators who justify *sea* in a more literal reading by reference to possible parallels in Irish legend or Persian history are introducing unnecessary hypotheses. More interesting is a second passage from Shakespeare, which has been discussed at length by Caroline Spurgeon:

> Was the hope drunk
> Wherein you dress'd yourself? hath it slept since?
> And wakes it now, to look so green and pale
> At what it did so freely?   (*Macbeth*, I, vii, 35–38)

This falls [she writes] under the main heading of "personification," and is so entered, but is cross-referenced under "drunkenness," "clothes," "sleep," and "turning pale." [4]

Had the passage read merely "the hope wherein you dress'd yourself," there could have been no real objection to reading it as a parallel with clothing, since it could be argued that *wherein you dress'd yourself* is sufficiently extended to represent more than one item. Yet obviously the picture of drunken clothing is ludicrous, and constitutes a genuine conflct. The comparison to a drunken man is founded on at least the following items, *drunk, slept, wakes, look green and pale.* The items are furthermore in order. There can be no doubt, even without counting the probabilities, that drunkenness is strongly supported, clothing is not. The only sensible conclusion would seem to be to reject *clothing* as an integral part of this

---

[4] *Shakespeare's Imagery and What It Tells Us* (Boston, 1958), p. 360. In this passage Miss Spurgeon speaks almost despairingly of arriving at consistent results in tabulating imagery: "any count of this kind, however carefully done, must to some extent be an approximate one, dependent on the literary judgment and methods of the person who has compiled it." See also p. 326 in the same work, where this passage is cited as one of those supporting the thesis that the character of Macbeth is consistently presented as a man whose clothes are too big for him.

imagery, by reading *wherein you dress'd yourself* as no more than the equivalent of *that you had*. Needless to say, redefinition of images by such methods would result in considerable revision of Miss Spurgeon's suggestive study of 1935.

While lack of support is generally a negative argument, leading to rejection of interpretations, the occurrence of support can often be used to establish a positive interpretation. An example is found in *Hamlet* I, iv, 23-27:

> So oft it chances in particular men
> That (for some vicious mole of nature in them,
> As in their birth, wherein they are not guilty,
> Since nature cannot choose his origin)
> By the o'ergrowth of some complexion.

A typical annotation on *mole* and *complexion* in this passage is the following:

mole: blemish, flaw
complexion: part of the make-up, combination of humors.[5]

The meanings given by the editor are possible, and if each item is considered alone, each is probably most likely. Yet a glance at the *NED* will establish the modern meaning for both *mole* and *complexion* as having been current in Shakespeare's day. The chance that they could have occurred together without reference to a figure based on the appearance of the skin is only one in four. The skin comparison is not contradicted by the larger context, so that reading both *mole* and *complexion* in accord with modern usage would seem to be a reasonable conclusion.

A second direction in which to develop the implications of the principles governing semantic parallels is in the relation of smaller sequences to larger contexts. The discussion given above should have established the fact that in general a larger context can be expected to take precedence over a short span. It is furthermore clear that items consistent on a short span can occur in fashions quite irrelevant to the design of the utterance as a whole. A good example of such a short-span consistency is one I recently heard in a technical linguistic discussion. The form "VP" had occurred quite frequently, always meaning "verb phrase." One speaker said "The VP can be . . . president," and then immediately corrected himself to "present." The larger context clearly ruled out the possibility that officers of government were the subject of discussion.

There is a problem, however. It seems necessary to assume that there must be a point at which the larger context can no longer contradict the

---

[5] *William Shakespeare, The Tragedy of Hamlet Prince of Denmark,* ed. William Farnham (Penguin Books, 1957), p. 50. I owe this example to the kindness of my student Mr. Saad Gamal.

smaller span. If there were no such point, then every instance of a part of an utterance inconsistent with the whole would have to be explained away as being essentially meaningless. Yet since we know that many such inconsistencies are indeed real. the existence of a critical deciding point must be assumed.

It seems to me that the critical point is precisely that at which order becomes a significant part of a suspected parallel. That is, when there is a minimum of three ordered items in the parallel, there is a nearly fifty to one chance (47 to 1, to be exact) that the parallel is significant. With two items only, order cannot enter, and the chances are only three to one that the parallel is significant. Since communication theory has pretty well established that human interpretation of language is a stochastic process in which the highest probability is always acted on as if it were a certainty, I should submit that when this sharp rise in probability is reached, we no longer question the significance of the parallel, but regard it as established.

If the approximately fifty-to-one point is critical, it has implications for the parallels consisting of unordered items. With five such items, the chance that the parallel is accidental is 1/32, and only when there are six items do we pass the fifty-to-one point. I suggest, then, that the outside limit of unordered items that we disregard because of inconsistency with a larger context is five. I am aware that the suggestion is not one capable of proof, but it is not without some slight empirical support. At least in my own experience I have met one parallel involving five unordered items which it is reasonable to reject because of inconsistency with a larger context; I know of no instances of such parallels with six items. The parallel I have in mind is one in which the less dignified meaning of *seat* in "seat of learning" was consistent with four other surrounding items, the most important of which was "fundamental components," yet in which the setting in a serious and humorless discussion of education either prevents the reader from seeing the possible meaning, or forces him to decide that it is an irrelevant accident if he does see it. Thus I should say for all parallels where the probabilities of significance are less than the critical point of approximately fifty to one, that we accept them unless they are contradicted by the larger environment. Further, it is in this area of parallels capable of being contradicted by the larger environment, that there is an important difference between metaphor and simile. That is, the overt statement of parallelism which constitutes simile forces the recognition of significance, where otherwise it might be rejected. As soon, however, as we pass the critical point at which a parallel can be assumed to be significant in any case, further difference between metaphor and simile becomes unimportant in calculation of probabilities.

The possibility that a parallel can be established, even though it may be inconsistent with the larger context, gives us a powerful tool for literary criticism and analysis. Literary critics have not generally, at least of late, had a very high opinion of Bret Harte's story "Tennessee's Partner," but all too often condemnation is expressed only in terms which express a subjective reaction—as when the story is called sentimental. Aside from its other faults, however, it is possible to establish, I believe, that a major portion of the story consists in an analogy inconsistent with the structure as a whole, and that this inconsistency is the basic weakness. In the end of the story, Tennessee is condemned by a mob. His Partner attempts to secure his release by a pseudo-legal procedure, and the attempt is rejected violently by the mob. Tennessee is then taken to a hill and hanged. His body is claimed and buried with honor by his Partner. The Partner (in delirium it is true) returns to the scene of the execution, and there meets Tennessee beside the "pine on the top of the hill," "sober, and his face a-shining." One needs only to enumerate these narrative items to realize that they parallel the story of the Crucifixion. There are certainly more than three of them, and they are certainly in an order parallel to the order of events in the Crucifixion. There would seem to be no real possibility of doubting the significance of the parallel. Further, since Tennessee has been presented previously as a thorough blackguard, the inconsistency is real, even shocking.

It is true that the analysis of the Harte story I have just given is often resisted by students. I need not attempt to guess why, except to point out that resistance often takes the form of insisting that parallels must be measured in terms of the closeness of the items contained in them, not merely in terms of the number of items. The objection is an interesting one, and leads directly to the last theoretical implication of semantic parallelism. Closeness of parallel can be quantified if an overall parallel is broken down into smaller items such that for each one it is then possible to say that the items are the same or are different. The number of items which are the same then measures the closeness of the parallel, and the number of items which are different is irrelevant. As an instance, we may use the scene in "Tennessee's Partner" in which the Partner appears before the assembled miners and attempts to buy Tennessee's freedom with his accumulation of gold dust. I have intimated that this scene is a parallel to the scene of Jesus Christ before Pontius Pilate. Stated in this undigested form, the parallel probably does not seem very close. Broken down into its component parts it is possible to measure its closeness. Both Jesus and Tennessee are in the presence of a hostile mob. A single man intercedes for both. The means is a legal, or near-legal device. Both intercessions are rejected by the hostile mob. There are four items in short, which is more than enough to establish the parallel. The items of dissimilarity are numerous enough, of course—among them is the fact that one intercessor is a powerful magistrate, the other a simple and unimportant follower; in one story the means of intercession is the custom of releasing a prisoner at a certain feast, in the other it is an attempt at restitution of stolen property; and there are many more. Yet it was said above that these dissimilarities are irrelevant. The reason is a simple one. All analogies and parallels involve differing things—if there is no difference, we are not dealing with parallelism but with identity. Therefore all parallels break down sooner or later, and the only measure of their closeness is how long they maintain themselves before likeness is exhausted.

The fact that it is possible to quantify and thus measure parallels is of importance in two ways. The first is that of most general importance, though unfortunately it is not yet possible to solve all problems which this conclusion raises. A number of students, particularly Eugene Dorfman, have been greatly concerned with the need for establishing some kind of process for segmenting literary narrative into ultimate units which would be parallel to phonemes in linguistic analysis.[6] The attempt at segmentation has not been completely successful, at least as yet. Consequently, the fact that narrative or other parallels offer an opportunity for even a limited segmentation process is one of real importance. It is too soon to say how far it may lead.

About the second implication of the possibility of quantifying and measuring parallels, it is possible to be more specific. In the pages that have preceded, I have tried to be careful not to use language which implied that I believe that number and order of items can establish that a genetic relationship exists, it can not define that genetic relationship. As a result, it is often true that a parallel may exist between a given utterance and more than one other utterance or event. When this happens, quantification and measurement of the two possible parallels are necessary, and the proper conclusion is that the more distant parallel is to be disregarded. The death of Tennessee, for instance, bears considerable resemblance to the death of any criminal who is hanged; yet only if we find some execution which is closer to the Harte story than is the Crucifixion, are we justified in assuming that this execution is the proper analogy for the story. Hunting for parallels and judging their closeness may seem a surprisingly indirect method of studying literary texts. In actuality parallelism, overt or hidden, is one of our most powerful tools for uncovering depth meanings.

[6] Eugene Dorfman, "The Structure of the Narrative: A Linguistic Approach," *The History of Ideas News Letter*, II (1956), 63-67.

61

Syntax and Literary Interpretation

W. NELSON FRANCIS

I TAKE MY TEXT from I. A. Richards--appropriately enough, since he has an impressive stature in both disciplines which are here meeting in tentative amity. In his book *Practical Criticism,* after describing four kinds of meaning involved in poetry, he suggests that readers of poetry may be trained by exercise in two kinds of paraphrase, "the one to exhibit the sense of the poem, the other to portray its feeling." The first of these, he goes on to say, "requires only an intelligent use of the dictionary, logical acumen, a command of syntax, and pertinacity."[1] I have observed that even those explicators and critics who stop to perform this more humble and pedestrian analysis before plunging ahead to the headier realms of paradox, tension, and symbolism, however gifted they may be in lexical intelligence, logical perception, and doggedness, are likely to disregard syntax almost wholly. Anything approaching 'command', even of the traditional Latinate kind of parsing, is rare enough. The newer syntax of suprasegmental morphemes, tagmemes, and immediate constituents and the newest syntax of kernels and transforms seem to be totally unknown.

This neglect of one of the principal keys to plain sense can be perilous. I cite only one example. It is from Kenneth Burke—ironically enough from his collection *A Grammar of Motives.* In the essay entitled "Symbolic Action in a Poem by Keats" he develops an interpretation of the "Ode on a Grecian Urn" which depends rather heavily upon a reading of the last six lines of the third stanza of that poem which seems to me to do violence to syntax in a particularly wrong-headed way.

The lines in question are these:

> More happy love! more happy, happy love!
>> For ever warm and still to be enjoy'd,
>>> For ever panting, and for ever young;
>> All breathing human passion far above,
>>> That leaves a heart high-sorrowful and cloy'd,
>>>> A burning forehead, and a parching tongue.

Reprinted by permission from *Monograph Series on Languages and Linguistics,* No. 13 (1962), Institute of Languages and Linguistics, Georgetown University. The author is Professor of English and Linguistics at Brown University.

[1] I. A. Richards, *Practical Criticism* (Harvest Books, New York; Harcourt Brace, n. d.), 213.

Mr. Burke comments as follows:

> The poem as a whole makes permanent, or fixes in a state of arrest, a peculiar agitation. But within this fixity, by the nature of poetry as a progressive medium, there must be development. Hence, the agitation that is maintained throughout . . . will at the same time undergo internal transformations. In the third stanza, these are manifested as a clear division into two distinct and contrasted realms. There is a transcendental fever, which is felicitous, divinely above "all breathing human passion." And this "leaves" the other level, the level of earthly fever, "a burning forehead and a parching tongue." From the bodily fever, which is a passion, and malign, there has split off a spiritual activity, a wholly benign aspect of the total agitation.[2]

It is clear from this that Burke takes the clause contained in the last two lines as a modifier of the "happy love" apostrophised in the first line quoted. This, in turn, forces him to read *"leaves"* with the meaning "departs from, leaves behind." This seems to me—and to several others upon whom I have tried it out—a violent wrench to the syntax of the sentence. Surely in placing the clause where he did and introducing it with the close relative *that* Keats meant this clause to modify *passion* and intended *leaves* to mean "results in, leaves as residue." He balances three lines about "happy love" against three lines about "human passion"; the unmoving, marmoreal, unsatiated, eternally suspended love memorialized on the urn is far superior to transitory fleshly passion, which, caught in the flux of time, inevitably passes into melancholy and feverish satiation. By wilfully disregarding the syntax, Mr. Burke has also upset the rhetorical balance of the lines, which Keats had emphasized by the triplicate rime structure, the indentation, and the semicolon at the end of the third line quoted.

Howlers of this sort are admittedly not very frequent. I am more concerned about the fact that an explicator faced with a difficult poem or passage almost never uses close syntactic analysis to match the scrupulous attention he gives to lexical matters. The assumptions seem to be that syntax can usually be taken for granted, and that when a favored lexical interpretation collides head-on with syntax, it is the syntax that must give. This second assumption, I suspect, was the cause of Mr. Burke's error about Keats. He wanted *leaves* to mean "transcends," which in turn required the clause of which it is the verb to reach back, across one very eligible antecedent and five adjective phrases in appositional position, to find its head four lines—rather than three words—earlier.

The native speaker can, of course, usually take syntax for granted as long as all goes well. For him, only syntactically ambiguous utterances are of even passing concern, and these he usually resolves on the basis of lexical, rather than grammatical, clues. So common is this habit—which is

---

[2] Kenneth Burke, "Symbolic Action in a Poem by Keats," in *The Critical Performance*, ed. Stanley Edgar Hyman (New York: Vintage Books, 1956), 266.

perfectly legitimate in easy poetry—that most people aren't really aware of how many syntactic ambiguities there are, especially in written English, where punctuation only partially makes up for the absence of prosodic features. But when the lexical clues fail, when the poet is purposely—almost, one sometimes feels, maliciously—avoiding the texture of lexical compatibilities and mutual reinforcements which characterizes most discourse, then the syntactic ambiguities come out from behind the mask of words to add to the reader's discomfort. No amount of dictionary grubbing seems to help; logical acumen is of no service in deciphering a writer who has abandoned logic; pertinacity leads only to frustration. The remaining avenue—close syntactic analysis—remains unexplored. I do not intend to suggest that it will prove the universal skeleton key to all difficult passages. But if it does nothing else, it will at least put the words in their places, and supply some kind of calculus of probability for appraising the validity of competing readings. I would like to emphasize the idea that syntactic analysis operates largely in the realm of probability; it seldom deals with either clear-cut decisions or heads-or-tails dilemmas. Mr. Burke's reading of Keats which I have criticized above is not an impossible one; it is simply highly improbable. Keats's passage, in other words, is syntactically ambiguous—not, however, with a 50:50 kind of ambiguity, but something on the order of 95:5. Mr. Burke's error was to pick the 5 side without sufficient justification from the total fabric of the poem, the exigencies of the diction, and the rhetorical structure of the stanza in hand, and without assaying, or at any rate clearly stating, what the syntactic probabilities are.

I should like to spend the remainder of my time with an example, chosen expressly for its difficulty. It is the first sonnet from the sequence "Altarwise by owl-light" by Dylan Thomas.[3]

> Altarwise by owl-light in the half-way house
> The gentleman lay gravewar with his furies;
> Abaddon in the hangnail cracked from Adam,
> And, from his fork, a dog among the fairies,
> The atlas-eater with a jaw for news,
> Bit out the mandrake with to-morrow's scream.
> Then, penny-eyed, that gentleman of wounds,

[3] This poem is by way of being a classic challenge to explicators. See, for instance, Elder Olson, *The Poetry of Dylan Thomas* (Chicago, 1954), 63-69; Ralph N. Maud, *Explicator* XIV (1955), 16; Bernard Krieger, *Explicator* XV (1956), 18; Erhardt H. Essig, *Explicator* XVI (1958), 53; Monroe C Beardsley and Sam Hynes, "Misunderstanding Poetry: Notes on Some Readings of Dylan Thomas," *College English*, XXI (1960), 315-22. Only Olson devotes more than a passing comment to Thomas's syntax, to which he gives up about a page of a ten-page chapter on "Techniques of Language" (60-61). It is, he rightly says, "full of pitfalls for the unwary." His discussion, in purely traditional terms, perhaps increases wariness but gives no clue to how the pitfalls are to be skirted.

Old cock from nowheres and the heaven's egg,
With bones unbuttoned to the half-way winds,
Hatched from the windy salvage on one leg,
Scraped at my cradle in a walking word
That night of time under the Christward shelter:
I am the long world's gentleman, he said,
And share my bed with Capricorn and Cancer.[4]

I should like to locate the syntactic ambiguities in this baffling poem, and see how (or if) they can be resolved. This will not, I hasten to add, lead us to a lucid explication of the poem. But it will supply the framework which such an explication, if one is possible, must follow, and set the bounds beyond which it must not venture.

The poem is punctuated as four sentences, the first two separated by the semicolon at the end of line 2, the second and third by the period at the end of line 6, and the last two by the colon at the end of line 12. All the lines are end-stopped; that is, they would be read aloud with some sort of terminal juncture at the end, though in each case the choice of which one of the three terminals might vary with the dialect and individual style of the reader, even if all readers could agree on a single interpretation. Each line is thus treated as a syntactic unit.

The first sentence, line 1-2, is unambiguous. Trouble begins in line 3, which is syntactically ambiguous because of the morphological ambiguity of *cracked,* which can be either a preterit or a past participle. The line is either a predication, with subject *Abaddon in the hangnail* and the predicate *cracked from Adam,* or a modification, with head *Abaddon* and modifier *in the hangnail cracked from Adam,* in which case *cracked from Adam* modifies *hangnail.* In other words, the problem is which IC cut comes first, that after *hangnail* or that after *Abaddon?* In the first case, the line is an independent predication coordinated with that in lines 4-6; in the second case, the whole line must be considered in loose apposition with *gentleman* in line 2, and the *And* at the beginning of line 4 coordinates the predication of lines 1-3 with that of lines 4-6.

The general syntactic structure of lines 4-6 is clear (introductory phrase followed by a predication), but they contain two ambiguities. The first concerns the function of *a dog among the fairies:* is it the subject of the predication, or is it in apposition with *fork?* That is, which IC cut has priority, that after *fork* or that after *fairies?* If the former, the noun-headed phrase in line 5 is in apposition with *a dog among the fairies;* if the latter, it is the subject. The second ambiguity is in the predicate which fills line 6, and concerns the function of the phrase *with tomorrow's scream.* Does it modify only the direct object, *mandrake,* or does it modify the whole complementation, *Bit out the mandrake?* That is, do we cut first after *out* or after *man-*

⁴ Dylan Thomas *Collected Poems, 1934-1952.* London: Dent. 1952. p. 71.

drake? Notice that this determines what screams, the mandrake or the atlas-eater-dog complex.

The broad syntactic pattern of lines 7-12 is also apparent. It is a single long predication, with a subject whose head is *gentleman* built up by a series of appositive and participial modifiers, a predicate which may be single and may be coordinate, and a concluding sentence-modifier filling line 12 and balancing the *then* with which the sentence begins. Apart from some minor uncertainties about the hierarchy of the constituents of the subject, there are three syntactic cruxes of some importance. The first concerns the function of *the heaven's egg:* is it coordinate with *nowheres* or with *Old cock?* That is, do we cut first after *cock,* making *nowheres* and *the heaven's egg* coordinate objects of *from,* or after *nowheres,* making *Old cock from nowheres* and *the heaven's egg* coordinate appositives, modifying *that gentleman of wounds?* From the point of view of meaning, is the gentleman of wounds also a heaven's egg, or did he just come from one?

Secondly, is *Hatched* a participle, in which case line 10 is one more of the loosely coordinated or pyramided string of modifiers of *that gentleman of wounds;* or is *Hatched* a finite verb, so that line 10 is the first of two predicates in asyndetic coordination, the second being line 11: In IC terms, do we cut first after *leg* or after *winds?* In terms of meaning, was the gentleman already hatched or did he hatch during the course of the poem, before he scraped and spoke?

The third ambiguity in this sentence is relatively minor, in that its effect on meaning is unimportant. Does the phrase *on one leg* modify the phrase *Hatched from the windy salvage* or only *the windy salvage?* Is the first IC cut after *salvage* or after *Hatched?* Does the line say that the hatching took place on one leg, or that the salvage was on one leg?

The final sentence, filling lines 13-14, is syntactically as perspicuous and unambiguous as the first. So far as syntax is concerned, therefore, the difficulties of the poem lie in the middle two sentences, occupying the middle ten lines. We have located six principal ambiguities, which may be thought of either as problems of syntactic relationship or problems of IC division, depending on how you like to approach your syntactic analysis. In either case, how, if at all, are these problems to be resolved? Can we arrive at some sort of estimate of the probabilities of the competing readings?

Assuming that in locating the ambiguities we have exhausted the information conveyed by morphology, concord, word order, and the unambiguous marking of parts of speech, there remain three sorts of clues. These differ in relative significance from one poet or one poem to another; I shall present them in order of decreasing linguistic validity. The first is punctuation, whose primary function is to suggest syntax. Compared with musical or mathematical notation, it is very sketchy and imperfect, but occasionally affords clues of primary importance to what the poet intended. It may also, of course, only indicate an editor's opinion—as in the usual editions of

Emily Dickinson. The second clue is the verse. This may direct us to the stress and juncture structure, which in turn supplies some indications of the syntax. Verse is thus a secondary indicator of syntax; that is why I rank it below punctuation, which is a primary, however imperfect. The third and least reliable clue to the syntax—however important and valuable it may be on the semantic, metaphorical, and symbolic levels of analysis—is the meaning already perceived. This is primarily a matter of the relative lexical compatibility of the words, and using it consists basically of bringing to bear on syntactic problems two of Mr. Richards's other tools, intelligent use of the dictionary and logical acumen. It should be a last resort, for two reasons: it is circular, since we want the syntax to tell us what words go together, rather than vice versa; and it is risky, since the metaphorical mode of poetry often attains its most striking effects by violating lexical compatibility altogether.

Assuming (perhaps a large assumption) that the punctuation of the poem is the poet's own and is in accordance with orthodox conventions, let us see what it can do to help us with our six ambiguities. In the first of them, the interpretation of line 3, the semicolon at the end of line 2 is of paramount importance. It is the strongest mark before the period at the end of line 6, and forces us to divide the first six lines 2:4 rather than 3:3. This in turn eliminates the reading of line 3 as an appositive to *gentleman,* and leaves us no alternative but to interpret the line as a predication, with *cracked* as a finite verb and the first IC cut after *hangnail.*[5]

Punctuation also virtually decides the assignment of *a dog among the fairies* as subject of *Bit out . . .* rather than as appositive to *fork.* The significant mark here is the comma at the end of line 5, which sets off that line as an appositive to *a dog among the fairies,* and would be definitely superfluous if this line alone were the subject. Note that lexical compatibility corroborates this judgment; *dog* goes much more consistently with *atlaseater, jaw,* and *Bit* than it does with *fork.*

The third crux, the assignment of the phrase at the end of line 6, receives no help from punctuation. Whichever way it is to be read, this punctuation would be conventional. (But note that a comma after *mandrake* would resolve the ambiguity by locating the first IC cut at that point.)

Our fourth problem is the exact nature of the coordination in line 8, and once again punctuation is of no help. The line as punctuated can be read either way: as a coordination of *cook* and *egg* or of *nowheres* and *egg.* A comma at the intended primary cut, either after *cook* or after *nowheres,* while not called for by the usual handbook rules, would have been very helpful.

---

[5] Krieger *(Explicator* XV) recognizes the significance of the semicolon only to disregard it: "Line 3: 'Abaddon,' in spite of the semi-colon after 'furies,' seems in apposition with 'gentleman.' "

In case five, the interpretation of line 10, we get a faint suggestion from the absence of a comma at the end of line 11 that our first solution—to take *Hatched* as a participle—is more probable, since if *Hatched* and *scraped* were coordinate verbs, the adverbial material in line 12 would presumably go with both and not be more closely associated with the second. But orthodox punctuation has no clear-cut way to indicate this. The comma at the end of line 10 is ambiguous, since according to one reading it ends the long modifier complex of lines 8-10, and according to the other it replaces the missing coordinator between the two predicates. We could presumably get some help here from studying the incidence of this kind of asyndeton in Thomas's early poetry; how does his usage compare, for example, with that of *Time* magazine?

In our last case, the assignment of the phrase *on one leg* to its proper head, neither interpretation is ruled out by the existing punctuation. In this case, furthermore, placing a comma at the primary cut, either after *Hatched* or after *salvage,* would not have solved the problem but would only have created a new one.

Turning to our second clue, the verse, we can take two of our four unresolved cruxes together. In lines 6 and 8 the problem syntactically and prosodically is the same: whether the primary cut, presumably marked by a single-bar juncture, comes after the second or after the fifth syllable. Metrically speaking, does the caesura come after the first foot or in the middle of the third? Either is possible. But a caesura as early in a deca-syllabic line as the second syllable is a rather shocking device, and on the assumption that the poet has an ear (certainly not an unwarranted assumption in the light of the evidence still available in recordings of his readings), we do not expect him to use it twice in one poem. Nor is there any metrical reason to expect it in one of these lines and not the other, since they are metrically virtually identical, even to the initial spondee and the grammatically weak or at best tertiary syllable under the third metrical stress:

> Bìt oût thĕ mándràke wĭth tŏ-môrrŏw's scréam
> Òld côck frŏm nówhères and the hêaven's égg

It seems clear to me that in both cases the verse calls for a feminine caesura —grammatically a single-bar juncture—at the midpoint of the line, with the consequent retardation compensated quantitatively by the following short, weak syllable in stressed position. This in turn leads us to interpret *with tomorrow's scream,* rather surprisingly, as a modifier of the whole phrase *Bit out the mandrake;* and, somewhat more satisfying metaphorically, to take *cock* and *egg* as coordinate.

The same line of analysis settles the disposition of *on one leg* in line 10. Here the caesura after *salvage* is a feminine one, followed once again by an unstressed morpheme *on* in metrically stressed position. To put a single-bar and hence a caesura after *Hatched*—the ictus of the inverted first foot—does metrical violence to the line. Note, by the way, that the pattern of feminine caesura followed by grammatical weak occurs in three other lines that are not ambiguous: after *owl-light* in line 1, *eater* in line 5, and *cradle* in line 11.

Our remaining crux, the interpretation of line 10, receives no help from the verse, since the question concerns the assignment of the whole line *en bloc* to either the preceding string of modifiers or the following predicate, and since all the lines are end-stopped, there is no evidence as to whether line 10 is to be read with a final double-bar, which would make it one more in the string that began with line 7, or whether it has a /232#/ contour like line 11.

It remains to apply the final test, lexical compatibility, to this one remaining syntactical ambiguity. Certainly the key-word *Hatched* belongs with *Old cock* and *heaven's egg*, and *windy salvage* with *half-way winds;* whereas a new set of images begins with *scraped.* This joins with our sense of the relative infrequency of this kind of asyndeton to incline us toward interpreting line 10 as one more in the string of appositive and postpositive modifiers of *that gentleman of wounds.*

We are at last ready for a syntactic reading of the poem:

> ²Ăltarwìse by³ ówl²- lìght²|² in the hâlf-wày hóuse²|
> ²The gêntleman lày³ gráveward²|² with his³ fúriès #
> ²Abâddon in the³ hángnàil²|² crâcked from³ Ádam²#
> ²Ánd²|² from his³ fórk²|² dôg amòng the fáiries²||
> ²The³ átlas-êater²|² with a jâw for³ néws²|
> ²Bìt ôut the³ mándràke²|² with tomôrrow's³ scréam¹#
> ²Then²|³ pénný-èyed²||² that gêntleman of³ woúnds²||
> ²Òld côck from³ nówhĕres²|² and the hêaven's égg²||
> ²Wìth³ bónes unbûttoned²|² to the hâlf-wày wínds²||
> ²Hâtched from the wìndy sâlvage oȋ one³ lég²||
> ²Scráped at my crâdle²|² in a³ wálking wôrd²#
> ²That nîght of tíme²||² ùnder the Chrîstward shélter¹#
> ²I am the³ lông wórld's² gêntleman¹|¹ he said¹||
> ²And shâre my béd²|² with Câpricòrn and³ Cáncer¹#

This is as far as syntactic analysis will take us; the more familiar modes of critical interpretation must go ahead from here. But it seems to me that they can do so now with a firmer ground under their feet than if the syntax had been taken for granted or left to intuition as it commonly is by the ingenious explicators of modern criticism.

62

Dialect Differentiation in the Stories of Joel Chandler Harris

Sumner Ives

DESPITE THE WIDESPREAD USE of literary dialect by American authors, this device for realism has been studied very little. True, George Philip Krapp included an extensive discussion of dialect writing in his *English Language in America,* published in 1925, but aside from this, very little original work has been done. And twenty years later E. H. Sturtevant and H. L. Mencken were simply repeating his conclusions: that all of our literary dialects are essentially alike, that authors did not succeed in differentiating them, and "that there are no true dialects in America . . . so far as dialects have been utilized for literary purposes. One may say that there have been only two forms of speech in America, the more or less formal standard and the more or less informal colloquial."[1]

I have already argued at some length that these conclusions have been unjust to many authors, especially such men as James Russell Lowell, Mark Twain, and Joel Chandler Harris.[2] This discussion is an extension of the arguments advanced then and a fuller demonstration of just how one of them, Harris, was able to use various white and Negro dialects in his stories and to show systematic differences between them. But first some review is necessary, for the recognition of differences between literary representations of dialects depends on agreement as to how dialects themselves are different.

We may apply the term *dialect* to the speech of any group, limited socially or geographically, which has certain language habits in common, enough so that there is an appearance of homogeneity within the group and an appearance of difference between this group and other groups. These distinguishing language habits, however, have individually their own sep-

Reprinted by permission from *American Literature,* 17.88–96 (March, 1955). Professor Ives is a member of the Department of English at Syracuse University.

[1] I, 243.
[2] "A Theory of Literary Dialect," *Tulane Studies in English,* II, 137–182 (1950).

arate and distinct distributions. The isoglosses, or lines bounding their distribution, extend horizontally across the country and vertically through the social structure of every region. Consequently, the social status of many nonstandard items is often different in different sections. For example, both *it don't* and *you was* are found nearly everywhere in popular speech. But all educated people know that both are condemned by guides to correct usage. However, a great many Southerners, knowing this textbook rule, use *it don't* in ordinary conversation, although the same people would not say *you was*. Thus the social implications of *it don't* in the dialogue of a story would differ according to the native region of the speaker. But *you was* in the dialogue of any character would at least separate him from the company of the educated or their more successful imitators. Another form, *it do,* is practically limited to the rural South and even there it implies a less educated or more rustic speech than does *you was*.[3] It is through the careful management of such items as these, with their different social and regional associations, that Harris was able to distinguish his dialects from each other and from other popular speech.

When all the characters of a story are residents of the same locality, use of dialect, or nonstandard speech forms, serves chiefly to identify the characters as members of different social groups. These social distinctions are indicated by two devices. One is the density or frequency of the nonstandard forms; the other is the choice of nonstandard forms. In general, the greater the density, the greater the rusticity or the lower the class. Thus, in Harris's stories, the speech of a "poor white" farmer has in it not only the nonstandard forms found in the speech of a middle-class tradesman but many others as well.

But just as the choice of certain dialectal forms can show a difference in social status, so can the selection of other forms give some indication as to the generation to which the character belongs. An elderly plantation owner may use archaisms which would not appear in the speech of a younger person, regardless of his social status.

Harris could indicate such differences in dialect in his stories of Middle Georgia because many distinct speech patterns actually existed there. Middle Georgia was a relatively isolated town and country section. Settlers had come in well after the American Revolution from both the lowland South and the mountain South.[4] These differences in origin must have been reflected in the local speechways, for they can still be discovered in field records of the Linguistic Atlas.[5] And differences in family origin correlated

[3] E. Bagby Atwood, *A Survey of Verb Forms in the Eastern United States* (Ann Arbor, 1953), pp. 27, 28, 41.

[4] J. E. Callaway, *The Early Settlement of Georgia* (Athens, Ga., 1948.)

[5] For a general description of the Linguistic Atlas and its methodology, see Hans Kurath, and others, *Handbook of the Linguistic Geography of New England* (Providence, 1939). All forms which have been cited from the Harris stories have been verified by examination of unpublished Atlas records.

to some extent with occupation and economic standing. Thus there were distinct social classes in town and in country, and town and country differed from each from each other. Both had their "poor whites" and their local aristocrats, with gradations between. And there were also the Negroes.[6] Thus the local speech mores were more complex than those of other areas with less diversity in settlement and culture. Harris must have had a keen ear and exact memory, for he used the distinguishing marks of the several dialects in his characterizations. Whether this use was based on deliberate and systematic analysis, I would not say.

Much of this social dialect is also regional. It is well known that all forms of popular speech are derived from earlier popular and cultured speech through the operation of the same linguistic processes as those which give standard speech. At the same time, each change of each word in each region and in each class is a unique event, and these changes are not necessarily consistent with each other. For example, in some dialects of eastern New England, the form *be* is generalized throughout the present indicative, regardless of the subject. On the other hand, the form *is* has been similarly generalized in parts of the rural South.[7] Thus, when Uncle Remus says *I is,* he is using both social and regional dialect. Such internal causes of dialect difference have been reinforced by education and other enemies of the local folkways. These have not been nationally uniform in their effect. Consequently, "relic areas" appear with distinctive traits, although these same traits might not have been regionally definitive a few generations earlier.

The grammar and vocabulary of local speech can be shown rather fully and with little difficulty, for the conventional alphabet will spell its forms, and the meanings are relatively clear. But the representation of pronunciations is another matter. The function of orthography is to identify the phonemes, or distinctive vowels and consonants, of a language. For it to show regional differences in the pronunciation of these vowels and consonants would be redundant. Although English spelling is defective and awkward, even in its representation of the distinctive sounds, an author is generally able to show which of the traditionally recognized vowels and consonants are used in particular words. Nevertheless, he very seldom shows purely regional pronunciations in the speech of educated people, even when he could do so, unless there is some immediate reason for showing that the character is not native to the locale of the story. He varies from the standard spelling only to show pronunciations which differ from standard speech in the region of the story. At the same time, pronunciations correlating with social class are nearly always circumscribed geographi-

[6] The Negroes in Middle Georgia had been born in this country, with rare exceptions. Negro slaves were brought in from the lowland plantations at the time of settlement. and the plantation culture was fully established within a generation of the time when the land was first thrown open for occupancy.

[7] Atwood, *op. cit.,* p. 27.

cally, just as nearly all social differences in grammar are geographically limited.

In summary, then, an author employs dialect writing to identify a character as a member of some social group to which neither author nor reader is presumed to belong. By exploiting the diverse occurrence and density of nonstandard forms, he is able to distinguish between social groups with some sureness. In dialect writing, structural, lexical, and rhetorical items can be shown rather fully, and generally are; for they clearly contrast with equivalent forms in the literary standard. However, this literary standard is not uniformly pronounced, and variations in the standard pronunciation are not ordinarily shown, even to the extent they could be. Only when pronunciations are socially indicative does an author represent them. Nevertheless, these socially distinct pronunciations, like socially distinct grammatical items, generally have regional as well as social limits to their occurrence.

The best known of all the dialects which Harris used is the Negro dialect of the Uncle Remus stories. I have shown elsewhere some details of how this dialect differed from rustic white speech, as Harris represented it, and shall give here only a few generalizations.[8] There are, it is true, many items which appear in both his Negro and his rustic white speech, but there are others which appear only in his representation of Negro speech. Among them are the use of *d* for *th* when it indicates a voiced sound, as in *the, that, them,* and *whether;* the use of final *f* for voiceless *th* in words like *mouth* and *tooth;* the omission of *r* in words like *before* and *sure;* and the omission of *h* in words like *what* and *why.* Also, the Uncle Remus speech shows far more assimilation, more loss of initial unstressed syllables, more leveling of preterit and past participle forms, and a greater density of archaic forms. Uncle Remus himself has a peculiarly ornate use of words, with such exotic formations as *sollumcholly, sustonished,* and *rekermember.* He has a rich imagery, with such expressions as *leg-bail* for escape by flight and *you'er thumpin' de wrong watermillion* for barking up the wrong tree. Furthermore, his speech is larded with such proverbs as *'oman tongue ain't got no Sunday* and such comparisons as *ez ca'm ez a dead pig in de sunshine.*[9]

Actually the field records of the Linguistic Atlas, aside from a very few Gullah records, show hardly any usages in Negro speech which cannot also be found in rustic white speech. And there are many similarities in usage as Harris wrote the dialects. However, the peculiarity of his Negro speech, in addition to the features already listed, consists in the greater density of nonstandard forms, and in the fact that the nonstandard items include, in

---

[8] *Op. cit.,* pp. 165–167.

[9] For many similar expressions, see the list compiled by Stella Brewer Brookes, *Joel Chandler Harris—Folklorist* (Athens, Ga., 1950), pp. 97–110.

greater number, features which are associated with Southern plantation speech rather than with Southern mountain speech. Since the same features can actually be found in the speech of both Negro and rustic white, Harris could more justly be accused of exaggerating the actual difference than of failing to indicate it. One additional point should, however, be mentioned. Some of the Atlas field records of rustic white speech show much closer agreement with the Uncle Remus dialect than do others. These other records show features which are neither in the records of cultured informants of the region nor in the records of Negro speech. Instead, they show characteristics of South Midland[10] or Southern mountain speech, and in this respect, their usage agrees substantially with that of the "poor white" as Harris wrote it. Although most of the animal fables are told by Uncle Remus, a few of those in *Nights with Uncle Remus* are told by Daddy Jack, who represents the Gullah Negroes of the coast. The dialect is quite different, in fact so different that any one complete line of text is enough to tell them apart. I shall be able to give only a few of these differences.

According to Lorenzo Turner,[11] Gullah speech has the same vowel in words like *pat* as in words like *pot,* and it has no post vocalic *r.* Thus *pat, pot,* and *part* would all have the same vowel. This characteristic is suggested by Harris in Daddy Jack's speech. For example, he spells *laugh* and other words normally pronounced with "short *a*" with *ah,* sometimes with *ar.* At the same time, he omits the letter *r* from those words which, like *smart* and *part,* have *ar* in their normal spelling, or he spells them too with *ah.* This spelling practice shows that Harris heard the same vowel in all these words.[12] In writing the dialect of Uncle Remus, Harris indicated no dialect pronunciation for these words.

Another of the peculiarities in the representation of Daddy Jack's speech is the use of a spelling for "short *e*" as in *met* for words which have "long *a*" in the speech of most Southerners, including Uncle Remus. Examples are *shekky* for *shake, yent* for *ain't, bre'k* for *break,* and *sem* for *same.* According to Turner,[13] *met* and *make* have different vowels, but the vowel of *make,* which is a diphthong in Southern standard speech, is a short monophthong in Gullah. There was no way by which Harris could show the actual facts with the conventional alphabet. But of course he may have thought that the two monophthongs were actually the same vowel.

Three consonant features will do for illustration, although there are many others. All these are corroborated by Turner's study and differ from the usage of Uncle Remus. One is the use of *t* for voiceless *th* in all posi-

---

[10] For the limits of this speech region, see Hans Kurath, *A Word Geography of the Eastern United States* (Ann Arbor, 1949), p. 36.

[11] *Africanisms in the Gullah Dialect* (Chicago, 1949), pp. 16, 17.

[12] This vowel was probably intermediate between the vowels of *pat* and *pot,* something like that in French *la.*

[13] *Op. cit.,* p. 16.

tions. For example: *troo* for *through, nuttin'* for *nothing,* and *mout'* for *mouth.* Second is the use of *f* for final *v,* as in *drife* for *drive* and *lif* for *live.* The third is the spelling of *young* as *noung.* This word occurs in one of Turner's illustrative texts with an initial palatal nasal,[14] a sound for which there is no precedent in native English.

Differences in grammar and rhetoric are quite obvious, but I shall illustrate them only by giving a portion of a conversation between Daddy Jack and Uncle Remus. Regarding one of the young plantation women, Daddy Jack said, "Da' gal do holler un lahf un stomp 'e fut dey-dey, un dun I shum done gone pidjin-toe. Oona bin know da' 'Tildy gal?"[15]

Uncle Remus replied, "I bin a-knowin' dat gal now gwine on since she 'uz knee-high ter one or dese yer puddle ducks; en I bin noticin' lately dat she mighty likely nigger."[16]

In giving examples to show how Harris differentiated between his white dialects, I shall draw from *Sister Jane,* a novel telling, in the person of William Wornum, the activities of Wornum's sister, Jane, and her associates. In it, some characters use consistently the standard colloquial of literature, deviating only in so far as consistent with occupation and personality. For example, the dialogue of the narrator, a mild and bookish man, is rather formal and old-fashioned.

On the other hand, the dialogue of Sister Jane herself has in it many nonstandard forms and local expressions which do not appear in the speech of her brother or in that of Colonel Bullard and members of his family. For example, she says *he don't, fetch* for *carry, chany* for *china,* uses *ain't* with subjects in all persons, and has such expressions as *it would look a heap better.* Next is a group of Jane's friends, middle-class townswomen, of whom Mrs. Beshears is representative. She uses all the nonstandard forms which are found in the speech of Sister Jane and many more. Examples of these additional usages are *done took; don't never up and tell me; I ups and says, says I; teetotal;* and pronunciations of the *ee* sound in *guardian, oblige, scare,* and *care; cuss* for *curse;* and *purty* for *pretty.* Such spellings as *bekase* for *because* and *natur'* for *nature* occasionally appear, but the standard spelling for many of these is more common. Next, there is the speech of Jincy Matthews, son of a well-to-do plantation family, but popularly regarded as a half-wit and vagabond. Some forms he uses, in addition to those of the persons already mentioned, are *ast,* preterit of *ask; I seen, I taken,* and *I know'd; jine* and *spile* for *join* and *spoil; allers* for *always; tech* for *touch, drapped* for *dropped,* and *hoss* for *horse.*

There are two further dialects which have all these features and many more. One is that of two elderly gentlemen, Grandsir Roach and Uncle

---

[14] *Ibid.,* p. 263. This sound is similar to that of *gn* in French *agneau.*

[15] Translated, this means: 'That girl shouts and laughs and stamps her foot right here, and then I see her walk pigeon-toed. Do you know that Tildy girl?"

[16] *Mighty likely* here means *well-favored* and *desirable.*

Jimmy Cosby, about whom it is said: "They owned land and negroes, horses and carriages; but back of their prosperity were the experience of the pioneer and the spirit of true democracy." The other is that of Mandy Satterlee, a young girl from a "poor white" settlement who is befriended by Sister Jane, and her brother, Bud Satterlee, of whom Sister Jane said, "He was born trifling and he's stayed so." Both dialects have a heavier concentration of nonstandard forms than is found in other white dialects of the story. That of the older people includes *holp* for *helped, mought* for *might,* and in general a greater density of other archaic items such as *ax* for *ask* and *desarve* for *deserve.* Additional forms which appear in their dialogue but not in that of the younger Satterlees are *nother* for *neither, oneasy* for *uneasy; hyearn* for *heard, her'n* for *hers, gwine* for *going,* and *cotch* for *caught.* Both they and the Satterlees have such features in their dialogue as *hain't; hisse'f; out'n* for *out of; e'en about* for *just about; a-nigh* for *near;* and the following phonetic spellings: *ef* for *if; hender* for *hinder; yan* for *yon; quare* for *queer; whar* for *where; arter* for *after; shore* for *sure;* and *creetur* for *creature.* These examples, of course, are only a few of the nonstandard usages found in each dialect.

The mere listing of specific items which occur in one literary dialect but not in others does not, of course, exhaust the distinctions between them. There are differences in syntax and idiom which are not revealed by this type of analysis; moreover an author puts more of such spellings as *sez* for *says,* which indicate no more than the normal pronunciation, into his writing of nonstandard dialogue.

From one point of view, this is an exaggeration of the dialect, an insinuation that it is further removed from the standard than it is. However, such exaggeration is probably defensible, for it adds to the illusion that actual conversation has been reproduced. Once the literary standard has been left behind, the author tends to suggest the actual rhythm and flow of speech as closely as he can. In doing this he is apt to indicate by spelling changes what probably occurs also in the speech of those whose conversation is not represented as dialect. Thus the dialects in literary transcription may actually appear more different from the regional standard than in truth they were.

But if this is a fault it is, so far as Harris is concerned, a happy one, for his writing of conversation in literary dialect seems truer and more natural than his writing of it in the literary standard. In fact, the more one examines the speech of Harris's folk characters, the more one admires the skill with which he worked. He has, in truth, done more than write a more or less informal colloquial, as Krapp put it. A shy man himself, he must have listened keenly and sympathetically, for he caught the various patterns of folk speech in great detail. And whatever his narrative ability, he handled the dialogue of his folk characters with skilful discrimination.

INDEX

(Boldface numerals indicate page limits of an article by the writer whose name occurs as the entry.)

Abraham, Leo, 104
adjective (*see also* part of speech), 30, 94
adverb (*see also* part of speech), 20, 30
Alford, Henry, 280
Allen, Harold B., **212–9, 231–241**
allomorph, 93
allophone, 86 ff
ambiguity, 111 ff, 139 ff, 516 ff
American College Dictionary, 242, 338, 434, 439 ff
analogist, 6, 20
Anderson, F. 104
Andrews, Schofield, Jr., 2
area linguistics (*see* linguistic geography)
Aristotle, 4, 5, 18–20, 23
Artin, Edward, 444
Atwood, E. Bagby, 156, 203, 210, 214, 226, 240, **242–51**, 248, 251, 524, 525
Avis, Walter S., 266
Ayer, A. J., 104
Ayres, Harry Morgan, 469

bahuvrihi, 121, 122
Baker, R. J., **303–6**
Ball, Alice M., 124
Bally, Ch., 123
Barnhart, Clarence L., 439, 444, **457–75**
base, 94, 373
Bloch, Bernard, 99, 123, 129, 156, 244, 275, 303, 347, 352
Bloomfield, Leonard, 2, 25, 28, 29, 38, 40, 99–103, 123, 128, 156, 159, 160, **274–81**, 347, 353, 354, 407, 424, 442, 469
Bloomfield, Morton W., 289 ff
Bolinger, Dwight, 173, 174, 185
Bolling, George Melville, 2
Brooks, Cleanth, 493, 495
Brown, Goold, 21, 23
Bryant, Margaret, 339
Bühler, Karl, 311
Burke, Kenneth, 515 ff
Burnet, MacCurdy, 382–8

Callaway, J. E., 524
Campbell, Alexander, 213
Campbell, N., 104
Cargill, Oscar, 280

Carroll, John B., 98, 349
(New) Century Dictionary, 242, 334, 435, 460, 461
Chatman, Seymour B., 493, **500–6**
Chomsky, Noam, 56, 140, 143, 148, 165 ff, **173–92**, 196, 405 ff, 415 ff, 425
Cobbett, William, 408
Cohen, M. R., 104
colloquial, 296 ff, 301–2, 368, 482–3
communication theory, 346, 447
composition, 282 ff, 362, 375 ff, 389 ff
compound, 120 ff
conjunction (*see* part of speech)
construct, 373
construction, 373
Cook, Daniel, **450–6**
correctness, doctrine of (*see also* prescriptive grammar), 388 ff, 400
Craigie, Sir William, 103, 203, 433
Curme, George O., 156, 419

Davis, Alva L., 214, 221, 251
derivation, 144–5
De Saussure, Ferdinand, 25, 37, 424, 430
determinant, 121 ff
determinatum, 121 ff
determiner, 157
dialect (*see also* linguistic geography), 40–1, 73–4, 203 ff, 208 ff, 217, 220 ff, 231 ff, 242 ff, 251 ff, 275, 316, 523
dialect, social, 251 ff
dictionary (–ies), 41, 433 ff
dictionary-editing, problems in, 457 ff
dictionary in the classroom, 435 ff
dictionary, information in a, 440
Dictionary of American English, 203, 450, 461
Dictionary of Americanisms, 434, 460, 461
Dictionary of Contemporary American Usage, 334
Dionysius Thrax, 4, 5, 20–2
distribution, complementary, 86, 93
distribution, contrastive, 86
Donatus, 11, 12, 21, 22
Dorfman, Eugene, 514
Dykema, Karl W., **3–15**

531